AMNIOTIC EMPIRE

Atropos Press
new york • dresden

Think Media EGS Series is supported by the European Graduate School

ATROPOS PRESS
New York • Dresden

THINK MEDIA SERIES:
EGS MEDIA PHILOSOPHY SERIES

AMNIOTIC EMPIRE

Death of the Sublime in World-Historic Culture

ANDREW SPANO

First Published 2020 by
Atropos Press
151 First Avenue # 14, New York, N.Y. 10003
Mockritzer Str. 6, D-01219, Dresden, Germany

Third Edition

ISBN: 978-1-940813-51-6

Cover: Hieronymus Bosch, "The Last Judgment,"
Permission: Gemäldegalerie der Akademie der bildenden Künste Wien

Cover and book design by: **maschinedasein**

In Memoriam:

Werner Hamacher

"When one doubt is followed upon another, the bubble, grown large from long-accumulated fallacies, threatens to burst .... Now is the time for doubt! The bubble of falsehood is bursting and its sound is the roar of the world."

– Anton Szandor LaVey

"Great indeed is the sublimity of the Creative, to which all beings owe their beginning and which permeates Heaven."

– Confucius

Contents

Preface

"The Deepest and most profound
Is the doorway to all subtleties."

–Lao Zi, *Dao De Jing*, Chapter 1

(ἀ)This book began as a post on a popular social media platform which I won't name so as not to become an unpaid promoter of it. Before I get to what the post was, I need to give it a little context. It was a time in my life when social media seemed like a useful tool. I was convinced that living in Brooklyn, having lots of interesting friends, working at my so-called dream job creating content and designing and directing an online media platform for a Major University, and maintaining dialogue with awesome international school chums was the epitome of human existence. Other people just *talked* about Brooklyn or wore Brooklyn t-shirts. I lived it. I *owned* it, I thought.

Not only that, but I had 450 (or so) carefully selected, fascinating, interesting social media friends who were political radicals, communists, right-wing nut jobs, poets, intellectuals, fabulists, gay poets, mystical charlatans, authors of unintelligible philosophical treatises, fire-breathing feminist theorists, bisexual artists, Antifa, avant-garde musicians, performance artists, code writers, anarchist hip-hop artists, post-modern scholars, Goa trance DJ's, university professors, and all the kinds of characters that made me feel that I had at last arrived at the topmost branch of the tree of modern human evolution. They all used this big corporate social media platform that sold all the information they surrendered to it to whomever could afford it (or whomever could get it with a court order) to launch their cultural revolution. I could hardly wait to hear the explosion. It didn't even occur to me, then, that about 1.2 billion persons in the world live without electricity, telephones of any sort, the Internet, or computers. It probably wouldn't have mattered anyway; they were the losers. We were the winners.

I was well paid. I had a great social and cultural life. I knew so many cool people offline and online. I was involved in a hundred radical projects at once. And it seemed to me that the glue holding it all together was this particular social media platform, and some others lending an assist. I wasn't naïve about social media, computers, and the Internet. Heck, I'd been using one form or another of social media since before the turn of the century (Twentieth, that is). Why, I'd used my first computer in fifth grade in 1969. In fact, I went so far as to dare to design and build computers. I'd been a member of this particular platform (that I'm not naming) since its users needed to have a ".edu" file extension to join and there were no ads or any visible sort of monetization. Long before its IPO, anyway.

Before I say much more about social media, and this one, I'd like to get to the point here so that I don't create the impression that this book is about social media. It's not. It's about what I consider to be a much bigger and more significant issue than some sort of Internet product that will one day seem quaint and old fashioned, if not downright unhealthy, like cigarettes. What really matters here is the kind of thinking I was engaged in, and what effect it had on the quality of the fabric of my life, particularly my sense of the sublime but in fact almost every other aspect of it, from sexuality to politics.

But before we go any further, I should say a few words about what I mean by the sublime. This book begins with the definition given by Edmund Burke in "A Philosophical Inquiry into the Origin of Our Ideas of the Sublime and Beautiful": "Indeed terror is in all cases whatsoever, either more openly or latently, the ruling principle of the sublime." Like the word love, the word sublime (if not the sublime itself) has been abused in modern discourse, especially in advertising copy where consumers "love the sublime taste" of spicy nacho cheese chips and vanilla ice cream, perhaps together. The promotional copy on the box of tea before me at this moment reads, "This sublime tea was first created for Scotland's famously soft water ..." Despite being the brand "by appointment to HRH Prince of Wales," this tea tastes like dirt. No abuse of the word sublime will change that for me or, I presume, His Royal Highness, though he likely gets royalties (origin of the word), whereas I must pay for my dirt.

My interpretation of the sublime in this book is an extension of Burke's. It includes Sartre's Nothingness, as well as Nietzsche's admonition in *Beyond Good and Evil*, Aphorism 146, that, "*Wer mit Ungeheuern kämpft, mag zusehn, dass er nicht dabei zum Ungeheuer wird. Und wenn du lange in einen Abgrund blickst, blickt der Abgrund auch in dich hinein.*" ("He who fights with monsters should look to it that he himself does not become a monster. And if you gaze long into an abyss, the abyss also gazes into you.")

There is another important position the sublime takes in this narrative. The sublime is not to be thought of as something we go out and hunt down and kill and then mount on the wall. Furthermore, it is not something only culture vultures get to enjoy because they are rich and have the leisure to do so. Rather, if it is something to strive for at all, it is only because we have lost the innate sense of it with which we were born. The right approach to the world is as one dwelling in the sublime. As I say below, it is something not subject to the distinctions of good and evil, right and wrong, interior and exterior, subjective and objective. Why? Because it is in itself the obliteration of these dichotomies which, at least in the vast religious and philosophical writings of the ancient East, represent not only the *true* state of the world, inasmuch as we can know it, but the true state of our Being.

This is not to say that it is precisely the same thing as what Heidegger means by "Dasein," or Lao Tzu (Lao-ze), in the *Dao De Jing* (*Tao De Ching*), means by "Dao De" (the Way and its Power). Such a philosophical reconciliation is a discussion for another day and another book (maybe even another author). However, let it suffice to say that the sublime is the tertium quid in our experience of dichotomies; better yet, it is the natural and symmetrical foil of duality. It unites our Being with the world and its power. Without this unity, we are lost. We suffer needlessly. We sublimate our terror into entertainment, prurience, narcotics, alcohol, consumer culture, acquisitiveness, depression, suicide, insincere religions, fundamentalist political beliefs, exploitation, the neural stimulation of digital devices, and, ultimately, that which is the cumulative sphere of it all: *the amnion*.

What we cannot face is that our natural state is *terror*. We will all die. That is a terrible reality for the fragile, narcissistic ego that would rather see the entire population of the world wiped out, except itself, than sacrifice itself to the only thing that is inevitable: death – its payment for its existence. Life is a burning house, as the Buddhists say. In this state of terror we make the right (meaning reality-based) decisions about our lives and our relationships with others. The haunting words of Psalm 103 say it much better than I can: "As for man, his days are as grass: as a flower of the field, so he flourisheth. For the wind passeth over it, and it is gone; and the place thereof shall know it no more."

The truth of this sentence from the Psalms is the sublime incarnate. It is only through the embracing of this terror, this haunting (which we so much enjoy in horror movies) that we will ever have a chance to experience the power of life present in the universe. A cruder way to put it is that life is not free. We pay for it with death. Those who want immortality, even in some afterlife Shangi-la, want a free lunch. And there's no such thing as a free lunch, as the Austrian economists like to say. Existence has its own rather inscrutable economy, but there is enough of it manifest through the sublime for us to intuit it if only we are willing to pay the price.

While I, with Burke's assistance, greatly elaborate upon the idea of the sublime here, there is an additional meaning that has a quite modern association: the terror of the "terrorist" who, judging by the "-ist" after his noun, is a kind of professional bringer of terror, like an optometrist is a professional measurer of eyesight. In this book I identify War as the ultimate expression not only of terror, but of the sublime. It doesn't matter if it is Holy War or nice friendly modern armchair war where a nineteen-year-old private sits in an air-conditioned trailer in Texas and obliterates a crowd of "targets" six thousand miles away in a dusty foreign street using a Hellfire missile fired from a UAV (a.k.a. military drone). War is war, just as death is death. It is a significant part of thesis of this book that the formation of the imaginary world culture now driven by digital technology and consumerism, expressed as the amnion, challenges reality. When it does so, war is inevitable as a kind of correction for the supposed "free lunch" the egotistical subject expected to get from his local big-box store, family doctor, or government.

But the distance between my comfortable, "rich" life in Brooklyn and the uncomfortable implications of this thesis is greater than the distance between the antagonists mentioned above because it cannot be measured in kilometers. It has no borders. And it is nothing less than the circumference of an invisible empire encompassing us all – even those without electricity – in a womb-like structure, an amnion, that increasingly determines the quality of our lives and what we can imagine about the near and far future.

The epiphany I express below that came to be the public post I'm talking about here came late in this period when I began to feel like I was living in this invisible sphere the three-dimensional geometric points of which were marked by the kind and function of the various gadgets I used to access the content of the Internet. These gadget points, as I'll call them now, allowed me to access this platform so that I could keep my amazing, awesome, enviable, hip, and all-around superior modern urban lifestyle together in a kind of unified digital field.

There was not a minute of my life where I couldn't reach out and grab one of these gadgets – be it a computer, desktop or laptop, a tablet or a "smart" phone. And as I lived in the Hippest, Coolest, Most Amazing Place on Earth: Brooklyn, New York City (in a brownstone no less), I was assured that all local friends, and all my cyber-friends on every part of the globe, were likewise connected to this sphere. Those who weren't well, they weren't worth keeping around, anyway, right?

But I started to notice that my feeling for people and things, for nature and mystery, art and literature, for ideas and beliefs, and for music and for beauty in general, and even for sex, was fading in some strange and chronic way. The problem really wasn't "computers," which is a pretty broad definition these days. Rather, it was the ways in which they were now being used that began to shock me, one who used his first not long before Dennis Ritchie and Ken Thompson compiled the UNIX operating system. These fading values had always been what I put above anything else, be it money, success, degrees, or possessions. With my ever-more plugged-in existence, my credo was that if it couldn't be encoded and transmitted as a hypertext packet or a bit stream, and if it couldn't be stored on some digital medium, it just wasn't worth my while. Why? Because it couldn't fit into the protocols demanded by my gadgets and the networks that linked them together. Therefore, the nasty, primitive analog world represented a threat to this sphere, this womb, this matrix, this … *amnion*.

Throughout this book I develop the idea of the amnion as a kind of digital womb formed from the convergence of many different technologies used deliberately, consciously, and intentionally at various critical junctures to form the consumer society. Nowhere in this book is this formation meant to be portrayed as some kind of conspiracy. What conspiracy theorists and their detractors and defenders often fail to see is that there are much worse things in human activity and behavior than anything a conspiracy can conjure. As Burns puts it in his ode "To a Mouse," "The best laid schemes o' Mice an' Men / Gang aft agley …" Put another way, the dynamic of the amniotic empire is no less or more of a conspiracy than the Roman Catholic Church is a cult.

The idea of a womb or amnion of digital technology is, of course, no new idea. It is expressed magnificently in the first *The Matrix* film, which definitely helped me form the concept in this book. Also, as the creators of that story well knew, the word "matrix" in Greek means "womb." This book is aimed at the restoration of the sublime more than it is at a matrix revolution.

Meantime, as these ideas were naturally forming in my experience, I was growing ever more paranoid about the security of these gadgets. Periodic brushes with malware, and the growing crop of phishing and Trojan horse messages in my email, as well as revelations by Edward Snowden and many others about deepening cyber-surveillance, made me feel that I had something to hide, even though I couldn't think of what it was. One thing I knew for sure, though: I had something to lose.

Worst of all, I realized that none of this was unique to me. I had come to regard myself as special, chosen, blessed, post-post-modern, even. Those who didn't go to the schools I went to and read the books I read and have the friends I had were just ignorant peasants. Cyber-commonality interfered with my ego's image of itself. It was a ubiquitous feeling among my awesome, amazing, brilliant, cool, and evolved comrades. They seemed to cleave into two groups: those who thought this was a problem, but didn't do anything about it except complain, and those who didn't care or who weren't even aware of it or who even thought it was the Greatest Thing Ever. Both groups, like I, only seemed to be digging themselves ever deeper into the world of this invisible sphere as they used more platforms, linked and networked them, or were the ones actually creating, developing, and maintaining them, as I was. Reality, for them and me, was becoming a contemptible, annoying, inconvenient, uncomfortable, and downright stupid and contagious nuisance!

I could at this point restore my sense of being better and more special than others by saying that I, and I alone, realized what terrible things the sphere of digital technology had done to my humanity, and that I, and I alone, had taken the brave action to change this. But that is not the case. Like almost everyone else, I just became more aware of it than I had been, shrugging it off as the price for being so amazing, awesome, cool, and evolved in a modern society. I thought that somehow the folks who created these platforms and profited from them were just like me. I quickly realized they were not, particularly as I learned more about the financial securities associated with them that were part of a great global economic system upon which I was not even a flea.

I knew how far digital technology had come, right down to the qubit, and how useful it was to me, especially as I made my living from it. I also knew that digital technology's level of comfort and convenience had gone far beyond those awkward science fiction days of computers that looked more like movie sets than machines. The more comfort and convenience, though, the more it seemed I was becoming like the machine itself at the expense of who I always thought I was, or at least who I believed I wanted to be.

Reacting to these vague intuitions and being subject to fits of sudden inspiration and also somewhat reckless and impulsive, I posted a thought, which I regarded as a proposition, a kind of throw-down, on my social media wall for all my smart friends to marvel at: "The Internet is the death of the sublime." Like most of what I imagined were profound insights that I posted there, it was (perhaps appropriately) ignored, until one day a former classmate from graduate school who was at the time in a new, bigger, and better graduate school responded with, "No it's not." It was clear to me that she was speaking ex cathedra, as it were. Considering the endowment alone of this august institution and all of the awesome politicians it had given us, I understood that she needn't condescend to actually argue with my statement. Besides, she might have even been invoking Hitchens' Razor – the unsupported claim that unsupported claims need not be argued with using support.

Frankly, I never held this person, Ms. No-It's-Not, in high esteem. She seemed to me to be the kind of person whom wealth, privilege, connections, arrogance, mediocrity, and shameless and shallow disregard for intellectual sincerity and integrity had gotten her perhaps too far in the academic world. I responded with, "THAT is an argument which cannot be refuted. I fall on my sword!" I still wonder if she felt my sarcasm, or if she just chalked up another victory to the institutional power that funded her. I suppose I'll never know. However, this little exchange on the servers of a social media platform lit a fire under me arse. Not metaphorically but literally, I became possessed by what Freud calls the "furor sanandi," or "healing frenzy" in an effort to repair the fundament, as it were, that had been scorched. The process was now out of my power. Part of the result of this conflagration, which led to many significant changes in my life, is now in *your* hands in the form of this book, comrade.

It suddenly became clear to me what had been happening: I had traded the sense of the sublime for the false sense of community and belonging the digital sphere of the Internet had installed in my psyche at my invitation. The sublime, rebuked and offended, seemed to be abandoning me. As I learned probing this idea, when the sublime meets an affront, it turns to war for a solution. I failed to acknowledge how it had sustained me unfailingly throughout my picaresque life, though not without quite a bit of fear and uncertainty, discomfort, and inconvenience during good and bad times.

I acted with an anxious sense that my mortal soul was in some kind of imminent spiritual danger. I shut down all social media accounts never to be opened again. On that day I "lost" the 450 (or so) friends whom I had carefully cultivated for their wit, accomplishments, interests in kind, affinities, connections, networking, and what I thought was mutual affection - often enough displayed during our in-person times together and professional and artistic collaborations. I also felt as if I'd lost 450 pounds of fat.

Alas, what I quickly discovered was that, at least in my life, this was a revolution of one. No one seemed to notice I was gone! However, I was not concerned about it. Instead, I was relieved. Besides, I was now an apostate to the digital media culture that sustained me and by which I was judged. I even left my job (it was mutual) creating online content and media and took off on a global adventure of book writing, travel, and teaching.

More than three years later only a handful of my former social media friends have stayed in contact with me through other means. Then of course there were those with whom, even if I were in prison writing letters, I would have stayed in communication with, such as my family. And, naturally, there are those who had never embraced this kind of communication, always preferring email, texts, or phone calls. Also, we must allow for what might have been my inflated sense of my own popularity, on or off social media, which was simply revealed for what it was when I was no longer a presence on the media platform. It's important, though, to emphasize again here that this book is not about social media. It could've been written had S&M never been invented.

Furthermore, digital culture is not "evil," and the "death of the sublime," as I call it here, is not the fault of technologists, Brooklyn hipsters, computers, post-modern doublespeak, or my cool present and former friends. Foremost, this death of which I moan and mourn is *my* fault for having allowed myself to lapse, as it were, into this amnion so completely as a consumer of goods, services, and information at the expense of that connection to nature and what has been called "the best that has been said and thought in the world." For at least half of the time of my experience with computers and digital technology there wasn't even an Internet to connect to!

I have more laptops, "smart" phones, and other digital gadgets and software than ever and various technology projects going on with them. Although I no longer have a full-time job creating online digital media content and systems as I did in those days, I still manage to spend a good part of my day online in one way or another using a broad variety of platforms and protocols, some quite exotic and sophisticated compared to those days, and am learning more daily about the minutest workings of my gadgetry. I am absolutely fascinated by digital technology, software and hardware, and its potential.

There is no doubt about it to me: the hardware and software of digital technology, theory behind it, and the uses to which it is put are beautiful too in a way that really has never existed in the history of humankind, such as landing a digital probe on a comet core. That is a masterpiece unequaled in the history of humankind's benign achievements, and there is little of it that could be monetized or weaponized. For now.

Also, as I am living in China as I write this, I am literally *required* to use the chief social media platform of this country not only to communicate with my employers and students, but also to pay for my everyday expenses, from utilities to food shopping, never mind provide the Chinese government with a record of my day-to-day activities, movements, health, ideas, proclivities, travels, thoughts, and associations. The other platform I refer to at the start of this preface is currently blocked here on all domestic servers by a government blacklist. If I learned anything from being forced to use yet another behemoth of a social media platform, it's that it's getting so that you may not be able to escape it unless you join the ranks of the 1.2 billion persons on earth with no electricity still burning cow dung in their huts and drinking amoebas who have no choice in the matter - something which is not their fault and is the greatest crime of history.

What this book is about is the so-called sphere I mention above and the effect it has on our sense of the sublime in what might be considered the more traditional domains of human endeavor, in particular philosophy, literature, and religion, which I define in some depth with examples taken mostly from the European tradition only because I know it best. The amniotic empire, which I call "the amnion" in this book, existed long before I did. Let me give you some examples.

I love to watch old movies from the 1930's, 1940's, and 1950's. I was struck recently how in those days newspapers, broadcast radio, landline telephones, two-way radios, movies, and in the latter part of that period television maintained what could perhaps be considered a far more effective and hermetically sealed *amnion* than anything we have today. What I call the "social degree of conformity" of those days in the United States of America was arguably much higher, in part because of the nature of the available and ubiquitous media, which was almost entirely a one-way form of communication, from the content creator to the public, in one vast, monolithic form. The only interactivity the public had was the on/off switch, which is powerful in and of itself, but also easy to overcome by the purveyors of content under any circumstances.

But we may go further in this inquiry. Using the work of communications theorists such as Marshall McLuhan and Claude Shannon, we may infer the structure of the formation of notional and nominal ideas back to Johannes Gutenberg and Hegel's and Fichte's triad of the *concrete, abstract,* and *absolute* in arriving at the discourse through a dialectical process. By making the printing of books relatively cheap and available, the discourse of authorized Christianity spread through (at first) the Bible, Latin and the vulgate. Shannon teaches us that the structure of communications remains the same throughout history: transmitter and receiver T(R) ↔ R(T), as with subject and object, inverting roles in a dialectical process to arrive at an agreed-upon discourse which we call *understanding*. The nominal-notional form of knowledge of the amnion, which is synthetic, remains to be verified by analytic intellect (logic), otherwise it remains, as Plato says of the categories of his Divided Line, *opinion* based on subjective empirical observation and not the process of intellectual (and abstract) knowledge. The word under-*standing* is related to the idea of the negotiated *state,* or ruling apparatus formed of a plurality of the polity, etymologically derived from the Latin *stare*, meaning "to stand." The result is a negotiated (nominal-notional) idea falling on the synthetic side of Plato's Divided Line at first (*eikesia/pistis*); it then must be independently (objectively) verified through the operation of a logical proposition (*dianoia/ noesis*). However, it seldom is in the amniotic empire, else it would implode from being revealed for what it is: a derivatives bubble of notional value.

Consequently, digital nets and webs are needed to *capture,* the way a spider or a fisherman does, the subject's use-value until such time as the subject can be cast aside or thrown into the dust bin of the Underclass. As Wordsworth says in his long poem the *Prelude* of his (unpleasant) time as a student at Cambridge, "I was ill suited for captivity." The subject begins to engage Hegel's negation of negation (Second Negation) when it begins to doubt what it formerly believed to be true about itself and its dreamworld. The pity is that if it happens at all, it is usually after some inexplicable personal catastrophe emanating from the amnion's nomological structure — such as suddenly finding oneself in prison but coming from the Apex Consumer class where prison is not the norm as it is among the Underclass. I am not saying that I am free of this capture, either; but I can say that I doubt the narrative discourse of the amnion (I hope you understand that at this point), and I know when to doubt doubt, too. I also know that the Second Negation is a *process*, not a *static state* in the past or to be striven for in the future; it is not an *event* like being born again in evangelical Christianity. I should wonder why I, as a person naturally inclined to be feral, if not something of a Fauvist and Flâneur, ever let myself be drawn into nets and webs as I have been, am, and for the foreseeable future will be. But then again, even without this technology, the social amnion exists, though in much weakened form. What once required swords, bayonets, scimitars, and burning at the stake - highly inefficient methods - to get people to maintain the amnion, now only requires the glowing logo of a once-innocent piece of fruit and a line of credit with an ever-expanding limit to accomplish.

What is the basis of this amnion? The thesis of this book is that there are two contributing human impulses converging to give it ubiquitous and almost omnipotent power: the subject's desires for comfort and convenience, which turn out to be much stronger than we typically assume; and the lust for infinite access to consumer goods. Naturally, such unbridled consumerism also requires access to credit and debt. And lurking in the background of this landscape is the craving for immortality born of the fear of death of the ego, which was once religion's bailiwick as incorporeal immortality but now belongs to the Cult of Scientism - the new religion of the modern state - as *corporeal* immorality. (I should mention now that throughout this book I have indulged in the figurative phrase "religion of Scientism"; by this I mean the *Cult* of Scientism, since a cult is not a religion, though I do want to point out, figuratively, that Scientism has this aspiration.)

Combine these impulses with a ubiquitous system of promissory notes, easy credit, and marketing created by those who are slightly smarter or at least less naïve and perhaps more ruthless than the average Jane and Joe, and you have the outline of this amnion. But as with all human impulses and desires, these must be effectively and efficiently contained by social, commercial, and political institutions, or else dissolve into the random distribution we now like to refer to as the Middle Ages in Europe between 500 and 1500 CE. It is here that digital technology, which I sometimes call electronica in the book, comes into play.

Considering these dates, I should mention that up until the beginning of this period (500 CE) the Unholy Roman Empire and its counter-valence the Holy Roman Empire, served much of the same function as the modern digital amnion, though in a highly inefficient way that, after an impressive and unprecedented run, finally exhausted itself effectively before that period - though its last gasps persisted in parallel with this period until the fall of the Byzantine Empire at Constantinople in 1453. Also, the Roman Catholic Church rose up during this period to attempt to fill the void during the Middle Ages. Despite its historical effectiveness in this sense, the Reformation belies how ineffective it was after all. It can even be said that one man, Martin Luther, was able to bring it to its knees, in large part because it turned the mercy of God into the commodity of an indulgence or a paper guarantee of a place in Heaven which we might consider an early form of today's modern derivatives market, in particular futures and forwards.

What the Church did manage to leave as its legacy from that era, though, is a paradigm for the new orthodox religion of Scientism preached in the halls of academe, worshiped in the towers of commerce and finance, sanctioned by the State, and purveyed throughout the amnion's shell network of political parties and campaigns, gadgets and services, commodities, and financial products and banks. My original idea for the subtitle of this book was *Scientism and the Overthrow of the Sublime*. However, what it's really about is the matrix of 21st Century culture in developed modern countries and what effect it has on our innate sense of the sublime.

As you shall see, I consider our sense of the sublime to be critical to meaningful existence. Without it, we are the stumps of trees long ago cut down and dead. It is the only sense we have that does not distinguish between subject and object, between being and non-being. I (with Burke's help) make the case that the most sublime event of all is death, and that the sense of our inevitable mortality pervades our psyche and psychology - right down to the apoptosis of cellular being. Furthermore, the sublime also does not distinguish between what Heidegger calls "ready-to-hand" and "present-at-hand." In other words, that which is manifest, and that which exists as an idea, both within Dasein, or the unity of differentiated and undifferentiated Being. The concept is well expressed by Lao Zi (*Dao De Jing*, Ch.1):

> The Being-without-form is the origin of Heaven and Earth;
> The Being-within-form is the mother of the myriad things.
> Therefore it is always from the Being-without-form
> That the subtlety of the Dao can be contemplated.

The word "subtlety" here is the material equivalent of what I call the sublime in this book. The sublime does not distinguish between rich or poor, high or low intelligence quotient, university degrees or the self-taught, or any of the, shall we say, biological distinctions between human animals. The sublime gives being meaning. It is the food of Dasein, the way a whale lives on plankton. Unfortunately, it is now nearly absent from what I call here default culture, or the nightmare of the modern technological consumer machine. Much of this machine is dedicated to extracting the sublime from the abdicated subject the way an exorcist extracts a dybbuk. Once the sublime becomes an unpleasant, far-off memory, the consumer is prepared for the onslaught of consumption arising as a displacement substitute for repression of the emotions evoked, and invoked, by the sublime terror of death.

In the presence of the sublime, the mechanism of the amnion, cannot function at the optimum level necessary to facilitate production of its ultimate expression: the Apex Consumer. Boats, houses, cars, and lots of "stuff" mark this top predator who, unbeknown to himself, is actually the prey of the demi-gods of the hegemony. "As flies to wanton boys are we to th' gods, / They kill us for their sport" (*King Lear* Act 4, scene 1, 32–37). He is the *nouveau riche*, the self-made millionaire, the dumb investor, the high-roller who bets the house, and the spender creditors like the most because he is always spending to impress himself and his peers. If he overspends, he has assets that can be seized and an income that can be garnished. The banks love him because he gives them an excuse to generate money through the fractional reserve system, allowing them to make something from nothing in the magic of the animal spirits of Keynesian economics - the amnion's most lucrative con game. It needs an iconic consumer that all the rest may aspire to so that they will keep signing promissory notes to get the things the Apex Consumer *seems* to own (though in fact most of it is debt and mortgage and is therefore owned by the bank). Meantime, the subprime subject's income does not justify this level of borrowing, getting him into an eternal indenture with the banks as if he were borrowing from Mob loan sharks and could not make the *vig*. None of this would be possible if the subject valued the sublime over this self-inflicted bamboozle. What he cannot understand is that death *is* life; it is the same thing seen a different way, as all phenomena arise from such apparent duality.

The world-historic part of the subtitle of this book refers to the persons, actions, movements, events, artistic creations, scientific discoveries, important ideas, and civilizations which have formed and informed what we see before us today in the guise of the world, developed to the satisfaction of the industrial empire's template or not. However, the emphasis is on the West, particularly Europe and North America. (Unfortunately, omniscience is not one of my many virtues.) To include the East, specifically, in this narrative would lead it far from the cultural references I need to consolidate in order to prosecute this argument in its present form. I plunge into the mechanisms of the global culture of the amnion in its Eastern manifestation in another book treating this matter specifically, so I do not feel the need to do it here to make my point. Moreover, much of what is said here applies to the manifestation of it in the East (and elsewhere) because of the viral (meaning poisonous) spread of global default culture - the chief excrescence of the amnion.

I am told by one of the "Oxford-powered" (that's what it says on the website) dictionaries that the term "world-historic" originated with Samuel Taylor Coleridge in the Eighteenth or Nineteenth Century, though it is not clear what he meant by it. In cultures which have enjoyed the intricacies of civilization for, perhaps, millennia, there has been a consistent emphasis on the sublime as the highest spiritual, aesthetic, and cultural value - even if it involved great suffering. This is not to exclude or excuse the vast slave populations of these same classical examples, though we must consider that those enslaved were often members of tribes which had themselves set out to enslave, but lost the battle. We are fortunate to have chronicles of these dramas, which include the Judeo-Christian Bible and the Koran.

One who cannot see what is sublime in these chronicles still has some work to do in learning how to appreciate the collective efforts of generations, centuries, and millennia of fellow beings just like himself reaching out to something beyond what can be found in the marketplace, treasure trove, or brothel (virtual or not). This is not to mention specific works of the religious philosophies of the East, a subject too vast for this narrative. History is also populated with world-historic characters who were *not* the celebrated leaders of their tribe. Their works abound, though without attribution. They are the unsung artisans, farmers, warriors, parents, artists, engineers, laborers, travelers, holy men, pilgrims, monks, mystics, witches, outcasts, mariners, functionaries, priests, and mere witnesses to history who were immersed in the sublime whether they wanted to be or not.

With every effort made to banish subjective romanticizing from my estimation of the situation (successful or not), I believe that the sublime has been man's common experience of Being until recently in his history, when it became the *enemy* of the industrial empire. The consequence is that it marks the end of an epoch that had endured for millennia, particularly of that quality of it that Julian Jaynes refers to as the "bicameral mind" of the ancients, a form of cognition capable of accommodating science and metaphysical mystery in equal measure.

The argument defenders of the amnion make – that their epoch is superior because it is not the benighted past, and that the future will be even better – is not supported by the works past epochs have left behind in abundance like messages or warnings to the future which have survived every sort of abuse, from burning and wars to neglect and vandalism. Where is the Johann Sabastian Bach of today? Where? Where? Where? *Show me*, and I will shut up and fall on my sword! The cultural medium in which he appeared, or even that in which Jimi Hendrix appeared, no longer exists for such apogees of art, particularly with the amnion's war on religion and ecstatic culture.

The war is not the result of debunking religious dogma or finding something harmful in religious and spiritual communion with the sublime world through art and music; on the contrary it is to eliminate competition with the *new* religion of Scientism, which has little to do with theoretical or verifiable science and everything to do with the new religion's favorite noun regarding scientific evidence: *consensus*. "A *consensus* of scientists say that … *X*," which makes it "true" in the global mass media, the narrative of the amnion, as if verifiability, theory, and theorem were a beauty pageant. The synthetic (unverifiable) proposition has become the new analytic (verifiable) proposition, and the verifiable has become the *enemy* of the dogma of the world's new dominant religion of scientific superstition.

If any scientist *verifies* a contrary finding to the consensus, he is hounded out of his profession, humiliated, shamed, and relegated to the lunatic fringe – the hegemony's form of what the Greeks called loathing where an individual was punished by complete social ostracism. The exception is when, under the aegis of some pharmaceutical company, he and his lab invent a marketable therapy, or engineers develop a new generation of a gadget. It seems to me, at 62 years of age and with much experience and study, that what is left of this state of being, this now atavistic ethical aesthetic, this sublime, can be found only in what academic eggheads call primitive or better yet indigenous cultures.

These natives, preserved like zoo animals if they are lucky, value the sublime of their ancestral ways and animistic gods over the trinkets of deceit vomited out by the robotic machinery of consumer culture. Therefore, in the language of the reigning *imperii* of the hegemony, they must always be referred to either in the pejorative as primitive or glorified as somehow saintly because they are innocent (meaning *naïve*) of the accoutrements of modern industrial-financial civilization. The abdicated subject has the pernicious habit of glorifying ancient cultures which have not (yet) submitted to the yoke of the amnion. This is done for the most transparent reason: as a kind of ad hoc *funeral* for the fatal abdication of their sense of wonder and enchantment about being alive in a dead universe in exchange for fleeting, and illusory, comfort and convenience.

The basis of the sublime, says Burke (more detail later), is *terror*. What is this terror? It is the fear of our inevitable *non-being*, which we repress with dire consequences. What we want is immortality, infinite access to credit, unrestrained indulgence in consumer goods and services, comfort, convenience, and progress. These are all the excrescences of the repressed terror of death. And yet, without consciously embracing death, as generations past had to do because it was constantly all around them, we cut ourselves off from the sublime. Instead, we have electronic gadgets designed to suck us dry of data and economic power through infinite distraction from the only event in life that is absolutely inevitable. THIS is primitive, not the belief in pagan gods, self-sufficient tribal culture, or languages without writing. I also make the argument here that *war* is the ultimate expression of the sublime; at all times, the subject *longs for war* to restore the sublime to his experience in the form of terror.

Therefore, it is interesting that the consumer's greatest fear is *terrorism*, variously defined but distinctly *bad*. To the so-called terrorist, it is war; to the terrorized, it is crime; to the hegemony, it is an opportunity to harden and expand its hegemonic powers. Like death, war is always inevitable among default cultures that have systemically murdered the sense of the sublime in order to exist in a seemingly deathless, imaginary media culture of commercial pitches and political propaganda. And what is the discourse of this propaganda? It may be expressed in two integrated propositions: 1) Because people believe in nothing, they are desperate to believe in something; therefore, they will believe in anything; and 2) Because people will believe in anything, it is impossible for them to believe in something; therefore, they believe in nothing. P1 and P2 form a recursive loop of unconscious pseudo-volition based on social pressures and constraints. It is maintained by official consensus, which is not consensus in its technical meaning as unanimity, but rather its *metaphorical* (or hyperbolic) sense as a coerced super-majority. The coercion is carried out (in the modern age) via economic token systems; it is a carrot-stick, funding-defunding ritual, the purpose of which is to maintain the symmetrical recursive loop of [(P1 → P2) → (P2 → P1)], or *if, if proposition 1, then proposition 2; then, if proposition 2, then proposition 1.* However, such a strenuous and infinitely inefficient regime must be enforced, sustained, manipulated, operated, prosecuted, funded, protected, defended, and perpetuated through an ethical aesthetic of infinite progress, or what I call throughout this essay the progressive fallacy: the unverifiable synthetic proposition that the mere passage of time discovers all mysteries of the universe and makes all things hoped and wished for and imagined possible (even unicorns; fear not: genetic engineering is working on it as we speak, comrade). Enter: Scientism. Ultimately, it is the Cult of Scientism, which is a sub-cult of the much larger and ubiquitous Cult of Mediocrity, and not what might be called *science itself,* that is responsible for the engineering and maintenance of the amnion and its digital empire. By contrast, what I call science itself has suffered as much as have the arts and Nature from this new religion, as so-called pure science, and certainly theoretical physics and mathematics, have always been concerned with the sublime as it manifests itself in the immutable laws of nature, reason, and what might be called the mind of God.

In this passage from John Ruskin's *Sesame and Lilies,* he makes the distinction between the commercial application of science and the idea of pure science, and what this distinction means in the social context:

> I say we have despised science. "What!" you exclaim, "are we not foremost in all discovery, and is not the whole world giddy by reason, or unreason, of our inventions?" Yes; but do you suppose that is national work? That work is all done in spite of the nation; by private people's zeal and money. We are glad enough, indeed, to make our profit of science; we snap up anything in the way of a scientific bone that has meat on it, eagerly enough; but if the scientific man comes for a bone or a crust to us, that is another story. (33, II)

Science has found itself divided into two distinct classes: what can make money for big corporations or make weapons for big government, and what can be discovered through the fundamental human desire to *know,* from which we get the word science itself. Recently I found an instructional video extolling Vincent van Gogh as an example of a successful entrepreneur, touting the ridiculous prices his paintings now fetch. It failed to mention, however, that he barely sold a painting his whole (short and miserable) lifetime. This kind of cultural amnesia produces myriad grotesques such as this, just as every new scientific discovery seems to produce yet another way by which humankind can annihilate itself in one fatal snap.

It seems to me that this book has a pretty simple thesis, hardly original, and one that doesn't do too much damage to other people's theories on similar and related concerns. It's not my objective here to change anyone's mind, clast any iconos, alter the way we do things, attack any theories, serve as a Luddite of digital technology, or shout the truth from the rooftops. My worst fear is of becoming yet another Cassandra in the digital wilderness of Wake-Up-America videos hosted by a DIY media platformed owned by what might be perhaps the biggest of all of the engineers of the amnion of which I speak, ignored by all except those who already agree with me.

Rather, I strive to give voice again to what I regard as the sublime which, though in the long run needs no puny human mouthpiece, nevertheless benefits from intellectual representation in what is thought and said in the world when it becomes part of our everyday experience. You might even say that I'm trying to prove to those who, like my colleague Ms. No It's-Not, that they may be wielding Hitchens' razor prematurely, and that speaking ex cathedra on such matters does harm to what we might discover and learn. But this is a positive, not negative argument. I attempt to show by assertion, by the extolling of the sublime, though some of those assertions do involve Occam's Razor – which is quite another thing than her rusty instrument, if hers is anything at all. I would go so far as to say that without a personal sense of the sublime, deeply felt, we self-destruct (choose your poison, or weapon), though war is, perhaps, the ultimate expression of the sublime when it gets pissed off at being affronted or ignored. It is better to give it a hearing now, than to wait for the nuclear explosion.

My objective here is a single, pointed object: the promotion of the sublime in art, literature, music, social culture, religion, and human experience as I define it in the text of this book, over what we may otherwise hold to be important. I will admit I have little mercy for the digital gadget culture of the Black Mirror with its enforcement of comfort, convenience, and *want* (as opposed to *need*) consumerism. In this book (which I insist that you *need*), as an expression of these ideas, the sublime is considered to be the life force itself; it is what Dylan Thomas calls "the force that through the green fuse drives the flower." It's what's behind the power of Nature and the human spirit, which includes the laws of Nature and of God, however, you may conceive of this God particle and its much-maligned parent: Nature.

"Ah ha!" the reader says, "A neo-Romantic argument! A metaphysician in analytic philosopher's clothing! Worse: a *Deist*!" That is hardly the case. I will admit there is a bias throughout this book for the literature and philosophy of what we now call the European Romantics, particularly Keats, Milton, Blake and German and French Romantic philosophers, such as Kant and Rousseau. And Emerson. What of the Enlightenment is in here also leans toward the Romantic side of it; whereas Descartes' notions, in as much as they've been twisted into the perversion of logical positivism, get dissected.

But that is only because the Romantics seemed to have made it their conscious mission to promote a sublime sensibility over what they saw as the rising influence of the Industrial Revolution – a preoccupation that I think fits our current demise and is a metastatic extension of that demise. Theirs wasn't a manifesto so much as a tocsin, a reaction, and an antidote as well as an expression of the sublime through their art and wit. The work of Shelley comes to mind as an excellent example, though Keats is favored here. The reader will also find much of what one Romantic called "the best that is thought and said in the world," though not so much of what another called "sweetness and light," since the sublime is, admittedly, a terrifying vision of the universe and includes the bitter darkness of war.

The dynamic throughout this book, and the two that are to follow (more about this in a minute), is between the forces described here as *realia* and *simulacra*. The former is simply reality as a sovereign force, represented foremost by Nature and what is discovered as the laws of nature by science and mathematics. The latter is what comprises the *amnion*, or the sphere, that today just happens to be largely sustained by digital technology but was sustained in other ways in other epochs as well as in other regions of the world besides Europe. The former consists of information that must be discovered by mankind. The latter consists of information that must be manufactured or not exist at all. However, it is today, in the world in which this book was written, that this amnion has reached its greatest and most powerful expression as an impostor, a simulacrum of reality itself, and a threat to our sovereign meaningful existence.

The reader needn't worry about having an elaborate explanation of these ideas here and now in this preface; the book itself it that explanation. I long ago realized that any work of philosophy – from Aristotle's *Poetics* through Heidegger's *Being and Time* – is a matter of taking a simple idea and restating it in thousands of different ways and in as many contexts, replete with examples of one sort or another, be they mathematical, empirical, or hypothetical, until the reader gets it (or surrenders in a fit of aporia). All such explanations and examples the reader will find here, perhaps ad nauseum.

Also, I should mention that the philosophical underpinnings of this book and the next two rely in significant part on the work of America's greatest philosopher: Charles S. Peirce, particularly his ideas regarding semiotics and linguistics, as well as his unique contribution to the logic of abductive reasoning in as much as it applies to the scientific method of hypothesis. He represents the side of science itself, or what has been called pure science (science for science's sake?) and theoretical mathematics and physics. This force is as opposed to its perversion into the religion of Scientism and the greater Cult of Mediocrity of the commercial, academic, and political branches of the empire.

Finally, something has to be said about the larger architecture of this book. *Amniotic Empire* is the Preliminary, in the sense of philosophical discourse, of a larger work titled *Death of the Sublime*, consisting of three books all together. This book, and the other two parts, is meant to be read as self-contained discourse. This book, though, being the *Preliminary*, lays out the whole elaborate argument. Therefore, the other two, which have not been published or even revised as of this writing, shouldn't be read without reading this volume. Ultimately, though, all three should be read together to get the full treatment of the idea of what the death of the sublime means to us. I could perhaps list what I see as the consequences of this death in a kind of postmortem right here, but I'd rather save that for a long and gradual unfolding in the books themselves. Ultimately it is up to the mind of the reader to flesh out the personal consequences.

Also, I've tried to keep citations to a minimum. For instance, I don't see the need to cite lines from Milton's *Paradise Lost* or Keats "Ode to a Nightingale" from which I quote extensively. Otherwise, the books I refer to and quote from can be found in the bibliography. If there are quotes from philosophical works or papers, there are citations indicating the page source or chapter and verse with corresponding works in the bibliography. As nothing in this book can be construed as being fact (though I overuse the phrase *in fact* as a kind of rhetorical *force majeure*), the reader will not find facts validated by cite, only by example.

I've tried to make this book, and the ones that follow, as un-academic as possible, seeing that genre of onanism as a blight on the sublime. Throughout, an attempt has been made to make this preliminary argument as readable as possible for anyone who is moderately well read and has the curiosity necessary to follow a sustained argument attempting to give proofs and examples. One might even consult the Oracle (Internet) now and again to amplify or clarify something I say here. There is a little mild algebra too of no more difficulty than what is met with in high school (my limit).

One final caveat: I understand that I might draw intellectual disdain from the reader for quoting from the "patriarchal" King James Bible as well as for daring to use the masculine pronoun (he, him, his) for the collective singular rather than "s/he," or "he or she," or the universal grammar error of the plural "they/their" for the singular. Or worse. Even pointing out that I defy the orthodoxy, by the sin of omission *or* commission, is itself heretical and may get my entire argument dismissed. In my defense, however, I use the pronoun "it" at least 7,822 times here mostly as a substitute for the gendered pronoun, requiring me to use the noun "the subject" as its referent, as it is entirely clinical and genderless. Where I do not use this noun to mean the abdicated citizen of the hegemonic state of the amnion, I revert to the Latin rule of using the male pronoun to represent both male and female persons.

My hope is that through our attention to the unfolding of the ideas in this book, we will become more conscious of what we are losing or have lost in our social and cultural rejection of the sublime and its terror. If we get even a glimpse of what has been lost, it should be enough to prod us into a sense of our critical mortality. We never have enough time left to do what we must do. So why waste what little of it there is? Perhaps then we may be moved to restore the supreme place of the sublime in our lives before we have forsaken our natural sense of wonder and awe to a life that will be, as a consequence, hardly worth living.

Andrew Spano
Shanyang City, Liaoning Province
China 2019

Amniotic Empire: Death of the Sublime in World-Historic Culture

It behooves us to say, before all, that philosophy lies closer to poetry than to science. All philosophic systems which have been constructed as a supreme concord of the final results of the individual sciences have in every age possessed much less consistency and life than those which express the integral spiritual yearning of their authors.

- Miguel de Unamuno, *The Tragic Sense of Life*

Indeed terror is in all cases whatsoever, either more openly or latently, the ruling principle of the sublime.

- Edmund Burke,
"Inquiry into the Origin of ... the Sublime and Beautiful"

PART 1: NEGATIVE CAPABILITY AND THE SUBLIME

1.0: Preliminary

Now more than ever seems it rich to die,
To cease upon the midnight with no pain,
While thou art pouring forth thy soul abroad
In such an ecstasy!

—John Keats, "Ode to a Nightingale."

(άά)The existential paradox in these four simple lines from Keats' "Ode to a Nightingale" leaves me in a state of mystery about the nature of death. What does he intuit about it that escapes me in my everyday conduct? These lines point to death as being life itself, rather than its antithesis. Is death not something *other than* life, which is the way I, my society, and my civilization typically and justifiably regard it? In my milieu, then, death is a *disease* to be cured by a priesthood of medical experts. If I pay my tithe, my medical insurance premium, I will live forever. If I do not, I will be damned to the Hell of mortality - like poor people are. I want death to be a sickness a doctor can cure and life to be a state that I, my ego, can cling to forever. Why? So I can keep on consuming the products of my culture in relative comfort, and fiddling with my digital gadget. Keats, conversely, seems content with his imminent crossing over to the *terra incognita* of non-being, a journey he regards as an occasion of rich ecstasy, signified by the nightingale. So the question is: why is *he* so content, without the aid of Morpheus, and *I* am in a panic over it? What is it about the nightingale's song that makes death rich for him, rather an occasion to express the surprise and frustration of the ego at having to be thrown into "The undiscovere'd country, from whose bourn / No traveller returns"? What seems paradoxical here is that in his intuition of the nature of death he finds what is significant, meaningful, and inevitable about life. Pain and ecstasy merge as *pathos*, the root of passion. Is it because the terror of death is the ultimate expression of our apprehension of the *sublime*, signified by the song of the nightingale? Those fortunate enough to have heard this bird singing in the darkness when no other bird sings are often startled, and deeply charmed, they say, by the sublimity of its solitary song. We associate the diurnal dying of the light with death. Night is the province of predators, human and animal. When we think of daytime we also think the birds around us filling the air with sound - a kind of affirmation of life. What, then, does the juxtaposition of the life of the nightingale's song with the rich inevitability of death mean to Keats? As thesis of this book asserts, it is the sublime (a term extensively defined here, dear reader, so fear not).

An ode traditionally trumpets a virtue, celebrates a precious object, or commemorates a significant event. Its Latin meaning is "lyric song." Keats writes (or sings) a song to a songbird. In a way they exchange songs that are out of time with each other. We are made to understand that the nightingale is the source of what allows Keats to invert our typical approach to the moment of death (here as signified by midnight). Rather than a loss of ego, it is a loss of *the pain* the ego feels about the loss of itself that will soon free him. The ego is its own greatest mourner. But of course it must mourn before it can mourn no more. We like to call this depression, anxiety, fear, self-pity, and horror. But is it *terror*, in the sense meant by Burke above? Conversely, when we think about ecstasy we tend to understand it as a letting go. Of what? Like the word eccentric, it implies a centrifugal movement away from a static core. While we do not share personalities with others, we do share the structure and function of the ego. We could say that the ego is more or less the same psychic construct in each of us, like the spleen. What we do not like to think about is how *alien* the ego is, not only to the id, but to the vast totality of our being, a holistic unit seldom expressed or recognized because of our flight from the terror of death and, consequently, from the sublime. We cannot even say that the ego is our personality, which is more a reflection of our unfathomable totality than it is of this single organ of the psyche. Nevertheless, what the ancient Greeks called the "persona" in drama, the mask, overtakes the personality as an expression of the ego and even the superego. Frank Bingo becomes Officer Bingo; Mike Dingo becomes Father Dingo. Each has a uniform expressing his transmogrification into an expression of the collective, societal superego, guardian of the *nomos* and, most of all, of the individual ego itself by extension. But seldom is the persona an expression of the id, except in certain kinds of saints, arch criminals, mass murderers, gurus, and serial killers - which is why we admire them. We envy their abandonment to the transgressions perpetrated by the id and, consequently, the resulting *jouissance* accompanying it. Perceiving this deviation, the prevailing hegemony, through its media channels, diverts such transgressions into impotent vicarious spectacles such as Hollywood movies and computer games where everyone gets shot, but no one really dies. Pornography, bless its heart, is another example.

The tendency cultivated by vicarious propitiation of the id is identification of the personality with the ego. Perhaps ironically, the hegemony is an expression of the collective egoic agenda of the polity it preys upon. Keep in mind that *contradiction* is the prevailing irrational state of mind of the subject. What is not contradictory and can be verified, is feared as a threat to the illusion the subject cannot live without. What the ego desires for the perpetuation of itself, apart from society, even at the sacrifice of others and, in the case of suicide, itself, is *immortality* - yet another stark contradiction. How, though, does the sacrifice of others lead to the sacrifice of the ego? *Because others are doing the same thing*, often enough resulting in the demise of the ego as other egos strive for dominance. This we call war. It is a shock to learn that quite apart from our hopes, dreams, and desires the ego has its own agenda: *to live forever*. This agenda may be incompatible with what gives life meaning, or even that rare a priori acceptance of death we find in extraordinary or fatalistic individuals.

However, in ecstasy we escape the gravitational field of the ego's agenda. Instead, we spin into that which lies beyond the ego's pale, like Dervishes. The ego does not like ecstasy. The collective social ego protecting the solitary ego constructs the *nomos*, the infinitely expanding body of laws enforced by an autonomous authority always already in a state of exception to its own proscriptions so that it may enforce them with absolute impunity. While the personality may be curious about ecstatic culture, the ego, by its nature, has not the slightest interest in it, as it is the negation of itself and is therefore always already a threat. It is only interested in itself. It is its only reality. All else is imaginary and symbolic. The collective expression of the confluence of the imaginary and symbolic, as an autonomous state of being, is the foundation of what I call here the *amnion*.

Ecstasy scorns pain and death. Saints possessed by religious ecstasy scourge themselves with iron chains in what seems like the erotic bliss of penance and release from sin (the self-centrism of the ego). Soldiers charge into battle intoxicated with honor and patriotism. Drugs, sex, music, and religious fervor all conspire to spin us out of the ego's grip. Therefore, what the ego fears is its dissolution in the throes of ecstasy. To be ecstatic is to be eccentric; the ego (guided by the *nomos* of its superego) functions as the core, the center, that which the id seeks escape *from*. But then again this is the ego's biggest mistake. It is not the core; if there is one, it is the id itself. The ego may encompass the id in some way, but it does not supplant the id's ultimate priority. What the subject desires most is freedom from the ego while at the same time being paradoxically driven *by* the ego (self) to this end. Herein lies the subject's fundamental state of contradiction aggregated into the *Cult of Mediocrity* - something we will hear about in some detail later. This fundamental conflict makes us *miserable*, a state and emotion not found in wild animals. Keats' "pain," therefore, opposes ecstasy. It is the nightingale's timely voice making it possible for Keats to transcend the ego. He apprehends the nightingale as the symbol of the *thingness* of things, of *realia*, and the *otherness* of the Other. It seems to us that just as animals do not seem to laugh neither do they seem to be miserable - unless we make them so in our own miserable image. The nightingale has all of the qualities needed for a symbol: its beautiful song, its nocturnal presence, and its power of flight. It also has historical precedent, such as the Holy Spirit, the phoenix, and the imperial eagle. Nevertheless, the ego would like it to remain *a symbol*. We do not want anything about it to become a reality, else we will (as does Keats), find ourselves confronting the sublime terror of death. Its night bird's song is a nagging reminder that we are not free. We reach a point where the personality becomes crystalized, fossilized, and we can no longer feel ecstasy. We are then no longer ourselves. We have abdicated our sovereignty in exchange for comfort, convenience, and medical immortality - provided we can keep up the payments for a lifetime without interruption. We have become this alien structure called the ego. And the ego itself has become an extension of a mechanism on an even more remote substrate: the social Discourse of the hegemony, embodied by the amnion.

Why, then, does Keats seem liberated from this fate? Why is death "Devoutly to be wished" like a religious awakening? Clearly the nightingale is the catalyst for his experience. It brings something to the apprehension of life the ego cannot. What is it? Compared to the core of Keats' identity, the nightingale is eccentric; it is the Other, outside of the ego's nimbus of self-interest. It lies entirely outside of the boundaries of his self-possession. But it is not just the nightingale inspiring Keats' ode. It is also death. The bird's song acts as a spark igniting a perception of death apart from the ego's belief that it will live forever. The bird pours forth its *soul*, not just whatever little birdlike ego it may have. The song helps Keats reconcile his personality with the ambitions of the ego. How is this possible? He tries to tell us that death can be "rich" rather than represent the impoverishment the ego fears as the irretrievable loss of itself which it is. Even if one has heartfelt belief in an afterlife, it is ludicrous to imagine that the same ego that went to therapy sessions and got nowhere, was addicted to antidepressants, picked up sex partners in a bar, ate junk food, sat in front of the TV all day, took illegal drugs, was a drunk, or robbed people in the stock market is what enters the gates of Heaven. Even if one makes amends and is in some way absolved of these worldly blemishes, *it is still the same infantile ego ascending to its divine reward*, leaving behind unpaid bills, a bewildered dog, and weeping friends and family.

The proposition of this essay is that the ego's desire to live forever brings about the death of the sublime in a collectivized way built from the superstructure of the nomos and the hegemony it makes possible. It is the collective will of the subjects' ego that defines the hegemony and its amnion. Together, they are only possible if they are *autonomous,* however, independent of their creators. We see this theme in much science fiction, starting with Mary Shelley's *Frankenstein*, continuing on into the imagined future when mankind will be destroyed by a race of anthropomorphic robots (also representing the collective ego in its autonomous manifestation). But of course, autonomy depends on the state of exception from the nomos the hegemony enforces to maintain its autonomy. Yet another paradoxical contradiction. As a result, the subject becomes a *node* of the network of the amnion it created through its selfish narcissism. At present, it maintains its dependence upon the amnion through the ubiquitous digital gadgets it always keeps ready-to-hand. The amnion the subject consequently serves is a kind of metaphysical womb (matrix); it keeps the subject just where the ego wants it to be: in an infantile, almost prenatal state of dependence. Infinite debt, taken on recklessly in order to leverage consumption, provides the *capture* necessary to enforce the subject's abdication of its sovereignty.

But the ego needs assistance. It gets it from the vast apparatus of civilization it has erected as a monument to itself. Civilization's laws, languages, customs, traditions, literature, wars, technology, media, food, corporations, government, and history conspire to create the Discourse of the ego's ode to itself. Its great terror is Non-being. It will create *any* illusion, start *any* war, bankrupt *any* economy, oppress *any* people, and exploit *any* resource in its quest for eternal life. In fact, it will even bring about the paradoxical death of the host individual it depends upon, or even itself, in its quest for immortality. To do so, however, it must coerce the organic personality arising from the natural unfolding of the subject's psychological development into abdicating its sovereignty to the assisting apparatus - its master. In so doing, it guards itself against the pernicious influence of what Keats calls the "soul" of the nightingale - the mortal expression of the sublime.

So let us start with the idea of what Keats might mean by "rich." To be rich in *death* is to be rich in a *negative* quality (the apprehension of which he later comes to call "negative capability"). To be rich also implies excess; we could say that the nightingale's song fills the moment with the emptiness of the sublime, rather than the maddening chatter of compulsive thought and civilization's steady and persistent buzz. Putting money aside, we also use the word to refer to a great quantity of something; a farmer could conceivably be rich in manure as well as heads of cattle or land. We also use it to refer to the greater density of something, such as in a *rich* chocolate cake or uranium enrichment. No matter how we have used it historically, we have not used it the way Keats does here: that dying - the loss of the burden of life - could be a form of richness. It is what makes this poem unique. We may long for the anticipated emptiness and oblivion of death the way we long for a lover. But even so, we do not see death as overflowing ripeness and richness the way Keats does in another ode: "To Autumn," which is also a direct address to a deified kind of natural phenomenon (the season). Even in our attempt to describe what he might mean by the word, we find ourselves in poverty. The best recourse, then, is to turn elsewhere in Keats' work to a more literal statement of what he thinks of the sublime.

In a famous letter of 2 December 1818 to Tom and George Keats, he refers to "Negative Capability" which he defines as "when man is capable of being in uncertainties, Mysteries, doubts, without any irritable reaching after fact & reason." Rich in nothing at all. *In negation*. In the absence of something. Nothing in place of something. That nothing and something are interchangeable, and in fact arise by their negation of each other, provides Keats with a kind of crux between life and death - another negation where the signs arise from their polar difference. The poem also seems to presage his death two years later 1821. His mother had died of tuberculosis. He had studied at a medical college at a time when the disease was a common cause of death. He knew the symptoms. A year after writing the poem, he had a hemorrhage in his lungs, a sure indication of the disease's advance. Time is suddenly compressed. Rather than being pushed out of mind (as if Keats were immortal), death is on his mind before his "pen has glean'd [his] teaming brain," as he says in the sonnet "When I have fears that I may cease to be." Impending death, one's own or another's, is the memento mori, debriding the unconscious of its layers of immortal delusion. It is replaced by the *resus sardonicus* of the lean human skull fingered by St. Jerome in early Renaissance paintings. It seems plausible that we can throw the term "sublime" at Keats' experience of the nightingale's song. If so, then how is it associated with pain, death, and ecstasy? For that matter, what does Negative Capability have to do with it?

We associate uncertainties and doubts with unpleasant experiences. To the rational mind the only function of mystery is to be solved like a puzzle or math problem. If it cannot be solved then it must be made to vanish, like the lady assistant in a magic show. As the so-called Age of Science dawned, mystery became a liability. Furthermore, it can be an impediment to the flow of cash, as profit demands a kind of predictable certainty. It is unteachable. It cannot be quantified. It does not get grants. Scientism, the new political religion of pseudo-science, must explain all mysteries in the universe from ghosts to black holes in its role as the guardian of the Sanctum Sanctorum of technology's gadgetry and prestidigitation.

What I mean by Scientism is the prevailing religion of the dogma of industrial production and universal quantification. Its aim is replacement of its chief rival: the Abrahamic (or Semitic) religions. It consists of an integrated system of *notional* dogma unchallenged by the global mass media and propagated by the Fischtean education systems serving the needs of governments and the industries controlling them. It is further combined with consumer- and product-oriented *robotic generation*. In other words, science that either strictly applies to the generation of consumer products, or opens the way for financial speculation in the imaginary (notional) derivatives markets. It has its own Apocalypses, renewed or recast with each credulous generation. We may ascribe this sort of pseudo-science (though it hides behind real science) to the imaginary order of what I call here the *Amniotic Empire*: the collective effect of the notional world in which Scientism resides like a holy relic in a cathedral. The religion of Scientism contrasts with *theoretical science* in a technical sense. Theoretical science meant to identify and probe that which deepens our understanding of the universe, great and small, typically does not produce anything to sell - though it may, indirectly. Though our knowledge of virology and microbiology is vast, applications of this knowledge lag behind every outbreak of disease. Why? Research into psychotropics and biologics has a much bigger payoff in the financial markets than tinkering with viruses - though viruses pervade the world. In poor countries, euphemistically called "developing" even when they are going backward into greater poverty, antivirals and vaccines are notoriously absent, even if they have been around elsewhere for a century. Further research and production to benefit these populations squelches, rather than inflates corporate shares in the financial markets. The Cult of Scientism therefore relegates research scientists involved in pursuing hypotheses lacking a distinct payoff to labs full of graduate students and grant writers. Naturally, there is a middle ground as well where their efforts eventually translate into a breakthrough in a medical product reaching the consumer, as the situation is not one of pure dichotomy - a fact which only obscures Scientism's pernicious effects. Therefore, we may say that theoretical science involved in the quest for the proof of a theorem for the advancement of knowledge alone belongs to the order of the real, or *realia,* in the Amniotic Empire, thus making it a threat to the imaginary order, or *simulacra,* needed for Scientism to be perpetually pulling rabbits out of hats to keep the consumer in thrall to its hegemony.

Scientism's sole concern, even above the verifiable truths it unveils from time to time, is what Keats calls "the irritable reaching after fact and reason." The important word here is the adjective "irritable." It implies that there is another kind of reaching, a *non*-irritable one, which we shall talk about soon enough. At the same time, the priesthood of engaged scientists guards their own mysteries selectively through academic mumbo-jumbo and a notorious love of jargon and needless technical specification. Any scientist - even Nobel Prize winners - who DARE to deconstruct the holy argot for the Common Man funding his research is branded a heretic, a popularizer, a dumber-down of the Mysteries - which are, often enough, not much beyond high school biology and algebra (II). In short, Scientism generates its own dazzling brand of mystical *arcana*. Serving the same function as the Latin Mass in the Roman Catholic Church, this obfuscation also converts the unbeliever who assumes that he is just too stupid to understand the metaphysical physics of the orthodoxy. Critics of pseudo-scientific dogma are ridiculed, belittled, ostracized, denounced, marginalized, and all but burned at the stake. As such, Scientism is the excrescence of all Keats finds "irritable" in the industrial-commercial order as found in his day and that has only enlarged today into the amnion of the hegemony.

Scientific reason is certainly critical where it is needed. It is the glory of our age. We live in a technical Renaissance. As da Vinci presaged, engineering is the new *techne* (τέχνη), the new Art. But as a cultural value institutionalized into an *ad hoc* political and economic religion, it acts as a deadly herbicide upon the feral weeds of the sublime. Scientism's mission is to rid the world of its foolish notions. It must dispel all mystery, quantify the unquantifiable, reduce everything organic to data and code, and establish a *novus ordo seclorum* (a "new order of the ages") based on coercive *consensus* rather than verification. Its ethical aesthetic is sold to a consumer through cheap digital gadgets the function of which is to get him to become dependent upon usurious monthly payments for a proprietary network. Aristotle's observation that nature abhors a vacuum may be amended to read that in the age of Scientism verification abhors a mystery, for it is the absence of the ego of man. It is as if the credo of modern man were "where there is no ego, there is no Being," a proposition which cannot be. Nothing has its own *thingness* except in as much as this thingness has been imparted to it by the ego of man as God inspired Adam with breath. The very idea that anything – a Grecian urn, a nightingale, or autumn itself – would have Being apart from man's ego is declared heresy, Deism, superstition. For what man has accomplished in killing God off with Scientism is that he has become God himself, which was the plan anyway. Under the guise of dispelling the superstition of god-religions, man has instead prosecuted the ego's ultimate desire against the metaphysical gods; the ego's ultimate desire is to become God Himself, with no other gods (even God) before it. And in the most ingenious propaganda mechanism of all time, the ego has set up a system whereby any critic of its regime is denounced by society as a troglodyte from the dark caves of atavistic superstition. But putting it this way endows the whole sordid business with more dignity than it deserves. It makes it seem as if this were some great ontological or philosophical upheaval, when it fact it is entirely motivated by profit excreted by robotic production; the resulting excrescence is then gambled in the casino of the financial system fueling the hegemony's power structure and robbing the peon of the economic value of his labor.

We live in the age of science, an age that never existed before. As such, it is a culture with all of the attributes such as a language (Latin, computer languages, mathematics, chemical formulas, the genome), music, food, costumes, customs, beliefs, social organization, and most of all a political-economic *religion*. Science's benefits and miracles aside, its sophistication, depth, and sublimity are not matched today by any other art in the sense of *techne*. Some of the deep (deepest?) phenomena of the universe hidden for all of the ages of mankind are now available to every school kid online. (Whether they look for it or not is another matter.) This is not the age of painting, opera, or the great novel. This is not the age of Beauty. There is no Rembrandt, Shakespeare, Bach, Wagner, or Dostoevsky. But there has been most recently the sublime Einstein, Planck, Turing, von Neumann, and Schrödinger. Furthermore, it is an age of collaborative invention, partly because of the unprecedented complexity of technology and partly because of the advent of corporate culture which rules the earth through its a-geographical city states funded by volatile public markets based on debt. The generative power of this massive system of robotic production is unprecedented and, ultimately, awesome. But not sublime. Being more than *techne*, though, science is a culture while also being integrated into the greater technological cultures of the hegemonic states. It is a kind of Mithraic Cult of Hope within the greater cults of national and global cultures. There is no culture without religion to unite the flock in awe of what it does not understand, reassure its members that they are in the hands of a beneficent higher power, and, in this case, maintain faith in the consumer market for gadgets and gizmos. Most of all, though, a religion must give its flock Hope. Scientism is a *hope cult* like the Semitic (Abrahamic) religions it is modeled after and that it vigorously seeks to supplant with its egotism.

Vilem Flusser, in *Vampiroteuthis Infernalis*, describes Scientism (with a little "s") as a displacement of traditional religion. He seems to think that it was a passing perversion of what science is and can be. If he had lived into the 21st Century he would have seen that Scientism as he understood it was just the nascent alpha test of what would become the Zeitgeist beta test, building strength for its battle with the Spiritus Mundi over what mankind would accept as reality. The example he cites is the role of Scientism in the debate over the competing models of inheritance between Lamarck and Mendel (though Flusser prefers to use Darwin in place of Mendel).

> The "scientific" basis of such feuds obviously does not come from science in the strict sense of the term, but from that vulgar science called "Scientism", which in the [Nineteenth] and [Twentieth] centuries substituted for the religious dogma of previous centuries. (p. 61)

He differentiates Scientism from "science itself," which we may consider similar to what American philosopher Charles Sanders Peirce (1839-1914) describes as "knowledge gained by … full consciousness of making an investigation ..." (p. 248). What it is not, he says, is "knowledge gained by instinctive processes and not deliberately ..." The prestidigitation of science's miracles, however, blurs the distinction between Scientism and science itself, as well as between knowledge from instinctive processes and deliberate investigation. It is, instead, predicated upon *possibility* (*Moglichkeit,* in the sense of *latent* potential) of data retention on an unlimited scale, even into artificial DNA structures. Science has found that a phenomenon can be encoded in one way or another, even if the process results in a *reductio ad absurdum* of the nature and spirit of that phenomenon; it is thus transcribed into *simulacra* rather than retaining its basis in realia. Big Data, big enough to have its own gravitational force, demands infinite storage media. The highest good become *more,* driven by infinite progress. What is therefore created, epistemologically, is the dogma and doctrine of the *knowing-more,* rather than Peirce's *getting-to-know,* which is a process only. It is not cumulative, but always set at 0 (null). Like the received information of the *knowing-of,* or the mere knowledge of something without understanding, the *knowing-more* is the *ethical aesthetic* of Scientism … *sans entendement.* (We will say more about this ethical aesthetic below.) The *knowing-of* (as noun or verb depending upon context) is the preserved excrescence of *knowing* (always a verb) called information or data. *Getting-to-know,* as a verb, is the process of *knowing,* whereas *knowing* is the action of the *getting-to-know* (as a noun). All knowing passes, at some point, into the *knowing-of,* where it becomes information. The difference between information and knowledge is that information is the quantitative form and knowledge is the qualitative form of the excrescence of the *getting-to-know.*

"Knowledge, once possessed by individuals, is now the property of corporations," says Hacking in *Why Does Language Matter to Philosophy*? (p. 184). This characterization reflects the transfer of ownership from the process of getting-to-know to the static state of the knowing-of. What changes? For one thing, the former is a process and the latter a "state." Nevertheless, both require a certain amount of *storage*. The saying "his mind is a sieve" refers to someone who observes, experiences, and thinks, but retains nothing. (If a thought falls in the mind and there is no memory to retain it, did it fall?) Phenomenology aside, storage - whatever its location - requires time, energy, effort, and even money. As the brain (and perhaps other parts of the body) has had untold eons to develop quick, cheap, easy storage, Civilization has been struggling with this problem on the most primitive levels for ages. Rote memorization. Sumerian clay tablets. Egyptian hieroglyphs and papyrus. The Rosetta Stone. Dead Sea Scrolls. Norse runes. Illuminated manuscripts. Highly inflammable Alexandrian libraries. Moldy books. Fragile hard drives. Accidental mass erasures of data. Hacking. Sabotage. Power failures. Data formats no longer supported. Data rot. The irony being that it was one of the earliest: clay tablets, that seem to have won the distinction of being the most durable record of socially-significant information, from state records and history to medicine and science. There are millions of such tablets left behind by the Sumerian and Akkadian civilizations, many still buried in the sands of Mesopotamia.

Today the clay tablets are the vast and redundant silos of data maintained by the wealthiest and most powerful corporations, though far more fragile. Moreover, such organizations are the corporate overlords of national governments through their importance to the economy and infrastructure – the measure of all political success today. Citing Karl Popper (*Objective Knowledge: An Evolutionary Approach*), Ian Hacking describes Popper's "epistemology without a subject" which Popper calls "objective knowledge" for short. He divides knowledge itself into three tiers which he terms Worlds 1, 2, and 3. The first is a form of "being known" which might be called the object of knowledge: *the physical world*, but not objective knowledge. The second is the world of our conscious experience which includes *thoughts and observations* and could be called subjective knowledge. The third, however, is true objective knowledge in that it treats 1 and 2 as objects by serving as a repository for what is *known of* them. In itself, however, what Popper calls the "world 3" of epistemology is not a form of knowing or *what-can-be-known*. It is what *is* known at any given time *X*. It does not matter if quantity *Y* expands or contracts. All that does matter is the aggregate quantification of what-is-known at time *X*. Popper specifically describes this knowledge as "theories published in journals and books and stored in libraries; discussions of such theories; and so on" (qtd. In Hacking, p. 184). For Popper, says Hacking, epistemology is "the ways in which world 1 and world 3 interact" (p. 185).

What makes objective knowledge categorically different from any other form of knowledge is that it is exchangeable. As such, it is a form of wealth. While it may be argued whether or not this characterizes what we call the Information Age, we know that it is the age where information has become the most valuable commodity. It may be traded the way corn was traded in 1850 in the Corn Exchange at Manchester, England. And unlike other commodities, it rarely loses its value. Being entirely abstract, it is not put up where, as it says in Matthew 6:19, "moth and rust doth corrupt," though it is uniquely susceptible to being put up "where thieves break through and steal" (but that is only because it seems to retain its value no matter who absconds with it). Also unlike other commodities, it would not have been stored if it were not inherently valuable. And it would not *be* stored for long if it did not *hold* that value. Data mining the riches of biologic, demographic, and psycho-graphic information pouring in from billions of telemetry channels is the umbilicus of the amnion. There are dozens of telemetry channels on the average cell phone constantly transmitting details of the user's habits while it is interacting with its gadget. When crude oil loses its value, one cannot delete it. And its very presence as a devalued commodity contributes to its depression in the form of unwanted overabundance. But when information becomes overabundant, redundant, or obsolete, deleting it *adds* value to the remaining information. In this way information is a unique commodity perfectly suitable to a culture that values the virtual (simulacra) over the real (realia). Moreover, such a culture soon comes to understand that the real, in its unholy alliance with the sublime, is a liability to its insatiable progress toward some undefined future which never comes because it must remain in the future to be valuable, like the notional value of derivatives. Information as Hacking's "property of corporations" is far more portable than diamonds or rubies. Much of the information valuable at time *X* could be stored in a satellite the size of a basketball, a briefcase, or spread out into thousands of redundant data centers near and far. The real, the sublime, even in the form of real estate, is subject to the vicissitudes of war, regime change, natural disaster, and the fleeting whims of public fashion. And of course moths and rust doth corrupt it. "World 3 is a product of mankind, and most of our corporate products of a more physical sort could not be fabricated without the third world" (Hacking, p. 185). Were this not so, universities – those shrines, citadels, and cathedrals of the virtual knowing-of - would not exist.

1.1: Overlords, hegemony, and the Imaginary (fasces)

So then what do we call this hegemony of information? It must have a cheerleader, priesthood, followers, and a police force. As Flusser remarks above, it is a religion. And that religion is called Scientism. But it is more than just the new a faith on the block. It is a *Cult*. As such it is less ecumenical and more fanatical than the Semitic religions it hopes to supplant. In all its ermine splendor, this Cult promotes the *knowing-of* while masquerading as the sacred process of the *getting-to-know*. When the basis of a civilization is the accumulation of information through the knowing-of rather than the pursuit of knowledge through the getting-to-know, the psyche of the subject becomes overwhelmed with a quantitative evaluation of reality. Reality, however, refuses to be *merely* quantified (except in the case of a quantum being the least quantity of radiation detectable in an imaginary perfect black body). The price of this orientation is the sacrifice of the qualitative appreciation of society and the world of things and phenomena. Reality loses the qualities of what Heidegger calls *thingness*. Seeing is believing becomes the subject's credo when the sign (*imago*) of a thing becomes *more real* than the thing itself. The term "Imaginary" refers to the *mode* of the hegemony's amnion in which it provides the *accoutrements* of the ethical aesthetic of *Genuss*: comfort and convenience on the part of the subject and expedience for the hegemony. "Amnion" refers to the matrix (womb) the subject sought in its exchange of sovereignty (and consequently the sublime) for comfort and convenience. Rather than undertake the journey from the womb to self-determination - its only path to *jouissance* - the subject abdicates this imperative in favor of a return to what it perceives, emotionally, as its amniosis. The amnion may also be described as that from which nothing is born, only aborted. Once having abdicated, regaining the throne of sovereignty is a violent affair. The amniotic matrix's psycholinguistics consists of the consumer discourse which replaces the subject's abdicated identity. It also includes the discourses of the Cult of Scientism and the *monad* of Big Data, which serve to support the consumer discourse. An umbilicus of networks keeps the subject fed with a dreamlike pablum of the imaginary and symbolic.

The discursive mode of the Imaginary is that the *imago* is "more real" than the real of bare life. When the subject abdicates, thingness vanishes in the vapor of its primal identity. The discourse of the hegemony and the Imaginary are both imperatives: abdicate and consume. Together they form the mighty algorithm of the unified discourse of the ethical aesthetic of Scientism: Abdicate, Consume, Repeat. What joins abdicating with consuming is the promissory note; in *borrowing* to consume the subject abdicates. The political process – whatever it may be – must needs mirror the economic enslavement through debt. V.I. Lenin said it rather succinctly: "The oppressed are allowed once every few years to decide which ... members of the oppressing class are to represent and repress them." ("The State and Revolution," Chapter 5, 1917). Unlike abdication of a king, though, this ritual must be repeated through infinite iterations of the algorithm. The engine of this algorithm is the ethical aesthetic of Scientism uniting the hegemony and Imaginary: expediency. What is ultimately inexpedient for the hegemony is to cast the subject aside or worse, throw him into the teeth of some contrived war. Such malign neglect is a common method of ensuring that the hegemony maintains the state of exception with or without suffrage.

When thingness vanishes, so too does the meaning of abstract ideas and the objective sovereignty of the corporeal. In the subject's abdication things lose their property of sovereign existence. Consequently, they are then subject to exploitation by the subject's, and the state's, narcissistic solipsism. Kai Hammermeister, in *The German Aesthetic Tradition,* elucidates Heidegger's use of the term *thingness* and how it applies to his aesthetics. Thingness is the *a priori* of our experience of the objective world, the reverse of the Imaginary's a posteriori:

> A thing [usually is] defined as the sum of all its properties that we can perceive, that is, see, hear, smell, taste, or touch. Yet Heidegger argues that this notion is *counterintuitive* .... Rather, to separate sensual perception from the perceived object, we must distance ourselves from our quotidian experience. Such insight is always the result of an abstraction. The fact is, then, that the *things themselves are closer to us than our perceptions. The thingness of a thing precedes the conscious perception of its sensual properties.* [italics added] (p. 176)

Why does the Imaginary strive to strip thingness from the world of things? In the quest for priority over the psyche of the subject, the Imaginary's chief competitor is the Real. If it can suppress the "counterintuitive" apprehension of the Object as a transcendental entity preceding perception then it will succeed in usurping the subject's sense of *being-in-the-world.* To "be" in the world one must have *some* relationship with the Real. To dwell entirely in the Imaginary, which is in fact not possible, abstracts one from the abstraction of the thingness of things. A thing and the Other become abstractions of abstractions when the subject regards the sign of itself as the world rather than the thingness and otherness of the living world and others.

Conversely, the subject in bare life dwells in the Real. Why? Because it is able to abstract itself from what Heidegger calls the "quotidian" or everyday life of one who believes what he sees. This stepping-back is necessary to suspend the ego's projection of itself onto the objective reality of the world. While this is not a direct denial of the empirical, it is a mode which allows one to acknowledge through action the *a priori* thingness of everything. People, cats, dogs, and even cows appreciate a person who regards them as entirely separate and sovereign entities with their own thingness - something they intuitively perceive, as they cannot but exist in the sublime of the Real. Dwelling in the Real, the subject contends with bare life. In so doing it is at all times threatened with the terrible majesty of the fathomless sublime. The Imaginary lurks on the sidelines of the subject's drama, ready to offer the consolations of comfort and convenience to soothe agitation, irritability, and bother of actually living life.

Why would anyone prefer the Law of the Jungle and Natural Law - which can be nasty and brutish - over the *luxury* of the Imaginary's air-conditioned amnion? In the Imaginary, however, the subject is perpetually dying "unto death," in the sense meant by Kierkegaard, of the sickness of its misprision of exchanging simulacra for realia in the ritual of its abdication through the signing of promissory notes. In the Imaginary, the subject is perpetually living *unto death* while regarding itself as medically (not spiritually) immortal. Those who prefer the bare life of the Real, despite its rigors, do find their reward in the sublime of not only the biological imperative, but in freedom from capture by the hegemony. Despite the glory of living in the sublime, it is not teleological but ontological. It has no purpose, no goal, no plan, and most of all, no future. Whatever meaning one can hope for in bare life comes through a simple formula: Life consists of problems and difficulties. Meaning is a matter of solving and overcoming problems and difficulties. Meaning is not static, which is why so few can honestly state that their life has any meaning besides being consumers. But the process of solving problems and overcoming difficulties, come as they may, is only possible through the intense mechanism of *curiosity*. It must be interesting, if not fascinating, to do so. It is something Einstein referred to as *Gedankenexperiment* - a special kind of thinking.

Otherwise, it is suffering, mere necessity, and perpetual drudgery. The Imaginary's proposition is this: "Imagine a world where all problems and difficulties are solved by the marketplace and the state through robotic production, narcotic consumption, and fiat. One need not lift a finger. You do not even have to think about it, for it is automatic and autonomic. The promise of eternal comfort and convenience (*Genuss*) are yours, if only you are willing to sign this promissory note. Abdicate. Consume. Repeat."

What the subject fears the most is what it has heard about the Law of the Jungle. It knows that primitive peoples live under its atavistic yolk, something civilization had sloughed off like a snake skin long ago. The *far-off other*, the "robot" who produces the Apex Consumer's electronica and other products, is only one click beyond the tribal native or displaced migrant living without electricity (1.2 billion in 2020) in the ordeal of Evolution. And the nearby Underclass in the subject's own state are the result of the importation of these same primitives and far-off others into the amniotic paradise of the hegemony where they just do not fit. They are denied access to the amnion because they refuse to grow up into the wonders civilization has bestowed upon those willing to abide by its nomos and prerogatives. The Underclass stubbornly resists the current of Evolution. The good citizen never thinks that the highly-evolved bipeds he calls its friends, family, neighbors, coworkers, and fellow citizens, under the right conditions, would tear him limb for limb for a crust of bread. The subject never considers that the state it supports as the Law Giver and Father perpetrates the greatest barbarisms ever known, quantitatively and qualitatively, on the subject's behalf in the territories of the far-off others and primitives. Finally, the subject condescends to become the institutional benefactor of the Underclass of Unfortunates and Less Fortunates, despite their barbaric behavior toward each other and sometimes his cohorts, by throwing unstable and stupefying social services at them instead of giving them equal access to the amnion. They are too much of a financial risk even for the hegemony and are therefore denied access to the loans and certificates needed to participate as full members of the amnion. Furthermore, this class is also denied access to an environment nurturing greater achievement and evolutionary development. They are seen as pitiful throwbacks to a barbarous age. They are always in need of the Apex Consumer's condescension, as barbarians not *at* the gates but *within* them. The subject shrugs its shoulder, pointing to psychometrics, birthrates among the unwed, substandard speech, crime and school drop-out rates, and what it sees as reprehensible vulgarities indigenous to the recalcitrant Unfortunate. Then, it clambers for the commandeering of its tax money to fund public assistance programs in lieu of granting the Underclass equality as members of the amnion. But is this to the detriment, or benefit of the Underclass? I cannot answer this question, as I was born into the amnion to a race of Apex Consumers.

What the subject is blind to is that the Law of the Jungle has not gone away; it has been *transited* (meaning "symbolically moved") to a more sophisticated level of supposed Darwinian and Spencerian natural selection and survival of what the hegemony of the amnion has deemed, by fiat, are the fittest. Aware but not conscious, the subject moves in darkness - but moves nonetheless, doing things, changing things, and making decisions affecting the lives of everyone in the social or national cohort - even beyond that into the far-off territories of the robotic producers. The hegemony's proxy wars, and the Imaginary's empire of vicarious thrills, are meant to serve as distractions from, or displacement substitutes for, the id's frustrated desires. Bereft of psychoanalysis and therefore living the unexamined life, and fed with a constant stream of its own narcissistic reflection through telemetry, the subject dwells in a fatal realm of the Unreal it believes is the portal to immortality. The id's symbolic communication with the ego, rather than being brought to the light of consciousness and direct action, is instead exploited for votes and cash, drown in alcohol, drugged, pornographied, and worked to death to pay off the promissory notes it signed - which is simply not possible.

Civilization based on the (lately) much-touted rule of law nevertheless makes the same demand for problem solving and overcoming difficulties to achieve meaning as the Law of the Jungle. The idealized world of the subject is its own jungle of jealousies, competition, subterfuge, and cruelty, but without meaning, curiosity, interest, and fascination. In their place is the compulsive lust for *more and more and more and more and more* of ... whatever. The significant difference is that its teleological goals are vicarious, which is what makes them imaginary; they are Lacan's *l'objet petit a*. When the subject achieves them, it finds the house empty, the car out of gas, the career unfulfilling, and social life fake, the government corrupt, the currency worthless, the retirement account bankrupt, the spouse a stranger, the children self-centered, and the ultimate destination of its life filled with toxic medication and life-support systems. Civilization, created as the answer to the Law of the Jungle, demands the subject accept it as the Law of the Concrete Jungle - only now it is called the "rule of law" (nomos) fabricated to capture the subject's labor and wealth and nothing more. The subject, ever impressed by concrete edifices, understands civilization as bastions of office tower blocks, highways, factories, police, bank accounts, loans, hospitals, busy airports, universities, apartment buildings, suburban houses, and frenzied crowds scurrying to and fro without any discernible purpose. The Law of the Jungle that civilization's nomos was meant to replace remains hidden in the crimes and wars of the hegemony. The meaning the subject could have gotten out of the struggle for survival in bare life through solving problems and overcoming difficulties itself, is displaced by the harvesting of its time and energy by working for the government to pay taxes and slaving away at meaningless jobs to pay off its loans.

Regardless, bare life is a powerful enticement for certain types of persons. There are those who come to it naturally by tapping into a vein of sovereignty running through the global refugee camp. There are others, however, who only know bare life because they were born into it with no escape or have been thrown into it like Christians to the lions. These three groups constitute the hegemony's perpetual problem. Sometimes they even attack the hegemony with pitchforks, rakes, homemade bombs, and guillotines. After a relatively brief period of the rebels' Pyrrhic victory, though, the hegemony returns with the swiftness and power of the tide to quash the rebellion. That which is needed to subvert the order of the nomos – a cryptic, covert, evolutionary subversion of the hegemony and its amnion – is always in the background, threatening to blow up the whole damn thing. Some of these agents are called terrorists. Some of them who *appear* to be terrorists, or who claim to be, are instead working covertly not for the overthrow of the nomos, but to create an atmosphere of social and economic chaos so that the nomos can tighten its grip on the polis. The ever-present advantage for those who "prefer not to," as Bartleby insisted, is that the hegemony, dependent upon illusion and vicarious existence, has no substance in and of itself. The amnion of the Imaginary depends upon vicarious palliation of the id's instinctive needs. Sure it has guns and bombs, money and political power. But it has now become axiomatic that a bunch of domestic guerrilla fighters in rags with no money or technology can fight superpowers indefinitely, just as Germanic tribesman slaughtered Publius Quinctilius Varus & three Roman legions in the Battle of the Teutoburg Forest in 9 CE. Action by proxy and vicarious experience have no substance in the sense of the thingness of the transcendental object – which is all there is. In the amnion there is no *thingness* of the thing and *otherness* of the Other. All is one big mirror of the subject's ego, represented by his ever-present digital gadget. When the subject apprehends thingness and the Other as the transcendental object, it exists in the bare life of the sublime and not the amnion of the Imaginary. Without capture of the subject's psychic energy, the amnion shrinks into a vulnerable state, like a deflating hot-air balloon, where it then plunges into the abyss of the sublime from which it issued in the first place. The hegemony's seemingly endless supply of the subject's time and labor, once it is converted into reckless financial bullying, eventually dries up through entropic exhaustion. There is hardly anything more real than the Second Law of thermodynamics.

The only possibility of the subject's release from capture is if it, through some accident or other, can *abdicate its abdication* or, as Hegel puts it, *negate its negation*. If that is even possible, particularly by accident, it is then inevitably followed by an almost irresistible desire to crawl back into the womb-like matrix of the amnion. In other words, it is not a hardened state. It is by nature friable; it requires a certain discipline and allegiance to self-determination lacking in the captive subject that must be learned or relearned. To the subject any alternative to servitude looks like a plunge into the Underclass of the Unfortunates and the less Fortunates who through no desire of their own must face the reality of reality. The subject believes that such a life is only fit for the far-off other slaving away in its atavistic hell hole to produce the consumer goods which keep the subject enthralled with the amnion. Overcoming difficulties and solving problems is something one does at work for money to pay debts, not as the basis of a meaningful life. At work, difficulties and problems are met with mediocrity, creating an even bigger morass of futile dithering. Though difficulties and problems abound and multiply nicely on their own, the subject's lack of analytical ability and fundamental consciousness impede attempts to make things better. As a result, the subject makes itself - and others - miserable. Regardless, there are gizmos, gadgets, drugs, entertainment, alcohol, junk food, cars, cigarettes, consumption, and a steady drip of propaganda to help ease the pain of a life without intrinsic meaning. Consequently, the subject's frustrated id sets up a sense of chronic ennui over its perpetually unfulfilled desires. The ominous *objet petit a* becomes a malign dybbuk possessing what is left of the subject's individuality and self-determination, driving it relentlessly toward self-destruction in the maelstrom of the consumer-driven economy.

1.2: Conscious and unconscious awareness

To apprehend the thingness of a thing the subject must embody the mineness (*Jemeinigheit*) of individual sovereignty. There is no "I" and "Thou" if there is no "I." Transcending the I-Thou duality, therefore, is a matter of first having an "I" to transcend. Once the subject abdicates its sovereignty to the hegemony through the agency of the Imaginary, it becomes impossible for the subject to apprehend the thingness of things or the objective reality of the Other. Meantime, the sublime insists upon the vectors of quantity and quality intersecting at the point of consciousness so that they may be understood as the unified fields of reality. Perception of quantity or quality alone is a form of awareness, not consciousness, just as the perception of the velocity or location of a sub-atomic particle alone is a form of data, not understanding of its complex nature as a superimposition of states.

But what is the qualitative difference between *awareness* and *consciousness*? The latter word is thrown around quite a bit meaning this or that depending upon context. For example, when we say of a person who has passed out, "He has lost consciousness" what we mean is rather vague. In movies the doctor says, "What is your name?" If the patient gives the correct name, he is "conscious." Is that all there is to it? At the other extreme is the neurobiologist's search for the part (or parts) of the brain responsible for "consciousness." The basic assumption of this quixotic search, however, is rather like what Catholic nuns sometimes taught in the golden age of Catechism: that the soul is in a little white sack just to the right of the heart muscle. In between these extremes we have the ideas of spiritual and psychological consciousness. In the first, this ineffable principle is used as meaning either "consciousness of God" or of a state of Enlightenment where one is aware that one is aware. Usually they are divided between the traditions of the West and the East respectively. In the second, there are some subtle gradations of what is meant by one psychologist or another. We could say, though, that psychology has had more to say about the *unconscious* than the conscious. In fact, even using "the conscious" as a suitable antonym for "the unconscious" (or subconscious) seems awkward because it is seldom used as such. The definite article is often only appended to "unconscious." The closest we come in the historical terminology of psychology is "the preconscious." Is this because to say what consciousness is *not* is easier than saying what it *is*? It is curious and perhaps a comment on the nature of consciousness that we will find the word *conscious* used far more as an adjective than a noun. The antonym of "the unconscious," therefore, is often "the conscious mind." We rarely hear "the unconscious mind." One reason is that it seems that the "unconscious" is not considered a "mind"! This is interesting because few would disagree (even neurobiologists) that what is *unconscious* comprises most of what we call "the mind." But historically the unconscious has been seen as a dumb beast. In it the "instincts" lie, dormant, forsaken, brooding over their rejection by the brilliant and civilized Conscious Mind. So we basically have three forms of the root of this word as consciousness (noun meaning a state of mind), the conscious mind (an adjective), and the conscious (noun), which is seldom used compared to the unconscious.

The subtleties grow when we consider the *absence* of consciousness in the form of the unconscious or subconscious. Even these two words have slightly different meanings we could apply to different psychological phenomena. Just as there seems to be a variety of types of consciousness, there is indeed a variety of types of *unconsciousness*. For example, Jung's concept of the collective unconscious has radical implications for the idea that consciousness is a manifestation of our individuality. It depends upon either the notion that somehow our genes pass on structured, meaningful, mandala-like images that connect us on some unconscious level. Such notions Freud found difficult to accept of Jung's theoretical schemata. Freud, though, came to appreciate the role in human consciousness of an oceanic feeling first brought to his attention in a letter from his friend Romain Rolland in 1927. In *Future of an Illusion* (1927) Freud argues that what we know as religion in the form of organized cults with distinct identities is based on the illusion of a world suiting the prerogatives of a particular sect. Rolland insists that although this may be true, there is an emotional side to religion millions share. It gives them a feeling of eternity, inspiring the useful belief that there is more to existence in the universe than working, procreating, eating, filling privies, and dying. Freud could hardly deny the possibility of some form of eternity. We might also call the feeling Rolland describes as a perception of the sublime. Considering Freud's reaction to Jung's concept, though, we can see that he was willing to admit that people do have this feeling, but not ready to assign it to a particular position in the functioning of the psyche.

He takes up the idea with some vigor in *Civilization and Its Discontents* (1929). Picking up on an idea from *Future of an*

Illusion, Freud equates religion with civilization. In the 1920's in Europe religion still had a significant grip on the consciousness of the population and the hegemony, despite the "*Gott ist tot*" theology which came out of World War I. So it is natural that he would make this association. Today he would have to revise that estimate, but only by replacing Semitic religion with Scientism. Deep in the "unconscious" of the world wars - if we can think about them for a moment as *beings* - was a battle of the Titans between Religion and Science for the hearts and minds of men. In this epic Titanomachy, Religion takes the part of the Titans and Science the Olympians. So there is nothing irrelevant about Freud's observations today except that there is a new crew running the game of civilization. The enormous transformation of technology which took place, from computers to nuclear weapons, assured the subject that science had Big Magic. By contrast, the doddering Domini of religion looked pathetic, even tragic. The slaughter of this Semite by that Semite, then that one by this one, pressed the point. The subject decided to put its bet on what looked like the faster horse: technology, which is not the same thing as science itself. In so doing the oceanic feeling of religion was lost despite the canard of network connectivity as socialization. Even machines do not take well to it. Eternity has been replaced by the enervation of the relentless buzz of personal technology aimed at the grossest parts of the brain. What was lost, then, in the rapid ascendancy of techno-Scientism? Referring to the Rolland letter, Freud in *Civilization and its Discontents* implies that that this feeling is a significant and mysterious element of the religious experience by acknowledging that it is likely what religion exploits in its own special assault on personal sovereignty:

> It is a feeling which he would like to call a sensation of "eternity", a feeling as of something limitless, unbounded - as it were, "oceanic". This feeling, he adds, is a purely subjective fact, not an article of faith; it brings with it no assurance of personal immortality, but it is the source of the religious energy which is seized upon by the various Churches and religious systems, directed by them into particular channels, and doubtless also exhausted by them. One may, he thinks, rightly call oneself religious on the ground of this oceanic feeling alone, even if one rejects every belief and every illusion. (p. 4464)

This feeling, then, can be separated from the apparatus of

religion but often is what attracts people to its apparatus. Why is one attracted to that which seeks to extinguish one's ability to be at one with God and the sublime? Freud certainly gives this question a good going over in his observations about the nature of civilization and what makes us discontent while in its grip. Submitting to the apparatus of civilization is as if we were birds caged into captivity where we are guaranteed all the birdseed we desire and therefore no longer need to fly. We are, alas, creatures relentlessly seeking out the bird-seed Apparatus. Our conscious effort to form families, groups, cults, clubs, societies, neighborhoods, organizations, and the contrived communities of social media belie our nature as creatures of the Cult. Just as language is an excrescence of civilization so too are the other signs and symbols we form to provide the mass of humanity with a sense of belonging to something other than the biological imperative to procreate.

All cults have emblems. These emblems can be seen as archetypes such as the Crucifix, the Nazi swastika, or more recently the logos of the corporations which provide online products people use in place of relationships. Language and our sense of identity cobbled together by this mass of signals forms the apparatus of civilization. Therefore, it is not apart from us, imposed from above (or from *behind* in the form of history). It requires our voluntary abdication of sovereignty to provide us with the benefits (birdseed) we seek. If we then look at the form and content of our thought we see that it too is constructed from the detritus of the apparatuses we submit to in our relentless search for belonging. And since we often associate consciousness with thought, we can see that what is generally meant by the idea of consciousness is really the bric-à-brac of civilization's discontents put into some kind of autonomous Other. For the Titans the Other was God the Father. For the Olympians it was Earth the Mother. One of the innovations of the Olympians over the Titans was that there was less emphasis on the *personification* and *anthropomorphization* of objective phenomena and values, and more on the values they represented to mortals, thus laying the groundwork for Christianity's saints.

Also, there is a dramatic shift from the *patriarchal* symbolic of the wrathful, authoritative Father to the *matriarchal* symbolic of the weak, wounded, but all-good-and-loving Mother. Capitalism (the Father) attacks the Environment (the Mother) through its Dark Satanic Mills and its maniacal search for plunder and booty. This rape of the world by the Father succeeds in vilifying the Titans of the Old Order. It is a bit of effective propaganda by the Olympians of Scientism in the temples of academe to hold on to their ascendancy to the throne – especially because it is not without truth, like all effective propaganda. The irony is that it is *Scientism itself* which makes it possible for capitalism to destroy the environment, enslave masses of people, control the population through surveillance, benumb the brain through enervating electronic distraction, isolate relationships into online chat groups, murder far-off others considered the enemy with proximal impunity, hook millions on drugs they do not need, make people obese with junk food and cars, and create wealth out of nothing by adding zeros to a number on a bank keyboard inevitably leading to the collapse of economies. And yet Scientism is seen by the masses as a benevolent Matriarchy (of mostly men) whose sole purpose is to wipe out hunger, bring medicine to the poor, make us smarter, help us get closer to our friends and family, give us a better education, make our cities more livable and beautiful, turn industry green through clever gadgets that make pollution go away, stamp out bad genes in our genome, protect us from our enemies, make energy renewable, increase comfort and convenience, and most of all save Mother (Goose) Earth from the bad, evil, wicked capitalists whose sole purpose is to create a Plutocracy of the Damned. If we scrape all of this fairy tale together and form it into a dense ball of stupidity, we have the misnomer of *consciousness* in the sense that it is used in civilization today.

The point is that when we talk about consciousness we also talk about a constellation of concepts which are fraught with contradictions and contraindications. Freud, apparently, was not happy with his friend and colleague Jung's idea that there is some metaphysical unconscious we all share. Nevertheless, he was willing to admit that we get something mysterious out of religion for which psychology cannot entirely account. But the most he could say about it is that he did not share this feeling, but he recognized that it is an important feeling to others which he cannot dismiss. And it is at this point where we might see the limitation of the scope of his thinking in *Civilization*. He does not account for the role of this oceanic feeling in consciousness. What he says above shows that he knows others are "conscious" of this feeling, but he does not go further into an investigation of what effect such a feeling would have on consciousness itself. Freud is honest about his limitations when he says, "Let me admit once more that it is very difficult for me to work with these almost intangible quantities." We can see in this statement that Jung's increasing desire to work without limitation in the realm of "intangible quantities" (which is what makes his work so compelling) was anathema to Freud's method as well as the ethos of his scientific work. As a result, though, he dismissed Rolland's more enthusiastic interpretation of the feeling by assigning it to an infantile impulse.

> Thus we are perfectly willing to acknowledge that the "oceanic" feeling exists in many people, and we are inclined to trace it back to an early phase of ego-feeling. The further question [is] what claim this feeling has, to be regarded as the source of religious needs ...

Could it be possible that the oceanic feeling does not necessarily refer to only one phenomenon? Could it be that perhaps Rolland and Freud were talking about different things while both being correct? The answer is yes. First of all, there is nothing mutually exclusive about the two views of the matter. There is just a kind of understandable misunderstanding - common when talking about intangible quantities as we feel our way into new territory. It seems unlikely that a person would be inspired to the levels of religious ecstasy recorded by the saints if the feeling were based only upon "an early phase of ego feeling." It seems improbable that in 1429 the teenager Joan of Arc would lead the army of Charles of Valois to victory over the English and Burgundians were she merely motivated by a desire to disclaim "the danger which the ego recognizes as threatening it from the external World." Her action seemed to be an all-around risky proposition, for which she paid the price.

Adler, in an unpublished manuscript "Childhood Remembrances and Lifestyle," gives a possible explanation. He says that there are many forms of consciousness that are not necessarily opposed to each other. And, consistent with his ideas, the purpose of each of them is to unite with what is unconscious to achieve what we desire the most. If that is conquering the Burgundians, so be it. If it is finding spiritual meaning and feeling in Religion, pagan or otherwise, then who is to say that this is not a conscious effort but is motivated only by neurotic regression to an infantile state?

> Undoubtedly very different forms of consciousness do exist ... but we regard them not as antithetical but only as variants. We do not find consciousness as opposed to unconscious to exist. We find ever the same movement-line; we find all the affects and actions, whether springing from the conscious or the unconscious, always seeking to attain one aim.

But this is also not to dismiss the more likely possibility that desire for a relationship with God the Father, in the case of the average worshiper, is at best a comforting return to inherent feelings of safety from the sting of death and threats of harm ingrained in the subconscious since infancy. In this mode the worshiper looks for *consolation* from religion for the bare life of reality. While scripture takes a rather harsh line on such consolation, the apparatuses of the religious Dominae manufacture a fantasy word of the Imaginary in which the subject may step through the Vale of Tears with relative ease. To say that there is more to the religious feeling than Freud accounts for is not to say that he is wrong. Even Rolland in his letters agrees with Freud regarding the illusion of religion. He is just trying to say there is more to it. So then what more is there?

The sublime as the horror vacui is not popular. It is rare to find anyone willing to rush out and meet it on what Matthew Arnold in his poem "Dover Beach" calls the "darkling plain" of objective reality. It is not what is sold to the consumer except as a safe video game. Instead, the consumer buys every possible means of *avoiding* the sublime which it sees as the horror vacui of bare life, the wretched Underclass, and death. Take your average Master of the Universe from a private equity firm in an office tower and drop him into the Amazon rain forest with nothing but his bespoke suit, wingtips, keys to his Porsche, and no digital gadget. The fact that his job *before* his existential crisis was burning down the same rainforest did not prepare him for this adventure. *That* is the horror vacui (and perhaps Nature's revenge). Fear of falling through the bottom of mainstream society into the cesspool of the Underclass is the subject's worst fear. Death is not a close second. As the horror vacui, then, the sublime demands bare life. Perhaps this is why saints have such a history of renunciation and even self-mortification. Surely Joan of Arc did not expect anything good to come out of what she did in terms of her own life as a young woman and career as a soldier. The secret of the intangible of the sublime is that without accepting it as one's state of being there is no possibility of what Rolland describes as a feeling of eternity. This is not the same thing as a feeling of immortality. The first is an ineffable blend of infinite loneliness and immense unity with one and all. It seems to be a paradoxical state, but only to those whose consciousness cannot accept the bicameral perception of subject and object. The Other is the transcendental object. If we respect its sovereignty by acknowledging our own, then we discover that we are infinitely and forever apart from the Other. This accounts for the loneliness. But in this discovery we learn that there are others and not just ourselves. In the state of consolation we live turned-into ourselves in narcissistic state of self-absorption. Others are merely extensions of expediency, which is part of the ethical aesthetic of *Genuss* pervading society. The only form of true consciousness is consciousness of the transcendental object as the Other. Otherwise, as Freud accurately shows, we live in a state of consolation where we believe that the ego will somehow persist past death, to be ushered into Heaven (as if there could be such a hellish Heaven full of disembodied egotists).

The sublime is the intangible which positivism and science are too embarrassed to admit exists the way apples exist. A better word would be ineffable. In science's relentless attempt to eliminate anything it is too embarrassed to admit is *incognizable,* it ends up burning people at the stake who were *metamotivated* by a feeling of ineffable power and inspiration that does not come from anywhere like most things come from somewhere. These *ex nihilo* feelings are what keep us all from killing ourselves tomorrow. Five minutes of reflection would lead most to conclude that life is, as Hobbes says in *Leviathan,* "solitary, poor, nasty, brutish, and short" (p. 78). And despite his claims that civilization and its discontents elevate us somewhat above this condition, it is not nearly high enough for people not to want to overdose on drugs, drink themselves into oblivion, and smoke and eat themselves to death. Just as we ignore the fact that the earth's magnetic field protects us from being broiled in the sun's microwaves, we also ignore the reality of *faith* that there is something intangible keeping us from suicide. The word is meant here in the metaphysical sense, not as a synonym for hope. In the ineffable reality of the sublime we perceive that there is more to the universe than our own egos and how tired and crabby we feel today.

Unfortunately for those with a hunger for the real, ethics and aesthetics belong to the qualitative function of reality and therefore are excluded by the hegemonic order in favor of the Law (Father). It supports the priorities of the quantitative positivism prevailing as the exalted ethic of the juridical and economic orders. Travesties of justice and crippling market crashes leave the scions of the hegemony unfazed. Why? Because they believe that as long as they cling to their quantitative universe of discourse they will always be able to calculate themselves out of any problem. Also, they have rigged it all so that they profit from chaos just as much as order. However, their approach is like being a cave man who refuses to use fire. For example, the governmental bank of the hegemony uses what it calls quantitative easing (a reckless spending spree of fiat currency to cover over fatal flaws in Keynesian economics) to solve economic problems that need precisely the opposite action, quantitative tightening, to be corrected. This madness is the result of the *dichotomania* of the hegemony. It sees qualitative concerns such as ethics and aesthetics - which would prevent such horrific errors in judgment - as obstacles to its relentless quest for total power. It vilifies and belittles the qualitative. While this strategy always leads to economic disaster and war, nevertheless the *subject* gets the blame for the disastrous errors the hegemony commits. "After all," intone the Domini of the hegemony, "YOU voted for us!" Herein lies the beauty of democracy for the hegemonic order and its corporate overlords. Just as it is the subject's fault if it buys a car and crashes it into a tree and dies, it is also the subject's fault if it votes for a regime which plunders the nation's treasure and plunges it into misery, destruction, and war. One need not cast about in more than a hundred years of history to find numerous unequivocal examples of this pattern. And yet the romantic dream of democracy persists because it plays into the wishful thinking of the subject's desire for power in a world where it has none. The subject, in turn, humbly accepts its role in its own destruction, maintaining its good will toward the hegemony and its corporate overlords. After all, who else would bring peace and prosperity to the masses? Only those who have the power to do it.

Therefore, it is always in the best interest of the hegemony to favor the *calculaic*, the quantitative, and all the presti*digi*tation that goes along with it. After all, it is the *digital* technology which keeps it in power through the ubiquitous gadgets and gizmos manufactured, advertised, and sold by its corporate overlords. Analog is too cumbersome because it is not easily manipulated. It works on *analogy* and is therefore qualitative. Even the workings of its most sophisticated devices and systems are accessible to those motivated to learn about, modify, and build them. Also, the Domini cultivate and exploit the subject's natural inclination toward *dyscalculia*. The subject says it hates numbers because they are too hard (exacting). In addition (so to speak), chronically mediocre minds thinking the same way to be of any effective help infest the school system. Besides, their job is to indoctrinate not illuminate. The subject does not see why it needs to learn math except to take what it considers to be meaningless tests. More importantly, though, by discouraging the subject's attempt at understanding the relationship between numbers (and values x and y) the Domini also preempt any possibility that the subject will a develop a meaningful sense of *ratio*. Of the qualities of reason ratio is the most important being the root of the word rational (but also ratiocination and rationalization). As Saussure says, what makes a word a word is its *difference* (ratio) from another word. Without this quality it has no value but most importantly *identity*. "The important thing in the word is not the sound alone but the phonic differences that make it possible to distinguish this word from all others, for differences carry signification" (p. 118). The word's identity is its sign or signification. Also, in numbers, Peano's 8th Axiom states that zero may not follow any number for that number to have identity. Or, for every natural number, S(n) = 0 is false. Therefore, a number following another number must have a value other than 0 and itself. The result, then, is a sequence of numbers regardless of their set. (For instance, it could be an integer each of which is +1 greater than the number preceding it, or it could be a prime number, each of which is greater than the previous number but only divisible by itself and 1.) And we can take into account Cantor's proof that numbers of different sets may nevertheless correspond and therefore follow the same rule. We can extrapolate from this that to have meaning we must have *difference*. As is said elsewhere here, 1 + 1 + 1 + 1, …, and so on has no meaning as the number 4 because it does not constitute a sign. Only signs may be subject to arithmetic, which is why the roman numeral system fell to the Arabic. Furthermore, it should be obvious that a workable language depends upon having enough phonemes to combine (computationally but also intuitively) to create a range of words which do not sound the same! Else we and up with the "signaling" of animals which, though in some cases quite impressive, never reaches the variety manipulated in the right way to form a language.

Therefore, ratio between X and Y (if not Z) makes it possible to use mathematics, communicate, and distinguish between the value of one thing and another - whatever the criteria for value might be. For example it is more *valuable* to have a screwdriver than a wrench if one wishes to turn a screw. Once one must turn a nut, then the screwdriver loses its value. If there were never another screw to be turned, only nuts, then in this universe of discourse the screwdriver would lose its value permanently. Its identity as a screwdriver would fade to oblivion. So for there to be *identity* there must be *ratio*. Although all men may be "created equal" in the eyes of law, when this concept is carried into places where it should not be (such as ballet schools) chaos ensues. The members of this devalued class lose their ratio (difference) between each other and therefore their identity. The one size fits all form of education prevalent here and there has always been a failure just as it would be absurd to provide only one size of shoe in a shoe store. However, it is *expedient*. Since expediency is closely allied with *Genuss* – the ethical aesthetic of perpetual, eternal, unassailable, sacred, and holy Comfort and Convenience – the application of this fatal strategy is common. Despite its equally perpetual failure, insistence upon expediency *uber alles* belies the agenda of the hegemony as self-serving despite its sanctimonious aura of altruism.

The problem, again, is the lopsided half-thinking of logical positivism as it is expressed by the discourse of the hegemony. Though we speak here of the need for analytical thought, we also speak of the need to distinguish the misprision of substituting rationalization and ratiocination for rational thinking. Rationalization is the *mea culpa* of the failed state. Ratiocination is the mental masturbation (onanism) of the apparatus of the hegemonic state which must extend its lust for quantification to every area of organic existence so that it may encode everything into the storage media of Big Data. To leave any stone unturned and therefore not encoded makes it dangerous.

Surely Russell would not recognize the positivism of the post-modern era just as Keynes would not recognize his economic theories distorted by today's financial marketplace of kleptomania and compulsive gambling. If the ethical aesthetic of the qualitative were a painting then quantification would be its frame, the painter's name, and the catalog number. In other words, quantification represents only the *metadata* of the thing. For example, Man Ray said he had a quarrel with the dealer of his art. When he switched from one medium to another as his artistic inspiration moved him, his dealer complained that he would lose the collectors of that particular medium and have to start over again. This was a quantitative problem. "I have an idea," said Man Ray. "YOU make the art, and *I* will sell it." The dealer got the point: without the qualitative *thingness* of Man Ray's art the dealer would have no-*thing* to sell. Starving artists have succeeded in creating great art that endures forever, but *no* gallerist has succeeded without an inventory of great art. Therefore, an ethical aesthetic is not just a matter of our appreciation of something. It is also a matter of the metaphysics of ethical significance and the physics of successful endeavor.

1.3: Automata and the black box

There is awareness in consciousness but no consciousness in awareness. We will get to this matter soon. In the previous discussion we looked at different ways the idea of consciousness is used. Like the word beauty it is more or less a special *noise* we apply to whatever we like as long as it fits the prevailing preconceptions about its various meanings. We also looked at how it is defined in the negative with such ideas as being unconscious (e.g. in a coma), the unconscious, and the subconscious (as well as the *preconscious* which is also a negative). So it is imperative that we do something about this here at the outset of this essay. First of all, here we make the distinction between awareness and what we will call consciousness. There are many different levels of awareness. But they all have one thing in common: their signal is a reaction to stimulus. In other words, awareness does not exist as such unless there is the mechanics of stimulus and response. Therefore, the only possibility for different levels of awareness is that they are either more or less sophisticated. No matter how sophisticated, though, they are not to be considered consciousness. We put the two modes of perception into their own categories which are related only in that consciousness contains awareness.

Unfortunately, in the fog of confusion about what is and is not consciousness the two get mixed up. Generally speaking, mere awareness is considered to be consciousness. This is a category error. It is easy to understand, though, why this error is the rule when it comes to defining consciousness. Part of the mythology of being human is that *we* are conscious and everything else is *not*. God (or reason) has endowed us with this divine attribute denied to the lesser organisms. This ridiculous idea is akin to the anthropocentrism which puts man and his earth at the center of the solar system and the universe. No other planet is so blessed. It is also a ridiculous idea, though, to imagine that other organisms are conscious the way we can be if we try. This idea is well suited to cartoons and literature (usually for children) where animals talk. In these productions the ability to *talk* signals the animal's anthropoid consciousness. Otherwise, when we are in the supermarket buying a chicken breast in its Styrofoam tray covered in plastic wrap with a label warning us to wash our hands after touching it, animals are just *automata* God put here so we can eat them. So animals are merely stimulus-response machines, as Descartes describes in *Discourse on Method* (and in *L'Homme)*. He uses the term *bête-machine* when describing animals as machines. This is not to say that he does not allow them to feel pain, have emotions, and even something resembling cognition. But the important word is resembling. He makes a distinction between human reason and thought as *cogitare (cogitatio) and penser (pensée)* and the *operations de l'ame*, or operations of the soul. These are strictly human characteristics. In Part V he says that, basically, a machine is a machine whether it is made of springs and gears or flesh and blood.

> You won't find that at all strange if you know how many kinds of automata or moving machines the skill of man can construct with the use of very few parts, in comparison with the great multitude of bones, muscles, nerves, arteries, veins and all the other parts that are in the body of any animal, and if this knowledge leads you to regard an animal body as a machine. Having been made by the hands of God, it is incomparably better organised - and capable of movements that are much more wonderful—than any that can be devised by man, *but still it is just a machine*. [italics added]

It is interesting to note here that Descartes looks at the idea of *automata* (robots) in the opposite way that we look at the problem of a machine controlled by so-called artificial intelligence. He marvels at how much a human can resemble a machine. We marvel at how much a machine can resemble a human. Maybe this is because he wrote just at the start of the Machine Age. We write just after it where the emphasis has moved from the machine to its programming. In his day it may have been as hard for someone to see a human as a machine as it is easy for us to see a machine as a human. Why? Because he was dealing with the intricate clockwork machines of his day, the emphasis was on the *hardware*. While his whole discussion of this leads to a meditation on the nature of thought, will, and consciousness, it is cased in the language of anatomy. In his characteristically plain and helpful way, he even advises an anatomy lesson: "To readers who don't know any anatomy: before going on, please arrange to observe someone dissecting the heart of some large animal with lungs (for such a heart is in all respects enough like that of a man), and get him to show you its two chambers or cavities ..." Today, though, we are dazzled by *Software*. The machine itself is just a black box with weird stuff in it that only has significance to the repair shop or the recycling bin. Nearly all consumers have no idea even of what the critical and historical difference is between analog and digital. But they know that the Big Magic in the Black Box is caused by Software, which they see as the *ghost in the machine*. This is enough for the subject to imagine that the machine can think, even though the subject often cannot adequately define what it means to think, sufficiently lacking the ability to do so. And as we all know, *cogito, ergo sum!* But one who cannot think cannot tell if another thinks or not. Marketing picks up on the subject's credulity regarding intelligence (which it mistakes for consciousness), exploiting it by using the adjective "smart" before every description of what is essentially a dumb device. This reinforces the subject's sense that the ghost in the machine is much like the Ghost in itself. Furthermore, the corporations which pay programmers to put this ghost in the machine are seen as godlike. Their names are on every subject's lips. Their logos are emblazoned upon the subject's memory as if they were the Star of David. They are loved, reviled, defended, and attacked as if their customers were members of religious sects bickering among each other rather than just consumers buying an appliance. They command devotion, fealty, faith, and tithing in the form of paying for constant upgrades. Like the automata of Descartes' day which were exhibited to the credulous public for their marvelous human-like behavior, the fancier ones of today walk, talk, and squawk just like the Real Thing. This bit of digital prestidigitation is enough to razzle and dazzle the subject made hapless by its abdication to the hegemony.

But under the divine plan for man and beast, it is only man who has the Godlike powers of reason and the vision to make it new in the realm of bare life and the *horror vacui*. In Genesis 2:19 God creates animals as "an help meet" for Adam, who at this point is still single. Animals are there for man thanks to God. They are not there for themselves. Therefore, they have no sovereignty. Without sovereignty they can have no consciousness at least in the sense of a self-conscious identity as "I am that I am" (הֶיְהֶא הֶיְהֶא רֶשֶׁא), the words God uses in response when Moses asks his name on Mt. Sinai. It is this *sapiens sapiens* which is supposed to make man Godlike. Since animals cannot talk, therefore they cannot *think* in the sense of *cogitatio* + *pensée*. By omission rather than assertion Descartes implies that to survive animals must have some kind of mental process. But the implication is more that they *scheme* in the sense of grasping the schemata they need to survive. This fits neatly within the mythology of Genesis. In the creation myth, God gives Adam not only the power of speech but also the power to *name*. It is not a Godlike power to speak and think; it is *reason* that makes man like God, for that is the *cogitatio*. When Adam names the animals, he gives them an identity apart from each other. While they have no sovereignty, they do have identity thanks to Adam. This is his Godlike power: to give the *signified* their *signifiers*.

> And out of the ground the LORD God formed every beast of the field, and every fowl of the air; and brought them unto Adam to see what he would call them: and whatsoever Adam called every living creature, that was the name thereof.

Here is a power that both animals and automata lack. Machines may be able to *listen to* or *read* a name as they do with creepy alacrity when we call a business these days where we have an account. However, no machine is able to name anything. This is a strange handicap. Could it be that these marvels of science and technology do not have a soul, cannot think, and (gasp) are not conscious? John Cottingham, in an essay titled "A Brute to the Brutes? Descartes' Treatment of Animals," Describes the importance of naming in the concept of the automaton:

> Notice ... how the language argument fits into all this. In pointing out that animals have no genuine language, Descartes clearly thinks that he has a powerful case for concluding that they do not think. Yet for Descartes to regard this argument ("non loquitur ergo non cogitat") as having such evident force, "think" (cogitat) here must evidently be used in the fairly restrictive sense ... (p. 556)

Cottingham makes a critical observation here. Although Descartes says that animals do not have language in the human, syntactical sense, and therefore do not think in that way, it does not mean that he also believes they have no feeling and therefore no sensibility. (*Non loquitur ergo non sentit.*) Here is a distinction between consciousness and awareness. Are animals *aware* (sensible), but not *conscious* (rational)? Do they not speak because they do not cogitate? Do they not cogitate because they do not speak? But perhaps they do not *need* to speak because of some wholeness we humans do not share. How, then, does this relate to the subject in its abdicated state?

To live one must be aware. To be aware one must react to stimuli. How one reacts is another matter. One may react in a way that complements the stimulus. If one does not, then chaos ensues. For instance, the nervous system is set up to have a specific reaction to the stimulus of burning. If an organism does not react in such a way as to avoid being burned, the consequences go against the organism's imperative to survive. (It is interesting to note that suicide is a *conscious* abrogation of this awareness.) Therefore, both animals and humans must have awareness - at least for this reason. Put a light in the window at night and insects will gather around the glass. They are attracted to what their awareness allows. Sometimes they seek the moon, since some nocturnal insects (e.g. the Diving Beetle, adult of the Water Tiger larva) use it for navigation. That they mistake the light in the window for something else is a symptom of their automation. No prophet insect will rise up and tell them that the truth will set them free. While in terms of their nervous system they are responding in a complementary way to the stimulus, because of their lack of reason (we may suppose) they cannot tell right from wrong. Why? Because when Adam was given the power of reason to name the insects in such a way that they could be distinguished from each other through language, they were denied the sovereignty of naming themselves. This self-naming is the imperative the *horror vacui* of the sublime forces on us in our isolation from others. We are given this faculty of self-naming by reason which, according to Descartes, is what makes man Godlike. The *horror vacui* is an emptiness of such incognizable vastness that it is a kind of vortex drawing us into it with the demand for an almost infinite creativity. In this imperative for infinite creativity we become like God. In as much as Adam was Godlike, he performed some of the duties of God which may be termed rational such as the naming of things. But while God saw it was good, Adam had yet to learn what good means! So even in his naming of things he was not fully conscious of what there was to be conscious of. In particular, he was unconscious of duality which, for our purposes here, will do nicely as reason. Nevertheless, Adam is the prototype of the sovereign man. He is not the First Man only because he was created first; he is so because he will be the first man to apprehend his sovereignty when he eats the fruit of the Tree of the Knowledge of Good and Evil. At that point he is transformed from the *prototype* to the *archetype*. And in so doing the responsibility of God is thrust upon him because he now knows what God knows (as the Serpent points out).

Therefore, consciousness is also a responsibility. It is not something that one is born with or that comes easily in the storm and stress of life. In fact, it is such a responsibility and hardship that it is easy to lure the subject away from this ordeal and into the matrix of the Imaginary where it loses all primal core identity. In this debridement of the spirit, the subject becomes the flotsam of the Imaginary, the hegemony, and its corporate overlords. And while this amniosis seems like bliss at first or from time to time, soon the price must be paid for it. In particular, we might say that God's imperative to go forth from the Garden and learn to rid oneself of the sin of duality ceases to be the cynosure of the subject's *raison d'etre*. As the path it was meant to tread fades into the weeds of oblivion so too does the subject's consciousness. Nevertheless, it persists. Mere awareness – like that of the sea slug – keeps it seeking food, safety, comfort, water, and sex. To make survival as a sea slug even easier, the Imaginary showers the subject with commercial appeals and retail opportunities to get these basic necessities. Meantime, the subject seals its fate hermetically by plunging itself into debt from which it will never free itself.

So what, after all, is consciousness? In *Logic of Statistical Inference*, Ian Hacking says that "philosophical inquiry into foundations has to begin with what everyone else takes for granted" (p. 35). Certainly, consciousness is taken for granted as what makes us human. However, this essay will *not* answer this question once and for all; such an attempt is a kind of hubris confusing knowledge *about* (the knowing-of) consciousness with the *possibility of* (*Möglichkeit*) consciousness. Moreover, it complicates the effort by throwing in the matter of truth versus knowledge. So any definitive attempt to answer such a question based on a word which in and of itself has no meaning can only end in more doubt. Furthermore, there is the matter of intelligence. Whatever it is, we speak and behave as if the formula "the more intelligence the more consciousness" (< I = < C) were a Law of Nature. But what that leaves us with is the need to measure intelligence using psychometrics so that we can find out how conscious a person (or machine) is. This dubious artifact of early positivism seems unlikely to also measure consciousness, though it does measure how well one can perform on a psychometric test. And yet we make this assumption that (< I = < C). What we like to forget is that the word intelligence, like the word consciousness, has been seized upon by the Imaginary as a commercial buzzword. This started to happen when it was appropriated for the creation of the oxymoron artificial intelligence. Unfortunately, intelligence must be *real* not artificial to be called intelligence. If it is artificial then it is something else. Furthermore, what has come to be its popular synonym: smart has been likewise appropriated by electronica marketing. If to be conscious is to be intelligent, and if to be intelligent is to be smart, and one owns a smart gadget, is one's gadget therefore conscious? Once the consumer would have laughed at this proposition. As these gadgets mimic human behavior better and better in the classic Cartesian style, though, the credulous consumer believes the corporate hype. It *wants* to believe it. Everyone deep down inside wants a slave. Sex slave, house slave, farm slave, work slave, school slave, sports slave, friend slave, and so on. This impulse grows as the subject loses more and more of its potency as a sovereign individual. Unconsciously it knows that it is powerless. The ego has a hard time accepting that it has become the ego of a slave. Therefore, it seeks out others to enslave so that it can negate the sense of its own servitude.

In *The Desperate Mission* (1969), Joaquin Murieta, a Mexican patróne (played by Ricardo Montalban), who has been burned out of his ancestral holding by American land-grabbing outlaws in California, says to a Mexican priest he finds on the road leading similarly displaced campesinos, "Freedom is a powerful wine, Padré; it only makes new tyrants out of old slaves. We sold the people immortality, but we should also have taught them to fight for survival." I would say that these lines do well in making a summary of thesis of this book.

The Imaginary capitalizes on the slave's base desire to see freedom as a transitional phase in his progress toward fulfilling his ego's most fervent lust: *to enslave*. Technologists scramble to make animatronic gizmos that drive cars, answer phones, fight wars, teach children and university courses, and even do automated robotic surgery. As none of these machines have human rights (yet), they make the *perfect slaves* from a nomological standpoint. Unfortunately, they are not as cheap and dexterous as the far-off other in his third-world hellhole waiting for a crust of bread from the master race of Apex Consumers across the ocean. Therefore, using the principal of regulatory and constitutional arbitrage, the hegemony and its banking and corporate *fasces* enslaves the far-off other on behalf of the subject who, like Pontius Pilate, can now wash his hands of culpability.

But for the technologists who regard themselves (with infinite hubris) as the Masters of the Universe, the best arrangement is to turn the far-off other into a consumer too, while bamboozling him into surrendering his minerals and ports, and converting his subsistence farming into foreign-owned agribusiness with the help of various development banks and NGO's. Then, and only then, can the far-off other have some credit (debt) to buy the food he *used to* raise himself from the hegemony's genetically modified and bug-proof cornucopia overseas. Even more important, though, is to keep these neocampesinos in a state of intellectual *torpor* through a steady feed of thought-killing nonsense and consumer pitches spewed from the ubiquitous digital gadget tied into on-message Big Data.

Like a priest with a special pipeline to God, the gadget has a special bitstream to politically sanitized Big Data. Its gadget voice even has a name (almost always female to go with the pitch of the voice, as women are considered by these enlightened, progressive technologists to be subservient robots), and uses the personal pronoun as in, "I understand you want to know the meaning of *anagnorisis*. Is that correct?" It addresses the subject as "you," or worse, by its actual name. "Surely *this* is consciousness," thinks the digitally-doped-up subject now suffering a fatal hallucination. Nevertheless, we also get the sense that consciousness, knowledge, truth, and intelligence are related in a special way. It even seems that if we were to break consciousness down into parts, they would be knowledge, truth, and intelligence configured in some way that they all work together to make us *conscious of our consciousness*. This is indeed a kind of self-consciousness, just as narcissism is. Herein lies some evidence for the idea that what is often considered consciousness is actually narcissistic self-awareness. As we know from the myths, Narcissus is in a state of permanent self-love where he is not even conscious that the reflection he sees in the water is of himself. He mistakes this reflection for the Other. Meantime he is also unconscious of the presence of Echo, the Other who loves him, whose handicap is that she can only repeat what she hears from her prospective lover. It would seem, then, that here is another way to bollocks any attempt to understand what consciousness is (the knowing-of), much less be conscious (the getting-to-know).

Part of our difficulty is isolating the *referents* for the components of consciousness. When we use the words intelligence, knowledge, and reality to what do we refer? What is *signified*? For our purposes here we make the distinction between a referent and a signifier. The former is *that to which we refer*. That latter is the *name* of that to which we refer. Later we will look at what Peirce has to say about the referent as a *Thing-presentation* as distinguished from the signified and signifier. Only the referent may be caught up in what Peirce calls cognition in the form of analytical thinking as *abduction*. Why? Because the thing itself is the referent apart from its signifier (name). We may only *refer* to the thing with the name. The referent adds a *tertium quid* to the process of language: there is the thing referred to (signified), the thing with which we refer to the thing referred to (signifier), and the referral to the thing (referent). In logic the referent is close to one definition of an enthymeme as *the thing referred to in a proposition which is not indicated*. This we could call an inference. A referent is *inferred*. So when someone says sarcastically "The Master of the Universe is coming over for dinner so make sure everything's perfect" the hearer knows precisely who it is that is coming to dinner even though that person was not named. However, that person was *referred to* by referent with some inference which could not be contained in the person's actual name (Bill). Another way to look at it is the use of *metonym*. To call Paris the City of Love is a metonym for its actual name. We know that City of Love is not its name (signifier). But we also know that the signifier is *inferred* by the metonym as well as being inadequate to adequately describe Paris not just in its name but in its *being*. This kind of knowing is not limited to the signifier and signified because it is a referent. In computer networking a metonym is a natural-language name representing a unique number or some unique string of often alphanumeric characters or even punctuation. The metonym is presented to the user in the user interface while the "true name" serves as yet another referent for other referents that different levels of the computer process understand (compute). That a symbol is *understood* as something specific, unique, and concrete makes it a word. Also, in computing, a "word" is the number of bits (8, 16, 32, 64) in the instruction set architecture processed by the central processing unit with each tick of its clock. For example, the difference between architecture processing 32-bit and 64-bit words is that the latter processes twice the instructions with one tick of the clock. Each tick is like a pull on the "arm" of a slot machine, but with a deterministic algorithm. What matters is that the referent is understood by something or someone, even in the case of the one-armed bandit: win or lose? When it is understood, the *argument* is successful. When something is understood, we call the event intelligence, a term adapted for the application *in all* cases but that is not anything constant and objective, or it would lose its functionality. The term artificial intelligence refers not to the science fiction of humanoid robots, but to this mechanical process of understanding within the limitations of a machine. By including the referent in the logical statement we infer a level of complexity absent in basal structures of signifier and signified. Inference brings communication closer to the reality it attempts to communicate. That language is infinitely adaptable means that there are greater and lesser approximations of reality in language. In computing, reality (such as the analog data of sound or image) can be sampled at a high or low bit rate or resolution, meaning that the computer can quantify *how much* reality will result as its output. Therefore, machines show us that if we are going to use language – for any purpose – it is always a matter of how much reality will be left over as the result of the processing of the input. Herein lie profound implications for human cognition.

Our consciousness of reality, though, is often to the contrary. Our first critical error is in thinking that what we say is the reality of what we mean to say. In other words, we tend to actually think that the signifiers spewing from our mouths (and on this paper here) are the material equivalent of the reality they represent. Statements such as "he is evil" are considered to be the equivalent of being (or not being) evil. If another person replies that "he is *not* evil" there is nothing different in the phenomenon of the statement. The only difference is that one is a negation of the other which is saying nothing at all except (A → ~A) – a self-negating tautology. And yet this passes for knowledge, information, intelligence and, yes, consciousness! A big problem for language is that concepts such as intelligence, knowledge, reality, and consciousness each by itself is almost impossible to define. Therefore, they are prey to those who would construct semantic worlds containing only synthetic propositions: politicians, advertisers, education, religion, and most of all Scientism. At best they construct statements which contain an analytic statement which can be proven so that they can point to this when challenged on the verifiability of their argument. "I am the right candidate for the job [synthetic] *because* I got the money to build a bridge over the river [analytic]." "Our product eliminates bad breath [analytic] *and* gets you the girl you want [synthetic]." "Go to college and learn a profession [analytic] *or* you will be a loser [synthetic]." And so on. The devil is in the conjunction: because, and, or.

We like to say, that one should get a grip on reality. It is common to observe that people lose their grip on it. Why? How? If reality is the Absolute, that which is apart from us, entirely objective, in opposition to our subjectivity, then how could we possibly lose i? Perhaps the problem is that it is not objective and that in fact nothing is except the fact that nothing is.

For example, the Doppler shift show us that, in sound (though there are other physical examples), what we think we hear as that sound is in fact the result of other forces such as distance and speed and not necessarily that sound itself (which perhaps we will never know). In short, as the sound approaches (A) the waves bunch up, increasing the frequency (or pitch). As the sound moves away (B) the opposite happens, lowering it. If we are in a position of continuity between A and B we know that the sound we hear before and after are the same sound even though they are different in an important way. But is this because we know something or because we have made an assumption based on what seems to be the case without any verification? If there are two persons isolated from each other so that one hears A and the other B, they will not agree that they heard the same sound because it would not be the same. How can this be? We are dealing with objective physical reality here. Surely the first person and the second person heard the same sound. If so, then how can we measure it? We might put them in separate rooms where they get to hear the sound without movement. In this case they are likely to agree that it is the same sound. What have we done, though? We have manipulated the circumstances to suit the objective of having both hear the same sound. Our conception of reality is that it is not manipulated. If it is, then it is artificial (which is why artificial reality is an oxymoron) and is no longer reality but rather someone's subjective reality imposed upon us. Furthermore, we may have eliminated speed, but we have not eliminated distance. Each person is a certain distance from the sound. We could further manipulate the experiment by fixing them in chairs so that they are both precisely the same distance from the sound. Now we have added further manipulation to what was supposed to be objective reality which did not need our subjective help to be so. Nevertheless, even if we are willing to accept this as reality, we are still dealing with two subjects in isolation. There is nothing guaranteeing that they will agree it was the same sound. When two or more persons see a crime it is rare that any two of them will agree on what happened although it happened in reality.

To get a grip on consciousness, then, we will have to subordinate reality, intelligence, and knowledge to this end. We will have to acknowledge - even if it is, as Wittgenstein says about a proposition, "for the sake of experiment" - that the only reality is that we really do not know what reality is. Furthermore, we will also have to admit that the words intelligence and knowledge are just grunts, noises we make when we are trying to show others that we belong to the human race. Then, we can use a kind of semantic trigonometry between the three subordinated ideas to try to get at a result which approximates something that we can accept as consciousness ... *for the sake of experiment*. They at least support the idea of consciousness in a way that any one point in this triangle cannot, whatever the expedient definition of consciousness is for the occasion. As we have mentioned, the idea that neurobiologists can find what is sometimes called the seat of consciousness in the wet brain is one of the great follies of the age of misapplied verifiability. It is positivism *in extremis*. The consciousness sought after by New Age acolytes is deliciously ineffable. Their attempt to raise consciousness is laudable. And of course evangelists always seek to raise the consciousness of the masses regarding their cause. (Sometimes they say *raise awareness*, but in either case the words are used interchangeably.) There is even a kind of conscious decision-making movement within the corporate self-help canon of seminars and buzz phrases. It is also known as presence of mind or *mindfulness* (as opposed to mindlessness?) for short. Again, these are laudable attempts to make the usually flaccid and inert state of the subject's mind into something that can help these companies make more money and fewer errors. We at least know that the word *conscious* is significant in a situation where a person is out cold and finally comes to (consciousness). This person's brain definitely crosses some significant threshold into a state where effective relationship and communication are possible. And we know that in relationship and communication there is a kind of intelligence which we might call consciousness.

To better understand this, we can consider a kind of *Gedankenexperiment*. In the Doppler example it is the *frequency* of sound waves which blurs what we might have considered the objective reality of a physical phenomenon. And this is only one parameter: sound. When we deal with events with many complex parameters such as reality itself (with the full input of the senses) the matter gets exponentially complicated. Nevertheless, just as the computer uses the ratio of two frequencies to determine its processing speed: 1) how many "words" processed 2) per second, we may look at the frequency of other phenomena as well to see how they affect our processing of reality in the form of consciousness. We tend to rely on frequency to give us the sense that life is consistent. It helps us exist with a sense that we can predict the outcome of things with some reliability. But is this so? Death, for instance, seems to defy predictability. The grave pronouncement from a doctor that he only has a few months to live can be seen as optimistic considering that the patient might be dead in a few hours after being hit by a car. Hacking says that our imagination of probability has as much to do with life as the actual frequencies of things. "Seldom are frequencies our only data. The world is too complicated, and men know too much. Only in the imagination do frequencies serve as the sole basis of action. But it is probable that laws governing imaginary cases operate in life" (p. 35).

Consider a video loop of a waterfall. This loop could be anywhere from a minute to several hours. Naturally, the interval will affect our experience of the waterfall. The goal of the experiment is to see how big an interval is necessary for us to lose consciousness of it being a loop and mistake it for the natural continuity of reality. To do this, we have to tell the subject that some show just a segment of time during which there is no loop (control). Others are loops of varying lengths. How many loops are in each showing of the video is random – if there are any. Without getting into minute details of this thought experiment, let us consider the possibilities. The subject watches a one-minute loop. After a few iterations, the subject notices some repetitive patterns in the fall of the water, debris over the waterfall, a passing bird, a jumping fish and so on. The loop is identified as such. We can say then that the subject is conscious of the video being a loop in *real time*. As the experiment continues, we lengthen the video but do not indicate whether it is a loop or one continuous scene. There is no doubt whatsoever that as the length of the video increases it becomes more difficult to tell the loop from the continuous scene. As the length grows to one hour, the strain on the subject to distinguish the real waterfall (which is, after all, only an image of one) from the artificial waterfall becomes ever greater. Extend this to a few hours and all distinction between reality and illusion is lost. Is this how life really is? Can we know?

So, then, where is consciousness in all of this? If the video were reality and not a video, at what point would we lose consciousness of whether or not we were watching a loop? How do we know that something like this situation is not in command of our experience right now? Do we not have the so-called *déjà-vu* experience where we swear we have seen something before when it is not possible? Have we not caught ourselves doing and saying the same thing we did and said before without realizing it? Have we not seen someone do the same stupid thing time and time again? Does the cat not roll over and want us to scratch its belly every time we pass? Do we not say the same thing at the checkout counter each time we pay for our groceries? "Again" seems to be a word we use quite often to describe our habits, behavior, and experience. When life is good, we are like children running from the exit of the roller coaster back to the entrance to ride again. When life is bad, we run to the forms of oblivion and consolation we have visited time and time again, from alcohol to God.

What if we are simply not conscious of reality being a loop? What if the loop is big enough to be just beyond the capacity of our intellect to seem like a continuous reality? Well of course we grow old and die. That is proof enough that it is not a loop. However, certain beliefs say that we come back again and again to live out our dramas in the wheel of Karma. This is not at all the "lucid dreaming" problem. This is a matter of the measurable limits of our supposed consciousness. If we are on a long unfamiliar drive, even without a map we "know" there will be a filling station up ahead, a diner of some sort, trees, roads, other cars, and so on. Walk through any city and there will be more or less the same distribution, block after block, of restaurants, dry cleaners, shoe stores, clothing stores, dog walkers, apartment buildings, dentists' offices, grocery stores, graffiti, trash, parked cars, and even homeless persons. It is as if all of life is made out of a small number of templates stamped here and there in just the right frequency to create the illusion of continuity and therefore difference. This world of templates seems to be populated with a handful of archetypes, the human form of which tend to conform to stereotypes. These stereotypes speak in clichés they all have heard as memes issuing from the media or their temples and governments. When we strip away the illusion of difference and continuity we are left with a tiny world with only a few ideas to hold it together.

In another experiment there is a public square which has a path to the left and to the right. Between them is grass. Both go to the same spot and are of equal length. Each time we approach this square we are presented with a choice: Path A or Path B. How do we choose which one to take? Whatever method, we will probably operate under the assumption that we have made a consciou choice. What are the possibilities?

We make the conscious choice to choose one at random each time. If the probability is greater that we take *A* rather than *B* then the choice is no longer random. Our conscious decision to make a random choice has been thwarted. We can argue that although we take *A* forty percent of the time and *B* sixty percent of the time it is still random. It just worked out that way. But an observer would say that "the truth is, she prefers *A* over *B*." Any argument to the contrary would seem disingenuous because "the evidence" says otherwise. If we come up with a rule that one day we will take *A* and the next *B* a definite alternating pattern begins which is not random. Already we are in a bind because almost any method will result in some kind of unintended, but not random, pattern. Admitting defeat, we decide to flip a coin each time we get to the square to determine which to take: heads *A* tails *B*. The best we can say, then, is that once we admit the impossibility of making a conscious choice of which path to take, we make a conscious choice to flip a coin, which is not the same thing as making a conscious choice to make a random choice. Most of the other possibilities are obvious. We decide to take the left path because it is closer to the wall in the shade. We decide to take the right path because superstition tells us that the left-hand path is sinister. We just choose one path and stick to it for no particular reason because we are creatures of habit. In the non-random choices which do not involve a coin toss, we cannot say that they are conscious choices because they are based on a predisposition to choose one or the other. Therefore it was not a choice of path but rather the expression of an already-existing state which we then impose upon the possible choice of paths. Ultimately, all of these possibilities are either 1) not a random choice (but a coin toss), or 2) not a choice at all but a predisposition to do one thing or another.

However, there is another choice which might meet a

definition of consciousness. In the first, the subject gets to the square and sees what the situation is. Deciding that it was stupid for whomever designed the square to put two paths of equal length going the long way around the square, he walks a diagonal path across the grass thus *creating* path *C*. This is clearly a conscious choice. The other is the person who decides that he will vary the reason why he takes *A* or *B so that life does not seem like a video loop!* The first day he uses strategy 1. On the second strategy 2. And so on. To make it even more interesting, he sometimes uses the diagonal across the grass (path *C*). Or avoids the square altogether. Maybe he even petitions the city to build a path which goes through the grass rather than around the square. In this situation he must make a conscious decision of some complexity each time he traverses the square in some way.

At the start of this discussion of consciousness we said that although there is awareness in consciousness, there is no consciousness in awareness. One must be aware or die. The concern of awareness is the avoidance of pain and the seeking of pleasure. It also involves the acknowledgment that data must be processed appropriately for the organism to experience and to take that experience and turn it into knowledge. Therefore, knowledge is the result of awareness not consciousness per se. As such it is the knowing-of but not the getting-to-know. Since awareness is part of consciousness, and knowledge is part of awareness, then knowledge is part of consciousness too. In its static state, however, it is *indirectly* relative to consciousness. Consciousness itself does not *need* knowledge. In fact, it cannot be predicated upon knowledge which is the gathering of information. The hunting and gathering of information is what simple Web crawler bots perform for data bases and search engines. Therefore, the gathering of information does not require awareness. It is a matter of quantity and category. But since it is a significant part of the acquisition of knowledge, it is the basis for the ethical aesthetic of the *knowing-more*. This aesthetic says that more is better than less. Why is it? Because when the concept of *more* is equated with consciousness, the simple formula of the more one knows the more conscious one is comes into play, leading to the illusion that Big Data is somehow conscious. If an automaton can only tap into this data, the fallacious thinking goes, it too will be conscious as a human being presumably is. This too is the origin of the legend of the learned man. It is also the origin of the character Professor Dryasdust whom Sir Walter Scott used satirically as a literary authority on his novels. He comes up again here and there in Carlyle (though not to be confused with the venerable Dr. Diogenes Teufelsdröckh).

Knowledge is a static-state proposition. No two persons know exactly the same quantity of knowledge. Standardized testing creates the illusion of equal knowledge quantization across test subjects. The obvious problem with this, besides the fact that illusions are not generally helpful when it comes to tests for medicine or law, is that subjects A and B could both equally demonstrate quantity X about discipline Y according to the objective test results. However, it is possible that subject A knows (n) times more knowledge about discipline Y than B, but the test lacks such scope to show it. So how is the quantification equivalent? The justifications are obvious and abound in the lore of standard tests just as they are and do in that of psychometrics. Still, the effect is that both A and B are considered to be equally qualified when medical liability and miscarriages of justice show they are not. While such quantification of knowledge has its place, it is not in the attributes of consciousness. In fact, since knowledge gets old fast a great quantity of useless practical knowledge may impede one's ability of transcend awareness. What was once the most important knowledge of engineering soon becomes useful only to amateur enthusiasts and historians. Encyclopedic knowledge of alchemy in the European Middle Ages may have been the foundation of modern chemistry and even physics, but it is not of much use today except to certain kinds of highly specialized scholars. This is not to say that if knowledge is old it is useless. Time is the best way to winnow out knowledge which may be passed down profitably through the ages. Unfortunately, knowledge is also like a screwdriver passed down from one generation to the next: when there are no more screws to turn the tool loses all use value. Its value may be reassigned (such as if it becomes an antique or is re-purposed) but like the perhaps millions of once invaluable objects it either becomes a curiosity or fades into oblivion.

Not so with consciousness. The process of the getting-to-know it is not a static state any more than a cloud is. Although the comment that someone has his head up in the clouds is considered pejorative it likely refers to a mode of cognition which consists of process only rather than the concrete, quantifiable objects of knowledge. While a glance into the sky may give one the impression that clouds or stars can be counted, we know this is an illusion. From time to time science comes out with a count of visible stars or some such cosmic quantification while at the same time announcing it has discovered new stars. Addicted to the knowing-of, the subject craves both the cessation of knowledge (the finite number of stars, the age and diameter of the universe, and so on) as well as its infinite extension (discovery of new stars, speculation about new dimensions). Both are the *knowing-of* because they presume to be the definitive *pronunciamentos* of the authorities who always know more than the subject. Therefore, the subject regards those whom it thinks know more than it does about subject Y to be more wise and intelligent. And considering that the subject does not know the difference between awareness, intelligence, information, knowledge, and consciousness, the knowing-more is sufficient priority to convince the subject to submit to whatever authority claims to possess this power. The priesthood of Scientism stands between the subject and Big Data the way that religious priests stand (or stood) between the believer and the divine. The subject imagines that it has access to the same mother lode of Big Data as the hegemony and its priests in the form of the Internet. While this is true in some marginal sense, the fact is that unless the subject is a master hacker all it has at its disposal is endlessly redundant information of dubious accuracy. Under the spell of the knowing-more, though, the subject feels confident that the vast amount of redundant, useless, inaccurate, unedited, infotainment it finds when it searches the Internet is actually some form of Big Data. In reality, its search behavior is tracked into the warehouses of Big Data where the subject is forbidden to trespass. The rest of the important, useful, significant data accessed through the Internet is proprietary. Only those with authorization may touch it. While the subject believes, by deduction, that it is accessing the greatest source of information in the history of humankind (which it is), it in fact has chosen a method to do it which only gives it the most superficial results. This is by design. Meantime, by induction, the owners of the Internet harvest the subject's unconscious impulses communicated by its fingertips at the input interface. This data is then gathered to form the subject's digital *homunculus*. This image is then associated with other images until patterns form which can be used in target marketing and for other applications serving commerce, the state, and the Black Hats who seek to steal the subject's image from the flimsy security of Big Data. While the subject may be concerned about the formation of this other self, it is of particular concern when it is hijacked. At that point there are two images: the more or less legitimate one and the rogue image which is bought and sold in the slave markets of the Dark Web. In all of this the subject is helpless and hapless. It never possessed even the understanding of the basic principles of this process much less the tools to do anything about it. The entire affair is just a Black Box full of Big Magic. As a result, the subject never reaches the point where it can bypass the priesthood. The idea that the Internet is free and belongs to everyone, like free-air radio waves indeed do, is a ridiculous children's fairy tale. Someone has to pay for the infrastructure, programming, and maintenance. And the subject must pay for access to it or lose it. The subject pays a fee, provides his consumer profile, or (usually) both.

More knowledge may even bring one farther away from the possibility of being conscious as consciousness always remains a possibility (*Möglichkeit*) and is never a probability. Anything quantifiable, such as knowledge, is always a probability and never a possibility in the sense that consciousness is. We cannot say that it is possible that a set of data are knowledge. Also, knowledge as a subject need not have an object to be considered knowledge. Useless and even unintelligible knowledge, such as we find in the mysterious Voynich Manuscript which no one has yet decrypted, is still knowledge until proven otherwise. Until the Voynich Manuscript has been translated or decrypted – or until it is proven that there is nothing to translate or decrypt – it remains *possible* knowledge. If it were necessary for information to be understood to be called knowledge then any book in a language the reader did not know would be disqualified from such consideration. So where is consciousness in this? For there to be knowledge there must be awareness. For there to be information awareness is not necessary. Herein lies the difference between the two. However, for there to be consciousness neither knowledge nor information is necessary. Its independence from the information apparatus makes it a constant threat to the power of the corporate fasces of both.

The first business of consciousness, then, is to distinguish intelligence from information through reason. To do so requires understanding of the mechanisms of positive logic. However, this modest task makes demands of the equipment of the intellect the subject does all it can do to avoid. Society aids it in this project of formal stupidity through the indoctrination of education and distraction of entertainment. What lies beyond this achievement, if it is attained at all, is understanding how intellect and knowledge work together to form true statements as meaningful language and other signs. While logical machines must also do this to function, they do so as a *tool*, not the *user* of the tool. Rocks existed long before someone thought of using one to smash a walnut open. Finally, the subject must understand what effect thought has upon reality, and what effect reality has upon thought, which is a complicated matter but nonetheless available to anyone who cares to learn it. Ask a fisherman. To begin with, intelligence is a *demonstrated attribute in action at the moment,* not a number like one's net worth. Psychometrics assumes that its snapshot of this demonstration is enough to account for the depth and breadth of living intelligence. Only those who cannot understand the difference between a living process and a photograph of it can accept the scores of psychometrics as being the *actual intelligence* of the subject. It can be argued that such quantification only *reflects* the subject's intelligence as a photograph reflects reality. Such arguments are true. But, within the phenomenological economy of quantification the statistic and the reality it represents are soon confused. This is rather like the situation where one is referred to by one's disease, nationality, or distinguishing feature: the Parkinson's in room 12 needs looking after; the Swede will know what to do; that redhead is back again. Even "bring in the birthday girl." By swapping the subject for an object outside of the signifying tree by which that entity is properly known identity is induced rather than deduced from the subject. The result is that the subject loses control of its identity. This is not quite the same thing as saying, "my brother will visit this weekend." The referent "my brother" is within the signifying tree of that individual as in:

X: Michael → Mike → Him → He
Y: (My) Husband → Son → Brother → Friend → Associate
Z: (The) Banker → Neighbor → Deacon → Mortgagee → Patient

NOT

X: (The) Lung Cancer; Y: Chicano; Z: Bankrupt

OR

X: (Score) Above average (+100); Y: Average (100); Z: Below average (-100)

While one may indeed be described as a bankrupt Chicano with lung cancer, that is not *who one is*. While it remains true, that, as Job says in 1:21, "Naked came I out of my mother's womb, and naked shall I return thither," our personality develops into a series of names based on our roles in society. Getting a disease, being called a Chicano, or being known for one's bad luck in the past is not *drawn* from the person deductively but is rather *imposed* upon the subject by induction. This is the origin of the dehumanization of an individual by the continual application of a pejorative epithet for either that particular person (the jinx) or what appears to be the tribe that person can be associated with by an attribute identified and stigmatized by the one who assigns this rogue signifier to the subject. The actual epithet is meaningless; in fact, some of the most demeaning and pejorative epithets are actually used by members of the target group as a positive reinforcement of their sense of belonging to that group – with the proviso that only members of that group may so use it. By honoring the protocol of the proviso members of the group neutralize the epithet's violence. In so doing the target subject takes back control of the signifier, bringing it into the tree along with the rule that makes it possible to do so. What is significant is whether or not the signifier is not transited into or exchanged for the signified. Sometimes this is done deliberately as a form of violence to the effect language (signifier) has on the signified. Otherwise it is done in a collusive way as a participant in but not initiator of the violence.

Either way the effect is the same because of the violation of the strict rule that the *signifier* shall under no circumstances become the *signified* in the inverse objectification of the subject. The imperative to regard the other as the transcendental object, and therefore a member of the category of the *real*, vanishes in the subject's narcissistic regard for itself. The other possibility is that the subject performs this violence on itself and others through its spectral orientation to itself as the sign of itself. Throughout history there are many examples of the consequences of this solipsism. Perhaps the most recent and iconic is the historical relationship – if it can be called that – between Nazis and Jews. It should be noted that although this association is often also considered the icon of hatred, such a simple-minded approach is rarely understood schematically and psychologically. It transmogrifies what is the fundamental paradigm of cruelty into a cartoon episode. Most of all, it succeeds in sequestering this cruelty into mythological event thanks to historians, the media, and the chitchat and bric-à-brac of our popular interactions with each other. We embrace this fairy tale because we do not want to believe the truth about ourselves and our relationship to others. Furthermore, it is a pernicious symptom of the indoctrination masquerading as education.

To understand this violence we must first see the difference between the *turning-from* and the *turning-to*. In the turning-from the subject enters into a state of *speculation*. This is a form of what Peirce calls "introspection" (but not the kind leading to self-knowledge). Speculation is structural, global solipsism. In this state the subject turns *from* the other and *into* itself. It is like when one turns one's back from someone in a conversation. Therefore, the turning-to is a process whereby the subject, through an apprehension of the sublime abyss between itself and others, turns-to the transcendental object in a desperate bid to overcome the feeling of horror generated when it realizes it will be forever the other to the Other. That feeling is the horror vacui of the sublime. Compared to the phantasmagoria of the Imaginary, this is no choice at all. It is like giving the subject the choice between cyanide and a candy bar because the subject has been indoctrinated into believing that the sublime *is death itself*. Furthermore, it has lost all courage in its abdication to the hegemony and therefore lacks the fortitude and will to face the wilderness of the sublime. Note the logical error the subject makes: if death is the sublime (A), then rejection of the sublime through abdication (P) leads to a state which does not include death (B). But of course death (X) is the only event which is *absolutely inevitable* (Y). Therefore, death is true (T) whether or not one chooses A or B. Consequently, P → B (-X) (if abdication then life without death) = F because the argument that (A or B) → X is T. One or the other but not both must be T. How do we know it is T? Because X → Y, then (A or B) = X is T. (If death is absolutely inevitable, it does not matter if we choose A or B we will still end up dead!). Therefore, death is the only event which is always true (T) because it is the only event which is absolutely inevitable (Y). The word "death" (X) is merely a signifier for the only event which is Y.

Here we have the motive for the crime: B (X-). But this proposition belongs to the universe of discourse of the Imaginary, not the real or even the symbolic; it is itself symbolic and therefore cannot belong to itself. The only thing we can be absolutely certain is real is death. As apprehension of the sublime is only possible in the desert of the real through bare life, life in the Imaginary, in usurping the sublime, excludes death. This is the fundamental mechanism of the apparatus (installation) of the Imaginary. By excluding death it also excludes any possibility of the real. Death, reality, love, the thingness of things, and the Other - the category of the signified - are reduced to signifiers in blatant violation of the rule of signification which states that each must remain in its own category to be true (T). Through this inversion the subject reorients itself in opposition to life, which is what Baudrillard calls a fatal strategy, resulting in one category negating the other, or a false (F) proposition. One cannot say that the signifier is the signified. This is the equivalent of stating that A = B, the fundamental error of Aristotle's Rules of Thought.

In the turning-from, then, the subject transmogrifies the other into a symbol of itself. The inverted orientation extracts humanity from the other. While this rids the subject of the nuisance of having to relate to anyone but itself, it also applies the ethical aesthetic of estimating the symbolic other in terms of its use-value only. If the other has a negative use-value, then it must be disposed of. If it has a positive use value (of varying degrees, which are trivial), then the other must be enslaved or exploited. This, then, was the ethical aesthetic of the Nazis which with great success they managed to make into an institution. The hegemony's corporate overlords were so impressed with the spectacular achievement that they have been emulating it ever since. The only difference is that 1) they avoided Hitler's greatest mistake: ultimately alienating the people from the illusion that they had a modicum of self-determination through the con game of democracy, and 2) they had the dramatic advantage of digital technology. By the networking of gadgets, it becomes possible to penetrate deep into the neuropsychology of the subject through an endless stream of meaningless bric-à-brac, chatter, and commercial and political propaganda. Combined with the unleashing of infinite debt through easy credit backed by the indenture of promissory notes, the subject inevitably chooses the candy bar of abdication over the cyanide of the sublime with all of its creepy memento mori. This is the Nazi legacy to the world.

In vilifying the Nazis and reducing them to cartoon characters, the bad guys in movies, and an epithet to hurl at one's enemies, the subject reinforces its sense that it could never be like them. Its vehemence on this point is usually in proportion to the degree that its speculation has isolated it from the transcendental object through fathomless solipsism. Such an orientation blinds the subject to the possibility that it is itself a Nazi. The subject is perfectly comfortable with the hegemony's strategy of engaging in the same inhuman practices of the Nazis except by proxy, robot weapons, and the paid or coerced conscription of brutal dictators who rule by terror and torture. The hegemonic powers that create refugee crises through their proxy wars even take in a token amount of these refugees from the countries they destroy to prove to the subject that their government is nothing like those evil Nazis. This does not mean that therefore the hegemony and its corporate overlords are Nazis. Nor does it mean that those who they dehumanize and persecute are Jews. The Nazis were the Nazis and the Jews are the Jews. They own their sovereign history. However, their historical relationship provides an apt example of the consequences of the subject's speculation. It cannot happen here, thinks the subject. History provides a neat excuse to believe that such atrocities are part of the stupid atavistic past, since in the ethical aesthetic of the subject's *progressivism* the world only gets better, smarter, kinder, and civilized through the mere passage of time. The subject knows, and has been told again and again, that *the future will always be even better than the present* because it is, well, the future. N'est-ce pas? It is the only possible outcome of the proposition that humans get smarter simply by the mere passage of time, like a fine vintage wine. A cave man, therefore, is the iconic stupid person. Popular history teaches us that the subjects of ancient cultures, despite their impressive achievements such as 3,000-year dynasties, millions of miles of paved roads, all forms of mathematics, elegant written languages, profound books, insights of astronomy, vast canals, magnificent architecture, global navigation by the wind and stars, and immortal art and music, nevertheless were "like an old-stone savage armed," says Robert Frost in the poem "Mending Wall." They moved, as he says, "in darkness as it seems to me ..." Atavistic cultures with their pretty carpets and tourist trinkets, worshiping cows and grotesque wooden idols, are pre Christian, pre TV, pre industrial, pre private equity fund, pre video game, pre fentanyl, pre digital gadget. What is worse, they are the festering repositories of the many wicked superstitious beliefs pagans, typically, abuse themselves and others with. Besides, people of the past carry exotic diseases which the subject's enlightened culture has managed to banish from its territory by fiat with the promise from the gods of Scientism that no new diseases will ever rear their ugly buboes again at the borders of their consumer culture. The subject never thinks that its belief in eternal life through consumerism and debt may be even more *primitive*, ignorant, superstitious, and deadly than anything even a cave person dared imagine. He could not afford to imagine such things.

Marcus Aurelius, in his *Meditations* (14), describes the error in the fallacious thinking of infinite progressivism that I am here calling the *progressive fallacy*: "The longest and shortest are ... the same, for the present is the same to all, though that which perishes is not the same, and so that which is lost appears to be a mere moment, for a man cannot lose either the past or the future; for what a man has not, how could anyone take this from him? These two things, then, thou must bear in mind: the one, that all things from eternity are of like forms, and come round in a circle, and that it makes no difference whether a man see the same things during a hundred years or two hundred or an infinite time; and the second, that the longest liver and he who will die soonest lose just the same, for *the present is the only thing of which a man can be deprived*, if it is true that this is the only thing which he has, and that a man cannot lose a thing if he has it not."

In particular, here, he points out the folly of the ego's narcissistic desire for immortality. "Though thou shouldest be going to live 3,000 years, and as many as 10,000 years, remember that no man loses any other life than that which he now lives, nor lives any other than that which he now loses." I would think that the irrational proposition of immortality would be self-evident to those receptive to the idea of death as the only certainty in life, and the price we must pay for it. Perhaps. But it is also evident that the promise of medical immortality in the video game of the amniotic empire (provided one keeps up with one's payments) is enough to enthrall the subject into a kind of hypnotic sense of infinite *Möglichkeit*, or possibility, of this metaphysical miracle, always in that land of happy unicorns: *the future*. As all miracles must defy sundry laws of nature and physics to *be* miracles, the fact that immortality requires infinite resources, meaning also infinite money, willfully escapes the subject; it would only spoil the fun. As Freud says, repression of such powerful psychic energy as the fear of death can only result in a *displacement substitute*, such as morbid fixation on murder, death, and war, such as we find to be ubiquitous in the casual amusements of civilizations grown moribund in their fatal embrace of hubris and mass psychosis.

Such a garden of earthly delights, however, is not possible in the bare-life world of the far-off other who is compelled by desperation to provide the Apex Consumer with the gadgets, gizmos, and bric-a-brac he needs to feel real in the fantasy world of the Imaginary. The strictures and rigors of bare life tend to pitch the far-off (usually brown) other into the sublime of the eternal moment Marcus describes above, but without the choice to live that way. What matters most to one is not how one lives, but if one *chose* to live that way. Why? In part because it also means one may choose *not* to live that way, which is not a specifically human right, but the biological imperative of all creatures to seek out that which is best for them and their fellows. Such an imperative transcends what Marx calls the *fetish* of freedom.

The far-off other, however, would not be the effective widget the hegemony of the Apex Consumer needs to power the amnion's lust for infinite power and resources if it were to have the option of *preferring not to*, like Melville's Bartleby. Despite being also pitched into the horror vacui of the sublime, the far-off other tends to long for what he sees a the prerogatives of these alien creatures jetting over his head in fighter planes, each of which is worth more than his nation's annual GDP, launching Hellfire missiles at his shadowy oppressor. Unlike his counterpart in the hegemonic empire, the far-off other longs for simple things the denizen of the amnion regards, at best, with contempt, such as food, water, shelter, and a living.

In Robert Bolt's screenplay for David Lean's *Lawrence of Arabia* (1962), King Faisal bin Abdulaziz Al Saud, of Saudi Arabia, then a so-called third-world country, upbraids British officer T.E. Lawrence for his seeming obsession with the arid territory of his kingdom. In a kind of colonial psychoanalysis of Lawrence and his compatriots' overtures, he says, "I think you are another of these desert-loving English .... No Arab loves the desert. We love water and green trees. There is nothing in the desert. And no man needs nothing. Or is it that you think we are something you can play with ... because we are a 'little people, a silly people ... greedy, barbarous and cruel'? Or do you know, lieutenant, in the Arab city of Cordoba ... [there] were two miles of lighting in the streets ... when London was a village?" Faisal does not fail to point out that the colonialists' low opinion of the far-off other merely shows their ignorance of history.

To the mentality of these various hegemonic characters throughout their adventures in this and the last century, the atavistic cultures of the far-off other are *bad* because they represent millennia of *tradition*, which is old (amortized), cannot be effectively monetized (self-sufficient), and are unscientific (in this case Muslim). To the hegemony, a cocktail of amortization of national assets, economic self-sufficiency, and a shared metaphysical ethical aesthetic holding that there is indeed a Power greater than mankind in the universe, *is cause for war*. How dare these cave men go against our commercial marketing and expedient political propaganda and geopolitics! Also, the far-off other favors *agriculture* and hunting-gathering (for obvious reasons) – occupations characterized by hegemonic bankers and industrialists as fit only for dumb rednecks, ignorant racists, genocidal nationalists, hungry cannibals, and other stupid poor people who look and act funny.

But finally and most importantly, these barbarians do not have the same level of comfort and convenience (i.e. civilization) as the mass of subjects in the land of the Fortunate. Such as sit-down toilets that flush. Therefore, the far-off other has a *negative* use value in the ethical aesthetic of the Apex Consumer. This is a dangerous situation for the far-off other. The subject's hegemony, that it claims it elected and voluntarily supports through ever-increasing taxes (it willingly cheats on), will act to *eliminate* the far-off other unless it abdicates its sovereignty, which is the only card it has left to play by design. As long as the Apex Consumer has access to cheap goods and the credit to buy them, it is largely content with the ethical aesthetic of the amnion. The Apex Consumer is satisfied with the status quo, despite its highly public displays of collective pity for what it regards as the subhuman races it professes to want to lift from the wretchedness and poverty it has exacerbated and even caused. Wrenched from its traditional agrarian society and incarcerated in a factory, the far-off other lives in terror of the corporate overlords who own the factory, often enough by foreign proxy, the overseers who run it, its government which is bought and paid for by these overlords, and the developed-world hegemonies ready to annihilate its territory to exploit its natural resources. Unless it keeps up with the Apex Consumer's demand for the blood and sweat of its sovereignty, it will be forced to become, at best, a refugee staggering through hostile nations, ultimately to be penned up in internment camps and forgotten. At worst, it will become a victim of a contrived genocide engineered to provide excuse and justification for military action by the Apex Consumer's hegemony in a wanton seizure and theft of its sovereign and hereditary territory.

Meantime, the subject is convinced that the fascist regime of the Nazis' could never happen again because of its government's quick action in suppressing what it calls tyrants in sovereign countries. It sees its armies as white knights crusading for democracy in god-forsaken hell holes. It is certain that a fascist regime would never really ever happen in its own nation – despite cries from one political party or another that its opponents are a bunch of Nazis. After all, the word Nazi is thrown around every day in the media as an epithet to the point that it long ago lost its assignment as the signifier of the actual *Nationalsozialistische Deutsche Arbeiterpartei* (NSADP). About the actual Nazi party the subject knows nothing. In school it learns that the word Nazi = bad, and that the swastika = evil, despite being one of the most common symbols in Hindu and Buddhist culture. That is all the subject needed to know in the special language of the hegemony. The word and the symbol would later be used as triggers for certain predictable behaviors in the subject by the hegemony which, ironically, has much in common in its actions and aims with the historic governments its vilifies. The hegemony knows that the gradual usurpation of the subject's sovereignty through debt and ever-greater erosion of its statutory freedoms will result in a citizen who will stop at nothing to preserve what he sees as his birthright as an Apex Consumer. If there is even the slightest doubt of this, we only have roll back the tape to news of motorists shooting each other over a place on line at the gas station. At even a hint of the slightest privation, the typically docile subject runs amok. A more general loss of public order, public works, and the comforting hum of commerce and finance would be a disaster. Nevertheless, the subject is goaded by the hegemony to take to the streets to protest against police brutality in the hope of harvesting its anger and frustration for weaponization against its enemies. Despite appearances, the chronically corrupt hegemony thrives in chaos, as chaos allows it to move about unseen through the interstices of popular belief and treasure behind a smoke screen of burning cars and calls for martial law. There is a risk, though, that chaos will get beyond control. The subject's gadgets and gizmos that depend upon a network infrastructure may stop working in such events. The plastic cards and automatic teller machines it depends upon for money may become unavailable. The sudden collapse of the amnion could shock the subject into a reflexive lust for fascism as it did to the German population after World War I. However, there is a significant difference between these comparative Zeitgeists. Western culture was *much better equipped* to deal with privation in 1918. Since the amnion has replaced the subject's culture, sometimes from before the subject was born, there is no time-tested ethnic or cultural aesthetic or self-sufficient agricultural infrastructure to fall back upon. The general standard of living before the war would be considered dire poverty to the subject. People expected far less from their government and from life in general in terms of basic necessities and creature comfort. Furthermore, most of these populations were engaged in agriculture which at least has the potential to feed them. Their amnion consisted of religion which for thousands of years had actually *helped* the subject through hard times and disasters, but is now vilified by its rival Scientism as superstition or even terrorism.

To avoid this horror, the subject continually elects exactly the same bevy of politicians who will help bring this disaster down upon its head. The elected officials' reckless spending of future tax money - most of which eventually finds itself in the digital vaults of the hegemony's international banking overlords - endangers the amnion's ability to remain a substitute for culture. It helps expand dependency on government handouts among the Underclass, condemning them to live at subsistence level just out of reach of the Promised Land. Meantime, the class of corporate overlords uses the profits to buy up the means of production, vast tracts of agricultural land, commercial and domestic real estate, and mineral and natural resources. Elected officials are candid about their agenda of restricting the subject's freedom in the name of national security, and the threats of human trafficking, gun violence, drug lords, pedophile priests, Islamic terrorists and other such nebulous media mythologies. With each diminution of the subject's degrees of freedom the culture sinks deeper into the corporate *fasces*. In the deep structure of the hegemony and its amnion, though, this fascist infrastructure has already been put into place. Surveillance, the most intimate personal details of the subject's life, and its fetal dependency on the matrix of the amnion, provide the perfect environment for a totalitarian state from which there is no escape as it is *ubiquitous*.

As its laws get more draconian, its prisons fill to far beyond capacity. Its miscreants find themselves on federal no fly and person of interest lists made public to terrorize the population into obedience. The apparatus configures itself so that all persons, no matter how Pollyanna and pure, will eventually break a law. The legal system becomes a minefield without a map. With justice mainly for the rich, the subject knows it is guilty even before it breaks a law. When it is charged and then fined or convicted, it is not surprised. It merely sees it as paying its debt to society which was long overdue since birth. Especially with the knowledge that throughout its life it has broken laws with impunity, such as underage drinking. While the laws are myriad, unintelligible, and draconian, the subject is actually encouraged to break them through the perception of selective enforcement. Its natural sense of statistical inference tells it that given the fact that the law is only enforced more or less at random it has an X percent chance of getting caught. Compelled by the discontents of civilization it seeks to satisfy its instinctive urges - which are the strategic target of the law - it even gets a thrill out of cheating on its taxes, buying and using illegal drugs, and breaking the speed limit. The *id* compels the subject to think that laws are made to be broken unless it becomes the victim of a crime. If it does, it demands justice to the fullest extent of the law. Among the many sins the subject's flesh is heir to is hypocrisy. In fact, it sees contradiction of its own values, breaking the law, and unethical practices to be the essence of the modicum of self-determination the hegemony strategically allows after abdication. Behind this miasma is the hegemony's strategy.

Selective enforcement targets the Unfortunates of the Underclass as scapegoats to keep the subject from having to confront the realities of bare life. Getting robbed of the precious acquisitions it has accumulated as part of its program of what Veblen calls conspicuous consumption makes the subject vote for more restriction of its own freedom. For the Unfortunate going to jail for these crimes it is as much a part of life as public school and collecting the handouts it gets from the compassionate largess of the subject's hegemony. Since the Unfortunate is often too disenfranchised and dispirited to vote, it makes an excellent scapegoat because it cannot influence elections in the direction of its own interests rather than those of the hegemony's corporate overlords. They need the "haves" to vote, not the "have-nots." No matter how terrible the Unfortunate's circumstances get, a little injection of public funds and benefits is enough to keep it from striving for access to the amnion where it is unwanted and feared anyway. The subject, smug in its amnion of *Genuss,* takes great pleasure in its superiority and relative immunity from the law. It knows that the more money and power it has the lower the percentage is that it will get punished for breaking the law. It may get caught, but it also knows that it will be able to pay its fines using the profits from its crimes. It is just part of the cost of doing business. Therefore, it breaks the law on a massive scale through white collar crime, corruption, and legerdemain. Despite the ever-increasing restrictions on freedom made into law by the lawyer-politicians they buy, the corporate overlords compel those same politicians to repay them by rescinding laws restricting *their* freedom to exploit the labor of the subject.

In this state of narcissistic solipsism the subject becomes impotent, incapable of relating to the Other as the transcendental object because it has reoriented itself from its natural position in the *turning-to,* to the *turning-from*. It *turns to* itself in specular orientation which is the same act as the *turning-from* the transcendental object. In the same event the subject loses its identity by assigning itself to a sign of itself. The amnion injects these alien signs through the media and memes transmitted by other subjects. While they have many appeals, the main discourse is: *abdicate*. (The sub discourses include *buy, consume, believe, vote,* and *belong*). This fatal strategy is part of the subject's undoing because it requires *a priori* abdication of sovereignty through debt in the form of signing promissory notes. Without the power to borrow, the subject would not be able to participate in the consumer amnion. It would have no mortgage, car loan, business loan, credit card, or, in some countries, higher education.

In turning-from the Other, it (A) deprives the Other of the possibility of possessing itself (B) as the subject in relation to the subject (A) as the Other. Therefore, the natural orientation of A → B, B → A becomes A → A, B → B. Obviously, in the first orientation there is relationship; in the second only isolation without the possibility of relationship. What is particularly pernicious about this objectification is that, again, it is imposed on the Other through induction; the Other has no opportunity to relate to the subject. Therefore, for there to be relationship there must be symmetry in the relational orientation between both sides of the equation because they are united in series (X) not parallel (Y). The requirement is that for X to be T then A and B must be

T: A(T) ^ B(T) = T. For Y to be T either A or B must be T but not necessarily both: A(T) ∨ B(T) = T. Therefore, if apprehension of the transcendental object were unilateral then even A(F) ^ B(T) = T. But that is not the case because for both sides of the equation to be relational they must also be true. Why? Because it is obvious that if both sides were false, as in A(F) ^/∨ B(F), then it is not possible for the outcome to be T unless it were A(F) – B(F) = AB(T). For this equation to be true, A must negate (destroy) B or vice versa so that one no longer stands in opposition (relation) to the Other. But once the Other is destroyed, the subject loses the potential to be the Other of the Other and therefore loses itself in the process. "For what shall it profit a man, if he shall gain the whole world, and lose his own soul?" says Mark 8:36.

Besides this infinite devaluation of the Other to *0* (null), psychometrics also manages to ignore what one instinctively takes for granted in one's relationships with others: the *distribution* of intelligence over different domains of cognition. Another effect of the exchange of the signifier for the signified is that it paralyzes instinct which is the origin of its inherent and pernicious frustration of the id. This is no accident; the hegemony's own autonomic mechanics tells it that it can control the cognition of the subject, but not what is incognizable in the subject which is primarily the functions of the id and the libido. The libido, as a kind of phallic extension of the id in psychological time and space, is subject to a certain amount of influence through repression. However, the id by its cryptic nature as being *prelinguistic,* evades direct attempts to repress it. Since all repression – except that which is prosecuted by the sword – is effected through language, the id cannot be seen by the thought of either the subject or object. If it could, it would not be unconscious! Still, it is vulnerable through its extensions such as the libido which must interface with the world in some concrete way to achieve its aim (principally procreation). We have been referring to cognition as if it were a monolith in the domain of awareness and consequently consciousness. This is a simplification for the sake of discussion. In fact, it is a highly complex collection of what might be called intelligences which by necessity, evolution, and the diversification of function in society and civilization are distributed over distinct domains. It is not possible to list them all; rather, what is significant is that these functions arise out of necessity through the fact of the need to embody contradictory roles, such as mother-lover in relation to the son. It is generally thought to be ineffectual for the mother to also be the lover of the son (or daughter). These relationships are in the vertical tree of hierarchical relationships requiring fundamentally different cognitive roles. On the horizontal plane there are the cognitive functions applying at every vertical level such as the computational, linguistic, visual-spatial, and kinetic intelligences. While the former are impossible to quantify (which has not stopped the fetish for quantification from inventing such interesting mare's nests as emotional intelligence or EQ), the latter are. The result has been chaos, confusion, misnomer, prejudice, misapplication, dehumanization, and a kind of smug resolve to let all arguments to the contrary to be dismissed as irrational. And all because we *can* quantify these functions with some demonstrable analog in the actual operation of the subject within their applicable context. Herein lies the problem. Under the ethical aesthetic of expediency if something *can* be quantified that possibility is seen as the determination that it *should* be quantified. If it can, then it follows this simple-minded formula for meaningless data. What drives this madness is the lust for *expediency* which began with an application of that which most of us can accept: the assignment of individuals to the specific functions in war. As war is the ultimate state of exception, expediency as an ethical aesthetic is good, right, and proper in a state of war for such obvious reasons that they need not be expressed here. After the first half of the Twentieth Century dominated by world war, the corporate and financial overlords of the hegemony observed that the state of exception is far more beneficial to their objectives than any other. Consequently, they began a covert campaign to install a permanent state of exception by aggravating perpetual *proxy wars* with what were once its client states. In many cases it was the cartel of the hegemonies which cut those states out of the dusty cloth of the desert only to find that under the sand untold riches of energy resources lied that were needed to fuel the next phase of commercial development their corporate overlords depended upon.

A result of the perpetual state of war was the encroachment of quantification into areas where it was either not needed or simply did not belong. While a case can be made for the correlation of cranium size and intelligence as the Nazis asserted, this kind of psychometrics is looked upon with abhorrence while others which are more or less the equivalent are embraced as the final solution to what is seen as a long-standing problem of figuring out who is stupid and who is smart. (As if it were not possible to figure this out from our social interactions with others.) A valid argument can be made that during a war there is no time to wait out this social selection process, particularly when the so-called clear and present danger erupts unexpectedly. Perhaps, then, such systems are needed – though it is hard to imagine the armies described first hand in Xenophon's *A History of My Times* going through pencil-and-paper tests before taking up the sword. The state, then, incrementally expanded the state of exception it so much enjoyed in wartime where there are no budget restrictions, no messy consultation with the public, and no deontological imperatives to do the right thing. Instead it has embraced the teleological as its sole ethical aesthetic while at the same time strategically inventing a kind end for its means: the means never reach the end because the end itself determines the means. Tomorrow never comes in perpetual war because the means *are* the end. As we shall see later in more detail, such a strategy creates an *ouroboros* with a circuit large enough to evade the subject's awareness of its cyclical nature. Like a video of a waterfall in a loop large enough so that the subject thinks it is a linear video of a finite segment of time played only once, this ouroboros of war is timed perfectly and is portrayed in the media with such skill and precision that the subject, whose attention span has been reduced to the "moment" and little else, accepts the "evidence" it is fed in quantities sufficient to maintain this illusion indefinitely. Meantime, the symbols of fear must constantly be refreshed to create the further illusion that beyond the pale of the subject's amnion lie vast hordes of unwashed barbarians and atavistic far-off others who, when not fabricating the bric-à-brac and gadgetry the subject cannot live without, plot endlessly to destroy the livelihood the subject's paradise of *Genuss* makes possible for them. That these propositions are absurd is not a problem for the subject. Absurdity is only perceptible when there is a basis for logical comparison of an efficient and rational system. For the Imaginary to function as it does it must preclude any possibility of this sort of cognition from reaching the subject. By reducing mandatory state education to *indoctrination* into this system and the media into the conduit for its corporate propaganda, the illusion is sustained despite occasional interruptions from trolls, hackers, and miscreants from the shadowy realms of the far-off others.

It is obvious to the subject and its society that the distribution of intelligence over the vertical quantitative (x) and the horizontal qualitative (y) axes poses insurmountable problems for the science of psychometrics. After all, the majority lie within the unflattering zones of the average and below average. Such distinctions are what the subject knows as undemocratic. Maybe even unfair, since they are not necessarily borne out in practice. Still, the subject accepts the sometimes cruel limitations imposed upon it by what amounts to a kind of social eugenics. Why? Because the entire system of endless *g*-loaded tests of more or less monolithic smartness favor those who provide the subject with the smart gadgets it cannot live without. Science and engineering – which are what in psychometrics are called g-loaded disciplines (STEM) – produce the cars, gadgets, gizmos, and infotainment the subject requires to feel part of the amnion for which it has forsaken its sovereignty. Also important are the arsenals of magical weaponry guarding the subject from the far-off other always on the warpath because, through the mechanism of relative deprivation, it sees what the subject has and wants it but cannot get it (although, presumably, it *makes* it).

It is also true that the amount of data necessary to accurately judge intelligence – if possible – is so vast that the ethical aesthetic of expediency will now allow it. The result is a *reductio ad absurdum*. There is nothing wrong with oversimplification when it is recognized as such. Certainly, intelligence should be measured. The results should be pondered. And in times of clear and present danger the data should be pressed into service for the good of all. But using the snapshot of a person taken during a test cannot accurately reflect that person's distribution of intelligence *over time*. So far we have analyzed this distribution as a static quantity present at any given moment. Also, as mentioned, that this state of intelligence is indeed present at any given moment does not allow, therefore, that it can and must be measured. But any attempt to apply such quantification to the outcome of one's life must neglect what Hacking calls the long-run or long-tail (ergodic) statistical potential "in some human scale of length" (p. 36). The quantities involved become astronomical. They must always prefigure a variable which is more or less "infinite" by being indefinite: time. The old saw that if you set a monkey in front of a typewriter forever it will eventually type out the works of Shakespeare is just another way of saying that T (time) is a variable which cannot be accounted for except when we limit it to a span of time for which we can manage to *make it* accountable. Therefore the only possibility for getting any kind of verifiable idea of how much intelligence there is in what someone does is in the *result*. If the smartest guys in the room collapse the economy, endanger national security, and ruin the financial lives of millions, were they *really* that smart after all?

We conveniently reduce intelligence to a quantity serving our *a priori* ends without taking into consideration how this methodology skews the result in favor of a predetermined outcome. Such behavior favors what Hacking calls *the rule for the unique case*. While this rule is essential for an accurate approximation of the probability of reality which is fraught with exceptions, it actually works *against* the idea of the quantification of intelligence. In terms of probability there is no error in saying that the rule for the unique case could apply to the person who shows great intelligence in the long run but not in the snapshot, although the snapshot itself has proven itself to apply to the outcome in the short run. If this were not so then it would be easy to pick out genius simply by taking a genius test. As ridiculous as the idea of genius is in the first place as something specific, denotative, and signified, we nevertheless regard it as inexplicable. It seems to come from nowhere, such as when it is the product of two unexceptional parents and a social milieu in which such precocity is not the rule. There is an anecdote about the Spanish virtuoso violinist Pablo de Sarasate. His assistant ran to him with a review of the previous night's concert in Cuba. "Master, they call you a genius!" he said. Far from pleased, legend has it that Sarasate said, "Genius? Genius! For 37 years I've been practicing 14 hours a day, and now they call me a genius."

A photograph of a person at a drunken party wearing a silly hat and dancing like an idiot does not account for that person's lifetime of experience, education, and achievement, as well as what Elizabeth Barrett Browning calls "the depth and breadth and height / My soul can reach ..." in her sonnet "How do I love thee ..." Again, though, the ethical aesthetic of expediency – which is the hegemony's equivalent of the subject's lust for comfort and convenience – reduces the incognizable complexity of reality to a simple formula which can be programmed into a digital system. This procedure *erases* the critical difference between the subjective and objective in our understanding of what might be reality. Once the transcendental object has been stripped of its otherness, the subject too loses its identity as a particular personality. With astonishing speed the subject soon strips itself of anything unique that might make it stick out among the herd. Of course there are those who secretly maintain their individuality through this ordeal. Sooner or later, though, they will be found out and punished – even if they become renegades and rage against the machine. Meantime, what Heidegger calls the furniture of the world gets robbed of its thingness. These are the things which are perceived which have their own *thingness* apart from perception. It may seem that it would be impossible to rob reality of its realness. If it were not for language, which is our chief interface with reality as thought and cognition, it would not be possible. Animals have little risk of this happening. In this state, they are blessed since they do not *need* to interface with the reality of the other and the reality of themselves through symbols. They remain members of objective reality even after domestication because of the fundamental difference between their thinking and human thinking. This does not mean that they do not think. Rather, they think in such a way where cognition is not burdened with the signifier and the referent. Why this is so, what its significance is, whether or not it is better or worse, what it has to do with God, and so on are all phenomenological questions which a philosophical essay cannot hope to answer. It is clear, however, that one of our great attractions to the companionship of animals and our admiration for them in the wild has to do with their apparent freedom from the need to assign signifiers to the thingness of things. Adam is given the task of assigning signifiers to *them*. Not long after that he discovers the Fruit of the Tree of the Knowledge of Good and Evil and his innocence dissolves in the catastrophe of the Fall from Grace.

After the Fall, we are left with the reality of the perception of things. We cannot say that our perception of the distinction between one thing and another is unreal. This has nothing to do with the thingness of the thing but of the process of our perception which begins with awareness and ends with consciousness. If one thing is red and the other green, is the distinction real? It is not outside of reality to say that they are different colors. Redness and greenness are part of the subjectivity of perception as a physical phenomenon of light, not of the thingness of the thing. That some animals see things in infrared light, which humans do not, does not mean that this more subtle perception of a thing is any closer to its reality. The air is cluttered with broadcasts over thousands of radio frequencies and RFI. Despite this, many persons today will go to their graves having never heard a real radio. Does this mean that the intelligence the waves carry does not exist? We say of course not. However, if we limit the subject's universe of discourse to what it can perceive without a radio and without anyone to tell it that there are radio waves, who is to say that they exist? Herein lies the value of predicate logic. If we are to make any kind of intelligent assessment of reality we have to understand our own limitations. While we scoff at the ignoramus who does not even know that he does not even know there are radio waves, we ourselves are the butt of some other cosmic joke based on what we do not know we do not know. It would be more accurate to call the human species man who does not know he does not know than the misnomer homo sapiens *sapiens* – which is more or less meaningless (even in Latin). How many members of the race can even be called sapiens homo, or the wise man? Kant's exhortation *sapere aude*, or dare to know, would not be necessary if it were an innate characteristic of the species. If anything, we can say that unlike other creatures man is given a *choice*. It is no use stating what that choice is here; there are too many answers to what it might be, from Yeats' "perfection of the life or of the work" to Moses' good and evil in the form of the Decalogue. It is sufficient to say only that it seems animals are not given this choice, and are, therefore, free.

Such distinctions do not make perception unreal, however. Whether one believes in fire or not one will still burn, despite insistence to the contrary by certain fakirs. Even the unreal is real because if it were not it could not be perceived as unreal. Something must be really unreal to be unreal. Trying to sort out the real from the unreal is like trying to determine if intelligence is the absence of stupidity or if stupidity is the absence of intelligence. Consciousness depends upon the right functioning of intelligence in the form of *choice*, the process of the getting-to-know, and the understanding of the objective and subjective qualities of reality. Without personal sovereignty any argument about intelligence, awareness, consciousness, knowledge, and reality is worthless. Why? Because there is no one to possess those qualities. The abdicated state is complete abstraction of the individual into a figment of itself. Without the sovereign identity of "I" there is no one to perceive the attributes of reality as the transcendental object. The "I" of the abdicated subject is the material equivalent of the "I" of the automated natural language processor (IVR) answering the phone at a business when it refers to itself as "I." It is not enough to throw around the personal pronoun to be considered conscious. However, it is enough to be considered responsible for one's actions by the popular mentality of the media, politics, education, and society. Therefore, democracy, egalitarianism, society, and even civilization only ever demand that one be aware enough to sign a promissory note. They are afraid that if they demanded consciousness from the subject it would expose certain already-existing modes of unpleasant stratification. It would also create a monster that would consider its own needs first before those of the hegemonic order and its overlords. In earlier forms of civilization where egalitarianism was not an ethical aesthetic the aware subject was best exploited for the ends of the state. The conscious subject was a liability. As a sovereign "I" that subject owed allegiance to itself first, then to the state. This is simply intolerable to the hegemony. Thanks to the efforts of a few conscious individuals of history – many of whom are admired for their martyrdom – it is fashionable today to allow the aware subject a modicum of self-determination. This little bit of wiggle room within the confines of the dungeon it has thrown itself into through abdication allows it to manufacture the illusion that it is free. Being able to choose between different cars, colleges, insurance policies, TV screen sizes, credit cards, and colors of peppers in the marketplace helps reinforce this illusion.

Of course this is only true for the Apex Consumer, admitted into full participation in the phantasmagoria of debt consumerism. The less fortunates of the Underclass only have illegal drugs, violence, religion, and alcohol as their freedom within the razor wire the hegemony has strung around the penitentiary of bare life. Without access to debt it is not possible for them to spin the web of materialism the Fortunates are fortunate enough to find themselves ensnared in. From time to time, however, the corporate overlords command the hegemony to loosen up lending rules regarding the less fortunates to allow them to have a taste of the good life. But this is not out of compassion for their lack of enjoyment of the full largess of civilization; rather, it is to harvest whatever savings or assets the less fortunates might have been able to scrape together in the meantime during their exile. On an even more fundamental level, it gives the corporate overlords of the hegemony access to whatever public money might have been just out of their reach because of quaint laws regarding the use of public money for private gain.

Considering its options, then, perhaps the choice for the subject is between consciousness and unconsciousness. But the paradoxical trap is that consciousness is consciousness of one's unconsciousness. As soon as one is conscious of one's unconsciousness one is no longer unconscious, but to be conscious of one's unconsciousness one must be conscious. How, then, does one bootstrap oneself into consciousness? It is simply not logically possible. In other words, the matter of the choice of consciousness is incognizable. Therefore, consciousness cannot be a conscious choice because it must come into being from unconsciousness, which is not possible through the willful action of the individual. At such an aporia the religious turn to God and the credulous turn to vain efforts at raising consciousness through *more* knowledge. Perhaps the first have more success than the second. Nevertheless, both do not take up the matter of sovereignty. Both also overlook the possibility that consciousness precedes knowledge, that it is not something which one attains but rather something that one loses. Peirce describes how children develop into self-consciousness:

> At the age at which we know children to be self-conscious, we know that they have been made aware of *ignorance and error*; and we know them to possess at that age powers of understanding sufficient to enable them *to infer from ignorance and error their own existence*. Thus we find that known faculties, acting under conditions known to exist, would rise to self-consciousness. (p. 29)

In other words, consciousness arises from the contemplation of ignorance and error. When one sees the error of one's ways, one becomes more conscious. When one discovers that one is ignorant of this or that, so too does one become more conscious. These are just other ways of describing the getting-to-know. The critical flaw in nearly all thinking about consciousness is the result of a kind of ethereal materialism. Consciousness is regarded as a *thing* to be acquired, just as unconsciousness is regarded as a thing to be gotten rid of. The oddity of this is that awareness is not regarded as a thing but a state. To say that one is aware of being conscious or unconscious would mean that the positive and negative forms of whatever consciousness is are both *things to be aware of*. Who can deny, however, that heuristics is not a concrete form of consciousness as a process? The materialism regarding thinking about consciousness is the result of ignorance about its nature as a process. It is not something apart from ignorance and error nor is it any different from the heuristics we apply in their correction. However, there must be a self to apply it. As the child develops self-consciousness the foundation of the sovereign self is laid. It is upon this foundation that the more sophisticated heuristics of reason prevail. Another meaning of sapiens is one who is reasonable. For a heuristic to be effective it must be guided first by awareness of ignorance and error – often pointed out by the wise men who have gone before the subject – and then by the correction of those errors and therefore the dispelling of ignorance. This process can only be practiced by a subject with a sense of identity in the form of recognition of the transcendental object in the form of the Other. Recognition and identity are the same phenomenon, just as the recognition of error and ignorance are not other than consciousness. Therefore, both identity and consciousness are not things in and of themselves to be had or found, really, but are rather principles which must be active in the form of processes to function. Just as life itself is not any one thing we can point to but a collection of processes, so too are these attributes which we believe we may ascribe to the subject. To dwell as the transcendental object one must apprehend it in the Other, negating the subject-object dichotomy by becoming the Other's Other. Sovereignty, however, is only possible when one has the power to live the bare life of the sublime. As the horror vacui, the sublime demands satisfaction of its creative imperative to fill its void with consciousness. In as much as we are *actively cognizant* of the sublime, we are conscious. To be cognizant without action is awareness. As such it is a passive attribute of being. Just as the horror vacui demands fulfillment in the creative imperative so too does cognition demand participation in the form of action to be considered consciousness. By *acting* the subject exposes itself to the getting-to-know. And in so doing admits that it does not *know-of* but that it *needs to know*. To admit that one needs to know negates the possibility (curse) of hubris. If Oedipus had not been so complacent about his shadowy past he might have discovered the truth before it was too late. The tragedy of Oedipus is that he remained in ignorance and error until it was necessary for fate to visit the disaster of the sublime upon him. He only became able to see his error when he put his eyes out, thus cutting himself off from the illusions of a world that so stealthily led him into his demise.

1.4: Ethical aesthetics of beauty and *Genuss*

What, after all, is beauty? Like the thousands of words indicating nothing at all, this one must be defined each time it is used. That is its chief characteristic. When we consider how many words *demand* this necessity to be more than nonsense, we realize that we hardly have a language at all. We are not really that far from hand gestures and grunts to indicate our wants and needs. Most of what is said need not be said. The chatter of a barroom or a party when heard in the aggregate is a noise containing no intelligence whatsoever. Most of what we do at work could be done in silence. Look at news cycles over modern decades. Stories repeat, but with different names and trivial particulars. Nearly all that is learned in school during the best years and hours of our lives is forgotten when the last bell rings and we go home for the day. Most propositions are mere tautologies. At best they are often enough synthetic statements allowing for no possibility of verification. When we say, I think this and that, we know we are saying that we *do not know* anything about it! So then why did we say what we thought? Our most intimate moments are lorded over by bankrupt phrases such as “I love you” which, if they ever did have meaning, they lost it long ago through overuse as chatter, platitudes, and advertising copy. At the end of a person’s life, even if he wrote hundreds of books, usually little is remembered of what he *said*. What we have produced by famous authors of the past, though seemingly abundant, is only a fraction of what was actually published and read. The rest is lost to us forever. Of the eighty plays Aeschylus wrote, only eight survive – and he was one of the greatest dramatists who ever lived, honored today and since antiquity. Is this some tragedy of civilization? Perhaps in the case of Aeschylus. But generally it is because we know that most of what we say and write (this writing included) likely need not be said. There is nothing in this book which should have to be said. The tragedy of it is that of all the sentences in this book, the previous one is the most important.

So then what of beauty? We will discuss what Keats has to say about it in his "Ode on a Grecian Urn." Perhaps in poetry we find what Matthew Arnold in his essay "Culture and Anarchy" calls "the best that has been thought and said in the world." (But then again who reads poetry but poets?) Before we get to Keats, let us look at some possible origins of the concept of beauty as we will discuss it below. While there are as many definitions of it as there are people to define it, few would argue that Nature is not beautiful. Few would look at a rose or a butterfly's wings and say they are not beautiful. Few would look at the Alps and say they do not inspire awe. Who would not say that the moon is beautiful on an autumn night when the air is clear and it bathes the trees in its cold grey light? When we look at nature there is hardly a thing we could not call beautiful. So why do we have such a hard time defining it if we recognize it all around us?

The matter gets more complicated when we think of the other applications of beauty. Foremost is the beauty of man-made things. There are many things that man makes that we call beautiful. Paintings, sculpture, music, movies, clothing, architecture, ships, furniture, literature, and many other things we can look at and listen to. Then there are things in an equally big class we tend to think do not have to be beautiful, but often are in their way, such as pyramids and CPU's. Bridges, roads, office towers, cars, rockets, machines, factories, school buildings, hospitals, football stadiums, garbage dumps, power plants, and the chaos of war can be beautiful or ugly, as we like. It is true that there are ways in which we can say that all of these things are beautiful too, even war. But that is generally not the way we think. We are happy to have a class of man-made things that we call beautiful, things that do not have to be beautiful, and finally things that we consider to be ugly. Such significations make life simple. These classes free us from the conundrum of the paradox that even ugly things can be beautiful, such as pug dog or Winston Churchill, *for such is the meaningless of the word!* We will not go into a definitive treatise on beauty here. There are just a few further points to make in order to understand what is meant by the term ethical aesthetic and how it relates to the sublime.

Taking what we have said above, and acknowledging that our task here of defining the beautiful is impossible, it is likely that we can agree that whatever beauty is has to do with some quality of nature rather than man. This brings up two problems when we think about the idea of something being artificial - i.e. man-made. We can also agree that nothing in nature is artificial (despite Oscar Wilde's observation that *life mimics art*). Therefore, if something is artificial it is man-made. Since it is not of nature, then, from where does it get its beauty? If it is in the category of things that we think are beautiful and is not in the category of things which do not have to be beautiful, from where does it get its beauty if it is the opposite of natural in being artificial? As is discussed below, there are certain principles in nature which might explain it. We can express the mathematics of certain things, such as the Fibonacci series in plants or the Mandelbrot series in geographical features. What we create out of mathematics seems to have some of the qualities of the beauty of the thing we are expressing. Therefore, it is possible to say that certain principles of form, color, smell, texture, taste, and sound - in other words the qualities which stimulate our senses - can give us the same sense of beauty as we find in some natural things. We are all familiar with the artist's painting of a beautiful thing, scene, or person. Masterpieces of this art are often regarded universally as the definition of beauty in the *techne*, or art and craft, of man. This regard for works of art and architecture often cuts across cultures and even epochs. Nevertheless, we are no closer to a useful definition of beauty here. Perhaps it is enough to say that it is the beauty we so easily find in nature that we look for in the artificial - whatever that natural beauty may be. A beautiful person, of course variously defined, is not ultimately artificial despite beautiful clothes. Just as a tiger may be beautiful so might a person (though it seems there are many ugly persons and few ugly tigers). Since a person is not man made, a person's beauty is natural. What, then, of these artificial things made by a natural person? What does it mean for nature to make something such as a beautiful person, and for a person to make something beautiful such as a painting? Is not the painting as an extension of nature not also part of nature's beauty? So how then can anything man creates be said to be somehow apart from all natural principles and be, therefore, artificial in the categorical sense? This conundrum will not be resolved here. Aristotle has much to say about beauty in the *Metaphysics*, *Ethics*, *Logic*, and *Poetics* which we also will not go into here in any depth. However, it is worth mentioning something that he says in *Poetics* regarding the beautiful in the plot of a story. He compares the wholeness and unity of a plot to that of a creature. In this way he sees no difference between the *techne* of man and the subtle art of nature's creation.

Beauty is a matter of size and order, and therefore

> impossible either (1) in a very minute creature, since our perception becomes indistinct as it approaches instantaneity; or (2) in a creature of vast size—one, say, 1,000 miles long—as in that case, instead of the object being seen all at once, the unity and wholeness of it is lost to the beholder. (Poetics, Chapter VII)

Which brings us to the matter of the ethical aesthetic. In the way that it is mean here and has been defined above, an ethical aesthetic may be beautiful or not. The ethical aesthetic of war is only beautiful when it reaches the history books or the battle reenactments. When they are happening they are not *beautiful*. However, they have a strong, distinct, conscious, and deliberate ethical aesthetic. To better understand the power and significance of an ethical aesthetic, we will take a glance at Keats' ode. Much later we will go into an extensive discussion of the poem. For our purposes here we will look at what are perhaps its most memorable lines where he states his *ethical aesthetic* of life:

> "Beauty is truth, truth beauty,—that is all
> Ye know on earth, and all ye need to know."

These lines might be called the proposition of an ethical aesthetic. So the first quality of an ethical aesthetic is that it is in the form of a proposition, or can be formed into one if necessary. Naturally, it must also include ethos, or that quality which we identify with a fundamental structural principle based in reality. For example, in oratory a person is said to have weak ethos if he exhorts upon a subject which he knows little about. Therefore we may say that it is unethical for him to expound upon something he knows nothing about (for instance, how to prevent a nuclear power plant from melting down or to do emergency heart surgery). We therefore say that his statements are not based on anything except his opinion, or worse. On the other hand we respect a person whom we acknowledge has much greater knowledge than we do about his topic and whom we consider a *bona fide* expert. Looking back to what we have said about information, the latter's information is *more valuable* than the former's because its ethos is stronger. (Note that we are not using the conventional idea of ethics here as meaning following the rules of everyday morality but rather the Classical concept such as we see in the rhetorical trinity of ethos, logos, and pathos.) But what makes Keats' proposition most powerful is its union of the ethical and aesthetic. It forces us to also define this term as it is used here. In its broadest sense the aesthetic of something may be beautiful or not. Either way it remains an aesthetic. The Nazi Party in Germany during World War II had a high aesthetic sense. Its Speerian architecture, its Hugo Boss AG designer couture, its snazzy Messerschmitts zipping through antiaircraft artillery fire, its flashy goose step, and most of all its iconic swastika reverberate down through their century into the next as the mass media's aesthetic of evil, though nonetheless admired for its bold graphic and symbolic power. Is evil therefore beautiful or ugly, as we are inclined to say when matters of aesthetics arise? In depictions of Christianity, why is the Devil often portrayed as handsome (in a devilish way), well dressed, a man of wealth and taste? Why is he often an aristocrat, known for his castles, capes, fancy signet rings, beardsmanship, and beautiful women? Why is Jesus a ragamuffin with no visible means of support except the charity of his followers? Why does he wear a bed sheet and walk around barefoot when the Pharisees and the Romans sport iconic raiment of success and power? Should not the Nazis have been ugly, dirty, with wretched uniforms, and a toad for an insignia? Should not the devil be a gruesome monster who lives in filth like the wretched peasants he so famously seduces into sin? The answers to these questions are often complicated and speculative. For our purposes here these questions are enough to point out that whatever an aesthetic is, it is nothing specific and must be defined in whatever context it pretends to be used. But it should not be limited to the simple-minded dichotomies of like and don't like or the commercially defined beautiful and the ugly such as we see in fashion magazines, despite Keats' use of the word beauty which nevertheless has value to all of us in some positive and concrete way because it is *his* aesthetic.

Keats finds the urn's beauty sublime in the sense that it undermines the standard dichotomy (duality) of truth and beauty by conflating them into a *single ethical aesthetic*. As mentioned earlier, truth and beauty belong to the qualitative axis of reality. They cannot be quantified in the true sense (i.e. measured in units). However, just as any quantitative value is mere metadata without the qualitative axis, the qualitative axis is without form and therefore without meaning bereft of its quantitative framework. For Keats, truth and beauty are as inseparable as the quantitative and qualitative axes of experience. (He died at 35 broke and alone.) The danger here is to lapse into a kind of ethical relativism by saying Nazi uniforms are aesthetically beautiful to Nazi sympathizers, as if this were some kind of test of one's fascist or anti-Jewish proclivities, and ugly if one loves communism, red, democracy, peace, love, and understanding. Hugo Boss AG designer suits still adorn manikins in shops in New York,

London, and Paris. And while we might presume that today's clothes horse would not wear an SS uniform, an SS officer would perhaps wear today's Hugo Boss suits with pleasure. However, when we speak of an ethical aesthetic such as Keats', the matter is absolute, not relative. In this case, "that is all / Ye know on earth, and all ye need to know" he says. It is a proposition. If x equals y, then y equals x ($x = y \rightarrow y = x$). The metadata structure of the proposition is irrefutable though its *inference* is not since we can always come up with propositions which contradict (but not disprove) Keats' proposition. Considering that x and y are quantities (because they are equivalent), we can be certain we have accounted for the quantitative axis of this qualitative proposition. Its analytic backbone supports, as metadata, the inference of the meaning of the relationship between truth and beauty, as ethical aesthetic.

So at least for Keats, the problem of ethical and aesthetic relativism is solved by proposing that there is no knowledge except of the fact that beauty and truth are one and the same thing. To say that they are not is ignorance, the absence of knowledge. That it is a Grecian urn, and therefore of great antiquity, is no coincidence. In the poem, the urn itself speaks to humanity in the voice of antiquity reminding those of today of the truths of yesterday which, like the urn, have come to us intact from the Classical past. When the truths of yesterday are the truths of today, then they must be – *ipso facto* – eternal and universal truths. To remove all doubt of the priority and significance of universal truth Keats leaves us with the proposition that *for something to be ethical it must be beautiful*. There is no such thing as an ugly ethic for it would then no longer be ethical and therefore an ethic. We can complain that ugly is as relative as beautiful. But that would ignore the fact that Keats is not indicating an adjective but a noun. Is Beauty the same thing as the beautiful? Can we say that Beauty is beautiful? Furthermore, while there is an antonym for beautiful there is none for Beauty as there is for death (life), love (hate), Heaven (Hell), and other metaphysical nouns. We can compare Keats' aesthetic of beauty to that of Oscar Wilde in his preface to *A Picture of Dorian Gray*. Wilde was a self-professed aesthete who prized the artificial in beauty as much as the sublime. This would not describe Keats, whom Percy Bysshe Shelly's Oxbridge friends referred to derisively as the cockney poet. In Wilde's aesthetic,

> The artist is the creator of beautiful things. To reveal art and conceal the artist is art's aim .... Those who find

> ugly meanings in beautiful things are corrupt without being charming. This is a fault. Those who find beautiful meanings in beautiful things are the cultivated. For these there is hope. They are the elect to whom beautiful things mean only Beauty.

Surely Wilde's vision of beauty transcends what is known in commercial discourse as a beautiful dining room set. There are five uses of the adjective and one of the noun. In the use of the noun he contrasts the meaning of beautiful things with the metaphysical principle of "Beauty." There are two kinds of aesthetes: the corrupt ones who find the ugly in beautiful things and those who only find beauty. To a certain extent Wilde was hedging his bet that his book would be well received. This is in the preface to the first edition. His mention elsewhere in the preface of critics shows that he is self-conscious about what they will find in his narrative of the unfortunate Dorian Gray. Therefore, he sets up a proposition which says that if cultivated (X), then the beautiful (b) in Beauty [X → (b = B)]; if corrupt (Y), then the ugly (u) negates (~) the beauty in the Beautiful [Y → (u ~ B)]. We must say, in the second enclosed part, that the ugly negates the beautiful because otherwise we will find ourselves in a contradiction. X finds beauty in beautiful things (T) whereas Y sees only ugliness in this thing that X regards as beautiful. So we cannot say that T is both beautiful and ugly because that is the equivalent of not saying anything at all about it. Therefore, if we are to say something *analytically* meaningful we must say that b = B, which is a tautology because beauty is Beauty only because it has the ineluctable quality of being *beautiful*. They are one and the same because they cannot be separated without losing all meaning. To be corrupt, then, means to have some ulterior (subjective) motive for denying the objective reality of a beautiful thing. It is so in what might be called a Platonic and absolute sense independent of what any literary critic might think of the book to the contrary in a review. Finally, then, there are two kinds of critics: the cultivated and the corrupt. The former "can translate into another manner or a new material his Impression of beautiful things"; the latter "[finds] ugly meanings in beautiful things ..." As aesthetes, the latter lack charm, which in Wilde's opinion is a fatal flaw.

All of this is highly relevant to the plot of the story, where Gray can be considered both ugly and beautiful when one considers that his outward beauty is the obverse of his inner ugliness which is recorded in his portrait hidden in the attic of his house. In truth his beauty is a subjective lie. The law of contradiction prevents him from being both if the proposition he is beautiful is to be true or false. But until his picture (the portrait) is revealed as reflecting his spiritual corruption, as it is at the end of the book, it seems - like Schrodinger's cat - that he is somehow in both states at once. The objective reality is that he *is* ugly, *but this cannot be "proven" until the portrait is revealed.* And if it is not proven, then it is neither true (T) nor false (F) from an analytic point of view. In Wilde's ethical aesthetic one's beauty depends upon *not* doing ugly things which hurt others as Dorian does while still miraculously maintaining his charming outward appearance. But there needs to be some objective proof for this to be true (T). The face Gray presents to the world as a gentleman rake masks the horror of his spiritual depravity, or what might be called his corruption. From the preface to the last word of the novel *A Picture of Dorian Gray* is a treatise on ethical aesthetics and explicitly *not* morality. "There is no such thing as a moral or an immoral book. Books are well written, or badly written. That is all," Wilde says in the preface. Ethical aesthetics, then, has more to do with whether or not a book is well written than with anything resembling the misnomer of the word ethics being synonymous with moral as it is in the popular mind. Wilde labors to make this clear in the preface *before* the critics and the public get their hands on the story of Dorian's demise.

This elevated definition of beauty and the beautiful features the artist, the one who commits the act of creation - "the creator." In this way the artist is like God the creator of Heaven and Earth. How? Flaubert, in a letter to his mistress Louise Colet, famously said, "An author in his book must be like God in the universe, present everywhere and visible nowhere." Wilde says, "To reveal art and conceal the artist is art's aim." Like Keats' axiom, this is an unequivocal statement of what the "aim" of art is. If this is all the aim is, then we can say that it is "all ye ever know in life, and all ye need to know." It carries the same axiomatic absolutism as Keats' dictum. Therefore, as we see in the story of Dorian Gray, Beauty is absolute. It is not to be corrupted because if it is, it is no longer beauty. For beauty to be beautiful, as Beauty must be to *be* Beauty, then it must not be "corrupt"— which is not the same thing as *ugly*. Those whose books are "badly written"; critics who have ulterior motives (e.g. jealousy and enmity), or the inability to perceive the beautiful); and Dorian Gray in his cruelty, are the "picture" of corruption in Wilde's ethical aesthetic. Wilde eschews the possibility of a work of art being either moral or immoral, but he does not rule out the possibility of an ethical aesthetic being necessary for there to be any morality at all. If anything is immoral in Wilde's ethical aesthetic it is the writing of a bad book.

One must understand beauty, says Stendhal in *Vie de Henri Brulard*. He calls it *"la promesse de bonheur,"* the promise of happiness. In such an aesthetic Beauty earns a capital initial as more than merely a sensuous pleasure or a way to decorate a hotel room. It becomes an ethos necessary for a meaningful sense of existence which, if there is one, is the only honorable definition of happiness. Those who know what beauty is are rare, he says. "[I]t takes the one hundred men in ten million who understand beauty, which isn't imitation or an improvement on the beautiful as already understood by the common herd, twenty or thirty years to convince the twenty thousand next most sensitive souls after their own that this new beauty is truly beautiful." Beauty, in its sublime form, is anathema to the prevailing social discourse. It is a *threat* which must be quashed at all costs to make way for what William Burroughs calls the Ugly Spirit - the Zeitgeist of the Imaginary age where the digital virtual is *more real* than garden-variety reality. Those who cling to the ideal of beauty are a threat because they refuse to accept the Ugly Spirit as their own spirit. Those who refuse such a gift from the hegemony are made into enemies of the state often without ever having a political thought.

Those familiar with Wilde's life know that in the end the Ugly Spirit of the social discourse had its way with him. It destroyed his life and career and left him loathed and destitute. So then what is an author to do? Does he pursue the beautiful only to find out how ugly and corrupt his society is? The odds are against anyone hearkening to his clarion call to the beautiful. And if they do, it is often after he is dead. A dead author is a good author. His corpus has had a good going over by the critics and academics. The secret underground reading his subversive novels, poetry, plays, essays, and philosophical works grows slowly as the rare devotees die off almost as fast as they are replaced. That is why, Stendhal says, it takes "twenty or thirty years to convince the twenty thousand next most sensitive souls ..." Add to that the (at *least*) twenty to thirty years it takes a writer to get his voice and you have an old man!

Why is Beauty perceived as such a threat? Perhaps it is its unholy alliance with the *sublime*. Worse is its insistence upon Truth to be beautiful. It must reflect nature's objective sincerity - even if it is, as Wilde says, artificial. "Life mimics art" he says, a credo embodied well in the plot of *A Picture of Dorian Gray*. Ultimately, for there to be humanity there must be its reflection in Nature and Nature's reflection in humanity. After man's ability to make fire humanity has always been artificial in a fundamental way. This only increased man's need for the *spiritus* of Nature in the mimetic exchange of mortal identity. In Act 3, scene 2, Hamlet reflects upon the most artificial form of human behavior, which is the taking on of a contrived identity in acting:

> Suit the action to the word, the word to the action, with this special observance, that you o'erstep not the modesty of nature: for any thing so o'erdone is from the purpose of playing, whose end, both at the first and now, was and is, to hold as 'twere the mirror up to nature: to show virtue her feature, scorn her own image, and the very age and body of the time his form and pressure.

If one *does* "o'erstep" the "modesty of nature" one forsakes the imperative to *make* life. One may *seem* to inhabit one's persona, but having failed to "hold ... the mirror up to nature" this persona is as ugly as Dorian's portrait in the attic. There is no Beauty without the mimesis of Nature. While the biological process of life begins at birth, what happens between is the horror vacui of the sublime. Nearly from the start, though, man tries to make a sortie back to the amnion of the womb. This zygotic need issues from the subject's somatic memory of prenatal oblivion. However, it is frustrated in this quest as the womb is a one-way street. Rather than face the sublime imperative the subject dramatizes its unconscious need for the matrix by seeking the imaginary utopia of eternal, immutable, immortal comfort and convenience, or *Genuss*. It is only natural and right that a class of overlords pops up to accommodate this need through the fabrication of the Imaginary. For this enterprise to be successful a hegemony is necessary to herd the subject into the waiting jaws of Jonah's whale. In its abdication of its identity the subject "o'ersteps" Nature. Of course it eventually gets what it wished for, but in the form of what it feared the most: the oblivion of death. But not before it suffers a *death-in-life* where there has been little or no movement of the soul toward becoming a Godlike maker of worlds. It has learned nothing. One great difference between mere awareness and consciousness is that the former has no memory of any knowledge it has discovered on its own since it has not discovered any. While it may be *injected* with information in the form of the *knowing-of* the synthesis of injected and apprehended knowledge never takes place. Without this synthesis there is no catharsis. And without catharsis the sublime simply does not exist for the subject except as an ominous shadow in its nightmares.

Truth is not the correct propaganda line, reckless honesty,

the dogma of the Church, or the result of positivist logic (unless we are talking about computers). Rather, it is bare life and all of the consequences of it. What distinguishes the Beauty of Keats, Wilde, and Stendhal from the beautiful dining room set of the common herd is that it is *sublime*. Above all the herd fears the sublime because the sublime is united with Death in the reality of bare life. The monstrous paradox of life is that what the subject fears as the intimation of mortality is precisely what it needs *to live,* not just be. This fear is *kenophobia,* or fear of emptiness, which is the subject's intuition of the horror vacui. The subject's fear of the chasm of mortality - life's only fact - drives it to the most expedient, comfortable, and convenient way to fill it (though it cannot be filled). The discourse of consumerism is the highest good in the ethical aesthetic of the Imaginary's discourse. Hearkening to its Siren call, the subject abdicates its sovereignty through debt, allowing the Imaginary to fill its emptiness with the meaningless chatter of social discourse, bric-à-brac of the media, indoctrination of the education system, endless commercial appeals, redundant nonsense from the Internet, financial notions, folklore-as-fact, sexual and violent pornography, and the propaganda of the Hope Cults of Scientism and conciliatory religion. In signing promissory notes, the subject signs its sovereignty away, becoming what is essentially an indentured servant. But rather than struggle to free itself from the chains of debt, it only digs itself in deeper so that it does not have to face the bare life of the sublime. It has been trained and indoctrinated into believing that bare life is only for *poor people* and the far-off other who makes its gadgets and rags.

What it seeks as protection from mortality through these trivial discourses is precisely what hastens its demise. This *delusion* makes the journey to the grave meaningless and corrupt. In bare life one *is living*. In the Imaginary one *is dying*. There is only the present continuous in the *process* of living. The simple present applies only the *fact* of existence as "I am." Living is a river not a stagnant swamp. Its proper verb phrase is "I *am living*." Those who run from death into the amnion of the Imaginary only *dream* that they have put some distance between themselves and the horror vacui of the sublime. In fact they have pushed themselves closer to the brink of what they fear the most but are entirely unprepared to face. Market crashes, hackers, wars, being sacked, divorce, chronic and acute illness, a crippling car crash, prison, and ubiquitous psychological depression plunge the subject into the alien world of bare life against its will. The tragedy is that its greatest fear is of that which it needs the most: to *be living*, to be "happy" in the sense meant by Stendhal, rather than to *be dying*. Tragically, the subject's Kenophobia preempts the process of life, leaving it without guidance, purpose, beauty, and truth. Those who value such things are seen as weirdos, kooks, and losers. The subject does not understand that this emptiness is what must be filled with the *turning-to* the transcendental object as the Other. Instead, it finds itself locked in a prison of the *turning-from*. The truth of this prison is that it is a mere specter of the Imaginary. It can be blown away either by catastrophe or volition in a moment as if it never existed – because it does not. The magnificent expediency of the Imaginary is that it keeps the subject imprisoned in its debt obligations and gizmos and gadgets with just the power of suggestion emanating from the thousands of media pores in its advertising, news, and entertainment matrix. It is true that the subject is surrounded; but it is also true that the subject at any moment can walk away from this illusory matrix. What really traps the subject is that it has abdicated its sovereignty through debt. It is powerless. If it leaves the matrix of the Imaginary it will have to go through a difficult adjustment to what the hegemony forces on those its disenfranchises. "I don't want to be poor" whines the subject to its therapist. Through the magic of pharmacology the subject has this fear benumbed through legal or illegal means. Which of them is immaterial for both operate in the same way with the same chemicals. Knowing that the police chiefly go after the Underclass to protect the hegemony from interference, the subject in the amnion of the Imaginary feels safe using illegal drugs (that it buys from the Underclass) to dull the pain of *Genuss*. And it always has alcohol to drown its chronic misery. As a result, its ability to dispel the illusion of its penury and strike out into the real world is crushed before it can even twitch. The copula "to be" must be an *action*, a *performance*, not a static state. One must hustle. As the Buddhists say, "The world is a burning house." There is no time to save the TV from the flames. The world is an urn which is still warm from the kiln (to mix metaphors). Its red clay has yet to be painted with the beautiful *imago* of Truth. The subject's imperative is to paint this urn. Its sovereign personality must fill this emptiness with meaning. Otherwise, the subject simply *does not exist* except as a slave to be exploited or a body to be thrown on top of a live grenade.

1.5: Wahrschoenheit as the getting-to-know

But is not ugly as relative a term as beautiful? "You are not pretty," says the callous man to the vain woman. "Then am I ugly?" says the woman. "No," says the man. "The truth is ugly." When we speak about beauty and truth in the *technical* sense, as Keats does here, we are obliged to make fine distinctions. The difference is that he aligns his ethical aesthetic with knowledge. By doing so, beauty becomes *techne* (τέχνη), the Greek word for the spectrum of craftsmanship, art, and even science in the sense meant by Peirce as the *conduct* of the creative process of logical abduction, or reasoning from percept (thing) to etiology (origin, or genesis). Religion, too, feels bound to this process, as we see in the Bible which of course starts with the Book of Genesis, or the creation of Creation. The mention of knowledge in Keats' poem is the *verb phrase* to know. He is speaking of the process of *knowing* in the getting-to-know, not the static state of *having known* in the knowing-of. *Wahrschoenheit* (truth/beauty) is the *getting-to-know*. It is Keats' ethical aesthetic. So what then is the ethical aesthetic of the knowing-of, or what Hacking calls the knowledge that "is now the property of corporations" (*Language*, p. 184)? If the knowing-of is the antithesis of the getting-to-know (just as a process is the antithesis of a state), then what is not true is not beautiful and what is not beautiful is not true. We could say that what is ethical in the monolithic sense is that which is both beautiful and true – true because it is beautiful and beautiful because it is true. This is *Wahrschoenheit.* The knowing-of leaves little room for the ugly truth. When we use this unfortunate phrase what we really mean to say is that such-and-such is a *fact at odds with our illusions*. Facts are not to be confused with truths. (Half this analysis is simply a matter of disambiguating common words that have found themselves corrupted by the barbarous use to which they are put in commercial discourse.) Then do we mean true as the antithesis of false? Of course. That something is *true* does not mean it is *the truth* (one is tempted to give the word a capital initial). Keats means truth in the metaphysical sense of the sublime, not in the binary sense of a truth statement (a = a) or in the sense of x + y = 4. Truth is one of the chief metaphysical abstractions which must always be defined in every context. This does not mean that there is not an absolute sense of the word, its kernel as it were. However, it still must be defined in every appearance it makes upon the stage of discourse.

Pilate famously questions the truth of Jesus' guilt or innocence. He is aware of the political nature of the Pharisees' accusations. But he is also beholden to Rome in the tracking and punishment of enemies of the state. "Pilate saith unto him, What is truth? And when he had said this, he went out again unto the Jews, and saith unto them, I find in him no fault at all" (John 18:38). It was presumed that Pilate's judgment against the accused was "the truth" since he was the adjudicator and therefore, as the representative of Rome, the final local word after the Sanhedrin. But he knew the Sanhedrin's mind although it was well within his authority to make such a determination of *truth* stick. If he pronounced that the "truth" was that the accused was innocent and therefore should be set free, the Sanhedrin would say that he lied. Therefore, stepping back from this no-win situation he resorted to the metaphysical truth that he found "no fault at all" with the prisoner. This meant that whatever was Jesus' innocence or guilt in the juridical sense, in the metaphysical sense he was simply *innocent*. After all, what they were accusing him of was not of stealing a lamb or of murder, but of something else even Pontius Pilate was uncertain about because of its political, abstract nature far beyond his civil purview. He seizes the moment to make the same philosophical point Keats does in the ode, though posing it as a question rather than an answer. "What is truth?" if it is not in the politics of the Sanhedrin, or the law books of Rome, or the teachings of the Torah, but in the heart of a man? We might paraphrase it thus:

Syllogism A:

1) To find fault is to find something unethical in a person
2) To find something unethical in a person is to find something ugly
3) Therefore, to find fault in someone is to find something ugly

Syllogism B:

1) To find "no fault at all" is to find something ethical in a person
2) To find something ethical in a person is to find something beautiful
3) Therefore, to find "no fault at all" in a person is to find something beautiful

As it is the Pilate's *perception* that the truth about Jesus is that he could find "no fault at all" in him, the truth was therefore "beautiful." Nevertheless, his dubious resolution of the problem vilified him for all time when he allowed the mob to choose to set free the man Pilate could find no fault in or the man who was clearly guilty of a crime. Naturally, they chose the latter, allowing Pilate to clean his hands of the matter. "When Pilate saw that he was getting nowhere, but that a riot was starting instead, he took some water, washed his hands in front of the crowd, and said, 'I am innocent of this man's blood. See to it yourselves!'" (Matthew 27:24). Now the question of guilt or innocence has been transferred to the mob *from* Pilate. Rather than seeking an appropriate verdict for the accused, Pilate pronounces *himself* to be innocent! Unfortunately for him, history has not been as magnanimous in this respect. But in his defense, *ex post facto*, the ugly fact is that the crowd had already been stirred up by the sacred Sanhedrin into the conclusion that Jesus was guilty of *something*. Therefore, the insurrectionary Barabbas gave them someone to vote *for* so that, in the same act, they could vote against the one Pilate had his doubts about. It was an extremely clever political and legal move by the Sanhedrin and the Pharisees. Pilate, a political appointee, sees that if he does not switch to Plan B (letting the mob make the choice, rather than choosing himself) he will have a riot on his hands and be in trouble with the Pharisees and, by extension, the hegemon (Herod) of Rome. Otherwise, Pilate will also have to put down a riot, generating much bad will toward the Roman government. Political chaos is precisely what Rome, via Herod, does *not* want. The only *Wahrschoenheit* Pilate might have been able to find in the trial is the possibility of *justice*, which is always beautiful in and of itself, even if it results in an ugly revolt. It is inherently beautiful because it is a matter of weighing evidence to determine the truth beyond a shadow of a doubt, acknowledging the limitations of epistemology, rather than acting on the impulses of man's natural inclination toward fable and fairy tale. Justice is humanity elevated by an elaborate process of manufacturing an objective process in an otherwise subjective fog of doubt. Lady Justice is supposed to be blindfolded to the socio-economic status of the accused and other irrelevant particulars (the political agenda of the Sanhedrin, Pharisees, Rome, Herod, and so forth), focused solely on the verifiability of evidence of innocence or guilt. Her beauty is not in any *state* (knowing-of) of judgment, but in the *process* (getting-to-know) of justice, as well as in the ethical aesthetic of justice itself.

Little of this argument, though, settles the issue of what makes something fundamentally beautiful, and, by inversion, essentially ugly. It is undeniably *true* that we all will die, but does this truth make death beautiful in the sense meant by Keats? Despite its marked emphasis on the afterlife, even the Bible admits as much about our ultimate fate as mortals. "For the living know that they shall die: but the dead know not anything, neither have they any more a reward; for the memory of them is forgotten" (Ecclesiastes 9:5).This sentence could easily have been written by Sartre. Though it nominates the truth, it is not beautiful in any sense that we would associate with the word beautiful. How, then, could justice be beautiful in a situation where there is the *ugly* injustice (for the victim, and society) of murder? For the answer we return to the urn.

Perhaps the greatest formal beauty of such an urn is in its *symmetry*, a quality an urn or amphora must have to be both useful and elegant. Symmetry is the characteristic we generally agree upon as being a common characteristic of the beautiful, perhaps in part because it seems to indicate a kind of material integrity or an abstract equality, though this principle can be pushed to the brink of ugliness too. We find support for the priority of symmetry in the disposition of everyday objects, buildings, art, music, fashion, faces, and even (of course) the balance of justice. (Winning a case does not mean the scale has tipped in our favor!) In a more abstract sense we find symmetry in mathematics, geometry, engineering, and physical and natural laws. What *about* symmetry deserves this honor? We tend also to have a sense that in symmetry there is a kind of *balance,* a principle we associate both with what is good and what is true. Generally speaking, we imagine that things in balance, literally or metaphorically, are healthy and in harmony in some way with universal forces. And of course for symmetry to assume this exalted place in our aesthetics, there must be *asymmetry* to provide a neat symmetric balance for the de facto asymmetry of symmetry itself! Nevertheless, we assign to asymmetry the idea of being ugly, unseemly, unsightly, or just plain bad. However, there is much aesthetic evidence in works of art, as well as in the outcomes of the best-laid schemes of mice and men, that asymmetry is, ironically, the counterpoint of symmetry. As such, it becomes symmetry's dialectical and generative opposite (Tarde's *l'opposition*). In Robert Herrick's sonnet "A Sweet Disorder," he exploits the ineffable delight we may discover in another's habits when we are in love, even if such habits are not what might be termed conventional:

A SWEET disorder in the dress
Kindles in clothes a wantonness:—
A lawn about the shoulders thrown
Into a fine distraction,—
An erring lace, which here and there

Enthralls the crimson stomacher,—
A cuff neglectful, and thereby
Ribbands to flow confusedly,—
A winning wave, deserving note,
In the tempestuous petticoat,—
A careless shoe-string, in whose tie
I see a wild civility,—
Do more bewitch me, than when art
Is too precise in every part.

What makes the object of Herrick's consideration so alluring is that the way she dresses ignores the *pro forma* requirement of civilization that everything must be tidy at all times or mere anarchy will be loosed upon the world. That symmetry can be too precise means that it can *bore* us. Worse, it can be perfunctory and therefore lose all meaning. It can even be perverse and tyrannical such as in the mindless quest for absolute and perfect civil and social equality in everything all of the time and at any cost. But this is not a problem. It is just a part of the heuristic of life which is always going out of balance and must be corrected again (cybernetics). It is a kind of circadian rhythm - with or without our mindless meddling. Like circadian rhythm, the getting-to-know is an autonomous process. All processes have built-in heuristic, else they would not be processes for long. They would simply collapse into complete entropy. For a process to continue it must stay in *balance*, like a bicycle rider. There is no static state of bicycle riding. When one is no longer moving on a bicycle one is no longer bicycle riding! One loses balance and falls down. The state of knowledge which makes it possible to say, "He rides a bicycle" dissolves when the bicycle itself is no longer in the process of being ridden. At that point rider and bicycle part ways to resume their separate, asymmetrical lives in proportion to each other as things: the animate and the inanimate. The inanimate must be animated by the animate. While bicycle riding we cannot separate the animate from the inanimate, just as we cannot separate truth and beauty when they are "all ye need to know" about the process of the getting-to-know as *Wahrschoenheit*. However, all processes are elusive creatures. They defy being made into commodities. When they are, they are called services implying that they are something the subject cannot or will not do for itself. A vendor must provide such services for a price. The knowing-of consumes the getting-to-know the way a TV consumes all attention in a room.

The inevitable result of the knowing-of is the amassing of data of every kind indiscriminately. Later it will be mined (parsed) for whatever is the expedient need at the time – whether surveillance or target marketing. As data accumulate, they swarm into the autonomous entity of Big Data. Hacking, citing Popper, says that "there is a sense in which this third world [of objective data] is *autonomous*," adding that the term and the italics are Popper's (p. 184). BD then coalesces into an idolatrous Icon worshiped by the hegemonic order and the public as the repository of the truth. Anyone who has had to deal with a bureaucrat who insists that these data on hand about one are true and that the facts one knows about one's own life are *false* because they misalign with BD, has experienced the existential priority BD has assumed in our lives. If anything is virtual it is these data.

However, the problem arises for the subject when its own *homunculus* (consumer profile) is considered more real than the subject itself. This mad *golem* is fashioned by the ready-to-hand expediencies of the Imaginary and its vendors and masters. Unlike the subject, it can be absolutely controlled and therefore, in the ethical aesthetic of the hegemony's *teleological* mission, it is a superior product. The only problem for the hegemony is to get the subject to *mold itself* to the homunculus. The hegemony knows it cannot completely control the subject without expending too much time, money, and effort. Furthermore, a happy subject is a good subject. By maintaining the charade of democracy and the choice of redundant products in the marketplace the hegemony, through the agency of the Imaginary, manufactures the illusion of self-determination. What makes this illusion so tenacious – since it seems that it would be easy to see through – is that it is hidden behind existential *obligation*. The promissory notes the subject has signed by its own free will are now obligations which no amount of self-determination can dispel. Because of the refraction caused by the ratio between self-determination and obligation the subject never quite sees its situation. When it looks into the water it sees that the reed is broken not that it is the same reed refracted by the effect of the light on the water. There is nothing metaphysical or mystical about the fact that the subject has signed all kinds of promissory notes. It has anchored itself to a bedroom community and deadly job through children it did not really want, married a person whom it is already tired of after five years of libidinal imprisonment, and committed itself (and sometimes its life) to the maintenance of the social and economic status quo – rational or insane. The hegemony makes sure the subject retains a measured modicum of self-determination to sweeten the hallucination of the subject's most treasured ideal: freedom to buy what it wants cheaply. At the same time, though, the subject's lord and master never fails to remind it of its obligation to its bank, political system, taxes, family, and social class. Thoughts of escape are met with threats of the most dire consequences, real and unreal. While cracks do appear in this seemingly hermetic situation they are quickly sealed up by a new loan, car, house, job, and even spouse. The bank happily funds these adventures with imaginary money it prints up on a computer keyboard which, despite being a mirage, is nevertheless an obligation from with the subject cannot escape.

But this is *still* not enough to maintain the illusion of prosperity which allows the subject to wallow in *Genuss*. Therefore, the hegemony *captures* the sovereignty of others in far-off lands and feeds it to the subject. Nourished by the blood of these far-off others in the form of cheap goods such as electronics and clothing (rags), the subject, despite its negative net worth, feels free to engulf itself in the frenzy of consumerism by the accumulation of more and more debt. As the measure of prosperity and even national security, consumerism is made possible by the nearly total capture of the sovereignty of far-off others in lands where their choice is slavery or starvation. Unlike that of the subject, *their* sovereignty is usurped without the benefit of abdication (which allows for a modicum of self-determination). It then enters into a *transitive* relationship with the subject through the artificially low prices of the goods the subject craves for validation of its abdication. "I can buy a cheap gadgets that work Big Magic, therefore 'iBelong.'" The transitive process follows Peano's 4th axiom: For natural numbers x, y and z, if x = y and y = z, then x = z, where the far-off other's sovereignty is x, the cheap goods it manufactures are y, and the subject's sense of self-determination is z. In other words, by usurping the far-off other's sovereignty through mortal imperative, the far-off (nominal-dependent) hegemony is able to produce cheap goods. In the subject's country these goods cannot be made without paying workers a wage commensurate with the inflated cost of living, the paying of which would spoil the hegemony's scheme of exchanging cheap goods for the subject's sovereignty. And since this has been going on for a time significant enough to have allowed the domestic infrastructure for the manufacture of these goods to atrophy, dwindle, and vanish, the hegemony finds itself in something of a double bind. It can exchange cheap goods for the abdication of sovereignty *if and only if* those goods are made by persons in cultures where sovereignty is usurped *without* abdication. Furthermore, it has more or less maintained this operation successfully for long enough so that the infrastructure necessary to manufacture these goods no longer exists in its immediate economic territory – if it ever did. Therefore, it is necessary to extend this economic territory in the land of the far-off other by proxy war, bullying, assassination, subterfuge, and bribery to ensure that the status quo there will be maintained. The subject becomes complicit in this operation by burying itself in the consumer phantasmagoria transmitted through the channels of its gizmos and gadgets. In so doing it 1) blinds itself to the reality of the crimes its state commits on its behalf, and 2) provides the revenue the state needs to commit these crimes directly and by proxy. Herein lies the primary cause of terrorism.

From birth, the subject is indoctrinated into the Cult of Mediocrity, history's most deadly cult, made possible by the fanatical-fundamentalist religion of Scientism. Within this cult, the definition of freedom is eternal and uninterrupted comfort and convenience, unfettered access to consumer goods and services, infinite credit and debt, and the pursuit of medical immortality. The cult's battle cry of "Death before inconvenience!", however, is confusing to the *kafir* (infidel). Just to be clear: it means "Death to those who stand in the way" of their compulsive and relentless pursuit of absolute collective narcissism in the Amniotic Empire. Woe unto those who present even the least obstruction in the pursuit of this idealized goal of a future of immortality and pleasure. No blasphemer will be spared. Toward this end, the hegemony, on behalf of its transnational overlords, bribes the poor into its military apparatus. They are then tossed as needed into the fray of foreign entanglements and adventures in the hegemony's relentless pursuit of minerals, wealth, power, and Securitas. The great disappointment of the hegemony is that for it to carry out its schemes, the subject must retain a modicum of self-determination to remain a member of the amnion. The paradox of the hegemony is that it must measure out self-determination in an amount which does not threaten its state of exception. The measure must be just enough to maintain the illusion of freedom while retaining total control over the subject's ultimate fate. The subject then becomes an expedient annoyance to be exploited and tolerated until such time as it is no longer needed. When it is no longer a useful tool, the state disposes of the subject through war, disease, poverty, disenfranchisement, and prison. Despite the abundant evidence of its status as disposable in the apparatus of the state and its corporate overlords, the subject nonetheless manages to sustain the illusion of freedom, and may, as Marx says, fetishize it into something it is not. This is the result of the Imaginary's prestidigitation through the proliferation of ever newer and ever more powerful gadgets and gizmos. The *narcotizing dysfunction effect* of the Imaginary is nearly impossible to escape except through congenital eccentricity or by falling through the bottom of the amnion into the feral wilds of the Underclass. The bread-and-circus of the political process and consumer culture reinforces the manufactured sense of self-determination by giving the subject a choice between *A* and *A*. Since a tautology is always true (Aristotle), the subject rests assured that it is participating in the sacred, holy, and enlightened exercise of its free will. It believes it determines not only the quality of its life but also those who will lead it to the promised land of medical immortality in an earthly utopia of perpetual comfort, convenience, and indolent mediocrity.

The subject's ritual of freedom, fetishized in the Marxian sense or not, however, is predicated upon the transitive differential between the *usurped sovereignty* of the far-off other and the *abdicated sovereignty* of itself and its peers. The critical part of the mechanism is that the subject has been trained to regard its modicum of self-determination, managed by others, as evidence of its individuation as a sovereign being. In fact, however, this differential is the *emblem* of its status as a servant trapped in a state of permanent indenture. Its only knowledge of the far-off other is what it is fed by the discourse of propaganda purveyed by media which are owned entirely by the corporate overlords of the state. In this discourse the subject sees that the far-off other looks different (ugly), seems less intelligent (stupid), is stuck in some anachronistic stage of human development (primitive), and is inherently violent (dangerous). The discourse of ugly, stupid, primitive, and dangerous is enough to give the subject a sense of its inherent superiority over these troglodytes its sees murdering each other on TV— but also making its cheap consumer goods. It then makes the transitive assumption that this inherent superiority extends to all dimensions of its life, but most importantly to what it sees as its fundamentally greater self-determination. At the same time it is ignorant of the fact that this modicum of self-determination has been bought by the *transitive dissociation* of the far-off other's own sovereignty which has been ripped from its grasp by the ruling proxy of the subject's own hegemony under the mortal-imperative.

Subtracting the differential from the far-off other's slavery equals the sense of freedom the subject's modicum of self-determination allows. The far-off other's sovereignty, therefore, transfers from x (itself) to y (cheap goods). The subject's sense of self-determination (z) then receives the cheap goods y(x) to maintain its bloodthirsty lust for what Veblen nominates as conspicuous consumption. Therefore, the far-off other's sovereignty x, in the form of cheap goods $y(x)$, allows the subject to maintain the illusion of the prosperity it was promised if it abdicated its sovereignty. In this way the usurped sovereignty of the far-off other *transits* to the subject's sense of self-determination, thus supporting the hegemony's need for a subject that *believes* it is free — whatever that may mean in the popular imagination. But all of this would be a risky proposition for the hegemony if it had to rely on the far-off proxy-hegemony to maintain this parasitic apparatus. Surely, the far-off other is not happy being the host of the Great Satan's voracious parasites. To buy the fealty of foreign *kleptocracies*, the hegemony dumps foreign aid and the taxpayer largess of nongovernmental organizations (NGO's) into the misery and poverty of the far-off other's dysfunctional and authoritarian state. This aid serves to keep the host alive just a little longer until the subject's hegemony can find another source of usurped sovereignty to exploit. It has another important function as well. This help (debt) is often paraded in media discourse as an attempt by a benevolent (but categorically superior) state to bring these savages into some semblance of the amnion of civilization. Naturally, they seem to resist this benevolence which makes its withdrawal easier for the subject to swallow when it happens. At the same time this spectacle of paternalism stimulates the subject's otherwise atrophied sense of the *deontological* in the form of altruism. Nevertheless, since these good deeds come with a price (more debt), they all ultimately serve the teleological interests of the hegemony and by extension its subjects.

By owning the means of production where the trinkets, gadgets, and gizmos the subject cannot live without are produced, the hegemony manages these far-off proxy states by hook, crook, carrot, and stick. Furthermore, if any leader of any state refuses to be part of this apparatus, the Imaginary forms a narrative where state X becomes a pariah state. Atrocities designed to appeal to the subject's weak *deontological* ethos are manufactured by the state and are then transmitted through the media relentlessly until the subject defaults to the position that this rogue state must be brought to submission or eliminated. When provoked, the cartel of corporate overlords commands its hegemony to deploy its arsenal of lethal gadgets which seem humane compared to the - usually - poison gas said to be employed by the dictator of the pariah state on his own people. And once again the world is safe for democracy until the next upstart dares to violate its people's human rights. None of this seems strange to the subject eager to remain in good standing with the Domini of the Cult of Mediocrity. The subject's own state is already engaged in perpetual war with sundry miscreants who will not capitulate to the overlords of the *transnational cartels*. Besides, it is no great loss to the world if the ugly, stupid, primitive, and dangerous far-off others are systematically exterminated by what the media portray as their own inscrutable internecine conflicts. Meantime, the transnational cartels manipulate the commonweal of sovereign states through a variety of means. These include meddling and interference by what are called banks but are in fact types of economic, transnational, *weapons* with their own supra-governmental powers, as well meddling in local elections, if there are any.

Enthralled by the Big Magic of its gadgets and gizmos, the subject becomes a kind of vampire with an unquenchable thirst for the sovereignty of far-off others usurped under conditions of mortal-imperative. Furthermore, any attempt to meddle with the subject's supply of cheap goods and ephemeral *Securitas* is met with an arsenal of lethal gadgets aimed at the insurgents. The gadgets do the subject's dirty work *teleologically* so that horror and suffering do not disturb the subject's state of comfort in the matrix of the amnion. The subject is perfectly happy with a teleological ethos where the ends justifies the means. Naturally, the subject pays ritual homage to the *deontological* ethos of do the right thing no matter what the outcome by being concerned about the environment and the poor. It applauds its government's weaponization of economic power made possible by borrowing from its own enemies (always good terms and fast cash) aimed at these trouble spots. But again it is vigilant that this secretly suspect ethos of deontology, which is sees as altruism, does not interfere with its teleological objectives. The transitive operation performed on the sovereignty of the far-off other is the parasite nation's greatest import in the form of y(x) – the usurped sovereignty of the far-off other transited into the wholesale cost of consumer goods for which the subject has abdicated.

At home, Big Data helps the hegemony maintain law and order through minute surveillance of the subject's every whim, proclivity, compulsion, desire, and fault. As it gains gravity by the knowing-more of the knowing-of, Big Data swells into an autonomous *substrate* with its own *Weltanschauung* and default culture of celebrities, criminals, politicians, facts, media, and corporations defining the amnion's Zeitgeist for its subjects. It also helps the hegemonic order establish itself as the aggregate identity of the public in the form of consumer culture. Big Data's bric à-brac of economic, social, and historic "facts" is disseminated by indoctrination in public schools and relentless discourse in the media. The pincer effect of Big Data's battle plan overwhelms the hapless subject. Weak, exhausted, depraved, the subject becomes receptive to the hegemony's propagation of dogma, seizing of taxes, contrivance of patriotic identity, dispensing of narcotics, and exhortations to wallow in the supposed social benefits of compulsory consumerism. To provide this service, the Imaginary *comes into being* (*le devenir*), creating a universal discourse (∀) superseding all lesser existential categories of discourse (∃). In other words, it forms a narrative maintaining the subliminal hum of the subject's belonging to some entity other than itself. The subject's mantra of identification, then, becomes the "iBelong, iBelong, iBelong, ...," chant of the Cult of Mediocrity. The psychic noise of it, or *massage* (not message) as Marshall McLuhan referred to it, replaces ratiocination in the subject with a repetitive effective association with the brands, products, teams, political parties and candidates, sub*cult*ures, infantile notions, protest movements, identity politics, and pseudo-cultural values of the amnion. Like a meditation mantra, its purpose is to interrupt thought. The difference is that its purpose is not to make room for enlightenment, but rather for a kind of benighted, chronic narcissism demanded by the amnion of all of its acolytes.

1.6: Installation of the apparatus of the Imaginary

To avoid reader fatigue, I abbreviate Lacan's tripartite constellation of the Imaginary (x), Symbolic (y), and Real (z) orders with letters. Also, I will dispense with the definite article. The constellation is discussed here as the psychic fencing within which the subject must dramatize its development through what Lacan describes as the Mirror Stage of psychological crystallization. Despite what must needs be a hardening of the subject's orientation to the objective world, it nevertheless remains in the *process* of development to some significant degree. Consequently, *xyz* never at any time exert the same proportion of influence upon the subject. One or the other may leap into prominence depending upon the subject's psychological and existential state, and the pressures and constraints upon it imposed by the community, the marketplace, the state, and what is needed within this environment to propitiate the demands of the id. Therefore, the matter of *jouissance,* transgressive and otherwise, comes into play as well. We will discuss the effects of jouissance later in this essay. When one order dominates the other two as a result of the prerogatives of the hegemony (such as the imperative of the Imaginary in the Amnion), it for a time defines the whole of the constellation. When an order becomes an *installation* in this way, it is then known as an *apparatus* as it develops its own schema, mechanism, means, and ends alien to the subject's indigenous psyche. As a result, a tense dialectic arises between the *constellation* of *xyz* and the *installation* of whatever apparatus the social amnion needs to stay in business. While the psychological, emotional, and even physical pathologies associated with this tension are easily palliated with drugs legal and illegal, the subject nevertheless degenerates into various states of robotic impotence readily exploited by the *kleptnotic* gadgetry of the Amniotic Empire's sprawling apparatus. Note there is no reason why *x*, *y*, and *z* must be in any specific proportion to each other. There is no ideal state in which this constellation is or is not in harmony. The constellation marks the boundaries within which the subject must operate in the mechanisms of its psychology and sense of being (*Dasein*). Nevertheless, an installation is not a constellation. An installation exerts a force upon the subject which may be called its *mode*. For instance, when the subject is largely under the influence of the Imaginary order its *mode* has certain characteristics which would be quite different - even contrary - if the mode were the Real and so on. Therefore we would say that the subject's mode is the Imaginary in the amnion. However, it is the *subject's* mode (mood), and not some imposition from without by government, society, religion, or science; the subject *volunteers* to abdicate its sovereignty to the apparatus of the Imaginary, and in so doing creates an installation within the confines of its psyche which determines its behavior and thoughts. The subject interprets this installation as, alternately, self-determination or inescapable *obligation*.

Can the subject abdicate to the Real or Symbolic orders? While one or the other may dominate from time to time - such as the Real in war or the Symbolic in theocracy - they are not the prevailing mode of the modern cult of Scientism. The cult provides a mode of living full of gadgets, gizmos, motorized wheelchairs (cars), lifts, junk food, stultifying jobs, stratified health care, throw-away furniture, and cracker-box mansions which make religion seem stupid and quaint and bare life terrifying and anathema to its ethical aesthetic. Bare life is for prisoners, poor people, and the far-off other. Its military utility, however, provides the illusion of Securitas, isolating the subject's imaginary enemies created by the media. Sophisticated flying robot warriors, dedicated reconnaissance satellites, and an obscene arsenal of nuclear weapons rusting in its silos, makes the subject feel all safe and warm, despite the catastrophic fragility of its *amniosis*. From time to time members of the Underclass are lured into sacrificing life and limb in combat with shadowy terrorists who have been armed by the hegemony's crypto *agent provocateurs* on behalf of arms dealers, oil companies, and corrupt domestic politicians guaranteed reelection and a cynosure on the board of directors afterwards. Therefore, the Real seems an improbable fate to the subject, though it is always at arm's length for anyone in the form of the sublime's annoying penchant for mortality. As for the Symbolic, it is more or less used as a tool by the Imaginary to help the subject transit from the mode of the *signified* to that of the *signifier* of itself. In the former, the subject naturally apprehends the thingness of things and the transcendental object in others. In the latter it sees only the reflection of people and things in the mirror of its own self-obsessed narcissism. In the great age of hegemonic Christian theocracy, the subject was under perpetual threat of being identified as a heretic if it did not make the right noises. What has changed is not this social pressure, but rather the *epistemological orientation* of the hegemony behind it. Today it is the Cult of Mediocrity and its consensus-based (rather than verification-based) religion of Scientism. As such, the tithing serf's servitude of yore resembles that of today's far-off other who supplies the subject with its sovereignty in the form of cheap goods ... or else! Meantime, the most the Apex Consumer can expect from this system (statistically) is *yeoman* status, with the its insurmountable debt-obligation taking the place of the traditional military service required of this class. The sovereign debt paid goes to fund proxy soldiers, human and robotic, taking the place of direct engagement with the putative enemy. The goal of the amnion's apparatus is a *rentier economy* for the few, and serfdom for the many. Nevertheless, from time to time the subject does find itself mired in the apparatus of the Real or the Imaginary as its prevailing mode when one or the other dominates the constellation, such as in a hot war.

What makes *x*, *y*, and *z* so significant to any philosophical discourse on the inferences of the psychology, logic, linguistics, and phenomenology of modern culture is that they are phenomenological *archetypes* in the repetitious and persistent *modes* of human behavior. In particular, we are concerned here with the installation of the Imaginary (a) as society's apparatus functioning between the hegemony and the subject. How the subject abdicates its core identity, and what effect this abdication has on the subject's sense of the sublime, are the foremost concerns of this essay. Other equivalent associations between Lacan's psychology and the use of these terms are as follows:

(*x*) Imaginary = extrinsic identity (Icon)
(*y*) Symbolic = signs and thought-signs (Signs)

(*z*) Real = bare life (Law, Index)

The enclosed words also represent Peirce's assignment of meaning to the three orders as he sees them. Note that one significant difference between Lacan and Peirce is that for the former it is the Symbolic which carries the Law as the Name-of-the-Father – the imposition of language (*langue et parole*) upon the order of the Real. For Peirce, the Real is the basis of law in part because the acting agency in establishing what one *must do* (not necessarily right and wrong) is Nature. "A law of nature ... [is] a legislative enactment, in that it exercises no compulsion of itself, but only because the people *will* obey it" (pp. 395-6). Herein again is the difference between a mathematical logician and a logician of the psyche. Nevertheless, they are both concerned with the mechanics of the psyche and how it is expressed in the world. The Law (nomos)– whatever its provenance – remains the foundation of every Thou Shalt Not standing in the way of the free fulfillment of jouissance and, concomitantly, our sense of the sublime in life and death.

Extrinsic identity as the *imago* is composed of corporate and governmental *memes* that replace the subject's intrinsic identity when it abdicates. The word meme derives from the word mimesis. A meme is an *imitatio* crafted by the *monad* of Big Data to form the Apex Consumer, which is based on the subject's surrender of its most personal information through the *kleptnotic* telemetry of its narcotizing gadgets. The apparatus works to mold the subject into the image of the *imago* of itself created by the accumulation of data about the subject's intrinsic persona. These data are then fed back to the subject as the mirror of itself subtly distorted by the prerogatives of the marketplace. The apparatus tinkers with this image to make it more amenable to the objectives of the hegemony and its corporate overlords. It then uses the gadgets and gizmos which enthrall the subject to make subtle neurological changes in the way the subject thinks and acts. The younger the subject the more effective. Most of all, though, it infiltrates the subject's malformed ego, shaping it into the perfect compulsive consumer and obedient citizen. Soon, the subject *must* have the rags, car, degree, house and so on to be happy, meaning experiencing a kind of symbolic jouissance lacking in catharsis. Since the consumer's desires are no longer governed by the natural economy of its indigenous core identity, its desires become wildly out of bounds of such simple facts as how much of this stuff it can actually afford. At this point of vulnerability the hegemony springs its rat trap, pushing promissory notes in front of the subject until it has mortgaged its imaginary future in the form of indenture. The subject signs with gusto, thinking that it at last has attained *l'objet petit a* that it always longed for and which, alas, by definition, it cannot have. Nevertheless, once upon a time the subject might have known what it could and could not afford. This time in the life-cycle of the human fly is often looked upon, in reflection, as the time when it was poor and struggling, when in fact it was the last outpost of reality in the subject's journey to the heart of the amnion. Here we have the start of the subject's voluntary abdication of its personal sovereignty. It is also the start of the subject's obsession with the imaginary future where all of the *accoutrements* of desire lie forever out of reach. This obsession with the future's imaginary state of being-in-the-world divorces the subject from the present. In so doing it also precludes the possibility of bare life. As Lacan points out, the developing child feels increasing anxiety as it gets farther from the bare life it was born into. While its language faculty develops it also develops *distance* from the object of the mother. The mother-object was the source of love, nourishment, and protection. Once the subject abdicates, however, its anxiety level begins increasing. Along with abdication must come an obsessive desire for the riches that await it *in the future*, that of course never comes. Anxiety propels the subject relentlessly toward a goal that it will never reach because the future is merely a psychological construct. However, such an illusion suits the Imaginary apparatus just fine. It is in fact the basis of its power over the subject. The Imaginary provides pharmaceuticals, alcohol, pornography, narcotizing entertainment and infotainment, and the hustle and bustle of jobs that rob the subject of the best hours of the day and the strength and health needed to escape. Attempts to violate the *civil* terms of the promissory note may result in a transubstantiation of it into *criminal* proceedings, particularly if nonpayment of taxes is involved, as it all too often is.

The matter is more clear when we look at Peirce's alternate conception of *xyz*. For him, the Imaginary is the Icon, the Symbolic the Sign, and the Real the Law (Index). While there is clearly a correlation between Peirce's and Lacan's definitions, Peirce gives more emphasis to the formal *mathematical* logic of these orders. While Lacan also presents a logical mechanism for x, y, and z, we could say that it emphasizes the *psycho*-logical rather than mathematical. They are both concerned with linguistics as well, though Peirce leans more toward Chomsky's schemata of *sentential* structure. Lacan favors Saussure's dichotomies of *langue et parole* and the signifier and the signified. Peirce's conception of the psychological is that it is a form of *collateral acquaintance* (CA) which includes the contents of the subject's memory and ability to reason as applied to its encounter with a proposition (p. 395). In a 14 December 1908 letter to his frequent correspondent Lady Welby, Peirce uses the statement "Cain killed Abel" as a proposition which will be understood (or not understood) in different ways depending upon the subject's CA. The subjects of the proposition, he says, are "Cain, Abel, and the relation of killing ..." It is entirely possible, now even in so-called Christian cultures, that a person has no acquaintance with the story of Cain and Abel. It is less possible that the person has no acquaintance with killing. But for a proposition to be called such it is not necessary that all of its parts are positive and absolute. For example, in a logical disjunction the outcome $p \vee q$ will be T (true) in three out of the four possibilities even though two of those three possibilities contain F (false): TTT, TFT, FTT, FFF. Only FFF is false. If we imagine two light switches connected in parallel where *on* is true and off is *false*, we see that even if one switch is off, the light bulb can still be on. Since TF (*pq*) and FT (*pq*) are material equivalents, the same is true for either configuration. Only FF (both switches off) will turn off the bulb. And so it is with certain propositions. If the subject has collateral acquaintance with Cain and Abel, it is likely that the outcome will be an understanding of killing. (Perhaps this is one of the reasons it is in the Bible as the archetype of sibling aggression and what the possible outcome of it might be.) Other configurations include "Cain killed" and "Abel was killed." It is enough to understand "to kill" or "to be killed" to understand what killing is. One need not have collateral acquaintance with both to grasp the full meaning of the proposition. A child is a simple example of a more or less wholly formed human being who might have no realistic idea of what killing is. Such knowledge is entirely dependent upon how the child becomes acquainted with the meaning of to kill and to die.

The Buddha Gautama's moment of renunciation of the world comes when, *at the age of 29*, he decides he is going to go outside the idyllic paradise of his palace and garden for the first time. To his existential dismay he sees the Four Sights: Old Age, Sickness, Death, and later, on his second trip, Renunciation of the World.

> Siddhartha asked Channa to explain the meaning of these strange sights. Channa responded that old age, sickness, and death were natural and unavoidable things that came to all people. They were to be endured. Shocked, Siddhartha returned to the palace and thought

> about what he had seen. *For the first time, he confronted the reality of life*: "Everything is transient; nothing is permanent in this world. Knowing that, I can find delight in nothing. How can a man, who knows that death is quite inevitable, still feel greed in his heart, enjoy the world of senses and not weep in this great danger?" [italics added] (Wangu, pp. 19-20)

As Gautama's enlightening experience shows, not only is it possible to be ignorant of what killing means, but also of such commonplaces as old age, sickness, and death – at the age of 29! He had a *negative* CA with what his charioteer Channa was acquainted with as the reality of life. It is negative because he either believes the opposite or believes nothing at all regarding these matters. His shock arises from his total lack of preparation for the revelation of reality. Gautama had been living in the Imaginary of the idyllic life of the court of a prince. The poor must live bare life. The acetic, however, chooses it after his own revelation. We do not know what his CA was before this, but his vision of reality leads him to *abdicate his abdication* to the Imaginary. In so doing he falls through the bottom of life, finding himself in the haunted vale of the bare life of the Underclass. But the Holy Man's vision of reality has convinced him that this is a way to regain his sovereignty while also confronting what nearly everyone else refuses to acknowledge, preferring instead to live in their version of Gautama's garden of Paradise. In so doing he applies his *collateral acquaintance* to the proposition that, as Buddha's first Noble Truth states, "Suffering consists of disease, old age, and death; of separation from those we love; of craving what we cannot obtain; and of hating what we cannot avoid." This is a radical proposition and certainly one pointing toward the abdication of one's abdication (Hegel's Second Negation) – which is precisely what Gautama proceeds to do.

> The man had shaved his head, wore only a ragged yellow robe, and carried a walking-staff. Siddhartha stopped his chariot and questioned the man. The ascetic told the prince, "*I am terrified by birth and death* and therefore have adopted a homeless life to win salvation. I search for the most blessed state in which suffering, old age, and death are unknown." [italics added] (p. 20)

Gautama sheds his royal *accoutrements*, telling Channa to bring them back to the palace and inform his parents of his decision. He then dons the rags of a begging mendicant. As it says in Buddhist literature, the world is a burning house. The *Genuss* of the Imaginary is but a puff of smoke and a fragile mirror contrived to create the illusion of something substantial. Whereas reality suffers no fools. It has Death on its side. And those who fail to heed its clarion call go to their graves never having really lived. The ascetic's terror is of the sublime.

Therefore, in attempting to understand Peirce's proposition "Cain killed Abel" we must have "collateral acquaintance" with the context of the story in which it is embedded, as well as some idea of what killing really means. This is Peirce's psychology in contrast with Lacan's, which requires no such a priori gnosis. Gautama's epiphany regarding the truth of life and death is a fundamental change in his psychology as well as his ontology. The *unfreezing,* as social-psychologist Kurt Lewin calls it, is the *getting-to-know,* which includes what he calls change, and not the *knowing-of,* which is the freezing or frozen psyche. Structural psychologist Lev Semyonovich Vygotsky's term for the frozen psyche is the *crystallized* or (worse) *fossilized* psyche. But if we are to understand the subject's predicament we must know where and how it becomes acquainted with the world. Typically, the environment created by parents comes first as the world, one that is arguably imaginary but definitely manufactured. But like carriers of contagion, parents bring the Imaginary's crude vision of life into the nursery for the budding neurons of the child to absorb. As soon as the child can hold a spoon it is holding a gadget or gizmo of some kind that begins to feed it the Discourse of the hegemony. Parents acquiesce to this abomination because they are too stressed out to notice or care. At the same time, they are unconscious of the fact that they are following a social script they are incapable of deviating from. This script does not arise from anything intrinsic, but only from the extrinsic programming of objective society which is not an organic social entity, but one informed and manipulated by the overlords of consumer culture and political economy. Nevertheless, it is powerless without the subject's voluntary abdication of its sovereignty to this power. Consequently, the subject unconsciously carries out the will of the Hegemony in the form of the *nomos,* which, after all, has supplanted its own will with its prohibited transgressions. In the chatter and bric-à-brac of this discourse simple but significant words such as love, kill, death, justice, freedom, guilt, obligation, terrorist, luxury, employment, education, sex, happiness, and economy are thrown around as signifiers with nothing concrete to signify. Lacking the capacity to discriminate between the signifier to the signified, the subject blindly accepts whatever expedient and cynical definition of these words the media happen to be using at the moment. For example, it is easy to say, in the media, that football team A *killed* team B. In this case it is used metaphorically (and hyperbolically). Then of course there is the differential between killing (in its various legal and illegal forms) and murder as a nomological adjudication. Finally, there is the mysterious difference between so-called justified killing in war, killing through accident, or killing beasts for food (usually indirectly by proxy). What we have in Genesis 4:10 regarding the killing of Abel by his brother amounts to the first murder in Semitic scriptural history after Cain's parents Adam and Eve were discharged from Eden. Out of jealousy of what he perceives as God's preference for Abel, Cain premeditates murder and in so doing not only carries out the first killing but also commits the first murder. His initial reaction is satisfaction. He is ignorant of the consequences of his action because his CA does not include knowledge and experience of the act he has just committed. This situation from then to now has been the subject of the most critical arguments in criminal justice regarding the culpability of the accused. Fortunately, in this case God intervenes, acquainting Cain with guilt, grief, responsibility, and personal sovereignty.

> The Lord said, "What have you done? Listen! ... Now you are under a curse and driven from the ground, which opened its mouth to receive your brother's blood from your hand. When you work the ground, it will no longer yield its crops for you. You will be a restless wanderer on the earth."

So reason is necessary to understand the imaginary, symbolic, and real implications of what now amounts to Cain's crime — a novel phenomenon at this point, and, at last, an example of evil. Peirce says that "the statement 'Cain killed Abel' cannot be fully understood by a person who has not further acquaintance with Cain and Abel than that which the proposition itself gives" (p. 395). For Peirce, the formation of collateral acquaintance is a matter of reason. It is based on the epistemology of what he calls an Index which is the collateral schema within which the subject's psyche operates as it interprets the world.

> To give the necessary acquaintance with any single thing an Index would be required. To convey the idea of causing death in general, according to the operation of a general law, a general sign would be requisite, that is, a *Symbol*. (p. 395)

For Lacan, the three orders lurk in the unconscious where they exert what might be called their "collateral" effect on the same principles in others. Dreams, artifacts from early traumas, desires of the id, the solipsism of the ego, and repression from the superego form a sub-constellation within the greater constellation of the Imaginary, Symbolic, and the Real through the manipulation of signs in the performance of language. As Giorgio Agamben says, *language is the first apparatus* (personal conversation). This performance is what Lacan calls the *signifying chain* forming the subject's world view, informing its behavior, and conditioning its relationship with *le grand Autre*. William J. Hurt in his paper "The Repetition Compulsion," gives a good description of the signifying chain's importance in the formation of the subject's sense of "I" (ego): "At the moment of entering language as Symbolic, the human being is 'subject' to the chains of signifiers in the flow; *it is indeed the effect of these signifiers*. The history of this subject begins at the moment of its insertion into this chain and its fate is in effect sealed" [italics added]. This description is similar to Peirce's conception of the formation of the thought process: "Every thought is a sign, and we cannot think without the use of signs, verbal or gestural. Signs stand for something to somebody. Hence every thought must address itself to something other than the immediate thought itself ..." (p. 16). In other words, thought must address itself to either the ego in the form of "I" and its conjugation (*I think, I am*, and so on) or the thing-in-itself (*das Ding an sich*) apart from the signifiers it consists of. Otherwise, it is narcissistic solipsism which is not thought but scheming. *Das Ding an sich* (not to be confused with Lacan's Das Ding), or the *thingness* of a thing, is its *noumenon* while the thing signified is the phenomenon of it. Therefore, thought is an excrescence of both noumena, and phenomena, expressed as the symbol (signifier) of what we know in thought as *the (this) thing* apart from other things. The contribution Lacan makes here is to bring a Freudian interpretation of the psychology of expressive meaning via symbols to phenomenological definition of the psyche. If he did not, we would be left with the signification of words as a mere utility in transactional communication.

> My research has led me to the realization that *repetition automatism* (*Wiederholungswang*) has its basis in what I have called the *insistence of the signifying chain*. I have isolated this notion as a correlate of the ex-sistence [sic] (that is, of the eccentric place) in which we must necessarily locate the *subject of the unconscious*, if we

> are to take Freud's discovery seriously. As we know, it is in the experience inaugurated by psychoanalysis that we can grasp by what oblique *imaginary* means the *symbolic* takes hold in even *the deepest recesses* of the human organism [italics added]. (p. 6 of Seminar on "The Purloined Letter")

Repetition automatism *irrupts* from the unconscious memory of a trauma which has wormed its way deep into the motivational regions of the psyche in a rather mysterious process. It is like a grain of sand in an oyster which it cannot expel and therefore manufactures an elaborate pearl around it transforming it into something rich and strange. Regardless of the mechanism of its repression, its position in the complex of the psyche gives it a certain amount of authority in the most literal sense of the word as being the author of activity. Lacan develops this idea into the *signifying chain* which is far more comprehensive. The critical link in the chain is what is possible to express in psychoanalysis: the significance of the *imaginary* in the formation of the *symbolic*. While the trauma of the *real* (sublime) takes on a cryptic symbolic existence deep in the psyche, the subject's thought patterns and dreams become the realm of the imaginary as a reaction.

The sense of existence residing in the "subject of the unconscious" becomes the ego's sense of "I." The authority of this "I" leads to an autonomic repetition of behaviors, ideas, thoughts, and dreams which, put altogether, form the subject's nominal *identity*. But we must question the integrity of this identity. The pearl is not the oyster. The role of thought as the cogito will help us in isolating what we could call the "selfness" of the self. Being apart from selfishness, the *noumenon* of our self belongs to the realm of the sublime. In Hindu psychology the distinction would be made between the self (phenomenon) and the Self, or Atman (noumenon). Like Lacan's Das Ding, the sublime is an emptiness which must be filled for there to be anything recognizing conscious life. The artist recapitulates this proximity in the creation of art from the blank emptiness of nothing (horror vacui). A piano does not make a sonata nor a lump of clay a bust. In the phenomenon of both there must be desire and longing injected into the process by a sentient being, even if sentience consists of programming a machine to carry out the effective procedure in the long run. But the significant difference is that Das Ding is the extrinsic (or eccentric) subject of consciousness, whereas the Self is the *object* of consciousness in what Kant calls the *transcendental object,* or the Not-I.

It is not necessary for the individual to be traumatized by

a "real" event such as the death of a parent, abuse, neglect, or a catastrophic upheaval; as the psyche develops through the mirror stage it reaches a point where the sense of object constancy with the mother breaks as the mother draws away. "You're a big boy now. You can do it yourself!" Initially the child has no desire at all to do it himself. A desperate longing for union results as he is forced from the matrix of the mother by the laws of the father. "Be a man!" he says, meaning be like me and not a mamma's boy. There are other inevitable traumas to rely on too, such as the birth trauma. So the child's first real sense of identity comes from these events to which the psyche assigns various symbols and then buries them in the recesses of the psyche. The child is usually unconscious of this process or even of the trauma involved in a specific sense. Nevertheless, the symbol lurks in the motivational regions of the psyche where it begins playing out the repetition automatism of the subject's drama. In effect the subject becomes an automaton, a slave to its own neurosis. Despite the illusion of volition this causes (the basic component of unconsciousness and the imaginary), at least it is *the subject's own trauma* which is the cause of its identity, such as it is. Therefore, it is accurate to say that the subject is sovereign despite its automatic and unconscious behavior. It is moving through a natural stage of development. When this stage crystallizes or fossilizes, however, neurosis sets in and the subject begins to suffer. It is here that psychoanalysis, by working with the signifying chain of the imaginary's representation of the symbolic, brings the subject *back* to the reality of healthy functioning as a conscious, autonomous adult.

What matters to us here in relation to the sublime is the sense of self. When the subject abdicates, it give up something to the hegemony in a psychological sense. This does not happen on a special day. It happens incrementally as the subject signs the promissory notes leading down the road to serfdom. At the same time its acquiescence to the parent state herds it into a subservient relationship with *le grand Autre* - the Father. What is lost and gained by this? Is it the symbol of the self, buried deep in the psyche, engendered by trauma, or is it the struggle of self-development during the mirror stage? At what point in this process does the subject acknowledge that it is an individual like others? The demands of the sublime, particularly in the admission to the self that the ego is finite, compel the subject to seek the *Genuss* of an imaginary world where everyone lives forever (if they can afford it) and all needs are taken care of by either a benevolent God or its material equivalent the parental state. In effect, then, the bewildered subject attempts to return to the womb to recover the sense of object constancy it remembers from its infantile relationship with the mother. At the same time it also finds the authority of the Father in the apparatus of the state. It is therefore pulled in opposite directions. The amnion of the Imaginary is the feminine principle and the hegemony (symbolic) is the masculine. The nagging symbol of its trauma seems temporarily propitiated by the struggle for reconciliation. What is most significant in terms of abdication, though, is that it resolves the conflict by *transferring* the authority for its autonomic behavior to the amnion of the Imaginary. The symbolic sense of self deep in the psyche is no longer the dominant motivator for the subject's drama. The drama is taken up by repetition of the fairy tales in the media which mirror the subject's compulsory automatism. All social fairy tales in the amnion have one rhetorical message: *accept the ethical aesthetic of consumerism*. The paleo-fairy tales of democracy, freedom, marriage, ownership, learning, religion, government, self-defense, community, and finance are all subplots at best and anachronisms at worst. Having abdicated, the subject has accepted the Imaginary as what Lacan calls the subject's "ex-istence" (sic) of the "eccentric place." Das Ding (*l'objet petit a*) is no longer the result of the vacuum the subject must fill as a result of the loss of its object constancy and resulting trauma. The subject now has no need of psychoanalysis. In the amnion of the Imaginary this problem is taken care of with pharmaceuticals, shopping, sports, entertainment, news, elections, advertising, and the catharsis of perpetual war.

The unfortunate presence of the repetition automatism gives the subject's behavior in the amnion of the Imaginary its seemingly unconscious, autonomic character. Permanently in a state of psychological trauma from the dismemberment of its core identity, the subject seeks the narcotic of what the French call the *métro, boulot, dodo* existence of the wage slave to pay its debts. This life of relentless commuting, dithering, frittering, and herding children makes the subject a *dodo*, a putatively dumb bird extinct because of its low score on the Stanford-Binet. The subject starts out as a useful tool and slowly (and then suddenly) becomes a *useless object*. It is then a *burden* to the hegemony. This dangerous proximity to power results in it being kicked aside, sacked from its job as redundant, pushed from the home it labored all its life for, and into a retirement home. After a brief time there, it is warehoused in a nursing home. Two to four years later (statistically) it finds itself *dying* in a hospital which drains off all the rest of its financial resources. Where is the medical immortality the amnion promised in return for the subject's sovereignty early on in this melodrama? The last stop is, of course, the crematorium where the amnion — in a great hegemonic tradition — disposes of its wretched refuse and lumpen proletariat. How did it all come to this after all of those bright promises of the amnion? Poised to dig itself into even more debt so that it can sustain its status in the consumer society, the subject puts all the money it has left on its lucky number at the roulette table of this artificial life. A remnant of the Machine Age, this *repetition automatism* is not an adaptation but a neurotic tick, a spasm. It is brought on by maladaptation to the inscrutable trauma of the loss of the *object*: mother's unconditional love and the comfort and convenience of the womb's sanctum sanctorum. Herein lies the formation of the phantasm of the Lacanian *objet petit a*. The subject loses all sense of object constancy *because it is no longer an object to itself.* What is missing from its collateral acquaintance with bare life is the realization that without apprehension of the transcendental object (Kant), the life of the sublime is impossible. Without the sublime there is no sense of oneself being a solid object in a world of things with thingness. The comfortably numb nimbus of the subject drifts in the cold wind of the Imaginary's heartless ether. *Sans puissance*, then, the subject flounders in the complicated world of debt and obligation it willingly threw itself into — all the while complaining that it was hoodwinked, bamboozled, hornswoggled, and flimflammed. Loss of core identity through abdication is the subject's second great trauma after birth. As a result, the subject dwells in the amnion, fearing the real as a threat to its haven of delusion and the pornography of vicarious thrills, until it is too late.

What grinds away at the subject's well-being is repetition automatism. It becomes wired to the amnion through the thousands of fibers of the umbilicus, any one of which, if cut, would cause an immediate hemorrhage of cash, status, and access to distraction from its fate. In "Remembering, Repeating and Working-Through," Freud describes the pathology associated with what he calls the "compulsion to repeat" which is, perhaps, what Lacan means by "repetition automatism" and its consequent *insistence of the signifying chain.* Just as Lacan describes the orientation of the subject as "ex-istence" [sic] at an eccentric position in relation to the Other, Freud describes the eccentric position in psychotherapy as "transference" (p. 2502). Compelled to repeat the same behavior with all individuals and in all circumstances, the subject is little more than a fleshly automaton, like Descartes' beasts, enslaved to the mechanism of its neurotic obsession. In this way the subject mimics the ideal industrial worker of the past Machine Age who was a flesh-and-blood part, or component, of whatever machine he operated.

Marxism in its original form may be explained as an attempt to migrate the worker's ontological role as a part of an industrial machine to being part of a social machine. Herein lies the object of material dialectics: to evolve, through struggle, the worker's application of his labor-capital from the private possession of the means of production to the public integration of his labor into the collective pool of the commonwealth. The so-called Information Age, however, replaces the old industrial machines with personal *gadgets* and *gizmos*. The new capitalist tools are in effect data terminals of remote soft machines owned either privately (once again), or semi-privately by various major shareholders and banks, which include governments. These sleek, warm, black slabs full of Big Magic do not have the cold alienating cogs, gears, axles, armatures, pistons, grease, oil, deafening clang and steam sirens, and billowing black smoke of the past's dark Satanic mills Marx and Blake reviled. Instead, they chortle with infantile glee at the worker's surrender of his labor-capital through monthly subscriptions and impulse purchases with credit, as well as the abdication of his personal sovereignty through consumer-data telemetry and kleptnotic neural states of narcotization.

Meantime, neurosis in the form of chronic fear of the loss of object constancy haunts the subject. It does not understand that in abdicating its sovereignty it has shut the door to the possibility of bare life in which it could abdicate its abdication and free itself from fear of the loss of the object. Such freedom is not possible in the amnion because it serves as an analog for the womb to which the subject desires to return. The best the subject can do is dwell in the amnion of the Imaginary where it finds a manufactured matrix (womb) in which it can wallow in the narcotic umbilicus of *Genuss*. While the abdication of abdication (Hegel's Second Negation) is a kind of return to a state of bare life through the process of *neoteny*, or biologic return to an earlier stage of development, it is hardly a return to the womb or even the object of mother love. Quite the contrary; it is a return to the moment-to-moment sublime *terror* of birth and its correlative: death. ("I am terrified by birth and death and therefore have adopted a homeless life to win salvation," says the ascetic to young Prince Gautama.) It is a return to the misery of being expelled from Paradise. It is a return to hardship, loss, and death. In short, it is a return to the sublime. Why would anyone want to do this? As it says in Mark 8:36, "For what shall it profit a man, if he shall gain the whole world, and lose his own soul?" This kind of religious scolding sounds quaint and old fashioned to the subject, having heard it from the nuns and evangelists. However, having already *lost* its soul, the subject also has lost its collateral acquaintance with what it means to *have* one, and therefore to love someone other than itself. The subject can no longer comprehend these propositions from books of wisdom honored through the ages for their fundamental understanding of what it means to live (rather than die). If the subject puts on sack cloth and scourges itself it is because it has been forced to do so by the hegemony when it invokes its wrath. It is done as penance for its sins against the Name-of-the-Father in the form of the hegemony. "Forgive me Father for I have sinned" is on the secular lips of the heathen subject bereft of any understanding of what God means. But this subject does not pray into the abyss of the sublime where the mystery of the *Spiritus Mundi* dwells. Rather, it prays into the mouthpiece of its gadget as it tries to make a new deal with the bank before it forecloses on its house. Or it sings to the jury before it is locked away and forgotten.

Snapping up the opportunity, the hegemony and its *amnion* of the Imaginary seize upon the subject's neurotic, obsessive psychology. The apparatus doses it with expensive drugs while crude forms of entertainment rat-trap it into dependency on the neural stimulation of the phantasmagoria transmitted by its ubiquitous black boxes full of digital Big Magic. There is no therapeutic value to this onslaught. Rather, it inaugurates the decay (decadence) of the psychological, emotional, and spiritual integrity of the subject's psyche. It also erodes the emotion of *empathy* toward others as real. After firing a worker for the crime of not being the right phenotype or being too honest, the boss-subject then makes a cash donation to the homeless, to whom it has just added another member, and feels that it has done its duty to society. This repetition automatism reinforces the subject's sense of itself as being a Good Guy (LaVey's *Good-Guy Badge*). Meantime, as grand martinet of the office tower, it exercises its petty imperial power over others with no conscience. Why are the weak and mediocre so quick to become tyrants of the office cubicles? Perhaps it is because they have made themselves powerless by accumulating debts and other obligations. Therefore they can only feel powerful when they terrorize those who suffer the misfortune of having retained some shred of their core identity, dignity, empathy, and sovereignty. Such apostates are the usual targets these subhuman creatures bully. This is compulsive behavior. It is the machination of the mad automaton. Of course, the side effects of this abrogation of all that is natural and sublime causes physical, psychological, and emotional violence in the subject and in those around it. Eschewing psychoanalysis because it takes work and imagination, the subject willing to admit something is wrong turns to Big Pharma or illegal drugs and alcohol. Though it may have a therapy (not a cure) for everything, the cartel of drug companies is not satisfied; it even invents diseases in order to prey on the subject's obsession with its imaginary aches and pains and self-centered anxiety and depression. The subject becomes a chronic *valetudinarian*, fixated on its health while destroying it at the same time – a perfect commercial cycle of repetition automatism bringing unimaginable profit to the drug cartels, legal and illegal.

Freud connects this cycle with a form of repression of certain ideas and memories. He says that the "compulsion to repeat" takes what has now become unconscious (memory) and transfers it to entirely inappropriate objects. This helps facilitate what Freud terms *resistance* to the symbolic meaning of the memory (trauma). To call it a form of repression is accurate, though in this case we have what Lacan calls an eccentric (as opposed to centric) transfer of the memory the subject is resisting. We all have likely seen the situation where one event – a car crash, a broken heart, a professional failure – permeates all the subject does after that in the form of remorse. As a result, the subject becomes obsessed with extrinsic objects as a displacement substitute for what is resisting, which is a terrifying understanding of its fate. As a complex, it tends to express itself as repetition because the psychic energy is *trapped*. It has nowhere to go. The canny psychotherapist is aware of this *sublimation*. Says Freud, he is able to use it as a way to eke out some self-consciousness in the subject of its inverted state.

> What interests us most of all is naturally the relation of this compulsion to repeat to the transference and to resistance. We soon perceive that the transference is itself only a piece of repetition, and that the repetition is a transference of the forgotten past not only on to the doctor but also on to all the other aspects of the current situation. We must be prepared to find, therefore, that the patient yields to the compulsion to repeat, which now replaces the impulsion to remember, not only in his personal attitude to his doctor but also in every other activity and relationship which may occupy his life at the time ... (p. 2502).

Outside of the kind of therapeutic environment where personal transference is possible in a clinical context, lie vast commercial propositions calculated to exploit this tragic situation. The subject allows itself to fall into the rat trap *willingly*, casting off whatever threadbare sovereignty it has left that it may be clinging to. Without the proper psychoanalytic treatment, it is unlikely that the subject will ever again acquaint itself with the real – unless perhaps if it finds itself in some kind of Armageddon of the ego. While the *memento mori* of death certainly fits the bill, the Imaginary has already hawked its cure for death – which is seen as an illness to be cured and not a natural and essential part of life. Therefore, St. Jerome's contemplation of a skull in Renaissance paintings no longer has its bracing effect on the subject as a reminder of what is and is not real. The automaton thrives on the lust for forgetfulness brought on by poppies (opioids) and the waters of Lethe (alcohol). If it did not, the legal and illegal drug businesses would not be the top money makers of the world. What it most wants to forget is the terror of death. As a machine that can be repaired ad infinitum, the automaton means to live forever, free as it is from physical corruption and the prerogatives of mortality that only the poor and other dumb beasts must suffer.

Is there no escape for our besieged hero? This neurosis is, of course, embedded deeply in the unconscious like a nail driven into the wet grey matter of the skull. It causes a *contraction* of the subject's symbolic orientation to others, turning its full force in upon itself. The subject becomes a symbol of itself and therefore nonexistent. Peirce makes it clear that he does not embrace what he calls the German sense of subject and object (such as we see in Kant's transcendental object). Rather, he sees subject-object as a linguistic matter. "[I] use 'subject' as the correlative of 'predicate,' and speak only of the 'subjects' of those signs which have a part which separately indicates what the object of the sign is" (pp. 394-5). It may seem that we are confusing the persona's proximity to the object with a simple use of subject to mean the noun or pronoun that acts through the agency of the verb upon the object of a sentence. But Peirce sees the subject as more than either the opposite of the object in the interpersonal sense or the necessary doer in a subject-verb-object string. The persona is a sign. Thoughts are a concatenation of signs of signs. And who we are is the result of this semiotic process *in vivo*, not *in obituarius*. In his description of what he calls the three Universes of Experience, Peirce holds signs up to be the *generative* principle of what we can know about ourselves and the universe. This is not such an alien concept when we consider that the only star any of us have come close to actually seeing is the sun. The rest are millions of light years away and may no longer even be there. The light reaching us emanated from them eons ago when there may have been no life on earth. What we see flickering in the atmosphere of a summer night may in fact have exploded in a vast cloud of gas and dark matter and is no more. The starlight reaching us is a *representation* of the star, its sign. The sun is itself first, as the sublime, ready at any moment to fry us with microwaves, and only then is it a sign of whatever the necessity of our sign formation demands. Peirce says that "The third Universe comprises everything whose being consists in active power to establish connections between different objects, especially between objects in different Universes. *Such is everything which is essentially a Sign* [italics added] ..." (359).

What does he mean by the "power to establish connections" between objects? Perhaps he means that anything at all can be considered an object or a thing, and that it has some kind of objective nature of its own apart from its predicate (attributes). Heidegger says that to discover what man is we cannot look to the attributes of Being which are after all extensions of the meaning of Being and not its soul. So something *is*. Therefore, it will attract to itself any number of attributes. They become a kind of encrustation, a shell, a persona, but ultimately an interface with the world and other personae with which we negotiate meaning and relationship. This is a purely psychological phenomenon. But along comes the pornography of the Imaginary. It showers bric-à-brac, chatter, noise, interference, delusion, notions, lust, and scraps of code which act like viruses (memes) within the cluttered content of what is now the subject's mind, which has abdicated mineness (*Jemeinigkeit*). While this process may seem rather chaotic, it in fact has a highly sophisticated organization operating invisibly within the everydayness of the subject's experience. This structure, as we have mentioned, is the ethical aesthetic of *Genuss* as the *summum bonum* of existence. Therefore this aesthetic is an existential argument with its own predicate logic continually interrogating the subject's repressed core identity. The memes (mental malware) infiltrate the operational structures of the subject's persona. There they become mechanisms of the apparatus of compulsive consumerism based on debt and hegemonic fiats. These fiats serve a union of two purposes: to keep the apparatus aligned with the commercial interests of the hegemony's overlords and to satisfy these overlords' lust for total power. Who are these overlords, and who, exactly, is the hegemony? There is no need to nominate them. If the reader has no sense of these things, he must look elsewhere (Marx, Thomas Paine?) for some wisdom. Once they are named, the argument becomes propaganda – which is precisely what I do not want this critique of discourse to be, though I cannot escape my opinions. (All is opinion, says Marcus Aurelius.)

To understand the apparatus we must understand *signs as a process*. What does this mean? The simplest example is thought itself, being a concatenation of signs overseen by symbolic relationships to the mythological discourse or narrative. Thought is sentential which means it is ultimately a *performance* just as a sentence is. *The* discourse is a fugue of ancillary discourses (nationality, gender, political affiliation, religion, occupation, and so on) with a *kernel discourse* which is a kind of caduceus of the chatter of the social and commercial orders and of the subject's bare life as subject-object. Signs do not normally refer to themselves, as that is not their function. But in the abdication of sovereignty that is precisely what they do. However, there are two quite different ways in which signs can be referential in terms of the subject's orientation to the Other. The first is the solipsistic, narcissistic inversion of the subject's sense of itself in relation to other entities. The second is the outwardly directed association with extrinsic signs emanating from other entities. In the latter there is active negotiation of meaning even of the simplest signs (words). "I'm feeling hot tonight" can refer to temperature and comfort or self-image and sex appeal. The matter becomes far more complicated when dealing with broad abstractions which have no *reciprocal meaning* between interlocutors unless negotiated. Despite the equivocal definitions of such words in dictionaries, they remain, in the fray of discourse, monstrous abstractions often used to mean the opposite of what, at least, the dictionary has to say about them or what children are taught in kindergarten that they mean. Take, for example, the word peace. This word is often used to justify war. Peace through war is a common concept in the mechanics of political thinking. Does security mean constant surveillance and curtailment of freedom for those whom is it intended to protect? What is the political difference between the left wing and the right wing? What does it mean to liberate people from a dictatorship by destroying their country and killing (murdering) the dictator so that chaos, looting, and rapine ensue? What can liberty mean to whose who have never read a book about the evolution of its meaning in Western thought? Does liberty mean escaping from jail so one can rob and murder again, or does it mean putting someone who robs and murders in jail so that one is free from being murdered and robbed? The sine qua non of meaningless abstractions is the word love. If it ever had a clear denotation in everyday use, that meaning has long ago vanished from any possible useful concept of what it might be. One loves to go fishing just as much as one loves one's spouse. A serial killer may love to murder, while a priest may love God. The everyday dialogue of the subject is based on a folklore which is at the kernel of the discursive narrative of being. Most of it, though, is filled with meaningless noises which nevertheless convey certain feelings and impressions too vague to articulate in any analytical sense. The fairy tale of the narrative infects even the most significant exchange of ideas through the agency of memes which now travel at (near) light speed through digital networks. The notion that those who do not vote have no say in government (often enough about fifty percent of the eligible electorate) do not understand that those who do not or cannot vote, such as children, felons, resident aliens illegal or not, invalids, and the incarcerated, all have rights and are in fact nevertheless represented by elected officials and by the legal code. This bit of brain-dead exclusionary folklore is not only synthetic, but also makes assumptions about democracy that are – using the definition thrown around in such debates – *undemocratic.* Still, it serves as a meme to dismiss the observations and opinions of anyone who believes that voting will change little or nothing, or who just do not care. Should we burn them, then? When we consider concrete words such as bread and fruit, we feel far more confident that we know exactly what is being referred to referred to. However, language allows us to say that man cannot live by bread alone, and that he is entitled to the fruit of his labors with meaning. But when we hear abstract words such as good or holy, we default into a realm of synthetic impressions that are, at best, marginally meaningful though more often simply meaningless. Still, if it is said that a person or a restaurant (interchangeably) is good or nice, we accept the adjective as a potential truth of some analytic, verifiable, denotative, concrete attribute of what is being described subjectively by the other. No further explanation or example is needed. And yet we all understand that what is referred to as bread or fruit varies enough so that both words can be used poetically as metonyms, or in the sense that there is bread, and then there is *bread* — as if A and A were not the same thing. "You call this *bread*!?" shouts the French *boulenger* to the American supermarket manager. The worker has to earn some bread. Business associations must be fruitful. And yet when it comes to such important concepts as *freedom* and *liberty*, it is quite difficult to find anyone who could explain the difference, much less define either one of them to the satisfaction of a dozen persons listening. Yet, more often than not, they are willing to fight, kill, and die for such abstractions, or at least pay someone to do it.

There are *thousands* of words which may be thrown into the volcano of verifiable meaninglessness that are nevertheless the bread and fruit of everyday political and economic discourse. (All the better! says the politician, the business, the mass media.) They are mere noises, signals, at best. Narcissism occurs when the subject *projects* the image of itself upon itself. Unless the subject is capable of negotiating these words in an extrinsic exchange of signs, chaos reigns. The words God, excellence, luxury, patriotism, faith, intelligence, security, terrorists, democracy, and even honesty are suspect. Therefore, the second form of sign exchange (where a sign refers to another sign) may properly be called *communication*. In its narcissistic, solipsistic form the subject's mental discourse consists only of signs of itself. This is the mechanism of the Imaginary, displacing the Real. While such thinking would immediately lead to death in the arena of bare life, the amnion of the Imaginary provides an environment in which such a deadly strategy actually works — as long as it is *others* who die, preferably the Less Fortunate or Unfortunate, not the subject itself and certainly not the Apex Consumer who has been guaranteed medical immortality (as long as he can make the monthly payments). The subject, in its narcotized state of kleptolepsy, consequently develops a paranoid horror of terrorists, human traffickers, drug gangs, global-warming deniers, and Republicans lurking under every rock. Despite its vociferous and even violent support of what it calls progressive causes, it compulsively fears beastly brown *poor people* smashing down the gates of its mortgaged Paradise. Meantime, the hegemony works tirelessly to convince the subject that there is nothing to worry about, as long as it pays its taxes and makes the monthly payments on its mortgage. For a fee, the amnion will provide a magic force field to protect the subject from the terror de jour, be it an invisible Chinese virus or a Russian hacker.

But the most iconic threat to the Imaginary is what the hegemony and its mass-media networks calls in their collective propaganda the *terrorist*. This cartoon character in the folklore of the knowing-of is defined as anyone who has somehow mastered the powers of bare life without dependency on the amnion's great big giant bag of technological tricks. It is even better if the terrorist professes some atavistic faith that fanatical Scientism sees as competition for the hearts, minds and most of all capital and labor of the subject. In its typically self-defeating way, though, the hegemony never understands that creating such bogeymen gives its enemies a significant advantage over the subject, who has never learned how to protect itself. It has always *been protected* by the amnion that *needs* the subject to sweat in its metaphorical gold mines. Most of all, the subject of the amnion is the bridge between the labor, minerals, and ports of the third-world far-off other that the hegemony needs to exploit. What the subject is often unconscious of is that the hegemony kills and destroys on the subject's behalf by proxy to maintain its role as the *bridge* between the exploited and the exploiters. The Imaginary deliberately keeps the subject ignorant of the true significance of murder by proxy by bribing and coercing the media into pumping its propaganda into the mainstream of public discourse. This is an effective strategy for the hegemony because it allows it to turn its military apparatus upon the subject if necessary – despite any constitutional injunctions to the contrary. Terrorists also serve an indispensable purpose in the schemes of the hegemony and the media. For the former they provide a threat scary enough to get the subject to surrender its freedoms and abdicate its sovereignty in favor of an imaginary force field that will protect its paradise of *Genuss*. For the latter they provide spectacular atrocities broadcast worldwide through every available channel, increasing ratings. If it bleeds, it leads, they say. These deliciously atrocious acts keep the subject glued to its gadget because 1) The subject feels that its safety somehow depends upon it being informed of this slaughter – even if it happens thousands of miles away in a far-off land the subject has not even heard of until then; 2) The subject's dangerously repressed id – the container of all the impulses its society and civilization consider criminal – lusts for a displacement substitute for the rape, murder, and mayhem that would release its fury. (The French Revolution of 1789 is a prime example of what happens when the hegemony fails to keep a lid on the id.) The id's repressed psychic energy has built up to a critical state. As such, it has so warped the subject's sense of its natural *being-in-the-world*, which includes the creation of reciprocal meaning, that it makes sociopaths out of the common individual. The hegemony exploits this too, providing an endless stream of the opium of the people by partnering with illegal drug cartels, Big Pharma, the alcohol industry, thought-paralyzing entertainment, and ever new and more magical gizmos and gadgets.

So far we have discussed what happens when signs refer to other signs inter-personally within the context of mainstream society. Behind and beneath this process is the semiotic significance of the exchange of signs versus the *turning-from* of self-referential signals which make the amnion of the Imaginary possible. As above, there are two directions the impulse to create signs as thought can move within the available environments and channels. When a sign becomes a sign of itself it stops being a *signifier* of the *signified*. It becomes a *signifier* of a *signifier*. In this configuration the subject loses all *consciousness* of reality while retaining a kind of animal *awareness* of what is necessary to survive by the rules of the hegemony. Under such circumstances, it is accurate to say that the subject is *not conscious;* we will develop the idea of *selective unconsciousness* later in this essay. Let it suffice for now to say that what is officially available to the subject is the *knowing-of,* also known as propaganda. The *getting-to-know* eventually becomes impossible, except for the most rudimentary and utilitarian applications, or in a cataclysm such as war, which is the sublime's way of throwing the subject *back* into the furnace of mortality and bare life from the delusion of medical immortality in the imaginary future. Scientists are thrown back upon the consensus of cults; the public learns to rely on hearsay about reality, having lost the ability to test it. The significance and meaning of abstractions soon elude the subject's cognition; it simply accepts whatever the media characterize in their steady stream of propaganda emanating from every pore of the Imaginary. The chief source of what has come to be known, quit accurately, as the *feed,* issues from the screens and speakers of the subject's gadgets and gizmos. In the turning-from, the sign ceases to be able to refer to any other sign except the sign of itself because it is no longer anchored to the signified from where it drew its power as an extension of that thing. Its anchor to the signified (even if it was an idea) had previously kept it visible to other signs. They could therefore discover the sign in the creative and sublime process of reciprocal meaning, or communication. New ideas that would have been born of this semination as the tertium quid of the subjective self and the objective other never come into being (*le devenir*).

The situation is far more severe when a self-referential sign is among other self-referential signs in a contrived social order, such as we see in so-called social media online. In other words, we see the spectacle of narcissists banding together to form a cult. In such a situation individuals become a herd at best, acting as one mindless stimulus-response beast without ratiocination. The herd takes on a wild, unconscious, bloodthirsty lust for destruction, even self-destruction, as the collective id dissolves into a force the super-ego and the nomos cannot repress. Giant sports arenas somewhat satisfy the mob's lust for violence vicariously in what is more or less a civilized contest. (This was not the case, however, in ancient Rome where such cruel entertainment was indeed barbaric, which was its main attraction for the hyper-civilized Romans.) What is not propitiated in the arena can be smoothed over in a violent video game or by watching almost any new movie with a leading male actor over 40; the studio casts aging heart-throbs in action-adventure films where they must fire a gun at someone as a substitution for what studio executives perceive as the male actor's loss of virility (diminishing box office) along with bygone youthful looks. Therefore, the gun becomes a kind of prosthetic penis spewing bullets instead or spermatozoa. Meantime, the audience is treated to endless spectacles of entertaining murder - by penis analog, no less. The abdicated individual alone is generally weak, listless, morose, and anxious. While he complains to his congressperson about the need for more gun control, he longs to watch the next movie featuring an orgy of gun-play, gang murder, genocide, drug overdoses, and rape at gunpoint. For instance, searching the inventory of one of the most popular movie-streaming sources, I find that there are 2,359 films with or about Nazis, but only 778 about Jews (if we are to pair them as adversaries, likes cats and mice). The reigning topical queen and king of this service's inventory are illegal drugs (6,350 films) and gangs and gangsters (7,532). Compare this to 984 about the economy - something the subject should be interested in since it will affect his access to the amnion through promissory notes and the ability to pay its monthly membership fees. How many of these films use gun violence? I might have to watch them all to tell you for sure. But odds are, many of them have to do with the violence, fist, gun, or knife, the impotent gelding of the amnion craves as a displacement substitute for his id crushed by civilization's nomos. As Freud says about "renunciation of instinct" in *Civilization and its Discontents*, "this seems the most important of all, it is impossible to overlook the extent to which civilization is built up upon a renunciation of instinct, how much it presupposes precisely the non-satisfaction (by suppression, repression or some other means?) of powerful instincts. This 'cultural frustration' dominates the large field of social relationships between human beings. As we already know, it is the cause of the hostility against which all civilizations have to struggle" (III).

The subject who has abdicated to the amnion immediately reacts to the loss of sexual potency and animal ferocity civilization demands from its vassals by a self-destructive program of compensation that is not without its cost. Fat, lazy, impotent (except for pornography), with multiple chronic diseases because of his inactivity, and usually addicted to some drug, the modern Roman citizen lounges before his big-screen TV ogling young, handsome, athletic men play football. He shouts his barbaric yawp atavistically at the glass screen: "Go go go!" as if players on the pitch could hear his voice echoing from Heaven above. He superstitiously believes that his worship of these sport personalities magically compensates for his inert state of capture. Furthermore, he exposes himself to tens of thousands of ingeniously crafted commercial pitches during these orgies of athleticism motivating him to spend - otherwise these spots would not cost $5.6 million per airing. If this is not enough, collectively he bets billions of dollars on the outcome of games through illegal bookies, from time to time borrowing money from underworld sources at an interest rate even more usurious than that of his credit cards, which are usually maxed out anyway. He then complains about how much he must pay in taxes for the proxy wars and surveillance he clambers for from the government to protect his national security and his decadent way of life. Or he grumbles about freeloaders on public assistance who, often enough through no fault of their own, cannot find work suitable for their level of skill, training, and education.

But of course sport is not enough. His innate weakness also leads him to worship the imaginary gunsel in entertainment, usually a middle-aged man like himself, while his preprogrammed progressive ideology prompts him to sacrifice yet another Constitutional freedom (the right to keep and bear arms) on the altar of social stability (a Chinese Communist Party term). But of course we assume here that he is in his right mind, which is generally not the case. Bookmaker's odds are that he is tanked up with alcohol and pharmaceutics, if not also illegal drugs, the sale of which eventually benefits those in power the greatest, with little economic reward for the doped-up population of peons. Meantime he lobbies for government to lock up the criminals from whom he buys his illegal drugs. This behavior also produces the cartels, gangs, murder, and prisons he fears without him seeing any connection between his recreational use of cocaine and what he pays the military and police to interdict at great peril to their lives. Furthermore, he sees no correlation between his abuse of alcohol and junk food and the rising cost of healthcare. In his turpitude, he also does not understand how these excesses wipe out the modicum of precious economic freedom allegedly bestowed upon him by the industrial and financial beneficence of his amniotic empire.

However, put the abdicated subject in a *mob*, and the ghost of his bygone sexual potency and animal ferocity seems to return. Whether the mob is a gang of hooligans at a sporting event, or activists in the street protesting the *cause de jour*, the subject, for a brief, transcendent moment, wallows in catharsis through the jouissance of the momentary transgression of the nomos. His mind clears. His adrenaline flows. He feels the thrill of the kill. What is happening? The amnion has engaged its pressure valve to let off the psychic steam libidinal repression inevitably generates. His capture by the amnion, however, blinds him to the reality that these events are, in the case of sport, sanctioned by one of the world's biggest capitalist industries united with advertising, and that his symbolic civil disobedience is not only guaranteed by the laws of his land, but is even *initiated and funded by its rulers* to palliate the subject and his comrades while duping them into causing the blood in the streets necessary for the acquisition of assets devalued by programmed social chaos. He is also oblivious to what should be self-evident: that the police state he begged for to protect his security against terrorists, gangs, sex traffickers, and the drug dealers he patronizes for his fix, can in an instant be turned on *him.* He is blind because he asked for it in order to maintain the social stability and law and order he voted for. He and his pseudo-revolutionary, middle-class comrades cross a certain line drawn invisibly in the pavement before their parade by the hegemony they imagine they are abusing.

What we have here is the subject's lust for self- and other- destruction with impunity to release the agonizing pain of pent up psychic (erotic) energy which has accumulated through repression in the troubled and now psychotic id. Socialization in the sense of reciprocal meaning is impossible. All that remains is the sign's impotent symbolic representation as a profile in the digital graveyard of (*anti-*) social media. Further tightening the screw, the self-referential signs are captured, surveilled, and then turned back in to the subject by its gadgets and gizmos. The turning-from here is the mirroring of telemetrics. The gadget captures the subject's demographic, psychographic, and consumer profile. It then creates a digital *homunculus* or *golem* of the subject which can be bought and sold in the cryptological marketplaces of Big Data. But what really affects the subject on a semiotic level is that this homunculus, which by definition is not the subject but a sign of it, actually *molds* the subject into the image of itself. By this mechanism the subject becomes *a sign of itself.* Such mimesis affords many advantages to the hegemony and its corporate overlords. Since they have control over Big Data (except for hackers), they can begin modifying the subject's sign of itself to conform to whatever they need from it. Soon the subject thinks it is staring at a reflection of itself in the gadget (its music tracks, its favorite website, its downloaded apps, its picture gallery, and so on) when in fact it is fixated on an alien persona contrived by the powers of political and commercial interest. The important thing for the hegemony is to get them when they are young. The closer the subject is to adolescence the better able the hegemony, through the Imaginary, is able to modify the neural pathways in the subject's brain to conform to its programmed configuration. As the subject matures, these pathways become hard wired (crystallized, then fossilized). The social goal is the formation of the functionally obedient *consumer* and law-abiding citizen of the hegemony.

1.7: Sign exchange as threat to the hegemonic order

The greatest loss is the subject's ability to negotiate meaning with the Other. Without this transaction there is no possibility of apprehending the transcendental other *in* the Other. The discourse of the hegemony twists the idea of everyone being created equal into the idea that we all understand the same signs and signals at the same time in the same way. Such conformity is policed by academics and their operatives acting as social justice warriors (SJW's). This is the hegemony's ultimate goal: a zombie army of obedient consumers who will tirelessly serve the hegemony's corporate overlords by borrowing money from them to buy the *accoutrements* of comfort, convenience, and notional prosperity. In the meantime, the goods the subject buys are manufactured by these corporate overlords who simply scoop up the money they lent to the consumer at the point of sale and then lend it back to him at interest. By ignoring its own lending regulations and borrowing from its enemies, it baits the economy with debt in pursuit of *capture*. The tragic irony of this scheme is that the citizen-subject must also pay taxes to service the interest on the hegemony's debt that was loaned to him at interest! If this is not enough to entirely ensnare the subject, however, the hegemony's last card is to devalue the currency by increasing its velocity (exchangeable quantity), causing inflation, so that the subject has no hope whatsoever of digging itself out of its own grave.

What has the subject given up? As stated above, the subject has given up the ability to negotiate signs freely with the Other. Why is this so critical? Because the hegemony's campaign to create a homogeneous psychic monolith over which it has total control is doomed to fail because of the nature of the autonomous and chaotic exchange of signs. Also, the id always wins in the end, one way or another, even if it means *totalen Krieg*. Finally, like the life of the subject in the Imaginary, the hegemony's entire enterprise is a mere chimera on the timeline of history. Empires upon empires built with far more sturdy materials and that endured much longer have wiped themselves from the face of the earth as if they never were. How much more fragile is the imaginary Amniotic Empire? But of course each new empire arising from the rubble of the last proclaims itself the next *Tausendjähriges Reich* - as Nazi Germany did in the ashes of the Roman and Teutonic empires — only to vanish in an *Augenblick* later. The fundamental problem is, again, semiotic. The fact is one person does not see what another person does. We can know this, but we can never know what it is that person sees. Herein lies the absolute limit of subjectivity. For example. If I show a sentence in Chinese characters to a person who cannot read it, that person will see something entirely different from what a person who can read it sees (semantic meaning). Perhaps there are some graphic agreements as to shapes and strokes, but since we are talking about writing and not pictures, such an objection is beside the point. To say that a person sees light is trivial. To say that the green one sees is precisely the color another sees is a highly complex proposition to prove because it is impossible, though we may talk about the physics of light, which is universal to all. Although a written word is a form of image (or *feeling* in Braille), its value as a sign transcends any other characteristic about it since it would not exist if it were not a sign. Turning to speech, the situation gets even more complex. Certainly, there are layers of signs in even the most simple language. They include innuendo, connotation, figuration, metonym, jargon, slang, and nomenclature. Add shorthand, Morse code, gesticulation, and the many grunts and other noises we make that seem to mean so much (the screams of orgasm?). Furthermore, there is a complex semiotics of the image which infiltrates, influences, forms, changes, and mutates language. It is no accident that we use see to also mean understand. Photos, paintings, TV shows, movies, video games, religious iconography, Internet content, and architecture all influence language. Finally – and this list is by no means comprehensive – we have the buzz words, memes, platitudes, slogans, and euphemisms of advertising, politics, and government. From all sides the call for the platitudes of peace, love, and understanding (p-l-u) enters into the discourse with a halo of progressive sanctity. While it gets it provenance from, perhaps, the New Testament (in which this was a novel idea to the peoples of the time), it has become an incantation reserved for sanctimonious occasions. Taken as a relative statement in which all parts reinforce each other, p-l-u, pulled from the subject's fast repository of platitudes, is a mood rather than a signifier. It is meant to trigger a solemnity which ultimately incites the subject to give money to a cause. It is similar to the reaction in the subject as when a hypnotist commands sleep to trigger the hypnotic state. Because the subject in its abdicated, unconscious state becomes a stimulus-response machine, the Imaginary and the hegemony use a lexicon of buzz words which initiate a response. By the endless repetition and redundancy of the subject's thoughts and life it becomes possible to train the subject just as a rat learns a maze or to push a lever to reach its food.

The subject is trainable but not educable. What passes for the subject's education is really an aggrandized form of vocational training and social indoctrination. Whatever mystique education seems to have is merely borrowed from its historic legacy. It was once regarded as a form of mental, spiritual, and even physical development necessary to create a more enlightened participant in the great cultural project of humankind. Consider John Dewey's description of the purpose of education. While it does have a certain mystique, it also indicates in precise terms those intellectual and spiritual qualities a person must possess to be considered educated:

> [The subject cultivates] deep-seated and effective habits of discriminating tested beliefs from mere assertions, guesses, and opinions; to develop a ... preference for conclusions that are properly grounded, and to ingrain ... methods of inquiry ... appropriate to the various problems that present themselves. (pp. 27-8)

While this is clearly a rationalist conception of education, which Dewey called Training of the Mind, it is entirely detached from, for instance, a master's degree in sport turf management (which really exists). There are two extraordinary things about his description. The first is that it is a philosophy which aims at the training of a person's mind and not the kind of lab-rat conditioning much of education has become so that its victims may be sold cheaply on the job market. Second, it is entirely in line with what Peirce would consider to be the necessary equipment for the exercise of abductive thinking. While Peirce seems to have many different ideas of education, as a philosopher of science and logic his distinct interest is in a kind of analytical thinking disengaged from any authority, assumption, belief, or dogma. In "Definition and Function of a University," he describes what might be called (in the Classical sense) the liberal education that the study of rhetoric, grammar, logic, poetry, art, mathematics, and science engender in those qualified to appreciate them. "[T] he only thing that is really desirable without a reason for being so, is to render ideas and things reasonable .... Logical analysis shows that reasonableness consists in association, assimilation, generalization, the bringing of items together in an organic whole ..." (p. 332). While Dewey emphasizes analytic discrimination through methods of testing tempered with a healthy doubt of one's assumptions, Peirce emphasizes the union of ideas which are the organic basis of analytical thought. *None of this comes naturally to a person.* And it is for this reason that the unnatural institutionalization of conscious, deliberate thinking applied to what Dewey calls problems is critical to the idea of being educated. Peirce also sees that intellectual, analytical development in the university must be tempered by personal and spiritual growth or what might be called maturity. "In the emotional sphere this tendency toward union appears as Love; so that the Law of Love and the Law of Reason are quite at one" (p. 332). Now here we have compelling idea: there is no reason without love and no love without reason. And we may presume Peirce speaks of a higher Love as well as a higher Reason by his use of the capital initial. Furthermore, both are Laws (again exalted by the capital initial). Is this so different from Keats' injunction about truth and beauty being *all we need to know* and (fortunatelyfor us) all we *can* know?

For the subject conditioned by its early Skinner-Box-like indoctrination into the wants and needs of the hegemony, all of this sounds like a bunch of high-minded hooey. Why? Because if learned in the way described by Dewey and Peirce the subject would become unmanageable. It would always put the interests of itself, its family, its friends, and associates first before it abdicated any of its power to some authority which must rattle sabers to get any cooperation. Bertrand Russell joins the chorus with some contributions of his own from his "Ten Commandments of Critical Thinking and Democratic Decency." The few quoted below – my favorites – show a distinct tendency toward the abrogation of the edicts and fiats of any hegemony. And they rely on a healthy sense of doubt to pry thinking away from the swill trough of complacency.

1) Do not feel absolutely certain of anything,
2) Never ... discourage thinking for you are sure to succeed,
3)Have no respect for the authority of others,
4) Do not ... suppress opinions you think pernicious,
5) [Favor] intelligent dissent [over] passive agreement.

The final commandment on the list alludes to a fool's paradise which just as well might be what we have been describing here as the amnion of the Imaginary. "Do not feel envious of the happiness of those who live in a *fool's paradise*, for only a fool will think that it is happiness." We are to keep our heads and our sovereignty. We must stop ourselves from feeling the pull of the Sirens of the amnion. Their borrowed prosperity, prestigious awards, corporate titles, grandiose degrees, expensive gizmos and gadgets, fathomless comfort and convenience, and access to medical technology cannot save the Apex Consumer from the perils of ignoring the Real and the Symbolic in the form of the sublimity and terror of death. These last two orders are merciless in their wrath. The first demands some semblance of bare life - from each according to his capability. The second is the key to understanding ourselves, others, and our place in the universe. Without understanding of our dreams, behaviors, thoughts, and beliefs - all of which are autonomic - we are as good as dead. Furthermore, we cannot grasp ideas without understanding their symbolic nature as signs pointing to ineffable abstractions. Without understanding of the symbolic nature of what we mistake for the Real, the Real itself forever eludes us. The result is mere awareness without consciousness. And of course absolute abdication from the possibility (*Möglichkeit*) of the sublime. Perceiving the transcendental object in the Other is not possible without 1) participation in bare life (the Real), and 2) understanding of the significance of signs (the Symbolic). Dwelling only in the Imaginary, despite amniosis, is not life at all. It is an opium dream of a journey from which we never return and in which we are forever alienated from the *Other*. Prospero, in *The Tempest,* describes life as "such stuff / As dreams are made on; and our little life / Is rounded with a sleep" (Act 4, scene 1). If this is the human condition, then returning to the womb (matrix) cannot be a good strategy for making the most of it. Prospero's words are meant to haunt us with doubt about reality. We are merely lucid dreamers incapable of knowing if we are in a dream where we dream we are dreaming. Dewey, Peirce, and Russell want us to sharpen our wits and turn them toward understanding what Prospero meant and how that affects who we are and what we do. Even if one finds that doubting what we think we know about the world is an exercise better suited for weirdos and eggheads, the greatest problem of them all remains. And it cannot be ignored no matter what one thinks: We cannot know how others see ourselves. It is frightening to think that we have as many selves as there are those who regard us. But we can be sure that what *they* think we are is not and never will be what *we* think we are. No one but ourselves will ever really know us, if that. *To go to one's grave unknown to even oneself is never to have been.* Others will only know what they think we are based on their subjective mélange of thoughts, experiences, notions, facts, feelings, and perceptions. Furthermore, we can never know how they see themselves. We can only know how whatever it is they are is filtered through our subjectivity. It is the greatest existential horror to contemplate the fact that no one will ever know us, and we will never know anyone else no matter what we do. We all assume that ultimately we know ourselves best. And yet this knowledge must remain with us and be taken to the grave. No matter how much we speak out, write books, make love, this Other that we are will remain isolated in the vastness of the sublime. It is only when we feel the chilling reality of this predicament that we are even capable of bare life and the experience of the mystery of the sublime. But who does this willingly? Who would enter a house of horrors at an amusement park if he knew that he would never come out again, or that it was on fire as the Buddhists say the world is? The essential feeling of the sublime is *terror*. And the origin of that terror is the understanding (not knowledge) that we will *die*. That this ego we cherish now shall one day *be no more*. It is more than most can bear to know, much less understand, that this *persona,* this mask, we know best and regard with love or hatred will, absolutely, inevitably, and by order of the facts of the universe perish forever. Just as a young child flees back to the safety of its mother's legs when scared, so too do we long to run back into the amnion where we imagine this terror does not and cannot exist. We desire to be *inside* the Other (mother), in a state of amniosis, borrowing our sustenance from the umbilicus of the financial-industrial hegemony.

It is only through reciprocal meaning in sincere communication that we experience *communion* with another. Therefore, it goes against the nature of communication to expect that the Other sees, hears, feels, thinks, and comprehends what we do. Reciprocal meaning unites us with others through communication which allows for a parallax between I and Thou that is symmetrical in its difference and incognizability. It is critical that we understand that the goal of meaning is to see ourselves through the *being* of the Other, which can only happen if we allow the Other to see itself through our being. In this way understanding and the getting-to-know become possible. The closest analogy is falling in love. Through a process not well understood, we undergo a fundamental change in our subject-object orientation when truly in love. This lyric from the Rodgers and Hammerstein musical *The King and I* expresses the matter in a delightful way, right down to the teacup:

> It's a very ancient saying,
> But a true and honest thought
> That if you become a teacher
> By your pupils you'll be taught
> As a teacher I've been learning
> And forgive me if I boast

That I've now become an expert
On the subject I like most

Getting to know you
Getting to know you, ... to know all about you
Getting to like you, getting to hope you like me
Getting to know you, putting it my way but nicely
You are precisely my cup of tea

Behind this innocent flirtation is (as the plot suggests) the phenomenon of falling in love with another, rather than with our own spectral imago. The getting-to-know not just of the phenomena and noumena of the universe but also the essence and nature of others is itself the *turning-to* (the Other). It turns us *to* the Other as it turns us *away* from the turning-from (to the sign of the Self). In the horror vacui of the sublime, we become possessed with the need to know the Other as the transcendental object. Without experience of the sublime of bare life, we carry on with the assumption that we do not need others in anything but a utilitarian or maybe symbolic way. We just see them as resources to be exploited. However, when we perceive the Other in the object it is enough to help us lose our longing for the deceptive solace of the amnion. We wake up just a little bit when something terrible happens that might affect us or that has affected people *like* us. When it happens to people *unlike* us, it is at best a curiosity. What we wake up to are the facts that others *do* exist after all and furthermore they may have *extremely* different views of life than we do – even when they are in our back yards so to speak. The herd is *shocked* by a mall shooting, murder spree, or the discovery of a serial killer's burying ground, despite their lurid frequency in the content of the media. We can be certain that these persons who shoot up the place with impunity, without conscience, and even with a certain amount of *joie de vivre,* had a Different vision of life which, perhaps, we cannot comprehend. The same is true for the so-called genius. His *eureka!* moment when in a bathtub he sees the mathematical reality of space-time may not be entirely unique in the course of history, but it is certainly *not* the common vision of the universe at the time of his epiphany. Later it may work its way into the thought and imagination of the masses. But at its moment of epiphany it is illuminated with a light few can see. Who does not know Einstein's most famous theorem?

So, what can we hope for from reciprocal meaning in a world of language where often the closest we get to it is reading a good book? How can we be sure that our exchange of signs with the Other is being read as we intend? Fortunately, there is a built-in redundant heuristic in communication (expressed well by Shannon). True dialogue approaches being an example, whereas a lecture is not unless there is a feedback loop to the transmitter (lecturer). On the most obvious level is the *interrogative*. In question and answer we find language's demand for understanding while at the same time allowing for negotiation of meaning through feedback. The so-called Socratic Method has come down to us in the form of the specialized dialogue of the examination and cross examination of witnesses in a criminal (or civil) trial. Analogies in computer networking include the interrogation *ping*, where a client computer sends a hypertext packet to a server to see if it is communicating with that client. If one is sent back, then absolutely, empirically, and analytically, the two computers are communicating (True). There is also the matter of the *checksum* in data-bit streaming. When an application is downloaded so too is a bit of information about what data are supposed to be in the application. These data are compared to the same data at the server end. If the two match, the download is complete (True). It is accurate to say that the machines are communicating with each other in a meaningful way since the conclusion of their interrogation (argument) must be either true or false. However, in human terms communication is a far more complex business, though it must involve this sort of reciprocity (Shannon, again). Computer analogies go farther than just providing neat models of a process which also takes place in communication between individuals. They show that logic, reason, and verifiability are critical to understanding — something few minds understand these days. Reciprocal meaning also can describe how machines understand each other, the input and output of their components, what they are processing, and how they interface with humans. What thinking and computing have in common is the use of signs to process and transmit a gestalt or a collection of signs with interrelated meaning which combine to form a larger single meaning of complex structure. Humans use words based on sounds and pictures strung together with syntax. Computers also use what are called words based on strings of binary digits (32, 64) carrying specific information about what operations the processor is to carry out each second. Therefore communication is not merely the mundane exchange of information. It is a complex *pas de deux* of meaning negotiated through a process approximating the complexity of the ideas and data conveyed and understood, verifiably, by both side of the exchange.

The Other's idiosyncratic sign processing and creation

are what we value in literature, interesting speakers, and the dialogue of movies and plays. We seek novelty in philosophers, teachers, and prophets (or we should). If agreement is *a priori* boredom sets in. It has its time and place. For example we would like a priori agreement during open heart surgery, the flying of a passenger jet, or managing a nuclear power plant. Under such circumstances there is no time for negotiation, though circumstances do arise when negotiation is pushed to the limit. But these are highly specialized forms of communication. Nevertheless we can see that narcissistic solipsism will not do even in a priori agreement under such circumstances. It is when the subject is more or less molded by the manipulation of its reflection in its gadget to want, like, need, and comprehend in unison with the abdicated masses that it must perforce fall back upon prepackaged notions of communication more resembling the signaling of animals. Clichés, idiom, boilerplate, and platitudes become the content of its memory and the signs of its thought. Naturally, then, a mashup of these forms of dead language will pour forth from its mouth. And in so doing it will reinforce its sense of belonging to the herd through signaling that *iBelong*. These noises signal this belonging. Those who actually utter meaningful language are often ostracized as threats because the unconscious subject instinctively feels challenged by the innate demand for reciprocal meaning — something it never developed and never will. In some rare cases they are elevated to iconic stardom by the marketing apparatus of the Imaginary to add a little razzle-dazzle to the otherwise morose existence of the herd. But even these interlocutors will eventually be pushed into a fall from grace by the jealous and ignorant subject of the Amniotic Empire.

PART 2: SOCIETY, THE INDIVIDUAL, AND SUBMISSION

2.0: Reciprocal meaning versus the Cult of Mediocrity

Reciprocal meaning is a largely emotional experience. The utterance includes more than just information in a mechanical sense that perhaps a machine would *process*, which is what machines do instead of *understanding*. Humans and other animals must process too, but they must also understand or perish. To say that a machine understands is to declare that one does not understand what a machine is. And here Descartes was right about the automaton. If a machine understood, it would not need us. As it is, most would not last a day without constant tending by their creators. "In a few words, please state your problem. You can say something like 'I can't access my account, someone stole my card, or I would like to apply for a new card,'" says the ubiquitous IVR, or interactive voice response system, a natural language (NLP) robot replacing old-fashioned, inefficient, expensive, cranky, unreliable, flesh-and-bone human customer service. In the natural language processing, or NLP-IVR, environment there is no room for emotion. Since the ultimate goal of meaningful communication is mutual or reciprocal acknowledgment of the transcendental object in the Other, human communication feels more like an epiphany than operating machinery. We are always a bit surprised, happily, that the Other is not *just* an abstraction such as a mechanic or doctor or clerk at a checkout counter. It is when individuals in a romantic relationship begin to look at each other as signs of themselves rather than each other that all emotional connection ends. Meaningful communication can feel magical. It certainly eases our angst about how alone we are in a vast universe of dark matter, black holes, and quasars. One only need compare it to the noise emanating from a crowded pub or the roar of sports fans at a game to understand the difference. There is also the strictly utilitarian language of the office job or the cryptic professional language of medicine and law. For these reasons reciprocal meaning transcends the meaning of logic in its verifiable, analytic form. (There are other forms such as fuzzy logic which we will not go into here.) That it also transcends the synthetic is obvious. Only certain occasions, applications, and subcultures draw out meaningful communication. They almost do it in a secretive way as if the authorities might find out that they are not talking about how to decide which is the best dish soap to use. Like the archaic pomp of weddings, funerals, and university graduation, meaningful communication has found its place in only certain sanctified and rarefied occasions and rituals. For instance, within the privacy of one's home one is expected to let one's hair down and get real. But how often is miscommunication cited as the reason for family strife and divorce, never mind physical abuse and murder? Like heretics gathering in a cellar late at night to summon the demons of the Hell, those who wish to be sincere in their meaningful dialog must be wary of when they do it and with whom. The subject is a representative of the hegemony. Its job is to protect the hegemonic order. Its form of knowledge is the knowing-of which it receives from propaganda pipelines feeding content to its gadget. It is told: If you see something, say something. The snitch is glorified and the person who minds her own business is considered a criminal. Betrayal is the mood of the narcissist. Since the workplace is often a suffocating micro-culture of incompetent, mediocre hacks whose only concern is their next paycheck, exercising meaningful communication in the form of sincerity is seen as a foolish vulnerability asking for bullying. Often the strong communicators are the *metamotivated* employees; the ones who can be counted on to do their job, please customers and clients, and generally compensate for the dead wood surrounding them. They not only work for their paychecks; they work because, as the old German proverb goes, "*Arbeit macht das Leben süß.*" Work makes life sweet. They instinctively know that the continual practice of mediocrity takes life's sweetness away, leaving nothing but the bitter quest for less work and more power and money. The hacks, however, find such workers a threat despite the fact that these workers actually sustain the company, making it possible for the hacks to get paychecks. But since the mode of the hacks is the turning-from of the sign of the self, they have no love for either their jobs or the company. Therefore, they must maintain their status as parasites by slander, innuendo, sabotage, bullying, and by cultivating the political favor of their overlords through sycophancy.

Curiously enough, they are often successful at prying the *metamotivated* workers out of their jobs and into unemployment. For this reason (and others) organizations, businesses, and corporations are like the rising and setting sun: they all succumb eventually to the deadly pall of chronic mediocrity until some snappy upstart usurps their position in the marketplace. We see that the turning-from is not at all a metaphysical phenomenon. It brings down financial markets, businesses, governments, and empires. What characterizes the disintegration of ancient Rome better than a plague of mediocrity from the leaders of politics, statecraft, war, and culture? The mode of the metamotivated workers, however, for whatever reason, can be called the *turning-*

to. They continually turn *to* the Other for that is their mode. Why they naturally orient themselves to this mode can be the result of a variety of influences, from home schooling in remote mountains by enlightened parents to immersion in a subculture insulating them from the memes of the hegemony's otherwise ubiquitous discourse. Some seem to be *genetically predisposed* to this mode, since their histories show nothing different from that of their peers who have abdicated to the hegemony's apparatus. There is a sense in which those who are so willing to abdicate their sovereignty and those who are not or will not seem to be different varieties of the same species *homo industrialis*. In any case, as Luke 6:43-45 notes, "Wherefore by their fruits ye shall know them."

Perhaps what we witness really is a territorial struggle for evolutionary change. Perhaps the mediocre sense that, like *homo neanderthalensis*, their day is passing. Perhaps they are indeed engaged in a life-or-death struggle against the rise of a new *species* of sincere, competent communicators. As they are systematically replaced by various forms of automata, the demise of the mediocre does indeed look like a giant asteroid is on their existential horizon. Meantime, the metamotivated either have something to offer which defies automation, or their mode allows them to adapt to dramatic social and economic changes brought about by technology. The chronically mediocre trapped in their prison of the turning-from regard this superiority with murderous jealousy. There was more than one revolution of the people during the Twentieth Century in which intellectuals and anyone else capable of leading the nation to the future were systematically exterminated by a mob of the mediocre. It is axiomatic.

Meantime, the mediocre rule. They destroy the economy, wage war, enable mass dependency on illegal drugs, pass laws to confiscate the citizen's economic power and right to self-defense, use surveillance to protect themselves from opposition, and favor their incompetent friends over those who are loyal to noble ideals rather than the Cult of Mediocrity. Shakespeare's Hamlet is eloquent about the effects of this cult on one's sense of well-being:

> For who would bear the whips and scorns of time,
> The oppressor's wrong ...
> The pangs of despised love, the law's delay,
> The insolence of office and the spurns
> When he himself might his quietus make
> With a bare bodkin?

Consequently, in such a culture attempts to communicate in a meaningful way immediately label one as a threat. Finally, kindness and a desire to live and work with others as a sovereign individual among other sovereign individuals is seen as a weakness. In fact it is a vulnerability. Sincerity demands a certain amount of transparency from the ego. Those who present an opaque facade immediately seize upon the intelligence they have gathered from the window into one's soul. With this intelligence they labor tirelessly to sabotage one's right to at least *pursue* happiness, win or lose. Why? Their ethical aesthetic of *Genuss* demands that they must be in ruthless competition with everyone or lose their undeserved, captured territory. They know that to accomplish this subterfuge they must form quick alliances with others to protect themselves from rival cabals as well as the competent and conscious individuals who make civilization viable. In short, it is the mentality of the prison. The subject, though unconscious, nevertheless dramatizes its sense of being trapped by the amnion of the Imaginary by seeing the Other not as an opportunity for sublime transcendence, but as a threat to its selfish, solipsistic, narcissism.

In the turning-from, it is as if the subject's sign of itself is looking at a reflection of itself as another sign rather than contemplating the Mystery of the Other. Signs as words refer to each other (not themselves) with meaning when they create new ideas out of already-existing ideas assigned to the preexisting words. This seems to happen most often in poetry, where it has been said that it is the poet's imperative is to *make it new* (attributed to Confucius, transmitted by Ezra Pound). The line "trip the light fantastic" from Milton's poem "L'Allegro" has somehow embedded itself into the English language seemingly for all time, whether one knows who Milton is or not. So too have so many of Shakespeare's lines, phrases, and words as to be (at least up until recently) axiomatic. What we are concerned with here, though, is the first definition. When the subject abdicates its sovereignty to the hegemony *it is a purely linguistic phenomenon.* Once the subject's personal discourse of itself began early in life as the stream of thought, so too did the subject's sense of identity. The fabric of thought is made of signs almost entirely in the form of words. Components of thought such as emotions, images, and memories are quickly mapped to words when it comes time for the subject to express itself *to* itself or others. Either way, once the subject has uttered a statement, it is fed back into the subject's thought process as an idea of itself. There it boards the train of thought as a distinct and specific memory. For instance, when a person gives his or her word we expect that this idea is as good as a contract. For this statement to take on that power it must be remembered by the interlocutors with precision. Furthermore, whatever it is it must be carried out as stated. How could this happen without a feedback loop into the thought process where such an idea is transformed into a linguistic image of itself? This snapshot of what was said will not fade because it is tagged, as it were, with an elevated state of importance in the which the memory feeds the thought process with images, ideas, and words. It is no different than when the dreamer wakes and recounts his dream or an analysand at last reveals the innermost content of his unconscious to the analyst through free association. Once it is expressed, it becomes an image of itself which is whole and as permanent as anything can get in the ever-shifting sands of the mind. It may even be committed to print so that the interlocutors can refresh their memories regarding the details of the utterance. Of course it is even possible that the written expression of the thought process ends up in the hands of an interested stranger where it then becomes part of that person's inner dialogue - perhaps forever.

2.1: "Colorless green ideas sleep furiously"

A collection of individuals is not ipso facto a society until it has rules and a common purpose, at which time it becomes an organization typically called a *state*. Submission to the state as a subject has meaning because it joins together two preexisting concepts: the individual and society. This is a meaningful union because both the individual and the other individuals in society derive mutual benefit from the action of their expression of collective identity. We hold these truths to be self-evident, they say. Conversely, when the subject abdicates its sovereignty it become useless as a member of the social organization of society. In trading its sovereignty for the trinkets of consumerism and the *Genuss* of the amnion of the Imaginary the subject becomes useless to everyone except itself in its pursuit of the elusive *l'objet petit a*. It becomes a kind of hapless parasite. But this is not strange to the subject because being parasitical is the prevailing ethical aesthetic of the corrupt fabric of society. At the same time, the subject points to the Underclass as the parasites of society because their anger at disenfranchisement must be bought off with social programs and handouts. Furthermore, they are denied access to that which allows a subject in the hegemony's favor to participate in the rodeo of the Imaginary: *credit*. The society in which the Underclass must struggle at great disadvantage has no need of its skills, intelligence, talents, and culture. The hegemonic social order's ethical aesthetic of ever greater comfort and convenience creates jobs which have no real value in the natural order. These "bullshit" jobs require a set of skills most easily acquired by those who also have access to opportunities such as higher education and loans. The former provides the subject with a meaningless piece of paper in the form of a degree. The latter makes the subject sign a piece of paper in the form of a promissory note.

While the hegemony would glibly elevate the Underclass to the status of *bona fide* consumers of the first order to exploit them, it cannot. Doing so would require a radical reorientation of the ethical aesthetic of the hegemony's apparatus to absorb the masses who have lived at the level of bare life for generations. The introduction of denizens of bare life into the amniotic bubble of the hegemony's Imaginary would be as if the barbarians had finally breached the wall. It is simply not acceptable to the Apex Consumer. Its worst fear is that these unwashed emissaries from the campuses of bare life will invade their imaginary paradise, contaminating it with discomfort, inconvenience, and mortality. It is far better to *warehouse* them in substandard confined areas and force-feed them with social benefits which prevent them from striving for independence from the teat of the hegemony. These areas include prisons for those who will not be domesticated and therefore represent the greatest threat.

The process of the subjugation of the Underclass requires an army of subjects that regard their quixotic pursuit of *l'objet petit a* as the kernel of life's meaning. Failure and catastrophe, personal, social, and national, leaves them undaunted and unfazed. The subject takes the pursuit of social status, comfort, convenience, and ready access to consumer goods and debt so seriously that when it actually achieves its goals they are always unsatisfying and disappointing. Why? Because what matters is the *chase*, not the *quarry*. It is a fox hunt, a hunting of the Snark, a battle with the windmills of their erotic fantasies displaced into a frenzied lust for *more and more and more*. This is far from what Hobbes meant as one's submission to the state as a useful and supportive member of the society it is convened to manage. It does not matter what kind of management it is, as long as it can only function when it manages a nation of sovereign individuals and not unconscious consumers. Submission to the state as a citizen of its laws and customs is a natural process in *Leviathan*. In this psychological mode the subject retains the symbol of itself *as* itself in relation to others – something it worked quite hard to achieve while an infant (as it strove to *stand*, the origin of the word "state"). In the modern totalitarian consumer state, however, the symbolic identity as a subject of the state is turned in upon itself. This sortie to the womb is what every natural process of development in the child struggles to prevent. It is a struggle because we forever retain this desire for amniosis. Maturity, then, is a generalization regarding a certain adaptation to what adults may regard as obedience to the nomos. But it is also supposed to be the culmination of psychological, emotional, intellectual, and spiritual integration in such a way as not to be found in children except as precociousness, and even then there always seems to be something missing: experience, for which there is no substitute. Society quantifies development in terms of years, and perhaps some testing. That infantile behavior in adults seems ubiquitous indicates that something is being overlooked and that more clinical research needs to be done.

The Imaginary offers a return to the womb in the form of the amnion of infinite debt and a perpetual flow of digital stimulation, alcohol, pharmaceuticals, and ritual consumerism. It promises that it will help maintain an egoistic bubble around the consumer so that he never has to actually enter into relationship with anyone except himself. Others are seen through a glass darkly in a whirling phantasmagoria of digital filters and interfaces. And as long as the subject pays its bills and taxes, this social order seems indomitable. That it is a mere chimera we need not belabor.

In Hemingway's short story "The Gambler, the Nun, and the Radio," the character Frazier finds himself in a philosophical discussion with a Russian and a Mexican in a hospital in Montana, USA, who have just been shot in a cafe. The topic is that of what, after all, is the Marxian "opium of the people." After some debate, Frazier concludes that it is "bread":

> What was the real, the actual, opium of the people? He knew it very well. It was gone just a little way around the corner in that well-lighted part of his mind that was there after two or more drinks in the evening; that he knew was there (it was not really there of course). What was it? He knew very well. What was it? Of course; bread was the opium of the people. Would he remember that and would it make sense in the daylight? Bread is the opium of the people.

This revelation comes only after he nominates religion, music, economics, patriotism, sexual intercourse, drink, the radio, gambling, ambition, and government. In short *everything* is (or can be) the opium of the people, not just Marx's materialist religion. Never mind that opium itself, legal and illegal, really *is* the opium of the people, quite popular, easy to get, and the plague of nations rich and poor in one way or another

Fiending for a fix, the subject immerses itself in the relentless and bloodthirsty pursuit of ever greater spiritual and mental lethargy. It seeks a morose state of semi-comatose unconsciousness. Life, liberty, and the pursuit of happiness fade into platitudes along with what the subject sees as the arcane incantations of superstitious religions and the mumbo-jumbo of philosophy, ethics, aesthetics, and law. More often than not the social discourse of *Genuss* dominates the subject's mental discourse, crowding out any possibility of an intellectual heuristic. Any criticism of this state of affairs is labeled a conspiracy theory, sparking slanderous attacks on the blasphemous apostates who dared utter it – until their lives are effectively ruined. A heuristic to this fatal strategy becomes more remote as the subject gets itself deeper in debt. Its mind, lacking nearly all analytic and creative capacity except that which is necessary to stay employed, gets less able to find a way out of the labyrinth the subject willingly entered to flee the ravages of the discomfort, inconvenience, challenges, and terrors of the sublime. Bare life has been left behind as the very *anathema* of its ethical aesthetic.

Egoic subordination as one abdicates to the state at first feels natural in the development of the alien, social persona replacing the possibility of the transcendental object in oneself necessary for dwelling in the sublime. However, as this Faustian bargain hardens through debt and the quixotic pursuit of perpetual *Genuss,* the subject's awareness of itself becomes troubled with anxiety and depression, civilization's *Unbehagen* as described by Freud. Such a wicked turn of events is not what Hobbes has in mind in *Leviathan* when he describes the reasons why man might want to organize into nations and civilizations. Only the well-ordered State can create a reign of peace and tranquility in which industry may thrive and man may pursue life, liberty, and happiness. Otherwise, says Hobbes,

> In such condition there is no place for industry, because the fruit thereof is uncertain: and consequently no culture of the earth; no navigation, nor use of the commodities that may be imported by sea; no commodious building; no instruments of moving and removing such things as require much force; no knowledge of the face of the earth; no account of time; no arts; no letters; no society; and which is worst of all, continual fear, and danger of violent death; *and the life of man, solitary, poor, nasty, brutish, and short.* [italics added] (p. 78)

We must admit he has a point, though it is also easy to argue that it is the *state* can make life nasty, brutish, and short too through war. Nevertheless, between Hemingway's deliberation of what constitutes the opium of the people and Hobbes' account of the perils of life without a state we have the subject's dithering melodrama as it stumbles through life seeking the *l'objet petit a* as the Apex Consumer, borrowing to pay off its loans. The result in the modern age is that life becomes nasty, brutish, and *long*.

When we regard a sign, it becomes a symbol to us of whatever associations we may have about it, whatever use it may be put to, and how others regard it in relation to ourselves as it is expressed in the various ways we communicate. In all three cases there is nothing disturbing the sign's "thingness," though it exists with the imposition of a symbolic order. This symbolic order is expressed well by the trivium of medieval education: logic, grammar, and rhetoric. The trivium derives from the concept of the *liberal* education (meaning education of the free man, not slave) in ancient Greece. In that context, liberal means either a freeborn person or, potentially, a slave who has earned his freedom (been liberated). In Attic Greek culture, the ability to reason publicaly in the arena of the nomos was essential to the proto-democratic ideals of Greece, particularly during the Attic period 500-300 BC and with the spread of Athenian democracy and rule of law. Rather than make the argument with the point of a sword, this logic implies, in a civil society it is better done with a wit sharpened with the liberal arts of the trivium. Here we find the basis of what Hobbes' conceived as the state. The development of Classical rhetoric had reached its peak; it was considered the foundation of a democratic republic. It was also practical, since one often had to act as one's own lawyer in court, civil or criminal.

Wittgenstein says that the search for meaning in sentential discourse (narrative) is meaningless. How language is *used* is what matters. "Do not ask for the meaning, ask for the use" (qtd. In Hacking, *Language*, p. 175). This is the inverse equivalent of the popular saying, "Do as I say, not as I do." We might say, then, that the latter is a formula for hypocrisy while the former points to an unconventional interpretation of what language *does* when no one is looking. Wittgenstein, however, points to the deep-structure action of language, as Chomsky does in *Syntactic Structures*. If I say, "I shot an arrow into the tree," the semantic meaning is trivial compared to the nontrivial action of the subject-predicate dynamic made possible by the copula of the verb. Why? Because the deep structure *creates the world* in which I, the arrow, the tree, and the possibility of shooting through space and time exist. Therefore, the grammar itself is the performance. It is incidental that an arrow was loosed or that the it was aimed at the tree. But the fact that *I*, and not another, acted does have significance in terms of establishing identity, or the distinction between I and Thou. The sentences "I am," "I shot," "I gave," or even "I sinned," have technical completeness, but do not cross the threshold of deep-structure significance in world-creation intended by Wittgenstein and Chomsky. Meaning is only possible when one entity acts upon another (person, place, thing, idea) with *effect*. Without effect, it is as if an action never took place. Why? Because there is no possibility of evidentiary verification that it took place if there is no effect resulting from a cause. The world comes into being through cause and effect. If we look at the two sentences often given as an example of what is newsworthy, we see that with the same words we significantly change the meaning of the sentence by swapping the subject for the predicate:

Dog bites man. / Dog bites dog.
Man bites dog. / Man bites man.

However, what both have in common is the verb, which, because of its role in the formation of the newsworthy event, determines the effect and cause even when they are inverted. This is only possible because there are two entities involved, both of which are affected by the action of the subject. A flip-flop of the grammar gives us the two definitions of news: one arousing concern and the other curiosity. This is not to say that the subject-verb-object sentence is the paragon of meaning; but it is the ontological basis of language and therefore of communication. Also, it does not matter what position in the sentence the verb occupies, as in these Latin sentences: A) Julius amat Julia; Julia amat Julius; Amat Julia Julius; Julius Julia amat; B) Et tu, Brute? Brute, et tu? Brute, tu et? Tu et, Brute? Tu, Brute, et? Et, Brute, tu?

The first expresses love and the second betrayal. Both love and betrayal have personal meaning to the entities involved, conveyed effectively, though not perhaps elegantly, by any arrangement of the subject and predicate. As such, they embody mineness (*Jemeinigheit*) and sovereignty in that one entity may act upon another effectively. To simplify the idea we can call it *reciprocal* meaning, as I have already mentioned. If this were not so, Chomsky's Universal Grammar (much debated) would not be possible. Nor would translation. Each language would invent an entirely new way of structuring communication with no reference to any other language — which nevertheless remains a possibility, as few truly foresaw computer languages as such, though analogs (so to speak) have been around for millennia. Furthermore, for a sentence to *mean,* it must be free of the need for bilateral action. In other words, even if subject and predicate are swapped at some point, nevertheless in each instance A(B) acts upon B(A). We can say it is *reciprocal* if and only if the utterance *does not* require bilateral action. If it does, then it is a description, which is always static, and not an action. ("The smell of the greasepaint, the roar of the crowd.") Such a rule emanates from what we observe about reality in time and space, the basis for the ontology of language. In effect, when one object (A) moves toward another (B), the object B toward which A is moving is only stationary relative to the moving object. With no force of its own, B will unite with moving object A as if B were moving too, but only because A, as the subject, engendered the need for a predicate (via the verb copula) to form meaning on a deep-structure level, not on the semantic level, which is merely a matter of substituting nouns as the occasion dictates.

What changes from one form of expression to another is our expectation of what the grammar should be (for example, interrogative, declarative, imperative). But this is an arbitrary expectation as long the grammar completes itself in the performance of a relationship between entities A and B. That a turnip is not called a dog, or a turtle a pencil, is purely due to a random assignment of sounds based on the principle that they are phonemically differentiated, so that we know that when one says turnip one does not mean dog. The arrangement of the elements of a sentence as subject-verb-object, as I have mentioned, is only one arrangement possible of those three elements, a matter which becomes more complicated with complex sentence structure and as it is used in different languages. The most we can say for it is that S-V-O mimics action in the spatial dimension of the phenomenology of "I" in the most efficient way. Grammar, rhetoric, and logic, and therefore the idea of the trivium as education, acknowledge that organic life itself is sentential. It is the determinant behind what Chomsky refers to as the *generative* grammar of narrative structure, or the story of the unfolding of expression and communication. Coordination between action and speech puts fundamental syntax in the same class as onomatopoeic words (e.g. hiss, pop, smash, and slither). Mimetic language, preferred in everyday speech for obvious reasons, tends to defy abstraction which always seems otherworldly (which is why it is so useful in religious terminology). Surely this is why Latin creeps into discourse that is more abstract than everyday speech, such as legal, medical, scientific, and even religious terminology — which is not mimetic but categorical; Latin terminology allows for a switch to a level of abstraction that helps reduce ambiguity and morphology.

Onomatopoeic words are perhaps the most ancient artifacts in language. They may have been the first attempts to convey an idea of something of importance in the concrete world simply by approximating the sound of that thing or that evokes an association with that thing. As such they are also artifacts of a time when language was almost indistinguishable from bare life. It was endued with the sublime as nature always is. The death of the sublime is a symptom of the artificial life of civilization which is a conscious and deliberate affront to nature if not Natural Law (whatever it may be). Great poets carry the torch of the sublime in language, which is perhaps their shamanistic role in the *possibility* of humanity within the *necessity* of civilization. Imitating the sound of something or approximating in syntax the schemata of action has no inherent meaning. When we use passive constructions we begin to see a more abstract form of syntax in English such as in "The vase was broken." Here there is no noun-subject acting directly upon the object. We could just as well imagine an entire language using only the passive voice - though academic discourse, and perhaps this book, overuse it. Nevertheless, "The vase was broken" and "He broke the vase" are close semantically but categorically different ontologically, as one lacks an actor. However, on the deep structure level they are mere tautologies: n-v-n, noun-verb-noun, which is true of most sentential communication. Therefore, is all of this n-v-n discourse really saying anything we need to know? As such, it is the nattering of the human animal, even father from being communication than birdsong.

We may take the noun of the predicate and substitute it for nearly any other noun, while keeping the subject the same: I go to *work*, I go to *school*, I go to the *doctor*, I go to the *fair*. "So what else is new?" is the retort of the bored bystander. It only takes an hour in a library going through old newspapers headlines to find that the same events occur over the years with only the proper nouns exchanged. A building (X or Y) burns down. A person (X or Y) is killed in a car accident. A budget (X or Y) is passed. And so on, to the point that we must conclude, as the prophet does, that there is nothing new under the sun. Considering this, what then is the semantic value of language? To tell us what we already know? There is more signaling and neural stimulation going on in most utterances than there is communication of anything worth telling or knowing. So how can there be reciprocal meaning in a simple S-V-O statement? If we expand the context of the utterance to include the neighboring sentences, and if those sentences include the interlocutor as an entity acted upon by the subject of the sentence, then we do indeed have reciprocal meaning. Sentences are artificial boundaries created to aid in the efficient packaging of content. Casual speech nearly dispenses with them altogether. The connective "and" is enough to create an hour-long sentence which is only broken off by a telephone call. It is most obvious that a page of a book is an entirely arbitrary boundary making it possible to have the advantages of a codex over a scroll. And yet we take these rectangles of paper rather seriously such as the page number in the citation of Peirce's quotation below. If it were not included, the reader would be uncomfortable – even if he or she had no intention of finding that quotation in the book from whence it came.

Occasion arises when the passive voice describes reality *in a more subtle* way than the active. For example, take the situation where one is talking on the phone when one is in a hotel room and the housekeeper comes to clean the room. What pronoun and voice is one to use in referring to the housekeeper to let the person on the line know there is an interruption?

1) *Someone* is here to clean the room
2) *She/he* is here to clean the room
3) *They* [error] are [is] here to clean the room
4) The room is being cleaned now
5) (The housekeeper is here to clean the room)

Although these distinctions are subtle it is often on the basis of such subtle distinctions that we make these linguistics choices. In 1 we might feel that "someone" is too impersonal since the housekeeper is now in an intimate situation with us. In 2 "she" or "he" might spark a question in the mind of our interlocutor as to who this person is. In 3 we are using "they" which has become the plural grammar error substituting for a genderless singular pronoun in American English. In 4 – the only sentence in the passive voice – the statement is accurate while avoiding having to use the pronoun since it is *implied* that a person would be doing the cleaning (though it would work for a automated housekeeper as well). Although case 5 uses a noun rather than a pronoun, it is included because it is a possibility though it has the same problem as case 1. Often *inference* is necessary, accurate, and appropriate. It solves the problems of 1, 2, and 3 and brings the matter to a higher linguistic plane. In this sense it is like the basic form of the *enthymeme* where the proposition of a syllogism (= c) is implied by the juxtaposition of the other two terms (a + b):

a) We must protect workers from getting sacked

b) Management sacks lazy workers

c) Inference: *We must protect lazy workers*

Statements *a* and *b* without each other would lead us to no specific conclusion. But together they lead us to the most likely conclusion (c). As Aristotle explains in *Rhetoric*, the enthymeme has its uses in oratory. In particular, it lets the listener come to the obvious conclusion rather than being *told* what it is. The advantage here over an explanation or a complete syllogism is that the listener's own cognition has worked out the problem, therefore making the listener think – and think in the way one wants him to think. So in this way *inference* is a higher form of communication because it encourages abstract thinking allowing for greater subtlety of meaning, while forcing the subject to come to the conclusion that we intend.

An utterance need not be confined to a sentence. In speech it is almost never confined to one self-contained utterance after another (though this is precisely how a computer generates language). In fact, it is rather almost a stream of consciousness not unlike thought itself. And in an essential way it *is* thought itself only gussied up for presentation to another entity through the miracle of syntax. It is for this reason linguists study spoken language over written. If only written language were studied, then what would a linguist make of the use of ancient Latin and Greek in science, medicine, and law? Would the stock phrases and *pro forma* discourses in legal code represent the language of a people? Philologists and not linguists study written ancient languages which have long since passed the point of further evolution. Professions employ their crypto languages to protect their territory, signal belonging, and create a more precise nomenclature. Of course the case could be made for these crypto languages being a significant part of the language of a people because they are spoken as well as written. None, I think, converse in technical Latin – even if, as lawyers, doctors, and scientists, they had to learn the Latin jargon of their professions. The closest we come to living Latin is what is still left of it as Ecclesiastical Latin in the Tridentine Mass of the Roman Catholic Church after the Second Vatican Council (though there's been a resurgence since Pope Benedict in 2007). Finally, children may learn spoken language organically without the aid of a teacher or textbooks, whereas few – even with those advantages – ever really learn how to write more than their name without tutoring. The point is, written language is a language of its own, quite divorced from spoken language, which is its virtue and its vice.

Russell believes that what he calls the Aryan languages contain the rudiments of Western logic. Note that he refers to the idea that the Germanic languages, of which English is one, are Aryan. He is not specifically referring to that branch of Indo-European known today as Indo-Aryan (Hindi, etc.). "It is doubtful whether [subject-predicate logic] would have been invented by a people speaking a non-Aryan language" (qtd. In Hacking, *Language*, p. 70). Here he mentions *predicate logic*, implying that perhaps the chief form of verification used by positivists is not after all a universal principle of every form of reason everywhere at all times but can be localized to a language group. As a logician, he hesitates to assert that *predicate logic* has that kind of ubiquity only because it is impossible to prove, though it is easy enough to follow its provenance back to Greek (closer to Indo-Aryan) and German – the putative languages of Western philosophy. Hobbes' view enlarges Wittgenstein's assertion that we should look to the *act* of communication and as well as the content of it if we want to understand its totality. In *Principles of Human Knowledge* (sec. 20), Hobbes says that what we regard as language is a vehicle for other types of communication which are at least as important as the literal meaning of the words:

> The communicating of ideas marked by words *is not the chief and only end of language* ....There are other ends, as the raising of some passion, the exciting to or deterring from an action, the putting the mind in some particular disposition. [italics added] (qtd. In Hacking, *Language*, p. 16)

In both Wittgenstein's and Hobbes' description of *sentential* meaning, either in deep structure or in non-verbal activity, we see the importance of the action of one grammatical entity upon another as the basis for meaning of the highest order rather than *semantics* which, after all, has a pejorative meaning too as quibbling over words. We say highest order because there are certainly other orders that produce what we can call a meaningful utterance, such as song and poetry. The foremost order is that which determines whether or not a statement is *true*. The second is whether or not it can be *verified* (which is more or less the same thing but aims at the process and not the result). And the third is a bit more difficult. It is one that natural language programmers wrestle with, in their inexorable pursuit of making machines that convincingly mimic human behavior. The first two are the noble extensions of Aristotelian logic. The latter is an interesting problem too, though it is more concerned with finding new ways to make products more comfortable and convenient, than with discovering any truth about meaning. It is the equivalent of an amusement park replacing its analog Animatrons in the fun house with digital robots. All three, however, function perfectly well with unilateral transmission from A(B) to B(A), either in the utterance itself or in cross talk between sentence strings.

As Russell indicates, English, as a descendant of Low German (and less Greek and Latin), relies for its power of forming a truth-statement on its underlying logic. If A = B and B = C, then A = C is a true statement as a syllogism, just as A = A is always true as a tautology. Peano's 4th Axiom states that the equality of natural numbers is transitive. In other words, when we have x, y, and z, if x = y and y = z, then x = z. That is, equality is transitive. For binary systems to work, what are called arguments (interrogation strings) must be resolved as either true or false. "It is raining." If this statement is true, then an umbrella will go up. If it is false, it will not. Of course this kind of interrogation can become extremely complicated, such as when one enters information into the bar of a search engine. Conditional branching and recursive loops add a dimension of intelligence to the process. A complex interrogation string ensures that search results will be highly specific, if Boolean operators (and, or/nor, not) are used strategically. Nevertheless, in predicate logic and machine processing meaning is reduced to 0 or 1, false or true They may be combined to form greater subtlety, however (TTT, TTF, TFF, FFF). Determining if a statement is synthetic or analytical, however, need not actually carry out the interrogation to arrive at T or F. Again the matter of meaning is binary; here quantity and quality intersect. The difference is that we wish to know if the statement contains a class of data that can prove itself to be verifiable, whether it is verified or not. If it can, then we may or may not verify it. But we know that we can if we want. And so we find that the statement has truth value. However, this does not necessarily mean that a synthetic statement is therefore false, even though, by definition, it cannot be verified. The binary does not have to do with the output as much as the input. The question is if the class of input data is positive. Output depends upon too many incidental variables, such as processing power and type, and bugs in the application. If so, then what meaning a statement has is dependent upon its truth value, which must be verified if it is to have positive meaning. If not, then it is some other class of statement (negative meaning, with the possibility of being a *false positive* – a critical problem in medical testing) which, for want of a better word, we call synthetic. The synthetic statement, however, may have much greater *qualitative* meaning (value) than the analytic statement because it is not beholden to the binary. "Do you love me?" (binary). "I love thee to the depth and breadth and height / My soul can reach, when feeling out of sight ..." (non-binary; Elizabeth Browning). In a lawsuit it is more important to know *why* one is being sued than it is to know whether one is or is not being sued. The *why* (qualitative) is what will be worked out in court, perhaps resulting in a settlement, which is non-binary. And although the ensuing child arguments will likely contain evidence of an analytical sort, the parent claim is qualitative - which is the whole reason why it went to court to be decided by a judge and jury, or negotiated between lawyers. One may hear from time to time the comment that "if he weren't guilty he wouldn't have been arrested." In this case there is confusion in the mind of the speaker about the nature of what is verifiable or verified and what is not. Under such circumstances justice is impossible. Analytical: the temperature 82 in Fahrenheit is 28 in Celsius. Synthetic: A temperature of 82/28 is hot. The first can be verified and is therefore quantitative and objective, while the second cannot because it is qualitative and subjective. However, it is the subjective which has significant meaning to the subject. Finally, we have the operation of words upon other words evaluated for meaning in two ways: whether or not those words are organized using the rules of the grammar of that language, or *relate in some other way* (as in poetry). The italics emphasize the problem computers have with human language. To put it too simply, a computer considers a noun a noun. It has a hard time distinguishing between the right and wrong noun, unless it operates with a selectively hierarchical (computational) algorithm and a comprehensive lexicon specifically integrated for this function, thus making the matter once again artificial rather than approximating some organic (natural) behavior. Figurative language presents significant problems for machine translation, with a metonym being difficult to parse in language strings though critical in the computer's interface with human language as long as its referent is a number the machine understands. Chomsky's famous sentence "Colorless green ideas sleep furiously" is an example of nonsense which is grammatically correct and is (or was) not likely to be flagged by an automated grammar checker. The computer application I am using now considers it a grammatical sentence because the parts of speech match the syntax of the sentence. But we know that the categories of the words are not matched correctly in terms of their reciprocal meaning. Therefore, reciprocal meaning is not just between two communicating entities but also *between individual words themselves as entities* just as it could be between sentences as entities. Of course we call this context, though that word does not go far enough to describe the non-linear phenomenon. Chomsky's words only have a relationship as parts of speech. Their denotations are not in compatible classes though their grammatical function in a sentence is consistent and correct. "Colorless green" of course is an incompatible pairing of two adjectives, the second an adjective-noun, resulting in an oxymoron or at least a logical contradiction. In this phrase the word acts as an observational limiter adjective (just as if I said "rare old book") imposing a limit on the main adjective which comes immediately before the noun. However, to say that something is "green" is a *positive* assertion that something has color. Therefore one may not modify the other because one limits what the other asserts. For the two words to be reciprocal (apophantic) they must be drawn from compatible categories of the lexicon. How could this be done?

Well of course we could make a rule that says that words with the suffix "-less" are negations and therefore cannot be used to modify a noun phrase in which an adjective of the same category is used as an assertion of that which it negates. We can presume that the word "color" is considered to be in the same category as "green." In fact it is the parent category: Colors: green, red, blue, yellow, and so on. But as soon as we add the suffix "-less," the rule prevents it from modifying an adjective which contains neither a suffix nor a prefix of negation (e.g. "un-," "ab-,"or "-less"). All adjectives are by their nature an assertion of a quality unless a prefix or suffix is appended to them which negates this assertion. Once this happens the observational limiter adjective becomes an assertion of a negation while the adjective it modifies remains an assertion of an assertion. Our rule is that an assertion of a negation (- > +) may not modify an assertion of an assertion (+ > -). Once we have cleared that problem up, we have the matter of "green ideas." Can an idea be green? This is a beautiful and complex problem which I will not go into here in full except to say that as language changes so too does the relationship between words, particularly in poetry. What once might have been nonsense – and therefore would have been characterized as a corrupt synthetic proposition – can later become analytic as the use of the word changes to make it so. (And vice versa, as sense is continually drifting into nonsense, particularly through commercial pitches and political discourse.) "Green" now also means "friendly to the natural environment."

Well, if an architect has some "green ideas" about how to make a new office building more energy efficient, who is to stop him? We need not go into the possible poetic uses of the pairing of the words which could have profound meaning in their context (Shakespeare's "multitudinous seas incarnadine," i.e. seas turned red by Lady Macbeth's bloody hands). No one except the factory owner has had any problem with Blake's reference to England's "dark Satanic mills" in his poem "Jerusalem." Would a computer's rules allow a mill to be satanic? How is this any different from a green idea? So we can see that the third form of meaning has issues we can work out by creating new rules. But it also has ones which will probably forever elude our positivist grasp.

In considering meaning in logical truth statements as they appear in language and the distinction between analytic and synthetic, we can see by the former example that similar complications arise. In one period of lexical categorization "green" cannot modify "ideas" because ideas cannot have color. In another period "green" serves as a useful description of a set of concepts and beliefs (ideas) as they pertain to the natural environment and technology. Even in an analytic statement with truth value the integrity of the statement's verifiability remains conditional - violating the mistaken concept that what is true in a logical statement is universally true (if and only if it is NOT universally true). This raises the interesting question of what truth is. Is not truth something that is true once and for all? If we could put Newton and Max Planck in the same room this topic would make an interesting debate regarding the physical universe. But there are plenty of examples in the literature of statesmanship, law, history, and science. For instance, in the Gettysburg Address Lincoln begins with a verifiable time frame conditional upon the day being 19 November 1863: "Four score and seven years ago our fathers brought forth on this continent, a new nation, conceived in Liberty, and dedicated to the proposition that all men are created equal." Much could be said about the logic of this extraordinary sentence. The part of it that can be called analytical because it can be verified is the time frame: eighty-seven years ago the country was founded by *our fathers*. On that day in Gettysburg in 1863 that statement was verifiable as true. But any number (n) of years later the same statement is not true *in and of itself*. Should it be continually updated? The once true, verified statement "the sun revolves around the earth" (Ptolemy) is now known to be false in our time (Copernicus). But in the time it was uttered every instrument of verification (until Copernicus) indicated that it was true. This was backed up by empirical observation and common sense. To say otherwise made one at best a lunatic and at worst a heretic because the anthropocentric universe was, if we may say so, a central part of Christian cosmology. If we update Lincoln's statement the way we have updated a long-held belief about the rotation of the sun, we would be tampering with the historicity of Lincoln's speech – as if no one has even been guilty of such tampering. The endless squabbles about the historicity of the Bible are a case in point. If we allow for dates in history to have a kind of reality of their own apart from the relentless arrow of time dragging us to our deaths, then it is possible to say that the statement is true. Therefore, in the universe of Lincoln's 1863 discourse the statement is true despite the fact that it is no longer true that the country was founded eighty-seven years ago.

The matter gets a bit more complex when we look at what he asserts regarding the founding of the state. Is it "true" that "our fathers" founded the country on the principle that "all men are created equal"? In this case we can absolutely say that at least in the written attestation of this fact found in the *Declaration of Independence* this statement is true. We know for certain also that it was transcribed by Thomas Jefferson in 1776. But as with statements about history in the Bible, there is also endless controversy over whether or not that statement is true if it came from a slave owner, which Jefferson was. As a purported statement of act, the idea that all men are created equal can also be debated. What did they mean by equal? Does it mean that they are equal under the law (nomos), in the regard and judgment of God, or that exact statistical parity should be maintained for the polity to be fair; e.g. there shall be the same number of girls in the Boy Scouts as there are boys in the Girl Scouts (this is actually happening today). While it seemed obvious to most Europeans of the early Middle Ages that the sun revolved around the earth, it also seems obvious to most of us today that all men are *not* created equal. Nevertheless, we still universally say that the sun *comes up* in the morning and *goes down* in the evening. Furthermore, it seems that the statement "All men are created *unequal*" is closer to the truth. In fact, we might even be able to verify it except for the fact that it is impossible to come up with a universal quantification of "all men" – even when we say that all men are mortal. We cannot verify that some men are not mortal, and we take it for granted that some men *can be* immortal given the right health insurance policy. We feel comfortable, though, in again allowing for multiple realities – in this case one in which the statement "all men are created equal" applies to the mechanics of the government they were forming at that time. We can say that it means that someday government will put all men on equal footing as citizens – at least in the way government affects them all no matter what their other differences. We need not go further into other forms of getting at the meaning of truth such as *falsifiability, incompleteness, undecidability*, and whether or not a tautology, which is always true, actually means anything despite being the deep-structure basis of subject-predicate statements. For the purposes of this discussion it is more useful to look at what happens to meaning when there is no reciprocal relationship between subject and object, only mere transaction and negotiation for various needs and gratifications. As said earlier, what matters is the meaningful effect one entity has on the other as exchangeable interlocutors (A[B] → B[A]). Between human entities it is recognition of the transcendental Other that is meaningful. Otherwise, language is merely utility or nonsense. Between sentences it is the expression of the meaning of this recognition. Between words it is the union of two ideas to form a new one so that the meaning of this recognition can be expressed in all of its glorious novelty and power. It is the psycholinguistic mission of the Amniotic Empire to subvert the meaningful recognition of the transcendental Other in communication. By doing so, it enforces the turning-from, inhibits the turning-to, promotes the knowing-of, and stifles the process of the getting-to-know.

2.2: Reciprocal meaning and the sublime

To understand what the sublime means on a personal level in our *everydayness* we must understand the importance of *reciprocal meaning,* or the apophantic (non-contradictory) employment of language. In meaningful communication subject (object) and object (subject) exchange their existential and phenomenological being in a process of convergence and divergence, notated (above) as (A[B] → B[A]). They negotiate meaning in a highly complex way with the tacit understanding that most of language has no meaning at all; it is a compulsive collection of markers and signals that are only considered words, phrases, and utterances because they are differentiated from each other. ("He's a real rotter"; "He's a little bit of all right.") Therefore, the dance of communication is a mysterious process that must somehow transcend the abyss of the infinite divide between one person and another. This process is impossible without the transcendental object perceived in the Other which is seeing that the Other is really *the* subject (definite), not *a* subject (indefinite), and that the subject of self is in fact the Other (not *an*-other). Really, how else could we possibly transcend the divide between subject and object? But to do so we must dwell in the sublime, the catalyst of transcendence, which begins with accepting the discomfort and inconvenience of bare life and the absolute inevitability death. Who is willing to do this? As I said in the preface, show me and I will shut up and fall on my sword as Ms. No-it's-Not advised. What deters them? Those who are willing end up being identified as heretics, scorned, scourged, and loathed, driven from the rainbow heights of the social-civil Imaginary into the bowels of the despised Underclass of poor people, drug dealers, gang members, sex traffickers, terrorists, and artists.

But truly we have no choice in the end. Since death will someday overcome us no matter how much money or power we have, we know, one way or the other, that the best life has to offer us as a reward for our lifetime of struggle is a trip to the graveyard in a fancy car with our best rags on. It is no wonder that religion arose at the dawn of Man to address this shortcoming. We get nowhere with our perception of the transcendental object if we do not begin to *doubt* all that brings us comfort and even joy (but not jouissance). It is no secret that drugs, alcohol, theft, exploitation, rape, and even murder can bring comfort and joy to certain kinds of personalities – and not necessarily sociopaths. Though there is transgressive jouissance, not all jouissance is transgressive. Those of us who feel above it all still spend much of our free time watching entertainment involving murder, war, fighting, killing, shooting, rape, drugs, drunkenness, theft, and exploitation. We eagerly participate in virtual (vicarious) forms of what are otherwise the same sociopathic behaviors that get people labeled felons and thrown in prison. We spend enormous amounts of treasure buying gadgets and gizmos that give us on-demand access to the virtual world of murder and mayhem in which we can be the dominant player with the most kills. Let us explore how this comes about and what effect it has on the possibility of regaining our personal sovereignty without rejecting society altogether.

The organic process of the development of the personality from birth through its various stages forms a symbolic order of the *self* functioning in conjunction with what Lacan calls the imaginary and real orders. In Peirce's description of the process of individuation the real, imaginary, and symbolic work together as one force forming the subject's sense of itself as a subject through the development and manipulation of signs – most of which are components of the tautological iterations of the copula "I am" as the grammar structure n-v-n. For instance, "*I* [n] *am* [v] a teacher [n]," "*I am* a police officer," "*I am* a criminal," "*I am* a student,"

"*I am* French," "*I am* Jewish," and so on. Tautology encloses the rudimentary attributes of the subject's being united by the copula *to be*, creating the subject's *sentential* narrative. Most of these attributes are environmental. The majority are random, being accidental and beyond our control (as gender *used to* be) Even so, how can one choose one's gender *at birth*? Perhaps later on the subject may find itself in an existential and phenomenological struggle with this *gender assignment*, but not at birth. In the general population, therefore, what constitutes the attributes of identity is, by and large, random and tautological in the grammar of its declaration. (*"Ich bin ein Berliner,"* says American president John F. Kennedy in 1963.) In Heidegger's phenomenology the sign of the subject extracted from "I am" must remain "in and for itself" else it forfeits its *Jemeinigheit* (*B&T*, p. 61). "Judgment" says Heidegger clouds our mineness through *hiddenness, burying, and disguise* (pp. 60-61). Why? Because the grammar of the subject's narrative is autological. Nearly every sentence uttered means nothing in the non-trivial sense because it is self-referent (A = A). "I am human" is not news, even to myself. If we look at the grammatical structure of the subject + copula + predicate we find that "I am a teacher" is simply (np) + n, or a noun phrase with a predicate appended to it. The only statistical variation is that n1 is a pronoun and n2 is a regular noun denoting a specific occupation. If this sounds a bit obvious, then it might be better to reflect upon the many times one has found oneself in a noisy room where everyone is talking at once, uttering such sentences in repetition, but where no specific conversation can be understood. In the collective noise we discover the hidden truth of the meaninglessness of chatter in the amnion. It is signaling at best, and vocal filler to dispel the demon of silence wherein we might reveal our emptiness at worst. Upon transcription and analysis we find that almost everything said in a social context need not be said, will be forgotten, is of no consequence were it not said, changes nothing, and may only mean something in a utilitarian sense. In the same way, if we take any predicate and divide it by an infinite number of possible real and imaginary predicates in the same category (e.g. jobs, colors, names of animals) we also arrive at 0 (zero) meaning.

It could be argued, though, that this oral and aural stimulation does indeed reinforce the subject's sense of being — a sense always slipping away because the subject feels that it ceases to exist when it stops talking or finds itself trapped in the dreaded situation of being alone in silence. But what kind of self is being reinforced with the tautology of *I am*? Once we look at the set of possible predicates we see that what Hacking calls the "long run frequency" (*Logic*, p. 1) reduces the predicate to meaninglessness – thus forming a neat tautology that is always true, but is a tale told by an idiot, signifying nothing. In the "short" or "medium" run the illusion of meaning is easy to generate. For example, we might find ourselves in a conversation where we say, "I am a teacher. What do *you* do?" The other replies, "I'm a carpenter. Thanks for asking." While "teacher" and "carpenter" are forms of differentiated information of a sort, what do they *mean*? What is really being said here on the surface level is, "I work." So what? On the deep structure level the utterance is "I am" (np + n). The only other possibilities are "I do not work" (its binary negation) or "My skill is X," a trivial fact, since everyone has some sort of skill, even if it is begging or professionally doing nothing (Baudelaire's *le flaneur magnifique*). If we are willing to reduce the meaning of meaning to simply showing that within the same category (kinds of jobs) there are equivalent differences of the most superficial sort, then we perhaps have stripped it of any meaning worth being called meaning. Besides, one's profession is not immutable; a teacher may become a carpenter and vice versa. If we look at it schematically the situation is obvious. There is not any greater ontological difference between carpenter and teacher than there is between A and A (job + job). All that could be said about A is that it is not B, but here that is not the case. All that could be said about a carpenter is that he is not teacher, just as he is not the other person (notionally and nominally), but is 99.9 percent alike biologically — also a form of logic. Even if the exchange is between two carpenters or teachers, does any fundamental bond form transcending I and Thou?

If we confine ourselves only to words which nominate various occupations, we end up with thousands of nouns such as teacher, criminal, clown — all more or less interchangeable at the moment and over Hacking's ergodic long run. This set can be extended infinitely by inventing imaginary occupations as well, such as necromancer or soldier of Satan, since there is no end to the invention of occupations or of synonyms of already existing ones (lawyer, advocate, counselor, mouthpiece). The bigger the number (n) the less the word teacher (t) means because its specific meaning can be divided by the number of nouns in the set occupations. This give us t/(n), with (n) representing an infinite number of occupational titles which could be used in the predicate. "Infinity is redundant," says Hacking (*Logic*, p. 6). Furthermore, as we have quoted elsewhere in this essay, "It is currently supposed that the world is a chance process" (*Logic*, p. 14). If the world is a chance process, then surely the language it represents and that is represented by it is random as well. But since whatever we think the world is can only reflect who we are and what we think, it seems to us that the world and everyone in it has the same kind of corporeal integrity we assume for the organization of our egos and the language of thought.

There is a great scene in the film *St. Martin's Lane* (1938), that says it well, where the street busker Charles Staggers (played by Charles Laughton) says to his lady friend and fellow busker Liberty (played by Vivien Leigh), "There ain't no answer. You're after justice and logic. There ain't no justice and there ain't no logic. The world ain't made that way. Everything's luck, see. And good temper. And if you can take a joke. The whole of life's a joke." If this is so, then all linguistic expression, including this one, is a kind of *scherzo*.

Peirce describes the reciprocal (apophantic) process between word and thought which serves to form our solitary, solipsistic account of what the world is and where we fit into it.

> Man makes the word, and the word means nothing which the man has not made it mean, and that only to some man. But since man can think only by means of words or other external symbols, these might turn around and say, 'You mean nothing which we have not taught you, and then only so far as you address some word as the *interpretant* of your thought.' [italics added] (p. 71)

When the subject considers itself in its *operant* narcissistic state, its being as the Object in relation to other subjects remains opaque. "[T]here is no element whatever of man's consciousness which has not something corresponding to it in the word; and the reason is obvious. It is that the word or sign which man uses *is* the man himself," says Peirce. Furthermore, "that man is a sign" meaning that "the man and the external sign are identical in the same sense in which the words *homo* and *man* are identical. Thus my language is the sum total of myself; for the man is the thought" (p. 71). Once again, language and its symbolic state of being in the form of the ego-identity is just as tautological as homo = man.

Like the infant it once was, the self exists in what it considers to be a universe contrived to satisfy its every desire, but does not and cannot. Underred by reality, the subject-self (ego) nevertheless pursues a policy of perpetual seeking after that which it can never have because it left it behind with its placenta. The delusional objective of this quixotic adventure Lacan calls, as mentioned earlier, *l'objet petit a*. But of course this operant state is impotent. No one satisfies any desire without effective interaction with the Other, and *real* reality, in a kind of transactional *pas de deux*. Rescue from this frustrating state of affairs dangles before it in the form of the mineness (*Jemeinigheit*) of potent self-determination, which, alas, the subject has vowed to forsake for trinkets of deceit laid out before it like a treasure in a dream by the amnion, or the likeness of the womb which its infantile orientation to life craves. Unfortunately, mineness must be earned because it is not a default state but a statistical *property* of probability driven by self-determination. What a wretched nightmare it is that the subject is born *leasing* the property of itself with an option to buy, but can never afford. But how else would it be possible to become the property of oneself? It requires a heroic quest in the forest of Others to take possession of what is *a priori* possessed by powers much greater than the subject's Being and that reside in and issue from the abyss of the sublime. While an infant, the subject could easily have been thrown into a ditch to die as a burdensome piece of human garbage. In some countries, such as the United States, the child is literally owned by the state, not its parents, until a certain age (16). During this period at any time for any reason the child may be wrenched from the parents and thrown into a maze of state childcare to be brought up as a ward of the state. If all goes well, the child runs immediately into the apparatus of state indoctrination in schools funded by the government in which it must enroll or go to juvenile hall as a truant and become, once again, a ward of the state apparatus but now as a social deviant. If it survives this ordeal, it is then baited and manipulated into the higher education system with the threat that if it does not get a college degree, it is a loser and will die in poverty along with the denizens of the wretched Underclass who are too stupid to go to college. Once in the system, it finds that its development is retarded rather than nurtured until it can be sold cheaply on the job market. One is tempted to say *like a slave*, except that slaves of yore had job security, such as it was, and no student-loan debt. Once in the real world, its freedom is immediately usurped by debt and more debt (student loans, car loans, mortgages, credit cards, and so on) which it will never pay off because it must always accumulate more debt to survive; the currency with which it pays off the debt is perpetually devaluing at the rate of the interest on the debt and some. Besides, it must pay the interest on the state's massive debt which requires many months of free labor (usually 1 January to 30 April) on behalf of the state, or else it goes to jail and, once again, is thrown into the miasma of the Underclass. What would have been its personal income for this labor is diverted into mandatory income taxes to pay the interest on the national debt over which it has no control, and which is always growing and never being paid off. With nothing left of its original quest for the comfort and convenience of the womb on its own (the American, Chinese, European ... and so on, Dream), the subject abdicates its sovereignty through the perpetual signing of promissory notes, repayment of which is enforced by asset confiscation, garnishing of wages, legal harassment, and denial of more borrowing except from the worst of the legal loan sharks.

What are the dynamic forces of the substrate of this epic bamboozle? Peirce begins with the movement of an object toward another object, whether it is a Universe or a teacup and a tea pot. Let us consider the latter and then make an association to our social relationships with others. To have a cup of tea the pot must meet with the cup so that it may be poured. Usually, the teacup stays in its place on the table so that we may pour hot water accurately and safely. What we observe is the tea pot approaching the teacup, pouring the water, and then retreating to its cozy. However, if we consider the *thingness* of both the tea pot and the cup apart from our associations (which include the idea of the tea pot moving toward the stationary cup), there is nothing to prevent us from saying that the tea cup and the tea pot approached each other even though it seems that the approach was unilateral. Objects, then, have the spirit of their thingness allowing them to defy the imposition of our symbolic thought. Their being in time is subject to varying interpretations moment to moment, allying them more with the imaginary than the real – though they are real, not imaginary. Consider a taxicab. When one enters the cab, the driver usually seems to try to drive as fast as he can to get us to our destination. Is he just trying to satisfy our impatience about getting from A to B quickly? Although we might fear for our lives, we also consider that it would be good to get where we are going fast and that therefore he is serving us well. At least that is what we are thinking in a symbolic way. As many drivers will say, though, this is an illusion at worst and a collateral benefit at best. In reality, the cab driver is trying *to get rid of the fare* as quickly as possible so that he can get his next fare. The more fares he gets in a fixed amount of time the more money he earns. We are a necessary nuisance standing between him and his potential profits. Again, there is the thingness of the situation and the imaginary reality of it as we perceive it. Peirce sees all relationships as symbolic, physical and metaphysical, and therefore the universe opens itself up to the forces of the imagination as much as it does to reality.

> [A Sign is] not the mere body of the sign, which is not essentially such, but, so to speak, the sign's Soul, which has its Being in its power of serving as intermediary between the Object and a Mind. Such, too, is a living consciousness, and such the life, the power of growth, of a plant. Such is a living constitution – a daily newspaper, a great fortune, a social "movement." (p. 359)

How does this apply to the social relationship between subject and object? We may presume that there is, again, the soul of the person's *thingness*. This is not so difficult to understand if we accept the fact that a sign or symbol is simply not that which it represents. The word dog is not the animal we call as dog. Nor is the word love any form of love. Therefore, a sign is a thing just as the thing it represents is a thing. A sign is a thing of a thing. The soul of the thing (signified or signifier) is its *being*; it *is*, one way or another. This being is Dasein, which has no attribute except that it has no attribute. It just is. But Dasein is what signifier and signified have in common, though phenomenologically they are different and therefore opposed in the schema of experience. However, it is what gives the signified its thingness, and what gives the signifier its power as an effective referent of the signified. And when either *is not* (or *is no longer*), then it has vanished over the horizon of Dasein and back into the infinite oblivion of its sublime origin. The subject, as a sign of itself, is therefore subject to the same rules of being, which is what it is most terrified of in a repressed, unconscious way. The subject, then, has two layers of thingness to contend with: itself and its referent. Surviving this contest requires, first of all, a true and healthy sense of doubt, which includes the capacity to *doubt doubt* (a matter we shall return to in depth later). Next it requires the ability to effectively distinguish between what can be proven and what cannot, or the power of verifiability. Finally, it requires the imagination to be able to conceive of the possibility of being without attribute and what that means for the thingness of the signified and the signifier. We may call this the analytical mind. The analytical mind, however, is seldom cultivated by cultures dependent upon consumerism and debt to survive. If it were, then the subject might refuse to accept the life of servitude the Imaginary offers through the apparatus of the amnion. Those who naturally possess such a mind are typically commandeered to work in research and development necessary to produce weapons to help the hegemony maintain its power status as well as the drugs, gizmos, gadgets, black boxes, and Big Magic the consumer craves.

Upon the blank screen of this thingness, the Other projects its symbols in the form of words, works of art, and actions (e.g. in modern times Martin Luther's "Ninety-Five Theses" viz-a-viz the Roman Catholic Church, the Russian and Chinese communist revolutions, the French and American revolutions, the world wars, and the rise of the industrial and digital ages). At the same time, the Other processes and then manipulates the signs it receives from the subject based on data from its own projection toward what is now the *other* Other who is also manipulating the signs *he* receives. Therefore, what is happening in both is that each perceives the transcendental object in the other, uniting them in the only possible way across the chasm of the sublime. As for the tea pot unilaterally approaching the cup, we may apply the same analogy to social communication. There are four possibilities of approach: physical, emotional, psychological, and intellectual. In the symbolic order, they are limited by the logic of statistical inference regarding the possibilities and probabilities of communication between A and B. We must remember that both have the attributes of subject and object, so that they would properly be described as A(s/o) and B(o/s). To understand exchange, we must look at what the possibilities are of its initiation. These possibilities we will call *approaches*. There are three possibilities of approaches in the negotiation of symbolic communication: A approaches B, B approaches A, and A and B approach each other. In terms of chance (probability) we can be certain that the odds of A approaching B, B approaching A, and A and B approaching each other simultaneously, are always variable. Whether or not A approaches B or B approaches A more often we cannot determine, though we can also be certain that in (n) number of approaches one will have a higher number than the other. However, it seems likely that A and B approaching each other will tend to have the weakest number of approaches only because there are two variables involved, both of which must be engaged at the same time to complete the approach. This sort of simultaneity is less common than unilateral initiation — otherwise every crush someone had on another person would result in a love affair. Therefore whatever probability there is of A(B) approaching B(A), the probability of approaches of a concurrent union of AB will always be less than the number of total approaches of A(B) and B(A) given (n) number of approaches (AB < A[B]).

How does this help us understand the symbolic relationship between subject and object? What we have just performed is a symbolic analysis of social relationship (physical, psychological, emotional, or intellectual) between subject and object in terms of how they approach each other in the process of symbolic communication. All of this is easily observed in any social situation, particularly when there are only two persons. It shows us that in our associations with others we must communicate on complex levels and in complex ways to find a connection, and be willing to accept whatever feedback we get from the other who is entirely independent of our will, except in forcible circumstances such as rape, robbery, and murder. Now, if we turn to the *thingness* of A(s/o) and B(o/s) we see that apart from the symbolic order of possibility and probability all things converge or diverge but always remain in relationship to each other to a greater or lesser degree but never in the same way and to the same degree. Apprehending the transcendental other is not a static, permanent state; it is, perhaps, the *least static* and *most impermanent* state always in need of inspiration and luck, not unlike romantic love. The relationship between subject and object - which both embody simultaneously - is a variable, random frequency of convergence and divergence. We cannot distinguish the dancer from the dance, as Yeats says. Our relationship to others on the symbolic level as the signs of subject and object preclude a limited form of communication in our understanding of how we communicate; whereas our relationship in our thingness constitutes what Peirce calls the "soul" of the signs where we are always in relationship whether we are diverging or converging — and it must always be one or the other and never a static state, which is only possible in death or death-in-life (crystallization or fossilization). After all, what would be the point of having a soul if this were not so? Without it, social relationships would be no more substantial than the abstract association between pieces on a chess board.

Since we are concerned here with signs, we are therefore concerned with language as the primary form of communication between subject and object. We might say that there is a subtle difference between saying subject-object and subject-predicate when we speak of *sentential* relationships of any kind. A sentential relationship is one where there is a perceptible grammar in the structure of that relationship. There are four basic *diads* which describe the copula "I am" in its effulgent form:

a) subject-object
b) antecedent-consequent
c) subject-predicate
d) *substance-attribute*

The last (d) is metaphysical. After all, what is substance?

And once we have fumbled with the answer to that question, we may compound the mystery by explaining what sort of attributes it may have. It could be argued that Being itself, as Dasein, has no attribute except that it has no attribute. If it did have any other attribute, we would have to call it something else (whatever); it would be a member of the set of the myriad phenomena we presume "to be," which is always already a posteriori of Dasein. But Being is not everything nor is it something. Perhaps the closest we get to understanding its inherent transparency is in Heidegger's concept of *Dasein*. "To work out the question of Being adequately, we must make an entity—the inquirer—transparent in his own Being. Thus in the very act of asking of the question, 'What is Being?' this inquirery [sic] becomes Dasein's mode of Being. Dasein therefore *gets its essential character* from what is inquired about: namely, Being" [italics added] (p. 27). As I said earlier, the interrogative – inquiry – is the closest we get in language to pure consciousness, which is why the Socratic Method is meant to get at the truth. Neither something nor nothing, Being (in the sense of Dasein) extracts its "essential character" from our acknowledgement of what is incognizable for us. Such a definition has an analog the Dunning-Kruger Effect in cognitive psychology where intelligence is defined as knowing the limitations of our intelligence. Surely the opposite – not knowing – must be some sort of stupidity. Without attribute, Dasein possesses no character of its own that would give it thingness. Its character, then, can only be a kind of attribute manifest as the result of inquiry into its character. For instance, the unanswerable question of if there is a God nevertheless pitches us into uncertainty about what it means to be, which, in that inimical way of the ego, always ends up referring back to our own being. Without an intelligent sense of being-in-the-world, which can only happen when we see and feel ourselves in relationship to others and other things, social life and therefore human life becomes intolerable. As it is the premier form of social interaction, procreation would cease were it not for the sense that Being possesses a rich fabric of character in need of perpetual continuation (not progress). Even this primal instinct is exploited by consumer culture in the form of the promise of robotic substitutes for children, a role often assumed by animal pets. It is well established that human life is possible without knowing the truth of its existential milieu. All that is needed is the biological imperative to survive and procreate to make it go on until it meets its own special rogue asteroid of extinction, political or natural.

Hacking, citing Locke, says that "The substance, before having any attributes pinned to it, seems to be what Locke long ago ironically called an 'I don't know what'" (*Language*, p. 80). Furthermore, Heidegger says that "Being is indefinable" (p. 78). It is neither a thing nor a genus and is therefore not subject to the categorization and quantification of predicate logic. Consequently, Being has no rules which could only come from a neat categorization of its attributes and perforce its effect on the world. If Being were capable of having an effect on the world, then it would be simple to explain precisely what substance is (rather than "I don't know what"). But since Being simply *is*, substance fades into, at best, a Platonic *eidos* of an ideal form. It is the magic of language that it can transmute this eidos into the flesh and blood of Galatea, the beloved of Pygmalion. It is no secret that the term "poesis" from which we get the word poetry means "to make." Make what? If there is any sublime magic in the world it is how language can embody, not just represent, that in which we have a fundamental emotional and spiritual investment. The sublime demands this investment, as Keats' odes show. However, the amnion of the Imaginary demands *divestment* of one's self-determination. At the same time the lost subject willingly abdicates its self-determination to gain access to the consumer phantasmagoria its magic black boxes (gadgets) vend in the Imaginary's gift shop. The ethical aesthetic of *Genuss* pouring forth from the digital interface provides a deadly soporific from which the subject seldom escapes except through what Keats calls "easeful death." Meantime, the Imaginary operates as a front for the hegemony which after all controls the whole *dark carnival*. This divestment preempts the possibility (*Möglichkeit*) of sublime union through symbolic language with what we refer to here as Being. Heidegger refers to personal sovereignty *mineness* and sees Dasein as the form of Being in which mineness manifests: "Mineness [*Jemeinigheit*] belongs to any existent Dasein, in the sense that how I regard 'my Being', creates the conditions that make authenticity and inauthenticity possible" (p. 78). Only language which is authentic conveys knowledge. Heidegger shows us that any attribute of Being comes from what he calls the "scholarly" inquiry into the nature of conscious existence. Perhaps the secret is that this inquiry itself *is* consciousness. Without it language becomes mere information to be stored up in the silos of Big Data to be used later for surveillance and target marketing.

Heidegger gives us three coordinates by which we may triangulate our understanding of being:

Being is not a genus
Being is indefinable

Being is self-evident

While we casually make *some* inquiry into the nature of our conscious existence before it is over, the most essential inquiry comes when we wax philosophical about love, death, and God, the big metaphysical topics. We also have to take into account what Heidegger says about the attributes of Dasein arising from our inquiry into being. Therefore, "substance-attribute" is primarily concerned with this trinity of metaphysical inquiry. Peirce, however, sees inquiry as a process of the imagination, particularly in the use of abductive reasoning (a form of hypothetical retroduction, as he calls it) as its primary tool. He sees the mind not as a repository of information and ideas but rather a collection of signs and symbols which eventually organize themselves into inner and expressed discourse. The discourse itself is further divided into belief and opinion. It is from our reflexive power of inquiry that we form the structure of our worldview in Dasein. Typically, it is formed of the bric-à-brac of commercial appeals, random mythology, childish legends, the antics of celebrities, the lies of politicians, and the indoctrination passing for the content of public education. Having abdicated its core identity through indebtedness and a neurological dependency on the noise of digital stimulation, the subject becomes a champion of the notions, beliefs, and opinions it has been told are the facts of life. To do so it must identify itself with this ragout of *exoteric* nonsense.

Then what is left to know? Keats informs us that all we can and need to know is the synonymous relationship between beauty and truth, or what we might call the ethical aesthetic of consciousness. The rest, says, Peirce, is merely opinion and belief. But does this mean that science in its quest for the verified fact somehow offers transcendence from this state of affairs? We eventually learn that much of what science dishes up as fact can be, for various reasons, as fanciful as a Russian fairy tale. "That the settlement of opinion is the sole end of inquiry is a very important proposition. It sweeps away, at once, various vague and erroneous conceptions of proof" (p. 100). Though we could go much farther back, we can start with Descartes' concept of the universe and travel up through time to today. Naturally, all of these theories – if they can properly be called that – cannot be true simultaneously unless we would like to invent yet another kind of universe (the popular multiverse?) here and now in which they are. We see in a short list of theories about the totality of the universe that if anything is true about it, it is the state of chaos: Biblical, Ptolemaic, Copernican (pre

Kepler), Cartesian Vortex, Static State, Einsteinian, Big Bang, No Big Bang, Quantum, Oscillating, Crunch, Inflating, Multiverse, String, Superstring, Parallel, M-Theory, and so on. Peirce would have found it wonderful that scientists today outdo the inventive imagination of their predecessors. Perhaps he likely should have had some doubts about the seriousness with which these theories are taken *as fact.* The credulity of the more or less ignorant public and the handouts of treasure from universities and governments for them seem out of proportion with the boundaries of the scientific sandbox where these theories are made like sandcastles. We could throw in the contrary theories of genetic inheritance by Mendel and Lamarck, both today in flux because of genetic engineering. Consequently, an existential question such as the personhood of a human fetus and its legal rights has befuddled and besmirched lawyers, scientists, politicians, and theologians since it suddenly became an issue with the use of abortion as a *legal* form of birth control. *At least* theological opinion and belief is consistent about it: yes, a fetus is a person, and is in God's hands, not the Latex-gloved hands of medical technology. But the nomological questions nevertheless remain unsettled.

Peirce describes three "various vague and erroneous conceptions of proof" hindering understanding of the truth as it is entombed within belief and opinion. Again, if all we ever know and need to know is the Keatsian Dictum, why not allow imagination in the form of abduction into the walled garden of science? And why not present the results of this inquiry as belief, opinion, and conjecture rather than ennoble it with the nouns of theory, fact, and truth? Why not accept that the majority of what we know about life is negotiable at best and simply wrong at worst? Have we entered an age apart from all ages where, at last, the scales have fallen from our eyes and every question has been answered by high school biology and algebra? Peirce does not fear calling opinion and belief truth, dispensing with what Keats calls the irritable need to subject anything and everything to fact and reason, as scientific consensus and Positivism have nominated this process to be. It is *true* that a fetus is a person at some point; if one kills an infant born prematurely at seven months, it is *murder*. If one aborts a fetus at eight months it is called a *medical procedure*. And it is true that a fetus is also *not* a person; its status after the day after conception is a theological and metaphysical debate at best. This is as close as language ever gets to the truth. The problem here is not scientific or theological; it is *linguistic.* Apply the need for absolute positive verification in either case and one becomes a mystic, a shaman, a soothsayer, a magician, and a charlatan using slight-of-hand (misdirection) to nominate what is real and imaginary. Peirce's list of epistemological errors is based on the need to use doubt *as a tool* to get at the truth, if ever we can:

1. [T]he mere putting of a proposition into the interrogative form does not stimulate the mind to any struggle after belief. *There must be a real and living doubt*, and without this, discussion is idle.
2. [A]n inquiry, to have that completely satisfactory result called demonstration, has only to start with propositions perfectly *free from all actual doubt*.
3. *When doubt ceases, mental action on the subject comes to an end;* and, if it did go on, it would be without a purpose, except that of self-criticism. (italics added, pp. 100-101)

What all three have in common is the emphasis on *doubt*. Doubt of what? As there is some contradiction here, Peirce seems to point to *doubting doubt* too. In this case it is doubting the tacit assumption about something in which we are interested, for one reason or another. It could regard a practical matter, such as doubting whether or not existing farming methods are best. It could be about the nature of something, such as if the sun really revolves around the earth. Even doubting if there is a God has led to social, cultural, political, and even scientific revolution. It may seem that using "real and living doubt" as a catalyst for inquiry conflicts with the idea that inquiry starts "with propositions … free from all … doubt." Here Peirce describes a process of inquiry, and as such it has stages or steps which lead to the truth, a belief, or an opinion. Therefore what he describes is a method which he sees as an alternative to the so-called scientific method used by those who are satisfied with what he calls "vague and erroneous conceptions of truth ..." It is what scientists seek today to make politicians happy so that they can get their taxpayer funding and prestige: verification based on unquestioned consensus and professional bullying. The whole point of doubting is to arrive at a stage in the process where that doubt has been satisfied one way or another, or is recognized as incognizable (such as final proof of the non-existence of God —Dawkins and Hitchens aside). Once this has happened, there is a need for some sort of demonstration, proof of concept, since all discovery must be followed by an argument and all argument must involve a demonstration to verify. But is this proof of anything? He could easily have used the word here, but chose demonstration. After all, this is a refutation of "erroneous conceptions of proof." Finally, the scientist infects his audience with his own original doubt, since it may be presumed that he has had little doubt about the object of his inquiry else he would not have embarked upon the process of its verification. Once he has the *disease*, the passion, the desire for truth, his demonstration resolves the cognitive dissonance he has engendered in his otherwise complacent acceptance of whatever was presumed to be the (erroneous or accurate) truth. However, when his new improved truth has had exposure to the world for a certain amount of time doubt naturally develops again, either through the lust for a new priority, or the need for a new application (bit versus qubit computing). This is precisely what happened to the Classical theories of physics when quantum mechanics came along around the turn of the Twentieth Century, driven by the need for a more efficient incandescent lightbulb.

Peirce's emphasis on the role of doubt in the formation of opinion has correlations in Hobbes' ideas regarding what he calls "mental discourse." In Chapter VII "Of the Ends, or Resolutions of Discourse" of *Leviathan*, he begins by describing the mechanics. He says that if one interrupts the "chain" of thought of another it will leave off with "thoughts that the thing will be, and will not be; or that it has been, and has not been, alternately. So that wheresoever you break off the chain of a man's discourse, you leave him in a presumption of 'it will be,' or 'it will not be,' or 'it has been,' or 'has not been.'" In other words, "being" is the primary concern of the concatenation of signs we call thought (Heidegger's *inquiry*). Why? Perhaps because thought's primary role in our psyche is to reinforce the notion that we exist. Its second is to doubt. Therefore, the sign of being arises from doubt. It is not enough *to be*, as Hamlet so nicely puts it. He must doubt its value against nonbeing. There must be the sign of being for being itself to exist as a *thing* in our minds. And what is this thing? The ego forms itself from the content and syntax of this mental discourse. And in so doing perpetuates the fundamental illusion of solitary existence: that thought is what Heidegger calls *being-in-the-world* or perhaps what we may call bare life, sans the bejeweled, constricting livery of civilization. From this monad of personality comes the tacit and indomitable sense that *We* are the alpha and omega of the universe, not God or Nature apart from us. That God makes the same claim in an ancient book seems almost quaint in an age where the ego is aggrandized over every spiritual, intellectual, emotional, cognitive, natural, and creative quality in the psyche and experience of man.

In describing the function of mental discourse, Hobbes creates a binary function that at last bases itself on the fundamental value in prepositional logic of a statement being true or false in the analytical sense. What makes such discourse possible – as it does in Peirce's epistemology - is the presence of doubt. It seems logical that without doubt there is only absolute acceptance in the form of *belief*. If there is only belief, then all propositions are synthetic (unverifiable). And while belief too can be the end of inquiry set in motion by doubt, it nevertheless exists as an independent process ready to be applied to any proposition about the world. What makes Hobbes' and Peirce's conception different from Positivism's brand of verifiability is that mental discourse, like abduction, may at last find knowledge in opinion and belief rather than a hard cold fact. Hobbes:

> The last appetite in deliberation is called the "will," so the last opinion in search of the truth of past and future is called the "judgment" or "resolute" and "final sentence" of him that "discourseth." And as the whole chain of appetites alternate, in the question of good or bad, is called "deliberation," so the whole chain of opinions alternate, in the question of true or false, is called "doubt."

We note that contained in Hobbes' analysis is the foundation of jurisprudence. The familiar term "beyond a shadow of a doubt" comes to mind. Doubt has its place in the cosmology of the sublime, as it opens its door. It is also clear that a world without doubt would be a static state of unchallenged and fixed ideas as *dogma*. It would be intellectual death in life. Like curiosity, doubt it is an agent of change, particularly when it comes to such scientific claims such as the Malthusian efficacy of eugenics and the humanitarian ethics of abortion.

Perhaps there is not enough doubt in current notions of artificial intelligence and genetic modification. We soon come to doubt whether this or that is good for us after having been told that we cannot live without it. Great social changes often follow the results of abductive inquiry. There are changes in the way people see the universe, too. The phrase "the speed of light" is on everyone's lips in a modern, presumably scientific culture. The public have a vague sense that all of their gadgets and gizmos depend upon radio waves conveying something called *bits* through networks really fast or not fast enough for them - though they have no clue what an electromagnetic wave is, what a bit might be, or how fast these waves travel. It is all just Big Magic to them. The consumer instinctively knows that it would not be able to enjoy the instant gratification these expensive toys promise without the prestidigitation of scientific and mathematical magicians in the priesthood of Technology.

They show their worship by tithing debt service and monthly service fees.

If we look hard at Hobbes' mental discourse, though, we see that it has two components: 1) thought's autonomic stream of signs reinforcing the ego's fragile sense of being, and 2) the application of thought in the formation of binary relationships to create a sense of ratio in the universe so that one thing can be distinguished from another. Above we mention the absolute reduction of the noun *teacher* when it is divided by an infinite number of like nouns until its cardinality is reduced to being infinitely small (0, or null). At that point we are left with only the copula: "I am a ..." since the predicate is now 0 (zero). In this way a tautology reduces language to a statement that is true but is without meaning, such as we find in A = A. There is no difference between saying "I am" and "I am that I am." We find the latter tautology in Exodus 3:14: "And God said unto Moses, I AM THAT I AM [הָיְהֶא רֶשֶׁא הָיְהֶא]: and he said, Thus shalt thou say unto the children of Israel, I AM hath sent me unto you." (I AM = *Tetragrammaton*, or the unspeakable name of God.) God speaks only in truths as He is the *arbiter* of truth throughout the Bible. If we take the phrase and concatenate it indefinitely, we have the basic structure of thought: *I am that I am that I am that I am that I am* … and so on. This can also be expressed in numbers. We may say infinity, or we may write 1 + 1 + 1 + 1 + 1, … and so on.

Once we step out of the safety of tautological discourse, though, we enter into the realm of the conscious application of thought to real problems of understanding through the agency of doubt. We may even *doubt* doubt, as I have said several times here already and will say again as it is consequential to this argument. Its application is universal. The journey of a thousand propositions begins with one step: the syllogism. In it, at least A may equal C, liberating it from tautology, but allowing for error. Also, it is never absolutely true in the way a tautology is because A could be 1 + 4, and C could be 6 - 1, ..., and so on. There are circumstances where while both equal 5, they could be regarded as significantly different, such as when the former indicates an addition to a ship's crew, whereas the latter indicates the death of a crew member. Hey, we say, there are still five crew members! Yes, but not as if the same five had departed on the voyage and returned, intact. Which brings us to various forms of epistemology affecting the way sentences *mean*. It also allows us to begin to see the difference between awareness and consciousness. The former is "I am" along with its autonomic mental discourse of "I am that I am that I am ..." In such a state the only epistemological possibility is the knowing-of. Knowledge accumulates in the subject the way barnacles find their way onto the bottom of boats. The subject is just aware enough to eat, copulate, work, borrow, and die. However, this awareness can be inflated into a grand showboat of the ego fueled by the possibility of endless accumulation of consumer goods and a perpetual supply of debt. There can also be intellectual and spiritual materialism as well. Examples include university degrees, publications, honors and awards, dignified titles, and fame. How is this spiritual? In consumer culture those with the most take on a kind of otherworldly aura of being superior demigods. After all, how could Lady Luck have been so generous to them if they were not destined by the Gods of Consumerism to climb to the heavenly heights of the academic, literary, artistic, financial, and social *summum bonum*?

But science's greatest effect on the way people think about the universe has been the replacement of theological order with the empirical and analytical orders. The common idea is that science has debunked religion. We came from monkeys, not from the Word, despite what the holy book says. "In the beginning was the Word [monkey], and the Word [monkey] was with God [evolution], and the Word was God" (John 1:1). However, as Darwin said (paraphrasing), I am theist because I believe God created evolution, but not man, and you do not. (Letter to John Fordyce, dated 7 May 1879: "I have never been an atheist in the sense of denying the existence of a God.") The monkey or the Word, however, seems like a ludicrous debate within the context of Peirce's framework for the employment of doubt. Even if a statement is true enough to survive any forensic test of its veracity, though, at best the public will come away from it with only the vaguest notion of what it really means. With facts, information, and understanding of such low psychic energy in the mind of the subject, what is and what is not tend to weave into the mythological fabric of the Imaginary dominating the subject's intrinsic identity. If this were not so, the public would heed the endless admonitions from scientists about the critical necessity for healthy diet and exercise, which few scientists practice, anyway. But in the womb of the ethical aesthetic of *Genuss*, the path of least resistance is exploited by the commercial interests the subject has already traded its sovereignty to for a hand full of ephemeral trinkets. This path becomes irresistible, even for those who know better. It is ubiquitous, pervasive. It is the amniotic sack in which the hegemony bags its prey.

In "The Marriage of Religion and Science" (p. 350), Peirce attempts an ecumenical union of what the Imaginary and the hegemony have put asunder. He begins by condemning what Big Data has to offer by calling the knowing-of "mere knowledge" which, though neatly systematized, is nonetheless "dead memory." Instead, he advocates a science that knows nothing at all. "[B]y science we … mean a living and growing body of truth. *We might even say that knowledge is not necessary to science*" [italics added]. He conjures the picture of Ptolemy under the stars with nothing but his eyes and thoughts to gather what he needs to create the mathematical methodologies that would define astronomy for centuries, until Copernicus superseded them but also made his own errors (which then Kepler dispelled, and so on). We may picture Galileo with his invented telescope challenging the cosmic anthropocentrism of the early Church. It seems that "eureka!" does not require a major grant from the National Science Foundation, the Department of Defense, or a major corporation seeking higher stock prices. Nor does it require an eternity of reading scientific papers in order to write new scientific papers, as Einstein's first Relativity paper shows, bereft of academic citation. "[T]he method of science is itself a scientific result" he says. The more self-contained science is the more free of the contamination of that which it seeks to overthrow. Moreover, mere analytics will not do; one must also be possessed by the spirit of doubt, curiosity, and compulsive inquiry. "That which is essential … is the scientific spirit, which is determined not to rest satisfied with existing opinions, but to press on to the real truth of nature." We see here the romance of science that perhaps was more available in Peirce's day than it is today with its desperate striving to deliver the gadget or pill to the marketplace.

His encomium to religion's role in the scientific process, however, extends the romance of inquiry into the subtle realm of the metaphysical. By doing so he reveals the need for sublime mystery, for spiritual dreaming, for the free play of imagination guided by the spirit and nature.

> In each individual [religion] is a sort of sentiment, or obscure perception, a deep recognition of a something in the circumambient All, which, if he strives to express it, will clothe itself in forms more or less extravagant, more or less accidental, but ever acknowledging the first and last, the A and Ω, as well as a relation to that Absolute of the individual's self, as a relative being. (pp. 350-1)

The subject, alas, has abdicated its "Absolute of the individual self" (self-determination). It is no more. In its place is the brassy chatter of celebrity gossip, infotainment, experts, sports, video games, and a plethora of meaningless distraction droning continually from the digital feed. Inquiry is limited to choosing one product over another based on how many stars and *likes* it gets from other consumers who have in turn done the same thing, ad nauseum. Religion becomes a tasteless side show patronized when such spectacles as weddings and funerals are needed to gratify one's sense of being a part of a more traditional social discourse than a social-media platform. *Mineness* becomes impossible, which in turn negates the possibility of the transcendental object as described by Kant. When *inauthentic* Dasein is (mis)taken for the authentic, being (awareness) without consciousness remains as the detritus of something that never was. Mere awareness of the surroundings, the food source, procreation, and the perils of the nomos are enough to convey the subject through a lifetime of uneventful *persistence* rather than *existence*. Even a virus, which does not really need to eat but has a much more complex agenda, seems more clever than the subject who has returned to this protoplasmic state. The subject is entirely ignorant of the *Möglichkeit* of Dasein, the only realm of infinite possibility where the imaginary, symbolic, and real integrate organically. At this confluence, one may win oneself back as authentic Dasein, or lose oneself forever in the nothingness of inauthenticity. Losing oneself in the nothingness of inauthenticity is *never to have been* (past perfect), which is the greatest spiritual tragedy. With the loss of Dasein's authenticity comes the death of the sublime and the birth of the Amniotic Empire.

2.3: Utterances as signs in the amnion of the Imaginary

A sign is not only a component of the unconscious, but also of what we utter. Peirce defines *utterance* as what we "put forth in speech, on paper, or otherwise" (p. 395). This of course includes the utterances of God. Though God Himself does not commit words to paper per se, He does *speak* to those who do on His behalf. Otherwise there would be no need for the word *scripture*. Speech always has priority in the utterances of divine personages. This should make us wonder. Jesus, Mohammad, Moses, Buddha, and even Socrates deigned *not to* pick up the pen, preferring live speech. Socrates even went so far as to criticize books as foils to the collective memorization of epic poetry. Therefore, we meet with what their chosen or incidental scribes have recorded for us from the master's lips, corporeal or incorporeal. As a result writers of books no matter how profound the utterances found therein are subordinated to scribes of their own inspiration. Even Hitler did not write *Mein Kampf*, preferring to *dictate* it (of course) to Emil Maurice and Rudolph Hess when he was incarcerated together in Landsberg Prison. Saussure's famous *Course in General Linguistics* was cobled together from the lecture notes of his students posthumously. Boswell was Doctor Johnson's scribe. A blind Milton, also, dictated *Paradise Lost* to his daughters. Milton's poem is regarded as one of the greatest poems ever *written* in English. The same is true of the works of Homer. While it is natural that a dictator would *dictate* his utterances to his quislings, in all cases it seems to give the written result of this dictation an aura of religious sanctity, profundity, and gravitas. Why? Perhaps it is because the fact that someone would be willing to take the role of the unpaid scribe endows the writing with an priority mere autography does not command as a do-it-yourself project. In various periods of antiquity the scribe was regarded with awe as well as suspicion for his ability to set discourse (narrative) in clay, papyrus, or vellum. There are many reasons for this. It seems likely that these reasons change over the epochs of history for practical reasons. We might infer, though, that it is because the power of writing has always been seen as the basis of civilization and the nomos, as well as of what Peirce calls the Index of thought. As Edward Bulwer-Lytton wrote in 1839, "The pen is mightier than the sword." But we must also remember that he wrote what is now considered to be the worst opening sentence of any piece of fiction ever when he began the novel *Paul Clifford*, published in 1830, with: "It was a dark and stormy night." It is only fair to say that sometimes the pen lacks the penetration of a sword. Nevertheless, suspicion falls on the scribe because throughout most of history we could never be certain if what "is written" is what was said or meant. At one time the *Encyclopedia Britannica* claimed that Edwin Armstrong, as he planted the first footprint on the moon, said, "This is one small step for *a man,* one giant leap for mankind." At the same time the *Encyclopedia Americana* claimed that Armstrong said, "This is one small step for *man,* one giant leap for mankind." This presents an interesting conundrum. The first is grammatically correct and meaningful, even poetic, while the second *is nonsense*. However, when we look at the newspaper reports of 1969 we read the latter which the recording confirms. The implications of this discrepancy are interesting. It is easy to resolve the matter by the priority of "following the flag" and choosing the latter, making allowances for the American education system's notorious murder of grammar.

What we see above is that the utterance, even when it comes at a great moment in history and is then propagated through the most respectable channels, nevertheless falls victim to confusion over what *was* real — as if anything that *was* (e.g. history) can be real in the present. Of course that is the problem: *was*. Reality *is*. It never was. Moreover it never *will be* in the future, which is entirely notional and imaginary. But since in the realm of the Imaginary past, present, and future are all cut from the same cloth of wishful thinking and self-indulgence, *is* becomes just as much of a phantom as was and will be. The case of Cain and Abel, then, is a good choice of example. First we see Cain in the state of the Imaginary where his growing neurosis regarding God's favoring of Abel's sacrifices, turns into paranoia. Although his motive is not made clear, what really matters is that whatever it is *he acted upon it*. Like speech, murder is an act. It is a transmission of one's innermost thoughts into action, just as language is. It is symbolic, significant, purposeful, and unequivocal. For language to be received and understood, however, there must be collateral acquaintance with its data and metadata. This means that the sender and receiver must encode and decode language by referring to the same lexicon, sentence structure, and possibilities of expression (imperative, declarative, interrogative, for example). This *synchrony* is usually a matter of the sender and receiver being from the same culture and speaking the same language. However, *asynchrony* occurs when the utterance becomes trapped between the Imaginary and the Real, the Real and Symbolic, or the Symbolic and the Imaginary. Therefore, the *mode* of the subject (x, y, or z) as sender or receiver must synchronize with other subjects in the same way (Shannon).

How then does the *indeterminate transience* of the utterance affect the discrepancy between Cain's *imaginary* interpretation of the significance of carrying out the First Murder and God's rectification of this error when he acquaints Cain with the *reality* of his crime? Indeterminate transience is a form of the transitive process of transferring one's sovereignty to another or of receiving the other's sovereignty. By killing Abel, Cain *negates* his brother's sovereignty irrevocably. He sees the negation as a negation of God's negation of his sacrifices. With Abel out of the way, his sacrifices will be better appreciated by God thereby making Cain a "better" person in the eyes of God, he imagines. Unfortunately for him, though, God retaliates by negating any positive which Cain may have hoped for from his double-negative murder. He is sent forth as a wanderer, eventually doing great things such as founding a city and the lineage of Enoch. Curiously, God gives him a mark which warns others not to kill him. As a person thus marked, he is also a symbol of God's will as it is imposed in the endless complications of man's drama. This story is sometimes interpreted as the beginning of evil in the world. Adam and Eve may have eaten the fruit of the tree of the knowledge of good and evil, but they did not *kill* anyone or anything. They sinned by learning the difference, or ratio, between the dichotomies of man's moral and ethical capabilities. But one of their progeny takes sin a step farther into *evil itself*. Much later at the end of the New Testament, the mark of the Beast (666) becomes the *sign* of evil in Revelation 13:16: "And he causeth all, both small and great, rich and poor, free and bond, to receive a mark in their right hand, or in their foreheads: And that no man might buy or sell, save he that had the mark, or the name of the beast, or the number of his name." (Today's credit score?) We may draw a direct line from Cain's sin to the gathering clouds of the Apocalypse. In both cases sin and evil are marks, or signs, subject to the *collateral acquaintance* of those who would read them correctly. In the first case those who read it must not kill Cain; in the second they may not "buy or sell" to those without the Number (credit). Such signs, says Peirce, have three possible ways to "appeal to its dynamic interpretant" (p. 393). In other words, the collateral acquaintance the receiver possess at the time of the utterance. These three ways are:

1) *Submitted* as something reasonable
2) *Urged* as an act of insistence
3) *Presented* as an interpretant for contemplation

The collateral purpose of the mark of Cain and the mark of the Beast is to advertise the will of a supernatural power. What can be submitted as reasonable is a proposition such as Cain killed Abel? What is urged as insistence is God's will and judgment in the form of Signs. What is presented for contemplation is the significance of 1 and 2 in the lives of those who are affected by the acts God notices, cares about, and acts upon Himself. What Peirce calls a sign's appeal to its dynamic interpretant occurs in the state space of the sublime. Outside of this state space, in the semantic void of the Imaginary, signs are alienated from their interpretant. The signifier no longer has significance in relation to the *thingness* of the signified. It is a detached sign, drifting like Cain through what Dante calls in Canto I of *L'Inferno* "the dark wood" (*una selva oscura)* where "the straight-way is lost" (*ché la diritta via era smarrita*):

Nel mezzo del cammin di nostra vita
mi ritrovai per una selva oscura,
ché la diritta via era smarrita

Cain and Abel, Peirce says, are in an *imaginary* relationship to each other "in so far as this relation was *imaginable* or imageable" (p. 395). Their relationship is a logical disjunction where if it is true that Cain suffers from the Imaginary in his relationship to Abel, then it is true that Abel suffers in kind. Why? Because to *be in relationship* means to mirror the other. One is truly in relationship when one mirrors the other (empathy) rather than projecting onseself onto and into the other. When one mirrors oneself *to oneself* or off of the other, it is said that one is narcissistic. The critical difference is that in the former, one sees what is (the other); in the latter, one sees what one wants (or does not want) to see *as* the other, thus obscuring the reality of the other, preempting the possibility of the apprehension of the transcendental object and consequently the sublime . One is now a sign of the sign of oneself. In such a state, it is *impossible* to apprehend the transcendental object in the other and in objects. Therefore, Cain's unilateral mirroring of his own jealousy – which in modern psychological jargon is called projection, or a character disorder – *prevents* Abel from mirroring Cain. When the other fails to mirror us, we are thrown back upon ourselves in isolation. We feel the pressure of this solipsistic mode even though it is not our doing as a psychological mechanism. Those sensitive to this feeling know when they are in the presence of a self-obsessed person. Such persons are aware, perhaps even in a malignant way, but are not conscious in the sense we have been discussing here. They are psychic vampires, living off the psychic energy of others to compensate for their own *lack*. Therefore, their behavior cannot be trusted, and their professed emotions can border on the psychotic. The tragedy is that in the land of gadgets and gizmos reinforcing the ethical aesthetic of comfort, convenience, expediency, as well as the promise of medical immortality for the ego and all of its untreated pathology, *the narcissistic mode is the norm*. It is the psychological foundation off the Cult of Mediocrity, with its weaponized forms of science, government, and mass media. Those who do not abdicate to this cult are, ironically, regarded with the same suspicion that they themselves regard the abdicated other.

Therefore, Cain *imagines* (projects) that God favors Abel, when in fact Abel merely takes the burnt offering to God seriously, sacrificing his best lamb, while Cain tries to get out of offering anything of value and so burns some chaff. He does not see the cause-and-effect of this behavior in his relationship to God. Cain's *imagined* relationship to God is one of doubt of God's omnipotence. Abel's is one of fear of and respect for God's wishes because to him God is *real* not symbolic. Herein lies the difference between the subject who dwells in the Imaginary and the one who dwells in the Real. The one who dwells in the real has need of God, since bare life has acquainted him with suffering and death as it did to Buddha Gautama. The prince in the pleasure garden has no need of God, whom he sees as merely symbolic, for he shall live forever first here and then in the glorified Afterlife.

The argument that God is only imaginary (Dawkins, Hitchens) troubles the matter needlessly with the old conundrum of faith versus reason, as if one could be without the other. Cain soon finds out, within the context of what he and his people believe, that his lack of metaphysical faith is actually a lack of faith in *reality*. He imagines that if there is any consequence of killing it will be of benefit to him in that it will please God. Such logic is madness. He learns that in no way is it beneficial; he discovers that he was *wrong* about his delusion regarding the reality of God's will. Cain's criminal defense lawyer would argue that his client did not possess the *collateral acquaintance* with killing necessary to prevent him from carrying it out. He would further argue that it is God's fault that Cain was ignorant of an unwritten law, *non est factum*. After all, the nomos of the Decalogue had not yet been propagated in its final form on Mt. Sinai. Therefore, God's punishment is based on an as-yet-unwritten law of "Thou shalt not kill (murder)," thereby exonerating Cain. The prosecution, however, would argue that both Cain and Abel were aware of sin, which surely includes murder. As early as Genesis 4:7 God says, "If thou doest well, shalt thou not be accepted? and if thou doest not well, sin lieth at the door. And unto thee shall be his desire, and thou shalt rule over him." Therefore, the prosecution argues, Cain was aware of sin and, by natural extension, murder. Murder is a sin. Therefore Cain was aware that killing is wrong in the eyes of God and man and shell be punished one way or another. God shows considerable mercy, however, acknowledging the *non est factum* nature of Cain's crime and perhaps his temporary insanity.

However, we must not be satisfied with the superimposition *our* logical understanding of man's relationship to the concept of God upon Cain and the people of his time, as I do above. It could be argued that the brothers had a kind of communion with God that we simply cannot understand, except the few of us who *do*. In *The Origin of Consciousness in the Breakdown of the Bicameral Mind*, Julian Jaynes describes the mind of the Ancients as having two conceptual and perceptual camerae. It is worth mentioning again here in this context. While for the Ancients both camerae were perceived within a *unified field* of reality, each was tuned to a different manifestation, or immanation, of it. The world of spirits and gods was perceived as real and even corporeal, while the other of the practical day-to-day conduct of life, or everydayness (*Alltäglichkeit*), which could be verified, did not possess a superior status and was just as spiritual. The remnant of this natural orientation we find living in the much-maligned (by Scientism) professions of psychics and clairvoyants.

Therefore, just as bicameral vision combines what are essentially two different images into one to create the perception of depth, the camerae of the ancient mind created one perception of reality which *included* the reality of spirits and gods without the sense of conflict between them (thanks to Scientism) we have today. Apophantic unity of the ancients conflicts with what Jaynes refers to as the subsequent "breakdown" of the camerae into a schism caused by imposiong a categorial ratio between them through reason, first by empiricism then logical positivism. Peirce recognizes this problem. In the same letter to Lady Welby mentioned above he says,

> One is often in a situation in which one is obliged to assume, i.e., go upon, a proposition which one ought to recognize as extremely doubtful. But in order to conduct oneself with vigorous consistency one must dismiss doubts on the matter from consideration. There is a vast difference between that and any holding of the proposition for certain. To hold a proposition to be certain is to puff oneself up with the vanity of perfect knowledge. It leaves no room for Faith. (p. 400)

In other words, the task of proving God does not exist is equal to the task of proving God exists using the tools positivism, a problem Popper later takes up with the principle of falsifiability. There is a category of phenomena which "passeth understanding" (Philippians 4:7) but can still nevertheless be categorized and is therefore categorical. The irony is that it is bantered around on the lips of the *kafir*, the unbeliever, as if it were as true (verified) as the temperature at which water freezes. Consequently, other metaphysical concepts follow as mere abstractions to be debunked: love, freedom, happiness, sadness, integrity, peace, loyalty, luxury, and with them all the absolute reality of death, which is abstract to the denizen of the amnion who has been promised medical immortality if he can pay his bills. Philippians says that it is "peace" which passeth understanding.

Yet the greater part of nearly every nation's treasure is thrown at this word in the form of armies and armaments as if it had the verifiable substance of the molecular structure of carbon.

The error of a person who answers the question about believing or not believing in God is that he supposes it is a proper question, with both parties knowing precisely what each other means. What is really being asked in such a situation is: "Do you affirm that *my* conception of God is also precisely *your* conception?" How can we know if it is? Whether we answer in the affirmative or the negative about believing in God, even if we have some sectarian approximation of this concept that we supposedly share, the best we can hope for is testament that we are or are not of like mind in this sense. If this were not the case, there would not be such murderous strife between Shia and Sunni Muslims over related issues, and those who did not share the same *name* of God would not accuse each other of blasphemy. There would be no need for the Tetragrammaton, or unpronounceable name of God in Hebrew orthodoxy. But we do not have to go *that* far to find insurmountable schisms. For example, is a Lutheran's concept of the church of God the same as a Catholic's? Martin Luther did not think so. It would only be possible to know what another experiences and perceives if we were that other person, which is absurd. What makes us ourselves is that we are experiencing our own perception of the perception of others, the world, and the interpretation of concepts and words, which is all we can ever do, being who we are and not being, by definition, someone else. Therefore, to say yes or no is nonsense, even a lie. And a lie is a sin. Apart from what is verifiable, we cannot hope to know if any of our conceptions are shared with others any more than we can see the world through another's eyes. We cannot even see our own eyes, except as a reflection where the original photons have been swapped with those of the reflecting surface, or in an image, which is no different, really, than a written description ontologically. Verifiability is indeed the only possibility where we can affirm, precisely, unequivocally, that A = A, but such forensics cannot, by definition, result in anything good when applied to metaphysical subjects. That does not invalidate them. But it does *obviate the proof of them*, throwing us back upon other forms of epistemology, such as intuition and faith. It need not be the *belief* asked for in the invalid God question. We base good jurisprudence upon this principle: he killed in cold blood in front of twenty police officers, on camera, with a signed confession and his DNA and fingerprints on the victim's throat. But the quantity of what in our experience can be verified in this way is scarce, even in the courtroom, which is why there is a courtroom.

Therefore, we must come to terms with what it means to believe something is or is not true. Is not believing just a form of knowing with an element of doubt thrown in? To solve this problem in a practical, civilized way we employ the intermediaries of the arts and religious ritual, for instance, to help convey a concept which brings together the Imaginary, the Symbolic, and the Real into the *tertium quid of action*, a third thing we can all point to and say, *That* is my conception in performance. At the same time, we now have a conception shared in the only way possible. Perhaps dance does it best, as those dancing together are indeed involved in an empirically sound activity as the *tertium quid* (the dancer is the dance). While the positivist may say, "I do not 'believe.' I either know or do not know," he may not be taking into consideration what the realm of *what we do not know* consists of by default and negation. Surely God is part of that incognizable realm. Or is God something like a chair, or an award, or a sunset? Is it not more likely what we do not know is infinitely greater than what we do know, meaning that we know nothing for sure? Where would you put your money, if you had to bet it all? Only a fool would say that it is the reverse, even if he cannot accept the proposition. Certainly, we cannot prove it one way or the other. It is not a quantifiable proposition. Even before Christianity, to puff oneself up with the vanity of omniscience was known as *hubris*. But as the quaint ideas of antiquity give way to advertising, TV, appliances, gadgets, gizmos, Big Data, and digital information, the caveat of hubris is forgotten. In its place is the smug idea that all of the universe's mysteries have been solved in the last two hundred years by scientists. But what is a scientist, for that matter? Is what we know today as a scientist precisely the same thing as what Archimedes, Da Vinci, or Galileo knew as a scientist? Even Descartes, a true modern, seems quaint, almost Medieval, contrasted with today's entrepreneur-celebrity-engineer-scientist-CEO.

Who has the arrogance to say that X, not Y, is reality? Consider the statement, The boss hates me. How may this be verified? Even if he sacks you, which you point to as proof, there is the (what your ego considers to be) remote possibility that you are incompetent, or redundant. Who is to challenge millennia of observation, thought, analysis, experience, experiment, art, literature, mathematics, intuition, speculation, and reason regarding the most fundamental concepts about the nature of reality by the most brilliant minds with which humanity has been graced, allowing for the impossibility of consensus as a valid proof of concept? How could the collective intelligence of millions of obscure men and women who believed in something fundamental about their place in the universe now be considered stupid and ridiculous? Which is more idiotic, to believe in what human beings have held as reality for millennia, or to cast it away overnight as delusion because someone saw a news report about it yesterday saying it is not so? The Cult of Scientism has no problem declaring that something is false if it threatens its hegemony, particularly in matters of metaphysics. As the New Religion on the Block, Scientism must bully every other religion into oblivion and doubt through press releases and, in the case of totalitarian governments such as China, fiat.

It could even be arrogance to single out the Imaginary as not true or delusional or the antithesis of the Real. The Imaginary as it is described and used in this essay is indeed real in the fundamental sense of this word. While it can blow away in a puff of smoke, so too can everything else in the world and the universe for that matter. This essay is about its effect upon the subject and its society. This effect has every bit of force as that of bare life on the individual. It is probably more accurate to say that there are those who consider the Imaginary to be the Real, and those who consider the Real to be Imaginary. Often they are one and the same person. And they account for the mass of humanity. The constellation of the Imaginary, Symbolic, and the Real cannot be torn asunder. Dreams, art, music, inventions, discoveries, literature, mathematics and most of all language and thought are impossible without the presence of all three in the processes of doubt and inquiry. It is not even accurate to imply that they can be separated. They are simply the Orders of the psyche in its relationship with the Word of the world. But as we have discussed, one or the other can be coerced into becoming an *installation*, an *apparatus*, to the detriment of the processes of doubt and inquiry. This, then, is the state the subject finds itself in the amnion of the Imaginary. Popper's challenge to positivism to prove that a proposition is *false* rather than true often brings verifiability to an *aporia* from which it cannot escape. Its minions will not accept the blatant fact (one hesitates to say reality) that sometimes one must dismiss doubts on the matter from consideration to maintain consistency in one's thoughts and actions. To dismiss doubts in this way one must be able to *doubt* doubt.

One who dwells in the imaginary has need of the contrivances of the hegemonic order as well as the gadgets, gizmos, and drugs of the amnion of the Imaginary which consume the social dimension of its existence. Through what Lacan calls the *insistence of the signifying chain* the subject leads itself along a concatenation of signs which only serve to bury it deeper in the catacomb of its hermetic narcissism. At the same time, and in an equal and opposite reaction, the signifying chain presents symptoms which are the extrinsic, eccentric expression of whatever the whole apparatus of the subject's resistance is formulated to forget. "That there are in the unconscious signifying chains which subsist as such, and which from their structure, act on the organism, influence what appears from the outside as a symptom, this is the whole basis of analytic experience" says Lacan (Seminar V, 21.05.58., p.7). By subjecting himself to transference, therapist tries to provide a mirror of these symptoms so that the subject might recognize itself as the Other does. Psychoanalytical *recognition* is an attempt to awaken the subject from itself reflection as a sign of itself. The subject becomes cognizant of itself as an automaton, which is the first step toward self-possession (sovereignty). What is interesting about this in terms of the ethical aesthetic of today is that people are more like robots than robots are like people. The quest for artificial intelligence is a reaction formation projected by the ego's own sense of its poverty and impotence. It is even more telling that it is always assumed that robots are (or will be) more powerful and intelligent than humans. Of course they will be! As reaction formations they represent the potency the subject has lost through its abdication and solipsism. The so-called singularity which will happen in the future where robots become conscious is, again, the subject's hapless projection of its lost consciousness. Trapped in a state of intermittent awareness (like a sea slug) it projects its idea of consciousness onto the machine in the form of the mimicry of intelligence. Never mind that the subject – as well as the wizards in the silicon towers of Scientism – have no certain idea what intelligence really is, considering the Dunning-Kruger Effect, much less consciousness. When pressed, the best they can come up with are standardized tests and magnetic resonance images (and so forth) of brain activity. Of course, all of this is extremely profound to the scientist. When challenged he backs into his corner of data and published papers. As a last recourse he will simply imply that he is *more intelligent* (conscious) than his critics. After all, he has the prestige, gadgetry, theorems, degrees, money, and patents to prove it! Reposing upon the seemingly solid ground of these inferences, the Fortunates look upon the Unfortunates and the far-off other as less intelligent and therefore *less conscious* and, consequently, disposable. In the ethical aesthetic of the hegemony and its corporate overlords this is yet another excuse to imprison and marginalize the domestic Unfortunates and exploit the far-off other by harvesting its sovereignty in the form of the production of cheap goods for the amnion in its manufactories overseas, free of labor and environmental laws and unions through regulatory arbitrage.

Ultimately, Lacan's (and Freud's) repetition automatism is self-determination as consciousness in an impotent state of unconscious automatism. The result is endless repetition of its the mythology of its traumas which have crystallized into symbols, usually a barn full of sacred cows. However, this lassitude in the face of reality does not preclude the subject from the benefits of therapy. In his spiritual weakness, Cain must turn to murder to carry out the obsessions of his emotional pathology. While this is a heinous act, it ends up acquainting him with all of the human qualities he lacked, such as conscience and remorse, and brings him closer to God and man, to which God ultimately attests. The therapist enables the subject to enact its trauma through symbolic expression without harming itself or others. It could even be said that had Cain gone through the regimen of psychoanalysis, Able would be alive today. He could have come to his realization about his relationship to the transcendental Other (in this case God and his brother) without the trauma of murder. Even the Bible is rather mysterious about his motives, which seems to indicate that they are deep-seated unconscious symbols of his rivalry *vis-à-vis* God with Able. His brother's almost fanatical devotion to God's will forces an inverse reaction in Cain in the form of the spiritual lassitude, or hubris, of putting the dictates of his own will in God's mouth, as it were. This too is a type of reaction formation which, taken to an extreme, we call rebellion. It allies Cain not with God but the Adversary, Satan, in a bond of evil. At least Cain did not take the coward's way out and say that Satan made him do it.

The actual murder, then, frees Cain from the tyranny of the Imaginary. He now sees the murder of his brother as symbolic of his own trauma of spiritual jealousy. Regardless of his greater awareness of the possibilities of his personality and the world - after all this is the first murder in history - Able nevertheless remains a *thing*. It is not until God ultimately intervenes directly with Cain in the form of casting him into exile that he begins to realize his unconsciousness, which is the first step toward consciousness or doubting his own motives and perception of his being. Thanks to Cain, we might say, a soldier does the same to avoid the trauma of realizing that he is killing another *just like himself*. The enemy has parents, family, friends, hopes, memories, pets, hobbies, a childhood, and dreams for a future that will now never come thanks to this patriot. The Other is simply turned into the enemy to accomplish the offensive objective. This type of objectification of the Other is not to be confused (obviously) with apprehension of the transcendental object. Quite the contrary. It is a systematic denaturing of the otherness of the other and the sacred thingness of things. Without this reduction mechanism war is impossible. But even in the prosecution of war, there is catharsis in the soldier as he becomes aware of death as something intimate and real and that he can cause, pushing him into the terror of the sublime. His experience as the prey of the enemy forces him into the present moment of bare life, or the animal world of predator and prey. It is only from the platform of the real that we can see the imaginary. Otherwise we are simply dramatizing the imaginary as repetition automatism of the real.

Cain has no feeling for the guilt and horror of his symbolic act which is only possible when the subject can perceive the object as the material equivalent of itself through *empathy*. He has a general sense of what death is in relation to life. "To convey the idea of causing death in general … a general sign would be requisite, that is a Symbol" says Peirce (p. 395).The idea of *causing* death abides in the "general" awareness of the social monad comprised of a mass of ideas commonly held. "For symbols are founded either upon habits … or upon conventions and agreements [monad of the nomos]" (p. 395). It is said that Napoleon defined history as "a set of lies agreed upon." History belongs to the symbolic not only because it is in the past, which does not exist, but also because it must be distilled into a mythical narrative reflecting the collective values, or prerogatives, of the *present* culture and its hegemony rather than the values of the battlefield in which it occurred. Bits and pieces of incomplete primary documents and random historical artifacts only fuel the process of the *mythologization* of the past. Through subjective selection and induction, they evade the imperative for forensic certainy that would pass muster in a courtroom but suffices in the fantasy world of academe and popular culture. Each successive epoch looks back on the history of the previous one with disdain for its errors and blatant biases. It then indulges in what it sees as much-needed revisionism based on the same data set, adding error to error, until we have scripture, dogma, mythology, and legend rather than factual history. It considers its own version of a place that does not exist (the past) as the orthodox one, only because it is its *own* version, not because it is verifiably more accurate than the version written by the defenseless dead – until the next epoch comes along and does the same thing and so on.

So what is real? Peirce says that law, the nomos, is real, meaning specifically the laws of nature (physics, mathematics), but also the Decalogue and civil and criminal codes inasmuch as they intersect with or reflect the laws of nature and of God. To the Positivist, the laws of God are the laws of man's fancy; to the Deist, the laws of nature are the laws of God; to the scientist, in Peirce's conception, the law is the law, provided it transcends the previous two distinctions, becoming a universal Index (as he calls it) of *conduct*. It is the basis for what he calls the Index of the real. It is an index because it is that which is wholly apart from the mind of man in as much as it has a life of its own transcending the will of any one individual. It is the *thingness* of things and the *otherness* of the Other. However, he distinguishes laws of nature (and those reflected in mathematics and science) from those canonized by civilization variously and over time. The former are absolute, while the latter are ephemeral, though real enough for their duration to mold and define reality. One nation's legal prohibitions are another nation's constitutional freedoms. One era's thou shalt nots are another era's thou shalts. Together, they form the Index, which is his version of Keats' all we ever know. The Index is, "A law of nature, which I insist, is a *reality* ..." [italics added] (p. 395). Again, the orders of the psyche and human experience which Peirce identifies as icon, sign, and law correspond to what Lacan describes as imaginary, symbolic, and real (again, from time to time here notated as *xyz*). It is easier to group the imaginary and symbolic together in Peirce's conception, though, as reality is the Index by which we determine what is and is not imaginary and symbolic. This is a mathematical view of the Real he calls the *ens rationis.* Peirce's conception of *ens rationis* is the truth of propositions (such as this one) either as affirmation of what is true or of what is false as a signifier of being. Such a concept is in contrast to the *ens reale*, or the being of things existing in nature as substance, man, or accident (such as illness). Here are two quite different ideas of what is real, though they do not contradict and are, therefore, apophantic. The first is the being of what is true or false; the second that of what is or is not a thing-in-the-world. Seen as such, this discrepancy is also analogous to Freud's idea of a Thing (*Ding*, imago, or Lacan's *Das Ding*), versus Thing-presentations (*Sache*). A Thing-presentation is the *referent* as distinguished from the signified and signifier. Only the referent may be caught up in what Peirce calls cognition in the form of analytical thinking as abduction or *retroduction*, Peirce's neologism. The signified cannot because it has being apart from man's cognition. The signifier is not the process of cognition (reason); rather, it is the sign which this process manipulates in its quest for what is true or false. Therefore, we can see that Peirce emphasizes the analytical whereas Lacan and Freud the *psycho*-analytical.

Peirce has some contempt for what civilization calls its laws, which he sees as being in opposition to the laws of nature. However, this opposition lies not in the *meaning* of those laws, or in the reality of that meaning (murder is a natural offense, for some do indeed coincide; rather, it is in the inescapable fact that the laws man makes are in the long run artificial and therefore belong to the synthetic, though they often intersect with natural law, whereas those of nature (such as we see in physics) are absolute and are therefore subject to analytical verification. I

While it may seem that *ens reale* would be better suited to the laws of nature, in fact it is *ens rationis* because the positive verification of the laws of nature as true or false lies in *reason* and not the empirical perception of things – as real as such perception may seem. Seeing is not believing to the blind man. St. Thomas (Aquinas) says that blindness belongs to the category of the *ens rationis*. To say that someone is blind is to assert that blindness is. Nevertheless, it is the absence, not the presence, of something that exists in the sense of the *ens reale*.

> [N]ot everything which is a being in the second sense [*ens rationis*] is a being also in the first sense [*ens reale*], for of a privation, such as blindness, we can form an affirmative proposition, by saying: "Blindness is"; but blindness is not *something in the nature of things*, but it is rather a removal of a being, and so even privations and negations are said to be beings in the second sense, but not in the first. (*Dinstinctio 34, Quaestio 1, Prooemium*)

To say that something is in the nature of things is not the same as saying that it is a law of nature. By nature here St. Thomas means the *thingness* of things – the referent – rather than the existence of things either as substance (signified) or sign (signifier). And what is the difference between a referent and the signified? The first is that which is the thingness of the thing to which we refer, such as *being* blind. But in the reality of the *ens reale*, blindness is the absence of the signified since it is an *affirmation of a negation*. Therefore we can say that there is a *sign* for blindness (the word), and a *referent* (the being of the negation of sight), but not the signified in the sense of *das Ding*. Nevertheless, in the most simple sense of the linguistics of the matter, blindness *is* the signified, or what we mean by blind where we use the word. It is not a frog or an onion. St. Thomas, however, is concerned with the *phenomenology* of what it is and is not. As signified, blindness is, but as referent blindness means.

Man's laws derive their power from fiat only because the

people will obey it. The laws of civilization (nomos), advertised as real, are in fact icons (imaginary), though they may intersect with the laws of God and nature. "Thus the *Icon* [imaginary, x] represents the sort of thing that may appear and sometimes does appear; the *Index* [real, z] points to the very thing or event that is met with – and I mean by an Occurrence such a single thing or state of things; and finally, the Symbol [y] represents that which may be observed under certain general conditions and is essentially general" (p. 396). The Occurrence is what Saussure would call the signified. Any signification belongs to the iconic and the signs it generates in accordance with the collective will of those who share a language. The Index, then, is always the Other. It is always the *Not-I*. The Index is never the vicissitudes of a shared language. The animal we call a *squirrel* in English, whether it is called *Eichhörchen, вбелка,* or *écureuil* in any other language, is still the same animal. Its squirrelness does not depend upon any name it is given or what it may symbolize (such as the animal spirit Mikew in the Wabanaki Native American culture); its Index transcends the semantic surface level which, as Chomsky and Saussure show, is trivial to that which is signified, das Ding an sich, and the signifier's ontological morphology. Furthermore, the real is the *container* of the sublime. It is a vessel for the sublime's horror vacui (or what the Strugatsky brothers in their novel *A Roadside Picnic* call a *full empty*). The real is the only environment in which the sublime can function without destroying all around it, as it is by nature anathema to the imaginary and symbolic if and only if they are used as its displacement. All humans, therefore, are cursed by what might be called the *creative imperative*: create, or live a death-in-life; make it real, or it remains unreal, impotent, false, evil. Unfortunately for the well-fed masses of the hegemonic order (not the Underclass and the far-off other), it is not possible *to create* without the personal sovereignty, or self-determination, they have tossed off like so much trash in favor of the trinkets of deceit. Creativity requires a *whom* who creates. Without sovereignty there is no whom, only an imposter formed of the clay of the meaningless bric-à-brac and chatter of the media, Internet, education system, and the prerogatives of the parasite classes of banking, finance, and government. For the not-so-well-fed, far-off other and the Underclass, though, reality is the constant misery of necessity. Their reward, if it can be called that, is dwelling ipso facto in the struggle of bare life. Their only contact with the Imaginary is as the conscripted suppliers of its accoutrements. Hermann Hesse's in *The Glass Bead Game (Magister Ludi)* describes how it is not so uncommon to find ourselves dwelling in the real and sublime when we are coerced by forces greater than ourselves that we can do nothing about.

> They are tremendously real, somewhat the way a violent physical pain or a surprising natural event, a storm or earthquake, seem to us charged with an entirely different sort of reality, presence, inexorability, from ordinary times and conditions. The gust of wind that precedes a thunderstorm, sending us into the house and almost wrenching the front door away from our hand – or a bad toothache which seems to concentrate all the tensions, sufferings, and conflicts of the world in our jaw – these are such realities. Later on we may start to question them or examine their significance, if that is our bent; but at the moment they happen *they admit no doubts and are brimful of reality*. [italics added] (p. 395)

Because reality admits no doubts, it is necessary to *doubt* doubt in order to engage the process of inquiry. But first we must open the door of doubt regarding what we have been told is reality. To do so, however, risks apostacy if we discover that what we were told is at variance with what we find to be so, the first discovery of which is this discovery itself. Then "we may start to question ... or examine" the significance of what Peirce calls an *Occurrence*. Doubting doubt is a creative process because it boostraps meaninglessness into meaning (which is the point of Dadaism, I would think). Furthermore, abdicating the abdication of one's sovereignty is also a *creative Occurrence*. It is not within the scope of this essay to define creativity, which would be an exhaustive expedition, and definitions abound. But we can say that without a void that needs filling (the horror vacui) there is no creativity. It is inductive not deductive, while the scientific process is inductive before it is deductive. The horror vacui is that which is filled with one's artistic imagination originating in an intuition of the sublime. The blank canvass. The block of marble. The blank page of sheet music. The empty page or screen. The new sketchbook. The sublime is a vacuum, a negative force, gaping in opposition to all that will not submit to it. It is hungry black hole deep in mental space. It demands negation of all negations for anything to *be*. What man feels as his *positive* role in the world as the namer, definer, metrician, and knower is in fact a *denial* of the mystery of the sublime. However, it must be done. We need to know how to make fire and grow crops. A knowledge of medicine that works is good to have. But the idea that man knows all the answers because he is man, homo sapiens

sapiens, is more of a form of hubris than any sort of epistemology. It is a result of a collective Dunning-Kruger Effect, or that what is known is all there is to know — the opposite of Socrates' *all I know is that I know nothing*. Science (a word that is supposed to mean knowing, without the mystique of it) has solved every problem and has provided every comfort and convenience to the citizen of the Amniotic Empire. The wisdom of the past - even fifty years ago let along millennia ago - is outdated like a carton of milk too long in the refrigerator and must be poured out into the drain. Everything in the subject's culture has an expiry date. No sooner has the Apex Consumer mastered a newfangled gadget than the vendor says it is outdated, flashing the new generation of it that the subject cannot resist, having been conditioned to salivate upon the rollout (as they call it) of such stimuli. The subject fears the scorn of its fellow consumers who it is trying to impress with its modernity and sophistication. Though he has no idea how the gadget works, which is usually pretty simple, he nevertheless believes that ownership talismanically transmits the knowledge of the techno-priesthood to his little mind, saving him a few clicks on that gadget itself to get the actual information from the Internet. Inside the black box is the Big Magic science provides through its cryptic incantations and wizardry. What science does not provide now is guaranteed to be provided "in the future." The subject's relentless desire for *l'objet petit a* keeps it hungry for more and more of whatever it needs to feel *real*. However, this desire is never satisfied because what the subject imagines as itself is not real in the sense of bare life being real. Its only notional reality is within the *installation* of the Imaginary's apparatus - not in the dynamic constellation of *xyz*.

It is true that the Imaginary has real effects on those who have been forced into or have chosen an existence of bare life. This effect is *exploitation*, which is an extension of the ethical aesthetic of expediency. It is *expedient* to transit the sovereignty of the far-off other to the subject's vampiric need for vicarious production in the form of cheap goods. These goods would be considerably more expensive if they were made by those with rights, medicine, clean water, food, job security, legal protection, unions, and at least some self-respect and self-determination. The hegemony exports exploitation and imports sovereignty. The imported sovereignty is then sold at malls, shopping centers, department stores, and online. Since the subject has abdicated its sovereignty, it must therefore feed, like a bloodthirsty vampire, upon this imported sovereignty ripped from the far-off other by mortal imperative and translated into the codes of the subject's default culture of consumerism, such as brand names and everyday uses of exotic products everyone and anyone could live without. Rampant consumerism in the ritual of exploitation is a symptom of the death of the sublime.

The far-off other begs to differ regarding the miracles of science. The far-off other would like clean water, food, medicine, and all the needless luxuries it imagines these gods of the First World enjoy as their birthright because they are superior creatures to the proles they exploit. The far-off other sees images of the subject wallowing in what looks like the unspeakable luxury of being able to turn on a tap and get fresh water, flush a toilet, switch on a light, or go to the supermarket and buy food. Meantime, the subject gets glimpses of the far-off other who makes his consumer goods suffering in misery it has clearly brought upon itself for being stupid. From time to time the Apex Consumer feels guity about this, only because fate has made it so, paying some NGO to do the dirty work of tossing the exploited a bone or two while loaning money to the warlords who enforce the robotic production the Apex Consumer craves above all else. Because the far-off other is seen to be ugly, dirty, uneducated, different, usually brown, and comes from an atavistic culture, the subject imagines that the far-off other has brought upon itself its miserable fate as the accursed of the god of Scientism. To ritually assuage any intellectual guilt, the subject indulges in various kinds of charity by donating to organizations purporting to help the swarthy far-off other by introducing it to highly technical methods of organic farming that even the Apex Consumer's nation cannot afford to use. Meantime, these NGO's see to it that the pesticides and genetically modified, disease-resistant, high-yield, patented agricultural products the Apex Consumer's own country uses to keep fat cannot used by the subsistence farmers of impoverished nations. They must instead subject their crops to disease, insects, drought, and depleted soil and seed stocks, so that the Apex Consumer does not feel that it is contributing to the destruction of the environment it is the most responsible for destroying.

The citizen in the amnion is told by its overlords that the high taxes it pays – which seem to vanish mysteriously into the drain of the international finance industry – somehow or other benefits these wretched creatures, though there is no proof of it. The subject feels it has done its part by paying the taxes in the first place, which are a kind of indulgence for the exoneration of its sins. Though the taxes have been seized from its income under the penalty of imprisonment, it nevertheless feels like it has somehow made a voluntary donation to help the far-off other and The Planet, just as the peasant of the European Middle

Ages felt washed of his sins by paying the church tithe. The subject also feels that by purchasing consumer goods made by the far-off other, it is helping that wretch buy the same goods for himself. When the Apex Consumer buys goods made in Third-World Hellhole X, he feels all warm inside and pleased with himself because he imagines that some of what he paid goes to make the life of the wretch who made the product more like his own glorified existence. Naive persons who imagine that they can export democracy (whatever it may be) to what they see as *undemocratic* nations by expatriating their own nation's means of production to those countries have been the biggest useless (not useful) idiots of them all. Part of the problem is that the subject's typically best definition of democracy is that there is the ritual of voting for leaders great and small. The subject fails to realize that nearly *every* nation, with any kind of government, has some form of voting, and that arguably the most vigorous exercises in popular voting in modern history were in Nazi Germany. As a ritual, popular voting allows the Apex Consumer off the hook for being responsible in any more direct way for the *conduct* (in Peirce's sense of the word) of his polity, state, and economy. Without the need to storm the castle with pitchforks and torches to get political results in the here and now, the subject is free to get into more debt and *consume*. Unfortunately, in the case of the matter of the far-off other's political freedom, the flaws in such a system lead to unimaginable cruelty and oppression. Inevitably, the Apex Consumer is goaded into a vague proxy war against what is advertised as the far-off other's domestic oppressor Dictator X. In this fairy tale, the dictator (who usually was elected), and his dastardly comic-book minions, typically uses what is nominated as poisonous gas (or even more abstract, weapons of mass destruction) to kill upstart ethnic enclaves of babushka-covered peasants running with babies and chickens in their arms. The far-off other is never consulted as to whether *he* thinks the Apex Consumer's beneficent and altruistic military-industrial apparatus might be seen as the actual oppressor, especially since the regime vilified by the international mass media often enough was the one installed by the consumer's own duly-elected regime. These campaigns cost borrowed treasure and destroy the fragile economic and environmental systems of the far-off other's impoverished homeland, forcing him to become a refugee in *other* lands where he is unwanted, shunned, abused, and reviled. While many of the innocent far-off others are also slaughtered in the melee, it is for their own good, thinks the denizen of the Amniotic Empire. It is necessary, he thinks, so that his benign and altruistic (read: progressive and liberal) hegemony can kill the bad guy and bring debt and consumerism to the far-off other's nation, even if the citizens of that nation have long since been killed or have fled in the resulting death, destruction, and chaos. Such an approach resembles in some significant detail that of the European colonial powers of the 18th and 19th centuries it was supposed to have corrected. Ignorant of even *recent* history, though, the subject has one less thing to worry about or to compare to its present circumstances which it simultaneously believes is all wrong and should be changed, and is perfectly ideal and should be maintained at any cost.

2.4: Consciousness, knowing, and the knowing-of

The order of the Imaginary is impossible without confusing the getting-to-know with the knowing-of, since the former would immediately lead to knowledge of the Imaginary, thus dispelling its illusion of reality. The knowing-of belongs on the side of Plato's Divided Line of the low and lowest forms of knowing: *Pistis* (πίστις) and *Eikasia* (εἰκασία), or belief and imagination. There are three epistemological possibilities: belief, knowing, and not knowing. When the subject cannot tell the difference between knowing and not knowing, the only form of knowledge left is belief. As mentioned earlier, belief is knowing mixed with doubt. "I believe that I have a virus," says the person with fever, not having gone through a polymerase chain reaction assay which might confirm his hunch. Although we tend to think of believers as those who have no doubt about what they believe, even a cursory look at how their beliefs are maintained shows that they require constant reinforcement from others who believe the same thing or they fall into apostacy. Without it, these beliefs unravel once they come into contact with the wicked world of the real. While Peirce's *collateral acquaintance* may form the context within which the real may be perceived and knowledge acquired, without it the subject is left with no Index by which to gauge what is and is not real. Without that faculty, it is impossible to know. It is only possible to know-of and to know-more, but the getting-to-know has been preempted by forsaking the Index of bare life for the amnion of the Imaginary.

Nevertheless, this mode suits the hegemony's agenda of control through debt and consumerism in the amnion of the Imaginary. The floundering subject reaches out for the nearest straw which of course the Imaginary offers in the form of an orgy of conspicuous consumption, endless distraction, promissory notes, and perpetual *Genuss*. Compelled by their masters, the media transmit the discourse of consumerism through various channels that inevitably reaches the subject and its progeny who are obsessed with life as represented by media products over the tedious, unmediated productions of the natural universe. Part of the message is that the subject must trust the banking system, education, science, corporations, and government to serve, protect, provide for, and shepherd their flock. For the Imaginary to survive, though, the quantity of information must be valued by the subject over the quality of it. This over-valuing becomes the ethical aesthetic of the pursuit of happiness as the quantitative *largess* of the Imaginary. The social order, itself the product of the Imaginary, must value quantity over quality by declaring the quantification of *more* as the official highest good (*ex summum bonum beatitudinem*). It evangelizes its doctrine through enervating electronica feeding cognition and memory with the *bric-à-brac* of information's spiritual and intellectual wasteland. But not in the form of the kind of dogma we associate with old-school text-based religions full of thou shalt nots; rather, it is the use of the *device itself* that is the dogma, making its catechism far more subtle and neurological than if it were ideas that could be accepted or rejected. The discourse is that 1) The device is real, 2) The world is imaginary, 3) Ethos is symbolic. The device, after all, is a Universal Turing Machine (UTM), a computer, which has no specific purpose other than to be *re-purposed* at will. It is the perfect delivery vehicle for the ultimate opium of the masses. While the content of the gadget hardly changes from the old circus and Vaudeville acts it is based on, the costumes, sets, lighting, and music do. Though the real attraction is that one may interact with the circus as a clown (rather than a lion tamer). To make the lure of the gadget's world more real and compelling than reality itself (which is usually quite boring), the Vaudeville shtick must be gussied up to look brand new with each iteration of UTM's capacity to deliver content. The subject, bereft of analytic cognitive ability which has long since atrophied, simply accepts this prestidigitation with the bedazzled credulity of a fool. But what spews out of the gizmo is more than just junk food for the mind, body, and spirit. The ethical aesthetic it transmits as memes takes hold in the empty interstices of the subject's indolent and unguarded mind, embedding itself like malware. There is nothing particularly complicated about this message. If it were, it would not fit neatly into the rudimentary container it seeks to fill. The simplicity of the content lies in its reduction of the world to binaries: this political party is good, that political party is bad; this ethnicity oppresses, that one is oppressed; heat is bad, airconditioning is good; bicycles are bad, cars are good; and so on. The introduction of a tertium-quid possibility casts the subject into a seizure of fatal dithering. The *techne* of the gadget and the simplistic nature of the content it delivers sever the unity of ideas necessary for creativity and epiphany. It is as Hobbes describes: when the utterance is interrupted, the mind is always left with a question of where it was going at the time, like a dementia patient lost in a labyrinth. Seeking any port in a storm, the subject quickly adopts a sports team as my team and roots for it, even though the team may be comprised of multi-millionaires usually not from any turf, or even nation, the subject might identify with. It becomes unaccountably depressed when its team loses and jubilant when it wins because this is the price it must pay for such an illusion of belonging sand identity. It chatters about what it sees as the subtleties and nuances of the management of the players on and off the field, as if it had any say in the matter regarding the conduct what it considers to be its own property but is in fact owned by investors and advertisers. It identifies itself as belonging to the team, going so far as wearing the jersey of a certain player it admires which includes the player's name. In so doing the subject adopts the persona of a character it has never met, just as the warriors of certain tribes eat the brains of their most worthy adversaries to gain their power. It enjoys the vicarious notion that it is somehow empowered by this association. Outside of sports, the subject has nothing to say. The space in its memory reserved for topics of free-ranging conversation have long ago been filled with the corporate bric-à-brac it considers the only knowledge worth knowing: the names of the players and their season and historic stats. Sports is of course not the only example. But it is a good one. Contrast the lethargy of consuming a media sport to the energy of playing one — the last thing even the sport enthusiast would ever dare to do past the age of twelve. There is hardly anything more thrilling and engaging than working with one's team mates to beat the other team on the pitch. In victory or defeat the game was well played and is the stuff of personal legend, truly lived. The loss or win is entirely the team's own doing and luck. They have thrown their bodies into the fray. They have tasted something of the real, and the real has tasted of them. But obese TV sport couch potatoes cannot ever hope to do this. If they tried, they would end up in the weekend warrior ward of the local emergency room. Perhaps they *did* have this bare-life impulse when they were children or teenagers. It soon becomes impossible to express it, though, when the *imago* takes over from the *ens reale* of action-in-the-world. However, this makes the subject the perfect consumer not only of the beer and junk food it ritually swills while engaged in this bread-and-circus, but also its tacit absorption of endless, intrusive, commercial propositions more clever than the subject can hope to analyze for truth value.

Each new state of convenience brought on by developmental technology turns the previous state of technology into an inconvenience. It does not matter that the previous state had turned the previous state before *it* into an inconvenience too. Therefore, the new state of convenience which has made the previously new state of convenience inconvenient is already inconvenient before it has had a chance to be convenient because it is *absolutely inevitable* that it too will become inconvenient when the next state of convenience emerges, which it most certainly will if product developers and marketers are doing their jobs. This algorithm escapes the subject's inert cognition. The subject does not realize that if the *previous* gadget was made obsolete by the new gadget, and that the *next* gadget will - absolutely and inevitably - make the *current* gadget obsolete, then the current gadget, despite its priority as the gadget that replaced the previous gadget, is, *ipso facto*, obsolete at the moment that it replaces the former obsolete gadget. Therefore, all gadgets are obsolete at all times. The only possible winning strategy in this game is to hold on to a worthy gadget for as long as possible, learn how to fix it, and learn how to resist the urge to buy the next big thing. But social pressure prevents it; who wants to be seen with a generation-2 phone when all one's friends have generation-4 phones? Surely this is the mark of poverty and stupidity. Furthermore, at no point in this shell game does the subject ever really own its gadget, anyway. It *leases* it, just as it is leases its car, home, education, drinks, dinners, vacations, and furnishings from the banks holding the promissory notes and leases it signed. The vendor's rationale to the subject for this rat trap is that if the subject pays a monthly fee for the gadget, it can get a new gadget to replace the old gadget on a schedule designed to prevent the subject from being embarrassed by an obsolete gadget. Never mind that this schedule is preordained by the vendor's actuaries and accountants to maintain the share price of its common stock, else the algorithmic trading mechanisms will *sell sell sell*, devaluing the shares in the sell-off as they flood the glutted marketplace.

Such algorithms are a stochastic process; in other words, they are predictably unpredictable, which is the hegemony's only concession to reality — that it still contains an element of chance. The present state of convenience is determined by the previous state of convenience but upon no other state of convenience (e.g. the state before the previous state, or predictions about the future, and so on). For example, let us take events the probability of which is seldom interpreted with any depth by the subject: being fired or accidentally killing someone. In both cases we can simplify things by proposing two possible previous states for each. In the first, one did something wrong or was simply displaced for a reason which had little to do with the one's activity at work (e.g. redundancy). In the second one, the subject has killed another through negligence or accident (wrongful death or manslaughter). The first state for both involves blame or direct action by the subject and is therefore deterministic. The second is random, or involves chance (even in negligence), which does not mean that there was no previous state before that which caused the present state. What fortune teller even knew the exact details of his or her death? Even if a novelist knows how the plot wraps up, he does not know precisely how many pages this will take, what the dialogue will be leading up to it, and what feeling he and most of all the reader will have when it is done. When the reader starts the novel but is ignorant of the conclusion even after reading considerably into the work, the ending is still difficult to predict, which is part of the charm of a it. Much of literature prides itself on this fact, though there are genres of fiction which lend themselves to a greater level of predictability *by design* through clues along the way planted as hints in a guessing game. Reality, however, leaves us no clues about its trajectory, as it has not been written. Its stubborn opacity is not due to the fact that we mortals lack the clairvoyance to see it but because the future is not there to be seen. It never is, because now is always the present. There is no other time in which what happens now also occurs (except in Hollywood movies), since what happens now only happens now because now is now; it is not in some alternate universe of experience (quantum superimposition nothwithstanding) where there is more than one *now*, just as there cannot be *reality* if there is more than one (*realities*? ... how ludicrous!), virtual included, which is more accurately termed artificial reality, or the *imitatio*. The future has no "being there" (Dasein) because for Dasein to be Dasein there must be only one Dasein which is only possible in an eternal present. Imagine trying to convince Heidegger that there is more than one Dasein, though it may change its empirical morphology depending upon our line of inquiry.

This is the simple algorithm of existence. Nevertheless, it is a stochastic process. Why? In both the deterministic and random states, which have to do with the "cause" of the event, the present depends upon the previous "present" and no other state. We could notate this by (p) or past progressive, and P', or present progressive. In the past progressive the action *is taking place* at a time in the past. It is important to remember that the past is not an actual state but an allusion to artifacts of the *past* present state (for instance a written document). The present progressive (P′) is taking place. Being-in-the-world (*In-der-welt-sein*) belongs to this state. As such the present perfect state is determined by Dasein - the *being there* which makes it categorical. If the present is categorical Dasein, could any other state (past, future, the afterlife) be real in the way that the present progressive is (or is not)? What makes the present categorical is that it is the only real state. If there is only one real state, then there is no other state. If there is only one state, then *anything* can happen in that state. There is no other state in which something *can* happen because no other state contains the potential of Dasein. If what one predicted would happen does happen, one's sense that the future is certain (X [now] → Y [the future *now*]) is reinforced, particularly because this reflex supports wishful thinking, which is the culprit behind the whole imaginary apparatus. We *wish* we would not die – the most impotent wish of all, and the most selfish – ergo, the Imaginary. If something unexpected happens defying all seeming probability (plane crash, earthquake) the subject gets uneasy, confused, and afraid because its wishful illusion of absolute predictability is belied. Soon, though, another miracle of predication ignites its wishful thinking, and its moves on and on into the imaginary future with its dreams of wealth, love, excitement, accomplishment, honors, power, and, ultimately, an life, physical or metaphysical, of eternal persistence of the ego with all of its neuroses and selfishness.

The present progressive is what Heidegger calls authentic while past and future are inauthentic. Regardless, they remain phenomena of the present as 1) the artifacts of the past (p) and the cause of the present as an effect (P′), and 2) as the future probability of the next present which we could notate as P″. The subject is encapsulated in what Husserl calls *Lebenswelt* or the life-world beyond the edges of which there is no world and no life. Therefore, the past and present are the wastelands of *non-being* in the forms of never having existed (not born) and death. They are the *terra incognita* and are therefore what Peirce calls incognizable. But, they are values in the present. They are absolutely necessary to define the present as the present. But that is their only function besides certain practical functions such as being able to produce and store written documents (i.e. data) and to design *that which will be built*. A blueprint, however, is not a cathedral. The present progressive therefore stands alone in time, an event in the Lebenswelt of its categorical Dasein. Being fired from a job or accidentally killing someone comes as a surprise to the subject; deterministic or random, it is an event existing in time only where the only time is now, therefore any glimpse into the future is at best a matter of statistical probability. We can argue against this proposition by saying that (p → P′)→ (P′ → P′′), in other words, *if* if the past then the present, then if the present then the future. What Lacan calls the *insistence of the signifying chain* here forces the psychological outcome, which is always at variance with reality which defies psychology as it is objective and psychology is subjective — even Adler's objective psychology is subjective.

The trauma of birth is the trauma of death. Being born sentences one to die. Death is payment for life. He who refuses to pay the vig, will be subject to collection proceedings of the harshest sort. Somehow, the embryonic self senses this in the first moment of self-awareness. The relationship of being and time is predicated on the same principle as that between time and space: one cannot be separated from the other. They are the same concept seen different ways. This type of *Gedanken* is extremely frustrating to the mind, which is used to signifiers representing only one thing as a distinct entity. To be cognizant of two concepts at once and yet have them remain different takes a form of thinking often only mathematics can sort out on paper, giving us a glimpse of reality's simultaneity united in one mortal container of Dasein. Once this paradox is grasped, it is not so difficult to also grasp that were it not for time we could not move around in space and vice versa. So what, then, is the difference between the two except semantics? In the case of being and time, however, the problem is more complicated, as Heidegger shows. Existence extends, through being, along the arrow of time and over the horizon of death into the incognizable. To simplify it for our purpose here, though, we can say that time *shapes* our being. That one person is a child and another an adult shows us that time has shaped the ontology of each, which then includes death over time. The first way it does this is in the form of the stochastic process of the present, which is predicably unpredictable. But the most important way is that it allows the ego to interpret itself as finite, though it resists this interpretation through repression of the idea. Herein lies the psyche's perpetual death trauma. Its autonomic behavior grows from this trauma into the inauthentic *Lebenswelt* as the abdicated subject. Time becomes the culprit that makes life itself suspect. "What kind of existence is this if 'I' must come to an end!" the ego cries like a baby. In Lacan's signifying chain the inauthentic becomes the amnion of the Imaginary as an extension of the subject's autonomic behavior motivated by the symbol of itself. In other words, the amnion of the Imaginary takes the place of the psychotherapist. Rather than help the subject (analysand) inch its way to the light of reality through the clinical expression of its speculation, the Imaginary (analyst) creates a symbolic dream world in which *Lebenswelt* is reproduced as a commercial proposition. Problem solved! All of life becomes transactional, making it unreal, a mere product, and therefore not subject to such filthy categories as mortal and immortal (though we still say, "My phone died"). In this complex, the subject seizes upon "the future" as its raison d'etre, not the present, which is just a nuisance. While *le flâneur,* the disinterested observer of life, saunters through the present, the subject scurries from the regretful or nostalgic artifacts of the past into the egoic wishes for the future. It sees what is between (the present reality, or authentic *Lebenswelt*) as at best a means to an end and at worst an annoying obstacle in its steeple chase to what will be. If this were not so, spouses would not murder each other for insurance money. One of the most pernicious exploiters of this compulsion is higher education which predicates itself upon the promise of a "brighter future" which never really comes because there is always one more sunrise over that horizon that will be brighter for some other reason (more degrees?). When it fails to produce this miracle, education falls back on the defense that the future *would have been* much darker without its social imprimatur – which of course cannot be proven which is why it cannot be disproven.

What we have, then, is a grammar rising out of the syntax of the relationship of the primary forces of the idea of the self with the objective structure of the psyche that is the same in each of us (barring pathology), or Chomsky's universal grammar. Just as we form a sentence out of nouns, verbs, adjectives, and so on we also form the narrative of our psyche from the constellation of the imaginary, symbolic: the focus of psychoanalysis. Where, then, is the *real* in all of this except in as much as we can say that this is what we *really* do? First, there is the reality of the complex of the imaginary and symbolic. Then, there is the reality of the analysand's neurosis which falls back upon the signifying chain of the imaginary and symbolic. When it does, it creates what Freud calls the compulsion to repeat. It must be compulsive to overcome the more natural impulses which inspire life to flourish stochastically, perhaps without any repetition where one conditional branch leads to another like in an acid trip or dream. The compulsive complex is morbid, meaning it is a kind of death-in-life where there is nothing but repetition until actual death comes along and breaks the cycle at last. Since death is the only event that will break this cycle, we long for it throughout life (the Freudian death wish), while fearing it as the end of that which in us can fear anything at all: the ego. The bare life of war, however, is an event that breaks this cycle by the immediate presence of death. As one sees one's comrades fall, one is pitched into the biological imperative to kill or be killed. Such a state of unequivocal ethical aesthetic wenches life's trivialities into perspective as inconsequential compared to nonbeing.

In this way war is sublime. It also brings into the present of bare life the thingness of things as they are systematically destroyed. There are few pleasures boys enjoy more than destroying things. Why? By killing and destroying we *own* what we kill and destroy, proving that *ego vincet omnia*. Despite the terror of war, our sublime exhilaration in at last throwing off the chains of civilization allows the id to delight in expressing itself freely with the least *anticathexis* from the superego's imposition of the extrinsic nomos. The imaginary and symbolic retreat into their foxhole as the Marines take the next hill of reality. In the contemplation of death and destruction the otherness of the other and the thingness of the thing are dragged (kicking and screaming) from the imaginary and symbolic realms of the past and the future into the bare life of the present. To suddenly exist in the present is always a shocking, though enlightening, experience. Those who dwell almost exclusively in the amnion of the Imaginary often only meet with reality in car crashes, robberies, bankruptcy, and fatal medical diagnoses. The amnion's substitutions for reality and appropriation of the symbolic get the subject to turn to gadgets, drugs, alcohol, junk food, and the conspicuous consumption of consumer culture for what it would have gotten from the psychotherapist. Consequently, nearly all of its pursuits, aspirations, and entertainment take on the logic and feeling tone of a lucid dream. The subject grows dependent upon the *narcotizing dysfunction effect* of this dream, loath to leave it for the cold bath of reality. Soon enough its internal dialogue begins to echo the external discourse until what were put asunder are again unified in an unconscious, and commercially exploitable, alliance.

When we think about anything at all what we are doing is using the imaginary, symbolic, and real simultaneously to process the abstract and concrete worlds as one holistic unit, as in a cold day. The day is concrete, but cold is a relative abstraction. The same is true of good person, and so on. To thought, though, the difference between the abstract and concrete is only a matter of degree. They are not separate categories, but rather ends of a spectrum of ontology. They repose in thought's compulsive narrative, which is: *I am*. The repository of I am is the ego sitting rather complacently upon the volcano of the id. The complications of this arrangement are what we have been talking about here. Born of this complex, the discourse of I am is entirely abstract. In fact, it does not exist in any sense other than as a notion of itself. Rather, it is an excrescence of the syntax of the signifying chain of the imaginary and symbolic. The psychoanalyst tries to get the analysand to open up the vault where this signifying chain lies so that both can begin to unlock and untangle it. The Imaginary uses it to chain the subject to debt and vicarious and prurient titillation of the id. Its relentless torrent of distraction from the reality of death, ironically through the constant portrayal of violent killing and brutality in its content, removes the subject from reality. The id becomes stupefied by this invasion of its secret realm. Meantime, reports of its dirty desires are sucked up into Big Data through the telemetry of personal gadgets, point-of-sale devices, and the Internet to be used for social control, criminal forensics, and target marketing. We must remember, though, that the subject willingly, intentionally, purposefully, and with full awareness of the consequences I have just described jumped into this science-fiction nightmare head-first by abdicating. It was not tricked or forced. There is provision in society for those who will not abdicate and go this route; they are either lionized as special if they can be marketed as freaks, marginalized as eccentrics if they get away with it, or are incarcerated or drugged, to keep them out of trouble. Meantime, they write books, go on TV, protest, create websites, make videos, teach it from the university pulpit, becomes stars, commit murder, become terrorists, are ignored, or shout it from the rooftops. They do what they can do. Worst of all, one must live among the possessed while struggling to maintain possession of oneself. Both are time and money wasted for nothing except the necessity of keeping the hegemony at bay and the Imaginary to itself. But asking the subject snug in its paradise of *Genuss* to accept the horror vacui of the sublime over the amnion of the Imaginary is fruitless. One's love of comfort and convenience will not permit it. The sovereign subject knows that without the surrendering of one’s self-determination the Imaginary is powerless. But since the mass of its fellow subjects have done so it sees that the Imaginary takes on great power based on the treasure at its disposal and the control it has over the subject’s id. Sometimes it takes a catastrophic defeat to wake up. By the time Hitler reached his 56th birthday in a bunker in Berlin on 20 April 1945, the entire illusion of the Third Reich had vanished as if it had never been. In its place was bare life smoking up from the wreckage of that dream.

Therefore, the amnion’s power lies in the voluntary, deliberate, willful, and complacent abdication of sovereignty.

Without this act it does not exist for the subject, though the subject may, as an outsider, regard it the way it would a movie. Surely, it has its effects on everyone equally. One must watch dumbfounded as one's government makes catastrophic mistakes. One must stand by while the financial system is plundered by the hegemony's transnational overlords. And one pays taxes to the hegemony or goes to jail. But the sovereign subject knows the difference between a difficulty and a problem. Choosing the difficulty of living within the amnion over the problem of belonging to it compares with the abdicated subject's choice of the difficulty of submitting to the amnion versus the problem of resisting it. Jesus' followers "marveled at him" when he said, "Render to Caesar the things that are Caesar's, and to God the things that are God's" (Mark 12:17). Considering his situation as a Jewish prophet in a Roman occupied territory, this seemed to make good sense to Jesus. So why are his followers so amazed at the idea? He is not being cynical; he is just advertising the fact that he understands the reality of the situation. Telling his followers to evade taxes will get them all punished and him killed; differentiating between what is God's and what man's is the lesson he is trying to teach that they do not seem to understand. He sees it as a difficulty while his followers see it as a problem. The one who becomes complicit is Judas Iscariot. The one who becomes rebellious is Paul of Tarsus who, most interestingly, was at first complicit and then later rebellious. Paul's iconic Road to Damascus experience could be interpreted as his fall from the Roman amnion into the bare life of joining the people he once brutally persecuted.

The mechanics of the subject's submission depends upon the interplay of being and time. If one identifies one's being with the imaginary homunculus of oneself created by telemetry and Big Data, what, then, is one's experience of time? The subject assumes that it is living a moment that is penultimate to the future at the head of a seemingly infinite queue of moments extending into the past. Moreover, this queue has a definite history with many threads including species, race, ethnicity, nationality, era, location, and so on. These threads come together into one confluence of discourse which the subject ultimately considers to be the narrative of itself. This narrative is the sign of itself. By relating to the sign as if it were the self, the subject becomes a sign of itself. It is perpetually divided, staring into the speculum of its own idea of itself. The subject's *speculation* puts it in a vulnerable state because it has identified with the Not-I of the ego's extrinsic accumulations. Such identity precludes actual self-determination. From what quarter is the subject to act? The subject's thought process develops into a concatenation of signs composed of fragments of the ego borrowed from these extrinsic sources, none of which have anything to do with the subject per se as an entity. It is susceptible to commercial, patriotic, rhetorical, and religious appeals in its desperate search for itself in the external world. But of course it is not there. The subject loses its entity through misidentification of itself as these extrinsic values, its self-determination rendered impotent by sublimating the imperatives of the corporate state into the substrates of the unconscious. The combination creates a being which is a sign of itself motivated by every alien interest except its own, giving birth to the extrinsic consumer. The species Homo Industrialis represents a dead end in the history of evolution. Such fatalism is of no concern to the hegemony and its corporate overlords; there are already too many people. Everyone must die some time. Besides, the ruling elite think of themselves as a separate species living perpetually in a state of exception. With the rise of automata and automation, the elite believe that these troglodytes will at least realize they are redundant and, God willing, eliminate themselves through opioids and suicide. They have become just more mouths to feed and not those who feed mouths, as the elite believe they themselves most certainly are in the eyes of God, history, and the universe.

The subject's history is a fairy tale of noble unicorns. And while it is difficult to prove that unicorns do not exist, no one has ever proven that they do. The subject seizes upon this problem, exploiting it to develop the heroic narrative of itself as victim or success within the nomos of the amnion. Worse, having abdicated and become a sign of itself, the subject perceives reality - all its birds, flowers, thunderstorms, symphonies, loves, and sublimity - through a glass darkly. This filter, which in and of itself does not exist but is a symptom of the subject's chronic speculation, creates a perpetual sense of *lack*: lack of understanding, lack of education, lack of luck, lack of money, lack of friends, lack of sex, lack of opportunity, lack of freedom, lack of security, and so on. The amnion's ethical aesthetic of consumerism jumps in to fill the gap between the self and the symbol of the self, creating a kind of unified, symbolic whole masquerading as the real. Sated, the subject recoils into itself. It enjoys lolling in this obesity of the soul. The state only requires payment of the monthly bills. Within the subject's culture there are a few reminders of what it may have lost, such as Mark 8:36: "For what shall it profit a man, if he shall gain the whole world, and lose his own soul?" But it is assured by Scientism that such nonsense belongs to the Dark Ages of man when belief in God clouded his ability to understand reality. There is no soul, says the savvy scientist, who has looked into the matter and even written a paper on it. Those who show no ambition to gain the whole world are considered slackers, losers, and even threats to the hegemonic order predicated upon infinite consumerism. They are shunned, penalized for not having borrowed enough money, ridiculed by their friends and families for not having a well-paying job, and often must accept living circumstances that are substandard and even dangerous — just nextdoor to the losers of the Underclass. Nevertheless, the sublime remains undaunted. It dwells in its own freedom as a stochastic process. The differential between its wild unpredictability (a probability of less than 1.0) and the subject's relentless quest for the absolutely predictable (a probability of more than 1.0) creates havoc in the subject's life. It reads books. It goes to therapists. It takes drugs (legal and illegal). It gets drunk. It grows richer or poorer. It goes vegan. It takes yoga classes. It votes. It fights wars to end all wars. And yet the gnawing sense of inescapable lack remains. It never realizes that Mark 8:36 is more than just benighted superstition; that whatever the soul may be, it is something one can lose in the sense of identifying with something else that is not the soul. If the stochastic process is the first state, and the following state is determined by the first state but no other state, then there can be no final state, creating a perpetual desire for consumption. What the subject craves, though, is a *final, static state*; unfortunately, the only permanent, static state is in the future is death; everything living is in the present, and everything in the present is in perpetual, stochastic flux. The present state is always the *penultimate* state in the mind of the mortal subject, never an end in itself. Therefore it is to be regarded as a necessary evil, a way-station (with a dirty bathroom) on the real journey to all of the glory promised to the subject by the Amniotic Empire *in the future*. The last thing the subject wants to confront is the ultimate reality: the ephemeral transience of the ego, which it assumes is the sum (*sum, ergo sum*) total of its existence, never mind the soul or even the body. Consequently, the sublime words of James 4:14 are seen as just more nonsense and superstition from the Bible, which is wrong according to Scientism: "Whereas ye know not what shall be on the morrow. For what is your life? It is even a vapour, that appeareth for a little time, and then vanisheth away." Cheer up, St. Jimmy!, says the network, or your show will be yanked this season and we'll insert some reruns of our most popular sitcom. Only in perfect homeostasis can the subject find what it is looking for. The tragedy of its quest is that there is nothing in the universe in an eternal state of homeostasis except death of the ego, which never existed anyway — the thing the ego (subject) fears the most and is willing to kill anyone to prevent.

I should mention here that when I use a quote from the (King James version, or KJB) of the Bible, I hear that inbred, censorious voice of Scientism echoing through the nautilus chambers of my brain, saying, "The reader will think that you're an irrational, Bible-thumping, superstitious, cretinous, religious, *lunatic* and not the fire-breathing, Marxian, atheistic, post-post-modern, Dawkinsian-Hitchensian ideologue who is taken seriously by readers of philosophy today." (Apologies to my publisher.) So be it. I do so because the Bible, particularly in the beautiful Elizabethan language of King James I, is an example of what has become a kind of symbol for the hegemony and the Cult of Scientism of *all that is stupid and bad* (i.e. a challenge to its priority). Therefore, it has become an emblem and vessel for the sublime. Never mind that it is a work of poetic wisdom vetted by perhaps billions of attentive human minds in the last 1,500 years. It is replete, in any translation, with beautiful poetry and fascinating, enlightening, historical, and sometime reprehensible stories of ancient peoples and cultures. Never mind that it also has manifestations as the Torah and the Koran, as well the Book or Mormon and other works, putatively divine in origin. Finally, it is the basis for the Western literary tradition in all of the literary genres, even modern, modernist, and post-modern works in abnegation of it.

In this essay, however, the KJB is used as an example of the sublime in common Western discourse, an indicator of the mysteries lying beyond the horizon of the incognizable. Even if you are a Satanist, variously defined, you are more likely to be on the side of the Bible, where Satan's story is actually told, than on the side of Scientism that says that all of it, including Satan, is a bunch of hooey —without providing any of its famous proof for this proposition, because it cannot. That Scientism *says* something is self-evident does not make it so, ex cathedra. Furthermore, the Bible is considered in this essay to be the core of Western world-historic culture. It predates the Golden Age of ancient Greece (c. 500-400 BCE), postdating in its present form the universal Semitic tradition begun in 1961 BCE when Abram (Abraham) left Ur. Nevertheless, the book you read now is about universal *Doubt*, in the sense meant by Anton LaVey on the dedication page of this book as the exhortation, "Now is the time for doubt!"

The disjunction between modern, altruistic, secular humanism, and traditional Judeo-Christian theology (as well as its analogs in Islam) reflects the subject's unconscious schism. It cannot reconcile the distance between the two, since they seem so much alike and yet the subject is told that they are categorically different, the former being, simply, *scientific*, and the latter bad, insane, stupid, dangerous, and superstitious. So then, life seems obsolete and new at the same time for the subject, always in a state of logical contradiction. The sublime is sought after in drugs and war, but condemned in government and school. Conflict of this nature, however, is the perfect environment for exploitation of the subject's lack of the ability to reason, which is apophantic. In such a world, the concept of ownership becomes a metaphor; it is transferred to the idea of being able to afford to lease something which does not really belong to the subject, but which the subject has been told does, believing this to be so despite all evidence before it to the contrary, such as repossession and foreclosure. The algorithm of the debt shell game (or mouse trap, to mix metaphors), and the redefinition of ownership as borrowing, form the economic illusion of the Imaginary. They cultivate a form of thinking which accepts a discontinuity between signified and signifier. Leasing something does not signify owning something. Something that is obsolete cannot also be new. Combine the two and the subject's thinking becomes ensnared in the apparatus of the Imaginary. It ceases to be apophantic. It comes to accept contradiction as being noncontradictory, and the unverifiable as the verified (and vice versa). Add inevitable debt accumulating under such circumstances, and the subject becomes obligated to the hegemony which draws its ultimate power over the government and media from the financial industry.

Naturally, there are some weirdos and kooks who would "prefer not to" abdicate. Such characters make good literature, or even scripture. The tale "Bartleby, the Scrivener: A Story of Wall Street," by Herman Melville, describes one of these kooks and weirdos. In it, a clerk in a Wall Street law office simply decides that *he will no longer do what he is asked*, and that is all. He gives no reason. Worse, he seems to think there is also no reason to move from his desk, much to the consternation of his boss, the narrator. "In this very attitude did I sit when I called to him, rapidly stating what it was I wanted him to do—namely, to examine a small paper with me. Imagine my surprise, nay, my consternation, when without moving from his privacy, Bartleby in a singularly mild, firm voice, replied, 'I would prefer not to.'"

But aside from an eccentric whom we assume does not know any better, and one we deem to have had a psychological break with reality and therefore cannot control himself, those who would *prefer not to* are rare indeed. Much of the reason is that most people want to do the right thing by their employer, family, friends, and society. They want to participate in the economy.

They want to give money to the poor. They want to pay their debts. They want to raise children. And they quite naturally want to have good things. These perfectly healthy desires however are their undoing in the end because they are not limited by a sense of what is not worth sacrificing to get them. Such aversion has been bred out of the modern domestic beast. Even though they start out more or less free from the tyranny of *l'objet petit a*, their good will and lack of suspicion about the institutions ruling over their lives put them in a prime position to be exploited by the hegemony. Alas, the rule of the universe is that if a person is willing to be exploited, he will be exploited. The hegemony, however, is not entirely evil or even to blame. It is just doing its job (to exploit). We could say that its corporate overlords are evil, but that would be bringing too much subjectivity into what almost anyone would do were he in the same position. The corporate overlords just *are*. That their mode is exploitation is in part because the subject has contracted with them to exploit others on the subject's behalf! What hypocrisy, then, to turn around and decry getting the same treatment. *The subject has a choice*. There is no end to popular literature, from Hawthorne to the Bible, making this clear. Martin Luther, for example, took on the whole apparatus of the empire of the Roman Catholic Church on 31 October 1517 when he posted "Disputatio pro declaratione *virtutis indulgentiarum*," known as the "Ninety-Five Theses," on the door of the Wittenberg Castle church – a simple act that led to the not-so-simple Reformation, as I have mentioned earlier. It was a clear throw-down to the Archbishop of Mainz, who then started the machinery for Martin's disputation and consequent fugitive status. Thus began the Reformation of Christendom and the first great schism in the Roman Catholic Church. What was his complaint? He had many (95, they say). But the icon of what he found wrong with the Catholic Church was that it had compromised its divine mission by selling indulgences, or certificates forgiving sins, as a kind of industry to raise money to repaint the Vatican and put in new gold toilets. He found this kind of brokering of spiritual futures reprehensible, though it was a boon for those who were congenital sinners in need of a sure place in Heaven at the right hand of God. A glimpse at Western history since then shows that he was successful in taking on the entire apparatus of a corrupt system that more or less ruled the (Western) world at the time. And this enterprise was headed by a CEO anointed as infallible by God Himself, since it is He who speaks *through* the Pope to the faithful. But the real problem is this: no one can stop the subject from selling its sovereignty except itself. And no one can abdicate its abdication except itself.

Later we will look at what happens when others try to storm the Bastille of the hegemony and release its prisoners when we discuss the French Revolution of 1789. For now we must focus on how sovereignty is usurped - one gadget at a time.

Gadgets and gizmos rely on the appeal of the promise of *ever greater convenience*. This reliance becomes the ethical aesthetic of the subject and therefore the society of subjects it belongs to. Gadgets would not be so important, as their use is limited and, perhaps, largely needless, were they not the basis of the most valuable stock corporations in the world at this time. Those who prefer not to embrace the whole package hook, line, and sinker receive the full wrath of their comrades' disdain, as well as the financial industry's ire via its governmental apparatus. For example, local opposition to a certain new type of high-speed digital network for *any reason* is written into the law in the United States as an *actionable offense* (FFC 18-133, 2018). It just so happens that this technology makes facial-recognition surveillance by the government possible, as it has so effectively in the People's Republic of China — the envy of all big states. The legislation is built upon the statutes and case law regarding *sovereign immunity* and *state immunity* (the state of exception), even though it is on the behalf of the wholly private telecommunications industry in the USA — an industry which, in China's defense, is at least owned by the state in that paradise of Marxian good intentions. The network giving the device its awesome power, then, must be a subtle infrastructure designed to draw every type of subject, high and low, into its matrix. The UTM, Universal Turing Machine, or modern computer, is perfectly suited for this objective. As mentioned above, the gadget accomplishes this feat in part through its constant renewal of itself so that the subject is always lusting for its next *build* — even though the electronic computer really has not changed much in its basic design since its inception. As this is happening in every part of the subject's life, it becomes the basis of its ethical aesthetic of perpetual convenience at all times and under any circumstance, even death. Its ethos becomes Death before Inconvenience! The possibility of infinite iteration creates a sense of timelessness. Like the repetition of an addictive drug, though, this infantile sense of amniosis comes with a price. The subject's energy, time, money, and sense of being-there (*Dasein*) are quickly consumed by the grinding iteration of this algorithm. What is left is a hungry beast longing for what it can never have while at the same time being intractably obligated to its creditors, *now,* for what it had borrowed *then*, for its creditors know more about the ontology of reality than the subject, which is how they exploit it. The credible threat is that if it does not pay *now* for what it borrowed *then*, then it will not be able to borrow *later* for what it wants *now*. Alas, what it wants *now* is often to pay the debt on what it borrowed *then*, though often at arm's reach by financial displacement of one obligation for another, which I call here the shell game. Since everything in the subject's life is one inconvenience superseded by another, total efficiency reduces to zero (0), meaning that borrowing often comes down to a negative degree of efficiency — like being robbed by oneself, but surrendering the proceeds to the mob boss but taking the rap when caught. Each current state is superseded by another in order to maintain the current one. Lusting for the opioid of convenience, the subject is forever frustrated in its quest by the total inefficiency of the economy of this sucker's algorithm. In mindless desperation, it digs itself deeper into the hole which opened up when it signed those promissory notes obligating it to the Mob. The subject is terrified that there might be a final state to the relentless algorithm. It never occurs to the subject that this final state - which is bare life - is *its only possibility of escape* while at the same time being what it fears the most.

The only possibility of there being *no final state*, then, is if each state depends upon a state that does not exist. A nonexistent state becomes an emblem of itself. It gathers itself to itself. What seems like something new is really the same old thing with a different sales pitch. People fall for the same cons (confidence games) time and again. Which is, perhaps, one reason why the annual revenue from theft and fraud on the Internet is estimated to be up to $6 trillion per year in 2021 (or maybe this figure is just a ploy in a con game run by cybersecurity IT firms). All sorts of economic and other traps labeled "THIS IS A TRAP" are blithely entered into by the subject with the esprit of a comic Vaudeville rube. Even feral rats learn quickly, according to behavioral science, to avoid an obvious trap. However, it seems that humans *crave* traps for the goodies they hope to find inside, judging by the impunity with which the retail, public, state, and OTC banking industries operate. Words from the wise are looked upon the way swine regard pearls; caveats fall upon the emptors' deaf ears. Young people see their older peers leaving university with surreal personal debt, maxed-out credit cards, strange worthless degrees, and some of the best years of their lives wasted in captivity, and yet they *still* buy the canard that if they do not follow suit, they will be regarded as Less Fortunate or Unfortunate *losers* in the eyes of society, a stigma they cannot bear and will pay any price to avoid. So off they go, ending up in the same mess as the others that went before them. Without a second thought, upstanding citizens allow themselves to become addicted to drugs prescribed by their own doctors. People sign finance agreements to get expensive cars to drive to work to pay for the expensive car to drive to work. There is simply no end to human folly in the amnion of the Imaginary. Many of these persons soon find themselves struggling unwillingly at the gates of bare life — if there is any good to come of this ruse at all — because of the essentially usurious nature of the deals they agreed upon to enter with gusto. Through the iron mesh of these gates they see the Underclass living their nasty, brutish, short lives. But if they are from the right socio-ethnic and socio-economic echelon of society the percentage chance that they will *end up* at the bottom are considerably less than the chance that those born there will ever escape — regardless, statistically, of ethnicity or skin color, the most superficial and irrelevant of all distinctions.

The imaginary order subsumes the symbolic order, positioning it in conflict with the real while exploiting it to provide the subject with an easy way out of having to face reality. What was once real behavior in the subject become symbolic. Its marriage, relationship to its children, religious observances, donations to charity, patriotism, political beliefs, and attempts to be altruistic and save the environment and so on become *ritualized* into impotent, symbolic behavior. The subject religiously avoids seeing if the outcome equals the intent of its actions, or if what it assumes to be true can be verified. Why? Because the *consequences of disillusionment* have become too terrible to bear, as they inevitably lead to discharge from the Amnion. When it *does* see that the results of its actions are aberrant, it is befuddled, turning to psychiatric drugs, legal and illegal, including alcohol, to dull the sting of reality and its consequent intimations of mortality. Lacking effective analytic capacity save a default ability to choose, more or less at random, between product A and B, it just simply cannot understand that in the end its actions are, at best, *symbolic*. The irony of the Cult of Mediocrity and its religion of Scientism is that it demands rituals of belief and consumerism while attacking metaphysical religions for the same thing. Canny marketers, perhaps not without a sense of cruel wit, have picked up on this, branding their clients with names such as Shop Rite and Rite Aid. Effectively unconscious, and merely aware, like an amoeba, the abdicated subject cannot see that symbolic action in place of real action results in a signifier of that action, and not the action itself being signified. Without effective language, there is no effective thought; without effective thought, there is no effective consciousness. Again, the role of the two, signifier and signified, are reversed or inverted in the logical propositions of thought, invalidating them. Furthermore, the law, or civil and criminal nomos, becomes strangely out of proportion to reality. An eye for an eye becomes a life for an eye, or an eye for a life. An inverse bias sets in based on social status (not race). The rich get justice and the poor prison. Laws that put people away for a decade are suddenly struck off the books because the financial markets see profit in them, while activities that were once regarded as innocent and legal become high crimes because they do not suit a subculture's idiosyncratic interpretation of right and wrong, becoming the law of the land overnight.

Patriotism becomes the imperative to *consume* rather than love and protect the land, its people, and its values. Politicians pretend to solve all the world's woes by writing bills, passing laws, enacting acts, and other forms of often self-serving paperwork to prove they "did something" about it without having to actually change anything, which would draw the ire of their various sundry overlords. Meantime, their edicts go unfunded, are not enforced, or worse – are *selectively enforced* by targeting the weakest and easiest to prosecute as scarecrows to the others and social scapegoats. The overlords of the hegemony who fund politicians' campaigns, meanwhile, expect enabling legislation transferring the commonweal into their private enterprises and bank accounts. Democracy becomes as much of a ritual as a maypole dance. The truth is that the subject's symbolic action was never intended to have any effect on anything except the subject's regard for its own sense of convenience and comfort. Unconsciously it *does* understand this, as the id is in crisis mode, which is why its conscious decision-making process is so grotesque by comparison.

By subsuming the symbolic into the Imaginary, *amniosis* arises where the real is regarded as imaginary and the imaginary as real. The amnion consists of symbolic iconography and signs signaling the subject's somatic memory of its life as a fetus *in utero*. Cast out from the womb like Adam and Eve exiled from Paradise, the subject naturally longs for return to fetal amniosis. Reality, though, bars the way back to Paradise with cherubim and flaming swords. Therefore, the subject seeks this state *in the world* – precisely where it does not exist. A state of being predicated upon what does not exist, does not itself exist and is therefore wholly imaginary. By necessity it must not exist, otherwise no state would exist so that it could not exist, which is necessary for *any* state to exist. However, it is extremely inconvenient to seek a state of perpetual convenience, as it is 100 percent inefficient and in fact *negatively* efficient, causing a constant and deadly drain on the subject's personal resources, which includes, alas, the resources of others around it. After all, no man is an island, but is part of the main. Despite this paradox, the subject nevertheless charges onward like the Light Brigade toward illusory fulfillment of its fatal ethos. The purveyors of gizmos and gadgets, cars and insurance policies, mortgages and credit cards, eagerly await the windfall of the tokens the subject has received *from them* in exchange for sacrificing the best hours of its short life laboring for the same imaginary entities of the Amniotic Empire. Having signed away its self-determination through promissory notes, the subject's capture is all but assured barring periodic economic catastrophes brought on by this fatally inefficient system. Nevertheless, the banks of the hegemonic order, and the state treasuries, consume whatever equity the subject has levered into the vig, leaving it destitute and clueless — a pariah in the amnion it created through its abdication.

Inconvenience is uncomfortable and discomfort is inconvenient. Therefore, the subject's ethical aesthetic becomes: *The comfort of convenience = good. The discomfort of inconvenience = bad.* Other than this simplistic dichotomy, the subject has no other ethical code than what the nomos imposes upon it but not itself through what it calls state and sovereign immunity (exception). This is the essential dichotomy or binary dogma of the amnion policed by the subject's neurological addiction to its digital gadget. What we have then is a perversion of the necessary animal functions of *Genuss*. Comfort is the organism's search for that which does not harm both the organism's ability to survive and its quality of life - concerns of all organisms from microbes to humans. Microbes made uncomfortable by light, shun it. Convenience is simply a way to conserve energy and avoid harm. Conservation of energy is a biological imperative the function of which is to extract maximum benefit from the least amount of available carbon. As it does with sex, the Imaginary exploits these imperatives, mining them for commercial opportunity and political power while swelling them into a monstrous juggernaut the subject is unwilling or unable to resist. The gadget is a utility. Its purposes are distraction from discomfort, diversion from boredom, to serve as a vessel for the storage of digital products (music, video, games), telemetry for the purpose of forming the subject's remote consumer profile, and the production of comforting chatter in the forms of text and speech that fill the gnawing void left by social isolation from the physical world. Traditional utilities, for instance a steel axe, are both inconvenient and uncomfortable, but highly effective and last forever. A *mattock* is inconvenient and uncomfortable because it is a third-class lever, meaning that its design actually reduces the potential efficiency of effort required to use it to perform the task it is designed for. But like the axe, it is affordable, paying for itself almost immediately through the sweat of one's brow — yet another biological function considered the mark of poverty and backwardness. It is used by the far-off other in third-world countries to farm. If the subject sweats at all, it is ritualistically at the gym, the symbolic Church of Health where it performs the rites of notional exercise on elaborate machines signalling that this is a serious undertaking sure to expiate all sins of lethargy and gluttony. The problem here is that the ethical aesthetic of utility is *utility*, not comfort and convenience. Also, a gadget that is perpetually obsolete through an iterative stochastic process of random improvement passes on its zero (0) efficiency to each new iteration, reducing the return on investment of time and energy to always less than zero. Such an procedure of ritual renewal creates a totally asymmetrical relationship between the buyer and seller, where the buyer is always getting less than nothing and the seller always more than something. This brilliant marketing scam is ubiquitous, from credit cards to car leases and even student loans. However, it is the only possible form of positive cash flow in a metastatic growth economy that must continually expand on the basis of increased debt, or implode (thank you, Lord Keynes). The gadget is the digital key to this zero-negative economic scheme. The gadget exists within the greater context of the *net-world* of the Imaginary, which is the Imaginary's macro infrastructure of satellites, microwave transmitters, fiber optics, servers, and nodes. Without it, the gadget has no ultimate utility and therefore is what is called in the business a brick. To cripple the gadget not connected to the network, perpetual updates badger and goad the subject into obedience or else face zero-day exploits of its gadget's software and firmware by the ubiquitous bad actor.

Its nature as *electronica* necessarily links it to an ever-expanding neurological *net-world* consisting of every medium possible, anchored in a Boolean universe of mechanical logic admitting no subtlety, managed by cybernetic (heuristic) control systems to prevent unpredictable outcomes — the essence of the sublime. It therefore excludes the sublime *mathematically*; there is no sublime function (despite Higgs' media-named God Particle), though theoretical mathematics is itself sublime as it expresses the laws of the natural world and even beyond. It also anchors the net-world to a commercial apparatus based on infinite data mining through the mechanism of surveillance telemetry. Content is only the *adjunct* of the device's true function. Its business is meme delivery, marketing and advertising, serving as a point-of-sale terminal in one's pocket, and consumer and psychographic data mining through surreptitious surveillance of the user-subject. Capture is made possible by what the subject sees as the Big Magic of science, which keeps it in thrall because it is loath to spend five minutes on the Internet looking up how the gadget works, what it does, and what it is for. The subject's curiosity about anything other than new products has been effectively killed off when it abdicated its self-determination, which demands curiosity (as cats demonstrate) if one is to be captain of one's own ship without sinking. Scientism has no ideas of its own, only the lust for more power. It has *methodologies* it purports to be sacrosanct, beyond the ken of the subhuman prole it lords over. Its crypto-incantations practiced in the *sanctum sanctorum* of the corporation's research and development department are not for the public. Their secrecy is justified by government laws regarding insider trading of the company's stock — which goes on anyway and is therefore a charade, or at best a nomological ritual. To maintain the awe of the public, Scientism broadcasts the misnomer that a person with a decent education could not understand the Big Magic of the products it buys, even though this presti-*digitation* is based on high school algebra, biology, or chemistry. So why bother explaining it? The sad thing is that this is probably true; whatever passes for education in the amnion is mere indoctrination, and indoctrination preempts understanding. Even though much of the information, at any depth, is available with a few clicks, the subject will NEVER try to find it because it is boring compared to a first-person shooter video game, football match, or (much maligned) cute cat video. To pull anything of scientific value from the Internet one must *recognize* what is valuable, and know how to use Boolean operators in the search bar to narrow the search rather than skim across the surface data, all the while shedding consumer information linked to the subject's personal identity and specific machines. To recognize what is valuable one must have had some fruitful contact with the big ideas on which the marvels of real science are based. But most of all one must *care* about them!

However, the mining of consumer data is cheap and easy, and pays for the infinitely expensive infrastructure the subject thinks it is getting for free. The search for meaning within it is expensive and hard, and takes an analytical mind — something reserved today for electronic and pharmaceutical product developers only. Despite the ever-expanding data of the Internet, users are like gamblers in a casino playing a slot machine: it is full of money, but they are *lucky* to get a payoff since there is no skill in the game they play. They know that the odds are against them. But this does not stop them from the thrill of playing, which is fine ... to a point. With anticipation that something stimulating will happen, but they do not know what, they skim over the surface of the vast, redundant, junk-filled, hodgepodge of promotional websites looking for the next fix of trivia to distract them from their existential nightmare. As they surf, they are more or less unaware that it is they themselves who are *being surfed* autonomically by the infrastructure itself. Each nervous twitch of the finger on a mouse or keyboard signals yet another immutable sign of their desires - desires they are often not even aware of - logged forever in the Iron Mountains of Big Data. As in most casino games, the house always wins in the end. But also like a gambler, the subject is more obsessed with the *gamble itself* than in winning it; perpetual loss is fine as long as it gets a periodic boost from a statistically calculated payoff it thinks is the random action of Lady Luck. What keeps the subject lashed to the deck of neurological distractions during the storm of the *knowing-more* is the hope that it will win the jackpot: eternal diversion from the unconscious terror that it will indeed die come what may. (We must also remember that Internet gambling, casino style or on sports events, is a huge global industry.) They hope that through a miracle of Lady Luck their Internet searches will return a distracting, prurient, meme which will reinforce their ever-crumbling ego with what seems like self-determination. What they get, though, is information that has been pornographied. These data have been scrubbed of their cumbersome potential to *mean* which would have made them boring to the lazy mind doped with chit-chat and bric-à-brac. As the liturgy of Scientism, the knowing-more plays into the natural indolence of the flock. It favors what they *want* over what they *need*. Soon the notion of need becomes conflated with that of want in an indistinguishable hash of random desire fueled by a perpetually repressed id in frustrated crisis mode, brimming with toxic psychic energy that must find jouissance in the worst place possible: online, for the marketers and government to see. In the larger culture of consumerism, the flock needs what it wants. It no longer wants what it needs, since the bare life of necessity where need is the name of the game is seen as stupid (if not contagious). If this seems like some sort of curse resulting from bad karma, that is an accurate perception; it is the *Curse of the Enslaved Far-off Other* (soon to be a motion picture) and the local native Underclass who must stand by suffering from chronic *lack*. The consequence of this imbalance is social disorder caused by a sense of relative deprivation in both classes.

Thanks to modern science, basic biological needs are easily satisfied in cultures rich enough to afford that luxury, putting the emphasis on the *want* rather than *need* economy. Technology allows the subject to ignore its needs in favor of what it wants and desires through *overabundant production* or idle excess. All seems well until the inevitable crisis such a usurious and inefficient system brings upon itself and everyone in it as the outcome of its invalid, fatal logic of contradiction at variance with nature, the spirit, and the universe itself. When the crisis occurs, the weak subject panics, surrendering what tokens of freedom it thought it had within the modicum of self-determination left to it after its abdication to the hegemony's hysterical alarm of national security. As the subject is infantile in its orientation to the world, it pleads to be saved by the Father, and be suckled by the Mother. Furthermore, it wants a guarantee that its irrational fear of the loss of object constancy *viz* the hegemonic Mother (consumerism) and Father (nomos) is unfounded. Answering its prayer, the hegemony's government floods the economy with fiat currency (which must be paid back through the subject's labor) to enforce the illusion that it is awash in Magic Mother's Milk, though there are no jobs, while at the same time showing the subject that the Great Father can pull prosperity out of his arse, as it were. There is no need for productivity, creativity, hard work, and plain old luck. The only biological imperative is *to consume*. The subject hopes that the sacrifice of its last remaining freedoms — even the ones legally guaranteed by its national Constitution for which the *blood of patriots* was spilled to earn — will give the hegemony more power to magically protect it from shadowy evil forces. These forces are the emblems of the flip side of the Imaginary's wonders the subject craves. The Apex Consumer sees this hellish realm remotely (and comfortably and conveniently) on TV, in the news, on the Internet, and in Hollywood movies. It consists of what the subject has been trained to fear as terrorists, pedophiles, gangs, drug dealers, serial killers, mass murderers, dictators, racists, Nazis, space aliens, fundamentalists, supremacists, virus plagues, human traffickers, nationalists, Christians, gun nuts, and dirty poor people lurking around the fringes of the amnion. The image of this horde of barbarians at the gate of the amnion threatens the impotent subject's illusory cocoon of comfort, convenience, and the promise of medical immortality (as long as it can pay bills) in the bowels of the Amniotic Empire.

PART 3: HOPE CULTS

3.0: Scientism's ascendancy to priority

The Industrial Revolution and the Machine Age which followed, signaled a fundamental change in the psyche of the West. It was comprised of lesser signals flowing from the corners and quarters of the socioeconomic fabric as it was torn apart and then sewn up again in a new materialist ethical aesthetic based on engineering science. The radical commercial-industrial vortex sucked in millions whose ancestors had for many centuries been farmers, tradesmen, and others plying what are known in economics, principally Austrian, as *real value* jobs in the fabric of communities which took many centuries to form from the raw material of their tribal affinities. Overnight (by historical standards) they found themselves in densely-packed company towns of strangers laboring at highly specialized jobs which, outside of the mill, had no real value except to keep the factories running *in situ*. What played a big role in this conversion of the ethical aesthetic of everyday life was a radical change in the basic idea of the ownership of land. In the American West during the Nineteenth Century grazing land shared for the growing of vast herds of cattle was enclosed by farmers who saw an unprecedented opportunity to obtain land that was for all intents and purposes free (yes, the term is *growing* cattle). Never mind that the original occupants of that land who had been there for millennia were pushed out by both groups into rugged territory few desired – free or not, until they found gold in some of it.

Meantime, in 17th Century England, the commons – land shared by all to raise livestock – was enclosed and turned over to the ruling elite to manage in a neo-feudal system. The previous feudal system established by William the Conqueror underwent a significant overhaul. They were to act as lord superintendents, and regional representatives in the House of Lords, effectively creating a new kind of serfdom among the now tenant farmers. This was done without consultation with those whose livelihoods depended upon the commons being free. Whatever the political and economic motivations, the fact is that the psyche of traditional agrarian culture had to get over the idea that *land can be used but not owned*. Farmers had to adapt to the paradigm that every inch of England was *owned* by someone other than those who used it directly. A new modern, industrial serfdom was born after centuries of struggle for liberation from Medieval fiefdom. Soon after this transition, the idea that the land could belong *to the people* of a nation (not to the people's government as in most Marxian states) became as subversive as the idea that factory workers could own the factory where they were employed. However, the rise of joint-stock corporations in England somewhat mitigated the sole ownership problem. IngSoc (English socialism) took care the rest in the 20th Century. It was not until the workers themselves began to understand that they did indeed *own the labor* they could provide that power started trickling back to the worker. While the few prosperous farmers could buy up their land, many had to rent it from the lord who now owned what was before land free for all to work provided they contributed to the manor's upkeep. This created what Hegel calls the lord and bondsman relationship (literal or metaphorical) which later evolved into the modern *creditor-debtor* relationship upon which all modern economies are now based. Furthermore, this new socioeconomic order put the country bumpkin in his place. Whatever democratic pretenses England's absolute Parliament or the the U.S. Department of the Interior professed, it became clear that representation was at best *selective*. It favored those with power and money as it always does and always will, because that is the nature of centralized power.

In addition, this change signaled a new ethical aesthetic. Now everything had a price tag on it because it could be quantified in the Age of Positivism following the Machine Age. The result, in part, was the birth of quantitative economics. Now everything could be *quantified* in a way that William the Conqueror's Domesday Book of 1086 could not have hoped. While he counted sheep, the new economy counted monetary value in numbers established in exchanges where goods could be traded. Nothing had intrinsic value as part of the *needs* of the local community; value became an abstraction, allowing it to enter into the Imaginary. The next logical step was the explosion of derivatives speculation — or notional value — commodifying everything, even the weather of the future. Derivatives had been around for millennia as forwards. Now they became a kind of exchangeable store of value, again pumping more air into the amniotic bubble of the Imaginary. The notional value of anything now depended upon the abstraction of exchange in arenas called exchanges (such as the Corn Exchange in Manchester). The value of commodity X now depended upon the value of commodity Y rather than the needs of the people who would otherwise have benefited directly from that commodity. Goods traded were also now subject to speculation (gambling) on which way the prices would go in the near or distance future. The economic casino was born with hardly a law to keep it in tune with the needs of the producers and the customers. This new economic order forced many farmers from the land they rented and into factory work they did not want to do but had to survive. They could not afford the rents which, as David Ricardo points out, were based in part on how good the yield of the land was. The harder they worked, the better methods they used, the cleverer they were, the better luck they had, the more promising the season, the higher their rent, as well as, of course, taxes on their income — a system of disincentive and a labor of Sisyphus. On the other hand, those with a low yield could not make the nominal rent. They were then pushed off in favor of someone else who could improve on what they had been doing, which makes sense but would not have happened had they owned their meagre property outright. While this logic is only natural in a free-market system, under the old system low and high yields were tolerated together because after all what really mattered was that people were fed and clothed by what they produced locally, offset by access to the value added by the commons which helped stabilize the business cycle. Nevertheless, Dickensian capitalism led to a shedding of tenant farmers into the funnel of the factories and the company-owned gin mills — a drug concocted by corporate chemists of Blake's dark Satanic mills for this purpose. Where members of the family would have worked around the house or on the farm, they now worked together tending the machinery which produced a perpetual supply of cheap goods for domestic and international consumption. The age of mass consumerism, the umbilicus of the amnion, was born. The engine of the consumer society was born along with the first inklings of the surrender of sovereignty in the form of bank debt to buy the farm, home, or the trappings of pseudo-gentility (the middle class). At the same time, the modern paradigm of lord and bondsman in the form of debtor and creditor also came into being as a form of neo-medievalism. For market speculation to occur, investors had to borrow money for leveraged operations. At the same time, since the value (price) of agricultural and even industrial goods was now dependent upon the vicissitudes of the exchange, sudden collapses of prices meant that the supply side had to borrow money until the bull market showed its horns again. Or, even more risky, depositors' money was loaned to speculators as leverage to gain advantage in the market, often enough leading to bankruptcies or runs on the banks (same thing). Bank credit, except perhaps in the form of a farm mortgage, was seldom extended to the lowly factory worker and tenant farmer. Far from being a hardship, it was all that saved them from complete abdication of their sovereignty. Meantime, though, the traders and speculators took command of the economy so that when they lost a gamble even the average person without a penny of debt would suffer as prices fell on goods they produced but debt service remained constant.

The *want* culture slowly began to creep into what was for hundreds of years a *need* culture. To have what one wanted but did not need, Veblen's conspicuous consumption, became the emblem of prosperity. Such an emblem became necessary for full participation in the culture of the new middle class of debtors. Herein lies the beginning of the Imaginary as an installation, grossly out of proportion to the symbolic and most of all the real. Herein also lies the beginnings of the modern middle class, the favorite target of the hegemony's methodology of exploitation through debt and the creation of jobs without real value to pay for it and therefore not translatable into survival. Those left behind in the need culture were now seen as the growing Underclass, on par with what Marx calls the lumpen-proletariat: prostitutes, drug addicts, criminals, drunks, the mentally ill, and the chronically unemployed or unemployable, impervious to "-isms" by their lack of wherewithal. Lacking the emblem of prosperity, the Underclass became particularly conspicuous in Victorian England, chronicled by such social reformers as Dickens, Arnold, and Ruskin. It had been around for a long time, as the New Testament attests, since Jesus seemed to have belonged to this class. These events helped ignite migration to new factory towns swelling in the once green and pleasant land of England which now, according to Ruskin, became a heap of coke cinders (Sesame and Lilies). There was a seemingly endless need for workers as these industries expanded along with the British Empire, which was now the biggest, most powerful, and richest in the world. America was slower to come to this point. But come it did, soon gaining in power at first equal to and quickly surpassing its former masters. All that stood in the way was the agrarian empire of the South. Once it had been destroyed and expropriated for private exploitation by Northern industrialists and speculators who funded Union forces in the Civil War — to the loss of 640,000 or so young men — England could not keep up.

What made this overnight transformation from self-reliance into mass dependency upon the umbilicus of the proto-amnion possible? Science. Technology. The destruction of agrarianism. Defrocking of the Church. Bank-controlled government. Massive public and private debt (their method). And finally, *the death of the sublime* as the result of this social juggernaut. The first victim was religion — the easiest target because it seemed to be the enemy of science. The loss of traditional God-based religion, however, was not due to the enlightenment that science proclaimed it had brought to the dark reaches of the human psyche and social consciousness. Rather, it was the result of a paradigmatic *coup-*

d'état. Scientism was born when technology had reached the point where it could be turned into a marketable commodity traded on an exchange as investment in joint-stock corporations. Money in unprecedented quantities poured into concentrations of wealth that would be known as das Kapital. Religion could hardly keep up with the riches consumerism seemed to bestow upon the mortal soul. While the Roman Catholic Church remained the biggest landowner in Europe, in the new economy land was not liquid enough to move with the financial markets. The age of morality replaced the quaint age of sin, quickly evolving into the nomological state. Secularized into statutes and code, sin would be handled by an infallible (absolute) parliament, the constable, the sheriff, and the courts rather than the priest and absolution, if not indulgences. Because Scientism now commanded such great wealth it was able to stand up to the once-powerful consortium of Semitic religions, which quickly went on the defensive in the form of evangelism, orthodoxy, and jihad. The old order had come to power professing its divine imperative to act as God's agent in the earthly realm. Its Big Magic was in the form of miracles. As Jesus says in John 4:48, "Except ye see signs and wonders, ye will not believe." Christ, an underestimated social critic and perspicacious psychologist, understood that exhortation to love God and one's neighbor has already been a failure. First the Noahide Laws and then the Ten Commandments failed to bring law and order to the selfish, rowdy hordes of heathens, Jews, and later Christians alike. But a few miracles and they would believe. Man in his boredom with the mundane mechanics of the Real longs for the magical, the mythical, the symbolic, the imaginary, and the prestidigitation of the conjurer and the charlatan. The modern miracle, then, is consumer society and debt that makes, as Stanley Kowalski puts it in Williams' *A Streetcar Named Desire*, every man a King, under a neo-Napoleonic code. Add to this the state's magic trick of pulling currency out of its arse, and the modern amnion could not be far behind, as it were. And who would not stand in awe of a state that can pull currency out of its arse? All that was needed to stitch it together was digital technology and high-speed networks. Their unifying power to shape the womb of the amnion and the conduits of its umbilicus was unique in history. Whether one believes in miracles or not is immaterial. Like the belief in God, it is no easier to *disprove* that miracles exist than to prove it, only because it is nearly impossible to define what a miracle is. Today's everyday gadget is yesterday's unthinkable miracle. And what is a miracle anyway except what it is defined as in the context at the moment for some, usually manipulative, purpose? Jesus' words, no matter which translation one reads, are laconic and even a bit cynical. The New International Edition brings this out a little better than other editions: "Unless you people see signs and wonders … you will never believe." The phrase "you people" and the hopelessness of the word "never" belie Jesus' despair over the failure of simply providing a good example and preaching the Gospel. If the straightforward approach does not work, or even the gravitas of the Ten Commandments and the whole Jewish tradition standing behind him, then what will make "you people" begin to see the reality of God? The words of Da Vinci in *Notebook XIX: Philosophical Maxims. Morals. Polemics and Speculation* come to mind (Richter):

> Some there are who are nothing else than a passage for food and augmentors [sic] of excrement and *fillers of privies*, because through them no other things in the world, nor any good effects are produced, since nothing but full privies results from them. [italics added]

Jesus' effort on behalf of what da Vinci calls "fillers of privies" costs him his life. Matthew 7:6 says, "Do not give what is holy to the dogs; nor cast your pearls before swine, lest they trample them under their feet, and turn and tear you in pieces." We often forget that it is the miracle of bringing Lazarus back to life that leads to Christ's crucifixion. It is only when he performs *this* miracle that he becomes a serious threat to the Pharisees and, consequently, the Roman governors. Why? Because even among miracles there are degrees of significance. The *sign* of undoing death is the sign of the Messiah, for only God could do such a thing. Wizards and charlatans could do some of the other miracles Jesus performs. Even those allied with the Devil. What the Pharisees do not know, of course, is that his *pièce de résistance* will be when he brings *himself* back from the dead — hard to refute or condemn, neutralizing their supposed negation of his messianic mission.

The subject in its spiritual, moral, and intellectual lethargy wants a miracle to stimulate it out the doldrums. Reading about miracles that happened two millennia ago just does not excite the imagination enough to assuage the monotony and boredom of *being-there*. Dasein is wretchedly boring, if not nasty, brutish, and short. Scientism offers miracles in the here and now through its cryptic Big Magic, the tricks of the trade of which it guards jealously. For instance, in the United States women have been convinced that natural birth is not only filthy and primitive and for poor people, but also that it will kill them. Therefore, caesarian sections are becoming the norm because, to the bean counters at the medical insurance companies, it is the least likely to result in a lawsuit. The miracles of the common digital gadget that likely would have impressed even Jesus, the subject thinks, are at its fingertips 24/7. Or at least that is what the ad says, and only if it keeps up with the monthly network fees. And these are *real* miracles not *fake* miracles, the subject thinks. They are empirically, verifiably *real*. They are not the ones probably made up by the universally credulous, superstitious minds of antiquity. With that level of stupidity it is a wonder they could even feed themselves or build a grass hut! The magical realm of advertising convinces the subject that technology, and its infinite progress toward ever greater comfort and convenience, will allow it to transcend the gross limitations of time and space, negating its worst fear: ego death. Since Scientism's advancement is unlimited, who is to doubt the outrageous claims made by the manufacturers of these gadgets and gizmos, never mind passenger rockets into space, flying cars, and robot surgeons? Anyone who does doubt, is a Doubting Thomas, and is regarded with suspicion as a Luddite or worse, a heretic. Never mind that the modern jet airliner has a top speed of the first one from the 1950's, that eyeglasses have not changed since the 14th Century, and medical error is the third leading cause of death in that paragon of modernity: the United States.

So-called smart gadgets are even brainier than people, the subject imagines, despite the fact that the human brain is considered to be the most complex creation in the universe. Your phone, comrade, is even more complex than this wet brain (with a battery lasting 80 years or so), meaning that you are stupid and it is smart. Gizmos that talk back create the illusion that inside that Black Box is an *artificial soul*, a woman (since most NLP voices are female, indicating the subservient nature of man's *helpmeet*). The ever-expanding artificial intelligence (an oxymoron) of the toy will someday provide us with more *helpmeets*, companions, slaves, and even sex bots. But most important, as smart gadgets evolve into anthropomorphic toys and slaves, they can be sent into battle to protect us from the heathen hordes at the gates of civilization threatening our cache of booty gathered in our frenzy of consumerism. The Unwashed are likely not to have the same level of gadgetry. It will be flesh and blood against micro-processors and solenoids. As with the smart gadget, we all know a man made of meat is no match for the Terminator. How, then, could the doddering *domini* of Semitic religion mumbling their monotonous incantations in antique buildings full of morbid art compare to *this* phantasmagoria? They cannot. The great Mystery of religion dies with the next app the subject downloads to make its life more comfortable and convenient. The litany of Thou Shalt Nots ... religion showers on the subject are uncomfortable reminders of the inconvenience of forsaking the empirical world for what religion claims to be a metaphysical reality. Scientism capitalizes on this discomfort by insisting that there *is no metaphysical realm*. Instead, these laws of Nature and God are really just man made by thousands of years of collective delusion, meaningless scripture, stupidity, and primitive superstition. Instead, medical immortality is dangled before the subject as the Real Thing. The atavistic Afterlife in Heaven (or Hell) is just bullshit. Want proof? Look at how religions are relative from culture to culture and time to time and therefore not absolute as they claim to be. The subject would do well to remember that each word issuing ex cathedra from the pulpit of Scientism is correct — or else! Meantime the real miracles of science, such as the applications of quantum mechanics, the intrigues of biochemistry, the sublime logic of computing, the beauty of mathematics, and the astounding achievements and discoveries of astrophysics are more or less ignored. The exception is Hollywood's distortion of them in horror, thriller, and science fiction movies — belying the public's ignorance of all of it. If the sublimity of physics, biology, astronomy, and mathematics appears at all in the subject's ken, it is rejected as the unintelligible mumbo-jumbo of nerds and eggheads. It is a pity that Scientism itself is partly responsible for the suppression of what could truly bring enlightenment to the mind and soul of man. Since the Cult of Scientism is more concerned with protecting the territory it has seized from old-time religion than it is with making any humble contribution to human knowledge, it fears that trying to make the fillers of privies *think* will chase them away. Furthermore, it has a special interest in maintaining the illusion that its dogma and liturgy are beyond the understanding of mere mortals. Its penchant for Latin and its priests in lab coats occupying the publicaly funded labs in the citadels of academe provide the awe that Gothic cathedrals and bishop's miters once inspired.

While the public has a hard time understanding the argot of hard science, it has an easy time understanding a person's net worth. In the case of the Scientist-Entrepreneur, his net worth is on everyone's lips. It is reported like sports scores. And with each report the public becomes more and more dazzled at the meteoric rise (as if meteors *rose*, not *fell* — another abrogation of scientific common sense) of the youthful so-and-so who started his scientific explorations as a teenager in his parents' garage and is now one of the richest men (why always men?) in the world.

The threadbare fairy tale of meteoric rise is a fashion template used repeatedly despite its obvious redundancy. Little allowance is made for the principal's appropriation of the Mad Scientists who actually invented, designed, and built the products in relative obscurity on an institute stipend.

The Scientist-Entrepreneur's vast wealth expands exponentially when his (why always his?) company begins offering shares to the public. This overnight rise to the status of *super-rich* is due largely to the financial industry dumping its clients' money into high-yield, high-risk ventures or levering its own bets with loans from banks that know if they lose the bet, their friends in the government will bail them out in exchange for do-nothing positions on the board of directors when they leave office. The super-rich are the worshiped (as well as reviled) icons of modern speculation-based capitalism where the majority of its value is notional, bubbled into the amnion of the derivatives market. These rock stars of technology are seen as either robber barons or benefactors to humanity depending upon which image they prefer to cultivate. Some like the black and others the white hat. Both have their place in modern cowboy mythology. However, this obscene success is portrayed in the media as the Scientist-Entrepreneur's genius for inventing gadgets which people never knew they needed – all presumably in his parents' garage at first, and later on in the world marketplace. What the public does not realize is that it is not the *gadget* itself that is invented; it is the presumed *need* for it which never existed before. Therefore, these so-called scientists are in fact hawkers, hucksters, and, at best, marketing geniuses or are rich enough to hire such capable advert-brains. The old adage in business used to be "Find that need, fill that need." In the realm of the Imaginary it is "Create that need, satisfy that need." This is a significant change in the basic concept of capitalism which, prior to this ethical aesthetic, could boast that it provided what we needed faster, better, cheaper, and more abundantly. Like a mark in a con game on a city sidewalk, the consumer gets hooked into the need for the gadget by getting it seemingly for free, with almost no credit check and then making monthly payments for the service provided by the carrier (drug dealer) of that service, indefinitely since he now cannot live without it. Even the thought of being disconnected from the amnion of the Imaginary is as unthinkable as a fetus cutting its own umbilical cord. Those who see what kind of trap they have fallen into and *do* manage to extract themselves from this con game are regarded by their peers, employers, society, and even the Authorities as suspicious kooks up to no good. Devil worshippers! Meantime, like sports and movie stars, the Scientist-Entrepreneur is held up to the population as the model of what *you* could be ... if you only had a brain.

The church of Scientism depends for its credibility and power upon the prestidigitation of Big Magic (magic from digital tricks) the entrepreneurial gadget maker creates a need for, which is his *real* skill. But, as a corporate ego, he is not satisfied with the tithing the gadget engenders; he also wants secular sainthood status, using some of his excess billions to buy vaccines for African countries or providing free gadgets and computers to poor people and schools so they can tithe too like their betters. Meantime, it was the Mad Scientists, often laboring in obscurity, who made it all possible by actually inventing something. Compared to the huckster capitalizing on his work and taking the credit as a genius, he is at best a footnote in a textbook or, worse, has an electric car named after him running on the form of electricity (DC) he invented an alternative (AC) — now the global standard. Who is Nikola Tesla (hint: not a car)? Who is Edwin Armstrong? (Who is John Galt, for that matter?) They might have lacked the marketing skills those who in one way or another appropriated or exploited (developed) their work. One of the differences between the old order of religious hegemony and the new order of scientific power is that the former seats itself in the *intrinsic* operations and the latter the *extrinsic* expressions of the accomplishments, wishes, hopes, prayers, and imagination of culture. The former is introverted, and the latter extroverted. While the former may have looked with suspicion upon the extroverted expressions of one's innermost impulses — rather hard to account for over its five millennia of recorded history — the latter most certainly regards the introverted orientation to social culture as the sign of a serial killer, mass murderer, or Devil worshipper. How often have we heard from the media that the bomber-gunman-arsonist-terrorist, cat-sacrificer, kept to himself and was a loner? Very suspicious indeed! 'Tis a pity he did not let it all hang out on a social media page for the authorities, big corporations, and strangers to mine for private data. Worse, Christianity, and especially the Roman Catholic Church (but strangely enough not Judaism), is regarded as a veritable font of child abusers, homosexuals, and psychopaths who "did it for Jesus." Could this blood libel have anything to do with the fact that Christianity, and especially the Roman Catholic Church, is targeted by Scientism as its biggest rival? If Islam had not come along with a more aggressive approach to self-defense, it might have spelled the end for it *and* the Christian branch of Semitic religion. However, it must contend with its own media libel that all Muslims are "terrorists," and that the Prophet was a child abuser because he took a a young wife after his first wife, who was much older than him when he was a teenager, died. It matters not to the media, ignorant of history, that an adult Isha took up the sword after her husband died and was the vanguard of battle for the cause of religious freedom — a cause that continues to this day. To a culture concerned with *extrinsic* appearances only, for that is the ethical aesthetic of the Imaginary, the *intrinsic* is nearly invisible. At best it is found in dusty books, weird old paintings in a museum treasure house, warbling from a cantata in a Gothic church, or drifting in the breeze over the minarets at dusk during the Call to Prayer. Those who value the intrinsic over the extrinsic are seen as losers. The occult (meaning obscure, hidden) treasure they have stored up where moth and rust cannot destroy and where thieves cannot break in and steal (says Matthew 6:19) is simply *not valued* by the prevailing extrinsic ethical aesthetic. Just as the tertium quid of eccentricity, allied with ecstatic culture, is viewed as something to be punished by the hegemony, so too is the ethical aesthetic of Baudelaire's *le flaneur magnifique* and Adam Smith's detached spectator. The eccentric's ecstasy in the sense of jouissance, *le flaneur's* indolent disengagement, and the detached spectator's personal disinterest are cause for alarm in the amnion. Suspicion is first aroused when they are not perpetually staring into the black mirror of their digital gadget. They have dared raise their heads from the forty-five degree angle of the slave and look at the others walking into traffic while texting. A big part of the problem is that the intrinsic cannot be properly quantified. What cannot be quantified does not exist in the ethical aesthetic of the amnion because it also cannot be encoded into data. Since value is always quantitative, the intrinsic is of no social or economic consequence, which, however, is his value to the few that have negated the first negation of their self-determination. Despite the fact that this discourse is easily found in narrative art from Melville to *The Matrix*, the person who dares to live it is the one who will do the most damage to the amnion merely by his presence and not any bomb-tossing or mall-shooting.

But there is push-back from the amnion, which does not take such behavior lightly. Religious or inspired art, tradition, literature, architecture, history, the occult, sacred music, philosophy, and even the idea of anything being holy are belittled as if they were a child's belief in Santa Claus. The modern Apex Consumer believes that by sacrificing his self-determination he has also shuffled off the coil of atavistic superstition and the need to worship in its benighted grottos. Domini of this cultural heritage are vilified as perverts, cat-sacrificers, and deluded idiots, a characterization which is a deliberately divisive move by the priesthood of Scientism to maintain its nascent hegemony. Despite the many real shortcomings of these Domini, of which they are well aware, they pursue the sublime, the hidden, the obscure, the intrinsic, while the Apex Consumer rejects all of it as a life that is stupid and contagious. Worse, they are portrayed by the media, which also means in the imagination of the public, as anti-social and therefore anti-amnion, which in the orthodoxy of Scientism is the worst possible form of apostacy.

The sanctity with which medical doctors are regarded is a good example of the creation of a priestly *cast* serving as an interface between the plain language of the corporeal, and the (surreal) argot of orthodox Scientism. They are the *demigods* of the hegemonic order, and therefore of the Imaginary — giving them a kind of otherworldly aura. In the form of the scalpel, between the fingers of their purple surgical gloves they hold the Power of Life and Death kooks think only God can wield. They can cause pain or make it go away. They can cut one open with impunity, something only serial killers and other murderers do without it. They can induce sleep lasting months, or awaken the dead with defibrillators and other methods of getting the heart beating. They can look at two millimeter slices of the brain with expensive machines. Their miracles are unceasing - for those who have access to health insurance. Their miracles cease when the insurance is taken away. Therefore, the logic of medicine is, by syllogism, that the miracle is the health insurance not the procedure. Just ask anyone in a third-world country which is the better miracle, to be able to afford health care, or having the Great White Father fly in on an NGO jumbo jet to give him an inoculation against a disease that does not even exist in this medical angel's country, only to fly back to it once the good deed is done.

To be treated as a human being with needs, one must tithe to the Cult of Scientism either directly, through an employer, or by high taxes. Miss a payment, and one is excommunicated from holy protection against the evil of destitution and the fate of the dreaded Underclass. Meantime, death and old age are regarded as diseases that can be treated, prevented, or even cured if one obeys the edicts, dogma, and commandments of the hegemony. The hegemony presents this canon through the media owned by its transnational overlords. The media products the subject buys parade examples of wicked apostates who disobeyed the dogma of the orthodoxy after being tempted by the devil's advocates of sovereignty and self-determination. How dare they! In the religion of Scientism chronic illness, genetic limitations, and freak injuries are regarded as the work of the Devil against whom no apostate may ask for protection. Only the anointed may receive the benedictions of the Great White Father of Scientism. If thrown into the wilderness of bare life as penalty, the individual must now make its way among the *Untermenschen* of the Underclass. In the dark Underworld of the Underclass, evil lurks around every corner in the form of drug dealers, prostitutes, criminals, sex traffickers, child abusers, dirty poor people, and last but not least the lumpen proletariat impervious to the nomos by their Bohemian misbehavior. Those born into the hegemony as full members of the Imaginary order but through some calamity or other fall into the Underclass are seen as *unfortunates*. Lady Luck was just not with them in the great casino of the amnion. Those born into the Underclass are the *less fortunates*. Those with more or less full access to potential indebtedness are the *fortunates*. The existence of these three strata of players in the great casino of what is supposed to be an egalitarian society show that civilization may not, as Terrence McKenna once said, be your friend.

Therefore, part of thesis of this book is that in modern Western-style civilization we live in a new Dark Age. Central to the social and therefore religious doctrine of the European Middle Ages was the concept of "fortuna." It is the idea that one is born into one's circumstances by random fortune which, even during one's lifetime, keeps spinning like a roulette wheel, driving us on to a predetermined, but occluded, fate. The Romans even had a saying about this: *amor fati*, love your fate. After all, what choice do you have? One may be born on a lucky number but after a spin of the wheel one might fall into a much lower state of existence. What makes this concept so significant for its day was that one's fortune was not necessarily because of what one deserved based on one's behavior in the eyes of God. It was a much more mysterious process which, at best, could be considered a reminder to renounce all worldly goods and love God because your life *will be* nasty, brutish, and short. If it is not, then you have sinned, because sin is the only way to make it less nasty and brutish, even though it may shorten it even more. It is fair to say that there were two views of the matter at the time (and it was a *long* time: 500-1500, more or less) consistent throughout Christendom: A) One may have some influence over one's fate by loving and being obedient to God, and B) Renunciation of the world, or asceticism, was the only path to liberation from the jaws of a wicked universe.

The matter of their contrasting psychology — one positive one negative — is anticipated by Job 1. Satan bets that Job, a fortunate man, will renounce God if he is stricken with misfortune and become unfortunate (negative). God bets Satan that Job will remain steadfast in his righteous faith in God come what may (positive). What we have here is a classic gentleman's wager. "Hast not thou made an hedge about him, and about his house, and about all that he hath on every side? Thou hast blessed the work of his hands, and his substance is increased in the land. But put forth thine hand now, and touch all that he hath, and he will curse thee to thy face," says Satan. Soon Job loses all his wealth and children, and more, and yet maintains his faith in God. "Then Job arose, and rent his mantle, and shaved his head, and fell down upon the ground, and worshipped, And said, Naked came I out of my mother's womb, and naked shall I return thither: the LORD gave, and the LORD hath taken away; blessed be the name of the LORD." Also, what we have here is a good example of *amor fati* in practice. On the other hand, the phrase "the Lord giveth and the Lord taketh away" is part of everyday fatalism. On behalf of the agenda of its transnational overlords, the hegemony wants its subjects to believe that the mechanized civilization it has built up and networked with digital gadgets has at least beat the system of fate. But when fate intervenes in its random way, the discourse of the hegemony suddenly tacks in the other direction, saying woopsi-daisy; you just got a bad number on the wheel of fortuna! So, are we to believe that Scientism's *Gott-ist-tot-Theologie* nevertheless contains the same injunction of *amor fati* that Job was supposed to embrace, to the loss of Satan's bet? Psychologically, this is a grim prospect. In the weak, it awakens fear of the loss of object constancy. As the mother has become the teat of consumerism, and the father the ferule of the state, when both fail, the subject feels *forsaken* by its ostensible parents. Abandonment anxiety produces a sense of the loss of object constancy, a clinical funk it cannot seem to evade without illegal drugs, alcohol, or psychiatric prescriptions. And even then it is only paved over with the hope, on the part of society, that the subject will just shut up and go away. Everyone hates a sore loser! At least the medieval peasant had God to fall back on, which is what the Church typically offered anyway, particularly with the parable of Job. The modern-day peasant only has bankruptcy at best and suicide, slow or fast, at worst. Nevertheless, the sentiment remains the same over the intervening centuries. It is expressed well in a poem from a Thirteenth Century manuscript found in 1803 in the Benedictine abbey Benedikbeuern south of Munich, Germany. This poem and others from that cache made their way into the work of Johan Andreas Schmeller in his poems of 1847 and consequently into the lyrics of composer Carl Orff's *Carmina Burana*.

> O Fortune, like the moon you are changeable, ever waxing and waning; hateful life first oppresses and then soothes as fancy takes it; poverty and power it melts them like ice. Fate – monstrous and empty, you whirling wheel, you are malevolent, well-being is vain and always fades to nothing, shadowed and veiled you plague me too; now through the game I bring my bare back to your villainy. Fate is against me in health and virtue, driven on and weighted down, always enslaved. ("Fortuna Imperatrix Mundi")

It is a cruel fate indeed that Scientism has taken away the modern peasant's refuge in God, spiritualism, or the occult, replacing it with pharmaceuticals, cars, toys, gadgets, and exotic vacations. If anything, science has given the subject half the story. Nature, though anthropomorphized into a sick and dying mother by the media, cannot be trusted. Its invisible microbes, sudden natural disasters, raging storms, deadly lightning, hot weather, cold weather, cloudy days, heavy rain, icy and snowy roads, stinging bugs, high winds, and suspicious wild animals make life inconvenient and uncomfortable. The soft, impotent subject depends upon the amnion the way a fetus depends upon the womb. Cowering in sterile suburban enclaves accessible only by car and fearing that the Underclass might leave its ghettos and rampage along Main Street looting coffee shops, the Apex Consumer wants *absolute quiet at all times*. Quiet = security; noise = ghetto. Silence is the emblem reassuring the Apex Consumer that the local government it pays high property taxes for has everything under control. At the same time, those high property taxes also reassure the subject that dirty poor people will never be able to contaminate its suburban paradise, bringing drug abuse and broken homes with them. "That's why we left the city and moved here," says the mother to her neighbor. "It's so *quiet* here." Her artificial environment must be predictably *deterministic* to offset her fear of random *fortuna,* which, alas, seems to be the nature of the universe. We cannot understand its complexity, therefore making it seem chaotic. Meantime, the Apex Consumer stares at nature on TV and screams that someone (governments, NGO's, activists — *anyone but him*) must do something about the environment before it is too late, but refers to an overcast day with rain as bad weather and calls the police if he sees a raccoon picking through the trash.

With nothing but a mountain of the booty of consumerism cluttering its garage to show for its existence, and having filled many of da Vinci's privies, the subject who falls from being *fortunate* to *unfortunate* is in some ways worse off than the *less fortunates* who adapted early on to their hopeless fate. Having no choice, they made it work. As a result, they do not welcome the Great White Father, now fallen from Heaven, into the nasty, brutish places they have carved out for themselves in order to feel part of civilization, albeit an unwanted one. However, this fear of falling through the bottom of the amnion, presumably through its rectum rather than birth canal, is exactly what the hegemony *wants* the subject to feel: the terror of being a *have-not,* so that social order is maintained and everything can be under control for the law-abiding citizen who still has a job. What the subject seldom realizes is that this is the terror of the sublime, just as is terror of the battlefield. It is an *opportunity* to be free of the amnion, but the subject perceives it as a *threat* to its pleasurable sense of life — which is its only ethical aesthetic (i.e. Freud's pleasure principle). Rather than aim its psychic energy at learning about life outside the amnion, it directs it into figuring out a way to climb back. A good concrete example of this is when the subject becomes a credit risk. At that point the loan sharks descend, offing it car loans and credit cards with especially usurious interest as a penalty for the poor credit rating acquired during its fall through the bottom of the amnion. As if this were not enough, in fearing the imaginary abyss of losing the ability to borrow money, the subject also fears the bare life of the sublime which, at this point, is his only hope for a meaningful life. Joining a church, Alcoholics Anonymous, going off the grid, writing a novel, or even reinventing oneself as an intrinsic rather than extrinsic are all possibilities that did not exist in the amnion. Now the subject is awash in *Möglichkeit,* but it has no ability to abide in terror or, as Keats puts it, abide in a psychological state where it is "capable of being in uncertainties, Mysteries, doubts, without any irritable reaching after fact & reason ..." Thus, the subject alienates itself from beauty and truth. While the subject is to blame for the choices it makes in life, its blindness to possibility in the face of terror has been ingeniously engineered by the hegemony in its fabrication of the amnion as a safety mechanism designed to defend it from the influence of capable apostates. By superimposing the terror of falling into the Underclass over the prospect of the sublime's horror vacui, the hegemony stops the subject from acting out the creative imperative of self-determination. The Imaginary, as an *apparatus,* can only exist when the subject's resident imagination has been immobilized, the way a wasp paralyzes its victim with its sting. To reactivate its cognition, which, after all, requires imagination to function, the hegemony of the amnion uses media content targeting the subject's consumer profile that its digital gadget has transmitted to the Big Data through telemetry. Otherwise, the subject may imagine that there is more to life than the amnion of the Imaginary. Free-ranging imagination belongs only to the *feral*, which is why they are either lionized or fed to the lions, depending upon the circumstances. The amnion also fears that once the subject begins to engage its active imagination, it will also engage its analytic function. Without it, the subject has no power to verify what is true and real for itself. It must instead rely upon the commercial and state purveyors of information which it cannot weigh against its own analysis and therefore must accept as dogma. Without the analytic function, consciousness is not possible. The first stirrings of consciousness may reveal the reality of the subject's circumstances — if it has the intelligence to do so. If this does happen, however, then the subject begins to act out its cognition as the *getting-to-know* rather than the *knowing-of*, which is now junked as the suspicious propaganda it is. In this mode, the getting-to-know soon reveals the reality of the cabal of the amnion's Imaginary, the hegemony's nomos guarding the amnion from the subject, and, if the subject is truly perspicacious at this point, the hegemony's transnational overlords (mostly global financial systems allied with the governments they have bought and paid for). At the same time, the subject has bankrupted itself, gone into default on its loans, and has seen its property foreclosed upon and its assets confiscated. Such spectacles are just the shock it needs to wake up, while at the same time what it first perceives as an unspeakable disaster may exonerate it from its intractable debt. (This is not true in every country, however.) By doing so the subject becomes free of the grip of the hegemony, at least temporarily.

Even in the bare life of the Underclass, however, the *Unfortunates* attempt to maintain their superiority over the *Less Fortunates* by the mere fact that they were not born into such penury. Also, they have something the Less Fortunates do not have: the mobility to climb back up into the mother ship of the Imaginary and be whisked off once more into the Shangi-la of consumer paradise. Those of the Unfortunates who were once fortunate Apex Consumers who go to prison for a white-collar (i.e. harmless, as opposed to black-faced, i.e. harmful) crime, write a book about it, becoming richer from the advance once the reduced sentence or sabbatical in a low-security prison has been served — options unavailable to the Less Fortunates of the Underclass. Those of the Less Fortunates who find themselves in prison know that once they have served their time, only the life of crime will sustain them since no one will hire a felon. And, if they do not end up dead in the process, they will find themselves right back in prison as statistics show. Once having been in prison, they are denied *all access* to legitimate forms of participation in the hegemony. Note that almost 10 percent of the US population is in prison at any given time; some credible estimates say that one in three persons in the US will go to jail or prison.

So why are these social deviants reviled by the system that claims to have rehabilitated them and wants to give them a second chance? Of course, that is altruistic rhetoric merely serving the purpose of reassuring folks in suburbia that not only does the government keep the criminals off their streets, but it also provides social therapy to get them back on their feet and working toward admission to the amnion. As citizens in good standing who have repented to the Cult of Mediocrity, which is the paramount ethical aesthetic of the amnion and its minions, they will teach others the path of the straight and narrow. This fairy tale is swallowed hook, line, and sinker by the Apex Consumer, just as is the fairy tale of the benefits the far-off other gets for making the consumer goods the denizens of the amnion seek as their reward for the abdication of their self-determination. Why so credulous? After signing the promissory notes that are the rite of passage into the state of capture in the amnion through debt, the subject enters into a psychology that can accept perpetual contradiction. The baseline contradiction from which all others emanate is the inversion of synthetic for analytic propositions, and the reverse. In its own quaint way, it is what John in Revelation calls the mark of the Beast. "And he made all, both small and great, rich and poor, free and bond, to receive a mark in their right hand or in their foreheads, *And that no man might buy or sell, save he that had the mark*, or the name of the beast, or the number of his name" (Rev. 13, v. 16-17; italics added). The italics highlight John's insight regarding the nature of consumerism in his own day, which is no different from today's materialism, except that now it is an extension of Scientism's imperative to borrow and consume. To be an Apex Consumer one must be officially recognized as such by the amnion. The mark, of course, is penurious debt taken on as a bond between the lord (banks) and bondsman (borrower). Throughout his sublime narrative, John berates those who reject the sublime for the Beast of materialism. I do not quote Revelation because I believe John's vision was some kind of prognostication. After all, a revelation is the *revealing* of something in the present, not the prognostication of something in the future. While John is describing the Second Coming, it is not any different than what has already been predicted in scripture and the Gospels — even in the scripture of Judaism which was already ancient when

John wrote the book. The point of emphasizing this passage in Revelation is to show that John understood the significance of the abdication of self-determination, man's God-given power to unite with fate in a meaningful understanding of death. Just as Darwin considered evolution to be the essence of God's creation, so too did John believe that self-determination was the essence of God's gift to mankind for the sake of his own salvation. He saw that this fatal strategy could only lead to a bad end for everyone. Adding up the wars, weapons, and conflicts of just the 20th Century is an Apocalypse enough, only it is spread out over a century so it looks like good triumphing over evil — the simple-minded rationalization for its vandalism and slaughter. However, I believe the wars of the 20th Century were *worse* than anything John describes with intense poetry, because they were *real*. The difference is that instead of getting a messiah out of the mayhem, history witnessed the coming of the *Gott-ist-tot-Theologie* of Scientism.

Consequently, forgiveness and repentance are handled by the apparatus of the state nomos. For this scheme to work, there must be a scapegoat. The odor of the apostate is a perpetual threat to the illusions of the Imaginary's consumer culture which wants only the sweet smell of success. The hegemony's autonomous macrophages snap into action to consume all attempts to pollute the purity of the Imaginary's promise of eternal *Genuss*. The fear is that if the amnion gets tainted with bare life, the subject will panic and regress back to the intrinsic order of religion or turn to the drugs and violence of the Underworld. Is this fear rational? Perhaps. Despite its occasional alliances with the Underworld, the hegemony remains at odds with it in order to maintain the illusion that it is not *also* a mafia. It sets up a public perception that there is a *good* mafia (the hegemony) and a *bad* mafia (criminal conspirators). Therefore, its biggest financial competitor today is the Underworld, in particular drug cartels that do everything right when it comes to economics, giving them a considerable edge over the hegemony's reckless exploitation of wealth through gambling in the derivatives market which is mostly notional (financial argot for *imaginary*). Drug cartel money is *real*. The cartels have proven that they can be big players, calling the shots, and even entering into secure alliances with the mainstream financial system of the world. And who can blame them for embracing this ethical aesthetic? Are they instead supposed to be moralists out to teach the wealthy a lesson about being good? Furthermore, are banks supposed to distinguish between dirty and clean money when the politicians who regulate them routinely accept dirty money for their pay-for-play enterprise?

What is most unfortunate about the Underclass is that it is stuck between two mafias: that of the criminal underworld and that of the transnational overlords of the *statist* hegemony.

Despite its loyalty to and faith in the promises of eternal *Genuss* of the amnion, the Apex Consumer is nevertheless in a wretched state of physical and mental health. Fat, drunk, drugged, semi-literate, and burdened with intractable debt, the subject struggles onward to its grave as if it lived in the jungle without a pocket knife. What happened to civilization's promise of a life that is *not* nasty, brutish, and short? Is the subject to accept only civilization's discontents (*Unbehagen*) and not its contentment in anything other than comfort and convenience? Most house cats live a life of comfort and convenience. Is the subject condemned to live the life of its own house cat, only cats do not have debt to pay? In fleeing the supposed terrors of the sublime, the subject finds itself trapped in an oubliette of debt and ill health which all of the marvels of Scientism suddenly cannot cure or even treat properly. Of course this condition eventually affects the subject's ability to earn enough money to make monthly payments on its debt and other forms of the umbilicus of the amnion, such as a car and network access. The greatest impact is on the subject's access to healthcare; it imagines going to the doctor to be like bringing a car in for repairs at a dealership. Unfortunately, cars can always be fixed, whereas humans can seldom be rid of their chronic illnesses that eventually drag them into the abyss of the sublime in the form of death. The aura of omnipotence projected by the medical apparatus vaporizes as soon as the patient runs out of money. Crippled by illness and impoverished by its economic consequences, the subject finds itself powerless to challenge the empty promises that once gave it infinite hope for a happy and healthy immortality - even *after* having been diagnosed with diabetes and heart disease. The subject finds that one pill it needs to live another day costs more than a week's worth of groceries and is not covered by its insurance. In some economies this expense is passed on to the healthy population in the form of taxes, as they must support a vast population receiving medical care as a social benefit.

More often than not, the subject simply regards its medical condition as a deterministic event, for instance being the result of its genetics or the widespread belief that old age is a disease for which we have not yet found a cure. In history there have been no violent revolutions over the matter of medical care, despite its modern roll as political football in debates and campaigns. Universal medical care, which is a rather vague phrase, is used by political hucksters as one more socialist morsel to throw at a hungry populace in return for votes. There are obvious reasons for this, which I will not go into here as I have tried not to make this discussion political in a direct sense. However, one of the less obvious reasons is that to the Cult of Scientism, illness, disease, and death are nevertheless seen as consequences of medieval *fortuna*. In this respect the new church resembles the Christian Semitic religion it has displaced. Herein we find the neo-medievalism of Scientism, sanctimoniously priding itself on being the peak of human achievement and progress, though without the beautiful triptychs, tondos, icons, illuminated manuscripts, and cathedrals. After Scientism did its best to smother the Christian and Muslim branches of the Semitic religions in their sleep in the West and Near East, the matter took on a more clinical guise reflecting the new religion's putative embrace of absolute Positivism. In this paradigm, 1) The subject punishes itself by not observing the contradictory hygiene and health practices proscribed by medical science and insurance companies, 2) Sickness and death take the place of Satan as the stalkers of men's souls, 3) Bad luck (fortuna) is not in the medical-industrial complex's control, so the subject must bear the yoke like a good peasant, 4) Death is a disease to be cured, but only if the subject pays its bills.

Meanwhile, the subject's paradise of democracy and civil society with at least *some* kind of chaotic healthcare system is far from the untreated epidemic diseases of the far-off other. The idea is that the worker who makes the subject's goods and gadgets, or hosts the exploitation of his country's natural resources for the manufacturing cartels, should stop complaining, and be happy he has any job at all. The rare subject who cares at all about this disparity assuages himself with tales of the symbolic beneficence of NGO's that buzz in, do their duty, and get the hell out — provided they are not part of an entrenched military occupation by the hegemony for the purpose of enforcing what it calls euphemistically *stability* in the region. Serious acute diseases of the most deadly kind, such as HIV, malaria, dysentery, and typhoid — all either preventable or treatable, are considered normal in these no-go zones covering huge parts of entire continents. Back home, millions are addicted to prescription opioids. Tens of thousands each year die of what are supposed to be third-world diseases such as HIV-AIDS. Nevertheless, it is seldom reported in the media, as it is an embarrassment to medical Scientism. It reveals its fundamental impotence as well as its subservience to industrial medical product manufacturers whose massive profits are traded on stock exchanges leveraged by central banks. Complicating the matter are the medical insurance companies leveraging their gambling in the derivatives market with their clients' insurance premiums. Note that, for instance, the Chicago Mercantile Exchange (CME) boasted on its website recently that it handles $1 quadrillion (twelve zeros) in derivative trades per year. Many people have never heard of the CME, or even have imagined there is such a sum of money in play.

Millions more are addicted to alcohol, tobacco, illegal drugs, overeating, and a deadly sedentary lifestyle. Tens of thousands die in car crashes, which is taken as the price of having such a wonderful thing as a car (something the far-off other seldom has and is therefore spared this form of mechanical death). Even more astounding, tens of millions in the subject's own progressive, modern, scientific, egalitarian, democratic, state where the rule of law (nomos) is paramount, lack access to medical aid beyond emergency services and charity care. Meantime, in a neighboring or allied state, healthcare may have been socialized by the government, causing the state's sovereign debt to soar, thus jeopardizing its national security and economy. While such dread diseases as bubonic plague are only found in story books in the Apex Consumer's state, heart disease, cancer, and diabetes are epidemic, bringing trillions of dollars into the market cap of medical product producers. They are also the socially acceptable ways to die, whereas death from such diseases as HIV-AIDS and drug overdoses are regarded as scandalous and are therefore ignored into oblivion. The subject regards the news that a person has one or more of the popular diseases as plain old bad luck rather than evidence belying the amnion's promise of medical immortality. Meantime, the subject has neglected its spiritual immortality in the afterlife, having lapsed in its faith and now, on an expensive death bed hooked up to life support in a hospital and attended to in its last moments of existence by paid strangers, the subject has nowhere to turn to make sense out of the only absolutely inevitable event in life: death. Was this worth the death of the sublime? Is this what escaping the terror of the horror vacui looks like? Did the amnion's nomological mouthpieces explain clearly enough that this was its prescheduled *terminus vita*? The subject's high regard for the advanced state of civilization that brought it to this end, however, remains unshaken. While its younger, healthier friends and family may regard the encumbered subject's fate with pity, they seldom see it as a wake-up call that something is wrong with the system to which they have sacrificed their life force.

Exacerbating the situation are persistent and growing economic and social ills which the subject's history books say were taken on, wrestled with, and conquered by canonized individuals touted by the hegemony as the founders, movers, and shakers of the state's progressive fairy tale. Why, then, is the word racism on everyone's lips? Why do millions live in poverty next door to billionaires? Why does influenza kill tens of thousands every year despite there being several vaccines (for virus types A, B, and C)? Why is the nation always on the brink of catastrophic economic collapse? Why is almost ten percent of the population in prison or under correctional supervision? It is astounding that the subject's faith in and devotion to the agenda of its overlords remains unfazed despite this overwhelming evidence that in fact the amnion is out of control and headed for some kind of catastrophe only a divine visionary such as John of Patmos could imagine.

A combination of fear of reprisal from the hegemonic order and disenfranchisement from the Imaginary order terrorize the subject into complacency. Millions default on their mortgages, loans, and credit cards. They go bankrupt after losing their jobs. Their marriages last only a few years. The jobs they were promised by the experts in business and academe vanish the moment they graduate from the training schools, colleges, and universities they borrowed huge sums of money to attend or pay high taxes to fund. They permit themselves to become utterly dependent upon the gadgetry connecting them to the amnion's nomos, and the hucksters and hawkers enforcing and selling this state of capture. They then complain, symbolically and impotently, that they have no *privacy*, the word that has euphemistically taken the place of *freedom* in modern discourse. Meantime, their expensive gadgetry is plagued with glitches, errors, bugs, viruses, malware, hackers, and half-baked builds that must be constantly patched to avoid *even worse* exploitation and customer frustration with malfunctioning products. As these miseries pile up, and the subject begins to feel the deadly stress of it all, it is given pills which make it all better but are extremely expensive so that only those with health insurance can afford them. Soon the threat of losing that insurance becomes *terrifying*. Not only do they fear a sudden fall into the Underclass, but also that they will lose their drug supply of happy pills and have to face the world with their under-developed psychological survival skills, called in the business *coping*. In states where the subject is guaranteed its pills even after its own ability to pay for them has ceased, the burden is shifted to those who *have* jobs and pay taxes, but are not entitled to the benefit they pay for. Consequently, even those with jobs struggle economically, pushing themselves closer to the brink of the same fate as the unfortunate former Apex Consumer who now receives the social benefits that they pay for. Such dependency upon the state means that *it must not fail*, even though providing these social benefits also pushes it closer to the brink of insolvency where it *will* fail. The consequence is that the state must sever the social programs the destitute subject depends upon, or reduce those services to a perfunctory level. Even a cursory count of failed states in the past one hundred years, never mind the past 4,000 years, should give anyone dependent upon the state for survival concern. I need not list any, as they are the brick and mortar of history and the news.

The new age of the amniotic empire is, ironically, the age of the failed state. How could this be? Digital technology has allowed the new paradigm of a *disposable state* to become normal. The network is a supra-national state, controlled by a kind of technocracy in the employ of the transnational overlords of the local hegemonies. A state made out of dirt and stone is merely a staging ground for military adventures or mineral mines. The folks tied to the earth there are either in the way, cannon fodder, or useful in sweatshops and office towers. The situation is hardly an example of normalcy to so-called developing nations rich in natural resources (e.g. oil, minerals), but without the funds and technology to extract them. What matters to the hegemony, and its transnational overlords, is the *digital transfer of wealth* from state to state to avoid surveillance, engage in regulatory arbitrage, and evade taxes on profits and capital gains. The Apex Consumer living in a first-world state once reposed on the notion that *his* state would be the successful *Tausendjähriges Reich* where the original one failed. But the success of this paradigm depends upon a perpetual lust for *Liebensraum* and its conquest — either in the form of outright occupation and exploitation, or remotely through capture of the industrial infrastructure of the target nation that has something the amnion needs (cheap labor, rare minerals) to survive in its infinitely inefficient political economy. In the dark of night, just before a holiday (typically), the lawmakers of the disposable state abdicate the subject's political and economic self-determination through the acquisition of sovereign debt. In doing so they sign promissory notes on behalf of the state and its polity, which must pay it back over decades and maybe centuries. The deals are made at the speed of light between the central banks and big investment banks of amenable nations, presumably with the subject's acquiescence. After all, it was the subject who voted for these policies represented by the politicians it put in office. So while it may seem that the subject abdicates its sovereignty to the disposable state, the actual mechanism of the apparatus only uses the disposable state as front for laundering money. The transnational overlords are the real and final hegemony. All of this is not a conspiracy, however. I am not setting up a kind of straw man here. There is nothing particularly shadowy about the so-called transnational overlords. Nearly everything they do can be found with a few clicks on the Internet. But no one does it because the Internet is for pornography, online gambling, random surfing, and self-diagnosis of hypochondria. Its transnational nature simply means there is no one nation where it is located. Explaining overlords is a more complex problem which I hope this book addresses by the horns. But what I mean specifically, quantifiably, analytically is just everyday investment banking — but within the bubble of the derivatives market consisting of notional (imaginary) wealth *in toto* exceeding the total GDP of the 180 or so states the IMF acknowledges as functioning political economies. The derivatives bubble may be considered the mother of all amnions. Therefore, when the subject abdicates, it is *by proxy* to the cartel of the banking systems managing and profiting from this leveraged casino, just as the mafia did from Las Vegas back in the good old days of Jimmy Hoffa. As the far-off other is forced to abdicate to the corporate needs of the Apex Consumer's hegemony by its cheap labor, so too does the subject in the hegemonic state abdicate by taking on insurmountable debt which becomes a perpetual tithe to the Cult of Mediocrity, the fanatical fundamentalist religion of which is Scientism.

Ironically, the captains of industry and finance bedeviling the subject are worshipped by it as heroes rather than tormentors. Members of political parties with a decades-long history of exploitation of the polity and support of the corporate hegemony (usually investment banks) at the expense of their constituency, spin fairy tales of benevolence and altruism in the media owned by the corporate interests they serve. Meantime, they rob their constituency on behalf of their powerful masters. To get away with such corruption, they apply a constructivist approach to law-making, being sure it hurts only the citizen, not the corporate interests they serve. When challenged about this, they plead not guilty because they are saving the economy so that the proles can keep their tentative jobs. It is easy to find politicians of this sort who have gone from rags to riches overnight serving their corporate masters in the investment banking industry. Unless they *prefer not to,* in which case they are marginalized by the senior party bosses but manage to keep their souls which appeals to certain perverse constituencies. The apparatchiks' corporate interests, surreptitiously installed, aid ambitious undertakings by the indoctrination and censorship system of public schools and public and private universities. In the amnion, the purpose of education is to retard the subject's mental development until such time as the subject may be sold cheaply on the job market.

Golden boys, stuffed with knowledge and armed with wits sharpened on the analytic whetstone, cost too much and tend to think for themselves. It would be better if they took up the violin. As it is in science today, the proof of truth value in this apparatus is consensus. Therefore, the goal of the propaganda and enforcement organs of the hegemony is for everyone to get on message, as approved by their corporate masters. The subject will never be able to take the wheel of the ship of its life unless it has, as Hegel says, *negated the negation* of its self-determination through doubting what it assumes is reality. Doubt is the first step to unraveling the amnion's imaginary inversion of analytic (verifiable) propositions and synthetic (unverifiable) propositions, where one takes the place of the other, so that they may rectify into their proper place in society and the intellect.

3.1: Abdication of the fillers of privies

A default culture of political and economic corruption is nothing new. A society of obedient serfs is nothing new either; it is the rule, not the exception of history. Therefore, da Vinci has some empirical and historical support for his observation that the masses choose a life where they live as nothing more than alimentary canals, or, as he puts it, "fillers of privies" (*Notebook XIX*). Plankton. For humans, evolution is not a priori; it is a posteriori, following the event of the evolution of consciousness. Persons useful only as political shills and compulsive consumers are immediately cast aside when the hegemony and its amnion have no more use for them. If use-value is *assigned*, it is not truly value because it is not intrinsic. It the same with power: If power is *given*, it is not really power; power must be *seized*. The typical subject in the amnion has neither intrinsic value to society except as a consumer *node*, nor any real power except what might be loaned it to perform some (at the time) perfunctory duty (e.g. schoolteacher-babysitter). At the end of its tenure it may be snatched away from this *pro tem* function and cast back into the passive consumer role, or even be absorbed into the dark cloud of the hegemony as a social dependent or worse, a prisoner of the justice system. As the industrial Machine Age burgeoned into the great period of mechanized world wars and the clash between socialism, fascism, and capitalism, variously styled, those who in one way or another found themselves on the fringe of the maelstrom looked in and reported what they saw with considerable misgiving for the future of mankind. Matthew Arnold's mid-Nineteenth Century poem "Dover Beach" and W.B. Yeats' early Twentieth Century poem "The Second Coming" presage Scientism's advance to priority cloaked in the bellicose realpolitik of banking wars. The first sees it as a loss of faith; the second as the fulfillment of a prophesy – much as John of Patmos does. Arnold identifies what Lyotard describes in *The Inhuman* as the "temporal gap" between the present and future in which the paradigms sustaining us now shatter to make room for the paradigms which will later (the *other* now) sustain us. This gap must be closed by the interests controlling the political economy of societies dependent upon the vicissitudes of the financial markets. In other words, the hegemony, through the prestidigitation of Scientism's Big Magic, must make time stand still. In *Libidinal Economy*, Lyotard says that,

> The more the temporal gap increases, the more the chance increases of something unexpected happening - the greater the risk. The growth of risk can itself be calculated in terms of probability and in turn translated into monetary terms. Money here appears as what it really is, time stocked in view of forestalling what comes about. (p. 66)

Arnold shows that the gap which opens in the Machine Age (roughly between the late Eighteenth to the late Nineteenth in Europe) is between Faith, which had an intrinsic political economy at the time, and an extrinsic one engendered by the Machine Age where there is no God because science has "proven" that religion is nothing more than pernicious humbug. But what really bothers Arnold is his hunch that machines, and the lust for self-destruction the loss of faith brings on, will conspire to make war more horrible. War is the inevitable outcome of the death of the sublime as it fights to regain its inevitable priority as nonbeing.

> The Sea of Faith
> Was once, too, at the full, and round earth's shore
> Lay like the folds of a bright girdle furled.
> But now I only hear
> Its melancholy, long, *withdrawing* roar,
> *Retreating*, to the breath
> Of the night-wind, *down* the vast edges drear
> And naked shingles of the world.

Faith withdraws and retreats into a Hades-like nether world from what was once the "bright girdle" enclosing the edges of the earth. Faith's modest beachhead is lost in the *anschluss* of Scientism's annexation of religion's political economy and intrinsic and eccentric culture. Perhaps there is an expedient reason for it which is not ideological or philosophical. The purpose is basically to take over religion's sales territory in the hustle to create more Hope through ever more fanciful promises of Heaven on earth. So what is the purpose of making time stop by paying capital forward by investing in promises of the future? Faith is a *sea* in Arnold's metaphor. In this sense it is rather like the oceanic feeling of eternity expressed by Romain Rolland in his letter to Freud above. While Freud was honest and said that he could not fit such intangible quantities into the framework of what he understood as the psyche, he did find what satisfied him as an explanation for the religious phenomenon. Arnold's "bright girdle furled" is not a feeling of oneness with the universe but rather a kind of somatic memory of the womb-like matrix of early childhood when a child is, or should be, immersed in the love and protection of the parents.

Freud stands between the intrinsic mysticism of the old religious order, and the extrinsic positivism of the new scientific order. Therefore, he has been rejected by both, which is as great a distinction as any man could want. He was reluctant to dismiss potential psychological significance in the myths of Classical antiquity, or the scripture of Abrahamic religion (meaning Judaism, Christianity, and Islam). He valued dreams when the medical establishment saw them as either excrescences of biological functions, or the province of the old mystical orders of the Bible and paganism. Nevertheless, in his work we can find a kind of argument with Arnold, who published his poem in 1867 thirty-three years before the publication of the *Interpretation of Dreams*. In Freud's paradigm, Arnold's "melancholy, long, withdrawing roar" is not the retreat of the feeling of eternity in oceanic oneness with the universe, because Freud did not consider *eternity* to be anything more than an idea. However, in those who claimed, as his student Jung did, that there is an unconscious connection between all beings and perhaps to the universe transcending individual psychology, Freud took the position that he was a scientist not a prophet. It is enough for our purpose here to show what is at stake in such a paradigmatic gap. Most important, then, is not the epistemological and phenomenological arguments arising out of this dichotomy, but rather the effect such arguments have on political economy and therefore the commonweal. *E pluribus unum,* the traditional motto of the USA, sounds suspiciously like a claim that there is also a collective unconscious we all share, despite our apparent isolation from each other. It implies that we should work together to create a state of freedom and justice for all if we want to live in such a state ourselves. For what affects the commonweal affects the possibility of the subject's sovereignty, just as it does in the lands of the far-off others. It is only a matter of degree. The real difference is that the far-off others are *forced* to surrender their sovereignty. The subject voluntarily *abdicates* its self-determination the way a king might throw away his crown.

Therefore, while in other ages collective versus individual psychology would have been a philosophical and theological gap, today it is *economic and political*. In a simple-minded sense, capitalism boasts that it protects the individual's right to self-determination; communism brags that it guards the wealth and power of that mythological beast *the people*. While it is not the purpose of this argument to choose a winner here, it is well within the scope of this argument to say that if capitalism and communism even exist as anything specific (which I do not think they do), then both make invalid arguments because they are economic rather than juridical systems. It is the *law*, the nomos, that gives or takes away the subject's freedom, not which system the prevailing government uses to skim off its cut from the commonweal and distribute to itself and its friends — which is generally the outcome of the systematic application of any apparatus based on an "-ism," communist or capitalist. The argument can be made that what we are talking about here is political economy, which presumes a union of the two. But that is *not* what we are talking about; rather, we are trying to find some truth in the idea that there is a de facto eternal, fundamental, transcendent connection interlinking all individuals, and if this connections may be called a Sea of Faith. It is part of the main argument of this book that the amnion, the amniotic empire it encompasses, and the amniosis the subject undergoes, follow a template nearly perfected by Christianity in particular, but that has been jealously usurped by the Cult of Scientism which seeks to become the single monolithic economic power. It hopes that by manipulating cultural and social behavior, it will consolidate its hegemonic grip on the subject's self-determination, particularly over how the subject chooses to value its labor. While it could again be argued here that this is a matter of political economy, the philosophical nature of this discussion tends to view it more as a matter of ontology and phenomenology. In short, it is a matter of *being*, of *being-there*, of Dasein. Not a petty squabble over which parent-state is going to handle our weekly allowance.

In the European Middle Ages the political economy of the Roman Catholic Church succeeded in preventing what Lyotard calls "the chance … of something unexpected happening ..."

(Libidinal Economy). The homeostasis achieved is extraordinary – a fact that did not escape the Cult of Scientism as it scrambled for power between its political and religious rivals. A peasant in the empire of 800 CE could expect that not much would change for his children, grandchildren, great grandchildren, and so on for generations, even including the invasions and acts of God all flesh is heir to. Prices remained more or less stable, except for inflation caused by the Roman debasing of its (then global) currency. Custom and tradition were more important than literacy and wealth. There were no media to speak of, not even the Bible at this point, to pollute the cultural purity of the community's chosen *Weltanshuuang*, no matter how ignorant it may seem today to the enlightened Apex Consumer of the amnion snacking on cheese doodles in front of the TV. The only books, if there were any at all, were religious and written in ancient languages and not the vulgate. Domestic architecture persisted for a thousand years in more or less the same form. Families lived in the family home, or at least on the same piece of property, for hundreds of years using the utensils, tools, and furniture of their forbears. Marriage was made in a highly formalized, mutually advantageous way benefiting the individuals involved and the community, rather than being based on the novel and selfish concept of romance born of commercial exploitation and adolescent wish fulfilment. Today, since one's house is called an investment in the future (which does not exist and never will), it is merely a symbol to be used by big banks as a bargaining chip in the casino of the amnion.

In short, political economy is the basis of the cultural sense of *time*, but not of being. Time is money, they say, but not being. The rise of capital which can be accumulated and then invested in the future rather than being spent in the moment to everyone's benefit, allows the investor to control *time* just as a central bank controls economic activity by manipulating the rate at which it lends money to other banks. "What is important for capital is not the time already invested in goods and services, but the time still stored in stocks of 'free' or 'fresh' money, given that this represents the only time which can be used with a view to [enforcing some future outcome] and neutralizing the event," says Lyotard in the book previously cited. He distinguishes between money frozen in an investment and money with liquidity which can be used to manipulate the future, the place where the amnion always already thinks it is. Buying bonds only affects the future payoff. Buying stocks has an immediate effect by the closing bell of the exchange that day. Under such a libidinal economy, as Lyotard would say, the cliche that time is money has assumed the truth value of such propositions as *space is time,* which can be proven mathematically. The force Scientism sought to neutralize in the late 19th Century was religion. If it managed to at least cripple it, then it could claim its sales territory as its own. Hostile takeovers leveraged by the relatively new power of liquid capital, depended upon getting religion, with all its thou shalt nots, out of the way. Meantime, institutionally, Scientism was reinforced by growing exchange markets taking the place of churches and cathedrals as places of worship. Despite capitalism's claim that it was *real* and religion was *imaginary,* commodities that were once real under theocracy became imaginary units (shares) to trade with no intrinsic value or, worse, imaginary future values gambled with. It did not help that at the same time modern communism rose up as a putative reaction to capitalism and started scrambling for the same turf. Therefore, Arnold is ultimately right in bewailing the death of the Sea of Faith in the 19th Century, as we should today mourn the death of the sublime in the 21st. In this horse race to Hell, religion, not communism or capitalism, was the loser. Why? Because communism and capitalism are, again, *-isms* that properly belong to political economy and not to the power of the nomos and the principle of being-there (Dasein). Today, with the rise of the big socialist state claiming to be a bastion of capitalism (the US), and the big capitalist state claiming to be a bastion of Marxism (the PRC), we see at last that these two political economies are equal and opposite forms of the exploitation of an all-too-willing proletariat. The predatory hegemony gets its mandate to prey from da Vinci's fillers of privies, the never-satisfied consumers of the modern capitalist or communist state who cannot see beyond the bezel of their own digital gadget. Their worst fear is that they will make the wrong decision in the process of choosing which of the two (or three) global operating systems they will have on their next digital gadget, or that the make and model of their next leased car might deflate their social status as they drive through town in front of peer-strangers. The decision about whether they would be better off under the flavor of communism rather than the flavor of capitalism has already been made for them, and is precisely the kind of inconvenient decision that makes them uncomfortable. So why ruin a perfectly good shopping day doing so? What drives Scientism, on the other hand, is not the pursuit of truth – though much verifiable scientific truth *does* come out of Scientism despite its ultimate purpose of being a secular religion; rather, its ultimate purpose is to provide a *metaphysical alibi* for the economic excesses of the hegemony it serves. Here again we may see the fundamental contradiction underlying the discourse of the amnion. The metaphysical alibi becomes the basis of a secular religion. The problem is that there cannot be a *secular* religion. The words together form an oxymoron, a self-negating phrase that therefore means nothing, more obvious when we juxtapose the words secular and sacred, which are supposed to be antonymous for there to be any sense to a language built on the principle of l'opposition. Though A = A may be trivial, it is at least a trivial *truth,* one a computer can live with, because both values are equivalent, leaving no room for one being in a contradictory category. Therefore, the phrase *sacred religion* is redundant because, as a tautology, it need not be said that religion is sacred, just as it need not be said that A is A, unless we are communicating with a computer, in which case it is important that such confirmation is consistent and ubiquitous (as *true,* or 1, versus *false,* or 0). However, the phrase *secular religion* violates Aristotle's principle of the excluded middle: the false claim being that A *is* B (the crooked confidence person's sucker pitch). What manipulates the unconscious psyche of the subject in the amnion is that the words as an adjective-noun phrase are paired correctly in a grammatical sense, but not in a semantic, or meaningful, sense, and therefore cannot be paired in an *ontological* sense (though the noun-phrase *green ideas* as meaning ecologically sound *has* become accepted, spoiling Chomsky's example of absolute nonsense). Ontologically, the mother of a human cannot be a horse, no matter how one feels about this mother, though one violates no rule of grammar when one says, "My mother is a horse." The category error, therefore, is fatal to the proposition. As for category, the adjective is drawn from the appropriate lexicon of adjectives that may be applied to religious matters. However, sacred and secular are *antonyms,* meaning that as such they may not allow for the same adjectives and verbs to be applied to them equally, because they mean opposite things. We may have a *hate* crime, but can we have a *love* crime? Are not both crimes of *passion*?

I hope the linguistic problem here is tangible, as it is also therefore a problem of the validity of the statement's logic as a proposition. Murdering someone you hate is probably far more likely in experience than murdering someone you love. It is like the problem with the all-too-common phrase for fast success: *meteoric rise*; meteors only *fall* to earth's gravity, not *rise* from it. Meteoric *fall* would work, but it is too late for that grammar lesson in popular argot. That *sacred* applied to religion is redundant, which is fine according to Aristotle because it is a true statement; but *secular* may not be applied to religion because the word religion itself, more obviously in its adjectival form as *religious,* includes or contains the sacred, but never the secular, its antonym.

Besides losing ten points on the middle-school grammar test, the subject also exposes itself to an epidemic of such contradictory memes infecting its thought process, sometimes fatally. Is it any wonder, then, that so many lives end in self-induced dementia?

What, then, does Scientism want from us? Of course everyone wants money. This pursuit is, in and of itself, necessary for funding any endeavor of science. However, because of Scientism's fundamental ethical aesthetic of *infinite progress all of the time under any circumstance come what may,* to get the *infinite* money it needs to flourish as an ideological force, it must have the acquiescence of the obedient subject. That the subject believes any scientific endeavor, even if conducted by Dr. Evil, contributes to the progress of mankind, Scientism need not make much of an argument. It has politicians and the media to make its case, anyway, since it gets its funding through government grants paid for by the taxpayer. The other sources are the corporations for which science finds the wherewithal needed to make new or better products. If the promise of the product made possible by the science arouses the company's share prices in the financial markets, then it is good.

To clear away annoying obstacles to these miracles, though, Scientism relies on the subject's religious, moral, and ethical belief that *infinite progress all of the time for any reason* is the definition of *good.* Anything to the contrary, especially if it is scientific evidence on the wrong side of the consensus of the hegemony's self-interested discourse, is *bad,* stupid, dangerous, primitive, religious, atavistic, and the hate-speech of right-wing troglodytes. Anyone who supports a view contrary to the hegemony's holy consensus (dogma) about anything, usually amorphously defined and described by the media, is labelled in the media as a Nazi. This vague allusion to the historical *Nationalsozialistische Deutsche Arbeiterpartei* (NSADP) of Germany, begun in 1919 and disbanded rather abruptly in 1945, has been weaponized by the hegemony into a way to exterminate opposition to its various schemes for power and wealth.

Synthetic propositions built upon fatal contradiction are considered to be a priori *safe* because they *cannot* be proven *false,* whereas analytic propositions that can be verified are considered a priori *dangerous* because they *can* be proven *true.* The ethical aesthetic of Scientism keeps us *hoping* for a futuristic paradise where: 1) we are perpetually in contact with all of our thousands of so-called *friends* (the social media euphemism for contacts), 2) our cars drive themselves via extra-terrestrial satellite signal but never get into terrestrial accidents, 3) government politicians protect us from terrorists and economic hardship by borrowing money from our enemies and printing money ad libitum, 4) our debts are either paid or forgiven in the future but never in the present, 5) our children grow up healthy and prosperous while addicted to opioids, 6) the education system turns out geniuses one and all who cannot find jobs, 7) the environment is protected while we enjoy consumer goods made from and that exude toxic industrial substances, and 8) other nations regard us as the beacon of peace and good government while we bomb their cities and loot their resources.

Further delusions born of invalid synthetic propositions include the assumption that our politicians are only concerned with our security and happiness, our foods are healthy and plentiful, our job security is guaranteed as is advancement through the ranks and ever-higher pay, the mass media's chief concern is our wellbeing and knowledge, and that comfort and convenience can be found *everywhere under all circumstances at all times* even in the wilderness and outer space. The grandest of them all, though, is that if we just keep our mouths shut and have faith, medical science will cure the disease of aging within our lifetime and our ego with its self-destructive pathologies and our flaccid, obese bodies will live on in a universe without death.

That little if any of this menu of infantile wishes never quite comes true is of course not the fault of Scientism, the hegemony, the Imaginary, government, or even the shadowy transnational overlords who otherwise are masters of the Amniotic Empire. No. It is *our* fault. Mea culpa! We are just *not good enough* for all of this divine splendor which the oligarchy and kleptocracy of the hegemony get to enjoy as their right as superior beings. But as long as we have *hope* that in the future this city on the hill will come to pass if we just try to be as good as our betters, we tend to overlook the reality of outcomes. The hegemonic order is well aware of the blindness of wishful thinking, just as the casino knows that the compulsive gambler who has lost everything will be back at the table with borrowed money to lose it all again. Hope overrides the instinctive reflex to act upon the evidence immediately before us. It focuses the eyes of probability upon the make-believe candy land of the future where anything that cannot happen now can happen then only because then is not now. Hope suspends analysis of probability by engendering unlimited fantasies of what we wish, not pray, will happen. Father Thomas Merton said prayer is a special kind of wishing; but he *did not* say that wishing is a special kind of prayer.

That there is nothing to this future except our hope that it will happen the way we want it to is not considered. We never consider that our greatest hope is not to die, and yet death is the only event in our lives we can be sure *will* happen and therefore should have no hope of preventing. It is even more sensible to believe in an afterlife, since this form of hope at least accepts the inevitable about which no hope is possible (death), while placing a bet on a number that *might* come up only because there is no way to say that it will *never* come up. If there is no way to know absolutely that something cannot happen, no matter how far-out it sounds, then it has a probability of 1. Whereas if there is a way to know, absolutely, that something cannot and will not happen and has *never* happened and will never happen given an infinite amount of time, then the probability is 0. But, you say, science has made great progress in figuring out how to make us all live forever. Statistically, though, the long-run ergodic probability of this happening is also 0, or is, using the most imaginative form of immortality (immortal aliens abduct us into the 5th dimension, or something like that, where there is no death), there comes a point in a long-run series where if the series runs long enough probability effectively becomes 0 — meaning that if there is such a thing as forever, the probability would always remain the same no matter how long the run. Since the afterlife is incognizable because death is the inverse of life but is not anything apart from it (because there can be no death without life), it is consequently as probable as it is improbable. Belief in the afterlife gets a rational boost from the fact that not only does it accept the inevitable, death, as the inevitable, which it absolutely is, but it also predicates its own probability on the inevitability of death. In other words, there is no afterlife for you if you are not dead first. As Keats says, "Now would it be rich to die ..." The order of the Real likes this kind of thinking. The order of the Imaginary does not. The order of the Symbolic is, as always, ambivalent.

Here is where Scientism gets into serious trouble as a religion. Belief in an afterlife is rational because we have no verifiable evidence that it is not the fate awaiting us. Furthermore, it hedges its bet with the fact that it accepts what Scientism cannot: *that we all must die*. In fact, it is predicated on the absolutely inevitable event of death for it to have any probability whatsoever. Without death the probability of an afterlife is 0 because such a form of life, whatever form it may take, comes only *after* the death event. Therefore, the proposition of an afterlife before death is invalid because of the necessary priority of the parts of the proposition (before and after). Scientism's proposition denies that death is absolute, but has no evidence to support this proposition except that some cells are immortal, meaning they exist longer than other cells, even indefinitely, *provided conditions remain favorable*. That conditions must remain favorable otherwise death will set in anyway is the material equivalent of the cells *not* being immortal. Therefore, the invalid proposition is that *immortality = mortality*. Considering the categorical difference in the probability of the two propositions, devotional, spiritual religion has the pseudo-religion of Scientism beat. Physical immortality of the body and ego has an effective probability of 0. A similar argument could be made, however, that if there is indeed an afterlife, it will not be the ego that gets to enjoy it. Scripture says as much, that it is one's spirit that migrates to the other side in some way or form. But as with Scientism, religion has played the card up its sleeve over the centuries by promising the faithful that they will enter the kingdom of Heaven with all of their neuroses, proclivities, idiosyncrasies, and bad habits intact.

When Scientism tries to ape religion by developing a fairy tale of technological immortality (that the subject would much prefer to the old fashioned one where it must die first), it fails. Even its own science — the law of the conservation of energy — states that this is impossible. If one person lived forever, then that person would consume an infinite amount of energy in order to do so, sucking the whole universe into himself as if he were a gigantic black hole (though it would take the better part of forever). But even if a person lived as long as 100 billion standard lifetimes, that single person would use as much energy as that number of persons just to stay alive. Multiply that by the over 6 billion persons already on earth, who all, we presume, would be extended the same opportunity of immortality even though most of them do not now even have basic health care, and the number becomes unimaginable or infinite. Why cannot Scientism even apply the physical laws of the universe learned in middle school to its own reckless claims? Even worse, why cannot *the subject*, whom we presume at least finished middle school, see through this bullshit bamboozle? If we imagine that immortality were possible in the way Scientism describes it, it is highly probable that it would only be available to the super-rich. They are the only ones who could possibly, or impossibly, afford to aggregate the energy into one place over an indefinite amount of time to make it happen.

A metaphysical afterlife solves all of these problems by accepting the fact that we must first die to enjoy its pleasures (e.g. 72 virgins, or, ironically, immortality). Therefore, it is something a reasonable person can hope for without entering into the invalid logical contradiction of hoping for something to happen that absolutely could never happen. We try to turn death into a festive occasion by pre-paying for a fancy funeral and taking out a big life-insurance policy so that some good will come of it, but we know, in a vague way, that we will never get to admire our good taste in hearses and tombstones or our generosity to those we left behind in the cold, cruel world. If we consider the probability of anything at all happening in the future, we find that it is almost entirely dependent upon what we already know about the present, or even the past. Past and present, by their nature, are *not* the future because in the case of the former we *have experienced* it, and in the case of the latter we *are experiencing* it. To say that we will experience the future is a nonsensical statement and may be classified, at best, as a kind of figure of speech along with simile and metaphor. In fact, it is a kind of hyperbole. We can never experience the future since the verb *to experience* means that it is *happening existentially in the moment*, and the noun signifies the memory of this once-continuous event *in the past only*. If it is something we could *never* experience, no matter how many clairvoyants we line up in a row or time machines we build in the garage, then how can we know anything about it? Even mathematical predictive models, run by super-computers, have a low rate of positive predictions.

We are going here through the pillars the amnion is built upon which have the imprimatur of its Cult of Scientism. Rather than knocking them down one by one, it is better to use the omnibus example of the amnion's favorite phrase: "in the future" which effectively takes care of them all. As I have already mentioned, one cannot go through an hour in the amniotic empire without hearing this phrase issue from someone's lips. It is a magical incantation that is supposed to conjure up whatever the subject hopes will happen, but has no evidence that it will or even could. Like immortality, the fantasy of a better life awaiting us *in the future* is yet another form of illusion and capture in the Imaginary. The real wonder is that this is not more obvious to the subject. Its masters can be forgiven to appear ignorant of it since they are using it as a tool to control the unconscious subject. Let us then look at the mechanism of this heuristic meant to capture whatever nominal value the subject might have to offer before it is cast aside as a spent vessel.

For example, if I have a bucket with eighty black and twenty white balls in the present then I am smart to bet that drawing at random will likely result in a black ball. Is this clairvoyance? Blindly accepting hope, of the sort peddled by institutional Semitic religion and Scientism, as the basis of probability, would be as if I had the same bucket of black and white balls, but still bet on the white ball turning up because I was told that either 1) it is God's will that I do so, or 2)like medical immortality and the cheating of death, technology and civilization will override the reality of probability; but first the nomos will tell me that if I choose the black ball, I will go to jail. I then choose the white ball to avoid prosecution and likely lose when I wanted to win, causing what Freud calls *Unbehagen*, or the discontent of civilization. This wanting to win can be called *jouissance*, as it is a joyful, transcendent moment when we beat probability, white *or* black balls. It is a mini example of feeling that maybe we can beat death too; but the sensible person soon sobers up by what Plato in the schema of the Divided Line calls *observation of the visible realm*. Consequently, we sooner or later arrive at analytic and intellectual (abstract) knowledge about death, through a dialectical thought process starting with doubt of the feasibility of this wish. We conclude with certainly that the odds are that in the whole universe there is, at best, only one white ball; all the rest are black.

Mathematical capitalism, as a unit-value system (not a kleptocratic weapon), cannot rely on synthetic illogic. If it did, it could not function in the mathematical way it does because, after all, *mathematics is the language of the rich*. It would have to be even more corrupt that it now is to survive; nevertheless, the majority of modern capitalism is based on notional wealth in the mother of all imaginary amnions: the derivatives market. But these gambles are hedged in various ways, the most common being credit default swaps that are a kind of insurance against losing the bet – something you cannot get in Las Vegas or Monte Carlo. Also, the system's army of quants and algorithm programmers puts a closed-system finger on the balance scale of free-space probability. Finally, as we have heard, the house always wins; therefore, the the role of the derivatives market in the amnion's financial bubble is not the only high-risk, high-stakes gamble. The house of cards itself is thrown onto the velvet, so that even if it loses, *it loses to itself*. The inverted logic of such an arrangement is breathtaking. As its own built-in risk is the enemy of the whole scheme, it must be hedged at every quarter so that the game is fixed everywhere, but is transparent nowhere. The financial branch of the loose cohort (not organized conspiracy) of transnational overlords seeks to reduce it by being sure that it can always recover its loses. It does this by setting up various hedges, from the moral hazard of government bailouts to the teetering Ponzi scheme of credit default swaps. However, it can exploit the credibility of the subject under such circumstances by a relentless stream of what seem like promises it can fulfill in the form of professional illusions of cause and effect: if you go to college you will get a good job; if you buy a car and a house you are making a good investment; the government and its central bank have the economy under control; debt improves your credit rating; perpetual proxy wars are needed to protect you and your dog from terrorists under every Muslim rock, and so forth. By shifting the risk *to the subject*, and the payoff *to itself* (perhaps an interpretation of Piketty's *rg* ratio) and its partners in government, capitalism unburdens itself of the volatile vicissitudes of nasty, brutish, and short reality, gaining the whole imaginary world of the amniotic empire while losing its symbolic soul.

Religion, on the other hand, always has nothing to lose, made possible by its metaphysical nature supposedly transcending these materialistic ambitions and hopes. All it has to do is promise that one will get one's reward in Heaven and then turn around and say that it is a sin to seek verification of Heaven's existence - which cannot be done anyway because of the incognizability of death. What exchange markets do is lure the subject in with the promise that although there are many more black balls in the bucket, if the subject puts its money on the risky white balls the payoff will be bigger. This is how hedge funds, horse races, and football pools, work. The problem is that it sets up a situation where the probability, and consequently the risk, is always B > W, but the payoff is meagre; whereas the desirable temptation for a big payoff — something the greedy and desperate subject cannot resist — is always W > B, representing the payoff, not the *risk* (a fact wishful thinking, by function, ignores). Once again, we see the psychological mechanism of the amnion of the Imaginary: the invalid, contradictory proposition. In this case risk (W>B) is swapped for payoff (B>W), as if it were a symmetrical, or complementary ratio with each side of the equation being from the same category. Risk and Payoff, though often found in the same tavern, hail from different neighborhoods: one dangerous, the other, safe. Both, however, are portrayed by the financial magicians of the hegemony's transnational overlords as being equal (W>B = B>W), which is simply Aristotle's excluded middle of A = B. The reality is that (W>B ≠ B>W) because of the category error, making the former proposition invalid and the latter valid though a negation. I bother going into this situation in detail because it reveals the psychology of contradiction the amnion needs to exert itself as reality, when in fact it is entirely imaginary and can vanish in an instant (just as the derivatives bubble can) — unlike reality, which is, by definition, permanent. The payoff of the Imaginary is always promised to be greater than that of reality. Unfortunately, the risk is also much greater because the subject has no way to account for the overwhelming variables it contains — a weakness the con men of the amnion's financial industry exploit. On the other hand, the risk of reality is always lower than that of the Imaginary. The problem is that the subject cannot accept this lower risk only because *reality includes the absolutely inevitable outcome of death,* whereas the Imaginary is like a roulette wheel where the subject's number may come up, making it immortal. As I said earlier, the subject believes that in the Imaginary the odds are at least 1 that it will live forever, whereas in the real, the odds are 0. Here the equation gets more complicated. What the subject cannot see, because of its abdication of self-determination, which affects cognition, is that the odds are reverse: the chance of immortality is 0, and of death 1. *This* universe, as I said, only has black balls in it when it comes to the probability of death (though ergodically we can say that there is some provision for what we do not, or cannot, know, in the long run, meaning that the odds are effectively 0 even though there is an infinitesimal, and even symbolic, chance that all propositions we have verified, including that death is absolutely inevitable, *could be* false in another unknown or even unknowable system of logic). Even if the subject also knows this, it is inevitably approached by the hucksters and predators of the amnion with a false proposition that it may *buy* white balls from the banks of the amnion and its medical establishment, which are casinos where games of chance are fixed. When I say capture, then, here you have it: a rat trap built to order for each mortal greedy for medical immortality and perpetual access to the consumer goods of the amnion. In other words, the subject is the sucker, the mark for the amnion's essentially predatory nature. However, we should not feel sorry for the subject (or ourselves). It is the subject's *choice* to play the game, even to get drunk and have its judgment impaired before it does. From the hegemony's point of view, forcing it to play the game places the blame on the hegemony, not the subject. Also, it dispirits the subject, thereby defaulting its use-value as well as its value as a commodity on the exchanges. Additionally, the hegemony has to spend too much energy *forcing* the subject to play the game. Put simply, the con man tricks the subject into voluntarily giving up its money, whereas the mugger takes the same money at gunpoint, thereby forcing the matter. It is too risky to forcibly fleece the subject, though there is also some risk in hoodwinking and bamboozling it, but far less. Finally, the hegemony, as the arbiter of the nomos, cannot afford to be too overt in its embezzling of the subject's wealth, or potential wealth in the case of debt. Even though it is always in a state of exception from its own laws through sovereign and state immunity, must maintain the illusion in the mass of subjects that they, not the transnational overlords, are running the show. It does not matter if it is a communist people's republic or a capitalist state of universal suffrage, the situation only *looks* different, but is at least equivalent in its teleological outcome in terms of its effect on the subject's ontology. That the amnion preys on these people is entirely *their* fault. It is the subject who has brought the amnion, the hegemony, and even the gang of transnational overlords, into being through its willingness to abdicate its responsibility for itself. However, it is also good news that it is the subject's fault, because that means it can also *prefer not to*, negating the negation of itself, and recovering its sovereignty which was, therefore, never really lost in the first place, only voluntarily *disengaged*. The subject has the control, even after capture, though capture in prison is definitely a bet lost to the amnion. While this process has its historical issues, the actual situation is a problem in itself. Instead of being the one placing the bet, the subject's bet is often placed *by proxy* through the transnational overlords' pay-for-play hegemony. It is also one ruse of the hegemony to maintain control by taking the responsibility, and therefore any possibility of choice, out of the hands of the subject. *Control-and-capture* is often sprung upon the unsuspecting subject, who just thought the government was going to *do something* about the vague threats the subject hears about through the hegemony's propaganda channels. They are a steady round-the-clock IV morphine drip of demi-truths aimed at boosting ratings, injecting manipulative inuendo biased toward a certain political party into mainstream discourse, and generating endless chatter (noise) to fill what used to be called dead air in the business. The 22-minute news cycle bores through 24 hours of daily broadcasting like an awl, until the narcotized subject is in no doubt of whatever the discourse may be (though it can be summed in one word: *consume*).

Media noise has value as a narcotic, one the subject pays dearly for. It is also critical to convey the nature of products we all want and need in an appealing and effective way. Moreover, media production is an extremely expensive enterprise full of creative professionals who need to be paid. Therefore, the mass media must get good ratings so they can charge a premium price for commercial spots to pay these costs and make a profit for investors. Publically traded shares in common stock the subject may be able to benefit from in other ways need robust earnings to stay competitive in the primary and secondary financial markets. The problem is that *persistent media narcotizing* leaves the subject with little analytic ability to process its role in this complex value chain. Furthermore, its ability to parse statements about what is, or can be, *real* remains undeveloped by the scheme of its social engineering. The result is a chronic state of *amniosis*, by design. Consequently, it cannot distinguish between invalid synthetic statements (or propositions) and valid statements supported by verification or that are at least, in theory, verifiable. It was for quite some time verifiable, but unverified, that the far side of the moon looked like the near side. However, it is *not* verifiable that extraterrestrial beings *will visit* the earth, though it may be verifiable that they *have visited* it. Consequently, the subject accepts invalid synthetic and valid analytic statements with the same degree of credulity or incredulity, depending upon the rhetorical power of their presentation and the receptivity of its emotional needs. At the same time it absorbs the bias almost unconsciously in the spin put on the tales told to get ratings and support the network's financial and political agenda. Once thus captured, the subject is then herded into a no-win situation. However, in the Imaginary it looks like its opposite: being a social winner (with 800 friends on a social media platform). Amassing contacts with strangers on Internet platforms *feels like* being accepted, nurtured, coddled, and even loved by these strangers experiencing the same social hallucination, which is made possible by the Big Magic of the subject's networked digital gadgetry. What the subject cannot understand, because it seeks only wish fulfillment (Freud's pleasure principle, without awareness), is that the house (amnion) always wins once the subject has been captured by debt. In its blindness, the subject usually either bets its winnings until broke, or its winnings never reach the break-even point of what has been invested in the game. Despite the reality of its losses, the subject points to its infrequent *negative* wins as evidence of its good luck, as well as the general all-around fairness of the apparatus that has captured it. Meantime, the promissory notes it has signed in haste and ignorance suck away the tokens of its labor, making escape *seem* impossible. As the subject strives to fulfil these obligations through the ups and downs of the business cycle caused by the hegemony's neo-Keynesian economic scheme of infinite debt, it is willing to accept *any* discourse that seems to make sense in such a way that it does not interfere with the subject's ethical aesthetic of comfort and convenience. Hence, proxy wars fought by career mercenary armies. Under such circumstances hope for a better world actually makes the *possibility* of a better world impossible, as the whole matter is conducted within an illusory framework categorically apart from the actual world that needs bettering. Bored, self-deluded billionaires, identifying themselves as progressives, and the myriad alphabet-soup NGO's and bogus foundations the state and the super-rich support, operate *within* the amnion, encompassed by the matrix of the Imaginary. Humility does not intrude into the obscene bubble of their narcissistic idea of themselves and therefore their schemes, where it would be ever so inconvenient, uncomfortable, and possibly even fatal. Reinforcing the public *surface* of the amnion as presented by the mass media (in which they typically own a controlling interest), is their *private* amnion limited only by the scope of their ego. The hegemony and its transnational overlords — associates and analogs of these moguls — require that they keep their vain, specular amnions within the boundaries of mythological personality cults with manufactured back stories about how they built everything from nothing in their parents' garage, or how they are certified polymaths who dropped out of Ivy League degree mills (an American-style fairy tale of the pioneer) because they were too smart for formal education which, as we all know, is only for intellectual cripples who need it as a prosthetic device. Despite these potential caveats, these individuals, some with an individual net worth greater than a third of the world's nations, become private quasi-governmental states unto themselves. As such, they believe they are somehow entitled to enjoy a taste of the *state of exception* typically the prerogative of the apparatchiks of the hegemony only, at least in relation to the hoi polloi, but only to a point. Despite being portrayed as Masters of the Universe in the media and in the boundless speculum of their egoic self-image, they are not, nevertheless, omnipotent, as we learn from time to time when we read their obituary in the *New York Times*.

What makes a better world, then, is *action in the present*, taken in situ, with a clear sense of the reality of the present as opposed to the fairy tale of the past and future. And it must be done by a person who is *like most persons*. To avoid hubris, this person, with a unique personality and family history, must embody a traditional and universal popularity, in the truest sense. This is not to dismiss the outré who are special and like to be treated that way. Many dangers, though, lurk in the dark corners of the amnion where predators conceal themselves and pitfalls abound. The most pernicious pitfall is the widespread belief in the future as the place where all good things happen, and the present as the place where all bad things are. While this schism is considered in advertising theory to be the best motivator to get consumers to buy products, it is the leading psychological pathology — defined as not having the effective ability to process reality — corrupting society with *Unbehagen* and its best friends: sovereign, corporate, and personal debt. The imaginary currency of the future is *debt*. It distorts the sense of the reality of the present — the *only* reality — by forming a kind of derivative, appropriately called a future. Guaranteed by the promissory note, which in itself is a kind of currency that may be traded for a price, the lender takes the risk of lending to the borrower in the expectation of earning significantly more back, in the future, than it loaned.

Unfortunately, built into this system is the so-called business cycle, though there are less polite descriptions of it. It has steady rounds of zeniths and nadirs, affecting the individual and let us say typical borrower by causing unemployment and underemployment during the nadir. Consequently, the person may no longer be able to pay back the lender as agreed upon in the promissory note. The point has been made, I think. Undaunted by the cruelty of this system, the subject paves over its misery with wishful thinking, and, consequently, the morbid and impotent emotion of *hope*. Being fueled by the subject's vague wishes rather than reason and determination, hope becomes the realm of personal fantasies which nevertheless make their way into the mainstream of social discourse, belief, action, and other behaviors. Also, where there is hope, there is hopelessness. As Swami Satchidananda Saraswati said when I was fortunate enough to be in *satsang* with him many years ago, "No appointments, no disappointments." Wishful thinking and the fantasies it generates is for the most part motivated by the same mechanism as wish-fulfillment dreams: a frustrated id, libido, and the resulting unresolved trauma of clinical depression. The more one relies on wishful thinking to cope with reality, the greater risk of clinical depression; the greater the degree of clinical depression, the more one relies on wishful thinking, exacerbating the situation into a crisis — though it tends to happen *en mass*, creating a social problem as well. Examples in history abound, so I need not mention any. Herein lies the symbiotic relationship between the Imaginary and the hope cults of institutional religion and Scientism. Belief in the future as the place where all good things happen, and the present as the place where all bad things are, paralyzes being because *being-there*, or Dasein itself, is systematically and tacitly rejected in favor of its simulacrum, which is the amnion. It also promotes an unhealthy relationship to the past. The subject figures that if the *future* is real (in the imaginary), then it follows that the *past* is real (in the symbolic) inversely, which is phenomenologically absurd One result of this kind of thinking, which is a good example because it involves mass fantasy, are endless stories and movies about time travel. As Goebbels noted, film, or the spectacle of the image in any form, is the most convincing medium. The presumption underlying this kind of story is that every nanosecond of the past is always operating at every moment in a parallel dimension to the present forever just as it was, and we may pick and choose which of those nanoseconds of the past we would like to visit in our contraption. That such an idea could even be entertaining, which it is, shows that we have no problem suspending disbelief for time travel, because those eggheads in the research lab will make a time machine in the future. In fact, it is just around the corner. All we need is the right quantum computer, right? These are fun stories, though, because they pitch two eras or epochs together, revealing much about present-day culture, as H.G. Wells' novel on the subject does. Such tales become a reality in the mind of the subject, who has little analytic ability except for choosing between Brand A and Brand B of the same kind of product. Choice is a component of the subject's ethical aesthetic in the amnion; the more choices the consumer has, the better life is. Scientism exploits this sort of credibility by bringing in the latest theoretical physicist or mathematician who has devised an abstract model of a multiverse. Spiritual mediums do the same thing, with their own spin on the idea, and with the same motive: profit. Of course the hegemony and its scientific priesthood frown upon these occult competitors as charlatans. They do not want rivals in this industry. Meantime, the result of this sort of intellectual mediocrity is that the subject does not feel the present is real until it is in a car crash or goes bankrupt. (Woopsie daisy!) The subject's sense of the future and past is forced into the present, causing a chaotic superimposition of the three ideas of time, only one of which is real. The subject then loses its guiding intuition of the velocity and trajectory of the arrow of time necessary for psychological wellbeing and creativity, if not effective productivity. By this unhealthy mechanism, then, nationalities and ethnicities hold grudges against each other centuries after the conflict has been forgotten. Politicians campaign for reform of the last reform that was a reform of the one before that, all the way back to the Stone Age. Worst of all, old age and death are seen as diseases that will soon be conquered in the future. Meantime, belief in the reality of the past and future but not the present interferes with the realization of the future better world progressives envision as a necessary replacement for the wicked present. It ignores the way reality works, and therefore how to be effective in it. Thus, the Cult of Mediocrity is born of such a delusion.

The important thing here is to see that reality works a certain way. To understand what way that is, one cannot be deluded about such fundamental components of reality such as time. Nevertheless, it is civilization's promise of the riches of its beneficence that keeps the subject chasing after the carrot. Meantime, it is pulling the cart for the farmer. Add to this situation what Freud calls the discontents of civilization, and the subject faces a serious problem with inadequate equipment to deal with it. Arnold presents a bleak view of human attempts to rely on civilization's promises of what he calls joy, light, love, certitude, peace, and the "help for pain" of modern medicine. How could he know that little more than sixty years after he wrote the poem in 1851 (or 1849) "ignorant armies" would clash as armies had never clashed before in World War I? First just across the straight from the cliffs of Dover and then, soon enough, in his own beloved country in the next world war. Furthermore, far away in the land of England's former colony, seventy years after its bloody founding, entities identifying as the Union and the Confederacy would be at war, for various reasons as yet to be properly defined, leading to the slaughter of as many as 1.13 million Americans (US National Park Service). How much more *ignorant* can armies get? Arnold, beseeching his love to be true, mourns the loss of the Sea of Faith that was once, like the moon, "full, and round earth's shore" when people believed in something other than the relentless pursuit of comfort and convenience — as if they were microbes. It "Lay like the folds of a bright girdle furled" around the "human sadness" of history. It is religious faith he refers to. Gripped in the frenzy of the machine age, Arnold witnessed the death of Faith and the birth of the Hope Cult of Scientism where everything good lies "in the future," never the present, which is always bad and defective and in need of infinite "progress." The 19th Century Machine Age promised that all would prosper under its yolk, when in fact slavery merely took on a new guise. Were this not so, why would have anyone wanted to form and join a workers' union as they did to right the wrongs of a kind of stillborn capitalism? This age, however, would soon be replaced by the Information Age where machines went "soft," grinding through algorithms the way the old machines ground through gears. This age made the next possible, the one we live in today (2020): the age of *financialization* where everything is turned into a commodity to be traded on the exchanges and OTC (Over the Counter, which are non-exchange trades). While science had been applying positivist principles to scientific research, art (such as architecture), and engineering with great success for centuries, it was the union of this success *with the industrial means of production* that made is possible for Scientism and its priestly cast to at last overthrow the ancient orders of metaphysics, mysticism, theology, and the occult. Of course this process began with the European Enlightenment in the 19th Century. But it needed cash. The 19th Century supplied it. The next step for the new industrial class of capitalists was monopolies, cartels, an international elite of industrial bankers, and the modern big government machine that serves them and they control. The proletariat was somewhat less enthusiastic about these developments, coming as it did from a more laid-back, self-determined, biological, traditional, and ancient *agrarian* order. By the middle of the 19th Century, the industrial and agrarian orders came to blows in the war between the Confederacy and the Union in the United States, officially known as the Civil War. As we know, the industrial interests won. They now had an opportunity to build themselves and their new religion up, with the help of big international banks, into the juggernaut that has made this book necessary.

Industrial bankers realized that their own physical, secular religion (oxymoron alert) was needed to get the prole under control, considering that a century earlier Luddites had been so aggressive that their name become the eponymous pejorative for anyone who tries to throw a spanner into the works of new-fangled gadgets, gizmos, apparatuses, and machinery. Today we call them hackers. What the investment bankers knew they needed was their own religion to get the industrial worker on board who still said his Pater Nosters at the Roman Catholic Church down the street. As the founder of that church, Paul of Tarsus, proved for all time, if you want to start a religion, you need a physical church. But of course there is no church without priests; answering the call, since it needed money to pursue its research, was the white lab-coated class of those who knew the rapidly expanding canon of physical laws, particularly about electromagnetic waves. The white coat symbolized a kind of secular enlightenment in the mind of the worker regarding this new creature who called himself a man (or person) of science, in contrast to the ominous black garb of the Christian priest who cultivated a sense of there being sublime mysteries behind the rituals, paraphernalia, and Gothic architecture of the established faiths. Universities, now even named after these industrialists who became their patrons, were the likely citadels, or monasteries, for the priestly class of scientists, just as they had been for the priests of the sacred Christian orders since the European Middle Ages.

A collateral transformation happened in government in Europe and North America. The man on the street did not understand the language of science, appropriately enough couched in the Church Latin of the Middle Ages; he did not need to. What he wanted to know was what he was going to get in return for the sacrifice his life force to this new faith. Surely not forgiveness of sins, divine intervention, a canon of scripture, cathartic ritual, and a promise of life everlasting for his soul. Promises ignite the hope of their fulfillment. The new positivist message promised that all would have a good job, a chance for advancement at work in jobs that were permanent, a generous pension, a suburban house, food on the table, a new car, stuff in the closet and garage, cheap technological medical care, superb public education, exotic vacations, a university degree for their kids regardless of their aptitude for it, a second home, investments in the financial markets, and protection from vague foreign enemies. Most of all, however, was the promise of medical immortality for their cranky bodies and neurotic egos once Progress had closed the gap of time lying between fantasy and reality. Unlike previous attempts at this hornswoggle, this one promised there would be no weird metaphysics, religious vows, prayers to memorize and mumble, vows to an omnipotent and terrible God, sectarian tribalism, and annoying interference from the Devil. All that, said Scientism, was now behind the subject like the nightmares of childhood.

What organization, sacred or profane, could resist exploiting its power over the herd by promising a glorious future in return for the sacrifice of the present to make it possible? After all, according to the doctrine of progressivism, there is always more and more and more *future* to be had for the medical immortal. Therefore, the mere passage of time will bring good fortune, including the money needed to pay back the promissory notes, which, though signed in the past, always exist in the present. There was also a need for the stigmatization of traditional, Semitic religion, particularly Christian and Muslim. The discourse of this blood libel says that these faiths are for the mentally deranged homicidal lunatic with an automatic weapon shooting up the mall in the name of Jesus or Allah (but never Elijah or Moses). Such revolutionary pronunciamentos as, “It is easier for a camel to go through the eye of a needle, than for a rich man to enter into the kingdom of God” (Matthew 19:24) made the new, super-rich industrial class feel threatened as it did the Judean establishment 2,000 years earlier. The ethical aesthetic of eternal and unceasing comfort, convenience, and medical immortality the amnion promised in the future, needed to come before the lure of what the subject's Good Book called the Kingdom of God. To the infantile, narcissistic ego of the unconscious subject, da Vinci's filler of privies, success came to mean being part of the status quo in some lesser way than the well-to-do, not just having a loving family, good friends, health, and food on the table. As I said earlier, thus the middle class, now nearly extinct, was born as a diminutive form of pseudo-gentility, just as modern higher education is a manifestation of this class's need to be considered learnèd, a condition which Sir Philip Sidney, it is said, defined as the mastering of ancient languages, in particular Greek and Latin.

Now that we may look back on this dramatic Titanomachy, we see it succeeded in establishing some universally accepted dogma about the nature of existence and reality itself. Foremost, as it is critical for the survival of the new orthodoxy, it established as fact the progressive belief in the future — the place where all promissory notes in the present must be paid off. The differential between the present, which is real, and the future, which is imaginary, is exploited through what Lyotard calls a *temporal gap* between the two; the former is infinitely *infinite*, while the latter is infinitely *finite*. To close the gap, it is easier to eliminate the goal than the rule since the goal has not yet been reached (and will never be reached, says Zeno) but the rule has already been established *in the present*. The stark difference between Scientism and religion proper is that religion has the decency to also offer *no hope* to those who qualify, rather than eternal candy for everyone regardless of their choices in life. *Lasciate ogne speranza, voi ch'intrate*, it says over the gate to l'Inferno in Dante's *Divina Commedia*. Conversely, the priests of medical science will offer the grieving family of an old man at the end of his life, dying of an incurable disease, hope that he might live longer - as if that were *the patient's* greatest hope under such circumstances. Again, death makes cowards of us all.

Returning to Arnold, he finds himself between the Sea of Faith of the old religion and the coming titanic revolution of science and positivism. While it might not be fair to say that he is defending the old order over the new, it is clear that he does not like what he sees on the horizon. Darwin published *The Origin of Species by Means of Natural Selection* in 1859, a period bracketed by Arnold's composition and publication of the poem. Surely this Titanomachy was in the air marking a theoretical and scientific breach with the past paradigm of divine worship and influence. But just as fast as it seemed that religion's clouds of delusion were dispelled by the winds of science, the accusation of Creationism soon became Scientism's battle cry in its witch hunt for religious fanatics. Boxed into a defensive position, religion made Evolution *its* war cry against the heresy that we descend from monkeys (and even squirrels). Meanwhile, regaled in the throne of its new-found glory, Scientism started cooking up creation myths of its own (too numerous to mention) which it had no conclusive way to verify except that they were *not* Creationism, and that they issued, ex cathedra, from the established church. By now everyone with a mediocre education has heard the canard that the chimpanzee's genetic profile is 99.9 percent similar to that of humans. Ergo, we descended from the chimp at the zoo. But what is usually not known is that we share 50 percent of our genome with the banana, 61 percent with the fruit fly, and 85 percent with the mouse. Here is a typical example of how Scientism allows the evolution of mythology while mythologizing evolution. Nevertheless, like Copernican heliocentrism, Darwin's application of real science opened doors for Scientism's intrusion into the territory once held for centuries by the Christian churches, Catholic and Protestant, though it was a collateral effect and not his main intent. As he insisted throughout his life after publication, he always believed in the conventional idea of God and saw nothing contrary to the will of God in his theories, just contrary to the religious and scientific status quo that set upon his work to slander it. By 1864, Herbert Spencer had used the phrase survival of the fittest in *Principles of Biology*, thus establishing a kind of evolutionary algorithm which was even harder to refute. By the 20th Century, the concept of the *survival of the fittest* was erroneously accepted as the sum total of Darwin's observations and theories, even though it was Spencer's concept. It bore only a passing resemblance to what Darwin meant by *natural selection* — a distinction I will not go into here. The die was cast for the misappropriation of these ideas as weapons to be used in Scientism's self-serving war on superstition. The undeclared war included the Positivist credo that *everything must be quantified* else it does not exist. It was then fashioned into a blunt cudgel to beat all religions back from the foreground of society so that Scientism may have its way with it. The only religion that would not budge, and has not, is *Islam*. Its punishment for its stubbornness is that it has been systematically vilified by Scientism's governments and mass media until it has become generally accepted in strategic Western nations (and Mainland China) that Muslims, of whatever ethnic derivation or nationality, and wherever they may be found, are fundamentalist Jihadi terrorists.

The goal of Scientism, the partner of the hegemony and a subset of the Cult of Mediocrity, which is the larger servant of the transnational overlords, is, of course, to replace the old religions — *all* of them — with itself as the one people would accept ecumenically, East and West. Everyone can understand the principle of consumerism because of its simplistic logic of infantile, narcissistic gratification. Also, since Scientism is based on consensus not verification, it is in a perfect position to speak ex cathedra, usually from universities, duping the credulous consumer, through the mass media, into surrendering his wealth to the hegemony, which then passes it on to its transnational overlords through the global financial racket. This is why the mafia has fallen into the background; it has been outdone. Furthermore, consumer debt can be cobbled into financial products, such as tranches in credit (now bespoke) default swaps, that can be traded in the financial markets by the cronies of the global Ponzi scheme. Such economic operations dovetail neatly with digital technology, the credo of which is *whatever cannot be encoded does not exist*, which includes the *Unbehagen* of the subject.

Darwin's *Autobiography* was published in 1887 after he had been dead five years. Posthumously, then, he made the evolution of his religious beliefs explicit. He explains how at first he wanted to become a medical doctor. Failing to qualify for the examination, he turned to theology with the idea of becoming a minister, for which he *did* qualify, but clearly did not pursue into a career. Consequently, history owes a great debt to the voyage of the HMS Beagle in 1831. He shipped aboard that voyage, never taking his religious vows. He explains that this was no attempt to avoid the question of God, but rather the seizing of an opportunity for the career he felt inexorably drawn to by its superior "miracles." The application of his training as a scientist during those five years brought him around to a new view of Christianity, not necessarily anathema to it:

> By further reflecting that the clearest evidence would be requisite to make any sane man believe in the miracles by which Christianity is supported,—that the more we know of the fixed laws of nature the more incredible do miracles become ...

(Note that in his day "incredible" was not a form of negative hyperbole, but meant what it is supposed to mean: *not credible*.) In his social milieu this was a profound disillusionment, as religious credibility and the orthodoxy it engenders were the norm. Fortunately for Darwin, he had what was for him the *fixed laws of nature* not available to Jesus, despite his omniscience, to take the place of the occult magick (sic) of scriptural Christianity. The phenomena he studied gave meaning to his work and life. However, his was not an attempt to overturn religion on this one point. Therefore, Darwin's practice of science differs categorically with that of Scientism, which has a socio-political mission. Moreover, it employs political consensus rather than verification as proof of its theories, so that it at once reinforces the strategic fairy tales of the hegemony and gets paid for doing so. Scientism ridicules out of existence the subject's belief in religion's sacred stories to make way for the fairy tales of the amniotic empire and the consumerism that fills it full of the hot air it needs to continually expand or implode. As mentioned above, Scientism deliberately tells only *half* the story. The good part, which Darwin turned toward when he turned away from religion's fairy tales, is seldom told to the rabble, and usually only in the monasteries and citadels of its fiefdom: universities. Hard science is considered to be, alternately, too hard for the average bloke to understand or not tantalizing enough to provide the ratings needed to sell beer and cars at prime time. While science programming abounds in the media, it is both oversimplified to the point of insipidly while being sensationalized into multiverses and time travel. What passes for science education today does more to satisfy the state criteria for standard curriculum, which is quantification for its own sake, than ignite curiosity in the fixed laws of nature that thrilled Darwin. All the subject wants to know is *what science will do to improve its gadget*. That is where it ends. And even so, the subject has no idea what that science is. Pitifully few subjects in the wilds of civilization can even tell you the difference between analog and digital. I have asked hundreds of my students studying communications what the difference is on the first day of class; not one has ever been able to explain it, as unbearably simple and fundamental as it is. All they know is *analog bad, digital good*. The consumer only asks one thing, which defines the boundary of his curiosity: is Generation 4 more comfortable and convenient than Generation 3? Yes = good; no = bad. The cost is immaterial, as the gadget is bought with credit. Meantime, the myths, legends, and fairy tales of advertising, entertainment, government, and history have flown in to replace those of the religion the subject has forsaken. The less conversant the subject is with the stories of Scientism's religious rivals of the past, the easier it is to recycle tried and true forms of control lifted from those religions' arsenal, such as guilt, fear, and hope. The result is that the *true* stories of the fixed laws of nature, which would bring reason and enlightenment to the subject (maybe), get muddled, at best, or go completely ignored at worst. How many among the generally educated public are at all familiar with anything Darwin said or thought? All they know is the catchphrase *survival of the fittest*, a passing phrase mentioned in one form of another by Spencer in his *Biology,* and not by Darwin in *The Origin of Species,* the subject of which is instead *natural selection*, which in some cases is the story of the survival of the *least* fit (using da

Vinci's latrine fillers as example). This phrase is not mentioned in the latter. Moreover, the popular understanding of its meaning is not what Darwin meant by the phrase natural selection. In his theory of evolution, the fixed laws of nature affect the organism's fitness to thrive in a changing environment, thereby selecting genetic differences too. What the subject seldom understands is that the *previous* adaptation, now extinct as maladaptation (as 99 percent of all species now are), was, at one time, *the one most fit for survival*! Therefore, we must conclude that 99 percent of all species that ever existed, that we know of, where *not* fit, according to the popular notion of evolution, and somehow bungled onto the biological stage to strut and fret their hour, only to be heard from no more. What, then, is consciousness? The definition need not be as nebulous as it often is; separating Darwin from Spencer, then their different ideas, from each other, and then doubting what amounts to one's misunderstanding of their critical concepts so that one may arrive at an accurate understanding of how one came to be, is a start. Discrimination of this sort is not just a matter of being an intellectual, or even a knowledgeable person. It is a matter of understanding perhaps the greatest transformation of man's understanding of his ontology in the modern era. The punch line here is that once one understands Darwin's and Spencer's concepts, then and only then may one consciously weigh them against the idea that God created each detail of Creation ex nihilo. From there, we may find ourselves involved in the possible paradoxes, such as if God created evolution, too, unpacking more *questions*, not answers. Physicist Richard Feynman is quoted as having said that it is better to question answers than to answer questions for there to be fruitful, meaningful scientific discovery. Scientism's mission, though, is to answer questions even if they cannot be answered because they are incognizable. Is there a God? Just ask Scientism (or Dawkins or Hitchens): no! Case closed. Here we have what Keats decried as the "irritable reaching after fact and reason" dominating the Industrial Revolution of his day, along with the *evolution* of Scientism. Then and only then may we, without being entirely unconscious, even dare to approach such questions as the existence of God (as God is variously conceived).

How this form of unconsciousness, which we politely call ignorance, came about, is, to me, something of a mystery, though I see how it can profitably be exploited. But to me one thing is true about it: what is taught, or at is least commonly known, about science, is worse than an illusion. It is a *delusion*. And yet Scientism strategically allows it to persist while at the same time taking on the ermine mantle of the dispeller of all illusion (with dogma) and delusion (with pharmaceuticals). The benefit of permitting and even propagating ignorance is that it tends to cloud the consumer's judgment in other important ways critical for the maintenance of the amniotic empire. Moreover, it softens the mark for the hegemony's mission of control and exploitation on behalf of its transnational overlords in the global financial system. Again, this system and the so-called overlords who try to run it, is not a conspiracy; it is just business as usual. But since the subject is entirely ignorant of the existence of such a system, at its peril, it brands any attempt to point it out or explain it as a conspiracy — which is precisely how the system protects itself. Even showing the subject that the notional (imaginary) derivatives market, which at least in size *is* this system and the mother of all amnions, is now greater than the GDP of all nations, and some, and will implode with the right provocation, dissolves into the emptiness of the subject's lack of deliberate cognition.

But even Darwin wondered late in life about what might have been lost in what was his own spiritual and intellectual evolution as a scientist within the confines of the Industrial Revolution, well underway in England at the time. He describes his youthful wonder when he still believed upon encountering what was then still more of a miracle than a marvel of the Brazilian rain forest.

> I well remember my conviction that there is more in man than the mere breath of his body. But now the grandest scenes would not cause any such convictions and feelings to rise in my mind. It may be truly said that *I am like a man who has become colour-blind* [italics added], and the universal belief by men of the existence of redness makes my present loss of perception of not the least value as evidence. (p. 91)

There is a plaintive note in this description of what he has lost along the way of being, as was called in those days, a man of science. Is it that one must be "ignorant and credulous to a degree almost incomprehensible," as he goes on to say, in order to even be accepted into the priesthood of Scientism, or at least its good graces? Is it that "the higher feelings of wonder, admiration, and devotion" we associate with the common idea of the sublime are obstacles on the path to being accepted as a scientist, rather than being dismissed as a dreamer, or worse: a kook? Keats says that to create great works of art which, after all, are not so different from great works of science (says da Vinci), one needs to be able to dwell comfortably in the "uncertainties, mysteries, [and] doubts" of the sublime. As Darwin describes it, he has lost the innate sense of the sublime, and therefore of the transcendental object, which made his discoveries, e.g. the biological consequences of continental drift – possible. Therefore, it is a productive intuition of the transcendental object which makes the transcendence of one's subjectivity possible as a prerequisite to scientific discovery – precisely what the Cult of Scientism perceives to be a threat and strives to quash. Early in life, Darwin's consciousness had been stripped of the fetters of Victorian society and its idea of what is socially acceptable, especially when it came to matters of religion, sex, and politics, the territory Darwin's (and Freud's) theories transgressed. After they were hailed by progressives in that society – the death knell for theories (just ask Einstein) – Darwin himself became lionized instead of the process (getting-to-know) of his ideas. Consequently, his ideas fossilized into the knowing-of. Once this happens, the next stage is popular mythology. I think there are no better examples of this devolution of discovery than those of theories of Einstein and Darwin. It is common in Europe and North America to know the catchy shorthand of Einstein's original theorem for the conversion of matter into energy, but few could even say what the letters of it represent in simple physics, much less be able to make the basic arithmetic calculation for which this expression of the theorem is a metonym. It is not generally taught, much less known. For his own fossilization, Darwin uses the metaphor of becoming color blind and as a "loss of perception." As such, it is an abatement of consciousness – a painful process in a man who was the most conscious of them all in evolutional biology, indeed its founder. We expect that if consciousness contains awareness but that awareness does not contain consciousness then as an experience consciousness would be so much more rich, spectacular, fulfilling, and meaningful. But it is not a football game, as wonderful as that can be. If this were the case, however, it could easily be packaged and sold as a new improved product offering twenty percent more reality free of charge! The wretched truth of the horror vacui of the sublime is that it demands constant attention *to draw us out of our solipsism* by intuition of the transcendental object. It *forces* us to stare into the horror of the Other, which is a galvanizing revelation of our isolation, requiring acceptance of the suffocating reality that we are forever apart from the Other and can never be at one with objective reality until we transcend our narcissism. It is not just on a personal level; it is also a cosmic matter. As Arthur C. Clarke said, it is as terrifying to think that we are alone in the universe as intelligent beings, as it is to think that we are not. The *terror* he refers to is the sublime. But who wants to feel this way? It seems better to stay in the chrysalis of solipsism than to burst forth as a luna moth, to be consumed by a dragon fly. Consciousness *lays bare* the fact of our abdication, pitching us into the dreaded state of bare life. Consequently, it takes the sublime of war, and the disciplinary fasces of the military campus, to force us into bare life, too often at the cost of the lives of all involved. It makes us *feel* what we have lost. Perhaps the extremity of death may give us a glimpse of this falling away just prior to the moment of death. That is the only tragedy. The haunting words of Whittier's "Maud Muller" come to mind: "Of all sad words of tongue or pen, the saddest are these, 'It might have been.'" But since *all* moments are the moment prior to death ("[we] give birth astride a grave," says Beckett), is it not imperative that our solipsism dies *now* and not moments before the coming of nonbeing? Once we have completely surrendered to the reality of the sublime, there is nothing left but the creative imperative to fill the void of the horror vacui with our effective, constructive imagination rather than accept the ignorant discourses of institutional religion or Scientism. In so doing, we engage the conscious process of the *getting-to-know* in the mode of the *turning-to* the transcendental object. As Theseus says to Hippolyta in Shakespeare's *A Midsummer Night's Dream*,

> And as imagination bodies forth
> The forms of things unknown, the poet's pen
> Turns them to shapes and gives to airy nothing
> A local habitation and a name.

3.2: Consistency of the *incognizable*

Whomever seeks to thwart the principle of the sublime, though, will suffer the wrath of war, destruction, famine, and pestilence. It sounds Biblical. And it is. Arnold and Yeats use a prophetic voice in "Dover Beach" and "The Second Coming." The Apocalypse to them is not the anger of an abstract deity but the misery human beings *bring upon themselves* by the abdication of their collective sovereignty – however they may conceive of being saved from this fate. Immediately upon surrendering its dignity and self-sufficiency as an animal to the artificial amnion of the Imaginary in exchange for the trinkets of deceit, the subject becomes an inert organ of the hegemony to be exploited and then thrown away. The tens of thousands of years of ancestors who led the subject to where it is in its present are forgotten, if they are even thought of at all, in the melodrama of its struggle to acquire the next shiny new digital gadget or car. Soon after capitulation, the subject is drained of life in the senseless struggle to accumulate more and more *stuff,* or die trying. It becomes the hapless victim of hegemony's internecine conflicts over power and money at home and abroad. The subject watches helplessly as the economy that it needs to pay off its debt collapses because of the corruption and greed of those who offered the subject the promissory notes to sign. With relative sangfroid, they watch epidemics of legal and illegal drug addiction sweep over their country, claiming the lives of their children and friends. Meantime, corporations that sacked them over redundancy in order to boost the price of their stock shares, and the hegemony they control, invent terrifying, mythical enemies, now at least stopping short of space aliens but priming the pump with illegal aliens. These threats, with some basis in reality, are sensationalized by the hegemony's mass media to create panic, and to sell ads profiting the corporations controlling the hegemony, circumventing whatever shred of deliberate thought the subject may have retained from the sacrifice of its self-determination. These threats, ever changing to avoid exposure as lies, typically have one thing in common: the potential destruction of the subject's access to consumer goods, eternal comfort and convenience, and the possibility of medical and psychological immortality.

It is inaccurate to say that the subject *is* a helpless victim, however. The correct verb is that it *becomes* one through its voluntary abdication, by a corrupt, infantile impulse. Make no mistake: it is a critical thesis of this essay that the death of the sublime in a state of capture is entirely the subject's fault. To the captive, this sounds like bad news; to the subject with a shred of self-determination left, such a bulletin about its status means that *it can act to protect its sovereignty*. Compared to the *guilt*, or culpability, of the subject in its obscene act of the voluntary abdication of its existential sovereignty, the sundry transnational overlords vying for power; the hegemony controlled; the fasces of the global financial industry and its leveraged corporate holdings; the priesthood of the Cult of Scientism; the hierophants of the Cult of Mediocrity; and the bishops and cardinals of the amniotic empire, are *innocent*. One always has the option to prefer not to, even in the most extreme captivity. One's dirty little secret, admitted to oneself in the dark of night, is that one *chose* abdication. Without the subject *choosing* to barter its self-determination for the illusory rewards of the amniotic empire, it is worthless to the hegemony's value chain. I should not have to explain, again, why *voluntary* abdication is necessary, as we should understand that *forced* abdication (e.g. traditional slavery, or *being abducted*) tends toward rebellion, which, to the hegemony of the amnion, is neither comfortable nor convenient. It certainly is not profitable in the end, in part because it provides leverage for one's competitors as it did in the Civil War of the United States. Let it suffice to say that involuntary slavery, wherever it has been tried, has failed in large part because it is inefficient; energy that could have been channeled into profit, ends up being dissipated in the mechanics of maintaining the apparatus of captivity. It is the difference between a cow in the pasture producing milk, and a cow in a zoo requiring food, housing, medical care, a support staff, and marketing to bring in zoo patrons, but does not provide milk that can be sold in the marketplace. Also, a slave in captivity makes a lousy consumer. He is to be paid in subsistence, rather than tokens exchangeable in the general economy. Moreover, he cannot be coerced into voting to maintain the hegemonic order of his captors, as the consumer can, and is a perpetual flight risk. As Yeats says in "The Choice," when all that story's finished what's the news? The subject feels no regret, no loss, no need to abdicate its abdication (Hegel's Second Negation). In fact, the prospect of doing so *terrifies* the subject far more than the idea that it is no longer the owner of itself. The terror-*ist* symbolizes this fear in the subject, made credible by a modicum of reality. It is also inaccurate to say that the subject is not ignorant of its voluntary capture. Even if it is *not* aware on some conscious level where it could articulate it, there is nevertheless the unconscious awareness of its predicament. This is sometimes called *neurosis*, though the DSM brims with other names for it. It is a perpetual unease lurking in the background of every pleasure and joy, even love, which, under the circumstances, is transient at best if found at all. *Jouissance,* except of the transgressive sort, is impossible because of this *unease*, or *dis*-ease, since, after all, the disease *is* the impossibility of jouissance, preempting transcendence of chronic neurotic amniosis. Sensing this, the amnion then becomes the purveyor of transgressive jouissance, lately in the forms of Internet porn, gambling, drinking and drugging, obsessive consumerism, and joining subversive revolutionary causes to destroy the "one percent" and the corporate fasces — while organizing this putative revolution on the platforms owned, operated, and censored by them. Their relative indifference to the rhetoric, and even action, calling for their overthrow is proof of how unconcerned they are that anything will come it. *They even join in*, ostentatiously embracing the subject's political and social causes. Meantime, the subject's teleological behavior as a *social justice warrior,* obsessed with the optics of its assumed identity, is harvested and sold to the enemy to target market what I will call for the sake of shorthand, Che Guevara t-shirts, or amnion-generated, wearable virtue signals. The subject even *knows* the drill, but only as the knowing-of, not the getting-to-know, and in an impotent way. Therefore, it goes ahead with the childish charade anyway, often because it is passively susceptible to what is now social-media peer pressure and pseudo-ideological triggering on an unconscious level. Here we have the emblem of unconscious — if not downright stupid — social action. In the forsaking of its own self-determination, the subject also forsakes the possibility, or potentiality, not only of real and needed social change, but also of the molding, motivating, and mortifying *terror* of the sublime and incognizable. I believe that terror of the sublime, through the recognition of death as the inevitable terminus mundi, is what is described more poetically in the Bible as the fear of God, who is not to be trifled with. The Tetragrammaton of the Hebrew Bible, or *Tanakh*, is incognizable, and therefore truly unnameable. What is unnameable remains, forever, the *signified*, if we can even call it that, as signification reduces the sublime to the mundane. It is not necessary to advertise that one fears God, or to join an institutional religion, or even profess to believe in the metaphysical universe of whatever is deemed holy. One would do just as well believing in what is considered to be *unholy*, or occult. As long as belief is not diverted into the cults of Scientism and Mediocrity, which are not occluded but are entirely visible as the signifier without the signified, or, in other words, the amniotic empire, the subject stops short of abdication, or rejects it altogether. Just *allowing for* the *possibility* of God - or Satan and whatever gods or demons one senses in the occluded universe - is enough to keep the door to the sublime open at least a crack. After all, it is rather sublime to think that besides the gritty world of traffic jams, digital gadgets, office work, TV, and bars, there is also an Invisible World far greater, more meaningful, unfathomable, and ripe with infinite possibility and power. Of course, Scientism says none of this is even a possibility, though its incredible fantasies of a multiverse, infinite dimensions, fusion power, God Particles, interstellar space travel, immortality, a race of androids, *in the future*, is already as good as done. In embracing the possibility of the sublime, however, the subject threatens the amniotic empire with exposure for what it is: like the derivatives market, imaginary. The ritualized, mundane drudgery of everyday existence yields to the sense that there is, influencing our thoughts, behavior, and destiny, what in Chinese traditional philosophy is referred to as *appointed destiny*, or the thought of the story of our lives in the realm of the mind of the transcendental Other (*Dao De*). Belief in what lies outside the materialistic realm of the amnion, and its imaginary spheroid, is a direct affront to Scientism. Try as it might, it cannot seem to root out the human tendency to believe that there is more to life than the nasty, brutish, and short struggle to *consume*. This Invisible World has a scary side too. Once embraced, it might also lead to belief in sin, for instance, the definition of which, like blasphemy, is ineffable, making it possible to also believe that one can *only* sin. What is sin, after all? Is it not the abdication of one's self-determination, one's soul to the fasces of the amnion? Indeed, abdication is *total envelopment in idolatry*, or sin, maybe even Original Sin, which is why Islam's contempt for the *kafir*, or unbeliever, is regarded by the hegemony of the amnion as proof of Islam's fundamentalist intolerance of the good, sensible, modern life of the consumer. Worse, it justifies deadly military action against innocent, unarmed believers who just want to get on with their lives the way their ancestors have. Ultimately, though, what *is* believed contains an element of doubt regarding what *is not* believed. If it did not, it would be the *getting-to-know*, which belief is not. But it is a start. And it is doubt that Scientism fears the most. While *knowing* is the elimination of doubt through verification or by what Peirce calls *retroduction* (abduction), getting-to-know is impossible without doubting. As Peirce showed earlier, the doubts we cannot resolve must be accepted for what they are: mystery, or what he calls the *Incognizable*. Acceptance of doubt does not preclude the knowing-of, since we need to *know-of* how to cut down a tree and turn it into a chair, fix a car engine, or split an atom, for that matter. Doubt does not preclude knowing in an empirical sense. If one sees a ghost it is an empirical experience which one may analyze (or which one's analyst may analyze). Was it real? That is the doubt. And who knows what conclusion that doubt may lead to; some have creative ideas about a spirit world, while others see it as a psychological phenomenon, while still others see it, perhaps correctly from time to time, as a parlor trick. What can be analyzed is empirical. What can be theorized is not, because it is logical. Between the two, we have some embrace of what Darwin calls the *fixed laws of nature*, as well as the empirical observation of biological phenomena that led to his apprehension, in a concrete sense, of what those laws are and how they manifest in the living world. Doubt may be analyzed without it being resolved into knowing. But in the process of analyzing, doubt is inevitable in the apprehension of that which we will come to know as *something*, even if it is that this particular doubt is incognizable. Nothing, alas, is something. We cannot escape it and still say we live. To know that something is incognizable is to discover the truth of that thing. If Occam's Razor has trimmed off every inch of fat from a proposition, taking its simplest explanation and expression, then what is left is True only because *nothing else can be* (if we did it right). Once one has reached the boundary of aporia, no further inquiry is necessary or even possible. Through the getting-to-know, one has uncovered the truth about something having the fundamental nature of being incognizable.

But what makes us assume that acceptance of something being incognizable is somehow irrational, superstitious, and a false proposition (as in the famous statement of such propositions: unicorns exist)? The *Copernican Principle*, also known by the less fetching though perhaps more descriptive name of the mediocrity or median principle, states that when drawing from a container with (*n*) amount of different objects, one greater (*A*) and one lesser (*B*) in number, the probability of drawing *A* is always greater than that of drawing *B*. Is the incognizable the greater or the lesser of the objects (*A*, or *B*)? If we believe that there is little that is incognizable because science has explained most things, as Scientism brags it has, though such a proposition is as unverifiable as the existence (or nonexistence) of unicorns, then the probability is that we are *not* going to find the incognizable more often than the cognizable. Even when we *do* draw the opaque mystery box of the incognizable, we tend to react to its impenetrability by endowing it with the quality of being cognizable *in the future*, which never actually arrives at our doorstep with the box of candy and bouquet of roses we had hoped for. Consequently, such speculative reasoning of this sort follows that of the notional value found in the derivatives market, which is the amnion's putative economy: Y > X, with Y being the *future* value of something (commodity, idea, information), and X being its *present* value. But because such a formula is entirely unverifiable, it is therefore based on the natural hope that tomorrow will always be better than today. Can it be, in any logical sense? No, unless we remove *death* from the equation, as medical death is the *only* future possibility of which we may be certain. For the derivatives trader to chortle, "Oh Death, where is they sting?" is a bit ludicrous, and yet his market itself is worth more than four times the present value of all private property on earth. As life is to us generally *more valuable* than anything else, and death is what we consider to be the loss of this value, the reverse of the formula is therefore verifiable: X > Y. The problem with the verifiable is that it dispels imaginary thinking; the beauty of the unverifiable (not to be confused with the incognizable) is that it allows us to generate illusions with little fear that they will be dispelled. We assume that what is cognizable *now* was incognizable in the stupid, benighted past before science at last pulled an explanation out its sacred arse. As with the survival-of-the-fittest notion, namely that 99+ percent of all species over aeons simply did not make the cut because they were too stupid and weak, the ludicrous idea that *we know more than we do not know* is equally unsupportable. Darwin proved (at least to *my* satisfaction) that some creatures evolve *out of* extinction, not *into* it, while others stay as they are because nature, through selection, has not called upon them to do so. Even as individuals we know, unless we are heavily medicated or locked up somewhere, that at any given time we know less than can be known. So how, then, does Scientism get away with pretending to be omniscient? The answer is that it folds the future into the present by saying that *given enough time and money*, all mysteries will be solved, packaged, and marketed as a new gadget or gizmo the consumer may buy on credit. Meantime, it vilifies the past as a benighted age of subhuman, superstitious savages dressed in sabertoothed tiger skins while skinning a squirrel, not in houndstooth tweeds, spectacles, and smoking a meerschaum while reading Milton. Therefore, its discourse goes, there is nothing special about the incognizable. It is just the lesser quantity because it is the absence of something and not the presence of something. In other words, defying the Copernican Principle, Scientism says that even if what it *does not* know is greater than what it *does* know, the latter far outweighs the former in terms of what we *need* to know. Therefore, whatever *is known* is what we need to know, and what *is not known* is either something we do not need to know, or will be know soon enough given unlimited access to funding.

From such closed systems of the *knowing-of* arises the formula that the amount of funding = the amount of knowledge. From this simple formula many misnomers grow, such as that poverty is ignorance, poor people are stupid, rich people are smart, money solves all problems (but is never a problem in itself), and so on. What we have, then, is a *genetic concept* of the kind that swells the bubble of the amnion to pregnant proportions with a tumor rather than life itself, which must needs acknowledge death as *real* to be called living. Such institutional arrogance is mortally self-serving. It denies us of the disposition of mystery necessary if we are to dwell in the clarity and power of the sublime, or what Pearse calls the *conduct* needed for discovery through the process of abduction, or reasoning from empirical effect to theoretical cause. That which we *do* know, the erroneous logic of hubris goes, is the precursor for knowing what we need to know but do not know now. All that is required is the (expensive) magical liquid of Progress, in the form of *money*, added to the dried powder of what little of the unknown we actually need to know, if anything. The greater the funding, the greater the payoff. A similar equation follows for political knowledge of the best way to govern, as well as improvements in social justice and a prosperous economy for all, but we shall leave that discussion for another day and book. Let it suffice here to quote American agrarian philosopher John Taylor of Caroline (1818): "Nations and individuals are universally promised wealth by political swindlers."

When we honestly envisage what we do not know, such as the nature of gravitational force, we discover, if we are honest and can see the difference, that there are many things we *cannot* know, as much as we would like to know it, because it is a fundamental, logical impossibility, such as the nature of nonbeing. This is not to say that we may not someday understand gravity as well as we do kinetic and electromagnetic force. However, I put my money on knowing the nature of gravity before death. Note that in statistics, and ergodic theory, if the slight possibility of something is *too slight* in proportion to its impossibility, it is therefore the material equivalent of impossible. The terra incognita of death is *incognizable*, despite conjecture by spiritual mediums and even the venerable *Tibetan Book of the Dead*. The reason is that it is not different from life; it is simply that which makes it possible for life to be, in Dasein, as life's negation. It is a *negative value*, meaning, by definition, it cannot be known. It is what we already see, but the obverse of it that makes what we do see possible. Therefore, by definition, it is something we can never know the way we know life. However, I do not mean to preclude a spirit world. As I say in the preface, omniscience is not among my many virtues. Even for me, Mr. Knowitall, life is a tangible mystery; I feel it every moment. I cannot even understand how it is I am alive, or even what I am. Part of the reason for my embrace of what has been called *divine ignorance* (Adi Da Samraj), is that I do not want to leave the orbit of the sublime, in which I am perpetually circling, seldom touching down except through the agency of ecstatic culture, the beauty of art and nature, and non-transgressive jouissance. You might think that I have said a lot about what death *is*, and therefore I am contradicting myself here; but that would be a misperception of what I am doing, after my mention of Occam's Razor. I am saying what it is *not*, which is how we may approach the incognizable. At such an aporia, we must accept the simplest explanation as true, as there is nowhere else to turn except to the prepackaged explanations in the form of the amniotic empire's *knowing-of*. Since the truth of the object has been discovered to be that it is incognizable, we set aside doubt at that point and accept what we have discovered through logic or spiritual intuition, aided by the great scriptures and works of philosophy of the ages. As Peirce said earlier, we cannot engage the process of getting-to-know (abduction) if we allow doubt, or not knowing, to prevent us from knowing that we do not know something. "One is often in a situation in which one is obliged to assume, i.e., go upon, a proposition which one ought to recognize as extremely doubtful. But in order to conduct oneself with *vigorous consistency* one must dismiss doubts on the matter from consideration" (p. 400). So what is this "vigorous consistency"? Here is an example. Suppose there is a person who has told two lies and three truths (2:3). Can we conclude from this evidence that this person is, categorically, a liar? If the person *mostly* tells the truth, does that fact bring us closer to the categorical, objective determination of the truth-value of this person's statements? In computing, the answer is yes. A logical, inclusive disjunction is true if A or B is true, but not if A and B are false; this is the OR Boolean function, found in conditional branching. In exclusive disjunction, a statement is true if A *or* B is true, but not if both are true; this is the XOR Boolean function. Between the functions we have or and not-or, a negation necessary for computing logic. The former is *inclusive*, and the latter is *exclusive*. The result is a binary pair of opposite that are, nevertheless, subject to some variability as such systems need to be to function. For example, if one forgets one's password, one way to recover it might be answering pre-answered security questions, such as where one was born, and so forth. In a fault-tolerant system, allowing for the *possibility* of the forgetfulness that also led to the forgetting of the password, answering three out of the five questions correctly will result in getting a new password. Therefore, three T answers out of five possible T/F answers are the material equivalent of T, even though two were F. Therefore, one's identity has been *positively verified*, at least enough to get a new password, and not accounting for fraud, which is another probability that is too complex for this discussion. In systems where there is low or no fault tolerance, all five would have to be T for verification. But again, that is a different discussion and not typical of the way we must determine truth value, for we cannot even answer such questions to ourselves about ourselves. "Am I good person?" The logic of a twelve-person jury, which needs consensus or else be "hung," is an example of a no-fault-tolerance system. But if this were how most decisions were made based on truth value, society, and consequently, civilization, would come to an end. That is why the present "consensus" system of science, which has replaced positive verification and proof-of-concept, requires massive bullying to work.

Herein lies the problem of pseudo-positivism as practiced by the Cult of Scientism, the mode of the Imaginary, and the nomos of the hegemony. For example, the government passes a law saying that it is protecting job applicants from discrimination by potential employers by giving the applicant the choice to indicate on the application whether or not he has a disability. If he says yes, then he dramatically reduces the possibility that he will get an interview, as he is now perceived as a *potential* liability not an asset. There is no other reason, such as the boss hates people with disabilities. And we shall presume the applicant's disability would not interfere with his job. For instance, he is in a wheelchair and he does desk work in a wheelchair-accessible facility. Despite the presumed intention of this law (which is the law of the land in the United States, by the way), there is no way for the applicant to prove that he was discriminated against for his confession of his disability on the application, even if he was perfectly qualified for the job but did not get an interview. On the other hand, if he is disabled, but chooses not to indicate this on the application in the hope that he will have a better chance of getting an interview, the law says subsequent to the submission of the *application* he cannot sue the employer or demand accommodation because he lied on his application. Furthermore, if the employer can *prove* that he lied on his application, he can now be fired for this offense with impunity. Therefore, the law put into place to *protect* him from discrimination, instead mouse-traps him into the choice of being discriminated against *or* waiving his right for civil or even criminal justice against the employer, as well as accommodation of his disability — rights he had that protected him *before* the law "protecting" him went into effect. We could get paranoid here and say that the law was *really* designed to help employers weed out the disabled, since in effect that is what it does; but in this case, I think it is the typical sort of nomological blundering of the mediocre class of parasite seeking legislative office. Such is the invalid logic of the nomos. Nevertheless, the benefit of such logic goes beyond enabling discrimination by the employer against the employee while purporting to protect him from discrimination. Invalid logic allows for the introduction of *any* proposition, verified, unverified, or unverifiable, into the operation of the apparatus of the state, thus lifting the burden of truth-value from its edicts, fiats, and pronunciamentos. Invalid propositions allow Aristotle's *excluded* middle to be *included* in the category of valid statements. Therefore, T = F; TTTTT = FFFFF; TTTFF = F; FFFTT = T. By extension, then, we have freedom through social control, peace through perpetual war, prosperity through debt, and justice through prison. While invalid logic fails in computing, it is the basis for the web and net of fantasy the amniotic empire spins to enforce its system of capture of the subject willing to serve its political and economic ends. Their reward for the sacrifice of their will and labor is infinite debt, obesity, drug and alcohol addiction, car crashes, perpetual war, divorce, chronic depression, diabetes, and a vast Underclass of have-nots that they must support.

In predicate logic there is room for conjunction, disjunction, and negation, which are employed extensively in computing. In these arguments and propositions total consistency is not needed because the logical outcome is based on rules which admit a great variety of *statements* necessary for the functioning of machines and other systems which cannot expect consistent input. The principle is what Peirce calls “vigorous consistency” because the *outcomes* are predictably consistent even if the *input* is not - as long as the input follows the rules, being vigorous. Sometimes this is also called a stochastic system of predictable unpredictability, which, however, is more often applied to a heuristic than a process. When vigorous consistency is applied to the values of everyday life, the complexity of its possible misapplication forces a kind of coward's retreat into the *reductio* of quantification — the bête noire of positivism. Knowing how much it is, not what it might be, is reassuring. A person would rather know exactly how much is in his bank account, even if it is not much, than to be told that there is *enough* in it. Dependency, nay, gentle reader, *worship* of quantification, is the mark of an idiot. Machines depend upon quantification. There is no consciousness or awareness in a machine, nor in a person who behaves like one. To such a creature and its regime, vigorous consistency becomes a threat because its output truth value is satisfied with uncertain input, and is, therefore, highly fault tolerant. The problem is that in the misapplication of consistency as mere quantification, as with enforced statistical parity in socio-mechanical justice, the assumption is that if the *output* is followed back to the *input*, the input and the output will always show statistical parity. There is no provision for the possibility that they may not, but still be true. In our earlier example, for instance, out of five possible states, if at least three of the five are one state or the other, then that is the state of all five in terms of their output. In quantification, the basis of consensus, there is no such tolerance for opposition states (viewpoints). Democracy, such as it is, would not be possible under consensus rule. How scientific proof is today based on consensus and politics rather than verification and proof-of-concept, is the wonder of our age. Then again, quantification extends to funding, as it is *x* amount of money, and funding is based on *p-value hacking*, or tilting the scale with one's finger, while delivering the outcome preferred by the funder or that is, at least, not damaging to it. In everyday language, this would be like saying "He wouldn't have been arrested if he weren't guilty," which we know is not justice, despite its almost universal acceptance as exactly what justice is supposed to be. Or "he lied once therefore he will lie again." Or, "He told one lie, therefore he is a liar and nothing he says can be trusted." If these statements were verifiably true, then nothing anyone says could be trusted to be anything but a lie. Furthermore, there is the semantic problem of the statement, "I am lying," which needs no explication to point out its paradox.

Perhaps this does not seem so unreasonable. After all, one lie does weaken our trust in someone. However, if we reverse the statement, we see that it too is an irrational proposition: "He has never lied, therefore he will always tell the truth." The second statement, which follows precisely the same logic as the first, is a non sequitur, as predicate does not follow from the subject in terms of cause and effect. We could say that as a police detective we checked out his alibi and it would have been impossible for him to have committed the murder in Las Vegas when he was at the same time playing guitar in a live concert in front ot 10,000 fans. Therefore, his proposition that he is not lying when he says he did not commit the murder is 100 percent verifiable. It is only under such a circumstance of verification, or the determination that something is verifiable, such as what the surface temperature of Pluto's North Pole is, when we can say with absolute certainty that something is what we say it is.

Furthermore, *trivial* positivism relies upon the truth determined by tautology: A = A. "He (p) is poor because he (p) has no money," or "He is rich (r) because he (r) has a lot of money," where → means "if, then ...," therefore, (p → p), (r → r). As such, nothing has been said, except that he is poor or rich. Quantification loves tautology because the input is always the same as the output, giving the operation 100 percent determinability in a universe where that is hard to come by only because of its complexity. As a result, in practical terms, although the applicant in a wheelchair is applying for a desk job in a building that is wheelchair accessible (by law), and is otherwise highly qualified for the job, the input: wheelchair (*disability*) does not equal the output corporate asset (*ability*), but, rather, corporate *liability*. Here is where Peirce's vigorous consistency steps in to save the day. For non-tautological input-output, of any complexity, adjustment must be made to *accommodate* (which is the word used in the disability law) input that cannot be predicted but that nevertheless still needs to be processed. What makes it possible to even have a common language is precisely vigorous consistency. We may say, for instance, that there are as many forms of English as there are speakers of it; no two speakers have the same lexicon, mastery of the subtleties of grammar, experience to inform it as knowledge, tone of voice, understanding of logic and figurative language, emotional expression, spelling and grammar errors, and so on. As long as there is reasonable presumption of cause and effect, or antecedent and consequent, what is built into the sentence depends upon what needs to be expressed and nothing else. Therefore, we may also have synthetic statements that are not verifiable as the tautology is, but that are also not trivial, such as, "He (p) is poor because he (r) is rich" ($r \rightarrow p$), or "He (r) is rich because he (p) is poor" ($r \rightarrow p$). While these are contradictory statements, and therefore are not apophantic as a propositions must to be valid, they at least ask the question of why he may be poor if he is rich, and vice versa, which is nevertheless non-trivial if it is also somehow sensible, which it could be. Language goes beyond the valid proposition, in the spirit of vigorous consistence, so that we may use it in, for example, a poetic way as Keats does, or in a revelatory way, as prophets do. In Matthew 5:3, Jesus says, "Blessed are the poor in spirit: for theirs is the kingdom of heaven." Here, the antecedent and consequent have a complex relationship which, to many, sums up Christ's teachings in one line. Despite its profundity as well as mystery, it is also the simple $p \rightarrow r$ synthetic statement we see above. Surely such a complex, interesting statement, the truth or falsehood of which may determine the fate of one's soul, but nevertheless cannot be verified, is preferable to the trivial tautology that may, but has no significance. In the case of both Keats and Jesus, both arrive at a truth, one regarding beauty and truth, and the other at the truth of the correlation between spiritual poverty and heavenly grace. Jesus' statement is especially surprising considering that one would assume that those *rich* in spirit shall enter the kingdom of Heaven. His statement is, therefore, unique in this way. It awakens a significant chain of philosophical thought about the nature of the spirit and the materialism we superimpose upon it. In his day, as in ours, we may suppose that rich people who observed the sacrifices, read the books, paid the tithes, built the temples, making sure everyone knew about it, were the ones expected to enjoy the grace of God. Whereas the hoi polloi, wretched on earth because of their inability to stop sinning and God's subsequent punishment of them, could only look forward to an eternity in Hell for their spiritual poverty. By introducing fundamental contradiction here — and therefore invoking a synthetic statement not valid in the logic sense — Jesus turns the society of his day and its religious oligarchy on its head, and, naturally, is made to suffer for it. The irony here is that in doing so he establishes a new rule of logic regarding the spirit, saying mankind dishonors Heaven by imagination that only rich people are admitted, like some kind of country club. Looking at the matter his way, it seems quite absurd indeed.

Therefore, what matters is not the orthodoxy of logic, or of what we may think, or of what we may say, but that what we assert as a proposition is consistent in its logic. If we all follow a rule, such as "a consequent cannot be a consequent of itself," then there will be consistency. It is the logical consistency of a rule (no number may be the successor of itself) that made integers possible, which we should not take for granted; there are many prehistoric cave paintings of antelope and buffalo, but none of integers. This is not to say that Wordsworth's famous phrase, "The child is father to the man," is not the key to a higher order of wisdom because it violates Peano's Second Axiom. Again, we see an analytic statement juxtaposed with a synthetic statement, where in both cases they get at the truth of that to which they refer. We can make any rule we want as long as it does not commit an error of logic within its own system. To violate the logic of one's own system is contradictory in a fatal sense; it is also precisely what the amniotic empire does in the formulation of its dogma and discourse. A common expression of such contradiction is hypocrisy, which seems to be the moral and ethical standard of social existence in the amnion. However, for an example we may look back to the law I cited earlier that is supposed to protect disabled persons by taking away their legal ability to protect themselves and opening them up to greater discrimination.

As we see above, it is possible to include the incognizable in the determination of the cognizable. That is not a fatal contradiction because it is the texture of existence for those who take it as it is. It cannot be disputed that there are some things we just do not know. But it is hotly disputed, by the *progressive fallacy*, that there is anything at all that we *cannot* know. Sooner or later, the faulty logic goes, science will figure it out. The ancient Greeks used to call this approach to godlike knowledge *hubris*, and wrote scores of tragedies using just this plot vehicle. Marcus

Aurelius, in *Meditations* (50), shows the logical error in such thinking: "Look to the immensity of time behind thee, and to the time which is before thee, another boundless space; in this infinity, then, what is the difference between him that lives three days, and him that lives three generations?" To believe that the mere passage of time will heal all wounds with anything but death is mere stupidity; furthermore, to consider that the mere passage of time contributes anything but itself (iterative, recursive change), demonstrates a fundamental lack of understanding of category logic. According to Marcus, to attribute a cumulative increase in consciousness and the getting-to-know, which is not quantitative in nature, to the mere passage of time, is putting us in the absurd position of either knowing everything, or nothing, all of the time forever. The only possibility left, then, which is equally absurd, is that we somehow know everything and nothing all of the time simultaneously. Therefore, we are left only with what Pierce calls "the incognizable," or *that which we cannot know*, throwing us into the position of admitting it to ourselves and others and leaving it at that, which is the greatest Sin in the ethical aesthetic of the amniotic empire. The problem is, though, that *the incognizable is the nature of the sublime*. Therefore, to rule it out of ontological possibility because you want a grant from the National Science Foundation or a consumer buy your new pill or gadget poisons the well of the sublime. Herein lies the meaning and value of being aware of, in an active way, the Greek caveat of avoiding hubris against what Marcus refers to as the gods, as well as what he calls the *daemon*, or spirit, within us. Need I point out the several and severe acts of heresy thus committed here by these Greek and Roman ideas against the dogma of the Cult of Mediocrity's ethical aesthetic? It cannot be argued that we know everything because we cannot know it. And yet the religion of Scientism, a belief not knowledge system, demands that we parse the universe into two pseudo-categories: 1) that which we know absolutely thanks to government funding, the corporate fasces, and Scientism, and 2), the trifling remainder which do not yet know absolutely but, with what we now know, we will absolutely know soon enough for you to buy the new product before next Christmas on credit.

Which brings us to the ultimate epistemological question of knowing we know. It could be (I do not know), that there is only the *getting-to-know*, but not the possibility of the *knowing-of*. Are knowing, the knowing-of, and the getting-to-know the same forms of epistemology? (Only a fool would answer those questions here and now.) Even the "the fixed laws of nature" from time to time mutate when we discover some critical aspect of them that we had overlooked, such as the equidistant orbits of the spheres around the sun of Copernicus versus the elliptical orbits discovered, and verified, by Kepler. What they both got right is that the Ptolemaic model was fundamentally in error. As I hope you can see, this is the process of the *getting-to-know*. If we choose any other path to knowledge, we end up at a dead end. Unfortunately, the so-called information age is just that: the dead end of static Big Data, a mass of rotting information that does not even lend itself easily to being processed into something useful or meaningful. Scientism solves this embarrassing problem by either giving a made-up explanation based on cursory analysis of these data sets, or cobbling together the opinions of "experts" who eventually come to a consensus about what it all means. Such a system of epistemology has an amazing record of coming to erroneous conclusions easily refuted by those who dare to verify; therefore, it has taken to *bullying* scientists into relying on consensus, which can be manipulated politically by destroying careers and withdrawing funding. Nevertheless, doubt remains. We have all seen that Scientism's particular use of the media as dissemination of its "truths" has the nasty flaw of the law of fatal contradiction, as the information propagated and the chains of logic by which it was reached do not follow Peirce's law of vigorous (meaning *living*) consistency. For example, in medicine it has come to the point where for every medical study there is an equal and opposite medical study. Let it suffice to say that there are many reasons for this, none savory, but that ultimately this strange phenomenon is yet another example of a departure from vigorous consistency, unless we consider being *consistently inconsistent to be a form of vigor and not rigor mortis.*

Consequently, an affirmation, such as "this is intelligence," is at best problematic when it is presumed that it can be quantified. Has the definition been created to fit the needs of the system of the metric, excluding any deviation as *noise* only because it does not fit the criteria? Or, worse, are the criteria defined by the intended use of the data output? If so, then they are, by definition and even purpose, biased. In such a case, the diagnostic should only be used in the application for which is was intended to serve as input, and not as a "g-factor" indicating, with absolute certainty and under all circumstances, a general value. Psychometricians argue that g-factor diagnostics is not meant for all applications; but then again what are "all" applications? Also, they tend to avoid this claim unless they are boxed into a corner; otherwise, such metrics as Stanford-Binet are highly profitable. They also solve the expensive problem for institutions and organizations of actually getting to know what a person can do in situ, not in the examination room. Where does it begin and end? Does it begin with who becomes a sergeant in the army and end with who is successful in picking up a sex partner in a bar? Therefore, such a claim is at best disingenuous and at worse hedging a bet that has a high risk of being lost if challenged by data conflicting the claim. One possible use of g-factoring is eugenics; this has been tried on a large scale here and there and no doubt will find justification again. Eugenics is one of those principles that makes perfect sense in terms of the popular conception of the "survival of the fittest" doctrine — it cannot be called a law of nature in the proper sense — mistakenly attributed to Darwin and properly to Spencer. And perhaps there is a time and place for it. However, at present it violates the prevailing concept of human rights, the first of which is the right to be different from others in ways that may include what is typically defined as intelligence. Again, eugenics is in the end a quest for statistical parity and homogeneity which, alas, is a quixotic quest since it merely sets up yet another hierarchic scale with someone once again at the bottom, only it is a bottom higher than that of the exterminated group, who, presumably, is now in need of extermination or subordination and so on. The certifiably brilliant have led mankind farther down the path of misery, self-destruction, theft, war, and corruption than those under the g-100 mean. It may be argued, though, that those under the mean would be even worse in this respect if they had the wherewithal of their betters. Considering this possibility, though, we must conclude that all men are indeed created equal in terms of what misery they may afflict on others. Furthermore, in quantification, which is abstract, empirical evidence must be ignored in favor of the data extracted. For example, people like to imagine that elephants and whales are intelligent “like humans” they say because their brains are about the same size. Oh really? Their lack of g-loaded signs of this parity is dismissed as evidence of their higher spiritual values. “They don't need civilization like we do,” goes the canard, “and they don't hurt the environment or fight wars” — two signs of intelligence in the popular imagination. Then there is the problem of the non-human primates ranging from tiny monkeys one can fit into the palm of one's hand, to gorillas significantly larger and more powerful than humans. Between is the chimpanzee, used as an example of the “fact” that humans really are not so different, since we share 99.9 percent of our genome with chimps. The outward manifestations of a potential difference between the two — such trivial things as language, technology, space flight, medicine, mathematics, and civilization for the past 5,000 years — are dismissed as mere ephemera compared to the far superior indicator: quantitative genetics. However, none of those who tout this nonsense, if blind, would trust a seeing-eye monkey. I have already mentioned that the genome of a banana is 50 percent and a mouse 80 percent similar, so I will not belabor *that* point. Also, as a geneticist will tell you, it is that .1 percent that makes all the difference anyway. And vive la difference! Finally, there is the definition of intelligence — really a kind of negative metric — of the Dunning-Kruger Effect whereby the lower the score on a Stanford-Binet metric, the more intelligent the subject tends to imagine it is. Naturally the reverse is not true: those with high scores *also* imagine that they are highly intelligent, though they have a number to "prove" it while the person under the mean has a number to disprove it (by comparison). The point here is that quantification of the incognizable — for example intelligence, which can only be variously defined by context — is the amniotic empire's substitute for the getting-to-know. It is perhaps the weakest form of the knowing-of. Once quantities, such as statistics, are compared, as long as there is no category contradiction, we may synthesize reason through ratio — something which psychometrics claims to also measure and does, but not as it is played out in the world as action that may be adjudged, by its effect, as intelligent. For the amnion to persist, however, something else must occur; quantities in contradictory categories are thrown together into the same set (e.g., race = crime; debt = wealth), leading to the invalid synthetic propositions upon which the illusion of its existence is based.

While it might be said that the matter of intelligence is debatable since the concept of it is defined by context or use, when it comes to life and death we generally tend to know what each is without much debate. If you offer those who wish to debate it the choice of being killed then and there, generally they will prefer not to, belying their lack of sincerity. Therefore, we may conclude that there is a category of concept which is less subject to negotiation than others. The elements of this category we call universal (∀) — such as being and nonbeing, as all things may be or not be — though any concept may be debated and so it is with such absolutes. It is when a universal is reduced to an existential (∃), and vice versa, that, again, we have the sort of category error needed for the amnion to function upon such propositions as debt is wealth, rather than its absence. While such an inversion is possible in language, for language is a creature of the symbolic order, it is not possible in the order of the real. While it is true that debt can be sold as wealth, that is the prerogative of the obligor only; it is not extended to the obligee, naturally. A vacuum is the absence of a substance, usually a gas. But it is not the absence of electromagnetic force, which is also a kind of substance, else we would not be able to detect it and quantum physics would not be able to measure it, though it is in a different category of substance from a gas which is a form of matter, whereas electromagnetism is a force. Nevertheless, for there to be a vacuum there must be a verifiable void — one we verify not by the presence but the absence of something. This category of phenomena we may define by absence includes death. The word makes it seems substantial, never mind all of the rhetoric associated with the word, such as tales of the afterlife, ghosts, and zombies; but the word *nonbeing* makes the true circumstance of the matter explicit as negation of being. On the other hand, matter must have mass and volume, which are subject to force and indeed are used to help us quantify and define various forces, such as gravity. For example, Newton's universal law of gravity states that matter attracts matter as gravity directly proportional to the product of their masses, and inversely proportional to the square of the distance between their centers. That Einstein proved there is a quantifiable, and constant, ratio between matter and energy further complicates our conception of these categories. Do life and death have this kind of relationship? The nature of their relationship is incognizable because, unlike these other phenomena, they are the *same thing*, one being impossible without the other as they arise as the same phenomenon in simultaneously different states that are nevertheless witnessed (not experienced) separately. While they may be ethe negations of each other, one is not the absence of the other. We might think that death is when life is no more, but would we ever think that life is when death is no more? There is an asymmetry here if we do; one we perceive as permanent (death), while the other we perceive as temporary (life). How could this be true? It cannot. Despite being incognizable in and of itself, we can say this much about life and death. Even if there is such a thing as a ghost, it will never have to die of cancer. Note that ghosts are found nearly everywhere in the house except using the toilet. The same is true of a vacuum or void and substance in the sense of matter of any sort. Like a ghost, a vacuum may be filled with ethereal electromagnetism, but it will never be subject to Newton's universal law of gravity because it is, by definition, the absence of what makes that law possible as what Darwin calls a fixed law of nature. In a sense they are negations of each other. A vacuum is not the absence of matter but the presence of a vacuum, which, despite being the absence of substance, is, in and of itself, something because, as I said earlier, *nothing is something*, in the phenomenological world as a phenomenon. Matter is not the absence of a vacuum but the presence of mass and volume. Although we think of something which has "no mass" such as a vacuum to be the absence of something, it is the presence of something else (void). Electromagnetic energy is without mass, and yet it has volume (amplitude) can be measured in frequency. One definition of "substance" is that it can be measured; what cannot be measured we term insubstantial. Therefore, electromagnetic energy has a kind of substance. It is probably better to be hit by a truck, which clearly has substance, than it is to be struck by lightning at a billion volts. As Aristotle said, nature abhors a vacuum; and yet in space it is what pervades the universe, and most certainly whatever lies beyond it. Its absence is the exception. Let those who argue otherwise (dark matter and so on) exit a spacecraft without a pressurized suit and see what happens. Therefore, we might amend his observation by saying that nature *is* a vacuum, from which all substance arises just as it is the emptiness of a bowl that makes it functional, not anything else about it. It is the argument of this book that that vacuum is none other than the horror vacui (Aristotle's term) in the form of the sublime from which all arises because, like life, substance cannot *be* without absence, just as life cannot *be* without death. Nothing, though, is more anathema to the discourse of the amnion than the idea that for there to be life there must be death. It is necessary to reclassified death as a disease in order to get people to pay for its cure. As part of its coercive nature, the amnion promises the subject medical immortality. The subject, in turn, must have faith, believe in dogma, obey fiats and edicts, and more importantly pay health insurance premiums - out of pocket, through a reduction in salary at work, or by taxes for the purpose.

The prerogatives of the symbolic world of language step in once we have signified a physical phenomenon which we presume works on laws of its own and not language. The phenomenon nevertheless remains a child of its parental laws and not those necessitated by the limitations and nature of language. Still, attempts are made to create a kind of linguistic symmetry distorting the often asymmetric nature of phenomena (such as life being temporary and death being permanent in the conception of the subject). If symmetry were in some way a fixed natural law, it would make the seeking of the truth of things less difficult. So much of natural and human life lacks symmetry. We find, its in execution and outcomes, that even justice, despite being symbolized by the symmetry of Lady Justice's balance, is asymmetrical a significant percentage of time, at least statistically. In the arrangement of features on our faces, our handedness, and the hemispheres of the brain a symmetry is the rule.

While we have been discussing for the most part natural

phenomena, it is in the realm of purely human constructions that we find the greatest discrepancy between what is supposed to be the equal distribution of values versus how our ethical aesthetics is played out in the machinations of civilized life. This is, perhaps, the sole topic of Freud's Civilization and its Discontents. Did not civilization evolve from our desire to be free of our discontents (*Unbehagen*)? For example, the Manichean influence brought into Christianity after its own independent influence waned after the late first millennium created a religion of endless concentric schisms. St. Augustine's vehement denunciations of Manichean philosophies in *On the Morals of the Catholic Church,* such as he understood them, calls for an equitable distribution of truth value to both Testaments, based on the idea that each is the word of one God, not the God of the Jews and the God of the Christians:

> What more do you wish? Why do you resist ignorantly and obstinately? Why do you pervert untutored minds by your mischievous teaching? The God of both Testaments is one. For as there is an agreement in the passages quoted from both, so is there in all the rest, if you are willing to consider them carefully and impartially. (Ch. 17)

In other words, consider them the way St. Augustine does. Like the ideas of the Gnostics, those of the Manicheans were superseded by the official dogma of the Roman Catholic Church which sought to allay schisms, particularly as notions of Protestantism loomed. Meantime, the Manichean schism of the mind-body problem (one sacred, the other profane) lingered in mainstream church dogma. Consequently, the Manichean influence permeated the thinking of Western philosophy and science as well as religion, Catholic and Protestant. Its grotesque expression today, perhaps, is in the dichotomy between the modern consumer's obese, sickly, ugly body and its high net worth. Net worth, credit rating, salary, and assets permit quantification – the god of the amnion – allowing the subject to base its assessment of itself and others on economic potential rather than physical reality. Also, what is quantified may be encoded. What may be encoded is real; may not be, is either worthless or illusory. Such dualism of course becomes embedded in the requirements of language though not necessarily in phenomena. While it is clear that the universe oscillates in various ways, often between poles, it does not mean that ideas need to also, despite the dialectical method which is nevertheless so variously defined as to be several distinct approaches to thought at odds with each other. There may have been a time when there were more words for concrete things than abstract ideas. But as the latter take over from the former computationally and statistically, it becomes less clear what is or is not concrete. Like the body of the obese consumer, the signified is looked upon with contempt, whereas the signifier is exalted to the status of the real. During the reign of the concrete signifier, abstractions such as God seemed concrete the society. The crisis comes to a head, though, with the matter of the nature of the Host, or bread, and Blood, or wine, of the Eucharist; do they *represent* the body and blood of Christ or *are* they such? This problem is quite an important juncture in the way Christians thought in general about the world, and has its antecedents in the philosophy of the Manicheans. A favorite fixture in the blood-libel of the Jews across Europe in the Fourteenth Century was the charge of the desecration of the Host. Woodcuts of the period show Jews stabbing the Host with daggers, settling the matter once and for all — unless they were merely slicing the bread. This was one of the ostensible reasons for such atrocities as the Strasbourg Massacre of 14 February 1349 where hundreds of Jews were burned to death on the pretense of various libels - including that they had brought the curse of the plague down upon Christians, presumably for not being harsh enough with the Jews in the first place. The fact that the plague *had not yet been seen* in Strasbourg by 1349 belies the ulterior motives of this slaughter, whatever they might have been. Host desecration might have been seen as offensive and yet another reason to hate them, but not provocation to murder them, had not the Host been regarded *as* the flesh of the Savior rather an symbolizing it. "Then Jesus said unto them, Verily, verily, I say unto you, Except ye eat the flesh of the Son of man, and drink his blood, ye have no life in you" (John 6:53). As he did not go on to explicate his meaning, as was his style, the job was left to posterity with the consequences I have just described.

As with the encroachment of abstract words upon the domain of the concrete, the ever-more figurative and euphemistic language of the Imaginary makes it nearly impossible to sort out what "reality" *means*, not *is* (which we leave to physicists and mathematicians who would rather verify than seek consensus in its place). The relationship between the signified and the signifier belongs to the symbolic order. There, it is properly managed for what it is. However, when the symbolic becomes subordinated to the installation (apparatus) of the Imaginary in the production and processing of language, backed by the fiats, injunctions, and edits of the hegemony, a fundamental change takes place in the way thought is constructed and consequently oriented toward the processing of objective reality. Darwin's comment in his autobiography that "the men at that time were ignorant and credulous to a degree almost incomprehensible by us" is another way of saying that they thought in a way equally incomprehensible to the modern mind, which we like to presume is more like Darwin's than the "ignorant and credulous" of his day. But are they? A quick survey of minds in some modern cultures will reveal, however, that the most ludicrous assertions of scripture are taken to be as much a "fact" as the boiling point of water. As psychologist Julian Jaynes argues, early ancient cultures in the West and Mesopotamia accepted and even perceived the denizens of the other world as "flesh and blood" when manifest, as mentioned earlier here. In this context, then, Christ's words at his last meal take on a significance our cultural narcissism typically does not allow. It is a good guess, though, that those who profess belief in God today and accept the fairy tales of scripture as scientific, historical, and mortal fact nevertheless are not visited by angels the way Mary most certainly thought she was by Gabriel. If she were not so astonished, she would have made tea. As it is she was dumbfounded. We cannot assume any mental pathology on her part, as there is no other indication that she was anything but a health person in mind and body otherwise. On the other hand, there is no evidence of a motive to make up the story — except in the lurid minds of those who might do so under her circumstances. Finally, there is enough verisimilitude of various sorts to her tale, vetted over the ages, to lead us to conclude that the visiting was not a later cynical interpolation. So then what was it? I think Jaynes' explanation the best: it was the bicameral mind of the ancients who did not distinguish, as we do, between the accepted and official superstitions of science and the those of the occult, in which I will include this event as it is, ultimately, incognizable and therefore occluded. As the story goes, she left the encounter pregnant. *How* she got pregnant, either supernaturally or naturally, is irrelevant. I have known some women who gave a less convincing explanation. It is interesting to note that it was the Manicheans in particular who saw "virgin birth" as one of the abominations of the Gospels; even among the premier dichotomaniacs controversy reigned regarding the "reality" of these scriptural claims. With phrases such as artificial intelligence, smart phone (gadget), and virtual reality – the three great oxymorons of the digital age – the phenomenological barrier between words describing the real and unreal become conflated by a kind of negating juxtaposition that seems less crazy than anything Mary alleged regarding Gabriel. *Meaninglessness* takes on new meaning as the prerequisite for advertising, marketing, and political and social discourse, particularly as it is found in the technology just mentioned. For something to have meaning in this newfangled way of thinking it must be meaningless, meaning that if it has a specific, concrete, verifiable meaning, all is lost. The Imaginary, required to hoodwink the consumer into spending his debt, dissolves into the ether of dreams from which it emanated. This is precisely the crisis of meaning that the Dada movement made fun of in the nascent, modern industrial culture they saw polluting the cultural environment around them in Europe. That they did so between world wars, in the deep background of which were industrial and banking interests, lent credibility to the criticism underlying their performances. In short, their message is that the real has become the *surreal*.

There is bound to be an emotional, as well ethical and aesthetic, correlative to this significant change in thinking from concrete to abstract, from real to imaginary, from simulation to simulacrum. About his countrymen, American poet Jones Very (1813-1880) says, in "The Dead," that "in their show of life more dead they live / Than those that to the earth with many tears they give." These haunting lines describe the chasm that was opening up in his day between the urban, fashionable, industrial, consumer and the agrarian farmer going about his business of feeding himself and the world as farmers had done since before recorded history. The former was attached to artificial life, with its coal, electricity, textile mills, and steam engines; the latter remained a part of the soil, dependent upon the cycles of nature and the labor and knowledge required to farm it. There are few if any romantic novels about passionate love affairs conducted using a plain old telephone line. But the handiness of the subject's new gadget and the deployment of digital channels devoted to so-called social media make this "imitation of life" more attractive than life itself. Therefore, any attempt to court in person is considered sexual misconduct because it preempts the online vetting process similar to an FBI background check, though more thorough (I know, I have had one). Mediated life is sanitized by being encoded into transistors. One merely needs to click a mouse to "defriend" those one wishes to dispose of. No murder is needed. No need to work anything out, even with family members and coworkers. Pathos of the sort we most commonly associate with shyness, anxiety, anticipation, infatuation, loathing, longing, heartbreak, excitement, and desire is replaced by the signifier. The *signified* is treated as if it had the plague, which it might, but which the digital persona cannot be infected by, though it may be hacked or serve as a Trojan horse for malware. Life reduced to data then becomes the signal for that which it has displaced, and that which it has displaced becomes the *copy of the signal,* not the original, which it is in an objective sense. Thus, what is then called relationship need not involve any relating at all, only a kind of online pantomime of it. Here we have mimesis as a virus, a word in Latin means poison. The subject, in trying to avoid the plague by not coming into contact with the real flesh and blood of Jesus, instead opts for the viral infection of the nominal imitation of communion – for that is what it is – with the transcendental object, or Other. In the process, the opportunity for transcendence of subjectivity is lost, since the digital medium feeds back to the subject its own profile, thus reinforcing its narcissism rather than circumventing it. Transcendence of our ego is why we are attracted to others at all, unless we wish merely to exploit the other for something we want or need, such as sex without love or friendship. This signal triggers a narcissistic copy of the original emotion. Eventually the chemistry of the brain adapts to the stimulus this signal sparks, creating a kind of three-dimensional construct of the original emotion so that it *seems* real, but is not, as the brain will often enough react to real or imaginary stimulus the same way. For example: fear in a nightmare cannot be distinguished from fear on the battlefield, in terms of its cognitive expression. Since the image has some of the same characteristics as reality – for instance a man with a gun – it fools the brain into an autonomic response. Nevertheless, the id will none of it, because it knows, at all times, what is real and what is not. For example, the libido may really need an orgasm, an ecstatic release of pent-up psychic energy in a moment of jouissance. If that real orgasm is achieved with pornography or sex with a partner, or even sex with a partner online as pornography, it is the same to the id: discharge. The same is true when killing someone in a video game. In the latter case, it is even more satisfying, presuming there is no pathology in the gamer, because the id does not invoke the censure of the superego in the form of sin (guilt), fear of the consequences of violating the nomos (murder), breaking social boundaries (sociopath), and possibly *really being killed* as the opponent defends himself or seeks retribution (fear). Free of the negative emotions and actions of guilt, murder, sociopathy, and fear, the id enjoys emancipation from the anticathexis otherwise keeping these impulses in check. Meantime, in the former case, while the subject may go ahead and have sex with a partner (these days and in Western culture), the lure of the smorgasbord of taboos online may satisfy the libido *more than* socially acceptable practices, or for that matter sex for the sole purpose of procreation, which nevertheless requires orgasm to be fulfilled, even in the most prudish. As a result, in both cases the subject enjoys the jouissance of the taboo of transgression in the virtual environment, but must abide by either the prohibition against murder, or the conventional ideas or even laws of erotic gratification. There is little evidence that taboo transgression in the virtual space leads to it being acted out in reality; in fact, the clinical data point in the other direction. From a purely clinical point of view, then. it might be better for society, as it makes the consumer all-around less potent in the real world and more amenable to purchase of digital products delivering ever-more-real virtual experiences. The chief benefit, however, is not to the subject but to the fasces of the corporate hegemony. The generally frustrated subject learns to act out its formerly subconscious fantasies *online* where they can be recorded through telemetry for mining by commercial Big Data and parsed (sniffed) by government surveillance for possible threats.

Here we will benefit from revisiting Matthew Arnold. Being at the incipience of the full installation of the Imaginary, Arnold feels the transubstantiation of what he calls Faith into a Godless world of consumerism, industry, and war. He dismisses civilization's pleasures and supposed benefits, such as peace, light, certitude, and help for pain as mere illusions. Even love is included, because he sees it as something other than being "true to one another." As I mentioned before, most murders occur between persons who know each other, are friends, relatives, family members, or lovers. We may presume that some of the departed loved or were loved by the assailant. There is ample evidence that love does not preclude murder. Love is more often a *prelude* to murder, statistically. As love and murder are in different categories — one an emotion, the other a legal term — it is not possible for love to *preclude* murder. Being in the relationship of a disjunction, then, together as subject-predicate they can only produce a synthetic statement which cannot be verified because of the category error. Love may *lead* to murder, but it cannot stop it, which is, perhaps, why Arnold includes love in his list of vacuous truths. Subject and predicate must be elements in the same existential category (∃), even if they are in different subsets. However, in Arnold's conception, *being true* to someone *does* preclude murder (and war-as-murder), because to murder someone is *not to be true* to that person. As such, we have a universal, verifiable, analytic statement. It can be proven conclusively that since murder is *not being true* to one another, it follows that being true to one another absolutely, universally, precludes murder (∀) in any circumstance or form. The murder being referred to here appears in the last line where "ignorant armies clash by night," in as much as war is a form of murder. To the victor, the vanquished were a bunch of murderers; to the friends, family, and countrymen of the vanquished, the victors are murderers. (Or perhaps I am mistaken, and each side sees the other as a tribe of saints.) If being true to one another precludes murder, and war is murder as defined above, then it also precludes war. The transcendent moment comes when Arnold intuits the other (his lover to whom the poem is addressed) as the transcendental object, thus inverting the subject-object relationship. In so doing he also transcends his narcissism; from such a vantage point, the preoccupations of humanity are seen for what they are: vacuous truths at best, and internecine war at worst. Therefore, *being true to one another* transcends the vacuous truths and selfish ideals he lists, which are valuable to civilization but worthless to him now as he envisages the true sadness of death in a state of bardic vision. As he has the courage to *feel* death, before the moment of death is upon him, as most of us choose to do, he finds the courage to also reject the comforts and aims of civilization for the horror vacui of the sublime. The resulting desolation of the absence of faith reveals the sublime in which somehow, somewhere, it shall return to those who can distinguish it from hope. The emotion of hope, as I have said, is a morbid emotion driving the sublime from its rightful place in our sense of existence, which is not always pleasurable. The sadness of death, which is a kind of suffering, pervades the poem. Only in the realm of this sadness, then, which is the haunting, lonely feeling that we absolutely *will* die (not maybe), and must some day, if we are lucky, say farewell to all we love and even who we have become, does the sublime reach out to us and give us a glimpse of eternity. Indeed it is paradoxical. But life itself is based on the paradox of life and death being one and the same *always already*. He need make no further argument than the lines immediately below. History has made it for him, posthumously. Ninety years later (after the original composition of the poem, 1849-1851) the very spot he stands on will be the scene of a world war.

> ... now I only hear
> Its melancholy, long, withdrawing roar,
> Retreating, to the breath
> Of the night-wind, down the vast edges drear
> And naked shingles of the world.

Being true, however, is not truth in the sense meant by Keats in his "Ode to a Nightingale," where it is an abstraction;

we may *be true* to one another, as Arnold says. But, turning Keats' material equivalent, beauty, into a verb, we cannot really say that we can *be beautiful* to one another without uttering pretty sounding nonsense. Arnold, well acquainted with Greek and Latin, knows that what he speaks of is *pistos* as found in the Greek translation of the Aramaic Bible, meaning faith, or faithfulness. To Keats, truth is the *episteme*, or the knowing, of beauty. Therefore, his proposition is aesthetic, and is, as such, also universal (∀), but in a different universe of discourse. In Keats' poem, beauty and truth are nouns indicating equivalent ideals that cannot exist without each other, and are therefore the *knowing-of*. In Arnold's poem, *being true* is a verb and is the *getting-to-know*, which is eternal, transcending the temporal. Being thus transcendent, Arnold's proposition is also universal (∀), only including the possibility of Keats' abstraction by implication. Arnold's objective correlative (Eliot) for existential emptiness and loneliness is the sea — as I say above, a form of desolation removing the obscurant layer of comfort, convenience, and illusion upon which civilization is based in its quest to repress the id and commodify jouissance.

> Listen! you hear the grating roar
> Of pebbles which the waves draw back, and fling,
> At their return, up the high strand,
> Begin, and cease, and then again begin,
> With tremulous cadence slow, and bring
> The *eternal note of sadness* in ...
> Ah, love, let us be true
> To one another!
> ... for the world, which seems
> To lie before us like a land of dreams,
> So various, so beautiful, so new,
> Hath really neither joy, nor love, nor light,
> Nor certitude, nor peace, nor help for pain ...

Arnold's vision of life, even *with* faith, is tragic, just as it is for Keats, as Unamuno says in *The Tragic Sense of Life,* hence "*the eternal note of sadness* ..." This lyrical poem sounds more like a eulogy than a lyric; it serves as a tocsin of impending loss while revealing the sublime to Arnold in the place of the Sea of Faith, which *is withdrawing* (not *has withdrawn*). It is not a jeremiad insomuch as a warning of what might come, namely ignorant armies clashing by night — which was indeed the case. It is inescapable to say that it is a "sea change / Into something rich and strange." Indeed it is strange, but also *rich* in the Keatsian sense in that there is a kind of imperative necessity to the transformation as a *process*. Like power, faith is not given, it is taken. It requires will to be more than hope, which is impotent and inert. As the world slips into two wars that will destroy Europe, the *Gott-ist-tod theologie* of Fichte and Nietzsche rises in the void left by the withdrawal of the Sea of Faith. Although Arnold invokes the sublime with his poetic voice, it is ultimately indicated only, as it can never be apprehended directly and remain *subliminal*. When willful faith in the transcendental object — the Other, God, or the spirits of the occult — is absent, the sublime rises like Juggernaut, destroying all in its path, usually in the guise of war. Therefore, war is always sublime because it is terrible, stripping away the narcissistic defenses the subject cultivates in its quest for egoic immortality. The carnage of war serves as a memento mori of how tenuous and brutal life really is underneath its nimbus of civilization's imaginary comfort, convenience, and promise of immortality — medical or spiritual. The less the sublime is a part of the ethical aesthetic of civilization, the less willful faith there is in the transcendental object as intuition, the more destructive and pervasive war will be, as it is today in the age of perpetual war. Pitching the faithful and the faithless into the same wretched abyss of meaningless nothingness, war wipes notional existence — as well as its imaginary economy of fiat currency and derivatives — into temporary oblivion. Only then does the subject, alas, wake up to the terror of the oubliette it has imprisoned itself in, but without faith in anything greater than his mortal situation. In the clash of what Arnold calls ignorant armies, the amnion of the Imaginary vanishes revealing the *truth* - whatever it may be, as this essay does not pretend to define it, only describe how it is lost and won. The subject, if it is lucky, then perceives the amnion for what it is: an illusion. The infrastructure it needs to maintain its perpetual expansion (progress) or implode has vanished. The resulting space, though it may be filled with the smoke of battle, enables the subject to see what matters, usually too late. The Other returns to the Real from the collective narcissism of the Imaginary. Language takes its place once again in the Symbolic order, as every word becomes an affirmation of life. We might say, though, that the subject does not quite appreciate this gift. Few would, concerned more with mere survival, which is the eternal state of all life anyway. Civilization's promise, in return for abdication to its hegemonic will, is that it will eradicate the Law of the Jungle and the struggle for survival even plankton must face, but cannot deliver on the promise as it always devolves into war as self-punishment for the forsaking of the ethical aesthetic of the sublime. No one celebrates the presence of a piece of wreckage to cling to after a shipwreck. One just grabs for it. Once afloat, instead of counting one's blessing, one typically bemoans one's fate, regarding others in the drink as competitors for the scant resources of the shipwrecked. While such a tragedy may make one think about one's life, it seldom brings about a reorientation to the transcendental other from one's state of narcissism, which is regarded as the norm of civilization's default culture. The sublimity of Arnold's poem in and of itself is enough of a demonstration of his appreciation of the significance of the transcendence of narcissism. The poem begins with a simple appreciation of the beauty of the Dover coast at night, and therefore of nature, which is always the other, working its way into the sea as objective correlative for faith.

> The sea is calm tonight.
> The tide is full, the moon lies fair
> Upon the straits; on the French coast the light
> Gleams and is gone; the cliffs of England stand,
> Glimmering and vast, out in the tranquil bay.
> Come to the window, sweet is the night-air!

The abyss of the sublime also brings him kinship with Sophocles, master of tragedy, whom he says "Heard it on the Ægean, and it brought / Into his mind the turbid ebb and flow / Of human misery ..." The central three stanzas rely on the *sound* of the sea. Arnold finds them to be a kind of voice, but in the sense of being the voice of the ancients, such as Sophocles, who appreciated the *sadness* inherent in nature. In this literal emphasis (after all, Dover Beach is a real place), the sea correlates, objectively, with his perception of the sublime. It allows the presence of the Other access to the subject's sense of being, thereby modifying the subject beyond the sign (signifier) of itself into the universal of the Other (signified).

There was a gathering spirit in English poetry in the time frame in which the poem was written. Theism — the last holdout of the Romantic period, which had pervaded the almost pagan nature poems of Wordsworth and the other Lake Poets — was yielding to the concerns of industry and science. Perhaps we may consider Shelly's poems, and his proto-communist manifestos, as an example of the transition. He did not shy from taking on industrial politics in a vigorous and aggressive way. Even Wordsworth gave in and wrote a (terrible) poem about trains. It is a unique and important time in art and science. The Spiritus Mundi, as Yeats later called it, took on the mantle of sublime the destroyer (like Kali), sowing the seeds of the chaos and unrest that would later lead to the toppling of ancient monarchies, socialist revolutions, and world war. The resulting *Gott-ist-tot theologie* works well into Scientism's eventual usurpation of Theism's dying grasp on productive imagination. Christianity, Judaism, and Islam remake themselves, taking up strategic positions that employ science and politics in opportunistic ways, compromising their faiths by working around their supernatural covenants. Fundamentalism in all three Semitic religions begins in this period, the early 20th Century, as a reaction to the denaturing of the fundamental tenets of those faiths. Briefly, the genie of the sublime is stuffed back into its bottle by superficial adaptation to inevitable change – only to come roaring back in two world wars, presaging the Cold War. What follows is the Zeitgeist we have now: an age of perpetual war on the battlefields of politics, economics, culture, territory, weapons, technology, and natural resources. The last words of the poem end in a despair anticipating the inevitable transition to this brave new world:

> And we are here as on a darkling plain
> Swept with confused alarms of struggle and flight,
> Where ignorant armies clash by night.

3.3: Sublime freedom of the *Weltgeist*

What does the Spiritus Mundi in Yeats' "The Second Coming" signal for the sublime? To understand it better, we must begin with Hegel's idea of the Weltgeist and the terror of what he calls *absolute freedom* – a value Marx would later label a "fetish" (cf. "Freedom and Fetishism," Marshall Berman, *Adventures in Marxism*, 1999). The first world war raged from 1914 until 1918. Yeats writes the poem in 1919, when the horrors are fresh in the form of experience: Irish squadrons suffered heavy casualties, and were more or less conscripted by the British. The spirit, then, of such a time is expressed in the physical, moral, spiritual, and existential devastation we find in the poetry of the time. In Yeats' poem, when "Things fall apart" and "the centre cannot hold," the robotic production and political powers of the hegemony, comprised of science, technology, and government, are commandeered for the anarchy of war for nebulous ends. To the grey-haired men who initiate these wars, it seems to them as if they are settling various scores and are "making the world safe for [fill in the blank]" and conducting, in history's most inaccurate prognostication, a war to end all wars. In fact, they are unwitting pawns of the sublime, which now conspires to destroy their amniotic empire *that hath forsaken it* for the trinkets of deceit: the accoutrements of bourgeois society of the day, its gross consumption, and the relentless imperialism that made it possible. The inversion of "the best" lacking all intensity and "the worst" being full of passion for destruction mirrors the inversion of civilization's epistemology and industrial and cultural *techne* for the purpose of its own annihilation at the behest of the forsaken sublime. In the aftermath, when all lies in ruin, the putative causes of war seem obscure, trivial, vague, as if they were at best an excuse for ... something. I have still not learned of a clear cause-and-effect explanation for World War I, much less America's involvement in it, despite research into the matter. I know the mechanics of it: poor, miserable Princip, a lousy shot according to his shooting instructor, shoots the Archduke and his wife while they are riding in a car in Sarajevo, after making a fatal wrong turn. The rest of the historical explanation ends up sounding, to me, like a family squabble between the Hapsburgs. The explanation, if it can be called that, in Charles O'Neill's version of the Irish folksong "Foggy Dew," says, sarcastically, "T'was England bade our Wild Geese go / that small nations might be free," when "Britannia's Huns" conscripted young Irishmen under threat of their "long range guns," who were much needed on the farms back home, to fight and mostly die in a war that could not be explained. By the way, it was the British in their propaganda campaign, much admired by Hitler (*Mein Kampf*), who vilified the German army as "huns."

Historians quibble over the priority of their interpretations of the amorphous mess of historical documents, artifacts, and scribbles already picked over by previous historians – sometimes 2,000 years earlier, when their memories were, perhaps, fresher regarding events of their own epoch (e.g. Herodotus, Josephus). The progressive fallacy, however, decrees that *those* ancient historians were not smart enough to apply the "scientific" principles of today's historians, who fight among themselves about the meaning of even recent events. Just compare Egypt's account of the Six-Days' War (1973) with Israel's. There is some overlap of inescapable facts, but it ends there. If fortunate, they will agree that Abraham Lincoln signed the Emancipation Proclamation in 1865. But they will keep debating whether or not he actually "freed the slaves," as the heroic fairy tale goes, without first having set up a situation for their re-enslavement as share croppers and third-class citizens. The best that eventually comes out of that debate is the contradiction of the excluded middle: "yes and no." That the slaves were nominally freed is what is called in logic and mathematics a vacuous truth: *x* is true because it *could be* contained in the set, but is not. Nevertheless, answering questions about the purpose of war is important for the creation of the collective mythology of ensuing generations so that they stay on message with prevailing hegemony over time. Heck, ask any American high schooler how many persons died in the American Civil War, which was fought, as the narrative goes, to "free the slaves." Of course, he will have no idea that about 646,596 died in combat and another 539,000 died as "collateral damage" for various reasons such as wounds, disease, displacement, and civilian casualties (military.com). However, he will tell you that every person on the side of the South died exclusively to defend slavery, and every person who died on the side of the North fought to end it. The North were the good guys, and the South were the bad guys, proto-Nazi racists all (the Rebel flag and the Nazi flag are together banned from the big retail websites). Deviate from this script, and you are branded the descendant of a slave owner and white supremacist, if not a neo-Nazi. Even if your descendants came from Finland ten years ago. Depending on how public it is, which is quite easy in social media, your life and career in mainstream society is over. Even as I write this I fear I tread on taboo territory and that this book will be boycotted or burned because of it; I will be denounced on major social media channels, which I no longer use, by self-appointed guardians of justice as a racist, with no chance for rebuttal.

Why is it that my blood runs cold when I write or say anything deviating even in the slightest detail from the prevailing discourse of the hegemony? Because I wrote this book, and others, about the matter, does not mean I am any more free of the capture mechanism of the apparatus than the reader may be. The answer is that *there is really something to be afraid of*; the mass of subjects have become robotic, programmed by their digital gadget to root out any dissent on behalf of the hegemony, while imagining that they are fighting it. Social media have become *weaponized*, to the delight of the hegemony because it brings in revenue and "shames" out true dissent – else it would be censored. The irony, if not hypocrisy, of these online crusades is that they are monetized by the major corporations running the websites – powerful media paid for by allowing the corporations they attack to mine their personal data, including their revolutionary pronunciamentos.

They do not want to feel that they have sprung from the social ether *ex nihilo*, or that they are the creatures of the very thing they hate. This is a pervasive mechanism not limited to DIY social justice warriors. Having lost its core identity through abdication, the subject conveniently and comfortably takes on the subtly manipulated, or refurbished, persona fed back to it from its consumer profile emanating from the networks of the amnion. This persona has been dredged from its own buying and browsing choices, as well as habitual behavior and political beliefs, covert or overt. This digital imago only marginally reflects who the subject might be to, say, itself, physical friends, and family. There is always the possibility, though, that the subject engages in transgressive jouissance online, such as cheating on a spouse in chat rooms, searching taboo pornography, or dramatizing a fantasy persona it is too timid in the concrete world to embody. In this case, the subject may be *more real*, at least in these ways, than at the dinner table with family, or at the work desk. Whatever the case may be, it is an indication that the subject whose persona is being reflected back in the black mirror of its digital gadget is confused about who it is. At an adult stage of the game of life, this is a true liability in the quest for psychological and emotional homeostasis, but a boon for the amnion, the hegemony, the Cult of Mediocrity, Scientism, and their transnational overlords: the global banking system. A subject with an undeveloped core identity (ego) will have chronic problems with object constancy, feeling abandoned if its gadget is not within reach, charged up, and connected to the network of the amniotic empire. Using the gadget, it indulges in reckless spending of credit, energizing the international corporate entities which have captured its once free will. Aggravating the situation is that an undeveloped ego is *infantile* in its orientation to others, seeing the world as a means to the ends of its organic gratification only, ever searching for the eternal teat.

Naturally, this orientation precludes the possibility of the apprehension of the transcendental object. At best the subject sees the world as the mother (consumerism) and the father (nomos). At worst it is a sociopath or psychotic to whom others and the furniture of the world are just a nursery full of playthings to be at bent to its will in order to fulfill the impulses of its unchecked id, or be destroyed. The subject without chronic pathology of this sort may still have object-constancy difficulties, but is stable enough to *seem* normal, hold a job, and have a family, struggling to wear the mask of marginal sanity. Herein lies the foundation of the digital persona of the Apex Consumer. Nevertheless, the void created by the absence of a strong core identity, and therefore a mature and effective will, leads the subject into onanistic psychotherapy, ineffective self-help, drugs legal and illegal, media distraction, alcohol abuse, or if not so daring and bold, simply accepting the consumer profile for what it seems to be *viz* an internalized imago entirely alien to the reality of the organic subject. (Ergo, the symbolic obsession with organic food.) Some choose a cocktail of a few of these products vended by the amnion to appease a vague but gnawing sense of not *being-there* (Dasein). I think I do not need to give examples, as they are the fabric of modern civilization itself. Look within, or around for them. If you have a digital gadget handy, which I will bet you do, you can reverse engineering your consumer profile, the other you. Adverts for diapers and statins? The geriatric set. Adverts for Caribbean vacations, new cars, and baby paraphernalia? Young couples. You will seldom see these profiles mixed on your gadget, because it has already adapted to this reductio ad absurdum of who you are. You can make a simple table of two columns, one for each conception: who you think you are and who you seem to be to Big Data. Perhaps they match about 90 percent; perhaps they conflict, overlapping only 10 percent. Consider the significance of each. Maybe make a third column and ask someone you know well to list her vision of who she thinks you are, without showing her the other two columns. This is one way to get at a basic understanding of what kinds of data are being gathered about you, what the machines (and the government — thanks Edward Snowden!) see as *you*, and maybe help you begin thinking about the health of your native core identity, absolutely essential for psychological wellbeing and what amounts to the same thing: apprehension of the transcendental object, which is the only path to the sublime acceptance of death. Do you think that the hundreds of strangers you have befriended on social media each have an idea of who you are that comes close to who you might really be? Maybe for whatever reason you have a persona online of *who you would rather be*, an alternate you, called an avatar. In this case you will have to make four columns! But one thing is for sure: if you use an avatar quite different from who you are (not including its practical use in the role-playing of gaming — you are not Thor), then you are then the kind of person who wants or needs an avatar. Why? What is the pleasure principle here?

Which brings us to the matter of the meaning, significance, and purpose of identity. Between the getting-to-know and the knowing-of lies the *narrative* of events, which is a thing unto itself as a sign, or signifier. You are part of this narrative as a character of some sort. Consequently, this character needs management so that the narrative your character inhabits, like a virtual reality game, does not end in jail or dead, for instance. But this management is difficult in the ever-shifting sands of the amniotic empire. Being *unreal*, its narrative is always in conflict in with the real. Thereby unstable, as it does not have the captain and rudder of reality to guide it, it is always changing randomly based on the vicissitudes of chaos, making decisions difficult (debt = wealth; war = peace; censorship = free speech; guns = crime), which is why we turn to the hegemony to make those decisions for us — helping it, voluntarily, to achieve its ultimate end of *total control*. The hegemony's disingenuous noises about the need for self-determination, prosperity, democracy, and equal justice are a cover for its role as the servant of the global financial cartels and the super-rich, who seem to have nothing better to do. Nevertheless, the mass of subjects *supports* the ever-expanding amnion by mistaking the signifier for the signified. The flimsy narrative of its character in this drama consequently labors in perpetual contradiction, hypocrisy, and chaos. From there, all propositions become either false, synthetic, or invalid. Even tautology, which is always true, becomes impossible when A = B. Journalism is never so shameful as when it tries to hide the fact that what it reports is a *story*, a tale, a narrative, and is therefore a signifier not the signfied. Unfortunately, a starving person was never nourished by a picture of food, though nations consider a treaty, a piece of paper, to be peace. The media, the purveyors of the narrative, abound with pictures of food, which seem to satisfy the hunger of the fundamentally symbolic nature of the subject's self-image while starving its need for organic integration with the world and its sustenance, which includes the sublime. Therefore, the distinction is phenomenological, not exclusively political, philosophical, or psychological. Moreover, built into this narrative is a critical element of *entertainment*, which should also make us wonder about how faithful the story is to the signified it is supposed to represent as a reliable mirror. When reports of unending war, murder, serial killing, mass shootings, premature death, destruction, robbery, car accidents, child abductions, sexual misconduct and other mayhem become a form of entertainment, we should not wonder, by reverse engineering, what is the true nature of those who find it so entertaining? Are they *really* the good citizens they purport to be, or are they latent psychopaths waiting for the moment when the state of exception touches them through social chaos brought on by the collapse of the economy or the sudden presence of total war? In their defense, as I was a journalist for ten years and needed to be paid, the media have to earn money to survive. Unfortunately, today they have been financialized, meaning that if they do not post excess profits that are ever-expanding, algorithmic trading will trigger a sell-off of their stock or that of their parent companies. The alternative, though, to this system is state-run media, such as the old *Pravda* (*Truth*), the present *Renmin Ribao* (*People's Daily*), and the *New York Times*. Also, in order to get people to take any interest in current events we must make the story as interesting as any story must be in order to lure and hold a reader. But to what ends do the media go in their quest for ratings and, as a consequence, ever-greater returns in the markets? The professional journalist's talent is to make the story seem true *no matter what* the pressures and constraints of the medium. A good journalist is a great storyteller. Anyone can gather information - even a machine. But a machine cannot tell a compelling story, even if the bare facts of it *are* compelling in some way. In other words, the reader cannot be bored into engaging with the media discourse. If the reader does not read, or watch, or click, then media vanish. Such power is in the hands of the subject, though it is usually wielded autonomically by consumer choice. Media once dominant can, in ten years, be a footnote in a communications textbook. The fact remains that the subject has this power as a consumer, but cannot use it unless conscious, not only aware, of it. To be power, it must *taken*, not *given*, presupposing will, which is the excrescence of the core identity in its healthy, homeostatic state.

As the history of Western institutional religion shows, however, boredom, as a soporific, is a viable state of mind for indoctrination, distraction, and the inculcation of default values and dogma. One of the strangest sights of the modern age is seeing someone watch hours of TV that he nevertheless finds boring, then next day go out and buy what he saw advertised. Communications theorists call this the narcotizing dysfunction effect of media. The subject is off guard, distracted, maybe even in a suggestive hypnotic state. In these states of distraction, the stories of the goings on of our fellow beings, and commercial pitches, bypass reason where they might have been filtered, analyzed, pondered, and perhaps rejected as not passing the test of reality or verification. Instead, they embed in the unconscious where they "set up" (*aufgezogen*), ready to take their place in the ever-shifting, expanding, and elaborating "uncreated conscience" as James Joyce puts it in *Portrait of the Artist as a Young Man*. The difference between Joyce's urge to "forge" a conscience "in the smithy of [his] soul" and the subject's indoctrination into the boredom of mediocrity is that the Joyce's vow of sovereignty allows him to approach the horror vacui through the creative imperative. The imperative is absent in the Apex Consumer, who has substituted creativity for consumption of the creativity of others. What animates the world spirit, then, is this imperative to *create* as action not idea. If we do not, then we are dead in life, uncreated, in conflict with our own genesis. Procreation is not enough to fulfil this imperative. The elite supplying the subject with gadgets, new-old products, and 24/7 entertainment and infotainment must have brilliant creatives in their employ. The creatives labor in the blacksmith's shop at least of the media they design, program, and for which they supply content. But where it the sublime in all of this? Does God live online? Does the Higher Power come to AA's in a chat room? Do we feel the power of the forces of the occult, the demons of old, and the flight of the soul to other worlds? Do we feel intimate with those of the past who have come before us? Are we moved to tears? Do we experience what Freud calls the *furor sanandi* (healing frenzy)? Do we even exercise online? Are we awed by a sunset seen on the gadget's little screen? These questions one must answer for oneself. I say no. The sublime must serve as the "smithy" where the sovereign individual, like a blacksmith, hammers out his own narrative if indeed he still retains the *creative imperative* in the active sense. The passive sense is mere consumption of the creativity of others, for instance great actors, musicians, astronomers, or technology engineers. In this comparison we see that there are only two possibilities of narrative: one's own, and that which is acquired through indoctrination into that of the hegemony's moment-to-moment need for power and money. As with power, the creative imperative must be taken, not given. If the amnion's need to first usurp the subject's power, and then dispense it back to the subject for a price, is not primed with abdication of one's sovereignty, it will instantly implode. For many great civilizations of the past that lost what in ancient Chinese political philosophy is called the Mandate of Heaven, there is left only, as Revelation 18:2 describes, "a dwelling place of demons, a prison for every foul spirit, and a cage for every unclean and hated bird." The status quo leading the population down this path to disaster can be stopped in its tracks by the subject. Not with protests, which are symbolic action and actually play into the hegemony's scheme for total control, but true action hitting at the heart of the its lifeblood. For example, if every person in the country, on the same day, decided that he would never make another mortgage payment, the amnion would instantly implode. At that moment, the mortgagor would be liberated from his servitude, disabling the hegemony's banking system from prosecuting the usually brutal action of foreclosure. Lenders would then be forced into negotiations with the borrowers, resulting in a far more equitable terms than they had previously — if there was even anything left of the financial system and its government. But the narrative of the hegemony is so powerful, that the slave would not *dare* run away from the plantation on which he has chosen to labor, suffer, and die. However, it is not the hegemony's apparatus preventing the subject from seizing its freedom back from its captors; it is the subject's *choice* to be enslaved. It *chose* to sign those promissory notes that built a cage of debt around it and its heirs. It could have chosen another far more modest path equal to its financial and social reality, but it strayed and likely will never find the true path again that was its rightful destiny, however, humble. Its egoic desire to live in a palace and have eternal access to consumer goods, as well as its bid for medical immortality, keeps it in thrall to its nominal captor. But the cage door remains open, because the hegemony needs the voluntary action of the subject to survive as the Imaginary.

Part of the subject's preternatural compliance with its own enslavement is due to its lack of the ability to analyze effectively. As I said earlier, its analytic ability is either considered something to be used to get a paycheck, or is confined only to choosing between Product A and Product B. While it has been processed through the state-mandated indoctrination of public education, it has come away from that symbolic ordeal with little learning. Its ignorance of propositional, or first-order, logic makes it impossible for it to verify a proposition for its truth-value. Never mind its ignorance of second-order and higher-order logic — all within reach of the person with an average intellect who has learned something from high school algebra. Add to this the subject's embrace of the invalid synthetic proposition as the foundation of the structure of its largely autonomic thought, where subject and predicate are in categorical contradiction, and the subject's mental activity become merely *reactive*, not responsive, effective, and creative. The Apex Consumer *reacts* by consuming. The cult of mediocrity (I will drop the initial capitals) does all in its power to quash any enthusiasm the subject might have to use propositional analysis except at work, else it will see through the veil of illusion the Imaginary of the amnion depends upon for its nominal existence, or, more accurately, its pervasive presence as a synthetic simulacrum of reality. Instead, the apparatus seeks to replace such enthusiasm with a dull sense of compulsive, gnawing, unfulfilled desire (the Lacanian *lack*) which *cannot be* fulfilled (*l'objet petit a*). The dullard makes an excellent consumer because he is bored with life. He is not engaged with it. Instead, he is enthralled with the sad little world the amnion pipes in to it through its digital gadget, which the subject keeps before its eyes at all times as if reality were contained in it, not the environment through which the subject must move and in which it must live. What, then, is in the real world that the subject fears, turning to the artificial world of the networks, or networld, in its place? I hope by now you could guess: *death*, the unspeakable, the unmentionable vulgarity in polite society. It is, paradoxically, the majority content of the entertainment the subject craves in order to feel that death is only part of a video game, unreal, not the end game of all life. In the networld there is no death; and if there is, one only has to tap on an icon to regenerate. The person who *prefers not to* — the outré creative artist, the feral coder-hacker, the apostate writer, the visionary engineer, or the theoretical scientist unconcerned with priority — is unpredictable and therefore hard to market and market *to*. The amnion must recuperate its vast expenditures on advertising and marketing. Wasting it on what it sees as the lumpen proletariat is inefficient and possibly dangerous. Even the dreaded Underclass is a more reliable, and safer, source of revenue than the rogue intellect who *prefers not to*. Wasting resources on a risky target demographic would be deadly to the amnion's mortal imperative of infinite expansion (which it calls *progress*). Homeostasis of the core identity, and a healthy sense of object-constancy, is the amnion's worst enemy. As a reaction, it appeals to the hegemony, elected or not, for ever-greater control of the mass of consumers in their personal and political lives with the goal of *total control*. Digital gadgets have made this dream a reality for the corporate fasces, and its footmen in the hegemony. It has also brought about the death of the sublime in the lives of the denizen of civilization — a prerequisite of total control. The result is chronic *Unbehagen* the subject tries to escape through opioids and antidepressants vended by the corporate fasces causing the feeling of chronic depression and social meaninglessness in the first place — to its unspeakable enrichment. The subject can *choose not to* narcotize itself, but it has not the courage, character, or will to do so because those faculties were never developed as they should have been by parents, society, education, and experience. Even in so-called primitive tribes these faculties are often developed to a highly effective degree in everyone. Why civilization cannot attain to the social accomplishments its past of 30,000 years ago belies its impotence and dissimilitude. The indigenous tribe dwells in the sublime. It has no choice. I do not mean this in the romantic sense that Rousseau does with his noble savage. I do not consider ritual cannibalism noble, even in the Eucharist, but I admire its audacity.

The sublime is all-powerful, being completely void and therefore an infinite *zero-width space* containing death, the obverse of life and is therefore one and the same with it in a way that cannot be adequately described and should not have to be. Like Dasein and Lacanian jouissance, it is unspeakable. We may only refer to it symbolically, or say what it is not.

Moreover, it is therefore the force revealing the transcendental object. Apprehension of the Other cancels the Imaginary with the order of the Real. It negate the amnion's progress into "the future," its perpetual, but never realized, Shangi-La, resulting in a fatal doubt of its reality as the simulacrum. What it needs is *metastatic growth,* like a cancer needs ever more healthy cells or it abates. The subject without self-determination is by reason of this shortcoming out of control in the social sense; it needs to be told what to do; it needs enslavement so that it does not have to make decisions about its life and labor. The hegemony steps in with an ever-expanding nomological code that eventually makes it so that just being alive is a violation of one of its ever-growing fiats and edicts. Pinioned like an etherized butterfly, the subject has no choice but to consume or die. Meantime, it is born a felon, a status that can be invoked at any time by the hegemony if the subject causes a ruckus.

How does the sublime react to this state of civilization? Violently. The reason is not metaphysical; rather, for this state to be maintained, someone, somewhere must be oppressed and exploited and even murdered systematically and preferably exterminated to make way for hegemony by proxy. But the subject would find it uncomfortable and inconvenient in its own land of rainbows and unicorns if there were some group, race, or class of persons thus oppressed within the borders of its paradise of social justice. True, there are select groups used by the dupes of the hegemony as example of either perpetrating injustice or being its victim; but these efforts are typically used by the hegemony and the fasces of its masters to let off steam and depress assets prices so that hedge funds can scoop them up and sell them high when the protests inevitability vanish as if they never happened. Rather than admitting the Underclass into its amniotic country club, the hegemony and its supporters in the cohort of Apex Consumers prefers to buy it off with tax revenue and money borrowed from foreign enemies of the state who are always happy to capture the hegemony with debt. The intention is to demoralize, incapacitate, and anesthetize the Underclass with weaponized social services. The hegemony turns a blind eye to the economy of illegal drugs made possible by the Apex Consumer, who buys its from the Underclass for recreation and narcotization; but the hegemony will not hesitate to imprison members of the Underclass at random to keep it in a constant state of fear. By making a spectacle of social order through imprisonment, the hegemony gets to keep its triple-A bond rating among the international central banks that lend it money so it can continue to enrich its friends in the corporate and financial fasces. The foreign banks now have a steady stream of revenue in the form of interest on the loans, which they do not want paid back for fear of the loss of this revenue (which they then lend back to the originating state) and which *cannot* be because the state has been captured by the obligation to pay the interest or lose its stellar bond rating. If it seems as if this were a terrible error on the part of the obligor, it is in fact a treasonous betrayal of the people since those who make it possible in the hegemony, elected or not, are rewarded by the powers benefiting from this embezzlement scheme.

Perhaps this scheme may be the only lesson Western civilization has learned from the story of Nazi Germany, or the American Civil War: exploit, destroy, exterminate *someplace else, not here*, then pinion the possibility of social freedom with sovereign debt from foreign sources. Hitler, for instance, in his persecution of his own citizens as political scapegoats, brought the war to his doorstep. He also shunned the foreign debt from the central and private banks of his enemies that would have staved the invasions off through signals to the governments they control. However, the real tipping point came on the Eastern Front with the USSR and Stalin, who, technically, saved the day by turning the tide of the war. Had Hitler *borrowed* from Stalin, he would not have been motivated to march east, and Stalin would not have been motivated to march west. There were even agreements to this effect; but Hitler could not accept the meddling the USSR would have demanded as a condition of the loans.

Therefore, the perfect solution in the 21st Century is *perpetual proxy wars*, while entitling minority groups with crippling social services at home rather than exterminating them. By portraying the Underclass in the media as weak, stupid, dirty, and even dangerous, the hegemony succeeds in getting the approbation of the Apex Consumer to ban the Underclass from the country club of the amnion in return for the commandeering of enormous treasure for their socialist entitlements. While socialism may seem contrary to the relentless profit motive of the corporate fasces, it is in fact a boon. Since the fasces pays only minimal taxes to support the Less Fortunates, due to the tax structure its footmen in the hegemony have arranged for it, it feels no impact from this social[ist] program, as it calls itself. At the same time, the fasces has managed to get its footmen in the hegemony to divert the Apex Consumer's taxes into the Underclass so that they too can be consumers. Unfortunately for them, though, they cannot be Apex Consumers (except for a few talented ones the hegemony allows to be rich to quash dissent) because of the disdain (stigma) the Apex Consumer has for lazy, shiftless poor people on what it pejoratively calls welfare. That it set up this system itself does not give the Apex Consumer any sense of hypocrisy. Rather, it craves charitable outlets for its chronic guilt at having abdicated its self-determination for a form of consumerism that ultimately keeps the poor in their wretched state. As I hope you can see, *capture is recursive*, or it is not capture, doubling back upon itself in an endless loop. Its iterations are the wheels of the amnion. Stop them, and it vanishes (if its autonomic microphages do not get you first). The loop depends upon the invalid synthetic proposition (A = B), as it ironically *prevents* social progress while at the same time *worshipping* it to cover this fact up.

What, then, does neo-colonialism and crypto-imperialism in the form of perpetual proxy wars bring to the table? It is a way to avoid the fury of the sublime at home; war is the sublime's way of poisoning the well of the amnion. By putting this event at arm's length, the hegemony falls under the illusion that it has solved this problem when, in fact, the sublime cannot be avoided *in any way* as it is the grim reaper, too. It has more tricks up its sleeve. Every civilization that has tried the tactic of proxy war to avoid the sublime has crumbled because of it, the fall of Rome being the best example since it is the template for the modern state and its corporate fasces, the fasces being a Roman invention anyway. *The tool the sublime uses when it is shunned is war.* It wipes away comfort and convenience in one brutal swipe, establishes terror as the prevailing emotion, and finally dispels any idea of living forever. It is most inconvenient and uncomfortable, and typically mortal. Living for one more day becomes the struggle even of the bourgeoise. As a result, the worst thing any civilization can do is try to avoid these effects by forcing them on some far-off nation and people who do not deserve it and did not ask for it. By so doing, the hegemony doubles the fury of the sublime at home, while forcing it to work in covert ways that are almost invisible and are therefore not apparent until it is too late to do anything about them such as sudden failures of major banks, unexplainable suicides, pervasive mortgage defaults, unemployment, an opioid addiction epidemic, crime sprees, mass murders in public, infrastructure failures, terrorist attacks, and so on. When they occur at the same time, it is a kind of Armageddon that the population nevertheless gets used to because it has to. The fact is, the father-nomos of the state is powerless to do anything about any of it, as history proves again and again, only because it is the state's impotence that has caused this problems in the first place. And what led to this impotence? The proxy wars and the exploitation of the far-off other and his national resources. That is when the empire starts to crumble. Complacency is the mother of the fall of civilizations. Everyone fiddles while Rome burns. Like the id, the sublime gathers more energy when civilization tries to sublimate it by proxy. The id does not take well to vicarious attempts to satisfy its volcanic desires. When they build up enough energy, like a flooded mountain lake or an overwhelmed dam, they suddenly burst forth as some terrible cataclysm. The irony is that this eruptus of chaos is exactly what the hegemony *was attempting to avoid* by forcing its self-serving, imperialist wars onto innocent lands and peoples. To make the matter worse, it is done not because the hegemony's corporate fasces have run out of resources, which even a native tribe can appreciate, but because of regulatory arbitrage and the drive to maximize profits to maintain high share prices in the exchanges. That is a fancy way of saying *greed*. Innocent cultures are invaded, plundered, and plunged into war to maximize profits of the corporate fasces in an economy based almost entirely on satisfying the Apex Consumer's infantile demand for perpetual comfort, convenience, and the hope of medical immortality — the three pillars of the amnion.

What the *Haves* of the amnion never seem to realize, is that if you fight a war by proxy, then *the proxy works both ways*; the obvious way is that it brings refugees from the countries that have been destroyed to the hegemony's doorstep, rightfully asking for a handful of food in exchange for their ancestral lands that it has turned into no-man's land. The other obvious form is the so-called terrorist, the sublime professional of terrorism, portrayed in the media as being crazed with some fundamentalist religion. Few of them taken into captivity, however, have shown any signs of mental illness, even if they were willing to be suicide bombers. Such self-sacrifice in the name of their god, aimed at presumably innocent civilians, is beyond the ken of the cultures they target. But the most devasting effects, which Rome learned the hard way, are the constant drain on the nation's treasure and the moral turpitude that sets in like a curse upon the people and their land. Another nation cannot be destroyed to the benefit of its destroyer without its destroyer suffering the disintegration of the moral fabric of its culture, inevitably bringing about its own collapse into chaos, terror, and death. It is merely cause and effect. Worse than being *invaded* by an aggressor, is *invading* other states in the name of greed. It is more devastating to the invader because it at first seems like its has been beneficial to it (as Hitler thought such action was for Germany). The canker of it, though, starts eating away immediately at the aggressor's sovereignty, as taxpayers feel the burden of funding these adventures, and their sons and daughters come home in a box. The first sign is instability in the domestic financial markets, followed by a soaring recovery, with the resulting gratulations to all concerned. As with the blindness of enjoying the benefits that come from the misery of others, the citizen is blind to the set-up (*aufgezogen*) these events have conspired to spring on him like a rat trap. Wallowing in the proceeds of what looks like a booming bear market, the rat trap snaps shut when the subject is least prepared for it. Overnight, the abyss of the sublime is upon the land. The main cause of this decent into what the subject perceives to be secular, corporeal Hell, is the *imitation of thought* arising from invalid synthetic propositions, such as "we must make the world safe for democracy." The subject cannot see that its thought process, fatally flawed in all its workings through contradiction, not paradox, is what leads it down the road to ruin. The less the subject understands its own psyche, which includes cognition, the more it blames its apparent bad luck on some outside force, be it the Devil, communists, capitalists, racists, or just Lady Luck taking a powder. Such propositions as making the world safe for democracy, bringing prosperity to poor nations by charity, or building up the military-industrial complex to maintain peaceful relations with other nations, are unverifiable and contradictory. For example, *forcing* people to use your system of government is what democracy was originally meant to *stop*, not perpetuate with missiles, UAV's, automatic rifles, and occupying troops. The same is true when the far-off other's homeland is used as a dumping ground for the toxic substances the amnion needs to make its gadgets and fuel its cars — which are the lynch pin of its consumer society. Never mind that the industrialization promised by the hegemony of another nation to employ what were formerly farmers in a poor country, ends up being owned and operated by the oligarchs of the foreign nations; traded as futures, forwards, options, and swaps on derivatives markets; and subject to the Keynesian business cycle, meaning they could vanish overnight and are, therefore, temporary. Meantime, the laborer of the country that is supposed to be the beneficiary of this foreign beneficence surrenders the sovereignty of its subsistence farming for the slavery of the sweat shop, only to be tossed out on the street when world markets dictate a downturn in demand or the need arises to find cheaper labor or more compliant governments and regulations (regulatory arbitrage).

What is evil? Here again we have a term meaning nothing, but which can also mean anything. I will define how I am using it in this context. Eventually this *evil* behavior, and I call it evil in the sense meant by Hannah Arendt in reference to the "banal" Nazi death machine, will result in a growing evil of the same sort back home. *Evil by proxy* is not any better than *evil itself*, though the Apex Consumer thinks otherwise. To the subject in the amnion, evil by proxy is not evil at all but is *good* because it does not impinge upon its prevailing ethical aesthetic of comfort and convenience *über alles*. Meantime, the subject is programmed to create civil unrest to blow off steam and depress asset values in the form of imaginary injustices at home invented by paid agent provocateurs and propagated by the mass media as sensational "movements." The charade of protest allows the unconscious subject to feel (not think) that it has "done something," usually on social media, to further social justice — which, like evil, cannot be defined and therefore can mean anything. Meantime, the depression of assets prices allows the financial industry to buy them up at fire-sale prices to be sold later on once there is some kind of artificial economic recovery. The tragic contradiction the subject does not see, because its entire being is a contradiction between the real and the imaginary, is that those it pities as the Less Fortunates, and that it purports to want to help by complaining about their plight on social media, are also those being exploited by the same subject itself to maintain its status as an Apex Consumer in the amnion. Moreover, if there is any social injustice here, it is that the protesting subject systematically, and constructively, *excludes* the Less Fortunates from access to the amnion's comfort and convenience that it enjoys ipso facto by its phenotype as an Apex Consumer, or by being the descendant of one, if not also genotype.

The point is that evil by proxy always come home to roost in the form of the decay of social values to the point where everyone becomes a theif, a con man, an embezzler, or worse. According to the doctrine of some terrorist organizations, the subject in a nation conducting proxy wars is also a murderer, or combatant (by proxy!), and therefore may be killed without offending God. Proxy wars demoralize the society that prosecutes them abroad, leading to that country's self-destruction. But what really brings the demoralized nation down is that proxy wars quickly become *perpetual and unstoppable*. It is their evil curse. They are like a hemorrhage that cannot be staunched. Sooner than later, the patient bleeds to death. Those who were watching from a distance as the nation destroyed itself in this way, come swooping in on vulture's wings to claim the spoils. Those who allowed their government to prosecute foreign entanglements on their behalf, not for self-defense, but for profit and to sustain an unsustainable lifestyle, eventually get their own taste of what their military had inflicted upon the far-off Other whom they pity as subhuman. Proxy war in the land of the far-off Other is the greatest affront to the apprehension of the transcendental object the subject and its government can make. Such ignorance is not without its consequences. The sublime's absolute, inevitable retribution comes slowly, then swiftly in the forms of strange outbreaks of disease, economic crashes, assassinations, rising crime, drug addiction, inflation, and the devaluing of the currency. If this sounds like a modern-day Revelation of an Apocalypse, it really is not. It has already been happening for over 100 years. In fact, it has been going on so long that what was once an apocalyptic vision has become what is accepted as everyday experience. It certainly is for the 1.2 billion persons on the planet without electricity, which is needed for medical care, clean water, and manufacturing, never mind the other advantages it brings that are taken for granted — when it has only been around 150 years.

It may seem like the sublime is something we can enjoy on weekends at the art museum, visiting the Grand Canyon, or watching a pretty sunset. It is, rather, as Burke describes, "terror ... in all cases whatsoever, either more openly or latently ..." Why? Because it is the abyss that is the obverse of life; it is a kind of zero-width space, described by Hamlet as that "undiscovere'd country, from whose bourn / No traveller returns ..." Death wins every coin toss, and yet the subject thinks that you win some, you lose some. It even thinks it can beat the house, given enough time, progress, and medical technology. Charlatans peddling medical immortality go after the rich first, because they seem to be the most desirous of living forever — as if immortality were another possession they could buy. They are therefore easier to dupe than the poor man on the street who cannot pay his phone bill, with a bigger payoff if the rich mark falls for the con. Cryogenic preservation of a corpse for future resurrection, once medical progress has reached the point where it can defy biology and physics, never mind God, is an example.

We may say war brings what Hegel in *Phenomenology of Spirit* calls *absolute freedom* as *objektive Geist*. The war's state of absolute exception permits anything, despite efforts to make war seem like it is run by the Marquess of Queensbury Rules. War is the great, sublime, secret desire of all men: to kill, to rape, to plunder, to let the id have its way in all things all of the time. As the Russian allies in World War II liked to say as they marched into Germany, it is permitted to rape any woman between the ages of 8 and 88 — which they then proceeded to do with memorable, and documented, alacrity. The other allied forces, according to the record, were not far behind their Soviet comrades in this respect. War is the lucid dream where one wakes up and realizes that there are no consequences for any action. The nomos, the bête noire of civilization and the cause of its *Unbehagen*, has been suspended. The result is a rapid erosion of the pent up mechanism of psychic energy Freud calls an *anticathexis*, as well as a repurposing of the superego into such abstractions as patriotism and the fight for freedom and so on. The urge for what Lacan (and Freud) call jouissance in war's orgy of violence and destruction satisfies mankind's deepest desire for Hegel's absolute freedom. Once engaged in the carnage not otherwise permitted by the status quo of the nomos, the subject is thrust into the sublime of terror for which it secretly longed. What is most interesting here is that the thing the subject's entire life was devoted to avoiding — the terror of death — now become what it wanted all along, only because of the boundless freedom it now unleashes, and the pressure it takes off from the misery caused by civilization's discontents. If this were not so, no one would volunteer to fight. The pay, lifestyle, and benefits are not great. Society looks upon the soldier who has put himself in harm's way to protect its freedom with a certain amount of contempt; it knows that the Apex Consumer rarely condescends to sacrifice its privileged access to comfort, convenience, and the promise of medical immortality for the rigors of military life and the risk of the battlefield. Therefore, those who do, must come from the Underclass, or that vague social space between the Underclass and the Apex Consumer. However, as it is pleased to fight these wars by proxy, it is also pleased to enjoy the soldier's jouissance vicariously — as all cowards do — through the pipeline of the mass media feeding it the narratives it most wants to hear. These narratives are the greatest hits of the hegemony's and the mass media's collection of justifications of war: making the world safe for democracy, exterminating terrorists east of the Jordan River, using weapons of mass destruction against innocent tribes, being ruled by a dictator, enriching uranium or at least buying the metal tubes needed for that purpose, and so on. The collection is only as big as it needs to be to avoid seeming played out on the record player of bellicose propaganda.

Who does not know what war really is? Is every volunteer an ignorant fool? Of course, I do not refer here to people who have war *brought to them*, leaving them no choice but to fight or, if that is not possible, flee. Could we possibly say that the volunteer was hoodwinked and bamboozled into joining the military? He may indeed have what could be called a genuine feeling of what the Romans called *patria*, or love for one's patrimony or paternal place of birth. In which case he fights not for the hegemony's expansionist adventures, but for what he perceives to be the protection and defense of his family, home, and property. Considering, though, that there are millions of well-armed combatants fighting here and there, and that there are millions more operating the sophisticated machinery of war, it follows there is more to the individual motive to fight than a heartfelt sense of patria – though that is how it is mythologized. Rather, we all ultimately, and often secretly, seek out the thread of our desire, which may lead to the point of least resistance in the id's pursuit of anticathexis and the release of psychic energy built up because of civilization's nomological *Unbehagen*. But in the case of war, obstacles to the feral expression of the id are swept away, so that in about 24 hours 50,000 young men can die on the battlefield of Gettysburg. Civilization's worst crimes, e.g. rape and murder, assault, robbery, abduction, arson, terrorism, imprisonment without justice, torture, mass and serial murder, and so on - are suddenly *rewarded, encouraged, funded,* and *commanded* by one's government. If one refuses to carry out these atrocities in the land of the subhuman, far-off other, one is court marshalled or even shot. Once back home, one is de facto a hero, no matter what one's exploits were abroad in the name of justice and freedom. What were once pedaled as heinous acts in the rhetoric of the status quo of the nomos are relabeled by the hegemony as heroic rather than sociopathic in the state of exception. As it is the hegemony that enables the military action, as it is called now, and as the interests the least abstract and vague in the whole matter are best understood by the grey-haired old men who are the hegemony and do the oligarchy's bidding, war is always in the interest of the relentless quest for wealth and power. For the person who actually has to get in a plane and be dropped into raging combat in a far-off land where he would have had difficulty even if he were on vacation there during peace time as a tourist rather than the enemy, the Commandment "Thou shalt not kill" becomes "*Kill and/or be killed.*"

Superficially, it may seem that the prospect of being hunted by another like oneself who has the complete support of the state and its people may seem terrifying. And it is. But, given the right gear and support of one's own state, it could be liberating. By the law of quid pro quo, as the hunted, one is given license to hunt. Hunt or be hunted. Once in this equation, life takes on new meaning because there are no more illusions. Yes, comfort, convenience, and the promise of medical immortality seem lost forever. But at the same time, the world is seen through new eyes free from the scales of civilization's pretention of safety and the law. The terror of war is a gateway into the sublime lost by civilization's suffocating nomos, perpetual debt, tedious jobs, demanding families, social conformity, and lifeless consumerism. Many veterans of war recall their battles with nostalgia for when they felt alive (in the way Genghis Khan probably felt most of the time). This is not to trivialize those who feel traumatized by their service. They are regarded as mentally ill, weak, cowards who just could not take it. Or, they are pitied as the price of freedom. It is simply unthinkable that they might be the only ones reacting to their war experiences as they should; it perhaps should seem more perverse to look upon killing others just like oneself, with friends, family, thoughts, feelings, and peacetime ambitions, as one's duty in order to stop communism or terrorism in far-off lands from bringing democracy in one's backyard to an end, whatever democracy and communism may be. Once the Other becomes the rhetorical Enemy, it enters into the fundamentally Semitic interpretation of the melodrama of life. The enemy is evil and on the side of the Devil; therefore, by default, one must be good and on the side of God, with or without evidence of it. Such empty belief is at best an enthymeme and at worst a vacuous truth. Even if one has disavowed the Semitic tradition as superstition, and accepts that those who believed in it for over 4,000 years to be complete idiots, one cannot escape its narrative. It has been repackaged, free of the baggage of God and mysticism, by Scientism and the hegemony as their story of the world. While there as been no shortage of Semitic holy wars over the centuries, at least they made some kind of cosmological sense according to the scriptures upon which they were based, which are full of entirely justified slaughter committed by God Himself. As above, so below. But when it is secularized into a defense of consumerism and the financial markets, bathed in the aura of idealistic abstractions, it becomes downright evil in the sense in which I have been using it here. Consequently, we witness the demoralization and dehumanization necessary for perpetual proxy wars which are the curse of such a society. Far from being obvious to the consumer, though, its belligerence by proxy only touches its ken when refugees wash upon upon its doorstep, or terrorists bomb its public places. Carried on long enough, it becomes the ethical aesthetic of the society. Once thus integrated into the subject's everyday life, mostly in the form of surrendering its treasure to the hegemony to prosecute these wars on its behalf — as if it had paid a hitman to knock off a rival — the subject is subtly demoralized into the creature it seeks to protect itself *from*, which more often than not *is a reflection of itself* in the black mirror of its digital gadget rather than an actual flesh and blood threat in some far-away part of the world well beyond the subject's postal code. War, on the other hand, gives the state unlimited treasure (because it can print money) and power to enforce infantile demands of the subject's narcissistic egotism; only the politician who successfully signals to the subject that he will do this dirty job on his behalf will be elected.

And in so doing we free ourselves from the horrible burden of having to treat the Other as a sovereign individual. While much is made of those who return from war with damaged characters, it is almost axiomatic that old soldiers must tell their Hellenica to anyone who will listen. But few who have not experienced this liberation from the bonds of civilization can appreciate just what euphoria it is to wipe out the enemy when the enemy is trying to wipe out us, our comrades, and our people as a "nation." This does not diminish the horrors of war for innocent noncombatants caught up in it machinery any more than it does the horrors of a plane crash. Horror here is not to be considered a synonym for terror. Life's significance is not a matter of eliminating its terrors, since we all must face the fact that we will die if we are to live the life of the sublime. In fact, the more we vainly try to eliminate terror through the relentless pursuit of the ethical aesthetic of *Genuss,* the less significant "bare life" gets. The less significant it gets, the more we wonder why we are even bother to live it. Drug and alcohol addiction, suicide, mass murder, rape, depression, divorce, neglect, gangbanging, obsession with money and possessions, and the insatiable desire for power are all the excrescences of reliance on the amnion for meaning. These pathologies are horror itself, but cannot be properly compared to the sublime terror of war.

Under the influence of the *objektive Geist* of *absolute freedom* the laws of God, Man, and Nature are suspended because they are all a posteriori. Nations no longer need to balance their budgets. Civil rights and privacy no longer need to be honored and guarded. By pushing a bunch of buttons the meek become strong, the weak become powerful, and the impotent potent. This otherwise unheard-of freedom is so exhilarating for the individual that he is willing to risk his life to experience it. He gladly puts down the bar-be-cue fork for the automatic weapon, justifying the insanity of his action by placating his doubt with vague, emotional platitudes of nationalism he has been fed as his mantra *de guerre*. Remorse is for "the future," which he claims he is safeguarding by his actions in the present. When he returns with no legs, his remorse brings him closer to what Hegel calls the "terror" of absolute freedom, but only in retrospect. If he does not return at all, remorse is then transferred to the survivors, who enshrine the memory of his sacrifice as part of the collective ethical aesthetic of protecting the present for the sake of "the future" but never for the present itself which under this regime is always threatened by terrorists, insurgents, radicals, death squads, juntas, coups, dictators, tyrants, and rogue states. The *subjektiv Geist* is something quite different. It is the world-historic character, such as Adolph Hitler, Joseph Stalin, Julius Caesar, Jesus, Mohammad, Buddha, and Columbus. It is not necessary for them to have forensic veracity (what is usually labeled "historic") to play a role in the drama of the Weltgeist. We might not have the birth certificate for Jesus as we do for Hitler, but Hitler is as much of a part of the Imaginary of history as Jesus is, just as Jesus is as much of a part of the Symbolic of history as Hitler is. One is "good" the other is "evil," all in a neat dichotomy that can be used as a kind of moral shorthand. There was a time when *someone* knew Jesus, presumably the Apostles of the Gospels and his relatives and friends, just as *someone* in the Twentieth Century knew Hitler as such. That their lives happened "long ago" is irrelevant only because what has happened "recently" will, absolutely and inevitably, someday be seen as "long ago." Therefore, stochastically, the present is *always already* in the past. Antiquity neither validates nor invalidates something. It just *dates* it. What the imaginary delusion of "the future" holds for the historicity of a world-historic personage will be revealed sooner or later, but cannot be predicted "now."

So we have the objective and subjective forms of Weltgeist engaged in a dialectic of activity which defines the multiplicity of the peoples of the world in an ever-shifting drama of identity and Universal Spirit, which is not to be confused with Zeitgeist. It is interesting to consider the difference between what we know as "the world" and what we know as "the time" we live in. To make it simpler we could think of the former as a kind of "space." When we think of "world" we first think of geography. There is, however, the topological "space" of the world and the psychological, and, consequently, the ontological "being" of the world. The latter is what is meant by Hegel as Being, though it is considerably influenced by the former in that it is the genesis of phenomena and, by extension, of Marxian *dialectical materialism*. While both might be called *objektive* in relation to the subject, in relation to each other we must concede that the Weltgeist, or what Yeats calls the Spiritus Mundi, is truly "*objektive*» also in the sense meant by Hegel. Inasmuch as the Weltgeist is "apart" from the subject, it belongs to the sublime realm of the transcendental object.

What is truly extraordinary, however, is the relationship of the Weltgeist to war. It is not hard to make the argument that war is a product of the Zeitgeist, as it eventually becomes an expression of it. Surely war was "in the air" like an escaped, inflammable gas when Archduke Franz Ferdinand and Sophie, Duchess of Hohenberg, were assassinated in Sarajevo in 1914. The shots from Gavrilo Princip which killed them were the sparks setting off the nebulous conflagration which followed as World War I. The "spirit of the times" was war, not peace. The Balkans were Balkinizing. Under the *Septemberprogramm* Germany was itching for more *Lebensraum* – ultimately a geographical proposition – which it would eventually get and then lose. The same is true for the tensions leading up to the United States Civil War. The only surprise is that both did not happen sooner than they did considering the amount of political tinder lying around at the time. But like all gasses, the Zeitgeist soon shifts with the wind and everything changes. Political memory being as short as it must necessarily be for the sake of practice, the new Zeitgeist instantly swallows up the old as a kind of ergodic expression of it, complete with historical amnesia. As Hitler is reported to have said prior to his, and Germany's, demise, "The victor will never be asked if he told the truth."

We do not find these characteristics in expressions of the Weltgeist, however. Its sublime expression is war, wherein the world-historic character *imposes his will* upon the world – Hitler's Triumph des Willens and the Will of the Nietzschean *Übermench.* In so doing the world changes forever after. It then seems as if life itself would not have been possible were it not for the world-historic character's exhilarating state of absolute freedom and reckless exercise of limitless power. In pondering the atrocities of this character, the good people who righteously abhor what he stands for in their public, *secretly admire and even may emulate its potency,* just as the weak, enslaved denizen of civilization secretly worships the arch criminal, mobster, or serial killer for their gross abrogation of the stultifying effects on the libido's agenda by the nomos. In their helpless, gelded, impotency as abdicated subjects of the new order which "saved" them from this or that monster, they are willing to be herded along as cattle until the next world-historic character comes along with a new, more ambitious spectacle of sublime slaughter. This is the sacred, cryptic, sacrificial nature of Man that must not be uttered – else one face the *auto-da-fé*. It is mankind's cellular apoptosis. It is Jesus as *homo sacer*, the man who may be murdered but not in a holocaust or ritual burnt offering to the gods – paradoxically murdered for mankind's original sin. It is the motivation behind every population's acquiescence and sacrifice to what they know are the contrived imperatives of the hegemony's quest for infinite wealth and power at any cost in the form of war, for which they secretly lust.

Hegel defines the absolute freedom of *Geist* as that "which grasps the fact that its certainty of itself is the essence of all the spiritual ‹masses, or spheres, of the real as well as of the supersensible world ..." (p. 356). This certainty is consciousness knowing *itself*. It is conscious of its pure personality and therein of all spiritual reality ..." But what is this really a certainty of? Is it of itself as phenomenon, and in this sense the perfect abstraction of consciousness? Hegel says that "This undivided Substance of absolute freedom ascends the throne of the world without any power being able to resist it." It is not hard to hear the echo of the imperial will here. It is no wonder that the world-historical character is often involved in these orgies of freedom. However, Hegel points to a state of being that is with us always and not during historical epochs of great upheaval. "For since, in truth, consciousness alone is the element in which the spiritual beings or powers have their substance, their entire system which is organized and maintained by division into ‹masses of spheres has collapsed now the individual consciousness conceives of the subject as having no other essence than self-consciousness itself." What looks like a contradiction between substance and essence is actually the dialectic which brings them together into "undivided Substance" which is then *indomitable*. War, not love, conquers all of what Hegel calls the *differences* between the masses of spheres.

This catastrophic "collapse" may make us wonder, then, what is in the head of the subject, *subjected* (as it were) to this necessary process. The answer is in what Hegel calls "subjective logic" or the "logic of the Notion" (*Begriff*). In *Science of Logic* he describes Notion as a kind of residual substance resulting from the subjects interaction with the objective world. This interaction is governed by necessity since we are all beholden to what he calls the "at first apparent other" (no man being an island, and so on). Being, essence, and substance are parts of what he calls the "genetic exposition" of Notion. As such, it has its own "subjective logic" which we come to know as our story of the world in a constructive sense – also known as "the truth."

> [S]ubstance is already real essence, or essence in so far as it is united with being and has entered into actuality. Consequently, the Notion has substance for its immediate presupposition; what is implicit in substance is manifested in the Notion. Thus the dialectical movement of substance through causality and reciprocity is the immediate genesis of the Notion, the exposition of

the process of its becoming. (§ 1281)

No war has ever been fought for anything other than "the truth" of whatever excuse there was for it. What is fascinating about war is it is often a battle between two absolute truths with competing (if not identical) validity. This matter is well thought out in game theory. (But it will not be so well thought out here.) Suffice it to say that this game in its fundamental form involves two sides, each of which is convinced that it must fight and defeat the other because the other is convinced of the same thing. There cannot be two opposing truths in a logical proposition. The resulting contradiction prevents the proposition from being valid, or apophantic. Therefore, both are invalidated in relation to each other as the two elements of the proposition. We are not so much concerned here with the logic of war - which is obvious - than we are with the *significance* of it. Hegel's "spheres" all contain the inflammable gas of "truth" but in different degrees of volatility. In short, there is no freedom without truth. And there is no truth without Notion. Its significance is its subjective logic as it is the subject which processes the signal or sign through what Hegel calls the "mode or relationship proper to the Notion."

We do not tend, however, to associate freedom with war. This is perhaps because of a certain amount of wishful thinking. We are all too ready to throw freedom into the company of such vague abstractions as peace, love, and understanding. But unlike its three cousins, freedom can be defined in a technical way, as in when we refer to the degrees of freedom of a machine such as a car (four: forward, backward, right, and left) or in a legal sense when we say that a person has certain liberties such as those found in the Bill of Rights. The fact is that war is a kind of freedom because - for instance legally - one can do things not otherwise possible unless war has brought about a state of exception. *Any* state of exception is significant, especially to those who otherwise feel oppressed (or simply put out) by the laws of the state apparatus because it is an abrogation of the nomos the chief purpose of which is to repress the libido so that civilization may pursue its infinitely "progressive" aims. We could even say that significance is born in the state of exception. When one is born into the rule of law one takes that law for the given environment of ones thought and action. However, remove that tacit superstructure and who one really is becomes apparent in precisely the way it does in a dream. The dreamlike state of exception allowing us to act out our repressed desires and savage impulses, particularly the most volcanic and therefore more repressed. This is what is significant about Notion in terms of understanding the subject.

It is even more revealing when the state - once the guardian of all the myriad Thou Shalt Nots holding civilization together like glue - reverses itself, exhorting the subject to indulge its every brutal, immoral, and unethical impulse to affirm its allegiance to the state. What is peculiar is how easily and quickly the subject jumps at the chance to live this lucid dream where everything is at long last *possible*. Even the higher probability of injury and death is not enough to deter the subject from betting its young life on these dicey odds. The subject might have been timid in school or at work about defending someone being bullied because of fear of in turn being bullied and therefore took no action to help another. But throw a vague abstraction at the same subject about "defending the Homeland" against a shadowy far-off other and suddenly it seems the subject has found boundless patriotic courage. While many do have the metamotivation to serve others in this way and do to the benefit of all, the attraction of entering a dreamlike state of bare life where one may violate mans most sacred covenants and taboos is a strong lure for those who do not. It seems a contradiction to say that bare life can be "dreamlike." It is not so strange, though, when we consider that if one is nearly always in a waking dream in the Imaginary bare life will seems as strange as a dream. The Imaginary is so far removed from reality that it is accurate to say that dreams themselves are closer to bare life than waking life with all of its honking, beeping, singing, ringing, and chattering gadgets and gizmos. The content they deliver is *only* a sign of the subjects sign of itself, whereas the symbolism of dreaming consists *only* of the signs of the self.

Therefore, Notion unifies the psyche as the genetic exposition of being, essence, and substance without which there is no sign and therefore no symbolic and linguistic life. The magnetic force in this process is necessity for without it there is no significance. Without significance there are no signs. Without signs there are no symbols. And without symbols there is no language. Notion itself becomes a Notion, then, as part of language. It is a floating concept which gets it bearings from what Hegel calls "the reflection of the transient into its ground ..." It is "grounded" in what is not transient, which, if we may be so bold, is the Weltgeist. When war disturbs the Spiritus Mundi through the action of the Zeitgeist, there appears when Yeats calls "that rough beast" slouching "toward Bethlehem to be born." In so doing the unity of Notion necessary for the assignment of signs to the thingness of the things of the world and the otherness of others meets with a schism. This is the only possible outcome of absolute freedom. The majority of the prohibitions against it arise out of Necessity. If a subject decides that he will kill all female subjects, no matter how good the reason (they all have the plague, for instance), nevertheless the freedom needed to carry this impulse out will create a schism in the biological process necessary for life - despite the Black Death. It eliminates the possibility that 1 percent may survive and therefore live to regenerate the human race just as the endless histories of genocide never seem to solve the problems the perpetrators insist are caused by those they murder. The Notion of absolute freedom, even by its unifying activity, must at the same time create what Hegel calls a *diremption,* or division, between the meaning of *utility* where "the predicate of all real being" becomes divorced from the subject. In war the individual and the mass are one; they must be to survive and certainly to conquer. In defeat, their fate is even more obvious. As a "mass" of losers they must all suffer more or less the same fate - the really bad ones "hang" while the rest are disenfranchised into the underclass of the victors. Among the victors, one may receive a medal for conspicuous heroics. But in defeat no one person is pitied.

Along with the exhilaration of the suspension of the rule of law, human, divine, and natural, comes the unburdening in the individual of the futility of self will based on consciousness of the death of the ego. In total freedom the ego ceases identifying with its own mortality, or with the masses of spheres separating it from the whole. By identifying with the seeming immortality of what is perceived as incorporeal Notion, it is now free to kill at will without killing being willful. Whatever act the individual is compelled to perform in the state of absolute freedom it does so for the whole and not the part. The part is mortal. The whole is immortal. No one can be free under the yolk of mortality. But in this diremption, the husk of its former state as a part, as a discrete ego, has lost all utility. In its uselessness it sinks down through the spheres of significance the way a dead sea creature sinks to the fathomless bottom. "The *beyond* of this its actual existence hovers over the corpse of the vanished independence of real being, or the being of faith, merely as an exhalation of the vacuous *Etre supreme*" (p. 358). Therefore, the significance of the Weltgeist for the sublime is that it is the arena within which the sublime emerges in a state of war as what Hegel calls the "vacuous supreme being." We are not to confuse "absolute freedom," which is individual and subjective, with the "state of exception," which is universal and objective. Nevertheless, they can be related as they are here. Despite the absolute freedom of spirit Notion and ego remain as the "ground" of the individual against which this freedom can be seen as freedom. What good is "freedom" if it is not freedom from something? This was the problem of Adam and Eve. They did not feel free despite the fact that they were save for a single prohibition. Under such circumstances (such is human nature) a single prohibition is enough for one to feel imprisoned. Why? Because this prohibition came from without. It was extrinsic. It was not component to the kind of embryonic sovereignty Adam and Eve were heir to.

The romantic idea of the intellectual scholar is the free individual whose purpose in life is the getting-to-know. Emerson in "The American Scholar" signifies the kind of freedom necessary to be what in his words is a scholar disengaged from the pressures and constraints from without. His view of the scholar is that his freedom comes not from being able to "to be" a scholar but from being able exercise his powers without being limited by the public, colleagues, university, students, or state. "Free should the scholar be, free and brave. Free even to the definition of freedom, 'without any hindrance that does not arise out of his own constitution.'" Despite what might be perceived as the hindrances of ego and Notion to the possibility of absolute freedom, since they "arise out of his own constitution" they are not perceived by the subject as limitations. Applying Occam's Razor, if we pare away every possible self-imposed limitation (which need not be listed) we are inevitably left with *the self itself*. For there must be someone left "to be free." So Hegel cannot possibly mean "absolute" to refer to a kind of selfless freedom. That is a romantic idea which seems to flow from the Manichean influence in the East and West. Perhaps one of the reasons Manicheanism, per se, died out is that it was based on this fundamental error of logic. The self is the ultimate limitation since it is comprised in part of the ego and its notions. Therefore, we are left with the absolute necessity (or what Hegel calls the truth of necessity) for there to be a self to be free from what is *not* the self. A man without legs can accept that he will not be able to run. This limitation is intrinsic. But a man with legs will *never* be able to accept that he is not allowed to run, as his limitation is extrinsic and therefore does not arise out of what Hegel calls the "truth of necessity." Since communication is a matter (in part) of using words in the transmission of ideas we must accept that when we say "freedom" it is a relative concept – despite the adjective "absolute." This ceases to be a conflict when we consider that the "absolute sovereignty" of the individual only means self-determination without the sphere of self-determination being usurped by another sovereign entity. If the man with legs can only move them when someone else gives him permission, or worse, orders him to move them, then moving them cannot be considered a sovereign freedom despite the fact that they can move. Pointing to his legs and saying, "See? Im free!" when they move is not enough for the establishment of sovereignty, though in the amnion of the Imaginary it is enough to impress the subject with its fantasy of being free. So-called intellectual freedom is often considered to be the greatest freedom. If a man is not allowed to *think* of moving his legs, or to advocate the free and sovereign right to move them, then he must move them at his peril and is therefore not free to move his legs. Emerson's concept of the Oversoul encompasses the universal possibility of the getting-to-know which he acknowledges is "obstructed" – though he does not specify by what. It is the universal analog of what he calls "the active soul."

> The one thing in the world of value is the active soul, — the soul, free, sovereign, active. This every man is entitled to; this every man contains within him, although in almost all men obstructed, and as yet unborn. The soul active sees absolute truth; and utters truth, or creates it.

What, then, obstructs it? We may presume that ego and Notion are not "absolute" limitations for reasons we have already discussed, in particular because they are intrinsic limitations. Foremost in the logic of this discussion is the idea that the abdication of sovereignty is the principal limitation of freedom. In Hegelian terms it is *bondage*. The enemy of absolute freedom then is bondage arising from total imposition of extrinsic pressures and constraints which usurp the possibility of self-determination. There are two caveats here. First, we have said that war in the state of exception can initiate absolute freedom. Second, obviously for human beings to live together there must be pressures and constraints in the form of Law. So the question is really how much of self-determination is usurped by the extrinsic imposition of war and the law? This is really a "trick" question when we consider what the central dogma of democracy is: that the law and war are the will of the people. If they are the will of the people, then they arise from the collective impulses of individuals exercising their freedom of self-determination. Moreover, war (A) allows the subject to be free of the law while law (B) allows the subject to be free of war. Far from being a paradox, this situation is symptomatic of the unconsciousness of the abdicated subject for whom both states (A and B) are one and the same. Furthermore, the unconscious subject does not see the difference between self-will and the will of the state. Through the illusion of the ritual of democracy the subject falls into a kind of narcotic state where vigilance against usurpation of sovereignty is suspended by design. If anything is the opium of the people it is democracy. By comparison religion pales. The "truth" religion promotes is now regarded the way the "history" of Homers Odyssey was regarded by Xenophon's time as fairy tales. The new *pravda* comes from the media. What it spews is regarded with the same unquestioned credulity that religion once enjoyed (and does enjoy still). One may argue, "But the difference is that the news is based on fact." Well so are scriptures. Is it then a matter of the *degree* of facts or of some special ethical aesthetic? Facts do not a story make. Consequently, there must be a certain amount of inference. For the modern to point an accusing finger at the ancient for credulity because his "news" was only twenty percent fact while the moderns news is nearly eighty is a category error. It assumes that because there is a difference in proportion therefore the ethical aesthetics are categorically different. The narrative parts of both are pure inference which is absolutely necessary to tell a story. And while we can and do accept this – even desire it, for who enjoys reading lists of facts? – it is mistake to consider that the moderns "story" is therefore not significantly a product of the imagination.

Part of what makes this state of affairs possible is that the subject cannot see the Weltgeist for the Zeitgeist. For democracy to function as the ultimate opium of the people it needs the news media to propagate its expedient messages, ideas, illusions, celebrities, symbols, and most of all *stories* which become the collective mythology of the Zeitgeist. Only in this way is it true that the news media "protect" democracy. Both democracy and its propaganda organ the news media work for the state hegemony which in turn promotes the interests of its transnational corporate overlords. That the word "time" (*Zeit*) appears in the name of so many of these propaganda outlets indicates the priority of the informational focus of their content. Their purpose is to obfuscate the subjects tacit absorption of the Weltgeist and therefore the sublime by replacing it with the Zeitgeist. This substitution facilitates manipulation. It makes is possible for the outlet to claim that the world "is" the way it says it is. The problem with this is that the Weltgeist is entirely a product of the objective state of the transcendental object. We may consider what we know of past ages when there were no media communicating the discourse of the hegemony. Even during the height of the European Middle Ages when the church ruled supreme few owned holy books much less were able to read. We might consider that for them the Weltgeist was foremost. They dwelt in it. Whereas today's subject dwells in the Imaginary which strives continually to establish the Zeitgeist through its time machine of the media. The Spiritus Mundi now must appear as a kind of specter as it does in Yeats poem. It arises like a monster wreathed in the dark, caustic smoke of the sublime, ready to strike out with misery, death, and destruction. This is certainly a far cry from Emerson's soul which "sees absolute truth; and utters truth, or creates." It could be this soul, but the state of affairs are such that it must be a kind of avenging angel come to claim the Weltgeist back from the manipulators of the Zeitgeist.

We might wonder why the Imaginary does not go after the Weltgeist as well. While this is its greatest desire and wish, it knows instinctively that it does not have to. Instead, it may create its own version of "real time." Why? Because what we know of it consciously is almost entirely psychological but not time in any absolute sense - if there is even such a phenomenon. Furthermore, the World encompasses time as part of its nature as a composite of space and time. The Imaginary's desperate bid for establishment of the oxymorons of artificial intelligence, virtual reality, and "smart" gadgetry belies its deepest lust for domination of the Weltgeist through the invalid propositions of befuddling contradiction. By injecting contradiction directly into the psycholinguistic vein of the subject's processing of reality, the techno-overseers of the amnion's hegemonic imperative form a schism in the structure of the subject's thinking, rendering it impossible for the subject to process the natural world as anything but a threat. For instance, rain is called "bad weather," though it is the manna of life. Moreover, there is some irony in the default names of the amnion's primary cybernetic structure: the Inter-NET, the World Wide WEB, NET-works, servers and clients (Hegel's lord and bondsman), WEB-sites, and CELL phones. With a little imagination, this jargon conjures up captured fish, predatory spiders, and prisons. The common phrase for a hand-held gadget's geolocation is that the subject is in such and such a "cell," or hex antenna array.

In their campaign against the reality of the sublime, the amnion's overseers vow to create their own bigger, better, snazzier reality with lots of razzle-dazzle. It may dominate this commercially viable world because its programmed, "virtual" nature allows for centralized control and harvesting of the unique elements of personal sovereignty by Big Data, forming what is called in the business a "fingerprint," "footprint," or consumer profile. Through the mechanics of telemetry and surveillance, Big Data autonomously forms the unique profile. It is complete with parametric demographics and psychographics, making it "addressable" and therefore a kind of *target* (another unfortunate term) for promotional rhetoric and discourse, commercial and political (which go hand in hand). The techno-overseers of the hegemony expect that someday the subject will simply be absorbed, unconsciously, into the amnion as a slave to its promissory notes and the displacement substitutes of infinite consumerism. In order to maintain status as an "apex consumer," the subject must maintain a steady "buying pattern" which eases into what Veblen calls "conspicuous consumption." Meantime, the amnion's marketing projections and computer models indicate that at some point the subject will be convinced, albeit unconsciously, to abandon that old, dusty, dirty, and most of all *mortal* reality for a new shiny, slick, corporate, *immortal* reality it can turn on and off - as long as it pays its bills. Do I need to say that all of this is hardly sublime like, let us say, a painting by Giovanni Battista Tiepolo or Tiziano Vecelli, or a three-day trek in the Rocky Mountains?

While we might say that the Zeitgeist tends to fog our view of the Weltgeist and may even masquerade as it at certain parties, its ultimate effect in time of war is that it ushers in a more menacing vision of the Spiritus Mundi. Like cowboys at a rodeo, the world-historic personage hopes to mount the Spirit thinking that his time has come. Always, though, at the end of the show he discovers (too late) that he was riding the Zeitgeist - and that no one rides that horse for long. This is not such a specious metaphor when we think how well it served St. John in Revelation. Yeats, the Celtic visionary and prophet, anticipates the drama which follows.

> Surely some revelation is at hand;
> Surely the Second Coming is at hand.
> The Second Coming! Hardly are those words out
> When a vast image out of Spiritus Mundi
> Troubles my sight ...

Christ himself remains a possibility (*Möglichkeit*). It is important here to distinguish between the possibility of Christs return (as he vowed) and Christ-as-a-possibility. When one accepts Jesus Christ as ones Lord and Savior, it is said that one is "in" Christ and that Christ is "in" one. We see this reflected in the Lutheran Sacrament where one is *in, with, and under* Christ. In the five lines above, Yeats invokes the Spiritus Mundi with the magic words "Second Coming" which we see repeated. "Hardly are those words out" he says than the daemon makes its appearance. Many who have read Revelation – strategically the last book of the New Testament – understands what is troubling about the Second Coming. Its nickname is the Apocalypse, the thing everyone fears. It is interesting to note that etymology tells us that the idea of an apocalypse being a global catastrophe is a modern invention, though the association is understandable considering the Seven Plagues described in Revelation. The role of the Spiritus Mundi as the soul of humanity in its most creative and active form is obscured by this apocalyptic vision of it. If we consider this reading psychoanalytically we see that what the subject fears the most about the Second Coming is indeed the release of the Kraken of the repressed id. At the same time, the subject – a deeply "dirempted" character – lusts everlastingly for release from its oubliette of bondage to the hegemony, the Imaginary, and humanity itself. If this seems abstract consider the morbidly obese individual whom statistics tells us is a fast-growing part of the worlds population. Is this person not in an oubliette of his own flesh? Does he not long to be released from it? At the same time he loathes the idea of giving up the habits and lifestyle which have made him that way. This character serves as both a metaphor and the reality of the subjects bondage. The bonds of the mind are harder to see except in the words and actions of the subject which are perhaps only fleetingly observed. In the obese individual we see the manifestation of the inner bondage that drives the corporal expression of it.

The Weltgeist and the Spiritus Mundi both have their start in Plato's anima mundi (ψυχὴ κόσμου), the idea that just as the soul and the body are one, so too are we part of the spirit of the world which is an objective phenomenon. For Hegel this is the source of the "rational design" of the world. We find similar ideas in the work of Paracelsus, Spinoza, Leibniz, and in Emerson's "Over-Soul." But all of these ideas go no farther than being similar. They each have their own role and purpose in the schemes of each philosopher and in our consideration of our place in the universe. Yeats' Spiritus Mundi is different from the Weltgeist in that it is highly personified, uniquely personal, rather anthropomorphic in a daemonic sense, having a distinct role not in philosophy *per se* but in the elaborate mythology of Yeats' poetry.

There are various stories about its origin and meaning in Yeats' life. In one, it is a being that can actually be communicated with through the medium of his wife's spiritual trances. But perhaps the most plausible is that it is Yeats' concept of the creative power of the world, which he describes as "a universal memory and a muse of sorts that provides inspiration to the poet or writer". Such sentiment supports Emerson's active soul which "sees absolute truth; and utters truth, or creates." Which puts us in a much better position to answer the question of what significance the Spiritus Mundi has for the sublime. And it is here where we see that in both Hegel and Yeats these spirits serve as the precursor for the influence of the sublime upon the individuals epistemological understanding of himself and others as subject and object. In both, the sublime is the horror vacui demanding creative action from the sovereign individual. To the subject, the sublime is a threat to its false sense of "absolute freedom." The sublime threatens to destroy the subjects sense of *mutual utility* (one hand washes the other, and so on) with other beings and plunge it back into its fear of the dissolution of its own ego and pleasurable sense of *Genuss*. "Universal freedom … can produce neither a positive work nor a deed; there is left for it only negative action; it is merely the fury of destruction," says Hegel (p. 359).

> TURNING and turning in the widening gyre
> The falcon cannot hear the falconer;
> Things fall apart; the centre cannot hold;
> Mere anarchy is loosed upon the world,
> The blood-dimmed tide is loosed, and everywhere
> The ceremony of innocence is drowned;
> The best lack all conviction, while the worst
> Are full of passionate intensity.

The drowning of innocence, says Hegel in "Religion in the Form of Art," takes the form of Oedipus credibility in solving the Sphinx's riddle, thinking thereby that he has overcome something when in fact something (fate, *Schicksal*) has overcome him (p. 446). This "shape with lion body and the head of a man," as Yeats says, looks upon the now deceived innocent with "A gaze blank and pitiless as the sun ..." And yet Oedipus believes he has achieved a greater state of *knowing* over ignorance (Hegel's "not-knowing"). After all, one who solves a riddle always feel a kind of enlightened superiority over the riddle itself, and certainly over those who are perceived as not being able to solve it because of their various shortcomings. "He who was able to unlock the riddle of the Sphinx, and he who trusted with childlike confidence, are … both sent to destruction through what the god revealed to them," says Hegel. The "god" here could be called Fate; Hegel calls it the god of the Oracle, which speaks in riddles anyway. An oracle is a unique category of epistemology representing the revelation of something what was previously hidden from mortals but was known to gods. In fact here we have the original meaning of "apocalypse" as *apokalyptein* meaning to reveal, uncover, disclose. In an existential sense, then, the information from an oracle is both known and unknown simultaneously. Scientific discovery, on the other hand, is supposed to reveal that which was not known presumably by anyone. The temptation, then, is for Scientism to claim status as an oracle. Access to information on the Internet through voice-activated search engines creates the illusion of a kind of oracle, particularly when these little black boxes reply to the interlocutor. We see here that anthropomorphization has more to do with the "shape" (morphology) of the illusion of humanity as the "ghost in the machine" than it does with the actual physical shape of a human being. These gadgets are the modern form of Wolfgang von Kempelen's "Automaton Chess Player," also known as the Turk. Von Kempelen was able to fool distinguished audiences (including Benjamin Franklin) into believing that his automaton had enough self-consciousness to not only play chess but answers questions about its personal life. The new gadgets, always female voiced for the proper level of subservience, become like family members, often placed in an honored and critical position in the center of the working household for easy access to the knowing-of. Meantime, they serve as agents of their creators gathering personal information to be used in creating the personal digital profile of the user as consumer.

What matters is not the knowing of the formerly cryptic wisdom or who knows it and when. What matters is that the mortal receiver of the wisdom has now been touched by the omniscient gods of information from who one may hide nothing. The revelation makes man like a god, just as eating the apple from the Tree of the Knowledge of Good and Evil makes Adam and Eve "like gods," at least according to the Serpent. Again, the bringer of revelation is a deceiver, while the "innocents," in gaining this knowledge, fall into another sort of *unknowing* regarding their fate – a fate caused by their act of knowing. "[T] his revelatory [sic] spirit could also be the devil," says Hegel. Their knowing of what they did not know they did not know leads them into not knowing the consequence of their knowing. This is what Hegel calls "the antithesis of knowing and not-knowing ..." But the ultimate effect of self-consciousness, says Hegel in "Culture," is that it "must concentrate itself into the One of the individuality and put at the head an individual self-consciousness; for the universal will is only an actual will in itself, which is a One" (p. 359). The universal will, which is the consequence of absolute or Universal freedom, endows the subject with knowledge of itself as an object. The experience is like a lucid dream of absolute freedom where one knows that in the dream world there are no consequences for one's action. It is the perfect narcissistic paradise. One can commit any act without consequence since anything is now possible in a state of narcotic exception. But the "waking up" to one's self-consciousness in a dream is merely the consciousness of one's unconsciousness, freeing one from the moral and ethical obligation necessary for real consciousness and therefore of perception of reality within the context of the universal experience shared with others and that is overseen by the Law. Hegel says this is being "cheated out of reality." Again, the subject finds itself in the "darkness" of not knowing the difference between *knowing* and *not-knowing*. Yeats mystical concept of the Second Coming is not what we read in Revelation. It is based on his idea of the "gyre," a period of 2,000 years of spiritual sleep and not-knowing. With the New Millennium looming, he has this vision of what it means to know the difference between knowing and not-knowing, which makes the event of revelation an epistemological issue, not ontological. It is, as we shall see later on, a matter of *ontological epistemology* – the ontology of the difference between *knowing* and the *knowing-of* in the phenomenon of self-consciousness.

The darkness drops again; but now I know
That twenty centuries of stony sleep
Were vexed to nightmare by a rocking cradle,
And what rough beast, its hour come round at last,
Slouches towards Bethlehem to be born?

It is impossible to understand these lines through the lens of Christianity, since theology is dramatically modified by Yeats epistemological mysticism which involves the Oracle of poetic inspiration from the Spiritus Mundi as well as his Celtic sensibility (he believe in fairies). The Spirit transmits *knowing* directly to Yeats in the bardic tradition of the poet as seer, prophet, and medium between the corporeal and incorporeal – whatever it may be. Yes, the "cradle" is the one that rocked in Bethlehem 2,000 years ago with the baby Jesus in it, but why would "twenty centuries of stony sleep" be "vexed to nightmare" by it? And what is the significance of the rough beasts "Slouching toward Bethlehem to be born"? Is not the Second Coming a matter of Jesus returning not the Beast (whom we may presume to be Satan) being born? And why would *evil* be born in Bethlehem where 2,000 years earlier the scourge of evil and the harbinger of *good* was born? The answers do not matter to the Bard. "But now I know," he says. What matters is the epistemological act of knowing whatever it is there is to know about this complicated and obscure situation muddied by the symbolic raving of John of Patmos in Revelation. The cradle is in a state of agitation. It rocks the lucid dream of the subject into the Nightmare of the sublime where the subject's worst fears come true with no understanding of why or what to do about it - an apocalypse in the modern sense of a catastrophe rather than revelation.

3.4: Returning to bare life through war

The grotesque events which inspired "Dover Beach" and "The Second Coming" mark the sublime's retaliation for its ever-increasing subordination during the *Fin de Siecle*. In a more romantic interpretation the period between 1850 and 1920 is seen by *Gott-ist-tod theologie* as the death of the sublime *by and in war*. But is it? To say that war is the cause of the death of the sublime is an *ad hoc ergo propter hoc* fallacy. The closest we can come to such an idea is to say that war is a symptom of it. Nevertheless, the fact remains that war ushers in the return of bare life. We rightly associate war with every privation. In such a state, illusions are nearly impossible. Even the sustaining one of the vilification of the enemy quickly wears thin revealing the absurdity of the *ex nihilo* nature of the war-game theory: you are my enemy because I am your enemy. Such enmity is created out of nothing, like fiat currency, and is used with the same cynical expediency by the hegemony and its overlords. The conflagration of war ignites at the moment when the imaginary has so subordinated the symbolic and the real that they seem no longer functioning, integral parts of what Lacan calls the "signifying chains ... which from their structure, act on the organism, influence what appears from the outside as a symptom" (Seminar V, 21.05.58., p.7). He calls the signifying chain "the whole basis of the psychoanalytic experience." That which can no longer be analyzed can no longer function. The first two world wars occurred at moments in history where it seemed self-knowledge was at its ebb. In retrospect it may seem that from 1900 to 1950 psychoanalysis made its greatest gains as a method of getting at the truth, ugly or not. But if we look at its effect on Western civilization in general (with almost no effect on any other civilization to date) we see that at most it entered into the nomenclature of pop psychology where all is by definition trivialized.

Attempted murder of the sublime by nascent Scientism was first thwarted by bayonets, gunpowder, and horses - artifacts of previous centuries of warfare - during the time

Arnold and Yeats were writing. This "temporal gap" helped prevent the future from overwhelming then-present which is the temporal equivalent of what Hegel calls the "at first apparent other." Conflating the two we get the *at-first-apparent present.* This phenomenon quickly becomes "the past" as "the future" takes the position of the at-first-apparent present and so on. Such a churning cycle of time found itself in a state of superimposition between the artifacts of the past and changes being brought about by the Machine Age, electricity, radio, telegraph, and Communism. None of these modifications of the present (which of course is what "modern" means) fit the prevailing paradigms of the existing hegemonies. As a result, the present began to slip from the grasp of the disparate hegemonies ruling Europe and what at that time were its far-flung holdings around the globe.

The most modern of thinkers understood that integrating the means of production with the supplies it needed in ever-increasing demand at the lowest cost would yield the greatest profits. The answer to this prayer was the establishment of firm colonial governments which could rule over the far-off others who were seen as Untermenschen who could only benefit from this kind of slavery. The ideas of economist David Ricardo had already been embraced; as long as the empires could maintain their holdings in the territories of the far-off others they could count on raw materials otherwise impossible to obtain such as cotton and rubber in England. And as Ricardo pointed out, obtaining these raw materials with the lowest labor cost would yield the highest profits. Such labor necessary to feed the machines of export could not be found domestically. One might say that the degree to which a nation can expect significant profit from the export of its goods is equal to the degree to which it is capable of importing the raw materials necessary to produce those goods. This was never the case until time itself sped up as the production power of machinery increased beyond what had ever been humanly possible before. We should keep in mind that this ratio depended upon what we would now consider a snail's pace compared to the speed of light at which digital commerce is now transacted. From this seed grew the possibility of creating an Imaginary where the hegemonic powers could fabricate a consumer paradise. Such dreams would never have been possible without machines and the limitless ability to power them. Therefore, the powering of machines became the most important dynamic force in the development of the modern age.

Consequently, "power" in every sense of the word became the most important objective of every government decision. While this had many implications, the one most significant for us here is within the closed economy of sovereignty. Power may be either distributed or concentrated. An engineering analogy is a train that is either a series of powerless cars pulled by a powerful engine (diesel or electric) or a series of cars each of which is powered by the electric "trucks" beneath each car. A train of six cars could have twelve powered trucks. In one power is concentrated. In the other it is distributed. Both have the same ability to pull the same weight at a certain speed for a certain distance. Some of the comparative advantages are obvious. It is enough to say that one powered engine is the best for freight while self-powered cars are the best, perhaps, for passenger trains. What matters for us in this analogy is the comparative dependencies. In the concentrated model, all cars become dependent upon their engine. In the distributed model if three or four of the trucks fail the rest can still pull the train. In fact, one car can operate on its own, a categorical impossibility in the other model. In the distributed model the individuals have no need of a central power base. In the concentrated model there are advantages such as pulling freight and not having to be concerned whether or not the cars are all part of the same power system. But the greatest advantage is that the cars are totally dependent upon the will of the engine. If the engine lacks fuel it can release some of the cars. If the cars do not carry what it wants, it can refuse to pull them.

We may carry this analogy to the development of the modern Western state. The rugged interdependence marked by endless Napoleonic skirmishes and trade disputes between European states was forced by modern technology to seek the consolidation and concentration of power and thereafter what the Nazis called *lebensraum.* European wars of the 18th and 19th Centuries focused on territory and treasure. The exceptions, perhaps, are the American Revolution and the French Revolution of 1789. After these events, any war which was not motivated by the seizure of territory and treasure came to be known as a "revolution." The great Marxian revolutions sought (at first) distributed power and the reestablishment of government by ideology rather than expediency. So there came to be a pattern in the writing of history where capitalist adventures were called wars and communist adventures revolutions. There has been the tacit assumption in history and the popular mind that revolutions are somehow a type of civil war. A revolution and a civil war, however, have some significant differences. It is no secret that the Marquis de Lafayette, once asked to be the "dictator" of France, was one of the greatest heroes of the American Revolution which was certainly a war with little in common with the US Civil War.

The problem in this overture for the concentration of power

through the acquisition of territory and treasure is once again the persistent superimposition of the past and future. In one building a telegram was sent in an instant across a continent. On the other wise of the street people lived much as they did in the Middle Ages, more or less with the same viewpoint though more likely to be a Lutheran than a Catholic. There is something beautiful and sad about those days. Visions of men in World War I mounted on horses or scattered in trenches like they were already dead fill us with a kind of gloom. This is the gloom of the twilight of the sublime. As in the days of old, troops in this period often had to rely on bugle calls, if any, to carry out their orders to charge or retreat. They lived in isolation with their comrades. The whole world was the trench they were in at that moment. Their loved ones might well have been on Pluto. They did not use satellite links to communicate with supercomputers thousands of miles away in their homelands. They could not "call in air support" in the form of helicopters, jets, and supersonic missiles when the going got tough. When they were wounded the best they could hope for was to be dragged bleeding from the mud of the battlefield over the dead bodies of their comrades. There was no doubt in anyone's mind – participant or observer – that this was bare life in its extreme form. The filigree of the imaginary world of martinets and dukedoms fizzled in the gunpowder baring the truth of the social and economic realities of Europe at the time. A century of colonialism, catastrophic family feuds among royalty, and a world-historic shift in the idea of sovereignty overcame the apparatus of the Imaginary until it had all but vanished from the stage.

Nevertheless, the sublime mystery is that the horrors of World War I did not seem to teach anyone anything. Not twenty years later a world war of exponentially greater proportion explodes partly because of the botched and harebrained "safeguards" put in place in Europe to make sure the "War to End All Wars" lived up to its hype. As fast as the Imaginary ebbed into its proper proportion to the signifying chain of the symbolic and real, it was replaced by even greater illusions dreamed up by the same persons who dragged Europe's and even North America's population into the first world war. This affront to the sublime immediately led to hyperinflation and, soon enough, the rise of highly organized and successful fascism. It was a strange time when two moons rose in the night sky: Fascism and Marxism. The great Marxian wars brought on regimes which redefined oppression as a form of government while serving to sweep away old ideas, things, and customs. In the process they deflated the Imaginary which has become grossly out of proportion to the symbolic and real in the signifying chain. By so doing they helped in great part to restore the sublime in the form of bare life. At last the Machine Age was being reckoned with using an ethical aesthetic appropriate to its dehumanizing nature. At the same time these wars redistributed power with the goal of restoring more than a modicum of personal sovereignty. This would have been merely a negation of the old order were it not for the communisms ideological imperative to then turn around and sublimate individual sovereignty to the dictatorship of the proletariat. Most of all, though, it gave the peoples of powerful countries a taste of bare life they would never forget.

So let us not delude ourselves into thinking that war causes the death of the sublime. It is the symptom of it as well as being its greatest expression. The sublime is only possible in a state of bare life. As far as the sublime is concerned, if it takes a war to accomplish this, so be it. If the outcome is communism or fascism, is that any worse than corporatism? The sublime does not discriminate when it comes to heads rolling from the guillotine. In an interview, the sublime would say that it gave them a chance to do it through art, architecture, science, music, literature, responsible custody of nature, philosophy, economy, simplicity, self-governance, cooperation, family, friendship, and simple religions worshiping Creation rather than themselves. It would say that man had the chance to ennoble himself in any way requiring the sane and sovereign sacrifice of his life for those he loves. Furthermore it would say that it provided the gift of the horror vacui to be contemplated as the Void – a source of infinite wisdom and creativity in the reality of death and bare life. As Emerson says, "this every man contains within him, although in almost all men obstructed, and as yet unborn ..." But no. Mankind again and again chooses the *other* path. The path of self-enslavement and death with no significance except to say that "I came, I saw, I consumed." Why? Because the subject prefers death in life than to have to face a life which ends in the death of the ego. What the ego wants is the perpetual and absolute reassurance of the infant in what Lacan calls the mirror stage of ego development. It wants a *specular* existence where it is never forced out onto the stage in the spotlight to face the Other as the other. The subject would rather watch itself on TV.

What then of the 21st Century ethical aesthetic of perpetual war? Does it restore the sublime in the way we have been discussing? Is it the same thing as what the ancients knew as war? In an attempt to thwart the sublime's dominance the Imaginary takes over the apparatus of war, adding it to its own elaborate digital apparatus. This is most easily seen in warlike video games, movies, and other forms of entertainment. It is at the forefront of the technological development of virtual reality which seamlessly benefits military applications of video gaming. But this is possible only by employing the transitive function also used in the displacement of sovereignty. By imposing such a displacement the Imaginary is able to protect itself from the bare life normally associated with war. This displacement is widely known as a proxy war, which is another way of saying that the bare life of war has been *transited* from the prosecutors to the prosecuted.

To those who know nothing other than the Imaginary, this seems to be the normal state of war. The subject's nation goes to war (and no longer declares it) in the Land of the Far-Off Other. It does not matter who these others are; they always have funny names and weird customs and a strange look in their eyes – at least on TV news. All that is asked of the subject is that it does not inquire about how these adventures are paid for. It is true that the subject knows (in the sense of the knowing-of) that a goodly part of the treasure it renders to the government somehow finds its way into weapons. It also knows that these weapons either rust in silos, magazines, or depots, or are exploded in the land of the far-off other. But it accepts this state of affairs because it also feels, tacitly, that the ritual of blowing off the explosives is like celebrating its own Independence Day where fireworks symbolize the days of derring-do when people actually aimed military weapons at each other *on the subject's own soil*. Such barbarous times are over, thinks the subject. Today, the weapons are dropped from the sky by robots into the land of the dark and swarthy, far-off, crazy-eyed other whose bizarre atavistic culture probably should not exist anyway. When the weapons rust in storage the subject sees this hemorrhage of cash as a symbol of the peace-loving nature of its far-superior and evolved culture. The subject is especially proud of the fact that the most expensive and dangerous weapons of all – nuclear weapons – lie in questionable readiness scattered throughout the domestic infrastructure of its life but are never even considered an option. Unless of course the enemy uses its nuclear arsenal first, spawning endless speculation about what would happen if one of these weapons were used by accident. Then what happens to the game? Despite the stakes there do not seem to be any significant rules about this involuntary move of the chess piece. Whether the weapons rust or are shot from a clear blue sky into a village suspected of harboring insurgents, they are being used in accord with what the subject finds to be good, natural, and beneficial to all – even to the far-off other. After all, this subhuman creature with no self-determination except terrorism and extremism needs a new culture anyway. The old one is getting *too* old. Its conspicuous consumption index lags far behind the subjects own quantifiable pinnacle of civilization. In the ethical aesthetic of *Genuss* old things, old ideas, and old ways are *bad* just like batteries which have lost their charge. Since the subject's relation to things and others is one of *mutual utility*, it seems only natural that this utility will fade over time into obsolescence, like all tools and machines. What is critical to understand about the economy of the abdicated subject is that with the loss of sovereignty the subject also loses intrinsic value or what may be termed real value.

So the question arises of why the hegemony would be so eager to facilitate this devaluation. If we stop thinking about economy in the usual sense of demand, production, and supply, then it becomes clear. By initiating a transitive relationship with the productive economy of the far-off other the hegemony enables a transfer of sovereignty by induction (force). This transfer comes in the form of the importation of cheap consumer goods which embody the transfer of sovereignty. If the far-off other had retained its sovereignty there would be no cheap consumer goods for the subject. Without them, it loses the possibility of participating in the consumer economy of the Imaginary. So as long as the subject receives the far-off others sovereignty in compensation for its own abdication it has value to the hegemony. Though this value is no longer intrinsic (as it would be if the subject possessed its sovereignty and was a net producer), it is enough that it is *associative*. After the far-off others sovereignty has been usurped its relationship to the subject is one of *dissociation* which we might call (somewhat ludicrously) "far-off otherness." A more sociological term would be that the far-off other is no longer seen as just human in the same sense as the subject sees itself. Otherwise it would not be able to accept the far-off others *dissociated* sovereignty as its own. In other words, the subject must be a like a thief who feels a sense of possession regarding the goods he has stolen. The fact that the thief came into possession of the goods by taking them from someone else rather than by participating in the official economic system of labor undermines the basis of the whole system from which he has stolen.

So how does the thief come to regard stolen goods as his own which he acquired through his labor in his underworld economy? Often it is by justifying theft as a *redistribution of wealth* from the haves to the have-nots (or from the Fortunates to the Less Fortunates or Unfortunates). The latter two classes are what

Victor Hugo calls les misérables. When we say that Jean Valjean in Hugo's novel "stole" (volé, pillé) a loaf of bread, we consider the social system under which it was stolen and how it may have necessitated that he steal it to live because the system itself is unjust. Of course this affects the whole psycholinguistic meaning of the verb "to steal." Or, just or unjust, is the punishment which follows *just* in an abstract sense in proportion to the crime? Of course, that conundrum is what the whole novel is about. But in the case of the "theft" of sovereignty by the subject from the far-off other this hardly seems to be the case. It is one of the rich stealing from the poor, the reverse of Jean Valjean's case. So how is this crime justified in the mind of the subject? By dehumanizing the far-off other as a dark, swarthy, strange, atavistic subhuman the subject actually thinks that it is *benefiting* not harming the far-off other when it buys products manufactured in the far-off others territory. The subject is entirely convinced that otherwise the far-off other would suffer and die without this largesse from the subjects much superior economic amnion. Therefore, the hegemony benefits from the transit of the far-off others sovereignty while at the same time gaining total control over the subject by enslaving it in the Imaginary's debt economy. It is not hard at this point to work out who benefits from what. If the subject had retained intrinsic value the transitive economy would be impossible. There would not be the *induction* necessary to usurp the far-off others sovereignty using the money the subject borrowed from the hegemony. This lack would frustrate the plans of the hegemony's transnational overlords to gain a monopoly over the collective sovereignty of all hegemonic orders. The cartel of corporate overlords forces the collectives (massed into trade zones, unions, and other paper agreements) to abdicate their sovereignty by signing promissory notes to borrow money from their enemies. By thus destabilizing their economies the transnational corporate overlords hope to gain complete control over the entire global economy. The anticipation of all possible states of function and dysfunction permits the cartels to profit as much (or more) from crashes as it does from booms.

But of course this scenario does not take into account the benefits of perpetual war. To really understand wars role in the economy of the cartel of corporate overlords we must understand its relationship to the ethical aesthetic of expediency. Once we bring up the matter of aesthetics we must consider what effect an aesthetic has on our appreciation of the sublime. For it is our aesthetic sense that either opens us to the possibility (*Möglichkeit*) of the sublime as the apprehension of the transcendental object of the Other or closes us off to the possibility of transcending our spectral orientation to the sovereign sense of self. If we already dwell in this state of apprehension then war *diremptss* its continuity, forcing us into a state of vigilance. If we do not, then war forces us into a state of bare life where the possibility opens up of entering into this state of apprehension. Either way war is a *challenge*. It is absolutely inevitable that the sublime will issue this challenge when the sovereignty of the individual is usurped or abdicated. Such abomination of the Natural Order will not go unpunished by the sublime. The speech made by the legendary Scottish character William Wallace in the movie *Brave Heart* embodies this spirit well:

Wallace:

> Yes, I've heard. Kills men by the hundreds, and if he were here he'd consume the English with fireballs from his eyes and bolts of lightning from his arse. I AM William Wallace. And I see a whole army of my countrymen here in defiance of tyranny. You have come to fight as free men, and free men you are. What would you do without freedom? Will you fight?

Veteran soldier:

> Fight? Against that? No, we will run; and we will live.

Wallace:

> Aye, fight and you may die. Run and you'll live – at least a while. And dying in your beds many years from now, would you be willing to trade all the days from this day to that for one chance, just one chance to come back here and tell our enemies that they may take our lives, but they'll never take our freedom!!!

Wallace and Soldiers: Alba gu bra!

As has been said here before, no one likes to have freedom *ripped* from his possession by force and intimidation. Therefore, it is more common to hear such brave speeches under such circumstances. But when the subject is *lured* by its culture into abdication … *that* is another matter entirely. It is difficult to fight a war from the womb (matrix or amnion). The subject acculturated into the canard of corporate and financial democracy must be approached in an entirely different manner than the people of Scotland in the 13th and 12th centuries! Threats are to no avail;

as an infant the subject requires lullabies, not imprecations. What is most reprehensible to the globalist-progressive who represents the world banking system's prerogatives is the idea of a "tribe." Although he romanticizes so-called indigenous, primitive tribes (while destroying their habit for minerals), he abhors the sort of tribalism Wallace espouses. Why? Because, he says, "it causes wars." How ridiculous, especially after what we have gone through here in our discussion of war! Rather, the globalist-progressive hates what he calls tribalism (a term defined as such in Popper's *Open Society*) because it forms a bulwark against the totalitarian ambitions of the hegemony, its banking system, and the apparatchiks it inserts into positions of control over the polity. In this way (and in Gibson's inimical way), Wallace is the tribalist and the burgeoning British Empire is a kind of proto-globalist-progressive, just as was the Rome it sloughed off in its indigenous kings' and nobles' quest for what we would call today a "United Kingdom," or in a larger and more disturbing sense, the European Union.

The idea that war is a kind of lacuna of the sublime is merely a romantic notion which has the further handicap of being the product of a logical fallacy. A common error of romantic thinking is the idealization of certain aesthetic ideas (which the sublime certainly is). This abstraction of these ideas amounts to a form of filtration; we see it already in Keats "Ode on a Grecian Urn" where truth must somehow reconcile itself with beauty in a world where the common idea is that "the truth" is ugly. In a time when bare life was that much closer to being everyday experience, to "know the truth," Jesus suggested, would "make you free" (John 8:32). Free of what? The words beauty, truth, and freedom have a strange history and relationship. They draw near and apart depending upon the ethical aesthetic of the Zeitgeist. Successive generations wonder what the previous ones could have meant by saying that truth is freedom in a time when telling the truth gets one burned at the stake or imprisoned. At other times "the ugly truth" – whether of ones marital fidelity or political corruption – can in no way be seen as beautiful. And how is freedom beautiful except in ad copy? Can freedom be "ugly"? One thinks of persons, not uncommon, who have been in prison for so long that once they are released they long to return, committing another crime to get there or even begging officials for their old cell back. In an "apocalypse" a prison would be the safest sanctuary if society runs amok; the inmates could protect themselves from the marauding mobs of murderous rioters that put them there in the first place.

Having a particular role in the cultivation of this ethical

aesthetic of cynical expediency is Scientism. Its first task is to show that such ideas as freedom, beauty, and truth have no basis in fact. As such, they are instantly relegated to the realm of the romantic which is a pejorative in the hierarchy of its specialized languages. All three words bear the mark of being unscientific. This is not because the hegemony supporting Scientism (and which it supports) has no use for these words; they are in fact glorified in the Imaginary. Rather, they are seen to interfere with the process of pure science which must ignore anything which cannot be verified or else be polluted with the superstitious thinking of the mass of wretched humanity it has been appointed to save by the hegemony and its overlords. Meantime, the hegemony must find some way to pay for the expensive adventures of science. Ultimately this requires borrowing from the lenders of last resort such as the hegemony's enemies since the more friendly lenders have since become net borrowers too. While this debt obligation is passed along to the subject and its descendants, the benefit of the research goes to the transnational corporate overlords of the hegemony which commissioned not only the science but the borrowing by fiat - implicit and explicit. Any complaint from the subject is silenced by the generous distribution of gadgets which, while nearly free in and of themselves, require ongoing monthly commitments of cash to function as they are ultimately nodes of a network though they *appear* autonomous. It is interesting to note that the Enlightenment conception of the automaton could not have anticipated this reality. Any machine which purports to think and speak autonomously in the moment of its function is in fact is only the extension of a network which relieves it of all autonomy. Such is the nature of an illusion. Even such a machine such as a train engine - which at first could function autonomously without any electricity inboard or outboard - now depends upon a complex electrical grid to function. The seemingly anthrobotic functions of the "smart" device are an illusion created by the infrastructure of a vast digital network to which it is completely dependent. To assume that a device is "smart" would be like assuming that a marionette moved by its own volition. At least in the case of the puppet it is true that something resembling intelligence does indeed operate it. As for the device, the puppeteer is nothing more than algorithms initialized by input with corresponding output *simulating* human interaction. A similar (in the truest sense of the word) illusion is behind the Big Magic of VR (and MR & AR) which would be accurately described as *simulated* reality. Such a disparaging phrase, however, would not be good marketing in an age where "simulated" and "fake" are more or less synonymous. "Fake" reality would not sell products which require the mystique of "otherness" signified by the nonsense word "virtual" (almost?) to seem more human than human.

If the sublime is part of reality (perhaps the basis of it) and reality is so flimsy that it can be reproduced convincingly as VR, MR, and AR, then the sublime must be as flimsy and insignificant as reality. Some have gone as far as to use the phrase "virtual sublime," thus adding to the heap of oxymorons upon which the Information Age is built. We could say that the sublime's "death" has a much to do with its being made trivial in this way as it does with any of the other causes we have discussed here. While the meaning of what is said is often trivial, language's power to trivialize reality is not trivial. A person can with a few words can be reduced to a thing. The distance from there to being a thing which must be gotten rid of is not far. For many centuries of Christianity whatever was not identifiable as orthodoxy was vilified as witchcraft, paganism, and superstition. Later, when science turned the tables on religion and nominated it as superstition, it too became a form of witchcraft in the eyes of Scientism. Between, Christianity itself lived to see its own hostile internecine divisions spawn sects fighting over orthodoxy as Protestant and even Orthodox churches. This development followed the same trend in Judaism where the Orthodox form was challenged by forms representing themselves as being either more or less "orthodox" than the Orthodoxy. What matters here is how language in these situations is used. It's clear from this one small example – which we could multiply exponentially throughout the day as we communicate – that language itself is a kind of friable medium blown by the winds of our momentary expediency. It is a bunch of elaborate and expressive noises approximating referents to the signified. The pairing of signified with its signifier is equivalent to thoughts formed from such chains of imagos. The signifier serves as a kind of place-holding intermediary between signified and referent. For example, a rock as a signified thing may be called a rock (regardless of adjective). Its referent, however, is that signifier *plus* whatever expedient (imago) we require to put that signifier to work. It happens that we want to use the phrase that a person in difficulty is between "a rock and a hard place" which allows is to use "rock" as a referent in a larger meaning of difficulty. While the bounds of the signifier are finite, those of the referent are not. The phrase itself refers to another, coming from Greek mythology where one is "between Scylla and Charybdis," a sea monster and a whirlpool. The Classical phrase is also associated with a particular rock

(Scylla), so that the "hard place" is the whirlpool. All of this makes language far more rich and expressive. Were it not for this linguistic friable quality poetry would be impossible. And so too would Humpty Dumpty's speech in Lewis Carroll's *Through the Looking Glass*:

> "When I use a word," Humpty Dumpty said in rather a scornful tone, "it means just what I choose it to mean — neither more nor less."
>
> "The question is," said Alice, "whether you can make words mean so many different things."
>
> "The question is," said Humpty Dumpty, "which is to be master — that's all."

Humpty Dumpty implies that it is possible to either master or be mastered by words. How this question is settled is another matter. But as we can see in the matter of orthodoxy, there is no orthodox meaning of the word orthodox when it comes to orthodox religion. Again, it is a matter of expediency. The various churches and temples are happy to observe what they see as strict orthodoxies regarding all aspects of life, from before one is born to after one is dead. The greatest minutia are delimited with the authority of no less than God Himself. And yet the free and easy use of the word orthodoxy makes the whole idea of anything being correct (for that is what it means) absurd. Scientism only asks to enjoy what powers its predecessors have enjoyed. It wants the Humpty Dumpty powers to have a word "mean just what I choose it to mean — neither more nor less."

So where then is language? The idea that it is some kind of precise instrument with which we carve up the universe into morsels of understanding comes from Genesis 2:20 when God gives Adam the power to give "names to all cattle, and to the fowl of the air, and to every beast of the field ..." This is Adam's first godlike power. It is at this moment where Adam ceases to be a beast himself through his naming of them. This objectifies him from the animal kingdom. Religion never let go of this banner of priority over the universe, marching deep into the territory of the abstract ideas it inherited from Classical and Hebrew antiquity such as "spirit." From there we get the grand dichotomies of spirit and flesh, the litanies of good and evil, the miracle of transubstantiation, and at last whole abstract worlds such as Heaven and Hell which exist on paper but cannot otherwise be found. In taking over the castle, keep, and kingdom from religion, Scientism was willing to overlook the accusations it had made when it was only a contender regarding religion's free and loose use of language to conjure something out of nothing. Taking over the controls, Scientism exploited religion's weaknesses by belittling its quaint language, funny costumes, and authentically sublime ideas about what is and is not. At the same time it commandeered the true great sublime discoveries of science as examples of its knowledge, wisdom, and power while promoting the illusions that those discoveries in part sought to dispel. Martyrdom of various sorts was required of many of the scientists who made these discoveries, just as it was of the many "saints" and countless others who strove to assert the truth of bare life and the sublime in the name of the spirit of humanity. Therefore it is particularly pernicious that the new religion then turns on those scientists who threaten its orthodoxy and dogma which are economic before they are political. While the *auto-da-fé* has fallen from fashion, it is enough to deny a scientist funding, publication, credibility, and a career to martyr him. He must then suffer the fate of the Underclass as an Unfortunate, scorned by his colleagues and regarded by society as a crank and a heretic.

The situation is all the more tragic when we consider that the extreme to which Scientism has pushed the world (need it be described in much detail?) not only anticipates war, it precipitates and necessitates it. We need not point to weapons proliferation, industrial pollution, and the psycho-social effects of its ubiquitous surveillance gadgetry. The overabundance of food, the pharmacopia of medications, and the psycho-social effects of its gizmos has as deadly an effect on humanity as a whole as the more obvious antagonists. Defying the Malthusian prophecy, the scientifically engineered food supply has far outstripped the population. It serves as a kind of hyper-stimulus for unmanageable population growth, obesity and even food allergies, and the use of food as a weapon in places where it is artificially withheld for this purpose. Medicine has created a population dependent upon its life-support systems, from drugs to surgery, so that those in the Fortunate countries live out most of their lives undergoing treatment for severe chronic illnesses such as cancer, diabetes, and heart disease at great personal and public expense. Meantime, the far-off other in the Unfortunate country must go without clean water and even the most basic medical care. The psycho-social effects of gizmos and gadgets, few functions of which serve any purpose except distraction from reality and surveillance, now permeate even the have-not societies. The result is that the world's population is drawn together into one global network where it is hauled in like fish and sold in the marketplace of consumer telemetry.

Therefore, war serves as a kind of correction for the sublime by pitching all of those involved into bare life. As we have mentioned, though, Scientism's great power wielded for it by the hegemony is to provide *transit* (in the transitive sense) for both the usurpation of sovereignty and the corrective power of the sublime. The far-off other's sovereignty is stripped from it by force and transits to the subject through the production and distribution of the cheap goods it makes to sustain the subject's conspicuous consumption. In return, the subject's state of exception through war transits to the far-off other in the forms of missiles, unmanned aerial vehicles, troops and equipment flown in by cargo and troop carriers, the covert funding of various insurgents, assassinations, and the manipulation of handouts of food and medicine from nongovernmental agencies. While the two transitives need not work together they often do because the combination is so devastatingly effective. The cartel of states with scientific power gang up on the state of the far-off other. They then claim to be usurping the state's hegemony for reasons which the subject does not really understand but has been conditioned to believe are just plain bad and are therefore a threat "to Democracy": religious fundamentalism, dictatorship, "human rights violations," terrorism, and so on.

The sublime, however, is not to be outdone. The hegemony's scheme to outwit the sublime and to feed the vampire lust of its hapless subjects can only be carried out in a closed economy where all of the values (energy, money, time, and so on) are finite. They exist within a closed system. As a result, the hegemony eventually undermines its own security and power by borrowing money from its enemies to fund its consumerism at home and its wars abroad. Of course, its enemies are happy to provide the means of the hegemony's own demise. Eventually, inevitably, mathematically the hegemony's ability to borrow even from its enemies will cease. When this occurs, the subject begins to lose its ability to participate in the consumer society at the Fortunate level. Soon, it begins listing toward the Unfortunate level – its worst terror because there it will encounter the bare life of the sublime. This terror is further fueled by the Imaginary which has taught the subject that bare life and the sublime are Death Itself. This mechanism is well concealed, though, in the Imaginary's method of *negative induction*: by offering eternal life in the womb (matrix) of the amnion the Imaginary *infers* that any loss of status brings the subject that much closer to the mortal and wretched condition of the Less Fortunates of the Underclass. Because of its lighter skin color and where it grew up the subject knows it can never be a Less Fortunate, for that is a fate of birth. What it fears is joining the Unfortunates it has seen or heard about who have fallen through the lower membrane of the amnion by the mechanism of foreclosure on a home, bankruptcy, or defaulting on loans.

To its shock, the subject learns that the hegemony has been sustaining the consumer economy artificially outside the bounds of economic reality. The sovereignty the hegemony fed the subject usurped from the far-off other by force evaporates like a dream on awakening. If there are no goods and services to consume then the subject loses the modicum of self-determination the usurped sovereignty of the far-off other provided. It can no longer choose between the red car and the green car. Worse, it can no longer make the payments on the promissory notes it signed for its old car. Just as the subject's illusory sovereignty evaporates so too does the hegemony's credibility and power when its enemies strategically refuse to loan it any more money to fight proxy wars in the far-off other's territory. The hegemony's corporate overlords have arranged the matter so that when the financing of proxy wars comes to an end the real objective is at last obtained: the bankrupting of the hegemony. In collapsing the hegemony's local economy its corporate overlords are able to seize assets at the lowest possible price. Sometimes in the shape of creditors seizing collateral assets. As the two pillars of the amnion collapse, the bare life the subject feared *as* death becomes its reality. It is only at this point when the subject has any chance of beginning to understand what the sublime is. In bare life narcissism results in a quick and painful death because it simply is not a survival strategy. It is an exotic excrescence of an existence in the amnion of the Imaginary.

3.5: Mad scientists, Big Magic, and the repression of the id

So far we have focused mainly on the Imaginary because it is the prevailing mode of the hegemonic discourse of consumerism. We have also seen what effect it may have on the experience of the sublime by providing a kind of displacement substitute for the real. The relationship between the Imaginary and real is one of displacement. The role of the sublime in such a displacement is acted out on the stage of war. What, then, is the role of the symbolic in this drama of displacement? We can begin to get an idea when we consider the content of the Imaginary, which is largely symbolic in the way that dream content is symbolic. In fact, the symbolic world of the Imaginary competes with dreams for priority in the subject's capacity to know itself. The enemy of the Imaginary in this sense is psychoanalysis. For example, when the powers of psychoanalysis are turned from the subject to the products of the media much is revealed about the apparatus of the Imaginary as an installation in the psyche of the subject. In fact, too much.

At one time it was the archetypes we found in Classical literature and mythology which provided a basis for the explication of their significance to the structures and motives of the psyche. Now nearly any media product will do. It is as if the subject's psyche has been disgorged into streets, through media, seemingly out of displays of gadgets and gizmos the subject can no longer live without for a minute. Narcissus, in falling in love with himself, has left the speculum of his obsession open for us to see. Once psychoanalysis was conducted in the private chambers of therapist. Now what might have taken a skilled therapist years to extract from the defenses of the reluctant analysand are divulged with the utmost candor and abandon by the subject through telemetry to every piece of marketing software grazing its psyche as it stares into the screen of its gadget. We live in an unprecedented age when even the word "literal" has become figurative. If one wishes to create hyperbole in a metaphor one need only add the adverb "literally" as in "the incumbent literally killed his challenger." What once might have been regarded as pathology is now a marketing opportunity not only for consumer goods and services exploiting these weaknesses but also the drugs purporting to "treat" them!

To really understand how this came to be, we have to understand how the relationship between consumerism and science developed after the period of the great wars. The wars themselves, which might be called the "revolt of the real," so accelerated the development of science that it was able to overcome and surpass the capacity of populations in Fortunate countries to absorb and understand it. The medium of television in particular and later its more fancy extension the Internet established an unprecedented channel or conduit for the psychological influence of the Imaginary's discourse. Nuremberg Rallies with banners and loudspeakers and a cast of thousands were no longer needed; millions more could be reached at any time anywhere there was access to the media. Radio lacked the overwhelming visual stimulus needed to properly transmit the new powerful symbolic order. Once accompanied by image, however, the narrative discourse now approximated a kind of extrinsic form of thought transmitted by the corporate overlords and governmental overseers of the communications infrastructure. Now that what was once intrinsic (thought) was now extrinsic it become a discourse which sought to mold the consumer to the economic and political priorities of the hegemony and the Imaginary. The amnion of the Imaginary was born as an ever-expanding network of communications channels tying together the collective psyche. What was missing was the abdication of the subject's sovereignty. This was soon enough accomplished through the generous apportioning of debt to the Fortunates and some of the Less Fortunates. As they signed away their sovereignty in promissory notes they at the same time turned to the *net-world* of the amnion which promised a return to the womb (matrix) through eternal *Genuss*. This transmogrification of the signifying chain was so successful that the ethical aesthetic of expediency was born to help the hegemony determine all political, financial, cultural, educational, and even religious decisions and choices. The combination of expediency and *Genuss* was enough to bring an end to any attempt by the subject to either retain or regain its sovereignty. This is a great deal to accomplish after 1950. Much groundwork had to be laid before this point for the effort to be successful later on.

Between 1850 and 1950 science begins to follow two distinct tracks: theoretical, based on pure mathematics, and applied, based on the needs of the consumer market and war. That there is more than one track to follow is made possible by the Machine Age which through negative induction creates the need for gizmos, gadgets, and bric-à-brac. In other words, Says Law is at last allowed its full expression: build a better mousetrap, as Emerson said, and the world will beat a pathway to your door. The sheer gravitational force of produced goods creates the consumer by induction. Supply at last creates its own demand. But this demand is *negative*. In other words, it is at first a paucity of consumers. This paucity, however, acts as a vacuum to suck in consumers desperate for *Genuss*: the pleasures, distractions, indulgences, comforts, and conveniences of the newly-forming secular amnion. Improvements in materials science, mechanical engineering, and the development of electricity which transmogrifies communication establishes an unprecedented age of gluttony and greed that now even the common man can wallow in.

Of course there is much traffic between theoretical and applied science. But their cultures diverge throughout the unique exponential growth of science during the Twentieth Century. Fueling this growth is the reciprocity between theory and practice. Soon a system is set up where if a scientist wishes to work on "theory" then he must produce something that can be sold in the marketplace. Meantime, the enormous financial rewards of this arrangement help feed more theoretical research and the growth of the research university. There are limitations, however. Theoretical science, though often based on simple concepts, nevertheless uses mathematical and other languages which in their raw state are impenetrable to the uninitiated. Attempts to "popularize" science often result in the *reductio* seen in schoolbooks and the media. The materials are created with financial and not intellectual profit in mind. In turn, they are taught by uninspired drudges whose only interest is in their next paycheck, generous benefits, and a long well-funded retirement. Seldom are these teachers actually interested in their subject. When pressed they may admit that they are interested "in teaching." But it usually goes no farther than that. As a result, so-called hard science remains remote for all except the initiated. The fact that all of its wonders and secrets in great visual detail and endless lucid explanation and animation is available on the Internet passes right by the subject because it thinks that science is just something to suffer through in school to get a grade and then forget about.

Whatever the public does not understand takes on a sinister shadow, in this case resulting in the "mad scientist" cartoon character in entertainment and pop mythology. In the language of Medieval alchemy theoretical scientist seeks the Philosophers Stone while the applied scientist seeks to transmute lead into gold. The cultural medium the subject swims through has not progressed significantly since the European Middle Ages by default and design. At best the subject has a vague notion of Newtons principles of the physical universe. That they clash fundamentally with the paradigm of such critical quantum concepts as the superimposition of states is at best portrayed as the most extreme fantasy in entertainment media. If such an idea is portrayed at all in the circus of the subject's cultural environment of notions and mental bric-à-brac, it is in a bastardized, comical, and ultimately misleading way. In frustration the subject merely dismisses it all as Big Magic and is done with it. "That is all ye ever know in life" thinks the subject "and all ye need to know." Therefore, theoretical math and physics manage to survive without much public scrutiny but with mush misunderstanding. The subject has a vague idea of "what is going on" in that laboratory up on the hill in the dark castle with the lightning bolts striking it. In the imagination of the subject the modern-day alchemist, partly allied with the Devil, works sleeplessly on his evil plans. Biological engineering, genetic modification, atomic energy, and robotics are portrayed as the Four Horsemen of the Apocalypse. In entertainment evil geniuses, often with British accents, seek to enslave mankind and take over the world. The applied scientists, of whom the computer engineers are now currently the greatest celebrities, are regarded as benefactors of mankind. They bestow the gift of gadgetry and "connectivity" on the stinking masses. The only possible way to dispel these misnomers is through a general culture of scientific thinking in the sense meant by Peirce when he says that

> No other occupation of man is so purely and immediately directed to the one end that is alone intrinsically rational as scientific investigation. It so strongly influences those who pursue it to subordinate all motives of ambition, fame, greed, self-seeking of every description, that other people, even those who have relatively high aspirations, such as theologians and teachers, altogether fail, in many cases, to divine the scientific man's simple motives. (p. 334)

The phrase "the scientific man's simple motives" sounds a bit idealistic and naive today. But it takes someone with the idealism and indeed the innocence of Peirce to have the nerve to describe what he sees as the true scientist. The scientific researcher's Nuremberg Defense is that someone has to pay the bills. A grant is a grant. And if he is not associated with a major research university and is not published in the best peer-reviewed journals what chance do his discoveries have of even seeing the light of priority? So much for theoretical scientist.

Applied science has quickly become a culture unto itself. It replaces the agrarian economy in rich countries, consolidating the work force, financial markets, education system, and consumer behavior. Soon the political system succumbs under the pressure, adjusting itself to the other changes. A new culture emerges with the speed of technological development. But it lacks a spiritual core, a uniting ethos, a transcendental aesthetics. Furthermore, world wars break the faith of the population; in the darkness of its plight, it searches for some kind of illumination that can be swept up with the Zeitgeist. It believes, momentarily, that theology of the Living God has failed them in the advent of nihilistic *Gott-ist-tot theologie* peddled by consumerism. Fed by their desperate hope, their financial resources surrendered through debt, and their willingness to believe the merest lie despite all evidence to the contrary, Scientism rises to take over the role of spiritual master of the masses. Their intimate embrace, however, is fraught with ontological misgivings. On a good day, Scientism brings snappy appliances into the home and snazzy cars onto the street; on a bad day it threatens all of mankind with nuclear holocaust and a totalitarian surveillance state (whichever comes first). It survives by alternating the carrot and the stick, while eliminating any possibility of alternative to its palliatives. Nevertheless, since the *Genuss* of applied science is in the present and nuclear apocalypse, like death, is "in the future," the subject accepts the risk. For former adherents of Semitic religions, the guilt of apostasy lingers in the unconscious, providing a bulwark for Scientism against defection to disturbing paradigms of self reliance and bare life.

In "Dover Beach" and "The Second Coming" we see the juxtaposition of the loss of faith and assumption of Scientism's threat of technological apocalypse alternating with its promise of infinite security and prosperity through the hysteria of political religion. Arnold mourns that the "Sea of Faith … / Was once, too, at the full, and round earth's shore … / [Laying] like the folds of a bright girdle furled." What makes his poem an elegy for the *Fin de Siècle* is that this faith is now trapped between the Scylla and Charybdis of Theism and Scientism. Arnold no longer has either the ship that sank or the safe harbor it sought in his journey from life to death. Now all he hears is the "melancholy, long, withdrawing roar" of Faith's retreat. Yeats expresses it in equally gloomy terms as the loss of the "ceremony of innocence …" In both cases there is the presumption of something *that was there but is now lost*, with no clear idea how to regain it or if it could or even should ever be regained. This sense of loss soon pervades Western civilization even before anything is really lost in World War I and what Auden called the "Age of Anxiety" is born. The collective mood disorder of loss and anxiety follows upon what Unamuno identifies in the romantic sensibility as the tragic sense of life. While this "mood" is not something new, for the heights of the Middle Ages and the Baroque have their share of it, never has it been so mixes with a pervasive feeling of angst. There is a perpetually unfulfilled sense of impending responsibility for something which never seems to occur. Here again we have what Lyotard calls the temporal gap where "the chance … of something unexpected happening ..." is neutralized by the excess accumulation of capital. It is further aggravated by the artificial production of capital by the lending banks themselves which increasingly flood the economy with debt.

Along with the establishment of the Imaginary through the endless supply of cheap goods the temporal gap allows for the culture of the Next Big Thing. As the subject drives its new car off the lot it is already thinking about trading it in for the new model which has not even been manufactured. What the Middle Ages achieves in the form of freezing time in the ascetic rejection of it along with the material world, the Age of Anxiety achieves by doing the opposite: creating an ethical aesthetic of *Genuss* where more is better. The price is the perpetually unfulfilled psychological state of *l'objet petit a*. The essential difference is that the former is qualitative and the latter quantitative. This is a distinct shift toward the Imaginary as it is concerned with fullness and not what Lacan calls "lack." Nevertheless it is driven by a manufactured sense of lack. Try as they might, the great Marxian states could not shield their people from the materialistic lifestyle of their neighboring capitalist states. Soon, their own people grew tired of the *lack* involved in bare life which for millennia before was simply taken as the state of life as it is for most animals. They wanted the phantasmagoria and prestidigitation it seemed their neighbors enjoyed in the casino economy of credit and consumption. Moreover, the power to shape the outcome of the future in the form of investment could dull the edge of the wretched "unexpected" which can only be bad for fiat capital and "planning for the future." By the time Auden publishes *The Age of Anxiety* in 1947 the Marxian experiment has created states which seem suspended in a kind of economic amber. In a time when theoretical science feeds applied science which in turn feeds the capitalist experiment which in turn feeds theoretical science the Marxian states almost seem to be going backward technologically. The USSR later catches up quite well at least on the level of weaponry but not on the consumer level. Meantime, the capitalist experiment which after 1950 or so begins adopting the leveraged capitalism of John Maynard Keynes fuels the Cold War's military metastasis, waste, and mutually assured death.

The problem of the temporal gap for the sublime is that it is a state of the knowing-of and the sublime is a state of the getting-to-know. Along with Big Capital comes Big Data, for capital is itself data. Just as the accumulation of capital seeks to diminish the unexpected so too does the accumulation of data. The idea in computer modeling is that if we just "had enough data" we would be able to predict everything. This idea is one of the follies of this age that in subsequent ages (one hopes) will be seen as ridiculous; the only data missing in the predicting of the future is what Madam Science sees in her crystal ball. Like the casino economy which predicates itself on great and more powerful computer betting models to predict outcome, so too does the monad of Big Data seek the omniscience of God which science has promised it "in the near future." Anyone with the latest gadget is thoroughly convinced that in his lifetime he will see walking, talking robots interacting with the human population as an everyday experience. There is even the possibility that it will take a "Turing Test" to discover if it is a robot or not. In "Computing Machinery and Intelligence" (1950) Turing sees chess as a likely application of a thinking machine anticipates out more ambitious projects.

> We may hope that machines will eventually compete with men in all purely intellectual fields. But which are the best ones to start with? Even this is a difficult decision. Many people think that a very abstract activity, like the playing of chess, would be best. It can also be maintained that it is best to provide the machine with the best sense organs that money can buy, and then teach it to understand and speak English. This process could follow the normal teaching of a child. Things would be pointed out and named, etc. Again I do not know what the right answer is, but I think both approaches should be tried. We can only see a short distance ahead, but we can see plenty there that needs to be done.

His machine would be all about the getting-to-know rather than the knowing of. What this machine would "do" is learn. Why? Because that seems to be what machines are the least good at. Therefore, to make one that can learn following "the normal teaching of a child" would be the most interesting and least trivial. The eternal problem with learning machines is that they do so in a proscribed way that is more or less a "learning program" following certain fixed and immutable algorithms which cannot be unlearned, relearned, or replaced except by more manual programming. Like a person challenged to distinguish a fake from a real fur coat, most humans quickly perceive these patterns and their limitation and the illusion of "consciousness" vanishes. Once we know how a magic trick is performed, if we have any sense of curiosity and wonder then we will nevertheless admire the magician's skill in fooling us. Turing says that the only arrangement that would make any sense is that the learning system is "like the Constitution of the United States": it can be amended but not fundamentally changed. These changes would be, he says, "of a rather less pretentious kind." But what the subject wants and at the same time fears can only be called pretentious sorts of intelligence such as consciousness, personality, and emotion. The Turing Test is more of a test of any signs of consciousness and intelligence in the man, the woman, and the interrogator interacting in the imitation game with a machine than it is of any such qualities in the machine. So Big Data's task is to be *so big* that the subject cannot see how the magic trick is done. If this illusion is maintained long enough to get some money from the subject then it has been a success just as it is in a magic show.

The enemy of the knowing-of getting-to-know. For there to be getting-to-know there must be Unknowing. Once man has all the answers there is nothing left to know. The historical state of Unknowing, with only an Oracle to point the way in mystical and poetic language, was the state of the sublime for millennia. Through "ignorant armies" and the "mere anarchy" of the "blood-dimmed tide" the subject-as-individual is torn from its anchor and set adrift on a sea without charts or a bright star to guide it. It is only in the recognition of what Peirce calls the "incognizable" that there can be any recognition of what can be known. As such, we all carry a personal version of an Apocalypse within us. It is the fear of the *unknown* of death, sublimated. We are not afraid of the *known* of death, such as eating a dead chicken, watching an action or horror movie with shooting and murder, or attending a relatives funeral. It is, as Hamlet says, "the dread of something after death, / The undiscover'd country from whose bourn / No traveller returns" that makes "cowards of us all." In our vigorous and systematic repression of this fear, enormous cathexis energy builds up in the unconscious that is expressed in our nightmares, neuroses, and waking visions of substitutes for the truth of our fear displaced into the unsuspecting environment as threats. In this way the extrinsic symbolic of discourse takes over from the intrinsic discourse of dreaming. At the same time psychoanalysis becomes impossible because what was once considered to be pathology, even psychopathology, is instantly absorbed into the "normal" of the Imaginary. In the Imaginary *anything* is possible. One need no longer dream that one is committing a sex crime or murdering someone. Now one can buy a game which exploits even the most minute of ones proclivities.

While this may seem to be the perfect solution to psychopathology, as it is sometimes described, it does violence to the signifying chain. Rather than the symbolic finally getting its equal time with the Imaginary in the chain of significant discourse, the fact is that this state of affairs *sublimates* the symbolic just as it does the real. As a result, sublimation forces an explosion of displacement substitutes in the form of consumer products. Reading these substitutes used to be an important tool in the method of the psychoanalyst. Most often found in Freuds analysis of sexual hysteria, this process is critical in gaining knowledge about the patients pathology and therefore is an epistemological issue for the analyst and analysand. Discovering the psyches *displacement substitutes* helps bring unconscious material into the *preconscious,* where it can be analyzed for its symbolic value through association. Dreams are an example of repressed unconscious material appearing in the *automythologization* of the process of the preconscious. It owes something to the conscious mind, which reinforces the symbols, story structures, and ethical aesthetic more or less inherent in it. Symbolic and structural values shared across a culture, such as the idea of an Apocalypse, are a collective expression of repressed psychical energy the conscious mind does not want to be cognizant of and therefore represses. As long as it is repressed it is *incognizable*. Through the association of ideas, Freud is able to manipulate the preconscious into giving up its secrets, albeit in a kind of cryptic form which he trained himself to read. He also uses the narrative automythologization of the dreams themselves to access psychical content cloaked in the riddle of the attempt to evade consciousness. The analyst's role, then, is to serve as a medium between the unconscious and conscious mind through the agency of the preconscious, either in free association or dream analysis. There is always an externalization of the neurosis. Sometimes it is well hidden. In other cases it is overt. In *Interpretation of Dreams,* Freud describes theory that one of the vicissitudes a repressed fear or instinct will undergo is its assignment to a displacement substitute.

> In the psycho-analysis of neuroses the fullest use is made of these two theorems – that, when conscious purposive ideas are abandoned, concealed purposive ideas assume control of the current of ideas, and that superficial associations are only *substitutes by displacement* [italics added] for suppressed deeper ones. Indeed, these theorems have become basic pillars of psycho-analytic technique. (p. 964)

Something in the psychopathology of the everyday environment will become the object of this displacement. It may be entirely alien to the repressed instinct when an attempt to conceal the connection occurs, or so closely aligned with it as to serve to cover up completely the displacement mechanism even entering into the appearance of being "normal." Both situations lead to the same conditions, which include neurosis, obsessions, paranoia, hypochondria, and depression. For instance, a person may have a terrible fear of foreigners (xenophobia) due to some traumatic idea or experience early in childhood that creates a maladaptation of the early childhood fear of strangers – a survival instinct. After being vigorously and autonomously repressed during the ensuing years because of its "irritable" interference in healthy functioning, that person may develop an obsession with helping refugees from foreign countries, work to ban them from his country on some irrational and virulent way, or find some entirely unrelated displacement such as an eating disorder out of guilt or an impulse for self-annihilation. In all three, the repressed early childhood fear of strangers is entirely masked by the substitute, which has now become a symbol of the repressed instinct. While psychoanalysis brings the condition to the foreground of understanding the displacement substitute condemns it to the "safe" ground of the commonplace.

In any event, the displacement remains in the realm of the symbolic until somehow, through psychotherapy or self-revelation, one comes to an understanding of its underlying psychic energy and structure. As Peirce points out in Questions 2, 3, and 4 of "Questions Concerning Certain Faculties Claimed for Man" (p. 16), we cannot think without the use of signs, for, according to Peirce, thought consists of signs. Signs of course are a significant part of the symbolic order particularly in the form of language and the Law. However, these signs may have many different types of roles in our intercourse with the world. Paranoia may alight upon random signs for the unconscious psychic energy seeking displacement that may be more or less understandable, such as fear that government seeks to persecute the subject through the Law. Conversely, it may alight upon a bizarre or irrational object, such as someone seen in the media, a loving familiar (often the father – *le grand Autre*), a benign stranger, or even an animal. In this case, says Freud, it may be a matter of deliberate distortion and obfuscation by the repressive mechanisms of the psyche to evade exposure of the root cause of the neurosis such as we see in "dream distortion." When a sign is so out of phase with the signified as to actually point in a misleading direction – like a street sign saying turn left when one should turn right – then we have a clear case of distortion. The matter is further complicated when a sign becomes a sign of itself, thereby becoming unintelligible to others. It is impossible to picture a sign pointing to itself, so it is an entirely abstract matter of self-regard known only to oneself and is therefore cryptic.

When a displacement substitute becomes a sign or symbol for the repressed instinct, as a thought or *idée fix*, it also becomes opaque because it cannot be a sign of itself. This neat arrangement gives life to the repressive mechanism which, like a cancer, has its own life and purpose apart from and even contrary to that of its host which is to live. Keats, in being overwhelmed by the evidence - not signs - of his impending death, loses the veil the rest of us more or less cannot live without: the illusion of immortality. This loss of illusion is akin to the concept essential to Greek tragedy of *anagnorisis* where the player drops his mask to reveal that he is not a man but a god (usually in yet another mask). While this example is taken from classical stagecraft, Aristotle uses the word to mean a "knowing again" in his one mention of it in Poetics. An example in Classical theater is when Oedipus learns that he is the killer of his father Polybus and consequently married his mother. The horror of his crime alights upon him as curse, even after revelation (anagnorisis).

PART 4: CONCLUSION; SUBLIME EPISTEMOLOGY

4.0: What *anagnorisis* reveals about *speculation*

Keats in his sonnet "When I have fears" expresses his anxiety about death not as the extinction of the ego but as the loss of an opportunity to "trace" what he calls "Huge cloudy symbols of a high romance ..." In the four lines below we see that the "nights starred face" is a surface upon which he may read these symbols which he describes as "shadows." The entire relationship between the parts of this constellation is semiotic.

When I behold, upon the night's starred face,
  Huge cloudy symbols of a high romance,
And think that I may never live to trace
  Their shadows with the magic hand of chance ...

As we have discussed, when a part of the signifying chain comes to dominate the others it removes itself from the constellation of that chain. It then becomes an *installation* or apparatus. As such it no longer need distribute its energy over the rest of the chain; instead, it may demand that other parts of the chain - the symbolic and real - pay tribute to its now imperial status. As we have seen with state power, it is a matter of whether it is consolidated or distributed. Examples of such distortions are states where nearly everyone is poor (real), rich (imaginary), or ideological (symbolic). Of course these are highly relative terms. Seldom is there a state which is so passionately and distinctly one or the other. There are even states where the values of the signifying chain result in a kind of mutual tension where a sustained balance results. Moreover, all states go through periods where there is balance (as in the "balance of powers"), disorder (chaos, anarchy), and order (dictatorship, tyranny, totalitarianism) if they have anything resembling a history.

In the sonnet, Keats regards the constellations of the stars. In them he sees the symbols which are shadows that the poet must trace with chance. (Only the quantitative machine could trace something with absolute certainty.) This is quite an extraordinary proposition. We may dismiss it as the belletrism of the poet compared by Theseus in "A Midsummer Night's Dream" to the madman and lover who both seem to make something out of nothing. But the poet is different, because what he produces has the specificity of reality, thus bringing together the signifying chain:

And as imagination bodies forth
The forms of things unknown, the poet's pen
Turns them to shapes and gives to airy nothing
A local habitation and a name.

Theseus indicates that imagination is the alchemy of the poet's techne embodying form from airy nothing. In so doing the poet *informs* reality by endowing it with "a local habitation and a name." This localization makes the poet's expression accessible to the Other as the Other's reality because it is a form of objectification (place and name, which must be shared by all). The madman and lover also bring forth something out of the symbolic shadows of language, thought, and idea but fail to make it real for the Other. It is only in this way that the poet engages in the process of "making" in the sense of *poesis*. Anyone can "make" a poem. But to make a poem *make* reality requires "the magic hand of chance ..." a process which at certain times in literary history has been attributed to the Muse. It is only through the process of *poesis* that *techne* results in *episteme*, or knowledge. This too is a significant (in the truest sense of the word) component of the signifying chain. In it, meaning "bodies forth" or, as Keats puts it, is the result of being "traced" from the nascent shadows of "high romance." When the constellation of the signifying chain is drawn along by the *techne* of *poesis* the result is *sublime epistemology*.

There is much in the phrase "Huge cloudy symbols of a high romance" pointing to the qualities of the sublime: its great scale in relation to what we have come to know as the world, its obscurity and cloudiness, its expression as symbols of "thought" in the sense meant by Peirce above, and its high elevation in proportion to other ideals. Keats' dance around the sublime here is necessary because, as Peirce points out, *we have no power of introspection.* The symbolic nature of thought prevents us from "reflecting" upon our own thoughtful reflection. While it is true that we may enter spectral orientation to ourselves just as we can look into a mirror, we must keep in mind that this orientation is not really a "relationship." *Relation* requires more than one entity which is not that entity itself as in A → B. The proposition A → A is false because A is not dependent upon A to be A. It is not the same as saying A = A, which is always true. For A to be A it must be in relation to "not-A" otherwise it has no identity. *A* alone is *A* in name only but not as an entity. As such it could just as well be B (or any other identity such as Ψ). If the identity of any entity can be any identity, then it is *not* in relationship to any other entity and therefore lacks identity. Its identity (a form of entity) is established in relation to another entity with equal sovereignty as an entity, such as B (or *XY*, *pq*, and so on). If the system allows, we may say that A → Ψ, which is true but in an abstract sense because they may not be in the same symbolic category. So the spectral self (the self-seen in the mirror of the self) is not a relationship of an entity to an entity though the self itself regards this proximity to itself as the paradigm of all relationships. In such as state the apprehension of the transcendental object as the Other is not possible. Under such circumstances "lack" arises in the subject's total isolation from others. This lack is the source of all of its self-imposed pathology.

A symbol cannot be a symbol of itself. "[T]here is no reason for supposing a power of introspection; and, consequently, the only way of investigating a psychological question is by inference from external facts" (p. 33). Such a limitation means that the perception of the process of introspection is an illusion, a kind of smoke-and-mirrors trick of the mind better suited to theatricals than epistemology. Peirce's approach to epistemology is original. It includes introspection as *one path* to knowledge. Keats cannot find the sublime through introspection either, where it becomes opaque. Instead, he turns to the nightingale to express his internal state as an objective correlative. Consequently, Keats finds the symbols where they must be: in the clouds of high romance. The word "romance" is a cousin of the sublime in that it invokes the narrative of the subject rather than the subject itself, which is not sublime. Ultimately the subject is a product of language. It is embodied in its narrative, from the words of God and its creation to the ceaseless concatenation of signs of its thought process all reinforcing the same idea "I AM."

"Romance" can be used as a nuanced synonym - if we eliminate the sexual connotation. As a noun, as a negative quantity, romance becomes the reason for doing anything. In other words, if there is no script (narrative, discourse) of our life then what are we to do in it as the actors? We hear someone say, "I left my job because there was no romance in it anymore," or "Isn't Rome romantic?" As with all abstract concepts we toss the word around depending upon application and context. But this is as it should be. Words do not exist in and of themselves as do that which they signify. It is an ineffable quantity that can only be apprehended by use of *negative capability*, which in turn is strengthened by what Pierce calls the "intuitive power of distinguishing between the subjective elements of different cognitions" (p. 30). These subjective elements, paradoxically, are found only in the objective world, perceived not by the senses empirically, but by the soul intuitively. The sublime may only be apprehended, intuited, not packaged, canned, and sold as a commodity. So in "When I have fears ..." Keats again pairs death with the sublime, while also adding "fear" to the list of what might be called states of being: "uncertainties, mysteries, doubts." One must be "capable" of not acting as expressions of these states, or what he calls the irritable search for comfort and salvation. The first twelve lines of the sonnet are a dependent clause modifying the couplet at the end: "Of the wide world I stand alone, and think / Till Love and Fame to nothingness do sink." Like Arnold, he is "on the shore," the Dover beach, of the abyss. The substitutes for the sublime - love and fame - again fall away in the unmasking of *anagnorisis,* a word etymologically related to *gnosis,* knowing in an intuitive and mystical sense. They fall away just as peace, love, light, and help for pain are seen as illusions by Arnold on the shore of Dover. "Surely some revelation is at hand" says Yeats. Note that revelation is not a proper noun here, nor does he directly refer to Revelation. Here it is meant as a pure *reveal,* the term now used in stagecraft as a synonym for *anagnorisis*. The reveal can be in the editing of the film and the structure of the plot; its effect is entirely psychological. It is revealed that the war hero is really a spy for the enemy. It is revealed that the evangelizing preacher is really a fornicating adulterer. In the work of Shakespeare a favorite reveal of his time has to do with the gender of the character; there are seven instances where female characters appear as men, later to be *revealed* as women.

But to have the Spiritus Mundi revealed is an epic moment in literature and in life, for it is here that the sublime becomes the Sublime, an entity unto itself of negative substance, an abyss, the existential "truth" which can only be found in the *horror vacui*. Irritable reaction to this fear of empty space leads to the fulfillment of that space with the unnecessary, the imaginary, and the illusory. Ultimately, it leads to the death-in-life of *specular* ontology - where the mere reflection of life is taken for life itself, which is the metaphor of Narcissus. His irritable pursuit of what he wants - love, romance - is what prevents him from getting what he wants. This double bind is the typical ontological experience of the specular, perhaps reflected in media products which are one and all the result of mirroring the demographics and psychographics of the subject else they would yield no profit. Keats fears that he may "never live to trace / Their shadows, with the magic hand of chance" and never "relish in the faery power / Of unreflecting love!" The key phrase here is "unreflecting love." Keats intuits that love, as an idea, must not be sought introspectively where thought, or the ideal of it, is mistaken for the *real* in a misprision where the symbol becomes a symbol of itself as the fatal strategy of narcissism. He rejects the specular. But the price is death because it is in the "shadows" that the sublime abides, often revealed only *in extremis*. Finally, when reconciling himself with love's caesura, he stands alone and "thinks." This act of thinking is Gedanken, which also has the meaning of to remember, recall, and commemorate, but not the meaning of *introspection* in the narcissistic sense Peirce rejects as the *knowing-of* oneself.

Now that Keats has been stripped of the specular, his thought no longer refers only to itself. Rather, he remembers *himself*, the one lost with the "fairy power" and the "magic hand" so critical to the poet in the process of *poesis*. This remembering is an invocation or what Yeats calls a "ceremony of innocence." For Yeats and Keats the magical and the romantic are activities, not static states or acquisitions. As such, the sublime is inductive, ingressive, negative, and void. In both poems, though, it comes at a moment of over fulfillment of the activity necessary for there to be life the way a virus will only attack a healthy, living organism. Death and apocalypse are the eschatology of a ripeness which brings about the tragic sense of existence. The metaphysics of this process is grounded in the physical economy of language. Compared to a noun a verb is "empty" of content, signifying activity and not a person, place, thing, or idea. It is a signifier void of thingness. It is by definition *transitive* in that its referent is less than or equal to what it signifies. Consider the difference between murdering and killing. One can kill without murdering but cannot murder without killing. In the first case killing is less than murder but in the second murder is *at least* equal to killing for we cannot have murder without it.

The linguistic possibilities are four: signified, signifier; inferant, referent. The implication here is that there is a correlation between the pairs so that we can further pair signified (inferent) and signifier (referent). An inferant is a phenomenon in statistics where a value is not present in the calculation but is inferred by the relationship between the numerator and denominator. For example, if there are 100 persons without health care out of 1,000, and we know that out of the total there are 200 persons over 50 years of age, if the distribution of those over 50 is greater within the group without health care, then we may *infer* that persons over 50 are less likely to have health care. What makes inference important in language is that it creates meaning in otherwise related but in-and-of-themselves meaningless facts. In other words, it is intrinsically "meaningless" to say that one in ten persons does not have health care. We may *impose* an extrinsic meaning on this figure by saying that our value system or charter or constitution or law demands 100 percent participation. But since the value does not come from within the relationship of the other values it is inherently meaningless to insist that it has meaning. We may impose any meaning upon it even going so far as to say that ten percent is as it should be. We can even say that there should be more than 10 percent if we factor in, for example, the limits of our budget or even those who refuse to participate. To attain 100 percent shall we force the nonparticipants to join? This becomes more clear when we consider statistics regarding epidemiology. If 10 percent of the population gets a certain disease, we know that at least the figure is possible. Insisting 0 percent of the population gets a disease is not possible because the probability is always 1 (or .1, .01, .001, and so on). When we try to kill bacteria we know we can only ever say that we can kill "up to" 99.9 percent of the bacteria. While this may seem like "bad" news, the fact is it is epidemiology's only hope. There is always the hope in an epidemic that if 99.9 percent of the population does get infected that there will be .1 percent that will not. This fraction may help us develop a cure or prophylactic or at least help us understand the mechanism of the disease. Otherwise, clearly, the only possibility is extinction.

The difference between the inferant and the referent is that the former is inductive and the latter deductive. When we use a signifier we *induce* the signified; when we regard the signified we *deduce* the signifier. If we say, as William Carlos Williams does in his poem "The Red Wheel Barrow," that something is "glazed with rain water," we infer that it is "wet." As "wet" is an abstraction it must be induced through our ability to interpret the evidence. Williams called this "Imagism." As such it is a kind of synthetic statement which nevertheless brings the abstract idea of something into being where it was not before. For example "communism" has always existed in some form or another but not in the form we know today as communism. This idea had to come into being so that, as the problematic signified it would have a signifier which others could recognize as this thing communism and not some other thing completely outside of its nature which could be regarded as communism too. (And certainly throughout the history of this ideology there has been this argument.) "Wet" is in the same class of abstraction as "cold." Water can be cold if it is frozen or if it is not frozen. Therefore, to induce "wet" from the evidence at hand is inconclusive because "wet" itself is not verifiable the way "frozen" can be. There is only one definition of the latter: the water has changed state from liquid to solid.

Furthermore, if we turn water into a gas as vapor it may also make the wheelbarrow "wet." But can we then say it is "glazed"? Conversely, if we regard ice in its solid form we can deduce that it is "frozen" because there are certain physical properties of this state which are distinct and incompatible with a liquid or a gas. Therefore, we refer to the water being frozen which in turn gives us the signifier "ice."

The sublime's greatest attribute as a negative value is, as we have discussed, its nature as the *horror vacui*. It seems probable that death and apocalypse are bound together by horror, but not terror, which we reserve for the ritual of war (as in "terror*ism*"), though the apocalypse is always "in the future," whereas death is always "in the moment." Both share a void, a nullification, of the amnion's architectural integrity. As the amnion becomes null and void in the advent of apocalypse and the event of death, the subject enters into the fullness of the dream of life which is, after all, a dream of a dream. (Thomas Carlyle is reputed as saying as his last words on his deathbed, "So this is death. Well!") But it is also the blank page, the white canvass, the still violin on the bench in a sunbeam, the dancer asleep in a bed, the unattended microscope. All of three are ripe with potential but devoid of action. Therefore the sublime is present in the stillness of death and the act of life. If it is an active, restless principle, though, what is it about death that is sublime? We might begin with the *coming-into-being* of life (*le devenir*) from the horror vacui of death. Beneath our sense of identity, time, and place there is a leviathan of unease churning through the black ocean of our unconscious in the form of our subliminal apprehension of the sublime. When life begins in the womb we seldom think of it as "coming from death." We can accept death as the negation of life (in that order) but not life as the negation of death. Why? Here we see our fundamentally negative view of the positive; we casually regard life as something entirely unrelated and even opposed to death. Life is homeostasis. Death is aberration, exception, disease, exotic, wrong, and bad. As such we limp along believing we can be cured by the magic waters bubbling from the font of life. Again we see the Manichean psychology latent in Western though. In particular, we see life cut off from death as if the two were enemies. And yet when we see a lion seize its living prey we know that for the lion to live the prey must die. We also see that life and death are inseparable. Between our denial of death's dominion and our observation of its priority we live in perpetual contradiction of reality. But the union of life and death remains seamless. Being what it is, then, the sublime is "sub" (beneath) the "limen" (limit or value) of consciousness awareness. Although it is something entirely apart from the mind of man, and man strives ever to make it so, it is nevertheless perceived subliminally. As such it is a powerful value in the economy of the psyche's energy system. Sometimes it is better, then, to say what the sublime is not so as not to stir the psyche into the protective action taken in dream distortion and self-delusion.

4.1: Phenomenological ratio of signifier to signified

Pierce uses the term "introspection" to indicate what occurs when the signs of thought turn in on themselves, inverting the ontology of subject and object so that the subject becomes the *subject of the subject* (itself). The extrinsic expression of such misprision is common enough. The Nazis, as a source of rhetorical invention overseen by Joseph Goebbels, were successful in transiting the signifier "Jew," through just such an inversion, into "enemy (of the state)," or Adversary of the Reich. To do so, the commonplace referent of a person who happens to merely belong to the Jewish faith, had to undergo this transformative operation. In other words, the introspective mechanism allows for a *narcissistic* redefinition of the referent, in an individual and collective sense.

First off, what is meant by "narcissistic referent"? When the subject inverts to what Pierce calls "introspection," the ego ceases to extract objective, or even collective, meaning from the idea, concept, or word. In other words, it gets what it has desired from infancy: a world fashioned only for itself, by itself. As the world is, in a special way, *created* by The Word (which was, as Genesis says, "in the beginning"), language, and the concepts it represents as the concatenation of signifiers, shapes our perception, serve as the schemata of our universe. If this is not obvious, then there is something wrong with one's perception in a generalized way. However, if this were all there was to it, then eventually the signified would be at odds with its representative utterance, causing both personal and social chaos. Fortunately, in a healthy, truly social sense, our personal language is weighed against agreed-upon meaning so that we may effectively communicate. A printed dictionary is an example of this, though online dictionaries are not – particularly "wikis" where fad neologisms and argot shared only by a small group are placed on equal linguistic terms consistent for millennia and that are critical to understanding. Such linguistic decay in the forms of argot, jargon, and slang is even seen as an improvement over the "social injustice" of dictionaries regarded as collections of etherized and pinioned butterflies. Nevertheless, we come closer to universal agreement with concrete words such as my favorite: turtle, than we do with abstract words such as justice (or Dasein, for that matter). The phenomenology of signifiers is arrayed on a spectrum, with abstract concepts being farthest from social definition and concrete concepts holding their own through onslaughts of fashion and casual usage. The barbarians at the gates, however, are the jargon and marketing of commercial digital culture. It robs language of even its concrete meaning with its fanciful appropriation of words such as "mouse," "server," "client," "Trojan horse," "worm," "spam," and so on. When someone refers to "the Web," what comes to mind is the World Wide Web, not the one Charlotte the spider weaves in the children's book by E. B. White and Garth Williams.

Generally speaking, though, we ascribe such a principle of definability to nouns, which are, after all, the ultimate signifiers, abstract or concrete. However, the same principle may be found in verbs, which are their own kind of signifier. They point to an action which, as it must also include the effect of time (whereas nouns merely indicate it, as in the noun "time" itself), therefore differentiates itself from nouns for this reason. More significantly, the verb allows formation of syntax. Starting with the king of all verbs – "to be" – the copula unites nouns and their descriptors with other words and phrases, forming the relation between subject and predicate. The relation is similar to that between our perception of subject (ourselves) and object (others, things, the world, the universe, and metaphysical or imaginary "beings" and "places"). Nevertheless, the ambiguity built into verbs serves the same purpose as that built into nouns: it allows us to adapt language to the infinite possibility of circumstance, idea, and fantasy. I think the phenomenon of verb definability also allows for jokes based on it. For example, there is the joke about the man who needs a place to stay. Every hotel he visits, though, has no more rooms. At last, he finds one with a room. But the clerk has a caveat: "This is the last room and we're very busy. Do you mind if you have to make your own bed?" Desperate, the man says, "No problem." The clerk then gives him a hammer, nails, and a pile of lumber. The "play on words," as it is called in the business, is, of course, on the verb "to make," which allows for such ambiguity in a well-established sense. There is also the catchphrase joke of comedian Henny Youngman; when he gives an example of someone's behavior, he says, "Take my wife" (as an example). Then, after a pause and with great timing, he adds "please!" Meaning, take her off his hands. Naturally, the play on words here affects the verb "to take." Combine verb and noun definability in the same utterances and we can "make" a joke or express subtle emotions such as irony.

However, what we find in the speech of politicians and advertising is the *manipulation* of definability. It is not always in the service of the truth as it is purported to be. Rather, in the case of public relations and politics (almost the same thing), it is to give the narrative a "spin"; in the case of advertising, it is to motivate the buyer with a sense of what Lacan calls *lack*. An unprovoked attack on a sovereign state becomes a "preemptive strike" on an (enemy) "asset." Despite one's high opinion of one's romantic viability, "body odor" threatens to condemn the handsome rake to a lifetime of sexual frustration and loneliness. Therefore, he must buy such-and-such deodorant, which, of course, is hawked with the synthetic proposition that it and it alone is the only product that will solve the problem of his personal *lack*. Whether he is afflicted with it or not, the idea is now living in his head. Eventually, at some pre-calculated marketing percentage called the ROI, or return on investment in the ad, he will buy the product whether there is some verifiable need for it or not "just to be safe." The ritual consumption then magically repairs the damage the ad did to his ephemeral self-confidence. His physiology remembers the pleasurable neural stimulation associated with the ritual purchase, initiating an endless repetition of the act euphemistically called "brand loyalty." Unless, of course, he is a sociopath, psychopath, or egomaniac. Then, we have another game altogether.

With greater abstractions we have more definability. One man's "freedom" is another man's "oppression," as the rhetoric of the Chinese Communist Party, extolling the virtues of the "freedom" from having to vote for leaders, indicates when it aims at so-called Western value of democracy. Also, we find this schism in the Marxian concept of "freedom" being a capitalist "fetish" in the Freudian sense, though not without some relevance to the captive subject of the amnion.

> The slavery of civil society [*bürgerlichen Gesellschaft*] is ostensibly the greatest freedom because it appears to leave the individual perfectly independent. The individual considers as his own freedom the movement (no longer curbed or fettered by a common tie or by man) of his alienated life-elements, like property, industry, religion; in reality, this movement is the perfection of his slavery …. (*The Holy Family*)

There is significant sense in what he says here when we regard the state of modern consumerism in the amnion. A telling example of it is the "freedom to choose" from dozens of permutations of dish-washing detergent, coffee flavors, breakfast cereal, frozen pizzas, TV's, and the colorful rags passing for clothing produced in third-world sweatshops. Moreover, each location of the modern supermarket or department store throughout the nation is organized and run in precisely the same way and sells the same products. The result is standardization of the "freedom to choose," turning it into an oppressive form of having no choice at all, except the awkward alternative of growing one's own food, which not everyone has the time or inclination to do. While the reader may balk at my criticism here, saying "it's better to have a variety to suit each of our needs," we must compare the situation to, for instance, the 1.2 billion persons throughout the world without electricity. When asked what they eat, they will say "maize," or "rice," or "beans" or some such staple their ancestors lived on for thousands of years. Is this any "better" than the "freedom" of the modern consumer and denizen of the amnion? I do not think this is a valid question, as "better" is entirely relative, being a commercial proposition and nothing more. What I am saying here is for the sake of comparison which, after all, is the foundation of reason in the form of ratio and ratiocination.

Also, as I have mentioned often here, the "freedom" of comfort and convenience is in fact mankind's prison in the womb (matrix) of the amnion. So before we condemn and burn Marx at the stake for his criticism of what is called freedom in a putative capitalist society, we must ask what it in fact *is*. Once we ask this question, we are immediately mired in competing and often contrary definitions. As Berman comments in "Freedom and Fetishism" (*Adventures in Marxism*, 1999), "If their whole outlook on life is 'fetishistic,' how will it be possible even to recognize that they are enslaved, let along make the efforts to set themselves free?"

Is it the amnion enslaving the subject? Is it "capitalism" (or Marxism, for that matter)? The answer in this book is NO: it is the subject's own pathological narcissism and its voluntary abdication to what it perceives as the *egoic gratifications* offered by abdication to the amnion, such as physical immortality through modern medicine and finite access to consumer goods through debt. Never mind that some estimate, in the United States, indicate that medical error is among the top five causes of death, and that debt robs the consumer of economic power through what Sharia Law calls the *haram*, or mortal sin, of *riba*, or interest.

In the turning-in of navel-gazing "introspection," then, language turns in on itself, ceasing in any effective way to be what would properly be defined as communication. It becomes an internal narrative that escapes from the confinement of the subject's hermetic solipsism, infecting those around it as they in turn infect the subject. The result is the deadly Cult of Mediocrity. It begins to reflect the prejudices and psychological and emotional shortcoming of the subject, rather than the world of the signified apart from its signifier – a categorical division made by Saussure. What is worse is when this fetish becomes a *cult*, such as in the Cult of Mediocrity, or the cult formed by the NSDAP leading to Nazi ideology and what Victor Klemperer calls the "*Lingua Tertii Imperii*," or "language of the Third Reich." And it is here, in the invention of such a collective narrative based on narcissism, that we enter into the machinery of genocide and extermination.

Again, what begins to form after the diremption of the signifier and the signified is just what the amnion needs to form itself into a virtual world and attract abdicated subjects to it like flies to a trap. By divorcing the subject from reality through language and debt, the amnion grows stronger as the subject feeds it with treasure, indebtedness, labor, political support, and even its life if necessary in a state of war. Marx's own phrase for the amnion, in the more abstract Nineteenth Century sense, is "illusions of the epoch," which I have been calling the Zeitgeist with, perhaps, less indictment. According to Berman, Hegel's term is the "illusory community" wherein freedom is a kind of excrescence of the "labor of the negative." Berman goes on to compare the fetish of freedom in the "illusions of the epoch" with Wittgenstein's "fly-bottle" where existence is reduced to the capture of an insect in a bottle children (used to, before the Internet) delight in. "When he describes capitalist society, Marx is constantly making the point that everything in it is … dominated by 'fetishism,' and hence is unfree …" (op. cit.).

While some members of Group X may be your enemies, not all members of that set will be. However, if we invert (pervert) the referent of Group X to be the material equivalent of enemy, then *all* members of Group X become a threat and therefore must be exterminated, suppressed, or subjugated. There was a period, perhaps just after the 2001 attack on the World Trade Center in New York City, when ALL Muslims were regarded, by American non-Muslims, as terrorists. The narcissistic inversion of the referent Islam became the synonym of the Adversary (Satan, as it has become in the dogma of Christianity). Of the three great Semitic religions, Islam, the newest, gets the most abuse. One reason is that enough of its adherents seem to actually practice what they preach, visibly engaged in the salat five times a day, that is publicly announced at those times. How dare they!

thinks the nominal worshipper of the other two seemingly more discrete faiths. As a result, Scientism seizes upon Islam as the icon of dangerous superstitious belief that must be wiped out by scientific consensus. At the same time, the progressive political structure *supporting* Scientism hypocritically holds Muslims up as victims of the bigotry of the other two Semitic religions, sometimes even protecting them with one law while persecuting them with another. In an Amniotic Empire, anything is possible; its nomos is based on a fundamental contradiction of invalid synthetic logic, which is like cracking open a boiled egg to get a chicken.

However, there is no reason to be found here, only what is possible when the state puts itself into a mode of exception from its own nomos. Is it in any way possible that all one billion Muslims wanted at that time to kill themselves in a suicide attack in the name of a jihad against America? Of course not. But we excuse such misprision on the basis of the exploitation of it; the expediency of making all members of Group X equal to the level of blood and treasure reserved for enemies makes war sweet, tolerable, absolute, and symbolic. The amnion, dwelling only in the imaginary and symbolic and abhorring the real, delights in promoting and perpetuating this misprision through its media apparatus and political mouthpieces in government office who have their hands on the valves of the public treasure. Consequently, social pressure enforces the subject to comply with the prevailing discourse – which is the blueprint of the mob mentality – in order to justify the ensuing death and destruction. The teleological result of this mechanism is usually the enrichment of select members of the hegemony, who we might refer to as the "hegemony of the hegemony," profiting from chaos while manipulating geopolitics in such a way as to help them maintain their hegemonic status. There is no shortage of Marxian and fascist dictators, warlords, NGO's, bankers, and arms dealers who can grease the way for the machine of the resulting carnage for personal political and economic benefit.

Today, the more broad term "terrorist" (indicating a vague group of far-off others and those nearby with whom they are associated) follow a complex transit involving manipulation of the inferant *and* the referent. The *inference* is the threat to "national security," in the popular imagination "Islamic," not Irish or German or American, as terrorists of old used to be, and hence a direct threat to personal safety. The new referent is to *far-off others* who refuse to abdicate their sovereignty. In their refusal, they disobey the standing order to capitulate to the reigning hegemony in order to provide the captured masses of the amnion with the gizmos and gadgets they cannot live without. Furthermore, stubborn "bad tribalism" (meaning Islam) of these miscreant far-off others deprives the hegemony of the minerals and regional stability needed to exploit them the hegemony requires to provide cheap goods to their expectant indentures. By maintaining a steady flow of goods globally, the hegemony is also able to speculate in the currency of the amnion: the derivatives market, which consist of futures, forwards, options, and swaps – the stuff of which dreams are made. Their relentless drive toward financialization of the first world and industrialization, as serfs, of the third world, enables them to join a transnational *supra-tribe* of financial manipulators and their operatives at the lower levels of the hegemonic machinery, such as politicians.

The complexity suits the geopolitical agenda of the hegemony's overlords in part because it always remains one degree beyond the comprehension of the largely unconscious and otherwise preoccupied and distracted subject who is merely "aware" that there is a "threat" and nothing more, though he may exhibit "strong feelings" about these things he really does not know anything about. But Peirce is concerned with the intrinsic *clockwork* of what eventually becomes an extrinsic expression once it has been thoroughly propagated by channels of social communication. In his day (the Nineteenth Century), these channels included books, periodicals, lectures, and speeches. It is pointless to list the many channels available today the entire infrastructure of which is owned and controlled by the corporate overlords of the hegemony. The idea that the Internet sets the user free is simply not borne out by the evidence; rather, the trillions of dollars stolen each year from users, corporations, and public services by fraudsters and hackers, as well as the obvious and seemingly infinite redundancy of the available data makes a thirty-year-old set of the Encyclopedia Britannica more valuable, and certainly safer and cheaper, than the entire Internet. Not a syllable escapes the filtration of government censors such as we find in China; and in the West, at best, these channels function autonomously as a kind of "capitalist propaganda" where everything and everyone is always for sale. These "nets" and "webs" and "cells" are the *carcerari,* as well as the nervous system, of the amnion. As some computer technicians will tell you, the only safe computer is one that is unplugged, disconnected, and off – preferably with the CMOS battery removed. All private social discourse which passes through electronic channels is subject to other forms of surveillance which mirror the values inherent in public media filtration. Since it would tend to disrupt the amnion's illusion of democracy to interfere with private communications, as well as stifle a valuable source of information about that the subjects are thinking, a form of passive filtration manipulates the subject into self-censorship. So, in the case of public discourse there is active and in private passive filtration. What do they filter?

Any attempt by the subject to reverse its *specular* orientation (upon which the amnion depends) is suspect or taboo. This includes discourse based upon curiosity, inquiry, and possibility (*Möglichkeit*). Learning from failed attempts to suppress thought signs in historic totalitarian societies, the hegemony uses a positive approach. It *injects* its symbolic structure into the discourse of its content on every level. The superstructure is parental: the hegemony is *le grand Autre*, the Father, the Law. The subject is the child. The amnion is the mother, the womb (matrix). The discourse has one message repeated *ad nauseum*: abdicate. (The primary sub discourses include buy, consume, believe, vote, and belong). It is as relentless as water wearing down stones in a stream. Of the totalitarian societies Nazi Germany was the most successful in this respect because it repressed one species of discourse while providing exciting incentives to participate in the preferred one. This example the hegemony and its corporate overlords have found most encouraging. Using the ruse of democracy with its ritual of self-determination, the hegemony has managed to lure the subject into compulsory participation in its financial casino. Addicted to this form of gambling and with a seemingly endless source of borrowing when it inevitably loses, the subject perpetuates the consumer culture which keeps the amnion inflated and expanding. Homeostasis (with the occasional embarrassing crashes) is maintained through perpetuating the modicum of self-determination. This modicum consists of the usurped sovereignty of the far-off other in the form of cheap goods. The hegemony's political economy inevitably survives its frequent crashes now built into its business cycle thanks to the subject's lack of consciousness regarding cause and effect. Were it not for the subject's turning-to itself in the form of abdication of its sovereign identity the amnion would be impossible. Rather than develop (build) out of the mirror stage the subject chooses to help build it into a Crystal Palace of conspicuous consumption. The first great scale model of the amnion was the Crystal Palace built in 1851 in London's Hyde Park for the occasion of the Great Exhibition. Formed of steel and glass, it resembled a bubble. It initially contained the wonders of technology capitalism had brought to the service of (Western bourgeois) mankind.

The subject enters the Crystal Palace of the amnion when it falls into a state of *speculation*. In other words, the thought process become specular; its referent is no longer the *thingness* of things or the *otherness* of the Other. This form of introspection is also known as solipsism. To be clear, Peirce does not consider the act of introspection to be what in modern psychology is part of the process of self-discovery. Rather, it is a turning *from* the transcendental object and *to* the reflection of the subject. As such, the psyche of the subject ceases engaging in *abductive reasoning*. It lacks the objectivity for such inquiry. In the modern sense, its new self is the digital homunculus formed from the aggregate of the telemetric data harvested from by the subject's gadgetry. This "self" is not conscious; it is a crystallized fossil (perhaps to mix metaphors) the subject regards as the sign of itself. This digital self-*injects* into the subject's psyche now exposed by abdication through the hypnosis of the frequency of inductive and deductive transmissions from the core discourse of the amnion. Injection is not to be considered a predatory act on the part of the hegemony and its corporate overlords, however. The subject is *completely and entirely responsible* for making the choice to abdicate just as any sovereign would be. In fact, we can consider the amnion, the hegemony, and their corporate overlords to be entirely innocent of this abdication. It is easy to point to the hegemony's real coercion, manipulation, baiting, and even entrapment and cry foul; the fact that the subject never does belies the truth of this statement. Rather, the subject cries out for more. It votes another and another and another and another regime of precisely the same overlords into the greatest positions of power over its happiness and even life and death. It does this with full awareness (consciousness is not necessary for this process) that nothing ever changes. That is because it does not want anything to change. It has abdicated and that is that. The thought of *not* abdicating, of facing bare life, of plunging into the horror vacui of the sublime is so terrifying to the subject that it fears it more than death. How? Because its requires effort, will, uncertainty, and bravery whereas death only requires being - something the subject already has by default.

That it is the subject's will (hence abdication) is the good news. It means that the subject 1) has the choice not to abdicate and 2) once having abdicated the subject can find the path to a new state of sovereignty in what Hegel calls the Second Negation - or the negation of the negation of the self. It is true that there is the possibility that it is not volitional; this we find in the wretched circumstances of the far-off other who lacks the resources to resist and is therefore put into the position, one way or another, or either relenting or dying. So it is possible for there to be a predatory abdication or what might be characterized as an offer which cannot be refused. But this is the exception in a state where it is possible to maintain the amnion. Furthermore, there are more isolated states where a religious or ideological hegemony has adopted the ethical aesthetic of abdication to the belief system rather than the subject's essentially financial Faustian bargain. However, these states are often religious or ideological authoritarian regimes where refusal to submit is seen as treason or blasphemy and are punishable by death. We are concerned with the subject in the phenomenological state of speculation where the turning-to the self from the Other is what could be called a volitional act. Both *speculation* (in the technical sense) and introspection use the root "spec," meaning "to look," from the Latin *specere*. In this state, the "feeling," as Pierce calls it, of the sublime is impossible. We become cut off from the source of life with all of its horror, for it is death itself that makes life possible. The inverted assumption in the specular state is that it is life that makes death possible. Death is a negation, as is the sublime. We seem to possess life, with science affirming it in the form of medicine as a product and service vended to us as the consumer or subject of possession. This illusion makes it seem that death is only the absence of life, when in fact it is life itself, as negation, for without death, life cannot come into being (*le devenir*), bursting into its phenomenal *res extensa*.

We can thank science for showing that the border between life and death cannot be drawn with a pencil. As we extend our perception deeper into space we see that more things exist. But they could hardly be called life. If we look at our surroundings, we see that it is populated with things that are as "dead" as a distant star millions of light years away in the phenomenological sense. Astrophysics even tells is that the stuff around us is made from the same elements as the stuff of deep space: cosmic dust as it were. We know that in the time it takes for the light to reach our eyes from a star in the existential sense it may no longer "exist" (though its light does exist as a member of the class of phenomena). But as with all members of this class, it is perceived using the telemetry of our empirical senses which always includes a kind of latency between the reality of the object and the machinery of the subject which, like a signal through a wire, has a certain amount of resistance to the transmission of the existential object of reality – in this case a star. While the scale is vastly different by ratio, we are generally ignorant of the fact that everything we see or hear, or even touch, only represents that thing, transmitted through a medium – space, air, reflected light, and then along nerves to the brain. As such, the difference between the latency of a light year and the speed of light that all electromagnetic waves are limited to no matter what the distance is only a matter of *ratio*, which is meant here as not only the difference between one thing and another (e.g. a magnitude of 2:1 or 2^{10}:1), but also the rational intellect which is able to divide them into differences, or discrete phenomena. With our native sense of time it seems instantaneous, but in the objective world there is no ruler for ratio that is not relative. Measurement is therefore itself a kind of ratio. *Big:small, up:down, in:out, high:low, good:bad* and so on are all then measured against the rule (law), which itself is no more of an absolute than the King's foot or a statutory brick. The time it takes for light to bounce off of the objects around us, find the pupil, swim through the aqueous fluid of our eyes, strike the retina, and be transmitted to the brain as electrochemical impulses might as well be millennia or a nanosecond; without the human measure of relative units of time, there is no difference between a light year and a nanosecond in the objective sense. We might even go as far to say that without human measure there is no time at all. Qualitative time is not what we consider to be "proper" time in that it cannot be used in machinery. Therefore, all time to be considered as such must be quantified. But when we look at how our experience orders itself we see that apart from our role in the prosecution of the prerogatives of machinery we naturally fall into – and prefer – qualitative time which, by the quantitative definition is no time at all. When we think of geological or even astronomical time then, as Keats says, "Of the wide world I stand alone, and think / Till love and fame to nothingness do sink."

What we *know* is that there is an *event* which must occur in a space we may call a state. We often do not even know we are thinking of time this way when we say, "She was in such a state" or that someone is in a certain "state of mind." In that state something occurs; what occurs is an event, mental or physical but if the latter then always both. But since these states arise of themselves we can say that they are outside the realm of temporal predictability. If we apply a burning match to a pile of dry hay the chances are strong that it will burn to the point that if it did not we would think we had witnessed a phenomenon the probability of which is "astronomical." On the other hand, our *a posteriori* our observations of events, usually in the form of analysis, give us a sense that this discrete event "arose from nothing" and sank back into the abyss. This is particularly the case when someone "dies suddenly." But like the absurdity of something happening "as soon as possible" – which is how everything always happens because if it were not possible then it would not happen – we all "die suddenly." The idea that someone experiences a slow death belongs to the romance of torture. If we are to consider time seriously enough to draw inference, then we must consider the state-space in which events occur and what their logical dynamics portend for the apprehension of reality. By bringing inquiry, curiosity, and possibility to the ratio of similarities and differences we are able to draw statistical inference.

What we infer from this, then is that everything "happens" in this space with no ratio between what is happening in this space at any one time and what has happened. In such a discrete-time state space an event *transits* to the next (future) state (T1) where its *probability distribution* depends upon the current state *it is in* and not on the series of previous events. The chain of cause and effect, which is our tacit thought paradigm when we consider an event, is at best a form of the *post hoc ergo propter hoc* fallacy. It is infinitely more comforting to think that what we are doing now will determine the future in the way we always hope it will when visiting a soothsayer. In this way we construct a narrative with our ego as the protagonist. The person who loses his story is considered "lost" or worse "crazy." Some simply and for no apparent reason lose the will to maintain their egoistical drama. Rather than choose to abdicate they choose to fall through the bottom of the amnion into a bohemian Underclass all its own and perhaps, alas, all but extinct. In French, this character is called *le flâneur,* much admired of the Symbolists and Surrealists. According to *Le Grand dictinonaire universel,* the many contributions of this period to the lore of *le flâneur* include *Physiologie du flâneur* by M. Louis Huart, *Journal d'un flâneur* by Jules Noriac, and *Le flâneur des deux rives* by Guillaume Apollinaire. The phenomenon is not confined to the precincts of Paris. There is also *La vie de Walt Whitman, le flâneur magnifique* by Cameron Rogers . In Nineteenth Century Paris there was just the right Zeitgeist for such a phenomenon to emerge. But after all required to survive (food and shelter in particular) became commodities to be traded as futures and other derivatives in the financial markets, the cost of living increased beyond the means of any self-respecting *flâneur* to survive. The animal lapsed into extinction along with other *Fauvists.* Baudelaire wrote the essential encomium of this exotic creature (in French; it's hard to translate):

> "Ô belles soirées ! Devant les étincelants cafés des boulevards, sur les terrasses de glaciers en renom, que de femmes en toilettes voyantes, que d'élégants "flâneurs " se prélassent !" (Villiers de L'Isle-Adam, Contes cruels, "Fleurs de ténèbres.")

(We will see more of Baudelaire later – his words bears repeating.) Balzac, in *Physiologie du mariage,* describes the habitat and mode of this unique being. "*Oh! errer dans Paris! adorable et délicieuse existence! Flâner est une science, c'est la gastronomie de l'oeil.*" ("Oh wander in Paris! Adorable and delicious existence! Strolling is a science, it is the gastronomy of the eye!") For Balzac to be a *flâneur* is to stroll (*flâner*) taken to the heights of a science where one sees but is unseen. A complex word, *flâner* also has the meaning of to lounge and loiter. It is movement in stillness. As Jones Very says in his poem "The Hand and Foot," "I mark them full of labor all the day, / Each active move made in perfect rest." There is no compulsion to move from the past to the future. One exists only in the moment, at which time reality gives up its secrets to the "scientist" of observation. This mode is not far from what Keats describes as that of negative capability where there is no "irritable reaching after fact and reason" to hinder observation. The sublime demands as much. To be conscious of it one must be in a sovereign state of bare life. This is only possible in the eternal present through hyper awareness of what the present contains in its otherness and thingness through apprehension of the transcendental object. Apprehension precedes comprehension, which is the getting-to-know. This movement from apprehension to comprehension is a form of digestion or what Balzac calls *la gastronomie de l'oeil.*

As we have seen, there is a significant distinction between the Zeitgeist and the Weltgeist. The former is temporal. It changes like the weather so that it seems "warm days shall never cease," as Keats says in "To Autumn," only to fall to winter where one wonders if leaves will ever again appear on trees, flowers bloom, and frogs call from the ponds and marshes. The latter is timeless; it is what it always is. It never was or will be. As an agent of the sublime it stalks the earth searching for the right time to assert itself. It is the Spiritus Mundi bringing on the Zeitgeist of the Apocalyptic, yielding to a momentary calm, then spiraling back into angry thunderheads of war. Why? The poetics of this process follow a logic based on the exactly the opposite of the narrative discourse of the ego. The reason is that the ego's sole goal is the preservation of itself as an immortal entity – even if that activity leads to the mortification and death of the body (ironically). The ego will drive itself into religious ecstasies by scourging its flesh and the flesh of others. It will throw itself into the *auto-da-fé* of martyrdom. It will plunge into the maelstrom of battle seeking glory. It will do all of this to achieve its own immortality – as if the body it has dragged unwillingly through life as its vehicle were a burden on the absolute immortal purity of its being as *cogito.*

What the ego cannot understand is that the macro events of the Weltgeist do not follow from the narrative of the history of those events. The event is unique, discrete, and only predicts (most often in the form of a fraction) the next event. It is a chain of events where each link is dependent upon the one before it – *but upon no other event*. Each event is unique and discrete. If this were not so, we would be able to predict everything. It would mean that all probability would always be set at 1.0. We would know the exact time and date of our death. If the probability of an event is anything less than 1.0 then anything can happen. We must accept that even if there is probability of .90 this does not mean that therefore this is the only possible outcome. We see this phenomenon in the outcome of elections and sporting events. A lottery, though, is not at all dependent upon any previous state. If a person bets each week on a different number (or the same number) the probability remains the same: 1 in (n), where (n) is how many tickets sold. We know life is not like this. Predicting the outcomes of our actions is more like predicting the weather.

For example, we can predict the weather with a certain probability based on a number of variables. We will use only one: the previous state. If it is cloudy one day the chance that the next day will be sunny increases. But the dependency of the state is between the first state and the next and no other state. Again, if this were not so then we would always have a probability of 1 in predicting the weather, the winner of a sporting event, or the outcome of an election. In an election even exit polls are often the reverse of the outcome because out of many polling places only a few can be covered. Therefore, all of the polling places that were not covered add a significant variable to the outcome of the event. Everyone knows from experience that official weather predictions are accurate enough to be useful otherwise they would not exist. However, sometimes they are grievously wrong and death and destruction result. The best example is a tornado. While it is as much of a weather phenomenon as clouds, rain, and sun, a specific tornado is almost impossible to predict. The best we can do is give a "tornado warning" which nevertheless leaves victims defenseless against the actual phenomenon once it hits.

So let us look at the difference between the dependency of the first state on the state before it. We will see if it is possible that any state *other than the next* state can depend upon the first state. For example we will use weather. This chart is based upon the proposition that "The more cloudy days the greater the probability that the next day will be sunny." Note that "1 cloudy day" equals a probability of 1.0 (100%) of being cloudy:

a) 1 cloudy day = a probability of .10 sun next day.
b) 2 cloudy days = a probability of .20 ...
c) 3 cloudy days = a probability of .50 ...
x) And so on … until the sunny day 1.0

The increments vary depending on how many days we are talking about. In an area known for a "rainy season" it may be 100 days; but each day increases the probability of sun anyway as the season draws to an end – *because the season cannot go on forever as a permanent state*. Each state *depends* upon the previous state, so that they relate to each other as a → b (if a then b). We can also express this as 1 → x, where x is the next state. Any state is always the first state. This is the mechanism maintaining the present as the only possible state. It relegates "the past" and "the future" to the realm of the Imaginary. It is like a relay race: each first state passes on the baton of being the first state to the next state. But we cannot say a → c or even if a → x. Why? Because it is not possible, or even allowable in this universe, to say that some state which is not the next state was dependent upon the first state of the next state. How can (c) depend upon (a) if there is a probability of .25 there will be sun in state (b) because state (b) depends upon state (a) and no other state? Or put another way, if there is sun in state (b) then we can say that the process is stochastic. We did not know (which would mean a probability 1.0) that there would be sun. Therefore, in any other first state the only state dependent upon it is the next state. Since it was more likely to rain in state (b), our presumed clairvoyance is confounded. Part of the problem is that when we look back on a chain of events we superimpose a narrative which makes them seem predictable and orderly. Again, though, this just leads us into the *post hoc ergo propter hoc fallacy*.

Nevertheless, we act, think, and speak as if (c) or any other state after (c) can be predicted by (a). If this were not so no one would go to college or get married saying "till death do we part" while knowing that the chance of parting before death is .50 or some other fraction. If the chance of parting before death were 1.0 no one would bother getting married. Still, the solemn vows taken in the presence of clergy in the house of God with the imprimatur of the state presume *a priori* that the probability of staying married is 1.0. As for college, one enters higher education with the idea that by doing so one "will get a good job" afterward. The propaganda of these institutions repeat this meaningless (and dishonest) phrase relentlessly. Never mind that "a good job" is so vague as to be undefinable. If one enters college with the sole ambition to learn, will it be the getting-to-know, or the knowing-of of the knowing-more? Are institutions really the best places for the getting-to-know? How can the human mind stand such contradiction and insensibility? Asleep in the dream of the amnion of the Imaginary anything is possible. So why think about probability? It we did, life as we know it would falter and halt. Civilization would be revealed for the con game that it has become. Chaos would reign. We would return to barbarism where only the fittest survive. The madness of civilization is that it is based on the ludicrous idea that if we just ignore the probability of reality it will go away. Is not marriage considered the pillar of civilization? And yet it is a ridiculous charade of insincerity and inevitable unhappiness. The danger is that reality is awfully stubborn. In fact, like a spoiled child it is downright vindictive when ignored. The more we ignore bare life, the farther from it we get, the deeper we dig into the *Genuss* of the amnion, the greater the probability that the sublime will forcefully intrude upon our paradise in the form of the Four Horsemen of some dreadful apocalypse. This is not a metaphysical proposition. Rather, it is simply the outcome of our activity which we only conscious of when it brings disaster.

Therefore, one cannot plan for the future in such a way that one can predict its outcome – no matter how sophisticated the modeling. Again, this is a discrete process wherein the next future state depends upon the present state but not the chain of previous states. When we look back on that chain we imagine there is a cause-and-effect story to them similar to a fairy tale. This story is not the property of those events. It issues strictly from the imagination of the subject, or even from the strictures of society and religion. The whole apparatus of sinning is a good example. The dogma states that if you sin and do not repent then you will go to Hell. This chain of events is highly speculative. Yet it is delivered with absolute certainty. The probability of going to Hell if one does not repent for one's sins is 1.0. Only in the imagination can such a realm exist where that kind of probability reigns. Life is a stochastic process. If there were a Hell, it would be interesting to see who ends up there. Dante did an excellent job of populating Hell with those who likely believed they were bound for Heaven. As a stochastic process each event is discrete or, in other words, predictably unpredictable. What this means for discourse is that any narrative except an *ex post facto* narrative is inherently fictitious. Nevertheless the ego perceives it as its own "true" story. It bases all of the subject's decision and behavior upon this imaginary story. While it may derive enormous comfort and convenience by doing so, it sets itself up for ever-repeating disasters because it is out of step with reality. The discrete events of the random walk are seen as chapters in the ego's heroic story either determined by Fate (Hitler made this fatal error), God, society, or one's own will. When in fact all that can be predicted about the future is that it is unpredictable. Again, this is good news. It means that we are not doomed to plod through the same dreary script we assigned ourselves or were assigned unless this is the path we choose. And even so, this path will and must be interrupted by the stochastic nature of reality. Even of, hypothetically, we were able to live out every detail in God's plan for us – without Him working in his infamously mysterious ways – we would still have to face the death of the ego. Nevertheless we would regale ourselves with fairy tales about an afterlife in which the ego persists with all its petty desires, flaws, delusions, and solipsism. The sublime abhors a narrative. Keats, Shelley, and Byron, the most sublime of poets, found their narratives cut far shorter than they would have ever wished. Why are we so surprised when the movie of someone's life seems to end midway through the story? The narrative is a product of the ego regarding itself as a sign of itself. It is reading its own biography while writing its autobiography. The latter is made of wishes and the former of the ego's self-aggrandizement as a celebrity within the context of its self-regard. The ego is its biggest fan. But in a stochastic process there can be no story. We take a random walk through life, buffeted by forces we hardly perceive much less understand. The sovereign individual in the state of bare life sees this. He knows that the present is not a result of the "past" which after all was only a random present identical in every respect to the *present* present. While the next state space is determined by the present state, it is a stochastic process where the present state is determined only by the immediate previous state (first state).

For example, someone is hit and killed by a car. We could say that it happened because the car ran through a red light. The driver ran the light because he was distracted by his gadget. Then we can trace the chain one state further and say that gadgets are causing drivers to be distracted, and so on. But what does any of this have to do with the *victim's* story? If it had continued, she was going to have children, get promoted at her job, and maybe grow old into her golden years. Soon after such a death we console ourselves by integrating the random event into a new story: little did she know that "being hit by a car" was the grand conclusion of her biography and autobiography. Every soldier in a firefight expects to fight another day, to return home to his family, and to parade down Main Street with a chest full of medals on Memorial Day with gray hair. What, then, is the logic of the chain of life's discrete events in the sublime? In this temporal sequence the probability of random phenomena in any event is always less than 1.0. While we can predict that the phenomena will be random with each iteration of event in the chain, we cannot predict what those phenomena will be based on any phenomena we have seen from previous states except the one immediately before the present. We can predict the probability distribution of the next state from the current state, but not from any other previous state since the state immediately before the present has already expressed itself *as* the present. In other words, its probability (always less than 1.0) is known. The race is over. The candidate has won.

4.2: *Le flâneur*, absurdity, and the sublime

One of the delights of life is continual wonder at the improbability of events. As Aristotle says in *Rhetoric*, "For what is improbable does happen, and therefore it is probable that improbable things will happen. Granted this, one might argue that 'what is improbable is probable'" (p. 27). This is a workable definition of a stochastic process. The significance of it to us here is the ratio of time as we have discussed it; in the sense of *discrete time*, how "long" it takes light to reach the brain as a signal from its source is trivial. Descriptors such as "long," "big," "hot," and so on are relative on such a "great" scale (which is itself relative on the same scale) that they fade into meaninglessness. If this property of time is trivial, then it does not matter if the light takes all eternity to reach the brain? Seizing upon this fact, Andrew Marvell, in "To His Coy Mistress," makes fun of her indecision about his amorous advancements:

> Had we but world enough, and time,
> This coyness, lady, were no crime.
> We would sit down and think which way
> To walk, and pass our long love's day;
> Thou by the Indian Ganges' side
> Shouldst rubies find; I by the tide
> Of Humber would complain. I would
> Love you ten years before the Flood;
> And you should, if you please, refuse
> Till the conversion of the Jews.

My vegetable love should grow
Vaster than empires, and more slow.
An hundred years should go to praise
Thine eyes, and on thy forehead gaze;
Two hundred to adore each breast,
But thirty thousand to the rest;
An age at least to every part,
And the last age should show your heart.
For, lady, you deserve this state,
Nor would I love at lower rate.

In a more somber tone he goes on to say that time in the human scale is limited. There is only so much we can do before we can do no more. In one of the most perverse lines ever written, he reminds her that the longer she waits the more likely that "worms shall try / That long preserv'd virginity ..."

It is simply impossible to appreciate the sublime without this perspective of the infinite relativity of time. We cannot go as far as saying that time "does not exist" because we cannot *prove* that it does not. However, we can say that what we perceive of it is entirely psychological. Not only is this easily proven outside of the clinic through acute observation of ourselves, but it also has a role in the drama of our everyday lives and in the marketplace. Those who produce movies, TV shows, and video games know that what people want is to *forget* time. The forgetting of time is psychological and not phenomenological. During the period of forgetfulness one still ages. Fall turns to winter, and we must face the fact of the human scale of time. Despite this physical evidence, the subject still lusts for a sense of timelessness. It longs for escape from the chains of time and death, for all psychological time is tainted with the stink of death. If there is even the hint of boredom the overstimulated, enervated subject will bounce to the next product that gives it the neural thrill it craves. Not only is this true of products, it is true of jobs, friendships, marriages, and even life itself in the self-destructive person and the suicide.

In the face of the evidence of time but constrained by only feeling it as a psychological phenomenon, we are forced up against the concept of the death of the ego. Says Job in 10:21: "Before I go whence I shall not return, even to the land of darkness and the shadow of death ..." Who, or what, is this "I" that "shall not return"? To the ego it seems improbable that it will die but not impossible. Between the improbable and possible lies an epistemology of alternating bouts of hope and anxiety interpreted variously by sages past and present. There is also the epistemological consideration of what Aristotle calls the probability of *improbability* we perceive through experience and observation. We make take it as a nuisance or a phenomenon of reality which brings us closer to bare life and the sublime. Miguel de Unamuno, in *The Tragic Sense of Life*, quotes Tertullian's assessment of the verifiability of the probability of Christ's resurrection: "*et sepultus resurrexit, certum est quia impossibile est!*" ("and he was buried and rose again; it is certain because it is impossible!"), resulting in his credo *quia absurdum!* (p. 68). What he calls "the scandal of the rationalists" is their mania for verifiability which can result in a mathematical affirmation of homeostasis. When an engineer builds a bridge the state wants assurances that there is a probability of 1.0 that it will not fall down. We can escape such demands by saying that there is a .999999999 ... (and so on) chance that it would happen. Such odds, combined with wishful thinking, result in the idea that .999999999 = 1.0. But does anything result in such absolute inevitability? Yes. Biological death. "But" says the savant. "Soon medical science will perform the marvel of reversing the aging gene so that we will live forever." Another canard is that we will be able to transfer our egos to the memories of machines. To be fair, we must give the dreamer a .999999999 ... chance that technology will advance to that point. This is the proposition of the monkey at the typewriter coming up with Shakespeare given an infinite amount of time, or at least until what scientists say is the "end of the universe" in five billion years. After all, we already live three times as long as the average person did only a century or so ago. Such statements, though, consider "us" to be those who live in countries where this is possible because of the standard of living. If we average it out over the world population to include those who have no medical care, decent food, clean water, and live in miasmas of rampant (though alas totally preventable) disease, as humanity we drop down closer to the age of death which has been the norm for human beings for millennia. Technology *always* reaches a plateau, sometimes where its stays. Eyeglasses for instance were invented in 1284 by Salvino d'Armati and yet they are the prevailing form of vision correction today - despite the risky and unpleasant alternatives.

Getting back to Tertullian's *quia absurdum*, we see that stochastic existence tends toward the absurd. It is preposterous that someone in the prime of health, intelligent, cautious, and aware, steps off the curb and gets run over by a bus. How? Why? It is not enough to mutter that is God's will and move on. It is absurd! The point he makes, though, is that the absurd is closer to the truth than rational plausibility. Herein we have the gap between the possible and the probable. It is one thing to verify that a person has cancer. It is another to "wage war" on cancer with the objective of absolutely preventing or curing the disease. Nevertheless, all organizations associated with this quixotic quest state this as their primary goal in all of their propaganda. Why? Because such nonsense allows those who fear death to take comfort in the hope cult of Scientism just as they did (and do) in the hope cult of religion. Also, it keeps the funds coming into the coffers of these organizations indefinitely. Why? Because they will *never* find a "cure." In fact, cures have fallen out of fashion because 1) not much can be cured, and 2) cures interfere with therapeutic use of treatments and drugs which are a perpetual source of revenue for doctors and Big Pharma. While all of this is obvious and jeremiads about it are legion, wishful thinking keeps us hoping that the fairy tales are true. In fact, we now can combine those of Scientism with those of religion, giving the ego a double chance of eternal existence. Even in Hell we live forever. If we give a person the choice between eternal oblivion and an eternal life of suffering in Hell it would be no wonder if he chose the latter. Many regard life here on earth a veil of tears. O Hell where is thy sting! Medical science and technology will enable us to live forever. If that fails, we will go to Heaven. And we are close to this outcome. Maybe even in our own lifetimes! We eagerly await the news story that scientists have found the Fountain of Youth. Meantime, we satisfy ourselves with creams in jars and yoga.

However, following Turtullian's formula of *quia absurdum* maybe we will see something resembling a dramatic increase (50 - 100 percent) in the lifespan of man through medical technology. Although it would likely only be available to the rich and would create a Malthusian catastrophe, still, anything, any circumstance, any catastrophe, any desperate attempt of immortality is fine with the ego. The ego has one objective: to preserve itself at all costs. It will pursue this objective even when it violates the biological imperative of the greater body-mind, which includes the enteric nervous system. It is this compulsion of the ego which strives for the absolute certainty of 1.0. Consequently the ego, which we consider to be the seat of reason when united with intelligence, predicates itself upon a proposition easily proven false. But since the ego operates in narcissistic speculation *to* itself as the sign *of* itself, all its great works should be suspect. "Vanity of vanities, saith the Preacher, vanity of vanities; all is vanity" (Ecclesiastes 1:2). What kind of hyperbole is this? Archaeologists will find a handful of bones and claim that "all of humanity" descended from this prototype.

The amnion, therefore, is dependent upon this sort mass madness of morbid narcissistic orientation to the self all done as a collective activity networked by the black mirror: digital gadgetry held in the hand as the speculum. While the glass of the gadget does reflect the subject's face, it is when the device is in full swing that the magic starts. At that time the full force of Big Data comes roaring back to the subject as the consumer profile that has been gathered in some cases now for decades through the ever-more-refined forms of telemetry these little gizmos are designed for. However, we have already discussed the speculum effect in depth. What I want to bring to the table here now is the summary effect of this speculation. As I have said, the subject is soon rendered into a state of amniosis, head bent at a forty-degree angle and oblivious to the world. But the most profound effect in a mechanics of the psyche is what childhood developmental psychology refers to as formation of a paracosm. In normal psychology a paracosm might be a child's imaginary friend or a special place often providing a sense of object constancy. It may be similar to a child's best doll or object . When the adult subject reverts to an imaginary world generated by the distributed power of the networked devices, with others similarly veiled by avatars and so forth, the result is an abrogation of objective reality. We experience such an abrogation as dreaming during sleep. But this is self-generated and regulated by the autonomous function of the mind. When it is imposed on the subject's mind by consumer interests, government prerogatives, and even bad actors in the form of hackers and confidence artists, the paracosm thus formed becomes a predatory, self-interested entity grotesquely aping the subject's consumer profile to exploit its infantile narcissism, usually found in ages six months to two years. The subject soon enough begins to show infantile behaviors in the cosmos otherwise regulated by Nature and, I venture, God. In this place of Otherness, infantile narcissism has no place except as a maladaptation to society, commonly known as the profile of the sociopath. While not all narcissists are sociopaths, most sociopaths are narcissists. Therefore, once the subject gets inured to its infantile paracosm through the form and function of the digital gadget and its neurological amniosis, it loses its ability to apprehend the transcendental Other. What it takes for media that are social are really a kind of discrete isolate of its own consumer profile. It no longer matters that there is another playing the game, because this other is performing too the same onanistic ritual, digging itself deeper into the amnion.

Social behavior unregulated by intuition is anthrobotic. Painting by artists who lived in dire poverty and seldom sold are bought at auction for tens of millions as investments, cash to sustain a city full of artists for a year. Governments plunge into wars they cannot afford based on vague civil rights crime and claims of weapons of mass destruction but with little verified evidence of either. Law enforcement wastes billions chasing drug lords and yet city streets brim with addicts and illegal drugs. Celebrities who produce nothing with mediocre and have no talent as if they were gods.

Additionally, the Internet chokes with redundant sites of misinformation, vulgar entertainment, and pornography. Whether it is the www, the so-called Deep Web, or even the shadowy Dark Web (.onion, anyone?), the seemingly endless redundancy of content plucked from the other websites and data bases gobbles up bandwidth in an orgy of digital noise, wasted resources, and bits and bytes of nonsense. It is worse thanhavinga dozen identical sets of the encyclopedia in one's home; would it not be wasting precious space and altogether useless, unless one happened to be selling them as inventory? And that is the key to this madness. Much is for sale on the Internet even scholarly research by taxpayer-funded scientists and those long dead whose work is in the public domain but has been captured by a Deep Web vendor of this researched data and is therefore absent from the fewer number of sites offering something (other than malware) for free.

While the myriad examples of man's intractable vanity born of solipsism seem absurd, in fact they are quite pitiful. They are signs of man's weak, impotent state as slave to the hegemony and its corporate overlords. The sublime, however, is absurd because of its stochastic nature. Its prototypes of humanity are le flâneur, Fauvist, mad scientist, ecstatic saint, visionary poet, and inspired engineer. We say not everyone can live up to these prototypes. That is true. Regardless, it is not necessary they do. They often possess possibility of the apprehension of transcendental objects as thingness and the Other. Once they choose abdication over bare life the possibility of apprehension vanishes. If lucky, then they will invoke the wrath of the hegemony which will cast them out of the garden of the amnion into the Underclass where they will discover the hardships of bare life. We can say that when the subject loses its low-wage job, the promissory notes it signed in abdication precipitate excommunication from the amnion. It has tasted, unwillingly, of the tree of the knowledge of good and evil. The fine print on the promissory note says as much regarding conditions which lead to this punishment for the sin of transgression against the ethical aesthetic of the hegemony. Doing the bidding of the hegemony's corporate overlords, the politicians the subject has voted for have put into place draconian laws penalizing the subject for the least violation of these covenants.

What follows is default, foreclosure, repossession, and disenfranchisement. Having lost its good credit rating and job, the subject becomes a pariah in the employment marketplace just as a felon does after leaving prison and therefore must turn back to a life of crime to survive. As the subject falls into the Underclass as an Unfortunate, it joins the Less Fortunates with prison records, no education, no skills, and often a bad attitude. But this is its great fortune! The subject has been released from the prison of the amnion. Though it is on parole, it nevertheless is thrown back upon its own self-determination. Also, it experiences the bare life of the reality of the hegemony's actual social and financial situation. If the hegemony did not have the ability to borrow unlimited funds from its corporate overlords, or print up fiat currency from central banks at will, in its own ritual of abdication the bubble of the amnion would burst along with the financial markets, which is always a danger. (Still, the hegemony shorts the failing markets and profits, while using the profits to buy up assets during the ensuing "fire sale.") During these periods, millions plunge into the Underworld temporarily until the debt system regains its liquidity and start preparation for the next economic crisis. Some wake up, some do not. Some feel liberated from the amnion, others crave reentry into the womb.

The absurdity of the flâneur's position of objective detachment, unlike the grim subjectivity of the specular subject, allows him to see the thingness of things and the objective nature of the Other. It also allows him to remain in society as an *outsider looking in.* He is an intentional misfit, happy not to belong as long as he is permitted to observe. He is too lazy to revolt and too much of a snob to accept the vulgar distractions of the amnion. Gadgets make him feel stupid and cheap. He would rather saunter along the Seine, his hand clutching the silver lion's head of his walking stick, and observe the pageant of humanity without judgment and scorn. What his society considers to be "work" – its frenzied shuffling of papers and pounding of keyboards in suffocating office towers – he considers to be enslavement. He would rather *not* have the money to participate in the amnion. He sees *no* value in rushing around in chariots of metal, glass, and plastic. He finds the billions of hours his compatriots waste surfing the Internet, chatting on social media, staring at distracting entertainment, pleasuring themselves with pornography, and stuffing themselves with junk food to be a kind of deadly crime, an abrogation of the imperative *to be*, the copula of language and the root of the sublime.

What, then, is sublime about absurdity? Atonin Artaud's *First Manifesto of theatre of Cruelty* points to the reality of language as chiefly a collection of primitive "sounds" which allow a far greater range of expression than the rationalist approach to the signs that they are. He understands that most words, particularly abstractions (such as "cruelty") are too often meaningless. Their only use is that they are different from each other and therefore can be used in the complicated sign exchange within a certain context at a certain moment. Once they are detached from context, written or spoken, they lose much of their power. This is particularly obvious in drama where reading the play has little to do with the expressive power of seeing it performed. The same is true of written music. Words by themselves are absurd. Seen this way, they are barnyard grunts which are nevertheless regarded as utterances of great gravity and importance. Armies scurry around killing each other over abstractions of which even their leaders have little understanding. The words for the values the Nazis held so dear are all but forgotten, such as *blute und boden* and *lebensraum*. What do they mean now? And yet it was the core of the *Tausend Jahre deutsches Reich.* Artaud envisions a theatre which takes seriously language's subordination to gesture and sound. He abhors the sanctity of the signifier as a mathematical symbol in the equation of expression. Why cannot the signified itself serve as a mute expression of *das Ding an sich*?

> Here too intervenes (besides the auditory language of sounds) the visual language of objects, movements, attitudes, and gestures, but on condition that their meanings, their physiognomies, their combinations be carried to the point of becoming signs, making a kind of alphabet out of these signs. Once aware of this language in space, language of sounds, cries, lights, onomatopoeia, theater must organize it into veritable hieroglyphs, with the help of characters and objects, and make use of their symbolism and interconnections in relation to all organs and on all levels.

The idea of creating a language of what Artaud calls "hieroglyphs" points to a form of metalanguage expressing *not* the prerogatives of the amnion, but the transcendental object of the Sublime. It is impossible for the hegemony to capture the absurd, the encrypted, the expressive, the artistic, the dramatic, and the *sublime* – for it is the horror vacui, the source of all terror, and the anathema of what the amnion is and represents. Its entertainment consists of horror, death, and terror in compensation for their absence in the drudgery of everyday life the subject prefers over the bravery and ferocity necessary to live under the sublime's Law of the Jungle. For all the razzle-dazzle of their products, generated like sausages in a slaughterhouse, online producers of entertaining and distracting content largely fail to generate anything resembling the "symbolism and interconnections in relation to all organs and on all levels" Artaud consigns to art that is in eternal flux, just as is the universe itself. As the amnion grows, theater wanes, or is consumed by predictable and obnoxious spectacles repeating themselves until the entire population is sick of them and their catchphrases and torch songs. The plays of Shakespeare and great operas are regarded as tourist curiosities, mainly frequented for the funny costumes.

I do not think it is necessary here to belabor the obvious: that what we treasure as classical visual art, music, architecture, subtle and beautiful literature and philosophy, elegant mathematical insights into the nature of the universe, the ineffable expression of a performing artist or actor, the physical beauty of a superb athlete or dancer, or the triumphs of man under great odds to achieve what was thought to be impossible are our ways of communing with the sublime that we intuit as the source of meaning in our otherwise barren existence. But there is no need to look so far and deep into the world to find the sublime; a sunset seen from the dusty window of an urban apartment building might do just as well as a Wagner opera, or the mysterious process of "falling in love" when the world is suddenly transformed into something "so various, so beautiful, so new ..." As I discuss in more depth in the two books following this one in the *Death of the Sublime* series, Nature is the overwhelming, terrifying, all-encompassing source of sublime power. Nature is at all times and under all circumstances infinitely greater than mankind or any of his contrivances. And all of this power belongs to those who are willing to face their greatest terror: the non-being of death, taking full responsibility for the self-determination of their fate. It is also the Abyss, the horror vacui, and what inevitably brings on our death if we are fortunate enough to evade war, accident, or suicide. Every deadly virus is Nature's calling card; every devastating earthquake is Nature shaking off a few fleas; every drought, tornado, hurricane, flood, and volcano is Nature reminding mankind of his insignificant place in a universe saturated with deadly radiation and absent of nearly all he needs for life, poised to intrude upon his little dream of civilization at any time.

The idea that mankind might accidentally "kill" Nature is ludicrous; it is far more capable of wiping out mankind without warning and for no reason except that he happened to be in the way at that time. The modern portrayal in the global mass media and by the political propaganda of the hegemony of Nature as a fragile, elderly, naive, weak, hospice patient on her deathbed, is in itself one of the greatest obstacles for our return to the life of the sublime. It subverts our potential embrace of the Law of the Jungle, the reality of real danger and risk, the personal value of health and strength, the thirst for direct justice sans the government middleman, for personal power and responsibility, for self-determination, and the satisfactions of the desires of the id lying just outside the battlements of civilization. Such a febrile portrayal of Nature preempts our love of ecstatic culture, wild music and dance, spiritual awakening, boundless creativity, and spontaneous invention.

Nature, on the contrary, is our greatest advocate in our return journey to the life of the sublime. Our best hope of doing so lies, first, in regaining our sovereignty, our tribal affinities, our innate ferocity, our capacity for wonder and devotion, and our libidinal potency. The chance of renunciation of the prerogatives of the amnion on any appreciable human scale is almost nil, except for when the orgiastic frenzy of war intrudes into the subject's petty dreamworld of consumerism, comfort, and convenience. War thrusts the sublime upon an unprepared and unwilling population of subjects dependent upon the discretionary largess of the amnion they worship as their Idol, the priests of Scientism who dispense its beneficence and the politicians and media who spin its yarn. However, even an isolated individual in the midst of civilization's most repressive regimes – and they abound today, aided by the digital gadgets and gizmos the subject cannot live without – still has Nature as his advocate, infinitely more powerful than any digital or political contrivance of the ubiquitous Cult of Mediocrity.

Today, however, there is scarcely anything "experimental" in the amnion because the subject just cannot afford it and still keep pace with the demands of membership – mainly the signing of promissory notes – in the hegemony's "illusory community" (Hegel), "illusions of the epoch" (Marx), fly-bottle (Wittgenstein), "technosphere" (Dmitry Orlov), "Matrix" (movie by the same name), Skynet (*Terminator* movies) and so on. The idea is out there. It is adequately expressed in some powerful entertainment such as that mentioned above, literature (Phillip K. Dick comes to mind), and philosophy (e.g. Baudrillard's Simulation and *Simulacra*). But it is clearly *not* of any primary concern to those who either profit from it, or are mired in its endless debt, digital gadgets, conspicuous consumption, comfort and convenience, "progressive" ideology, aggressive financialization, derivatives markets, and virtual interactive electronica. The amnion, as a virtual world of default culture, offers a computer-generated environment where no one can (really) die, everything is provided for at the push of a (virtual) button, government solves all problems, enemies are subdued, sexual partners acquiesce at the click of a mouse, and interpersonal complications and friction are mitigated by (un-) "social media." It is all neatly packaged in devices bought online or in fancy stores that look like temples of worship staffed by priestly pseudo-technologists. The gizmos and gadgets of this trivial world can be turned off, upgraded to the latest "generation," and networked in a timeless, deathless state of infinite consumerism.

Artaud's manifesto may sound *absurd* to the rationalist of language whose goal is to make a better natural language processor. However, that is his *point*. Is his vision any different from our actual semiotic experience of life as meaning, expressed in the physical hieroglyph of the reality that is *not-us*, rather than the twenty-two-minute news cycle? Is it somehow alien to the autonomic encoding of our reality into language so that we may share in the transcendental object of the Other, as the Other does in us (for instance, through poetry and music)? Does it not point to dissolution of the diremption between "I" and "Thou" in our everyday interactions? In such a life, there is no need for the amnion and the abdication of sovereignty required for membership in it. There is a visceral revulsion for the amnion's vulgar default culture and infinite debt. It is not possible for Baudelaire's *le flâneur magnifique* to abdicate, for he is the eternal apostate of the hegemonic order's religion of Scientism. Le flâneur stops psychological time, which is in his control, instead working outside of it where he can see the moment in all of its profound absurdity, realizing that past and future are not places but delusions. The hope-and-wishful-thinking cult of "in the future" is not part of his consciousness. As an existentialist, a fatalist, even a nihilist, he tacitly agrees with Confucius, who says in the *Analects*, "How can I know God when I cannot know man?"

Through indifference, arrogance, political and social disinterest, impulsiveness, disregard for safety and future prospects, non-action, distrust of civilization, and laziness, and uselessness, le flâneur magnifique's presence in the amnion presents a noisome affront to its hegemony. His tacit understanding that the price paid for Being is Non-Being, relegates his perception of time to the present, not the future. He cares little for development of the body. His disordered dress mocks elegance. He needs a good haircut. His "net worth" and credit rating are abysmal. The self, the ego, and the world his mind has defined for itself, are irrelevant to him. He has no choice but to let his libido run free (where possible), caring not for the approbation and ire of the status quo. He rejects the life of robotic production and obedience to civilization's social codes and repressive nomos. He bases his "conduct," as Peirce calls it, on the prerogatives of his innate feelings of wonder, curiosity, interest, and daring experiment. The sublime and the sublime alone is what he lives for, making him a threat to the hegemony and its amnion. His mood is one of perpetual doubt. He even doubts doubt.

We tend to think of le flâneur as an urban creature, sauntering along the Champs Élysées, people watching; but we forget, if we knew about it at all, the brief artistic movement contrived by artists who called themselves *les Fauves* in the early 20th Century in Paris: Fauvism, or the "-ism" of the *fauve*, the wild animal, the feral beast. Their art and especially their unique concept of color lived up to their manifesto; it echoed the aesthetics Picasso and Braque, who saw that what art needed was the gift of the sublime from so-called primitive cultures that, at least during the reign of the Montparnasse artists, had not given it up for the trinkets of European civilization. What they did, then, was bring the terror of the wild into the galleries and salons of Paris. They had the vision to see that without the sublime, which is always feral, life drains from civilization which is not anything other than the people inhabiting it. There is no civilization apart from the people; the artifacts are, again, the *trinkets* and monuments to their vision they left behind from their ambitious or humble daily activity. Always at the Ishtar Gate is the tribal barbarian, the wild beast, the sands of time covering over the works of Ozymandias. The terror of being alone with nature, or of being deep in woods with the haunting signals of wildlife echoing among the trunks of trees rising into the gloom of the nighttime canopy like the columns of the Duomo in Milano, conquers one with the *feeling* of the sublime. Nature, portrayed in the media as a sick, old, dying mother, is in fact more powerful than mankind can even conceive. In one day the estimated fifty-million-year reign of the dinosaurs was wiped out forever by a big meteor. Hurricanes are charged with more power than many atomic bombs put together. One bolt of lightning is five times hotter than the sun. An earthquake can submerge the landscape under water or destroy a city in one minute. Tornados routine ly wipe out whole towns in fifteen minutes. The Mariana Trench, an underwater canyon, is 36,000 feet deep, about the maximum altitude of a passenger jet, and filled with life forms we know little about. Oceanographers say we know more about the surface of the moon than the bottom of the sea. Therefore, nature, like war, is indifferent, brutal, powerful, unfathomable, and deadly. Unlike war, though, *it cannot be stopped* from doing whatever it will, making it far more terrible. The trivialization of nature by the media and progressives is a psychological reaction to their fear of it. They cannot admit that they are nothing and nature is everything; and that is how the matter will remain. Between war and nature, the puny human has little chance of being master of the universe. At least not today. But of course, "in the future" it will, given enough "progress," says Scientism.

Without self-determination and doubt, the chance of the renunciation of the prerogatives of the amnion on any appreciable human scale is almost nil, except for when the orgiastic frenzy of total war intrudes upon the petty dreamworld of consumerism, comfort, convenience, and the delusion of medical immortality. Natural disaster, too, is an agent of the terror of the sublime, when it is brought on by nature itself and not anthropogenesis, which is rare, improbable, and always localized. In contrast to nature, is the amnion of digital networks that has swallowed whatever had been expressed in Western (and now Eastern) culture that still had the radiance and life of the sublime about it. There have been many attempts to describe the amnion since it began to be recognized as such with the rise of industrialization and mass communication. Some include Hegel's "illusory community," Marx's "illusions of the epoch," Wittgenstein's "fly bottle," dystopias such as Orwell's Oceania and Butler's *Erewhon* (Nowhere, or Utopia), Dmitry Orlov's "technosphere," the Matrix in the movie(s) by the same name, Skynet in the *Terminator* movies, and so on. We may even go back so far as Plato's *Republic* — a familiar amnion of nightmarish proportions (though well meant).

The idea of preferring not to accept the Imaginary of the amnion as reality is out there, and has been for longer than anyone today has been alive. But it is clearly *not* of primary concern to those who either profit from it, or are mired in its endless debt, digital gadgets, conspicuous consumption, comfort and convenience, progressive ideology, aggressive financialization, derivatives markets, and virtual interactive electronica who can no longer escape its gravitational force. The amnion, as a virtual world of default (unintentional) culture, offers a simulacrum of reality where no one really dies, everything is provided for at the push of a virtual button, government solves all imaginary problems, enemies are violently, or magically subdued, vicarious sexual partners out of the subject's league say yes at the click of a mouse. Interpersonal complications and romantic frictions are mitigated by "defriending" the discarded friends and lovers in the sterile environment of social media platforms. It is all neatly packaged in devices bought online, or in fancy stores that look like temples of worship, staffed by priestly pseudo-technologists, as if they were the who are just hired hands. The complex gizmos and gadgets of this trivial world can be loaded with software, upgraded, networked, but not ignored; they offer a timeless, deathless state of infinite consumerism responsive to our every *twinge*, as Lacan would put it — for a price. If this offer of eternal comfort, convenience, and medical immortality were only true, I might have had to rethink this book, since, at least, the customer is getting what was pitched. Caveat emptor! The lure is so great for this return to the infantile and even fetal state that we are willing to get into any amount of debt, even if it means mortgaging our future, to have what is being sold to us by the corporate fasces, even though we are aware that there are better values to have in life.

Who, then, is this character who prefers *not* to sacrifice his self-determination for these empty promises? Who is this Bartleby, this *flâneur magnifique* of Baudelaire, this Ideal Observer of Smith and Hume? In a state of what Hegel calls the achievement of freedom through the "labor of the negative," the horror vacui of le flâneur's *negative capability* (Keats) swallows him whole like Jonah's whale. Application of Hegel's Second Negation, or the negation of the negation of our abdicated self-determination, depends upon *doubt* of what one has come to accept about oneself as a subject, a serf, even a slave, through the system of debt, promissory notes, and financialization. Through a willful and self-directed process of what Peirce calls *retroduction* (abduction)—following the chain of logic of an accepted proposition back to its start to test its truth-value — we begin to turn our doubt into thought and action. First, though, we must understand what it means to test the verisimilitude of a proposition or statement, including the many in this book (none of which I present as anything more than my opinion, save the tautologies). Next, it is critical that we doubt the amnion's promise of eternal comfort, convenience, and medical immortality, seeing it for the illusory, and deadly ruse it is.

Once one doubts in this way, one begins to *negate the negation* of one's self-determination upon which the amnion and the hegemony depend. At the same time, the amnion begins to reject you, often in a rather painful and brutal way, I need not list them. It must be worth it to suffer these humiliations. The brave, the conscious, then witness their umbilicus to the amnion severed by the exertion of their free will, if they are not burned at the stake first. At the same time, one enters, by default, into the company of those whom the amnion and its interests, near and far, large and small, seeks to grind into oblivion before any further damage can be done to the authoritarian imago of their fasces by the spectacle of apostacy.

But where would you rather be when the illusion of the amnion is pitched suddenly into the sublime of total war, or nature brings about the next cataclysm? Such events inevitably occur within one's lifetime. Their cycle is typically within the natural span of human life. Therefore, the umbilicus is severed *anyway* by default rather than will. But if it is by default, one is left without the self-determination needed to guide one out of the resulting chaos. It is necessary to develop the spiritual, intellectual, emotional, and cognitive resources to turn such events into an opportunity for liberation from the fasces of the corporate hegemony.

Would you rather have already adapted to the abyss of the sublime as the source of life's meaning and beauty when at last it arrives on the scene to reclaim its territory, or would you rather flee from it in terror of the death you will not be able escape anyway, no matter what your credit rating happens to be? It is not necessary to be an iconoclast, unless that icon is *the narcissistic imago of oneself* reflected in the black mirror of the amnion's ubiquitous digital gadget, head inclined at a forty-five degree angle in obedience to the will of the fasces. The sublime is the apprehension of the transcendental object, without which we are not truly alive but trapped in a state of amniosis, unborn. It is not necessary to put technology down; it is necessary to pick doubt up, however inconvenient and uncomfortable it may be, and embrace the truth that one day we shall be no more. (ώώώ)

BIBLIOGRAPHY

A note about this bibliography. Works mentioned for which no page numbers are cited in the text (for good reason) generally do not have specific editions and publications described here, such as Plato's *Republic*. Where there is specific quotation, there will be some citation (such as chapter, verse, or section). This is true also for literature which can be found anywhere (e.g. online), as well as quotes from the King James Bible, though book and verse are given. Sources of commonly found poems are not listed. "Shakespeare" will do as a reference in the text along with the name of the play, act, and scene. Throughout the text the last name of prominent figures and authors is given without the first name, such as Lincoln and Hitler. All quotations are cited in text. References to popular works that can be found anywhere (online) and in uncountable editions are not listed or cited to reduce academic clutter. Where possible, I've tried to use original editions (such as Burke's 1789 edition). Where it matters, I indicate translator.

Albran, Kehlog. (1981). *The Profit Kehlog Albran: Albran's Serial.* Price/Stern/Sloan.

Arendt, Hannah and Amos Elon. (2006.) *Eichmann in Jerusalem: A Report on the Banality of Evil.* Penguin Classics.

Aristotle. *Poetics.* (1979.) Malcolm Heath, trans. Penguin Classics; Reprint edition.

Artaud, Antonin "Theatre of Cruelty (First Manifesto)."

Auden, W. H. (1948.) *The Age of Anxiety: A Baroque Eclogue.* Series: *W.H. Auden: Critical Editions.* Princeton University Press; (27 February 2011).

Augustine. (388.) "de Moribus Ecclesiae Catholicae." ("On the Morals of the Catholic Church.")

Balzac, Honoré de. (2017.) *Physiologie du mariage.* Independently published (20 May).

Barlow, Nora ed. (1958.) *The Autobiography of Charles Darwin 1809-1882.* With the original omissions restored. Edited and with appendix and notes by his grand-daughter Nora Barlow. London: Collins.

Baudelaire, Charles. *Villiers de L›Isle-Adam, Contes cruels, Fleurs de ténèbres.*

Berman, Marshall. (1963.) "Freedom and Fetishism." *Adventures in Marxism*, Verso, 1999.

Burke, Edmund. (1789.) Chapter I: "On the Principle of Utility" of *An Introduction to the Principles of Morals and Legislation.*

Burke, Edmund. (1756.) "Philosophical Enquiry [sic] into the Origin of our Ideas of the Sublime and Beautiful."

Carroll, Lewis. (1871.) *Through the Looking Glass.*

Chomsky, Noam. (1956.) "Three Models for the Description of Language." *Theory*, Vol. 2, No. 3, Nov.

Christodoulou, G.N. (1986.) *The Delusional Misidentification Syndromes.* Karger, Basel.

Darwin, Charles. (1859.) *The Origin of Species by Means of Natural Selection.*

Debraye, Henry. (1913.) "*Vie de Henri Brulard*, [par] Stendhal. Publiée intégralement pour la première fois d'après les manuscrits de la Bibliothèque de Grenoble.

Descartes, Renee. (1637.) *Discourse on Method.*

Dewey, John. (1910). *How We Think*. D.C. Heath & Co. Flaubert, Gustav. (1980.) *Letters 1830-1857*. Belknap Press.

Freud, Sigmund. (2000, 2007, 2010.) Complete Works (CW). Ivan Smith, All Rights Reserved. PDF copy: Holy Books. (Quotations and citations from volumes below are taken from the Smith online collection named above.)

Freud, Sigmund. (1930.) *Civilization and its Discontents. CW*, Smith.

Freud, Sigmund. (1900.) *Interpretation of Dreams. CW*, Smith.

Freud, Sigmund. (1939.) *Moses and Monotheism. CW*, Smith.

Friedland, Paul. (2012). *Seeing Justice Done: The Age of Spectacular Capital Punishment in France.* Oxford University Press.

Hacking, Ian. (1976.) *Logic of Statistical Inference*. Cambridge University Press; Revised edition.

Hacking, Ian. (1975.) *Why Does Language Matter to Philosophy?* Cambridge University Press.

Hammermeister, Kai. (2002). *The German Aesthetic Tradition.* Cambridge University Press.

Hawthorne, Nathaniel. (1853.) "Bartleby the Scrivener."

Hegel, G.W.F. (1967.) *Phenomenology of Mind.* J.B. Baille, trans. Harper Torchbooks.

Hegel, G.W.F. (1977.) *Phenomenology of Spirit.* A.V. Miller, trans. Oxford University Press.

Heidegger, Martin. (2000). *Being and Time*. John Macquarrie & Edward Robinson (trans.). London: Blackwell Publishing, Ltd.

Hemingway, Ernest. (1938. 1995.) "The Gambler the Nun and the Radio." *The Short Stories of Ernest Hemingway*. Simon and Schuster.

Hobbes, Thomas. *Leviathan*. (1651). Andrew Crooke, at the Green Dragon in St. Paul's Church-yard.

Hurst, William J. (2014). *Modern Psychoanalysis*, 39(1):38-55. "The Repetition Compulsion; the Repetition Automatism; the Insistence of the Signifying Chain."

Jaynes, Julien. (2000.) *The Origin of Consciousness in the Breakdown of the Bicameral Mind.* Mariner Books.

Jung, C.G. *Psychological Types.* (1976.) The Collected Works of C. G. Jung, Vol. 6. (Bollingen Series XX.)

Kant, Immanuel. (1998.) *Critique of Pure Reason.* Edited and trans. by Paul Guyer and Allen W Wood. Cambridge University Press.

Keats, John. "On Negative Capability: Letter to George and Tom Keats," (21, ?27 December 1817).

King, Stephen. (2010.) *Danse Macabre*. Gallery Books; Reprint edition.

Klemperer, Victor. (2013.) *Lingua Tertii Emperii (LTI): A Philologist's Notebook (The Language of the Third Reich).* London: Bloomsbury.

Kropotkin, Peter. (2010). N.F. Dryhurst, trans. *The Great French Revolution 1789-1793.* Red and Black Publishers.

Laplace, P. (1951, 1820). *"Essai Philosophique sur les Probabilités,"* introduction: *Théorie Analytique des Probabilités.* Paris: V Courcier; repr. F.W. Truscott and F.L. Emory, trans. New York: Dover.

LaVey, Anton Szandor. (1969.) *The Satanic Bible.* Avon Books.

Leibniz, G.W. *Monadology.* (2017.) CreateSpace Independent Publishing Platform.

Lyotard, Jean-Francois. *The Inhuman.* (1991.) Geoffrey Bennington and Rachel Bowlby, trans. Stanford University Press.

Minger, J.D. "Jacques Lacan: Kierkegaard as a Freudian Questioner of the Soul avant la lettre," in *Kierkegaard's Influence on the Social Sciences*, Ed. Jon Stewart, Aldershot: Ashgate, 2011. 195-216.

Moles, Abraham A. (2011.) Forward to Vilem Flusser's *Brazilian Vapyroteuthis Infernalis*. Atropos Press.

Morelly, Etienne-Gabrielle. (1755). *Code de la Nature.*

Neitzsche, Frederick. (2012.) *Nietzsche's Notebooks in English: A Translator's Introduction and Afterward*. Trans. Daniel Fidel Ferrer. Opensource upload to Archive.org by D.F. Ferrer.

Orwell, George. (1945.) *Animal Farm.*

Pape, Helmut. (1995.) "Abduction and the Topology of Human Cognition." Review of Ansgar Richter, *Der Begriff der Abduktion* bei Charles S. Peirce. Europäische Hochschulshriften 20, Vol. 453, Frankfurt a. M., Berlin. Verlag Peter Lang.

Peirces, Charles Sanders. (1966.) *Selected Writings.* (*Values in a Universe of Chance*). Dover Publications, Inc. New York.

Poe, Edgar Allen. (1845.) "The Descent into the Maelstrom."

Rousseau, Jean Jacques. (1762.) *Du contract social.*

Saussure, Ferdinand de. (1959). *General Course in Linguistics*. Wade Baskin, trans. The Philosophical Library, Inc.

Schmitt, Carl. (2005.) *Political Theology: Four Chapters on the Concept of Sovereignty.* Trans. George Schwab, University of Chicago Press.

Smyth, William Henry. (1920, 1921). *Technocracy*. Reprinted from the *Gazette*, Berkeley, California.

Spichal, Slavko. (2002.) *Principles of Publicity and Press Freedom*. Series: Critical Media Studies: Institutions, Politics, and Culture. Rowman & Littlefield Publishers.

Topell, Edward. (1599.) Sermon XXIX from, *Times lamentation: or An exposition on the prophet Ioel, in sundry sermons or meditations*. London: Printed by Edm. Bollifant, for George Potter.
At London: Printed by Edm. Bollifant, for George Potter, 1599.

Turing, A.M. (1950). "Computing machinery and intelligence." *Mind*, 59, 433-460.

Unamuno, Miguel. (2017.) *The Tragic Sense of Life.* CreateSpace Independent Publishing Platform.

Wangu, Madhu Bazaz. (2006.) "Buddhism," *World Religions*, 3rd ed. Facts on File.

Watts, Alan. (1969.) "The Game Theory of Ethics." Lecture.

Weijer, Charles, et al. (1887.) "Bioethics for Clinicians: 10. Research Ethics." *Canadian Medical Association Journal*, Apr 15; 156(8): 1153-1157.

Wilde, Oscar. (1891.) *A Picture of Dorian Gray.*

Wilhelm, Richard. (1969.) *The I Ching, or Book of Changes*. Princeton University Press.

Wittgenstein, Ludwig. (2003.) *Tractatus Logico-Philosophicus*. C. K. Ogden, trans. New York: Barnes & Noble.

Xenophon. (1979.) *A History of My Times.* Rex Warner, trans. Penguin Classics; Reprint edition. [QED+]

www.ingramcontent.com/pod-product-compliance
Lightning Source LLC
LaVergne TN
LVHW010050110826
845155LV00028B/271

* 9 7 8 1 9 4 0 8 1 3 5 1 6 *